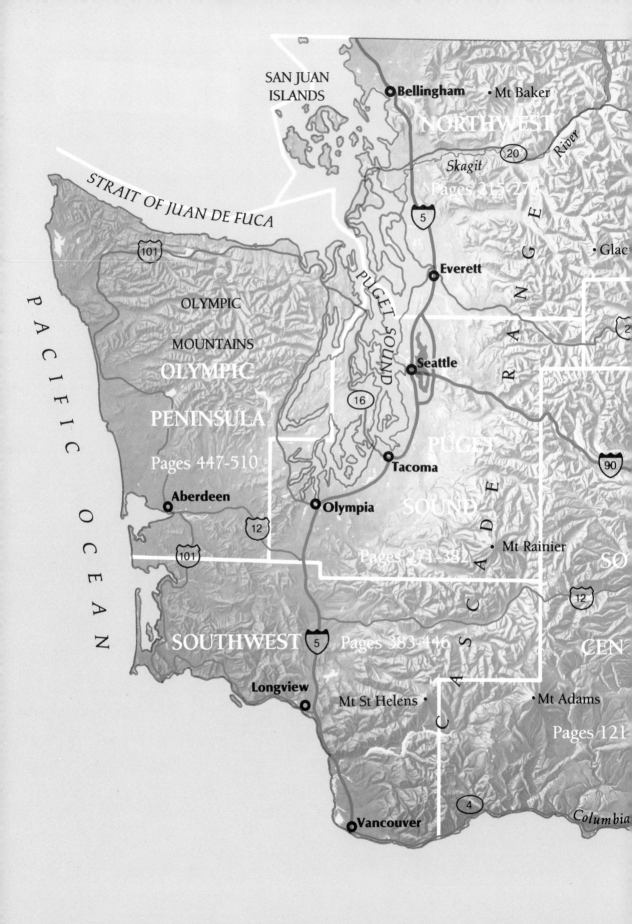

SAN JUAN
ISLANDS

STRAIT OF JUAN DE FUCA

PACIFIC OCEAN

OLYMPIC

MOUNTAINS

OLYMPIC

PENINSULA

Pages 447-510

Aberdeen

●Bellingham

• Mt Baker

NORTHWEST

Skagit

River

20

Pages 315-270

5

Everett

• Glac

2

PUGET SOUND

Seattle

16

PUGET

Tacoma

SOUND

Olympia

12

90

Mt Rainier

SO

Pages 271-382

101

12

SOUTHWEST

5

Pages 383-446

CEN

Longview

Mt St Helens •

CASCADE RANGE

• Mt Adams

Pages 121

Pages

4

Columbia

Vancouver

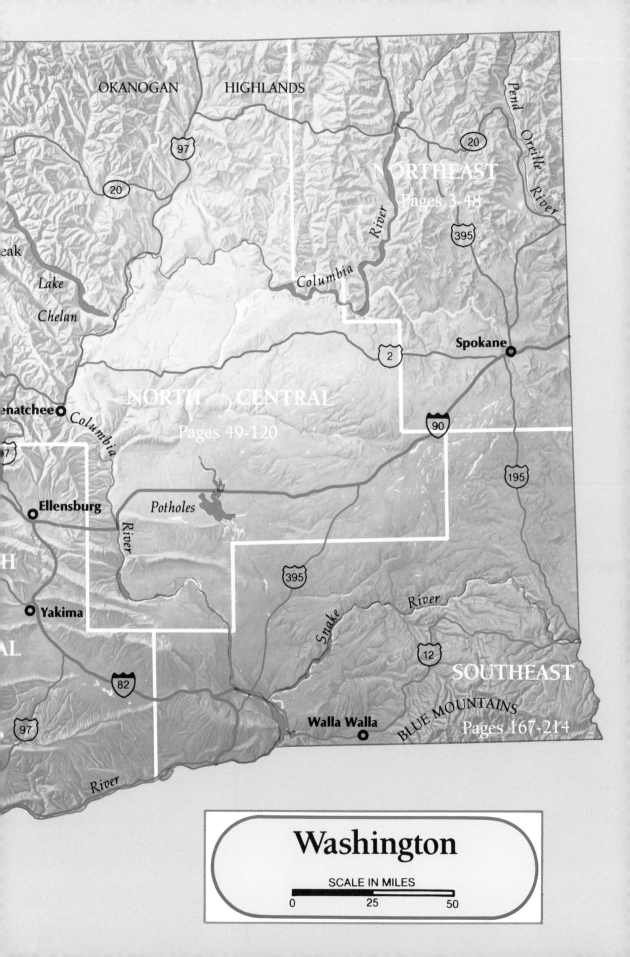

OKANOGAN   HIGHLANDS

Pend

Oreille

River

97

20

20

NORTHEAST
Pages 3-48

River

Columbia

395

eak

Lake

Chelan

2   Spokane

NORTH   CENTRAL

Pages 49-120

90

enatchee

Columbia

97

195

Ellensburg

Potholes

River

395

Yakima

River

Snake

12

82   SOUTHEAST

97

Walla Walla

BLUE MOUNTAINS
Pages 167-214

River

Washington

SCALE IN MILES

0   25   50

Exploring Washington's Past *A Road Guide to History*

Revised Edition

Ruth Kirk and Carmela Alexander

INTRODUCTON BY DAVID NICANDRI

Photographs by Ruth and Louis Kirk

University of Washington Press

Seattle and London

Copyright © 1990 by the University of Washington Press
Third printing (pbk.), 1991
Revised edition copyright © 1995 by the University of Washington Press
Designed by Roz Pape and Judy Petry
Printed in the United States of America

Library of Congress Cataloging-in-Publication Data
Kirk, Ruth.
 Exploring Washington's past : a road guide to history / Ruth Kirk and Carmela
Alexander ; introduction by David Nicandri ; photographs by Ruth and Louis Kirk.
— Rev. ed.
  p. cm.
 Includes bibliographical references and index.
 ISBN 0-295-97443-5 (alk. paper)
 1. Washington (State)—Guidebooks. 2. Washington (State)—History, Local.
3. Automobile travel—Washington (State)—Guidebooks. I. Alexander, Carmela.
II. Title
F889.3.K56   1995
917.9704'43—dc20   95-41635
                                                                          CIP

Cover photo: Max Steinke barn near St. John, in the Palouse (p. 199)
Half title photo: Cloverland Garage, near Asotin, southeast Washington, 1918.
Title page photo: Homestead cabins near Republic, northeast Washington.

CONTENTS

PREFACE to the Revised Edition

ONE MIGHT EXPECT a road guide to our past to need little revision after just five years, the time from original publication of this book to issuance of a revised edition. But these pages now include hundreds of updates and small changes, most of them not immediately noticeable.

Ten photographs are new. Scores of additional cross references have been inserted. And there are dozens of new or altered mentions of historic structures and interpretive centers. These range from the moving of Seattle's historic steamship *Virginia V* from one dock to another (p. 296); to the opening of Curlew's quaint 1906 Ansorge Hotel for viewing (though not lodging) because of the public-spirited dedication of the family who owns it (p. 32); to completion of Stevenson's splendid Gorge Interpretative Center, a triumph of a small county historical society (p. 164); to the eagerly awaited 1996 opening of the new world-class Washington History Museum in Tacoma (p. 334).

Other events relevant to a book of this type have also occurred. Weyerhaeuser Real Estate Company has deeded the Hudson's Bay Company 1843 Fort Nisqually fur trade site at DuPont—once on the Washington Trust for Historic Preservation's "Ten Most Endangered Properties" list—to the Archaeological Conservancy, a national nonprofit organization (p. 305). The M. J. Murdock Foundation has provided a large grant that will turn Vancouver's historic Pearson Airpark into a major aviation center complete with restored hangars and historic aircraft (p. 409). Centralia is restoring its railway depot (p. 387). And Port Townsend has reopened its 1904 nickelodeon Rose Theater (p. 498).

How to see—and savor—our past has changed in these and other ways in the period from one edition of the book to the next. So has what we call ourselves. The Klallam people of the northern Olympic Peninsula now spell their tribal name *S'Klallam*, and the Yakama Nation has changed the former *i* in their name to an *a*. They are the Yakama, not the Yakima. Regrettably, it has not been practical to make these changes in the book. Nor has *African American* replaced *Black*, which was standard five years ago. Similarly, *Latino* continues to be used in these pages, not *Hispanic,* and despite recent political changes ethnic background is indicated here by *Yugoslavian* rather than by *Croatian, Serbian, Montenegrin,* or *Slovenian*, the old-country names with which many of these people first arrived in Washington.

Methods of making changes on the pages have themselves changed since 1990. New type is no longer set and stripped in. Instead, entire pages are computer scanned and alterations are then entered onto the scans. Unfortunately, however, the scanner "reads" somewhat imperfectly. Italicized words may arbitrarily appear in roman type and apostrophes lower themselves into commas, errors that are tedious to catch and correct. Other scanner errors are amusing. As scanned, Seattle's Pike Place Market entry (p. 292) commented on the joyful sounds of "skeet musicians," not street musicians; at Grayland, cranberry conveyor belts connected to "boogied trucks" instead of bogside trucks; and—our favorite—for the dour, abortive Keil idealistic colony at Menlo, livelihood came from "fanning" rather than farming (pp. 439-40).

For yeoman service in entering changes onto scanned pages and correcting the scanner's own contributions, Veronica Seyd, production manager at the University of Washington Press, has our deep appreciation. So does Julidta Tarver, managing editor, who patiently edited pages to be corrected and read the resulting proof, in some instances catching errors and typos that had remained undetected through the previous three printings.

One further note of change within a mere five years: certain words rooted in our past have taken on new connotations. *Salmon. Owls. Hanford.* In the mid-1990s the general public has become environmentally aware in ways that were the province of specialists as the decade began. Not that the problems of Washington's fisheries and forests and nuclear contamination are new. On the contrary, the causes have been gestating in attitudes toward the environment as well as in field practices since before statehood. As early as 1883 John C. Tidball, accompanying General William Tecumseh Sherman, commented that Indian fishing at Kettle Falls, on the upper Columbia, had been greatly harmed by the huge catches of salmon supplied to canneries at the mouth of the river (p. 45; see also p. 417). Today, dams and habitat degradation threaten to complete what that overfishing began. Solutions will be slow. Despair seems to outpace hope.

In a comparable manner, our "endless" forest now unmistakably shows the vulnerability it has always had. *Trees* still grow and supply our economy, but—as the small owl with the big eyes symbolizes—a *forest* is more than trees. The task of wisely managing our 1990s mosaic of natural and commercial growth can no longer depend on simply retuning existing practices. It will require an entire redefinition of values, objectives, and budgets. On both sides of the Cascades, our back-up of untouched forest is essentially gone, taking with it the chance to fully understand what we have systematically altered (see pp. 466-67). Only now are we beginning to realize the intricate linkages that comprise the natural whole of the forest.

Hanford (pp. 172-73) fits much this same pattern of painfully sharpened awareness. Utilization of what seemed a single resource has proven fraught with ramifications that refuse to ease. Fifty years after World War II, public release of formerly sealed documents outlines the appalling magnitude of what we have done. Hanford's earth holds staggering quantities of toxic materials, some so "hot" that engineers dare not disturb them lest their hazards be compounded rather than controlled. Cleanup has begun; it is the highest-funded public works project in the state.

What has become clear in the last few years is that, as Paul Hawken says in his book *The Ecology of Commerce,* the best things in life are no longer free. We must pay in dollars and in discipline to hold onto—and restore—the environmental legacy we inherited. *Economy* and *ecology* share a common root that means simply *home.*

Our hope as authors has always been that this book will limn highlights of the story of our state as home.

RUTH KIRK, *Lacey*
CARMELA ALEXANDER, *Wapato*

PREFACE to the Original Edition

A SENSE OF PLACE is the focus of this book, a human tale of how we became as we are and also of where to find the evidence. The pages weave historical information and themes into suggestions for seeing the state. Particulars, tied to place, provide a cumulative, broad tapestry of events and landscape. This book should serve as a guide for vacations and an enrichment for other trips. U.S. 2 takes no longer than I-90 when driving between Wenatchee and Spokane. And to *see* the I-5 region, rather than merely drive through it, spend an hour or two windshield viewing the Victorian homes in Bellingham or the 1920s planned community aspect of Longview; turn off into the old river town of Woodland when the lilac garden is in bloom; or visit the historic coal country of Wilkeson and Black Diamond.

The time is right for such a look at ourselves. Washington's first century as a state is complete; the twenty-first century of the world's present calendar is about to begin; and interest in history flourishes. Phone books in Wahkiakum County (Southwest Region) recently have offered more pages of local history than of phone numbers, and two history museums in minuscule, isolated Molson (North Central Region) annually draw 100 times the entire population of the town and its hinterlands.

Does it matter? Yes. A sense of connectedness provides valuable—perhaps crucial—guidance amid today's instant-everything, which turns swamps where frogs croak and herons nest into shopping malls, and changes sagebrush slopes into productive vineyards as if that were a natural metamorphosis. We drive freeways, move frequently, and lose linkages without even knowing it. Actualities dim into stereotypes. Awareness of Northwest pioneering becomes limited to covered wagons and log cabins and isolation, without regard for the men and women who came by train and steamboat to found towns, never intending to live on homesteads or to work at logging camps or gold claims.

Awareness of ethnic and racial history grows equally blurred. Hawaiians came here with the late 1700s maritime expeditions of Captains Robert Gray and George Vancouver. Blacks accompanied the celebrated 1805–1806 overland exploration headed by Lewis and Clark and the 1841 Wilkes naval expedition. French-speaking Canadians as well as Scotsmen and Englishmen worked for the Hudson's Bay Company. A Japanese photographer documented late 1800s Okanogan mining camps. Hindu workmen endured the same brutal treatment accorded Chinese workmen from Puyallup hopyards and Palouse railroad camps to urban Chinatowns. And archaeologists find that our Native American heritage is more than 10,000 years old—an antiquity known all along by the people themselves.

No book can perfectly capture all of this. But the experiences that we, as authors, have had while compiling this sample have led, for us, to discovering a wondrous variety of Washingtonians, a host of new favorite corners in both cities and countryside, and dozens of outstanding back roads. For example, some day try the Mabton-Bickleton-Goldendale-Klickitat-Lyle road instead of hurrying between Yakima and the Columbia Gorge. Or follow the twisting Kettle River Valley, which previously served as a major travel route with Marcus as its gateway. Or visit Oysterville and Port Gamble, now almost like life-size museum dioramas but once major links between our budding 1800s economy and the necessary "outside" capital of San Francisco and New England.

The inevitable decisions of what to leave out of these pages have been difficult. Equally challenging has been deciding how best to organize what is included. Final resolution: alphabetize individual place entries within natural travel areas to make the material readily accessible yet avoid the need to read backwards, as guidebooks often require. Endpaper maps show this division along with modern highways and historic routes. Individual area maps cover places discussed in each particular section.

Museums and festivals tied to local history are included; accommodations, campgrounds, most public parks, and commercial entertainments are not. Buildings and districts listed in the National Register of Historic Places are often identified as such but not always—and some that are mentioned may soon vanish. For example, the largely abandoned farming town of Elberton (Southeast Region) and the Broughton lumber flume (South Central Region) are likely to be demolished soon; Spokane continues to search for a way to perform CPR on the venerable Davenport Hotel. Seattle repeatedly battles to save the Pike Place Market. Listing in the National Register indicates significance but provides neither operating funds nor broad legal protection.

From the outset, we have been encouraged and helped by innumerable persons as enamored of this state as we are, and therefore unquestioningly willing to share information and check manuscript. They range from university professors and historic preservation planners to librarians, county historical society members, and rural postmasters contacted for local specifics (one of whom answered a phone call, saying "Wait a minute. I'll call you back as soon as I get the mail sorted").

The book is a story of people. It has been produced by far more than the two of us whose names appear as authors. Indeed, our job has been to look and listen, travel and read—and savor the beauty of scene and the human richness that comprise this state. Acknowledgments and mention of sources could properly fill as many pages as the Index itself. That being impractical, from among the much appreciated

many we would like to especially thank: Craig Holstine, Glen Lindeman, and Cort Conley for immense help with the initial gestation of the book; Jeanne Welch for endless patience—and cheer—in searching out obscure historical data; Jeanne Engerman for repeatedly leading us to pertinent state library material; Jacob Thomas, David Hansen, Sara Steel, Leonard Garfield, Greg Griffith, and Marie DeLong of the state Office of Archaeology and Historic Preservation for consultations, clarifications, and access to files.

In addition, David Stratton, professor of history at Washington State University, and David Nicandri, director of the Washington State Historical Society, have read and criticized the entire manuscript. Individual sections have been checked by regional and local experts, which include: for material in the Northeast Region, John Fahey, Scott Brooks-Miller, Glen Lindeman, and Madilane Perry; for the North Central Region, Bruce Mitchell, Wilfred Woods, Mark Behler, Nathaniel Washington, Craig Holstine, Allen Gibbs, and Rebecca Haeberle; for the South Central Region, Tim Equate, George Martin, and Ted VanArsdol; for the Southeast Region, Alex McGregor, Mary Reed, Larry Dodd, Nancy Pryor, Robert Weatherly, Nathaniel Washington, and Ted VanArsdol; for the Northwest Region, Keith Murray, David Dilgard, Michael Sullivan, John Douglas, and Reed Jarvis; for the Puget Sound Region, Murray Morgan, Charles Payton, Florence Lentz, Al Elliott, Patricia Sias, Gary Reese, Cecelia Carpenter, Trish Laughlin, Shanna Stevenson, Greg Griffith, Berwyn Thomas, Ralph Munro, Dick Linkletter, and John and Elsie VanEaton; for the Southwest Region, David Freece, Marian Osterby, Ted VanArsdol, John McClelland, Irene Martin, Larry Weathers, and Pat VanEaton; for the Olympic Peninsula, Rosalie Spellman, Harriet Fish, and Peter Simpson.

We have been helped, too, by Harvey Rice, who shared long-accumulated knowledge of back roads and enticing sited, and Richard Daugherty, who gave access to his extensive files and checked specialized archaeological and ethnographic information and concepts. Scores of other friends, acquaintances, and contacts supplemented the overall research. They include

Bob Abshire, John Brown, Jill Carlos, Susan Carter, Jim Carty, Emmett Clouse, Ivar Dolph, Molly Erickson, Lou Foster, Chris Hentgess, Frank Johnson, Mary Kline, Mary Koch, Bill and Kathy Lester, Mildred Ludwig, Rick McClure, Sheila McLean, Carolyn Marr, Dick Reed, Kirstin Ravetz, Joan Robinson, Les Rowe, Robert Ruby, Susan Schwartz, Ed Sherwood, Claudia Shobert, Stephen Stout, Dale Stradling, Howard Stradling, Don Tracy, Gil Turner, William Winn.

Extreme generosity in providing personally owned photographs has come from Mary Randlett, Ira Spring, Larry Bullis, Betty Jo Neils, Juanita Walter Therrell, Clifford Ott, Alex McGregor, and Tom Murray. Hedy Hartman of the Washington Museum Association provided a directory of museums. Robert Peters and Harold Garrett of the state Department of Transportation gave moral support and suggested sources. Public librarians Laura Boyles, Carolyn Ferguson, Sandy Lauritzen, and David Dilgard responded lavishly to phone pleas for help; so did Charles Sigo, curator at the Suquamish Museum. Joe Garcia and the late Frank Buck agreed to special interviews and Edie Hottowe authorized including excerpts from an earlier interview with her mother, Ada Markishtum.

Larry Cort brought great skill and seemingly endless hours to preparing detailed maps for this book; Stuart Wallin helped plan the maps and drew the cartouches; John Sherman drew the underlying shaded relief of the endpaper map. Margaret Foster-Finan coped lovingly with a peculiarly difficult editing job; Julidta Tarver tied up the loose ends and shepherded the manuscript through its transition into a book. Lorri Hagman compiled the index, a demanding task that requires a knack for creating and remembering cross references. Roz Pape not only did the design but patiently revised layouts to meet shifting demands. Veronica Seyd presided over the long, complicated process of typesetting, pasting up, printing, and binding. Don Ellegood, Dick Barden, Naomi Pascal, Pat Soden, and Maura Craig helped to shape early concepts into this final product.

To all of these persons, our abiding thanks and our awareness that any lingering inaccuracies are our responsibility—and regret—as authors. To Washingtonians past and present and future, our admiration and heightened awareness of what a varied and splendid state this is.

RUTH KIRK, *Tacoma*
CARMELA ALEXANDER, *Wapato*

INTRODUCTION

WASHINGTON is a place of surprises, as tourists, newcomers, and even long-time residents discover. Born and raised in upstate New York (and as a youth thinking of Michigan as "Western"), I was amazed to learn when I first moved to the Northwest that such a large portion of Washington is semiarid, if not outright desert. The Evergreen State? In part, yes, but if gray, green, and blue (water) are the dominant colors west of the Cascades, yellow and brown characterize eastern Washington.

Exploring Washington's Past by Ruth Kirk and Carmela Alexander introduces the reader to many such surprises and celebrates the state's marvelous diversity. A fine and exceptionally useful addition to the body of literature offering new insights into and summaries of the human experience in Washington, the book provides a rich tapestry of history.

By definition, a sightseer's guide must be oriented toward place, as opposed to theme or chronology. That does not mean, however, that the broad pattern of Washington history is absent here. Each crossroads hamlet, town, or city has its own topography and pattern of human factors, faithfully highlighted in this book. Fundamentally these pages are about people and provide something akin to a group portrait, showing a diversity that is ethnic and cultural as well as geographic. The range is from Basque sheep herders in the Channeled Scablands to the Hawaiians employed by the Hudson's Bay Company and black pioneers such as George Bush, who settled near Olympia, and George Washington, the founder of Centralia; from the chewing-gum Wrigley family and the Canadian-beer Molsons, who invested in Washington mines, to a dozen utopian colonies that sought the good life through pooled assets and efforts (a few Hutterites and Mennonites still endure). Let me offer a few examples of the people encountered here:

Chief Joseph of the Nez Perces is one of the most famous of Native Americans, evidenced by the fact that he is claimed by four states: Oregon, Idaho, Montana, and Washington. He is buried near Nespelem. His gravestone image faces toward his Wallowa home to the southeast, where he was never allowed to return.

Comcomly of the Chinooks served as a pilot for Hudson's Bay Company ships entering the Columbia River. His daughter married the company's chief trader Archibald MacDonald, and their son Ranald became a world traveler who played an indirect role in the 1853 opening of Japan to world trade. MacDonald now lies buried on a lonely hill above the Kettle River, north of Spokane.

At several points in Washington's history, people have become strongly linked with specific places. One notable example is Sam Hill. The son-in-law of the better-known railroad "empire builder," James J. Hill, Sam was an advocate of road construction and experimentation with new surfacing materials. He is best known as the creator of Maryhill, now a fine arts museum, and of a replica of Stonehenge built above the Columbia as a memorial to those from Klickitat County who died in World War I. He is also the father of a distinctive landmark at the other end of the state: the Peace Arch near Blaine.

These discoveries and more await you in this book. For example:

What resident of the Northwest has not pondered the origin of The Dalles place name?

We learn here that the term means "paving stones" in French, a reference by the early fur-trading voyageurs to the outcroppings of basaltic slabs so common in the Columbia River gorge.

Grand Coulee Dam has loomed so large in the region's history that it has taken on legendary qualities—"the biggest thing ever built by a man." To construct this high dam and make the desert bloom on the Columbia Plateau, the fishing community of Altoona on the lower Columbia paid a heavy price. Grand Coulee Dam destroyed the summer Chinook salmon run (known as "June bums"), upon which the town had staked its reputation. And as early as 1883 a young lieutenant accompanying General William Sherman wrote that native fishermen at Kettle Falls were finding salmon scarce because of "the great numbers taken for the canneries near the mouth of the river."

In the boom days of the 1880s whole communities catered to the whims of the Northern Pacific Railroad, whose decisions could make or break fortunes. In central Washington, David Guilland continued to operate a hotel, renting rooms and offering meals, while his building, pulled on rollers by mule trains, took a snail-like month-long trip from Yakima City (now Union Gap) to North Yakima, where it could better serve the Northern Pacific's traffic.

I always wondered why the Northern Pacific put such an emphasis on completing a little jerkwater line from Kalama to Tacoma in 1873, when the main line westward had only reached Bismarck, North Dakota (and would not be completed for another 10 years). Now I know. The rail line had to reach salt water by December 31, 1873, or lose its generous land grant from the public domain.

Exploring Washington's Past is nearly poetic in saying much with an economy of words: "The area around the Columbia River mouth is geographically small but historically large." Nearby "Cape Disappointment is the opposite of its name: it delights anyone interested in landscape and history." "The pavement leading [to Tokeland] from Raymond seems as much a road through time as a geographic link."

Not too many states can be said to have had successive frontiers. Washington did. Most western states have had a single distinguishing and enduring stamp placed on them by their initial settlers. Arizona and New Mexico are the prime examples, but even Oregon to this day has the steady reserve and mien of the transplanted New England town builders who established aptly named communities such as Portland and Salem. In Washington, by contrast, the principal cities have names with an indigenous flair—Seattle, Spokane, Tacoma. And whatever cultural "establishment" Washington's early pioneers managed to build was completely swept aside in the tide of new immigrants that began to swell in the 1880s.

The completion of the Northern Pacific Railroad in 1883 transformed Washington from an economic backwater to the leading state in the northern West. Between 1880 and 1890 the population of Washington grew by 380 percent, a demographic movement so large that it completely swept away what little of a cultural establishment the relatively few overland pioneers had put in place. Thousands upon thousands of single men, many of them foreign born and living alone, came or were brought to Washington to harvest and fashion wood products. In eastern Washington, hosts of field hands moved from farm to farm to help with the harvests, just like the loggers who moved from camp to camp. This hetero-geneous, itinerant, and unattached population, when galvanized by the new radical political currencies of the late nineteenth and early twentieth centuries, laid the foundation for that famous aphorism, "the 47 states and the Soviet of Washington."

Only two presidents have ever had a tran-scendent interest in the Northwest. Thomas Jefferson was one and Franklin Roosevelt the other. Jefferson, one historian has argued, took more pride in being President of the American Philosophical Society than he did in being president of the United States. As the quin-tessential product of the Enlightenment in America, Jefferson, like his contemporaries (such as Captain Cook), was fascinated by the great geographic questions of the age. Though what we know as the Lewis and Clark Expedition (Jefferson himself always referred to it as the Lewis Expedition) had significance in the areas of Indian relations and international diplomacy, it was primarily a scientific reconnaissance. Among other things, the Corps of Discovery provided the first practical view as to the width of North America and, in the decade after the seaborne Northwest Passage faded into mythology, it established a riverine version, with its Missouri-Columbia rivers headwaters explorations.

No state was more favored by Franklin Roosevelt's New Deal than Washington. This state had its fair share of local problems during the Depression, but Roosevelt and his operatives also saw Washington—specifically, the Columbia Plain—as a new promised land for the refugees of the Dust Bowl. For that reason, Washington received a disproportionate share of that first big round of federal expenditures that included, most notably, Grand Coulee and Bonneville dams. From 1934 to 1939 Washington received four and five times as much money for public works and welfare as it sent to the nation's capital as revenue. No state with a population greater than a million people received a higher per capita expenditure of New Deal federal dollars than did Washington.

With the succeeding years of World War II, Washington became the first military industrial state. The vast reservoir of cheap hydroelectric power attracted a swarm of aluminum plants, whose product was transformed by the Boeing Company into the wings of America's war machine. Henry Kaiser's shipyards near Vancouver, and those on Puget Sound, also availed themselves of the power that created whole fleets of Liberty Ships. Even the selection of Hanford as the site of the army's experiments in the military application of nuclear physics has its roots in the developments of the 1930s. The American West abounded in the remoteness that this dangerous new work required, but only Hanford had the requisite supply of potential hydroelectric power—the waters of Lake Roosevelt behind Grand Coulee Dam just 120 miles north. Washington as we know and see it today is still largely the product of the years between 1933 and 1945.

Now that the twentieth century draws to a close, and historians begin to bring it into focus, the history of Washington will stand in greater relief. For the new history of the West will not rework developments that largely passed by nineteenth-century Washington—the cow towns and mining camps and Indian wars (though we had a little of each). Modern Washington will become the front line of historical investigation into the pattern of this century's West—urbanized, increasingly sculpted by human hands as well as natural forces, reliant upon technology and federal investment, and conscious of its distinctive environmental qualities. *Exploring Washington's Past* serves as an excellent guide to the events and forces that set us upon this course.

DAVID L. NICANDRI
Director
Washington State Historical Society

Exploring Washington's Past

A Road Guide to History

Exploring Washington's Past

A Road Guide to History

NORTHEAST Region

Deep Creek School, west of Spokane.

THE NORTHEAST corner of the state is a major crossroads. Each summer for at least 9,000 years, Native Americans traveled long distances to fish for salmon at Kettle Falls on the upper Columbia River. In 1810 Canadian fur traders opened a post on the Spokane River—the first commercial structure in what became Washington. Travel through the region to British Columbia mines began in the 1840s, and by the 1850s the lure of gold had drawn prospectors to the Pend Oreille, Columbia, and Kettle rivers. Their increasing encroachment touched off warfare between native warriors and the U.S. Army.

In 1858 a new era opened. Proportionately small acreages were reserved for native people, while immense opportunities were available to those white settlers and miners suited by attitude and physique for frontier life. Arrival of the Northern Pacific Railroad in 1881 assured Spokane a role as queen of the "Inland Empire." The rails linked mines, sawmills, and farms to markets—and to Spokane financiers.

English was not the only language spoken during these first decades of regional development. French Canadians, Metis (French-Indian), Iroquois, and Hawaiians worked for the fur trade companies. Chinese men arrived to wash gold from placer claims and later helped to build the railroads, joined by crews of Irishmen, Italians, and Greeks. Finns worked at sawmills and struggled to establish backwoods farms complete with saunas.

In the 1930s the Pend Oreille Valley barely lost out to Grand Coulee, on the Columbia, as the site for a federal irrigation project—and, ironically, at the beginning of the 1940s water backed behind Grand Coulee Dam drowned the region's first centers at Kettle Falls and Fort Colvile and destroyed orchards on the river benchlands. Logging and, to some extent, mining have continued. Recreation has joined commerce as an economic mainstay.

Spokane Area

The city of Spokane offers urban attractions on a scale still pleasantly manageable. The outlying countryside embraces a merging of fertile wheatlands, rocky scablands, and a vast carpet of pine forest. It includes the sites of crucial clashes between the U.S. Army and native people who were trying desperately to hold onto land and customs. Here, too, were the first fur-trading post in the state (Spokane House, built in 1810) and the last frontier army post (Fort Spokane, garrisoned beginning in 1880). An annual encampment held at Spokane House each August recreates trading-post life during the period from 1810 to 1814.

Protestant missionary effort in this area is represented at Tshimakain, today no more than a site at the crossroads community of Ford. Catholic missionary effort includes Gonzaga University in Spokane (and also Cataldo Mission just east of Coeur d'Alene, Idaho, built in 1840 and now beautifully restored; well worth visiting).

Power dams crucial to regional development—and part of a network intended for the export of hydroelectricity—are at Nine Mile Falls and Long Lake, northwest of Spokane.

The **BATTLE OF SPOKANE PLAINS** is marked by a monument standing beside U.S. 2 just west of the main entrance to Fairchild Air Base. Near this location on September 5, 1858,

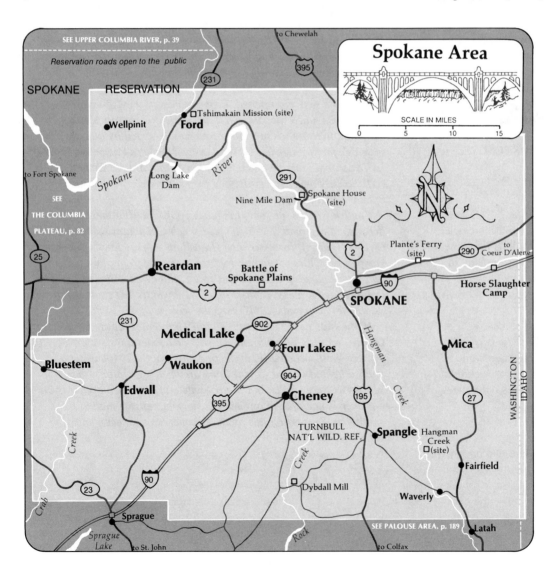

Early-1900s college students boarded at the David Lowe home in Cheney (Third and F). Lowe, a semiretired farmer, still owned acreage outside of town and was active in real estate.

destiny played a crucial act in the story of regional native-white relations: warriors of the Spokane, Palouse, Coeur d'Alene, Pend Oreille, and other Columbia Plateau bands clashed with troops commanded by Colonel George Wright.

(Also see SPOKANE BATTLES sidebar, p. 10.)

BLUESTEM. (See under CHENEY, p. 6.)

CHENEY (Chee′-nee) holds reminders of the town's close ties to both education and agriculture. The south end of town hums with the around-the-clock operation of an imposing flour mill (First Street) built by the F. M. Martin Milling Company in the early 1900s and later owned by Clarence D. Martin, Washington's governor in 1932. For a time, this mill was the largest and most prosperous of its kind anywhere in the state. A handful of houses from that era remain nearby. Notable are an elaborate Queen Anne home (Third and F streets) built in 1904 and a brick home (Fourth and F streets), which has old-style windows set low to the ground.

Cheney's largest remaining farm building is the "Big Red Barn," a mortise and tenon structure that now houses the Eastern Washington University campus police department (west edge of the campus). Built in about 1884, the barn—which is listed in the National Register of Historic Places—is exemplary as adaptive reuse of a fine old

building. Also listed in the National Register is the interurban railroad depot of the Washington Water Power Company (Second and College; built in 1907), a brick building that appears unchanged from when electric trains linked Cheney with Spokane and Medical Lake. Excursionists rode to Medical Lake. Farmers with city business to attend to tied their horses at special sheds and rode to Spokane.

Cheney began simply as "Section 13," a designation for land available to homesteaders. Then the name changed to Willow Springs. A new phase began when rails reached the town, newly renamed Depot Springs. Soon it acquired still another name—Cheney—while courting favor with the Northern Pacific Railroad Company. The first choice had been Billings, to honor Frederick Billings, company president. A Montana town already had that name, however, so someone suggested Cheney to honor a Northern Pacific director.

The idea soon paid off. Benjamin P. Cheney gave $10,000 to go with eight acres donated by the company for an academy. In April 1882, a year after the railroad arrived, classes opened with two teachers from Boston who had been personally selected by Cheney. The academy later became the state-supported Cheney Normal School and went on to evolve into Eastern Washington University.

For a look at the countryside that was once farmed, but is now again much as it was when

Norwegian immigrant Ole Dybdall's gristmill, south of Cheney, operated from 1897 until 1955.

whites first arrived, drive to **Turnbull National Wildlife Refuge** (6 miles south of town, accessible via Cheney–Turnbull Road). Ponderosa pines surround ponds frequented by wild ducks and swans; flowers brighten sagebrush hillsides. Native people traditionally dug here for camas, bitterroot, biscuit root, and a variety of other staples.

Also search out the **Dybdall Mill.** (Follow Cheney–Plaza Road south from town; stay left at the fork in 8 miles, then left again in one-half mile.) Until 1955 farm families brought grain here to be ground into flour. The mill is still privately owned and is not open to the public.

North of Cheney a "back-door" drive leads to the minuscule towns of **Waukon, Edwall,** and **Bluestem**—now pinpricks of time and geography. The entire area is a scenic merging of wheatlands, ponderosa pine forest, and rough, basalt scablands. (From Cheney, go north on Salnave Road; cross I-90 and continue 1 mile to Malloy Prairie Road. Turn west 2 miles to Tucker Prairie Road; then turn north and continue as Tucker becomes Stangland Road. At Stangland's junction with Fancher Road, turn west into pine forest. Waukon is 2 miles farther.) A false-fronted general store and post office look much as they did decades ago. A "flat-house" by the railroad tracks remains from the era of

sacked grain storage, and cribbed elevators and concrete silos mark the shift to modern bulk storage. (See WHEAT STORAGE sidebar, p. 192.)

Edwall, a more substantial town, is nonetheless also on the fringe of existence. Peter Edwall platted it in 1892 just before the arrival of the Great Northern Railway. Several typical boomtown commercial buildings still stand, and turn-of-the-century houses are in various stages of rehabilitation.

Bluestem, farther west, has a cluster of grain elevators and collapsing frame buildings. It began as "Moscow" but was renamed for a high-yielding, disease-resistant variety of wheat developed in 1896 at the State Agricultural College and Experiment Station in Pullman (now Washington State University).

EDWALL. (See under CHENEY, this page.)

FORD. (See TSHIMAKAIN MISSION, p. 21.)

FORT SPOKANE (trading post). (See SPOKANE HOUSE, p. 20.)

FORT SPOKANE (U.S. Army). (See p. 41.)

FOUR LAKES is a "bedroom community" about 10 miles southwest of Spokane and the

site of an 1858 defeat of native warriors by the U.S. Army. A stone monument on Electric Avenue, just south of the freeway, commemorates the battle. (See SPOKANE BATTLES sidebar, p. 10.)

White settlement at Four Lakes began as an irrigation promotion called Meadow Lake, but growth was slow until 1908 when a development firm bought 1,400 acres along the Washington Water Power Company's electric railroad between Spokane and Medical Lake.

HANGMAN CREEK. (See under SPANGLE, p. 9; also see SPOKANE BATTLES sidebar, p. 10.)

HORSE SLAUGHTER CAMP, just west of the Washington–Idaho border, is where the U.S. Army in 1858 killed about 700 horses owned by a Palouse chief. (See SPOKANE BATTLES sidebar, p. 10.) A monument commemorating the event stands 20 miles east of Spokane city limits, near the west side of the I-90 truck weighing station. The actual site, 1 mile to the northwest, is now fenced and inaccessible to the public.

When **LONG LAKE DAM** was built by Washington Water Power Company in 1910, it was a major hydropower project that could boast what then was the world's highest spillway— 208 feet—and also its greatest electricity output. Washington Water Power brought in about 500 construction workers and built a model community with four-room cottages for families, a school, and a "commodious club building" with a reading room, a gymnasium, and baths. Little of this remains, and the dam itself is best seen from an overlook slightly to the north. (On the west side of State Route 291, about 1 mile from its junction with State Route 231, park at an unpaved pullout and walk to the edge of the cliff.)

The dam spans the Spokane River at the approximate crossing of the historic road between Fort Colville and Fort Walla Walla, a 200-mile route pioneered in 1859 by Major Pinkney Lugenbeel (who, of course, actually followed existing trails). Formerly the river here teemed with so many salmon that native people would ride into the shallows and spear them from horseback. When the dam was finished, the salmon came no more. Fish ladders seldom entered into dam construction during that era.

MEDICAL LAKE nestles amid gently rolling pine hills about 15 miles west of Spokane. Legendary curative powers gave the lake its name and led to development of one of the state's first popular resorts during the early 1900s. Today's town library displays advertisements from that time. For example, Allen's Sanatorium proclaimed:

We can cure you of rheumatism, skin diseases, stomach and kidney trouble by the use of Medical Lake Mud and Water Baths—each mud bath consists of steam bath, hot fresh mud bath, shower, blanket pack and massage.

Men in rowboats scooped up a "gelatinous substance of dark reddish color" and stored it in pits dug in the middle of town. Wonder remedies also came from residue collected in evaporation pans and used in soap and tablets, which would "effervesce slightly and form a pleasant wholesome beverage."

In 1905 an electric rail line from Spokane to Medical Lake allowed recreation to eclipse the therapeutic trade. Tourists walked from the depot to the Coney Island Pavilion Boat House at the foot of Lake Street and there boarded a launch for Camp Comfort or Stanley Park. In an era when doing business on the Sabbath usually was against the law, the Camp Comfort dance hall seems to have had the state's only Sunday license.

One of Washington's most whimsical homes is a three-story brick "castle" (Lake and Stanley) now converted to apartments. It belonged to Medical Lake's first mayor, "Lord" Stanley Hallett, a transplanted Englishman who designed and built the house himself. Workers lived on the property for three years. They included one entire family hired to round the edges of bricks for the ornamental detail.

While serving as a county commissioner, Hallett was instrumental in bringing Eastern State Hospital for the Insane to Medical Lake (west edge of town). The first patients—called "inmates" at the time—arrived in 1891 and were committed involuntarily, kept for years, and given no more than custodial care. Cures were not expected. Today, treatment in the hospital typically lasts only a week or two, and many patients are treated—and cured—at Medical

Medical Lake's Hallett house was built in 1903 by the town's mayor. It is now apartments.

Lake health centers without entering the hospital. Interlake School for the profoundly handicapped and retarded now occupies several former hospital buildings, which were designed by the prominent Spokane architectural firm of Whitehouse and Price in 1915.

At **MICA** Charles P. Oudin established the American Firebrick Company, which produced high-quality brick used throughout the Northwest. Remnants of that plant, built in 1902, stand immediately north of today's town; modern brickmaking continues at a plant east of the highway.

At the time Oudin opened for business, fires had destroyed the wooden downtown sections of communities in the Spokane area, and builders were turning to brick and stone for a sense of permanence and prosperity. Production at Mica included the West's first high-temperature fire brick for smelters and for lining fireboxes on board Great Northern locomotives. A brick company "hotel," or boarding house for single men, still stands on Mica's main street (east of the general store), and the plant superintendent's house—not of brick—dominates a hilltop overlooking town.

Perhaps the oldest ranch in Spokane County lies immediately east of Mica. It was established about 1864 and soon became one of the few

stops where lodging and supplies were available along the Kentuck Trail—a main route from the Snake River to Montana gold mines (named for Joe "Kentuck" Ruark, a ferry operator). An impressive hand-hewn log barn and granary still stand at the ranch.

NINE MILE DAM (visible from the highway bridge across the Little Spokane River) is easily overlooked today, yet it contributed mightily to the region's development by providing power for efficient transportation. The Spokane and Inland Empire Railroad began work on the dam in 1907, soon after incorporating. President Jay Graves dreamed of "highways of steel" to link the entire region, and he achieved his goal by organizing several small interurban lines into a single system that reached from Spokane to Coeur d'Alene and through the Palouse to Colfax and Moscow. Nine Mile's hydropower let people, freight, and mail ride the electric cars. Furthermore, it permitted communication by postal telegraph and provided communities along the line with their first electricity.

Washington Water Power Company bought the installation in 1925. They built neat brick operators' cottages that rimmed a shady, central lawn near the dam.

PLANTE'S FERRY began in the 1850s when a French-Canadian man named Antoine Plante established the first commercial crossing in the area. Travelers en route to the Great Plains via the Mullan Road, or to British Columbia mines in the Kootenai Mountains, crossed with Plante, who continued his service until the mid-1870s. By then a bridge had been built near the Idaho border.

The site now is included in Plante's Ferry County Park, reached via Upriver Drive. (From the first lot at the east side of the park, walk downhill from the picnic shelter to the water's edge.) A concrete post marks the location of the original wooden post where Plante anchored his ferry cables.

REARDAN consists of venerable brick buildings downtown; a classic, high-steepled church set on a hill; and streets lined by comfortable homes with spindled porches and chimneys rising from the center of their

ridgepoles, signatures of an era when fireplaces provided household heat.

Early 1880s efforts at creating a town here faded soon after starting, then revived when a branch line of the Northern Pacific Railroad arrived at the end of the decade. Residents platted the town, named it for a Northern Pacific civil engineer, and dug a well to convince company officials that the community was permanent enough to warrant a depot. Grain elevators beside today's tracks indicate the economic base, unchanged from the time of original settlement.

SPANGLE, situated in the Palouse wheatlands just south of the forested Spokane area, is a town with grain elevators, pleasant homes, and scattered businesses barely able to withstand the nearby city competition.

The Spangle family settled here in 1871 on what three years later proved to be railroad land. They then moved and filed for a government homestead. The first year after breaking sod, their wheat harvest provided enough grain for feed, for the next year's seed, and to grind into flour. The flour required a trip to Walla Walla, a two-week journey, which included time to unload, buy supplies, reload, and return home.

East of town is **Hangman Creek,** so named because of army "justice" in the form of as many as nine hangings as the Indian battles near Spokane closed in 1858. Witnesses disagreed how many had been executed. (Drive 4 miles southeast of Spangle on Spangle–Waverly Road, turn east on North Kentuck Trail, and watch for a road fork in 2 miles. Stay left there for another mile, still on North Kentuck, then turn left onto a dirt road a short way after crossing the creek.) A stone marker commemorates the hangings. Colonel George Wright's camp was on the flat by the bridge.

(Also see SPOKANE BATTLES sidebar, p. 10.)

SPOKANE began deliberately: James N. Glover of Salem, Oregon, came here in 1872 intending to build a city. He was 36 years old, had come West by wagon train as a youth, and had made a modest fortune merchandising apples in California and mining in Idaho. Advice from the aging Presbyterian missionary Henry Spalding, who extolled the merits of

waterpower and Chief Garry's "friendly Indians," guided Glover to Spokane Falls.

He liked what he saw—thundering water, rich bunchgrass, stately pines. The only disappointment was smoke rising from a chimney and a minuscule sawmill (about where Spokane Falls Boulevard and Howard Street now intersect). Glover soon bought out these interests, which belonged to J. Downing and S. Scranton, who were posing as cattle ranchers but more likely were actually rustlers, and to Richard Benjamin, who had set up the mill. Glover settled. He expected government surveyors to come through "soon" and lay a baseline, which would permit a proper land claim and eventual title. He also expected a railroad.

In 1878 Glover filed a townsite plat and that same year sold a half interest in it to John J. Browne and Anthony M. Cannon, who so energetically promoted the infant community that within a year the population jumped to nearly 100. In 1881 a Northern Pacific locomotive puffed into town along what became Railroad Avenue, and suddenly land became easy to sell. Describing Spokane Falls, as the new city was called, H. P. Robinson commented in an 1884 issue of the Northern Pacific's publication *The Northwest:*

Nothing in all the strange ways of the wild West strikes an Eastern visitor as more curious than the manner in which cities are planted and grow out here. A man plats a townsite much as he would break a few acres of farm land, and then proceeds to raise a city as if it were a crop of potatoes.

Half a century earlier the area had lost out to Colville when the Hudson's Bay Company moved its trading post from the Spokane River to the upper Columbia. The Mullan Road, connecting between the Missouri River and the Columbia, went *through* the Spokane country but led to Walla Walla, which remained Washington Territory's center of agriculture, shipping, and population growth. Lewiston, Idaho, was a third center with a head start on Spokane Falls; it might have become the largest city in the region had the Northern Pacific opted for Lolo Pass instead of following the longer but easier grade of the Clark Fork. As it was, the first transcontinental rails arrived at Spokane

SPOKANE BATTLES

In May 1858 Colonel Edward Steptoe marched north across the Snake River in violation of a promise made by Governor Isaac Stevens at the Walla Walla Council three years earlier. Ostensibly he was en route to the Colville country to protect border surveyors and miners.

Near present-day Rosalia, a combined force of Spokane, Coeur d'Alene, Palouse, and others attacked and thoroughly defeated Steptoe's troops. The victory exhilarated the natives. It humiliated the army. General Newman Clarke, newly arrived on the Columbia as commander, ordered immediate retribution: Colonel George Wright was to march north from Fort Dalles, Major Robert Garnett to march east from Fort Simcoe. Wright set out from Walla Walla with only a month's worth of supplies. He was in a hurry.

Jesuits warned chiefs that the troops were coming and urged peace, but their words availed little. On September 1 fighting broke out near Four Lakes, west of today's Spokane. Native warriors charged Wright's men, but were overwhelmed by the troops, shooting with long-range rifles far superior to those used by Steptoe four months previously. At day's end, Lieutenant Lawrence Kip wrote that the natives had been "panic stricken by the effect of our fire at such great distances."

On September 5 the troops again fought—and won—near the present Fairchild Air Base. Wright took one chief hostage and hanged a warrior who had killed two miners. He also met with native men who asked for peace, including Chief Garry, whom he told:

You must come to me with your arms, and with your women and children, and everything you have, and lay them at my feet. . . . If you do not do this, war will be made on you this year and the next, and until all your natives shall be exterminated.

September 9, en route to Coeur d'Alene country, Wright captured about 900 Palouse horses that were being driven out of the army's way. Because he could not manage such a large herd while on the march, he told his men to select about 200, then ordered the rest shot. The slaughter lasted for two gory days. Skeletons lay in place for decades, and the site was referred to as the Bone Yard. The wanton destruction stunned plateau natives, who measured wealth by their horses.

After Coeur d'Alene, Wright turned back to camp on Latah Creek, east of today's Spangle, and there many chiefs and leaders came to meet with him. On September 23 Chief Garry and 34 others signed a peace treaty, even agreeing that hostages would be held at Walla Walla—well treated—as an assurance of "good behavior" by their bands. Despite this "peace," however, when Owhi (an Upper Yakima chief) arrived, Wright seized him, angry because two years previously Owhi had not brought in his people as promised following the Yakima War. The colonel then sent a message to the chief's son Qualchin who was hiding nearby: unless he appeared, his father would be killed.

Qualchin came the next morning. Wright considered him directly responsible for the deaths in Yakima territory of six miners and Indian agent Andrew Bolon in 1855. He seized Qualchin, and later reported officially, "Qual-chian came to me at 9 o'clock this morning and at 9-¼ a.m. he was hung."

That evening Wright also hanged six Palouse men. While en route to Walla Walla, his soldiers hanged four more and shot Chief Owhi as he tried to escape. On September 30 Wright noted tersely in his report: "The war is closed."

(Also see YAKIMA WAR sidebar, p. 148; and PUGET SOUND WAR sidebar, p. 326.)

Falls—and what a Colfax newspaper called "a fair country village" mushroomed into the chief arrival point and dispersal center of the region.

Miners, lumberjacks, and construction workers soon jostled each other on the wooden sidewalks. Outlying settlers joined city folk in the stores and theaters. And at a livery stable on Riverside Avenue, Chief Garry made a final protest at losing land. Spokane Falls seemed to be fulfilling James Glover's expectations. Then came 1889 and a fire. How it started is uncertain, but 32 blocks of the business district flamed—and vanished. Leaky hoses used in vain to fight the blaze cost the water superintendent his job (although he was hired back as a private contractor to rebuild the entire water system).

A stronger, more ebullient city quickly developed from the devastation. Neat tents lined streets, and businesses resumed while architects and contractors rebuilt with brick and granite, albeit along streets that varied seasonally from dust to mud. Five hundred buildings went up in one year and, by August 1890—the first anniversary of the fire—the city council could order all remaining tents removed. Population zoomed to 25,000 as workmen pocketed inflated wages. In 1891 the city dropped "Falls" from its name.

Devastation in a different form came in 1893 with the nationwide financial panic. Seven out of 10 Spokane banks collapsed, and the Dutch-owned Northwestern and Pacific Hypotheekbank (which means "mortgage bank") began calling in its loans. It had formed 10 years earlier specifically to finance the development of the city and its hinterland, backing local optimism with Netherlands capital because of the potential for waterpower—and therefore industry—and also because of plans for extensive feeder railroads. British insurance companies covered Hypotheekbank losses from the 1889 fire, and the Dutch financed the city's reconstruction, a sound investment with dividends at first as high as 44 percent. Then came 1893. A few years later representatives of Dutch stockholders began foreclosures, and the banking company declared bankruptcy—apparently a ploy to permit reorganization, for it actually remained a major force in Spokane finance until World War II.

As the 1890s depression eased, several forces began restructuring the economy. Perhaps chief among them was the Washington Water Power Company: it expanded to serve outlying communities, helping link them with Spokane, and to supply the mines at Coeur d'Alene with power. In time it bought out a total of 85 small electric companies in the region (even as distant as Chelan). This gave the company a monopoly, and it could—and did—determine which industrialists and which sites were to be served. Urban people felt well served. Farm families felt bypassed and often tapped onto powerlines near their houses to help themselves to electricity.

Men with capital made fortunes from Coeur d'Alene, Idaho, and (later) Kootenai, British Columbia, gold, copper, lead, and silver; from building railroads to reach those districts; and from the white pine forests opened up by the rails. By the late 1890s fine mansions began to line the bluffs above the Spokane River. No one among the newly rich lived in mining towns like Wallace or Rossland; all that was necessary was to nurture profits from mining the ore. Those who could afford to live in Portland did so; others settled for Spokane. Elegantly bustled and beruffled wives, who ordered their clothes from Paris, called on one another by carriage, while husbands puffed cigars and gestated deals. (Also see NORTHPORT, p. 46.)

The mines affected Spokane's wealthy elite and built the mansions but were not the whole of the city's economy. "Working stiffs" flowed in and out more in accord with the demands of the logging camps and mills than of the mines. They formed a customer base for boardinghouses, clothing stores, saloons, barbershops, and employment agencies. Labor organizers, especially among the Industrial Workers of the World, recruited members and staged street-corner rallies urging reform within a stratified society and protesting kickbacks at the hiring halls, unsanitary living conditions and poor food at the camps, and the unwillingness of company managers to deal with unions. (See WASHINGTON WOBBLIES sidebar, p. 255.)

A "China Alley" developed behind the old city hall at Howard and Front (now Spokane Falls Boulevard). Italians lived in the Liberty Park area, blacks a little north of the Italians (and for a few years, beginning in 1910, also at Deer Lake, where they arrived as a colony from Midwest cities intending to demonstrate Booker T. Washington's philosophy that blacks could gain power through owning and farming land). Union Park and Peaceful Valley were strongholds for Finns, Irish, and other immigrant groups clinging together in a new land. Jewish businessmen and professionals lived in large, comfortable homes south of Browne's Addition mansions. And elite families who could afford ever more opulent homes moved to Summit Avenue overlooking Natatorium Park at the northwest side of town; to Sumner on the ramparts above the central district; and out past the country club on the Little Spokane River. Glover had dreamed well.

For the best look at remnants from these early days, sample downtown Spokane on foot, walking both at street level and along the pedestrian "skywalk" network that connects 15 blocks (including parking garages at Main and Howard and also at Lincoln and Spokane Falls Boulevard). Either on foot or by car, also sample the gracious neighborhoods where city elite from James Glover to D. C. Corbin and Patrick Clark lived. And for a look at Spokane's unique setting, drive along the river northwest of the city, winding among basalt outcrops and ponderosa pine (Aubrey White Parkway), and also to the Indian Canyon municipal golf course (S. 1000 Assembly at West Drive) for an overview of the city (especially striking as viewed from the balcony of the clubhouse, a public building complete with snack bar).

East of the city, visit the Riblet Mansion (see p. 17) for a 300-degree view of the Spokane Valley. To the north, drive along the Little Spokane River to enjoy spring wild flowers or fall color interspersed with modern houses—or at any time of year for a look at the distinctive texture of the Spokane area.

(For sites connected with 1858 battles between Native Americans and the U.S. Army see individual entries for BATTLE OF SPOKANE PLAINS, p. 4; FOUR LAKES, p. 6; Hangman Creek under SPANGLE, p. 9; and HORSE SLAUGHTER CAMP, p. 7; also see SPOKANE BATTLES sidebar, p. 10.)

Late-1800s army posts such as Fort Wright incorporated suburban qualities in their design.

Points of interest, keyed to the Spokane map:

1 Today's **City Hall** (W. 808 Spokane Falls Boulevard; built in 1929) represents a fine example of adaptive reuse of a building, in this case a former Montgomery Ward store turned into municipal offices. The architecture is a particularly ornamented version of the company's stock design. From the skywalk, notice the Art Deco floral motifs, hand-painted in pastel shades of red, blue, and yellow.

2 In some ways **Riverfront Park** (Spokane Falls Boulevard) epitomizes Spokane. The city began along the riverbank and burgeoned as railroads arrived, but by the mid-1900s trackside squalor had cut off commercial and civic activity from the river and the north side of the city. In 1974 Spokane cleared derelict buildings and readied the river site for a world's fair, leaving only the 155-foot clock tower from the Great Northern depot (built in 1902) as a symbolic monument.

As a souvenir of the fair itself, the lacy structural skeleton of the U.S. Pavilion now houses amusement rides and winter ice skating. Near it the wooden, hand-sculpted horses of a 1909 merry-go-round brought here from the erstwhile Natatorium Park still invite reaching for the brass ring.

3 The **Levy Block** (N. 118 Stevens; built in 1892) represents Spokane's brick and masonry reconstruction immediately following the devastating 1889 fire. The technology of the time required walls to be thicker at the base, tapering as they rose. This limited the height that was practical for buildings.

4 The **Old National Bank** (W. 422 Riverside; built in 1910) rises to 15 stories clad with lightweight, gleaming white terra-cotta. The noted Chicago architect Daniel Burnham used steel framing, still a somewhat new technique, especially in the West. Its strength allowed openings for the many windows that gave light and ventilation.

5 The **Fernwell Building** (W. 503 Riverside; built in 1890) is a true cast-iron storefront building, a product of the transition from masonry construction to the use of structural steel. An iron front carried the weight of upper-story masonry walls while allowing street-level display windows and a wide entry-way. Notice the manufacturer's plate on this building: "National Iron Works, Spokane Falls."

6 Observe the **Sherwood Building** (W. 510 Riverside; enlarged in 1916) from across the street to study the full decorative detail. Spokane's premier architect, Kirtland Cutter, wove Gothic elements into a basically Chicago-style building: pointed arches provide an overall motif; terra-cotta gargoyles guard the door; lions and griffins accent the corners of both the roof and the street level. Construction features steel framing with a concrete facade.

7 The Classic Revival **Hutton Building** (S. 7 Howard; built in 1907; three more stories added in 1910) is listed in the National Register of Historic Places. It is equally prominent in the hearts of Spokanites. May Arkwright Hutton and her husband Levi (nicknamed Al) financed this building and bought the Fernwell Block soon after arriving in the city. May had worked as a cook at a Coeur d'Alene mining town, Al was a narrow-gauge railroad engineer. They struck storybook wealth in silver by grubstaking the miner who happened to find the Hercules "glory hole," the richest ore of the entire district.

Polite society could not ignore the newcomers—the Huttons had too much money—but neither did society accept a couple so obviously of the "working class." May campaigned noisily for women's right to vote, and in 1910 Washington added such an amendment to the state constitution; a decade later federal law followed suit. Poor as children (Al was an orphan, May came from a fatherless home), the Huttons also poured energy and wealth into labor union causes and into helping unwed mothers and homeless children.

8 The Art Deco **City Ramp Parking Garage** (W. 430 First; built in 1928) was built at the east end of the downtown district in response to construction at the west end, which threatened to draw away customers. Actually the garage was ahead of its time; parking on the street was not yet a problem. The building is of cast concrete, Spokane's first use of "slip forms." This was a new technique that made it possible to pour concrete one section at a time by simply moving along the form for each additional section. The result was an integral joining impossible with mortar, which deteriorates as it weathers.

9 In designing the **Davenport Hotel** (W. 808 Sprague; begun in 1914), Kirtland Cutter successfully incorporated several styles. By the time of its construction he had honed his imagination and experience as an architect—and Spokane had honed its taste and finances. The result is a cosmopolitan gem.

Cutter drew plans for a flamboyant Mission-style restaurant for Louis Davenport in 1902. A decade later Davenport commissioned him to build an adjoining hotel. Its lobby fairly dripped with detail: greenery, caged birds, aquariums, elaborately "sculpted" (plaster) beams, rams' heads, and knights' helmets. Beyond, were—and are—a Bourbon dining room, a Venetian ducal hall, a Tudor chamber, a Turkish bath, and a mirrored ballroom. A basement flophouse accommodated down-and-outers with a meal and a blanket, and guest rooms cosseted such luminaries as John F. Kennedy, Dwight Eisenhower, Theodore Roosevelt, Haile Selassie, and Mahatma Gandhi.

Spokanites and people throughout the Inland Empire remember the hotel for its Friday afternoon tea dances with a live orchestra and its lavish Sunday morning champagne brunches. But fond memory and sound economics are not the same. Cut off from Riverfront Park and the business-district skywalk system, the Davenport closed in 1984. Expectations are to reopen it as a modern luxury hotel. First to be renovated and opened are the magnificent lobby and the Isabella and Marie Antoinette rooms.

10 The red brick **Review Building** with its five-story corner tower (W. 927 Riverside; completed in 1891) stands as a beloved landmark, although the tower, with its grand view of the city and the river, is no longer open to the public owing to possible liability suits. The *Review* began in 1883 when Frank Dallam arrived from California. Ten years later it merged with the *Spokesman* as a means of financial survival for both papers. Middle floors of the building originally served as apartments.

11 **Riverside Avenue**'s sweeping crescent is graced with stately buildings designed by different architectural firms, in varying styles, over a period of nearly 30 years, yet all in splendid harmony. Street plantings and a grassy median strip with linden trees and traffic islands with statuary add a parklike quality.

Spokane

Key to Numbered Locations

1	City Hall
2	Riverfront Park
3	Levy Block
4	Old National Bank
5	Fernwell Building
6	Sherwood Building
7	Hutton Building
8	City Ramp Parking Garage
9	Davenport Hotel
10	Spokesman Review Building
11	Riverside Avenue
12	Monroe Street Bridge
13	Spokane County Courthouse
14	Flour Mill
15	Broadview Dairy
16	Gonzaga University
17	Royal Riblet Estate
18	Saint John's Cathedral
19	James Glover Mansion
20	D. C. Corbin Mansion
21	Undercliffe
22	Austin Corbin House
23	Patrick Clark House
24	Fotheringham House
25	Campbell House/Cheney Cowles Museum
26	Peaceful Valley
27	Fort George Wright
28	Jamieson Frequency Changing Station

Before 1900 Spokane's main architectural interest had been in commercial buildings and showplace homes for the wealthy. In contrast, buildings along this part of Riverside Avenue belong to the city's religious and social life. On the north side of the street, conveniently close to the Monroe Street Bridge, is the Georgian Revival **Spokane Club** (built in 1910). The club was organized in 1890 for men only, a retreat for camaraderie and behind-the-scenes decisions. Escorted women could enter only through the lower-level door leading to the main dining room, a requirement that kept them safely apart from such masculine retreats as the smoking lounge and paneled library.

The **Chamber of Commerce Building**

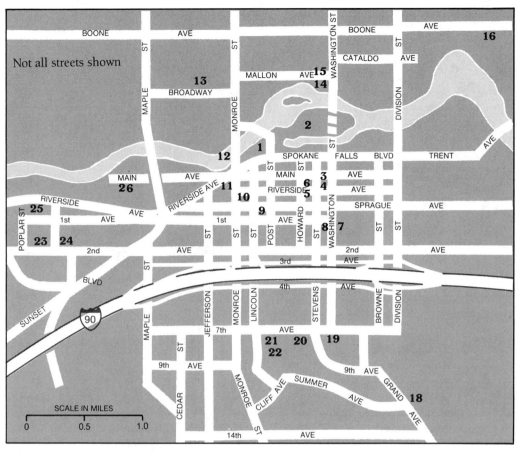

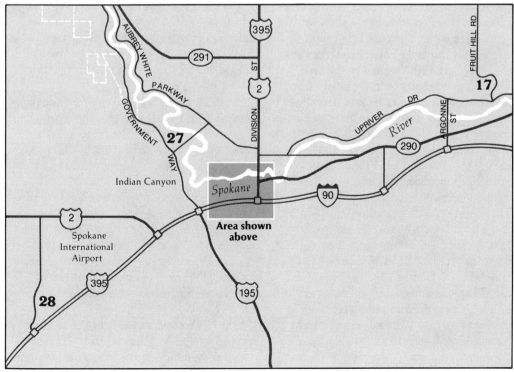

Riverside Avenue's historic district architecture epitomizes early-1900s City Beautiful ideals.

(opened in 1933) stands next to the Spokane Club. At the top of its columns notice the rather romantic and stereotypical masks of Native American chiefs. Its tile roof echoes the copper alloy roof of the grand **Elks Club** building to the west (begun in 1919), separated from the Chamber of Commerce Building by the even more grand **Masonic Temple** (begun in 1905, enlarged in 1925). Magnificently colonnaded, the Masonic Temple curves along the avenue for 222 feet. Its gray cast stone harmonizes with the gray cut stone of the adjoining Elks Club.

At the west end of the curve stands the French Second Empire **Smith Funeral Home** (now closed), built with apartments on its second and third stories. Farther west, the San Marco apartment building (dating from 1904) of buff-colored brick provided additional fashionable housing. Near it the Classic Revival **Carnegie library** (opened in 1905; now used for offices) completed the architectural elegance of the avenue's outside curve. Facing these stately buildings on the inside of the curve are **Our Lady of Lourdes Cathedral** (begun in 1902) and the Catholic diocese chancery (built in 1924 as the Great Northwest Life Insurance Building).

The entire group of buildings is listed in the National Register as a historic district.

12 Walk onto the **Monroe Street Bridge** (completed in 1911) for a vantage point above the seasonal white thunder of Spokane Falls (most dramatic in spring). An 1889 wooden

bridge here was replaced in 1891 with a cantilevered steel bridge, which developed such a severe tremor that elephants leading the 1907 circus parade refused to cross, a well-publicized indication of a need for replacement. Kiosks along the sidewalks of the resulting concrete-arch bridge include decorative terra-cotta bison skulls designed by Kirtland Cutter as symbols of the frontier, and plaques listing dates and personages from David Thompson in 1811 to J. Downing and S. Scranton in 1871. Immediately upriver from the bridge, notice the brick **Washington Water Power Company substation,** another Kirtland Cutter building (dating from 1909).

Ideally, from the north side of the Monroe Street Bridge, circle to the east and recross the river via Riverfront Park footbridges. The **Upper Falls Power Plant** (built in 1922) stands at the site of the 1871 sawmill purchased by city founder James Glover.

13 The wondrous **Spokane County Court-house** (W. 1116 Broadway; built in 1895, altered in 1953 and 1973) is the Chateau-style product of Willis Ritchie, apparently self-trained as an architect through correspondence courses. Splendidly turreted and ornamented, the exterior delights the eye. Inside, all original character has been lost.

In 1881 Cheney had won election as county seat and forcefully abducted records and the county auditor himself one night when most of

Spokane's elite were at a wedding dance. Six years and a new election later, Spokane regained the honor—and the records.

14 Spokane's brick **Flour Mill** (W. 621 Mallon; built in 1895, remodeled as shops and restaurants in 1974) sits directly above the middle falls. The building was saved as a landmark during the clearing and revitalization of the riverbank in connection with Expo 74.

For its first five years after completion the mill stood idle, tied up in legal suits and countersuits that carried to the state supreme court. Operation finally began in 1901.

15 The **Broadview Dairy** (Washington and Mallon) began operation in 1897. It is one of the state's oldest continually operating dairies, a functioning remnant of a type of enterprise once fundamental to Washington's economy. Allen H. Flood came to Spokane from Maine in 1889 right after the city's devastating fire. He moved to the outskirts; did some surveying; operated a lumber business; then started a dairy herd and milk business. He was the first commercial dairyman in the state to get rid of cows that tested positive for tuberculosis and was also a pioneer in urging the pasteurization of milk regionwide. In 1910 he bought the brick dairy warehouse that still serves as a processing and distribution center.

A viewing room permits watching today's commercial operation, and displays range from the nostalgia of to-your-door milk delivery to how cows' multiple stomachs work. A winery in the same building is open for tours and tasting.

16 **Gonzaga University** (E. 502 Boone; established in 1877) began just ten years after Father Joseph Cataldo had opened Saint Michael's Mission. Jesuits had planned on a school for native boys, but white Spokane families wanted education for their boys—and somehow Gonzaga never served its original intent. Classes opened with just eight students. The stately **administration building** (1903) and **Saint Aloysius Church** (1909) are points of interest on today's campus along with the **Crosby Library,** which exhibits memorabilia of Bing Crosby, Gonzaga's best-known alumnus.

17 The **Royal Riblet** estate (4505 Fruithill; built in 1925) has become a winery, its mansion restored and used by winery guests and rented for private special occasions. The grounds are open to the public daily and in themselves convey a sense of the earlier sumptuous living here. Landscaping includes a rock and cement croquet court, a lawn checkerboard, and a basalt swimming pool. The estate is perched dramatically at the edge of a cliff overlooking the Spokane Valley. Royal Riblet was an inventor, as was his brother Byron, from whom he was estranged. It was Byron who invented the tram mechanism used for ski lifts and still manufactured by the Riblet Company.

To reach the mansion/winery, follow Upriver Drive northeast from the Gonzaga University area, or drive 1½ miles north of I-90 on Argonne, turn east for 1 mile on Upriver Drive, then north again up the hill on Fruithill, and continue for less than a mile to the grounds and parking lot. The site of historic **Plante's Ferry** is within 2 miles of the Riblet Mansion. (See p. 8.)

18 **Saint John's Cathedral** (E. 127 12th; begun in 1925, completed in 1954) achieves an effortless, upswept effect though it is built of stone. Rich detail inside and out ranges from an almost lacy Gothic tower to exquisite stained glass and heraldic shields representing the historical development of the Episcopal church.

Fine homes of eras from the 1890s to the present surround the cathedral, their winding streets a part of the City Beautiful plan designed for Spokane by the Olmsted Brothers, renowned landscape architects. Part of the land for **Manito Park** (17th and Grand) was given to the city by Jay P. Graves, who made a fortune from the British Columbia mines, then organized the Spokane and Inland Empire Railway. The park's exotic lilac garden, rose garden, formal sunken garden, and Japanese garden are justly famed. Prosaic, but evocative of the past, is the original watering trough for horses (just off Grand Avenue), one of two remaining in Spokane. The other is at Fort George Wright.

19 **James Glover**'s 22-room, half-timbered mansion with a broad view of the entire Spokane Valley (W. 321 Eighth; built in 1888), is now the manse of a Unitarian church. It was the first opulent home Kirtland Cutter designed in Spokane, somehow fitting since Glover was literally the city's first resident. Its splendor assured Cutter as the architect of choice for anyone planning a mansion. When built, the house stood outside the city, accessible by a pine-shaded lane along the base of basalt cliffs.

The Panic of 1893 broke Glover financially; he mortgaged his $100,000 mansion for $30,000 to the Hypotheekbank, which foreclosed. (The house he then moved into still stands at W. 1725 First Avenue.) At the time of the Panic, Spokane's population had reached 20,000. By only a decade later it had quintupled.

20   **Daniel C. Corbin** selected a fine hillside site and built a huge, yet austere, home (W. 507 Seventh; completed in 1898). Kirtland Cutter served as architect; at the time he was Corbin's son-in-law, a relationship ended by divorce. To save money Corbin left the third floor unfinished, used ordinary brass hardware for door knobs and other fittings, and chose plain glass for the windows—simple touches unusual in a mansion. His rolltop desk sat in the huge living room along with a billiard table.

D. C. Corbin, a New Yorker, first built a railroad serving the Coeur d'Alene mines, then took a contract to build the Spokane Falls and Northern Railroad along the upper Columbia. That brought him to Spokane. The home of E. J. Roberts, his indispensable engineer who laid out the railways and supervised construction, still stands in Browne's Addition at W. 1923 First Avenue. Corbin's house is now owned by the Spokane Parks Department and used as an arts and crafts center.

21   **Undercliffe** (W. 701 Seventh; built in 1896) was the home of F. Lewis Clark, who made a fortune first in speculating in Spokane real estate, then in milling flour, and finally by gaining control of the Last Chance mine (albeit through a banking maneuver and without even so much as visiting the mine). Notice the landscaping behind the house where head-high "beehive" outcrops that look like volcanic plugs are incorporated into a seemingly "wilderness" garden. A rustic stone gatehouse and rock rubble wall further carry out the theme. The home is now part of an office complex and publicly accessible.

22   The **Austin Corbin House** (W. 815 Seventh; completed in 1898) was known throughout Spokane for its splendor and lavish parties—doubtless to the chagrin of Austin's penny-pinching father, D. C. Corbin, living just two houses to the east. From huge fluted

columns to arched windows with spiderweb leading, the house is a visual feast. Now an office building, it affords some public access. Decorative exterior friezes are echoed inside by similar treatments above foyer doorways, and the grand staircase, with its polished banister, still sweeps elegantly toward the door.

23   The **Patrick Clark House** (W. 2208 Second; built in 1898) has become a restaurant (and diners are welcome to tour the premises beyond their own table). Mining gave Clark his fortune. Irish by birth, he came to the United States in 1870 at age 20. He built the house while in his 40s, which coincided with a period of Spokane's growth and the flowering of its wealthy class. Clark lived up to his status by commissioning architect Kirtland Cutter to build his house. He even sent Cutter abroad to gather furnishings and inspiration.

The result is a three-and-a-half-story extravaganza of buff-colored brick with a red "tile" roof that actually is fabricated of metal. The architecture suggests Spanish and Moorish influences, with rounded corner towers and arched loggias. For interior appointments, Cutter apparently turned to the East Coast firm of Louis Tiffany. Onyx fireplaces, carved stucco ceilings, elaborate lamps and chandeliers, and 14-foot stained-glass windows in the stairwell create the desired opulence.

Yet in the 1970s the house barely escaped demolition. The new owners knew they could sell its furnishings for more than they had paid for the whole house, but they (successfully) held out for a city zoning exemption to allow converting the venerable mansion to a restaurant. Authorities agreed in 1981, providing parking problems were solved and that neither interior nor exterior was altered to the detriment of its historic value.

24   The **Fortheringham House** (W. 2124 Second; built in 1891), across the side street from Patsy Clark's, is where the Clark family lived while their mansion was under construction. It now offers bed-and-breakfast lodging. Across from it, **Coeur d'Alene Park** dates from 1891 and the time of ladies in crinolines carrying parasols.

25   Visit the grand **Amasa Campbell House** (W. 2316 first; built in 1898) and the adjoining **Cheney Cowles Memorial Museum** of the

Eastern Washington Historical Society for insight into the development of the region from prehistoric native life to Spokane's Age of Elegance. In the Campbell House, Oriental carpets feel thick underfoot, the hall clock chimes in mellow tones, the bubbling of a Chinese fountain carries musically into the sun porch, master bedroom windows look out across the river—and the house as a whole seems dark and remarkably closed-in compared with today's glassy construction and brilliant lighting fixtures.

26   **Peaceful Valley** is a workingman's residential district at the edge of elegant Browne's Addition. Here contractors built rental houses with kitchen, living room, and two bedrooms plus a toilet perhaps in the house, perhaps out back, and a dirt basement. The houses—many of them little changed—are now occupied mostly by owners rather than tenants. (An easy way to reach this neighborhood is by driving down the hill on Main Avenue, immediately behind the Riverside Avenue Historic District.)

27   **Fort George Wright** (W. Randolph Road) opened in 1897 as a replacement for Fort Spokane. Among its first troops was a regiment of blacks assigned in 1899 when fort buildings consisted of little more than a single barracks. The men had come from service at the Coeur d'Alene mines where they quelled labor violence and from duty in Montana arresting members of "Coxey's Army" en route to Washington, D.C., to protest unemployment. The troops had also served as a Bicycle Corps, sent as a test first from Fort Missoula to Yellowstone National Park, then from Fort Missoula to St. Louis, only to have the War Department decide against forming such a "wheeled cavalry."

As a means of expanding the city's economic base after the fire of 1889 and the financial depression of 1893, Spokane businessmen lobbied earnestly for establishment of the fort. Partly for comfort and partly to protect slate roofs, Quartermaster Captain W. H. Miller carefully oriented buildings away from prevailing winds. The fort remained an active post until 1958. Present use is as a Japanese-operated center providing an American cultural experience and intensive English instruction for Japanese women students.

The grounds are open at all times and well

The Clark mansion in Browne's Addition is now open to the public as a restaurant.

worth visiting for a step back to a time when regimental posts enjoyed a strong social link with the nearby community. The old commons and chapel buildings are used on special occasions. Plans call for restoring **Saint Michael's Mission,** a small wooden church building that sits quietly among the pines at the northern end of the fort grounds. Originally the mission stood across the river on a site that now hosts a housing development. The mission, too, will eventually be open to the public.

28   The **Jamieson Frequency Changing Station** of the Washington Water Power Company stands—appropriately—on Electric Avenue, near the Spokane International Airport (take Exit 272 off I-90 and turn east on Geiger, north on Hayford, then east for about a mile on 53rd). The building served as a substation from 1905 to 1922, then changed to use as a taxidermy, a House of Horrors, and Spokane's most popular Halloween "haunted house." Another frequency changing station, once owned by the Spokane and Inland Empire Electric Railway, stands near Liberty Park in southeast Spokane (E. 1421 Celestra). A handsome brick structure dating from 1908, this substation has been rehabilitated into townhouse apartments.

Washington's early power installations developed to supply the demands of interurban railroads; households used electricity for only a few hours of light in the evening, and industry had not yet developed. "Changing stations" were needed because electricity cannot be transmitted over long distances as direct current. The stations stepped down the incoming high-voltage alternating current that electric railroad engines, cable cars, and trolleys ran on, changing it to the much lower-voltage direct current needed for urban use.

Appropriately, Spokane's 1930s milk-bottle buildings began as ice cream parlors (W. 820 Garland and S. 321 Cedar)

SPOKANE HOUSE began as an early 1800s fur-trading post (not to be confused with the U.S. Army's Fort Spokane; see p. 41). No buildings remain at the site, which is within Riverside State Park (three-fourths of a mile north of the community of Nine Mile Falls). A state park interpretive center is usually open in summer. Wooden posts outline where fort buildings stood. The grave of North West Company trader Jaco Finlay is near the southeast corner of the fort, marked by a concrete slab.

Three separate companies operated here beginning with Spokane House in 1810, the earliest fur-trading post in the state. Jaco Finlay and Finan McDonald of the Montreal-based North West Company picked the site, at the confluence of the Spokane and Little Spokane rivers. It was the company's fourth post, following Kootanae House, Saleesh House, and Kullyspell House to the north and east (out of Washington). After two years the rival Pacific Fur Company opened a competing post only about a half mile from Spokane House, naming it Fort Spokane. Their motive in settling so close was for mutual protection in case of a tribal uprising, an unnecessary precaution.

The following fall, the American-owned Pacific Fur Company decided to close their entire Northwest trade. Using ocean vessels to provision posts and collect furs had proved to be less effective than the overland operations of rival firms. The Pacific Fur Company sold to the North West Company, and the Canadians moved into their rival's more commodious post. There they continued to trade with Spokane natives until that company, too, went out of business in 1821, absorbed by their more powerful competitor, the Hudson's Bay Company.

Soon after that event, George Simpson, Hudson's Bay Company governor, moved operations from Fort Spokane to Fort Colvile, a new post at Kettle Falls. Trade with the Spokane had fallen off, leading the chief factor to comment in 1823 that the Spokane "do not bring us One hundred Skins in the Course of the Year." By 1826 men had transferred every potentially valuable article to the new post, including even iron door hinges. Jaco Finlay remained but no longer traded. He was married to a local native woman, as was customary among Canadian traders.

SPOKANE RESERVATION. (See p. 48.)

TSHIMAKAIN MISSION (Chim´-uh-ken), located near today's community of Ford, was abandoned in 1848. The two couples who built it knew they had achieved little either in winning converts to Christianity or in convincing native people to settle down as farmers. Even so, Cushing Eells and Elkanah Walker and their wives might well sigh over today's total disappearance of their 10-year effort. Only a lilac bush endures as a possible physical remnant from the mission. A granite shaft marks the approximate mission site (east side of the highway just beyond the north edge of Ford).

In 1838 Protestant missionaries Eells and Walker arrived at Tshimakain ("Place of the Springs"), a major camping place on the trail between Walla Walla and the Upper Columbia River. Archibald MacDonald, trader at the Hudson's Bay Company post at Fort Colvile, had recommended the site. The earnest young couples experienced little except discomfort and discouragement during their first few years. In 1842 Henry Spalding, visiting from his mission at Lapwai, Idaho, wrote:

Messrs Walkers and Eells have done almost nothing in the way of building or farming (Mr. W. being a very feeble man). [They] live in very inconvenient cabins and pack their [provisions] from the station of Messrs. Gray and Whitman, a distance of 160 miles.

Visiting again the following year, Spalding found an adobe house, "well finished," and a blacksmith shop. A flour mill had recently burned. Spokane native people accepted the Eellses and Walkers well, and the missionaries, in turn, tried to "improve" life for their followers. This included an effort to stop their seasonal migrations, for how could instruction be effective among people who did not stay at one place long enough to hear successive lessons?

Farming seemed an answer, but it never really succeeded despite the fact that Walker was the only one of the Congregational and Presbyterian missionaries in Washington and Idaho who had a farm background. Gathering roots and berries, fishing, and hunting were basic to tribal culture and, though native people added grain fields and potato patches to these traditional food sources, they felt no urge to change their timeless pattern. Furthermore, the Tshimakain farm was largely a failure. Summer drought caused trouble. So did killing frosts, which came even in August. Fields were not fenced until the spring of 1843—a huge job—and cattle and horses often ruined crops by grazing.

Nonetheless, the missionaries preached and set an example as best they could. They learned to speak Spokan, a Salish language, and translated a primer, which was printed at the Lapwai Mission, as an aid to teaching natives to read and write. Then trouble overwhelmed the Eells and Walker households. In 1847 hundreds of native people died of measles, and many blamed whites for the tragic toll. In addition, that year's winter brought severe flooding and cold, which devastated livestock throughout the region. Worst of all, disillusioned and angry Cayuse men killed Marcus and Narcissa Whitman and others at the Waiilatpu Mission, near Walla Walla. The following spring, the Eells and Walker families left Tshimakain for the Willamette Valley. Their mission never re-opened. Ironically, the site is now a successful farm.

(Also see WHITMAN MISSION, p. 186.)

WAUKON. (See under CHENEY, p. 6.)

Pend Oreille Valley

Entering Washington from Idaho, the Pend Oreille River (Pahn-do-ray′) flows north through a bucolic valley formed by the silting-in of an ice-age lake. North of the valley, the river continues through a deep mountain gorge as a raging torrent. The name is said to come from the French vernacular *pendant d'oreille,* "earring," a designation given to natives who wore shell ornaments in their ears. No evidence bears out such a custom among the people of this region, however. Why the name came to be applied here is unknown.

Several dams now supply hydropower for the region, and a major irrigation project nearly went in near Newport instead of at Grand Coulee. Railroad buffs will enjoy the spectacular Idaho and Washington Northern Railroad trestle at Box Canyon north of Ione; also the annual excursion aboard the Pend Oreille Railway (inquire through the county historical society at Newport). Historical society museums are at Newport and Tiger.

The Pend Oreille drive is ideal in the fall when trees have turned golden, their glow bright enough to illumine even a gray day. A Kalispel Salish Fair held each August draws Native Americans from British Columbia, Idaho, Montana, and Oregon as well as Washington. It is open to the public.

BOUNDARY DAM. (See under METALINE FALLS, p. 26.)

In 1903 **CUSICK** (Kew′-sik) opened its post office, a mark of success for any pioneering community. Choosing the name was easy: the Cusick brothers, Joe and Frank, owned and operated a fleet of five Pend Oreille River stern-wheelers, which carried freight, passengers, and mail. About 1910 trains largely replaced steamboats. Only the Cusicks' luxurious *Ione* continued in service, popular for its dining and dancing amid spectacular mountain scenery.

The rail connection to outside markets brought prosperity as men fed virgin white pine into the saws of successive lumber mills. Local forest giants, nearly the size of western Washington's Douglas fir, became literal

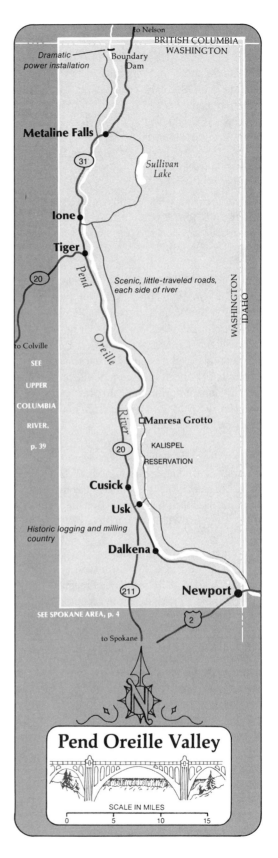

Pend Oreille Valley

SCALE IN MILES

0   5   10   15

matchsticks after the Diamond Match Company bought the mill of lumber baron Burton Willis about 1920. Match-company operation continued until 1961.

Little remains of the vast log booms that once floated on the river, sorted and positioned by steam tugs and sturdy men in logger's boots. Hundreds of mooring piles now line the river, utterly useless. They stretch for a mile. The present economy depends on construction work and local service companies plus newsprint and aluminum fabricating plants.

DALKENA (Dal-ken′-uh) today consists of a false-fronted building with faded white paint, a handful of homes, and proud memories; but until the 1930s a bustling railway depot here handled passengers and freight, and a huge mill whirred and hummed. River pilings testify to hundreds of thousands of logs supplied to local mills for decades. The concrete foundation of the last mill now sprawls between highway and river, a mute symbol.

Rapacious logging exhausted the forest, although the highway now winds through second-growth pine, fir, and red cedar interspersed with larch, aspen, and paper birch (which is rare in Washington overall, but present from near Tiger, north). Large-scale logging began near the end of the nineteenth century when Great Lakes lumbermen began to eye the Northwest after having turned their own forests into board feet. Among these men were Henry Dalton and Hugh Kennedy, who picked a hamlet called Glencoe as the site for a new company town. They built a large sawmill and decided on Dalkena as the name, a combination of the first syllables of their own names.

Administrative offices, two bunkhouses, a cookhouse, and a general store rose beside the railroad tracks. Surveyors laid out three city blocks to accommodate businesses and homes. The company also sold 20-acre lots on the outskirts of town to millworkers who attempted ranching while also working shifts. The mill whistle told men when to get up in the morning,

Snow let early loggers skid out pine and larch from northeastern forests.

Spokane architect Kirtland Cutter designed the home of Metaline Falls's town founder.

when to report for work, break for lunch, end the day—or work the night shift. Occasionally its shriek signaled fire, a dreaded occurrence that brought devastating loss. The flames of the 1910 "Great Blowup" not only roared through the forest but destroyed much of the town as well.

At its peak, the Dalkena mill spewed out lumber at a rate of 100,000 board feet per shift.

IONE (Eye-ohn′) was larger than Metaline Falls for years, but this no longer is true. Commercial buildings still line the main street downtown, however, and an old school struggles to belong to the present.

Steamers began tying up at the landing here in the late 1880s, although regularly scheduled stops waited until after a post office opened in 1896. In 1910 an engineer from England located nearby limestone suitable for making cement and opened a plant, which operated only a few years.

Until the late 1930s, lumber poured from Ione mills, one of which was the biggest and best equipped in northeast Washington. That mill,

which belonged to the Panhandle Lumber Company, has been replaced by a smaller mill on the same site.

North of Ione about 4½ miles, pull off into an informal picnic area to view Box Canyon, spanned by the Idaho and Washington Northern railroad trestle.

The **KALISPEL RESERVATION** actually dates from 1914 but, in a sense, its story begins 70 years earlier with the arrival of Jesuits who were the native peoples' first steady contact with whites. Fur trappers had come through the region earlier but never stayed. The Jesuits founded Saint Ignatius Mission in the Pend Oreille Valley in the 1840s. Then, because of severe winters and poor agricultural prospects— and to be nearer the main group the Jesuits hoped to serve—they decided in 1854 to move their followers to Montana. Many families who went soon drifted back.

Left out of nineteenth-century treaty negotiations, Kalispel people received no reservation land, yet refused to leave traditional territory. Hoping to gain time, they simply withdrew to the part of their land they most wanted to hold and lived by hunting, fishing, digging roots, and farming. They were poor, but at home. Finally President Woodrow Wilson signed an order granting the Kalispel 4,629 acres as a reservation. Within it individuals were to select their own 40-acre allotments. That land policy, begun in the late 1880s, was intended to turn natives into citizen-farmers "like everybody else."

Kalispel people have preferred, however, to succeed as tribally oriented individuals. They buy up individual allotments that come onto the market so as to return as much land as possible to communal ownership.

The tribe now owns a bison herd as a source of meat, reminder of bygone hunting trips to the Great Plains, and a possible asset for tourist development. They also own the aluminum fabricating plant at Cusick, and they encourage the employment of Native Americans at the newsprint plant. Decades of shaky economics seem to be stabilizing.

MANRESA GROTTO, a natural rock shelter, has five rows of flat stones arranged as seats facing a simple altar of mortared rock. Since the mid-1800s, Kalispel people have held services here, a practice that still continues with an annual Easter Mass. The missionary priest Pierre Jean DeSmet named the grotto for a famous cave near Barcelona, Spain, in which Saint Ignatius (founder of the Jesuit order) had meditated before writing his treatise "Spiritual Exercises."

The main grotto, about 60 feet long by 25 feet deep and high, is hollowed out of conglomerate rock. Smaller caves are nearby. Apparently wind-driven waves lapping a huge glacial lake formed the caves by splashing against the cliff and enlarging breaks already weathered and eroded into the rock.

To reach Manresa Grotto, cross the bridge at Usk, then drive north for about 6 miles on LeClerc Road (paved), passing Our Lady of Sorrows, a high-steepled white and blue chapel built in 1914 by Father Edward Griva. A steep path leads 100 yards from a parking area to the grotto, which is on the east side of the road. The quiet river valley and distant mountains seen from Manresa "chapel" appear timeless. A

rough trail to the top of the cliff offers a still more sweeping view.

(Also see KALISPEL RESERVATION, p. 24.)

The town of **METALINE FALLS** (Met´-uh-leen) slumbered until 1910 when F. A. Blackwell built his Idaho and Washington Northern Railroad. Activity and population then shot up. They have held fairly steady ever since, although many downtown buildings now stand forlornly empty. Potential customers are too readily lured elsewhere by today's ease of automobile travel.

Metaline Falls always was a predominantly one-industry town: cement. Massive silos still loom skyward, symbols of what once provided a fairly stable financial base. The cement also spewed out powdery dust, which all but forced

A cement plant provided a steady payroll for Metaline Falls beginning in the early 1900s.

residents to use a weak muriatic acid solution when washing their cars; otherwise, the accumulated dust hardens disastrously into cement when wet by rain or snow. A multistoried dormitory near the cement plant is mostly empty now, but rows of workers' cottages remain, very much lived-in. Their facades have changed over the decades, but several still show the original stucco ground floor topped by a small, shingled upper story.

The spacious 1910 home of Lewis P. Larson, Danish immigrant and founder of the town, overlooks the river (at Fifth and Pend Oreille). Designed by renowned Spokane architect Kirtland Cutter, the facade is shingle combined with cobblestones from the river. At the opposite end of Fifth (next to the railroad track) is the Washington Hotel, which Larson built as the start of the town's commercial district. Its steam heat and readily available porter service made it a marvel in its day. Both the hotel and the Larson house are in the National Register of Historic Places.

Larson, and others, persuaded the Idaho and Washington Northern to lay track as far north as Metaline Falls. That assured, the Portland Cement Company built a plant and employed 400 workers. For power, they dammed Sullivan Lake (6 miles east of town; worth visiting for its setting at the base of glaciated peaks). The installation demonstrated the promise of its era: a bright future for all, through technology.

North of Metaline Falls a high overlook gives a striking view of rugged "Z" Canyon and Boundary Dam. (Follow State Route 31, then turn off on a marked, 2-mile side road.)

On the west side of the river, a side road winds toward Crawford State Park (a limestone cavern; tours only in summer), and a branch from that road leads to **Boundary Dam,** which is a Seattle City Light installation. First proposed in 1914, actually completed in 1967, the dam rises 340 feet and spans a deep canyon. That much looks as a dam "should." The rest could be from a James Bond movie. A tunnel 76 feet wide and 477 feet long penetrates the solid rock of a towering cliff and, below a glassed-in display area, six throbbing turbines drive generators. Their electricity goes to a Bonneville Power Administration substation for distribution through the Northwest power grid.

NEWPORT has a divided background: it started in Idaho, yet is a county seat in Washington. Further confusion comes from the position of the state boundary, which was determined longitudinally, not topographically by following the river.

The Idaho town began in 1889 as a small store near what now is the western approach to the Pend Oreille River bridge. A year later the store added a post office, and homesteaders met to pick a name. They decided on Newport, confident that steamboat companies would develop a full-fledged port at their town. The next major event came in 1892 when the Great Northern Railway laid track past the store and installed a boxcar as depot. It soon burned, and a replacement depot went up three blocks west—in Washington. A town mushroomed around the new depot, and postal authorities are said to have officially explained that "Newport, Idaho, moved 3,175 feet to Newport, Washington." The original Idaho part of town is now called Oldtown. Newport boomed as mines opened nearby. An 1897 Spokane newspaper article on the town reported:

"Have you heard the latest about what's his name's rock" has taken the place of "good morning" and "that ledge will be alright" is the last [word] at night.

Railway depots predominate Newport's historic architecture, which otherwise leans toward contemporary false fronts layered on top of earlier false fronts. A half-timbered, concrete depot serves as offices for the logging subsidiary of Burlington Northern Railroad. Directly across the tracks, a smaller, brick Idaho and Washington Northern depot now houses the county historical society museum. F. A. Blackwell, already owner of an electric interurban line serving Spokane, Coeur d'Alene, and the Palouse, built the Idaho and Washington Northern to permit shipping lumber from sawmills he had invested in.

For the railway, Blackwell hired 1,500 Italians, Greeks, Bulgarians, and Montenegrins (Yugoslavians) to grade a roadbed and spike steel onto crossties. This led the Newport paper to editorialize that the mix of languages would "make the Tower of Babel wish that it had never posed as one of the wonders of the world." By

1907 the track connected Newport with the main line in Idaho. Three years later it also extended to Metaline Falls, near the Canadian border.

In the 1920s Newport nearly became headquarters for the Columbia Basin Irrigation Project. The Washington legislature funded study of a "gravity flow" system, which called for low dams to increase the size of Idaho's Flathead and Pend Oreille lakes. From there water would follow its natural drainage into Washington via the Clark Fork and Pend Oreille rivers. Near Newport, a dam would control release of water through a 130-mile system of natural lakes plus tunnels, siphons, and canals.

DAVID THOMPSON

David Thompson (1770 to 1857), renowned partner in the North West Company, led a canoe exploration of the Pend Oreille River in 1809, immediately after establishing Kullyspell House on the east shore of Lake Pend Oreille. The following spring he again explored the river, this time investigating whether the Columbia could be reached by water. He gave up at Box Canyon (north of today's community of Ione), however, correctly deciding that north of that point the Pend Oreille really was not suitable for canoe travel.

In 1811 Thompson entered for a third time what became Washington. At Spokane House, which the North West Company had established the previous year, he borrowed horses, then rode to Kettle Falls. There he gave natives British flags as gifts and, with their cooperation, built a large cedar canoe. In it, Thompson started down the Columbia to claim trading rights for the company. With him were five French-Canadian voyageurs, two Iroquois boatmen, and two Sanpoil interpreters.

Disappointment climaxed the effort. Thompson rejoiced at the sight of the ocean but his men, already used to huge Canadian lakes "with high rolling waves" had expected "a more boundless view, a something beyond the power of their senses," Thompson wrote. Still more disappointing was the sight of smoke wafting from four new cabins. *Tonquin,* the supply ship of an American-owned rival—the Pacific Fur Company—had crossed the river bar four months earlier. Thompson commented, perhaps bitterly, that the company had picked a poor location (today's Astoria, Oregon). Furthermore, he judged the quality of their trade goods as "low," probably an accurate assessment, for American trade goods were then inferior to those made in Great Britain, the industrial giant of the era.

Rivalry between the two companies proved short-lived. The *Tonquin* soon sank while trading off Vancouver Island; and uneasiness during the War of 1812 caused the Astoria post to be turned over to the Canadian North West Company.

For David Thompson, the journey to the Pacific ended a quarter century of exploration. He had mapped British Columbia's vast Thompson River, named in his honor; untangled knowledge of the Pend Oreille–Clark Fork drainage; mapped part of the Columbia's confusing headwaters; and found Athabaska Pass, the fur-brigade route between eastern Canada and the Columbia region. Thompson also was the first to map the entire Columbia and the second white man to reach its mouth. (Joseph Howse, a Hudson's Bay Company officer, beat him by a few months.)

Thompson had been reared and educated in a London charity house. He apprenticed to the Hudson's Bay Company at age 14, taught himself mathematics, and learned surveying during winter isolation at a prairie trading post. His Chippewa wife Charlotte and three children often accompanied him on his travels.

The resulting irrigation would turn the thirsty sagebrush lands of Grant, Lincoln, Adams, and Franklin counties into productive farms.

Stormy local debate raged between Spokane interests, which supported the Pend Oreille gravity-flow plan, and Ephrata/Wenatchee interests, which favored a large dam and pumping plant at Grand Coulee. In 1931 the matter was decided. Grand Coulee won.

TIGER now consists of little but a highway junction. Ione—only 4 miles distant—swallowed much of Tiger's identity when good roads and dependable cars lessened the need for hamlets. Homesteader Jennie Wooding, remembering an earlier day, wrote about the trip downriver to Tiger:

[The boat] left Newport once a week on Sunday, if nothing happened to it. The day we started . . . it rained pitchforks and Captain Cusick nailed tin over the worst leaks to keep us from getting drowned. . . . There weren't any docks, but it was high water so the boat pulled right up to the bank and landed us about where Tiger post office was built later on.

South of Tiger (11 miles), a historical marker commemorates Welsh-born David Thompson, the first white man known to have entered the region. He was an explorer for Canada's North West Company and was regarded by one historian as "the greatest practical geographer the world has ever produced." (See DAVID THOMPSON sidebar, p. 27.)

USK was named in 1892 by its postmaster, who felt nostalgic for the Usk River in Wales. The area now drowses, but pilings—topped by osprey nests—evoke a lively past. They line river shallows for a mile, remnant moorings for "rafts" of logs en route to sawmills. The best view of them is from the bridge crossing to the east side of the valley (and connecting with LeClerc Road, a scenic alternative route between Newport and Ione).

For millennia, Native Americans have dug camas bulbs here and baked them in shallow pits heated with coals and rocks from a fire. Archaeologists have found hundreds of these ovens, some measuring nearly 10 feet across. They date as much as 5,000 years old. The Salish word *kalispelum,* meaning "young sprouting camas" or "great camas digging-place," accounts for the name of the local Indians. (Also see KALISPEL RESERVATION, p. 24.)

Logging at Usk began as soon as the railroad arrived in 1909. Two or three decades later, families moved onto the stumpland and tried to turn sweat and hope into a living by milking cows or raising beef cattle and sheep. Poor soils and distant markets complicated success and, by the despairing years of the 1930s, federal projects amounted to the only bright star in the economic firmament.

Usk's project called for a 7-mile diversion canal to drain 2,000 acres of soggy camas meadows and divert Calispel Creek to irrigate other, drier land. As many as 150 men worked on the canal. Some brought mules or horses to hire out for a small additional "wage." Most worked only 15 hours per week so as to spread income among as many families as possible. They built flumes and dug ditches, which they lined with rock or packed clay—techniques that were deliberately labor intensive. Jobs! About $100,000 later, the time came to test results. Water shot from the head gate, boiled through a flume, and burst a ditch where the lining had not yet been sealed. Meadows supposed to be drained, instead lay flooded. The project ended.

By then the regional economy was picking up, and workers could return to mines and mills, logging camps and farms. This was fortunate. Usk's climate never would have permitted profitable wheat, potatoes, or other crops, except for hay, even if the canal project had succeeded. Part of the would-be canal still skirts trees at the edge of the meadow. Watch for it from the main highway about 2 miles south of Usk, near the entrance to the newsprint mill.

Anyone who enjoys local festivals will want to sample the buffalo barbecue and fair held at Usk each August.

Sanpoil and Kettle River Valleys

Follow the glaciated gorge of the Sanpoil River, strikingly scenic because of high, sheer cliffs. Also drive along the twisting, unfettered Kettle River as it loops from headwaters in British Columbia's Monahsee Mountains to the Columbia River at Boyds, an indirect crossing and recrossing of the international border, but integral with regional history.

This is mining, logging, and ranching country, with the state's second largest Indian reservation, the Colville (the Yakima is larger). Log cabins still stand, and towns are small and isolated. The "Hot Air" railroad grade (Spokane and British Columbia Railway) remains intact near Republic, and two venerable train depots linger in Grand Forks, British Columbia. The historical society has a museum in Republic, and the Stonerose Center there interprets local prehistory through world-class fossils found

locally. A Kettle Falls museum highlights 9,000 years of human presence.

Various abandoned mines are accessible by unpaved National Forest roads; check Forest Service maps. Backcountry roads on the Colville Reservation are highly scenic (no services); passes at about 4,000 feet lead from forested eastern slopes to grass-and-sagebrush western slopes.

BOYDS depended on a ferry operation, logging orchards, and farms in its early years. Little but the mood remains. To sample it, turn off U.S. 395 into the Kettle Valley Campground near Milepost 248 (a little south of Boyds). Herons, geese, kingfishers, coyotes, deer—and empty space—seem to suspend the effects of time and create a balance that stirs empathy for people forced to leave this place, by treaty or because of a rising reservoir. Three valleys—hence, three travel routes—converge here: the Kettle, Colville, and Columbia.

Four native villages stood at the mouth of

The historic Kettle River Valley provides a travel route twisting along the international border. In mining boom days it gave access to the interior of British Columbia.

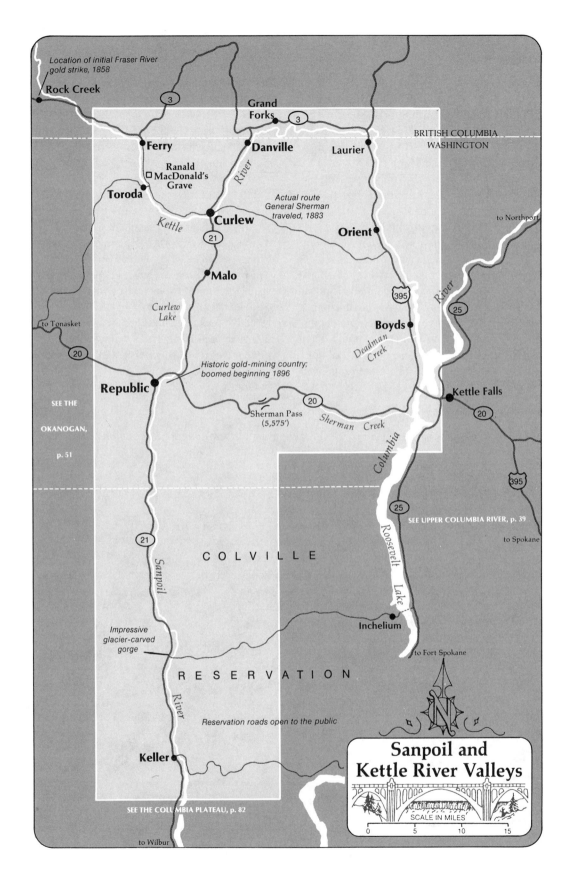

Location of initial Fraser River gold strike, 1858

Rock Creek

3

Grand Forks

3

BRITISH COLUMBIA
WASHINGTON

Ferry

Danville

Laurier

Ranald MacDonald's Grave

Toroda

Actual route General Sherman traveled, 1883

to Northport

Kettle

River

Curlew

21

Orient

Malo

395

Curlew Lake

to Tonasket

Boyds

25

20

Deadman Creek

River

Historic gold-mining country; boomed beginning 1896

Republic

SEE THE

OKANOGAN,

p. 51

20

Sherman Pass (5,575')

Sherman Creek

Kettle Falls

20

Columbia

395

25

SEE UPPER COLUMBIA RIVER, p. 39

to Spokane

Roosevelt Lake

21

C O L V I L L E

Sanpoil

Impressive glacier-carved gorge

Inchelium

to Fort Spokane

R E S E R V A T I O N

River

Reservation roads open to the public

Keller

Sanpoil and
Kettle River Valleys

SCALE IN MILES

0   5   10   15

SEE THE COLUMBIA PLATEAU, p. 82

to Wilbur

the Kettle River. By the 1880s several of the villagers owned ranches where they raised "grain and vegetables in considerable quantities—no less than 4000 bushels of wheat . . . last year," according to Lieutenant Henry Pierce, who passed through the Boyds area while seeking a route across eastern Washington to Puget Sound. Fort Colvile, a Hudson's Bay Company trading post, stood directly across the Columbia from the mouth of the Kettle River. Its site now is underwater. (See FORT COLVILE, p. 40.)

A major ferry operated at Boyds, but quit when a railroad bridge was built in 1901. The train assured access to distant markets, a basis for success in any farming community. Boyds thrived, then declined. Its best agricultural land—close to the river—vanished beneath 30 feet of water as Coulee Dam gates were closed and Roosevelt Lake completed its rise in the winter of 1939–1940. Small-scale farming and logging continue today.

For a look at remnants of early white settlement in the area, drive up **Deadman Creek.** It is reached by an unpaved road that turns off the highway 1 mile south of Kettle Valley Campground. (Stay high—right—at the road's first fork and low—left—at the second. Signs are few, so expect confusion.) Watch for several venerable cabins and fruit trees, the roofless remains of a log stage station, and a school that has vanished except for its floor.

Early 1900s advertisements widely circulated in the Midwest attracted homesteaders to eastern Washington. In *Reflections,* the Kettle River book of pioneer reminiscences, Ruth Davis Lakin tells of arriving at Deadman Creek from Oklahoma in 1903:

Mother hated the thought of going up the narrow steep trail but we kids all piled in the buggy with her and off we went. It was a cold and muddy day and the trail was slick. . . . Ernie got scared and screamed to get out and walk. Mother gritted her teeth and vowed that if she ever got to the top she would never drive down . . . and she never did.

COLVILLE RESERVATION regulations allow the public to drive paved and unpaved roads but not to picnic, camp, hunt, cut wood, collect rocks or plants, or drive off the road. Reservations are not public lands.

President Ulysses S. Grant signed the order establishing this reservation in 1872, although Colville people had not signed a treaty. Instead, Congress had voted that tribes need not be recognized as separate nations and dealt with by treaty. Control could be by executive order. Land would belong to native people by sufferance, not by inherent right.

Reservation boundaries started changing three months after they were drawn. Land east of the Columbia River, where white population was greatest, was split off first (although natives there eventually were given the relatively small Spokane and Kalispel reservations). In 1896 another stroke of the pen abruptly flooded the northern half of the reservation with hundreds of prospectors who staked thousands of claims.

In 1900 the northern half of the reservation also opened to homesteaders and timber cutters. Until then, only mining claims were permissible, but many whites actually had picked land for farms by simply camping on it until they could legally post a location notice. Some whites married native women because the government would allot 80 acres to any native willing to accept individual ownership and give up tribal rights—an exceedingly wrenching decision.

The southern half of the reservation—1.3 million acres—soon met the same fate as the northern half. It opened for mining in 1898, and men immediately depopulated the town of Republic. They staked 5,000 claims the first week. After all, placer gold could lie along streams lined with flat, open land ideal for farms! Legal homesteading began on reservation land in 1916.

At least 11 separate groups now form the Confederated Colville Tribes. At first, relations between them were difficult. Chief Skolaskin, leader of the Sanpoil and Nespelem, bitterly opposed the arrival of various rival bands such as the Sinkiuse led by Chief Moses and the Nez Perce under Chief Joseph. (Also see CHIEF JOSEPH'S RETURN FROM EXILE sidebar, p. 64.)

Skolaskin also refused government money or farm equipment, which he saw as seduction by handout. He would neither fight whites, nor make agreements with them. For this, in November 1889—the same month that Washington gained statehood—he was sent to Alcatraz Penitentiary without trial. General John

Curlew's Ansorge Hotel offered early-1900s guests the very latest in modern amenities.

Gibbon, commander of the Department of the Columbia, described Skolaskin as a "pernicious influence . . . interfering with the design of the Government." After a few months the chief returned home, subdued.

(See also INCHELIUM, p. 43; NESPELEM, p. 64.)

CURLEW stretches along the riverbank in a valley of grasslands and forest. What seems like the junction of two valleys at this point is actually the base of a river loop, a key topographic location commanding access to both the northwest and the northeast. The National Register of Historic Places lists three Curlew structures: a 13-room hotel replete with jutting corner bays and sheet-metal siding stamped to look like cut stone; a one-lane, wooden-decked bridge; and a frame schoolhouse.

A British Columbia firm built the school, an example of the international commerce that is traditional here: the United States–Canada border cuts east-west, but the land and the flow of human commerce trend north-south. Railroads formerly carried Republic gold to a smelter near Grand Forks, British Columbia. The cooperative creamery of Curlew operated branches in Grand Forks and Nelson. And, until national prohibition brought a tightening of border formalities, local people traveled in and out of Canada as casually as those elsewhere might crisscross a county. Even today, regional

Kiwanis Clubs occasionally sing "Oh, Canada" as well as "The Star-Spangled Banner."

Curlew got started when Guy Helphrey arrived with an early wave of prospectors and opened a store. A few years later, the right-of-way for the Great Northern sliced off the store's front, and merchandise had to be piled beside stoves to prevent freezing while a new building went up. School classes had been meeting in the store, but townspeople financed a new school. This "white school," as it is fondly known—the one built by a British Columbia company—still stands. A new, consolidated school stands at the south edge of town.

The Ansorge Hotel no longer operates but is open to be admired on summer weekends, or whenever volunteer docents can find time to be there. Original furnishings remain intact, picturing an era frozen in time. Built in 1906, the hotel still faces railroad tracks, yet both it and the train arrived late: gold mining had already peaked. Even so, a pay phonograph flooded the lobby with music and patrons enjoyed a gravity-fed water system and the only long-distance telephone for miles around (or, as some old-timers remember it, Helphrey's store also had a phone). The Ansorge's greatest glory came in 1917 when Henry Ford checked in while visiting relatives who lived in the area.

Less than a mile north of Curlew is the squared-log home and store of Chief Tonasket (west side of State Route 21, just north of the Vulcan Mountain road junction). The building now is dilapidated and used as a barn. Tonasket was born about 1822 at Lake Osoyoos on land eventually pioneered by the legendary Hiram (Okanogan) Smith. When the government "reassigned" natives living in the Okanogan region to the Colville Reservation in the 1880s, the chief moved to Curlew Creek to be near his wife's brother Joe Somday. At the time, Curlew was part of the reservation. The two families raised livestock, hay, and oats—the first sizeable ranch operations in the area. Tonasket also had a mile-long horse racetrack, as did his son Baptiste.

The Somday house—a two-story Victorian with dormer windows, once the showplace of the county—is now slowly self-destructing on the river flood plain (below the road bank about 4 miles south of Curlew, near the foot of the Empire Creek Road).

DANVILLE streets are excess to present needs. One would suffice, yet a grid of hushed streets and more than a score of commercial buildings and houses—many of them empty—testify to a lively past.

The town began when Peter B. Nelson and his brother O. B. opened a store in 1889. Ostensibly the two traded with native people, which was legal, but more likely they antici-pated the opening of reservation land to whites and wanted a head start on mercantile success. Seizing opportunity, the brothers even moved their store in 1897 to a building that straddled the United States–Canada line and had doors opening into each nation. Border formalities were simple in those days, but not *that* simple. Customs officers told the Nelsons to close their business or move it. They moved it.

With the store again south of the international line, Peter Nelson became the only postmaster in the 2,000 square miles that are now Ferry County. His delivery costs were minimal: he sent letters with anyone heading in the right direction. As was frequent, the town at first carried the name of its postmaster, but in 1901 this changed to Danville—the name of a prominent local mining company—so as to avoid confusion with Nelson, British Columbia. By that time town population justified several

stores stocking everything from kerosene lamps and mining supplies to fine velvets, silks, and button shoes. Land locators, assayers, horse breakers, and lawyers opened offices. A saw-mill employed turbaned Hindus from British Columbia as cheap labor, but dismissed them after a few days when local people protested. A Japanese barber lasted for a year.

Livery stables prospered because most freight for Republic came through Danville in pre-railroad days, shipped from Marcus aboard six-horse wagons that followed the meandering Kettle River. Drivers changed teams every few miles, including at Curlew and the Somday farm.

At **FERRY**, the trim brick border station (and its white-frame Canadian counterpart) marks the international line. Today's isolation is deceptive, for gold mining, "tiehacking" (cutting railroad ties), and bootlegging each have boomed here although half a dozen collapsing houses and a broad flat, now empty, are all that remain of the formerly rollicking town.

The mining began a few years before the international border was firmly surveyed. In 1858 prospectors spawned a boom at Rock Creek (northwest of Ferry), an area of uncertain nationhood until 1862 when the official boundary survey placed it within British Columbia. Years later, Spokane and Butte financial titans, who regarded the border as no barrier, pocketed fortunes from mines at Rossland and Nelson, British Columbia. (See NORTHPORT, p. 46.)

By the early 1900s Ferry had a branch line railroad and 27 saloons, stereotypical measures of success for any frontier town. Sheep and cattle took over grazing lands as wild horses were rounded up and herded as far as Dayton for auction. Former Colville reservation lands were opened to logging, and portable mills whirred their saws in one drainage after another.

In the 1920s and 1930s hard times thwarted expansion, and a U.S. Customs agent who transferred to Ferry from Bellevue found that all accommodations were on the British Columbia side of the border. He stayed at a hotel in the town of Midway, which offered rooms "heated" only with Hudson's Bay Company blankets. Prohibition was officially in effect, but stopping liquor traffic amounted to a courageous farce. Local people gave no support, and officials' cars were those they seized from bootleggers. Of them, "the brass got first pick," leaving only rattletraps for the agents. Earlier customs problems had been with opium, which Chinese smugglers hid in quarters of venison and shipped by packtrain to Curlew. From there the opium was sent on to Portland and San Francisco.

KELLER today consists of grocery, tavern, post office, school, and modern housing. The town began in 1898 when the southern half of the Colville Reservation officially opened for mining. That year, a man named J. C. Keller moved from Almira to the mouth of the Sanpoil River and announced himself in business as a storekeeper. Boats had already been ferrying miners onto reservation lands, so Keller felt sure his location would bloom into a town once legalities were attended to. By 1904 several businesses and a sawmill provided payrolls at Keller; two stage lines ran south into Lincoln County; and steamboats stopped three times a week. The steamers never played a major role, however. Both Congress and the state legislature appropriated money to clear the river channel between Bridgeport and Kettle Falls, and crews dynamited several rapids. Even so, the mountainous land of the upper Columbia attracted few farmers and, with neither people nor crops, river traffic dwindled.

Ferries remained an exception. At least 16 operated on the Columbia between the mouths of the Methow and Sanpoil rivers. Many were highly individualistic. Thomas Seaton, downriver from Keller, would refuse service to anyone who drank alcohol or differed with him politically; he simply told them to "go back to Keller for your crossing." On the other hand, he ferried native people across the river at half fare. Chief Moses had suggested free service, reasoning that reservation lands extended to mid-river, but Seaton countered with free transport across the reservation side of the river, full fare the rest of the way.

Keller prospered as a typical river town until the winter of 1939–1940. Franklin D. Roosevelt Lake then drowned the original site and gave birth to the new one, 8 miles away.

(Also see INCHELIUM, p. 43.)

MACDONALD GRAVE. (See TORODA, p. 37; RANALD MACDONALD sidebar, p. 36.)

MALO (May´-loh) set its early beat to the rhythm of train wheels, and the country store here—built in 1903—still bears unusual witness to the era. What seems to be the front door opening to the highway is actually the back door; and what seems to be the back door is the original front door, facing the train track. The Spokane and British Columbia Railroad apparently laid steel through Malo in early 1902; the Great Northern arrived a few months later. David and Goliath.

Local people called the Spokane and British Columbia the "Hot Air Line" because company promises continually exceeded performance. The railroad tied Republic mines to a smelter near Grand Forks, British Columbia, but it had problems doing so, owing to shoddy construction. Regardless, a superintendent of the Colville Indian Agency spoke of the company as "a plucky little road" and of the Great Northern as "that King of Bulldozers and Lawbreakers." (Several miles of the Hot Air grade remain intact near Republic. From Curlew to Danville the old right of way has become State Route 21.)

Malo no longer aspires to the big time. It is farming, ranching, and logging country and contentedly so. In the little store, which virtually is the town, a ladder gives access to upper shelves where goods range from canned tomatoes to kerosene lamps. The old oak-fronted post office that stood by the erstwhile front door (now the rear door) has closed, and safety regulations have put out the fire in the classic wood stove. Even so, the store remains a timeless place of warmth and neighborliness.

Clearly **ORIENT** slumbers, despite previous bustle. Trees planted to give shade on hot, dusty summer days still line streets, and the ornate bell cupola of the handsome brick school (built 1910 and listed in the state Historic Properties inventory) remains the highest and by far proudest structure in town. But "First Thought"—the name of a rich mine in Orient's boom days—is now the name of a riverside tract development, and the Big Nine Mine Building (Main and Fourth) sags forlornly.

The name Orient probably came from Chinese placer mines common here following the 1858 Fraser River gold rush. The town developed later to serve mines in nearby mountains.

When hard-rock prospectors staked the Never Tell Mine in 1902, the town of Orient came alive. Those first mining efforts sputtered out, but a syndicate known as the Orient Improvement Company filed on the property and renamed it the Orient. About that same time, word spread that the Great Northern Railway was on its way. No longer would supplies have to come by ferry and wagon from Marcus. More important, ore could be shipped to Granby, British Columbia (near Grand Forks), for smelting.

For a while, expectations came true as mines paid their backers millions of dollars. The First Thought alone averaged a half ounce of gold per ton of ore, with secondary values in silver and copper. Sawmills added to the overall prosperity. Then ore gave out, trees were cut, and people moved on.

In **REPUBLIC** a western mining-town ambience lingers; houses and pines dot steep hills, and businesses line a gully barely wide enough for three parallel streets with alleys. Early 1900s buildings adjoin each other on Clark Avenue, the main street (which is named for "Patsy" Clark, owner of a splendid Browne's Addition mansion in Spokane and president of the Republic Gold Mining and Milling Company). The buildings include a fire hall, with roof tower and bell, and a drug store with hand-cranked street awnings and a pressed tin ceiling in proud and perfect repair. Facades—except for the drug store—have undergone "rustification," a face-lifting that town fathers hope will appeal to tourists.

The stone Episcopal church at the uppermost end of town was built in 1909. The Catholic church, on a hill at the east edge of town, went up in 1913 modeled after the village church of Italian Jesuit missionary Edward Griva. Financial underwriting came from Irish brothers who owned a local bank, meat market, and contracting business. They sent to their hometown in Minnesota for molds in which to make concrete blocks, fashionably shaped to look like cut stone. They used the resulting blocks both for the church and for their own homes (which are still standing on Delaware, across from the courthouse).

Republic burst into existence when the northern half of the Colville Reservation opened for mining in February 1896. Prospectors staked the first claim slightly north of today's town. Within weeks 64 men had arrived, and freight for them already was piling up at Marcus and Nelson (now Danville). The Panic of 1893, associated with a shortage of silver, had occurred only three years previously; that gave gold an extra allure as a means of rebuilding national credit. Furthermore, gold let a poor man dream of getting rich. Republic burgeoned. Tents and canvas-topped shacks gave way to frame buildings and, when the reservation's southern half also opened to mining, the town's population quickly soared to 2,000. Homesteads and sawmills soon followed.

Most of the mines and mills are memory now, although tunnels and tailings mark a patchwork of claims. A history museum displaying vintage tools and the town's first log cabin stands next to the Stonerose Interpretive Center (Kean Street).

RANALD MACDONALD

Ranald MacDonald was born in 1824 at Fort George (Astoria, Oregon) the son of Archibald MacDonald, Hudson's Bay Company trader, and a daughter of Comcomly, a high-ranking Chinook chief at the mouth of the Columbia River. His mother soon died.

As an adolescent, Ranald became fascinated by three young Japanese fishermen who had drifted helplessly across the Pacific before washing ashore near Cape Flattery in March 1834. Makah men captured them, and the Hudson's Bay Company made one or two unsuccessful rescue attempts before finally bringing the men to Fort Vancouver. In school at Red River, Manitoba (headquarters for the Hudson's Bay Company's western trade), Ranald found people excitedly discussing the castaways and the virtually unknown land they came from. Japan became fixed in his mind. As these were the first Japanese ever contacted by the British, the Hudson's Bay Company's chief factor John McLoughlin sent them to London so that they might "convey to their countrymen . . . the grandeur and power [of England]" when they returned home. MacDonald never forgot the seamen.

After graduation, he went to work for a banker friend of his father, but suffered from racial prejudice because of his Chinook blood. Even his father bluntly cautioned him against joining the British Army because he could never expect promotion. No profession would fully accept him.

Pained, Ranald was determined to see something of the world and to learn about crosscurrents of national interest, then go to Japan. He knew Japan was firmly closed to foreigners but he reasoned that the authorities would not kill him if he arrived as a shipwreck victim. He roamed widely as a seaman, then bought an English dictionary, grammar, history, and world map—and signed onto an American whaling ship, which he fully expected to enter Japanese waters. When it neared Hokkaido, Japan's northern island, he insisted that the captain give him a small boat. He rowed, then gathered his books, and deliberately capsized.

Ainu, the aboriginal natives of Japan, pulled him from the water. They knew he was foreign and dutifully turned him over to authorities, who hustled him to Nagasaki. There, under what amounted to house arrest, MacDonald achieved his

---

SHERMAN PASS is misnamed, as are also Sherman Peak and Sherman Creek. Lieutenant Henry H. Pierce, not General William T. Sherman, crossed the mountains via today's highway route in 1882. He reported "numerous ravines [which] rendered the progress slow," and also "plenty of grass, wood, and the purest water, but . . . no level space for tents." The illustrious Sherman, commander of the U.S. Army during the Civil War, came through the region a year after Pierce. Making a final western inspection trip before retiring, the general crossed the mountains by a rough trail north of "Sherman" Pass. (Boulder Creek Road between Orient and Curlew now follows his

route.) The pass named for the general is the highest on any major highway in the state: 5,575 feet.

For a glimpse of both virgin ponderosa forest and pioneer logging, stop just east of the Bangs Mountain campground (about 7 miles before the Sherman Pass road reaches the Columbia River). A Forest Service interpretive trail leads to vestiges of a flume used for floating logs to a mill and also to a "dry flume," a ditch gouged out for convenience in dragging logs.

TORODA (To-roh´-duh)—not to be confused with Old Toroda near Wauconda—is an area rather than a town. Conspicuous elements

dream. He taught English to Japanese youths. The Shogun opposed the presence of all foreigners except Dutch traders, yet also wondered about alien goods and

Ranald MacDonald, remarkable mid-1800s world traveler, lies buried on a hill above the Kettle River.

technology and welcomed English instruction for a small corps of interpreters. After a year MacDonald was sent out of Japan with other captive seamen. He again traveled, then returned to America in 1853—by chance the same year that Commodore Matthew Perry of the U.S. Navy cracked open Japan's closed door by successfully negotiating a trade treaty. MacDonald's pupils participated as interpreters.

By the time of his return, MacDonald's Chinook relatives had fallen victim to epidemics. Scottish relatives, however, lived in the vicinity of Fort Colvile, where his father Archibald and great uncle Angus had each served as trader. Ranald homesteaded. On New Years Day, 1894, he wrote to his niece Jenny Lynch at Toroda Creek saying he had been ill and apologizing for having failed to make a Christmas visit. "The next time your team is here," he added, "I may be able to muster courage to make the attempt."

In August he finally made the visit—and died in Jenny's arms whispering, "Sayonara, my dear. Sayonara." Farewell.

Monuments to MacDonald were erected in 1988 near where he landed in Japan, and at Astoria, Oregon (15th and Exchange).

include collapsing log barns and roofless cabins, predecessors of today's miscellaneous houses and mobile homes. There also is a Jobs Corps center.

The area is a point of historical pilgrimage because of Ranald MacDonald, eldest son of a Hudson's Bay Company trader. His grave, beside the road to Ferry, forms an improbable link to far-flung world stages: MacDonald endured the ostracism of being half Chinook, half Scottish; experienced Washington's transition from British domain to American; and unwittingly served aboard an African slave ship, yet lived to see the end of slavery in America. Above all, he witnessed the emergence of Japan into the world community—and knew that he had played a part in the transition.

To reach the grave, cross the Kettle River 12 miles northwest of Curlew, then turn north immediately beyond the bridge. Watch for a cemetery above the road (almost 1 mile from the bridge). The cabin where MacDonald died (now converted to a horse shelter) stands on private property across the river. It is visible from the roadside a half mile south of the grave; use binoculars and look for two adjacent cabins on the first terrace above the river. MacDonald died in the cabin to the right, which is built of carefully squared and fitted logs.

Upper Columbia River

The highway north from Davenport to the Canadian border follows a scenic transportation route that dates back to the earliest fur-trading days and the preceding long era of native culture. Roosevelt Lake attracts fishermen and campers—and supplies water for Grand Coulee Dam's turbines. Abandoned buildings and remnants of orchards survive on benchland above the reservoir. North of Northport, the Columbia River still flows and ripples!

Points of interest include the reconstructed pioneering Catholic mission Saint Paul's and the sites of the Hudson's Bay Company's Fort Colvile (now underwater) and the U.S. Army's Fort Colville and adjoining Pinkney City (where nothing remains, although the two served as a regional center before Spokane had even begun). There are history museums at Colville and Fort Spokane and near Kettle Falls. The LeRoi Mine and museum at Rossland, British Columbia, will intrigue mine buffs—and everyone.

At Kettle Falls a July celebration called KnKanna-Xwa Day honors the last of the native salmon chiefs who directed the fishery here for thousands of years. Marcus holds a September cider festival, reminiscent of prereservoir days as a fruit-growing center. And at Christmastime the Keller House in Colville is open for special candlelight tours.

Today's **BOSSBURG** is a "new" town. It moved to higher ground as Roosevelt Lake backed up behind Grand Coulee Dam in 1939 and 1940. On the river terrace a half mile below the highway, assorted remnants of the earlier Bossburg now slowly disintegrate.

In the early 1800s the Hudson's Bay Company pastured horses here. Town life began in the 1880s as a camp for the Young America Mine, a lead-silver property profitable enough to warrant opening a wagon road to the (short-lived) smelter at Colville. Between 1889 and 1893, the future seemed promising. The mining company had opened a mill in town. Spokane railroad magnate D. C. Corbin was pushing his tracks north toward Canada. Population stood at 800. About this time a traveling merchant named Chester Boss opened for business in a tent, liked the area, took up land, built a proper store, and soon became postmaster. His name, combined with that of pioneering resident John Burg, became the town's official name.

In 1893 hard times set in nationwide. The price of silver plummeted, and the Young America Mine closed. Only the post office and a few diehards hung on at Bossburg, although ferry business picked up briefly when the northern half of the Colville Reservation opened to mining. Soon, however, both the mining and the town dwindled. The ferry continued until 1940.

CHEWELAH (Chuh-wee´-luh) hosted the beginnings of Protestant Christianity in the region when Cushing Eells, in 1838 one of the founders of the Tshimakain Mission, preached his first sermon in the Northwest. A plaque under the bell by the First Congregational Church (Park and Webster) commemorates the event and lists Eells as the donor of the bell. Seven years after Eells' sermon, the Northwest's most famous and well-traveled Jesuit, Pierre Jean DeSmet, picked a site near Chewelah for Saint Francis Regis Mission. A second mission of the same name (located about 5 miles west of Colville) replaced DeSmet's mission in 1869.

By then Chewelah was becoming the heart of the agricultural settlement in the Colville Valley. Consequently, native people who took up farming tended to concentrate in the area, and this led the federal government to open an Indian agency there in 1873. Its staff taught farming methods, distributed seeds and farm machinery, and operated a small flour mill. Twelve years later the agency moved to Nespelem, present headquarters of the Colville Confederated Tribes. The original Chewelah agency cabin, built of hand-hewn logs, still stands (309 Third Street).

Slag piles and rusting metal buildings from a huge magnesite plant are conspicuous along the highway south of Chewelah. During World War II, the plant employed 800 workers to refine ore brought from a mine by aerial tram. The end result was magnesium, needed for airplanes.

(Also see NESPELEM, p. 64.)

The town of **COLVILLE** occupies pleasant wooded terraces and hillsides overlooking a fer-

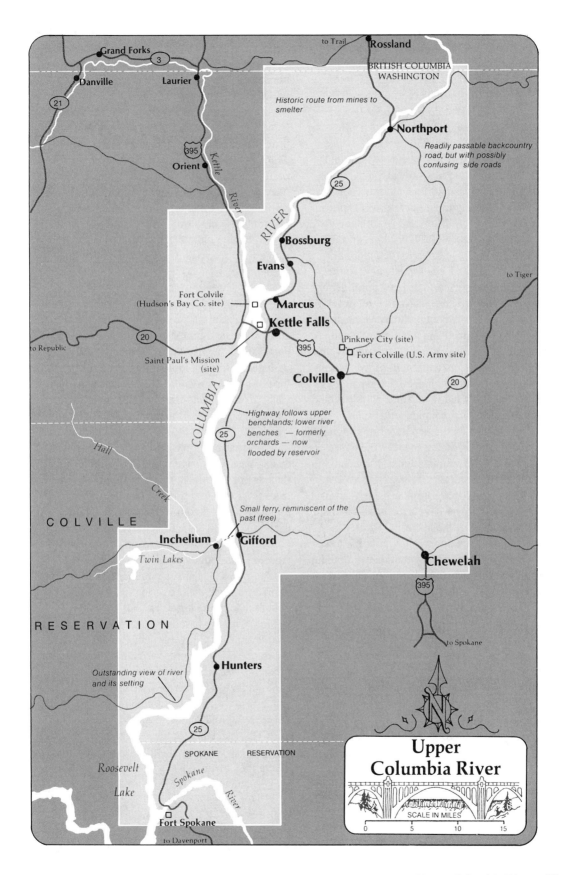

Grand Forks

Danville

Laurier

3

21

to Trail

Rossland

BRITISH COLUMBIA
WASHINGTON

Historic route from mines to smelter

Northport

Readily passable backcountry road, but with possibly confusing side roads

395

Orient

25

Kettle River

RIVER

Bossburg

Evans

Fort Colvile
(Hudson's Bay Co. site)

Marcus

Kettle Falls

Pinkney City (site)

to Tiger

20

to Republic

Saint Paul's Mission
(site)

395

Fort Colville (U.S. Army site)

Colville

20

COLUMBIA

Highway follows upper benchlands; lower river benches — formerly orchards — now flooded by reservoir

25

Hall

Creek

Small ferry, reminiscent of the past (free)

COLVILLE

Inchelium

Gifford

Chewelah

Twin Lakes

395

RESERVATION

to Spokane

Outstanding view of river and its setting

Hunters

N

25

SPOKANE   RESERVATION

Roosevelt

Lake

Spokane

River

Fort Spokane

to Davenport

Upper
Columbia River

SCALE IN MILES

0   5   10   15

tile river valley. Several early commercial buildings still stand; a bank with gleaming white columns (Main and Astor) and the Odd Fellows Hall (W. First) are perhaps the most impressive. At the county courthouse, grindstones from the Arden flour mill now form a lawn sculpture. The mill itself stood 7 miles east of town on Little Pend Oreille River.

Old street plantings and overgrown garden shrubs are among the signs of early-day homes; so are multiple chimneys and decorative fishscale shingles remaining under eaves despite overall re-siding. (N. Main and E. First streets have several of these older homes.) A spacious bungalow-style house listed in the National Register of Historic Places stands next to the county historical society museum (uphill from Fifth and Wynne). The house was built in 1910 for a prominent local businessman who had made a small fortune from a mine at Nelson, British Columbia. Oak floors gleam with walnut inlay; birch beams run the length of the living room; wooden columns flank the entry to the music room; and windows sparkle with beveled glass—graceful details typical of the early twentieth-century Craftsman movement. Inquire at the museum concerning tours of the house, usually led only in summer and as a special holiday candlelight tour.

A school, blacksmith shop, trapper's cabin, and fire lookout tower have been brought to the museum grounds by the historical society. Summer visitors are allowed to climb the tower, which is typical of the many that once stood on peaks to guard Northwest forests. Aerial surveillance now replaces that system.

Conspicuous near the museum, but not open to the public, is the large white Harvey Hospital built in the early 1900s (now converted to apartments). The construction came at a time when hospitals were just beginning as separate structures; previously, patients were treated in their own homes or were brought to extra rooms in the doctor's house to be nursed.

Colville got its start in 1883 when the army closed Fort Colville and moved its troops to Fort Spokane. Pinkney City had adjoined the fort, but residents and businessmen decided to move a few miles west to a site with riverboat access. They ripped apart buildings at the fort and carted them off before the army could salvage much for their new post at Fort Spokane. Even the flagpole got moved to town.

Five years later surging optimism prompted boosters to open an office in Spokane Falls where they could answer questions for prospective new citizens. At the time, railroad magnate D. C. Corbin was circulating 50,000 copies of a promotional booklet, which extolled Colville as "An Open Door to a Magnificent Country." At first, response came slowly, for land surveys were not yet complete and only "squatters' rights" were available. But at dusk on October 18, 1889, the first train rolled into town, and townspeople greeted its arrival with a 42-gun salute fired from rifles and pistols. Colville was on the map.

(Also see PINKNEY CITY, p. 47.)

EVANS is now a score of houses, a Grange hall, and a store surrounded by small farms and large pastures. Its heyday began with gold and ended with cement. For a look at this economic gamut, turn into the National Park Service Evans Campground, then take the first lane to the north. The ghostly silos of the cement plant stand amid young cottonwoods and wild roses, and old quarries notch the skyline on both sides of the river. Extensive mounds of cobbles (at the edge of the forest, south of the silos) remain from the sweat and hope of Chinese placer miners who worked the riverbank for gold during the 1880s. A half century later crews clearing land for the reservoir behind Grand Coulee Dam found occasional small caches of gold or coins buried beneath these men's doorsteps—poignant, overlooked reward from patient, backbreaking work.

Most Chinese first came to America as laborers for the California gold mines. As that boom played out, some drifted into Washington on their own; others were brought by labor contractors to work at newly opened mines, or at canneries (which began on the lower Columbia River in the mid-1860s). Later railroad jobs also drew Chinese laborers. Once in the Northwest, many of the men gravitated to rivers and creeks, where they gleaned placer gold from sands and gravels abandoned by white prospectors.

The site of **FORT COLVILE**—a major Hudson's Bay Company fur-trading post and farm, which occupied a large river terrace—now forms a Roosevelt Lake bay with a 6-mile shoreline (State Route 25, about 2½ miles from the bridge across the Columbia River). Nothing of the old fort remains visible. Governor George Simpson, dynamic head of the Hudson's Bay Company's western operation, personally picked the location in 1825 and named it for Andrew Colvile, a company director. He then ordered all trade transferred here from Fort Spokane, an earlier post 70 miles to the southeast.

Fort Colvile stood at the upper end of the 2-mile portage around Kettle Falls. Chiefs here had welcomed Simpson, and their cooperation boded well for trade contacts throughout the surrounding area. The post and adjacent Saint Paul's mission quickly became the largest European center between the Rocky Mountains and the Cascade Mountains. Travelers stopped for supplies and sociability—and advice. Shipments of beef, pork, cheese, and vegetables from the 340-acre farm provisioned other inland Hudson's Bay posts, and Fort Colvile employees built most of the company's river vessels, including canoes and 30-foot, cedar-plank riverboats capable of carrying up to 10 people and three tons of freight.

In 1854 prospectors found gold near Fort Colvile, harbinger of change for the surrounding region. Hopes of striking it rich brought men surging back to the Northwest from California, where they had flocked after news of discoveries at Sutter's Mill a few years before. With this strike on the upper Columbia, Americans began insisting that the treaty signed with England a decade earlier be implemented. They called for a survey of the international border, a necessary first step before anyone could hope for a clear title to land. The new boundary established Fort Colvile as deep within United States territory, although the Hudson's Bay Company continued to operate it for 25 years.

Finally, the post manager, Angus MacDonald, packed records and valuables and on June 8, 1871, closed nearly half a century of trade. Company fields, cattle, horses, fur presses—and singing, roistering voyageurs—began slipping into memory. MacDonald stayed on, living as though the property were his own; after he died, a son filed on it as a homestead. While the family still lived at the old fur-trading fort, the U.S. Army built their Fort Colville a few miles to the east (and slightly changed the spelling by adding one more "l").

FORT COLVILLE, site of a U.S. Army post, can be reached by turning north off the main highway a mile east of the town of Colville, then following Aladdin Road for about 2 miles to a gravel pit. There look for an inconspicuous granite slab, which reads: "Here stood Fort Colville protecting the Last Frontier, 1859–1882."

Establishment of the fort came in the aftermath of battles that began in 1855 as native people tried to prevent intrusion by white miners and ranchers. When the bloodshed ended three years later, Brigadier General William S. Harney, commander of the Department of Oregon, chose a site for Fort Colville. He reasoned that a military presence would encourage continued peace in the region and also facilitate escort for boundary surveyors. Consequently, in the spring of 1859 Major Pinkney Lugenbeel arrived from Fort Walla Walla with two companies of infantry.

For the next 20 years, army regulars—and, during the Civil War, also volunteers—spent their energies trying to move native people onto reservations and to arbitrate disputes concerning land rights and the frequent inability of government agents to honor promises. Largely owing to this role as interlocutor, the army in 1880 decided to close Fort Colville. Its location no longer was central. Within the next five years the entire garrison moved to Fort Spokane.

The inner eye today struggles to visualize the 45 or more structures that were here—officers' quarters and enlisted men's barracks, store, guardhouse, stables, hospital, theater. Absolutely nothing remains. The ear hears little but wind and song sparrows.

(Also see PINKNEY CITY, p. 47.)

FORT SPOKANE stands at the confluence of the Spokane and Columbia rivers, administered by the National Park Service as part of the Coulee Dam National Recreation Area. The old quartermaster barn built in 1884 remains, a mammoth structure that sheltered up to 98 mules used to pull cannons and supply wagons. The original 150,000-gallon reservoir still provides fire protection for the barn. The fort guardhouse has become a museum. Plans call for clearing brush from the foundations of additional buldings, marking the corners of others, and erecting "ghosts," skeletal structures that do not recreate buildings but faithfully evoke their scale and locations.

Events of the 1880s led to the establishment of Fort Spokane. Activity in the Colville area—long a hub—began to wane as Northern Pacific advertisement lured trainloads of immigrants to what now are vast wheatlands. Anticipating the new center of activity, the army in 1880 closed Fort Colville and opened Fort Spokane, housing the first troops there in tents. At the time, the running battle against Chief Joseph's Nez Perce had only recently ended, and the army hoped that a well-placed military presence would prevent similar tragedies by quieting trouble before it could fester. Their goal was to keep whites off land set aside for native people and to discourage natives from continuing to use root grounds and potato patches beyond the boundaries of their new reservations.

For its new fort, the army chose a river bench close to the main salmon fishery on the Spokane River—a crossroads of ancient trails—and close also to the main village of Chief Skolaskin, a leader of the Sanpoil and Nespelem people. Conservative and bitter, this chief practiced the Dreamer religion, preaching that white people would disappear and the old days return if natives followed certain practices. Army officers believed in surveillance.

In addition to affecting—and sometimes managing—"Indian affairs," Fort Spokane men helped to restore order during the riotous strikes at Coeur d'Alene mines in 1892 and also during the nationwide labor unrest associated with the financial panic of 1893 and 1894. To forestall protesters from confiscating trains, Congress in 1894 ordered troops to run the railroad and safeguard the mail. Men from Fort Spokane briefly handled rail traffic in and out of Sprague (55 miles to the south). Later they guarded the transcontinental track from Missoula, Montana, to Tacoma, Washington.

By the 1890s Fort Spokane consisted of about 50 frame and brick buildings. For the most part, officers stationed here were veterans of the Civil War; enlisted men were predominantly new recruits, especially urban Irish and German youths from the east who detested the stillness and emptiness of the fort's setting. The entire U.S. Army then numbered only 25,000 officers and men thinly scattered throughout the nation. By the turn of the century, Fort George Wright (in the city of Spokane) had replaced Fort Spokane.

GIFFORD started when James O. Gifford settled here in 1889. By 1900 the community had become the site of an important ferry crossing to Inchelium—an automobile ferry

Men of the Second Infantry parade in German-style dress uniform at Fort Spokane. The fort's air of permanence signaled to native people that whites had come to stay.

The army garrisoned Fort Spokane—Washington's last frontier post—from 1880 to 1898. Three original buildings still stand; others are outlined. The site is a national historic park.

2 miles south of the town store is one of the two ferries remaining on the upper Columbia. Hours of operation usually are 6 A.M. to 9 P.M. The crossing takes only about five minutes. No charge. Great scenery.

Gifford's population stood at 39 when Grand Coulee Dam was built; the economy depended on orchards and poultry. Inchelium, across the river, had a population nearly five times greater.

Men surveyed **HUNTERS** and, in 1890, platted a townsite on river benchland that James Hunter had settled a decade earlier. Moved to higher ground above Roosevelt Lake in 1939, the community has survived. Of architectural interest is the 1915 Catholic church (converted to a store) at the northern edge of town. Its belfry is shaped like a bell.

During the early 1900s Hunters was a major town with the only newspaper in southwest Stevens County. Apple orchards tufted the riverbanks, irrigated with water brought for 2 or 3 miles by flume. The orchards employed about 150 people to prune, cultivate, harvest, and pack the crop. Two huge processing sheds boasted the latest in apple-sorting machines.

Orchards covered river terraces from Hunters to Kettle Falls, nearly 40 miles. But people moved away as reservoirs rose behind Grand Coulee Dam. Slopes remaining above water are not suitable for commercial orchards.

INCHELIUM (In-chuh-lee´-um) is an English rendering of a Salish name that translates

"Where Small Water Meets Big Water," specifically, the merging of two creeks into the Columbia River. The old site is flooded by 135 feet of water, a situation somewhat glibly summarized in a guidebook published shortly before Roosevelt Lake started its rise: "Inhabitants are beginning to move to the benchland, where the town, which is an Indian agency, will take new roots." But "roots" are not actually that simple, especially for people whose ties to a location reach back for generations. Tribal councilman Joe Kohler testified at a hearing in 1975:

Families and communities were close together geographically and in extreme close communication in times of sorrow and festivity. . . . [How a man] stored and preserved salmon and other foods, and his function in the salmon ceremonies—these were matters of importance and status. Suddenly, within a period of four years, all of this was wiped out.

Fish came no more after the dam was built. People could not cross the flooded river at will to dig roots or hunt. Horses that easily forded shallow water shied when put onto a ferry. On the other hand, power from Grand Coulee Dam was crucial for the production of airplanes needed during World War II and it facilitated the atomic bomb project at Hanford. Furthermore, irrigation made possible by the dam has transformed Washington's economy.

A sense of countryside—and of time— remains here. To sample it, drive the Colville

Native people fished at Kettle Falls through the 1930s, following ancient traditions.

Reservation road that follows the bend of the Columbia River from Inchelium to Keller. Note especially a classic mission church (about 23 miles south of Inchelium) and a river overlook (8 miles south of the church) with a view to Fort Spokane and the mouth of the Spokane River. The highest elevation of this road is 3,200 feet.

Today's **KETTLE FALLS** conveys no obvious sense of its past. No landmarks show from the bridge spanning the Columbia River. The falls lie submerged. The salmon come no more. And generations of people whose lives centered here are long dead. An interpretive center operated by the Kettle Falls Historical Society depicts events.

Quite possibly the first people in the area came about 13,000 years ago while glacier ice near the mouth of the Okanogan River was blocking the Columbia and forming a lake

deeper than the reservoir now backed up by Grand Coulee Dam. Certainly people had arrived by 9,000 years ago, for archaeologists find stone net weights of that age. The weights are heavy, suggesting use in fast, deep water. They lie on an island, indicating that the people who used them knew how to maneuver watercraft through the dangerous river currents near the falls.

By the 1800s about 1,000 Colville native people gathered at Kettle Falls each summer to fish, joined by three or four times that many from other groups. Probably half of the calories they ate came from the salmon catch, which is estimated at one million pounds per season. Takes went as high as 3,000 fish per day.

In 1811 David Thompson, eminent explorer for the North West Company, arrived with his party at Kettle Falls, the first white men to enter the area. Fourteen years later chiefs agreed to let the

Hudson's Bay Company build Fort Colvile just above the falls, but they insisted on keeping rights to the salmon for themselves (although they usually were willing to supply fish to company personnel and to white travelers). Native control of the salmon proved short-lived, however; as early as 1883, John C. Tidball, who arrived at Kettle Falls with General William Sherman, wrote:

[The falls] were from time immemorial a famous fishing place for the Indians. It is, however no longer so; the salmon [at Kettle Falls] have become scarce by reason of the great numbers taken for the canneries near the mouth of the river.

Two rivalrous white communities sprang up near the thundering cascades of the ancient fishery. Speculators from Rochester, New York, in 1889 platted a town and named it Kettle Falls. They assumed it would be on the route of the Spokane Falls and Northern Railroad, which was then building north from Spokane. They were wrong. The rails bypassed their town and left both dream and newly completed hotel to die the death of errant speculation.

Even so, Kettle Falls clung to life and by the 1930s had a population of 500, which was sizeable for inland Washington at that time. Soon, however, "Camp Kettle" rose along the banks of the river, and men hired by the Works Progress Administration began to clear railroad tracks, bridges, farms, cemeteries, and even entire towns from what would become the bed of Roosevelt Lake after the floodgates at Grand Coulee Dam were closed. Kettle Falls' fate was sealed.

Three miles to the east, an older, smaller, unincorporated village called Meyers Falls stood on a bench above the Colville River where the Hudson's Bay Company had built a gristmill in 1826. Proud of their identity, people there rejected a proposed merger with neighbors at Kettle Falls who were doomed to watch the rising reservoir flood their homes and businesses. Kettle Falls citizens nonetheless accomplished their goal: they simply engulfed Meyers Falls by annexing all the land around it.

For a look at the cascading waters of historic **Meyers Falls,** drive south on Main Street in Kettle Falls; then turn right on 11th, left on Juniper, and continue a half mile to a bridge. Park in a gravel lot by the southwest approach to the bridge and walk to an overlook.

To see what remains of the original **Kettle Falls townsite,** drive west of today's city limits for 2½ miles, turn south on the last road before the Columbia River bridge, and continue 2 miles more to the National Park Service information center. From there walk the interpretive trail among ghostly streets, sidewalks, and building foundations.

(Also see COLVILLE, p. 38; FORT COLVILE [Hudson's Bay Company], p. 40; FORT COLVILLE [U.S. Army], p. 41; and SAINT PAUL'S MISSION, p. 47.)

LAKE ROOSEVELT. (See ROOSEVELT LAKE, p. 47.)

MARCUS seems from the highway like a hundred houses, a couple of grocery stores, and a big brick school, derelict now that kids are bussed to Kettle Falls. One glance seems enough—but Marcus has been a regional center.

The community began in the fall of 1860 when a team of 45 engineers, surveyors, astronomers, geologists, and naturalists appointed by Queen Victoria built a dozen log buildings and settled in for the winter. With them were mule packers and woodcutters needed for clearing a wide swath of trees and brush along the 49th parallel. Fifteen miles away, a similar American team moved in at the U.S. Army post of Fort Colville. Since 1818, the United States and Britain had formally shared land between 42° and 54°40′ north latitude, adhering to a "joint occupancy" treaty.

In 1846 Britain acquiesced regarding where the final boundary should be; the government was overextended coping with other international tensions. From the United States' standpoint, the pressing need was to assure a boundary far enough north that American ships would be guaranteed entry into Puget Sound, the only port of potential consequence north of San Francisco. The issue was settled—but given little actual heed. Then increased mining necessitated a survey: each government needed to know where to enforce its laws and which mines to tax. In 1862 the survey crews completed their work.

Marcus Oppenheimer almost immediately filed for a homestead on land where the British Boundary Commission buildings stood. He platted a townsite and turned one of the buildings into a store. Three years later a riverboat captain named Leonard White cannibalized a decrepit steamer and created the *Forty-nine,* the first paddle-wheeler to churn the river above Kettle Falls. For a year, the new vessel carried hopeful miners into British Columbia as far as Death Rapids (Revelstoke). They found little ore and paid Captain White insufficient fares to cover his costs. He went out of business, and the Oregon Railway and Navigation Company took over the operation; but in a few years they, too, gave up.

Miners on their way to Canada were then forced to ferry across the Columbia River at Marcus and follow an ancient native trail north. Business and population therefore stayed strong because reaching British Columbia mines was much easier via the north–south valleys of inland Washington than by crossing mountain passes from the coast. Men by the hundreds continued to throng into Marcus.

A new chapter began in 1880 when the Spokane Falls and Northern Railroad linked the growing town to the outside world. A few years later the rails extended to Northport, then to the rich mines at Rossland in British Columbia. An additional railroad—which became the Great Northern—crossed the Columbia at Marcus and followed the Kettle Valley in and out of Canada, connecting the mines and agricultural lands of the Okanogan to Spokane. This line made Marcus an even greater shipping center. Its roundhouse and train operations alone employed more than 100 men.

Logging provided additional payrolls. Early sawmills in outlying creek valleys turned out ties for logging and mining railroads and massive timbers for trestles and bridges. By the 1920s a spectacular aerial tram crossing the river carried logs to a railroad landing at Marcus. The population stood at 600; then the reservoir started backing behind Grand Coulee Dam.

Marcus was one of the largest towns forced to move. Today it thrives on higher ground as a pleasant residential community, the oldest continually occupied white settlement in Stevens County.

NORTHPORT nestles between the base of a high cliff and the Columbia. The tall smokestack of a defunct smelter rises from a flat above the river. Brick buildings wait by the railroad track, lonesome for past glory. A tavern retains colored glass above its windows and door, signatures of a proud identity. A blacksmith shop with a double door built high enough to accommodate teams and wagons sags forlornly on a side street.

In the 1860s miners churned up the Columbia River past the future site of Northport on board a paddle-wheeler, seeking a bonanza in placer gold with no investment beyond energy and prayer. Few succeeded. Twenty years later mining entered a new phase: instead of simple equipment for washing gold from river gravel, men needed machinery for tunneling into rock to blast ore veins. Machinery required capitalization, which in turn depended on investment houses and mining conglomerates.

Spokane wealth had begun with gold and lead production at Idaho mines in 1883, but it nearly strangulated four years later because of labor problems and litigation there. New discoveries at Nelson (on Kootenai Lake 50 miles north of the border) came just in time to restore cash balances.

To benefit from the boom, Spokane's renowned railroad builder D. C. Corbin extended his Spokane Falls and Northern Railroad north from Marcus to the rapids of the Little Dalles (15 miles below the international border), from where steamships ran on upriver. At the same time he picked a base for further expansion and bought the townsite of Northport. In the fall of 1892 a passenger train puffed up to a boxcar standing on a siding there as a temporary depot. The next day a second train arrived pulling a combination post office/saloon loaded on a flatcar. The postmaster at Little Dalles had simply rolled north as the tracks lengthened.

Corbin's next step was to lay track to the mines in British Columbia. On June 26, 1893, his rails reached the border and six months later—despite a nationwide financial crash—Spokane welcomed the first ore from Nelson. Three years after that, Corbin's Red Mountain and Columbia Railway twisted from Northport up to Rossland. To gain the 1,500 feet of elevation, he had his chief engineer build five high trestles and three half-mile loops, which included 22-degree arcs. In fact, the line avoided every possible obstacle, even large boulders and trees. Because of the railroad, Spokane financiers such as Patrick Clark, William Ridpath, George M. Forster, and other titans could keep the profits from their Rossland mine investments flowing south, not west to Vancouver.

Corbin also donated land to Northport for a smelter. The sight of smoke wafting from its new stack set off general rejoicing, although the *Northport Miner* cautioned that "fumes are getting in their deadly work on Mr. Walters' orchard." Mere months after the smelter opened, however, Spokane investors sold their interests at Rossland to Toronto and London interests—perfect timing, for the Klondike gold rush was drawing attention farther north, and labor strife soon crippled Rossland production. Income from the sales financed new buildings in downtown Spokane and built mansions in Browne's Addition and on Seventh Avenue. (Also see mansions listed under SPOKANE, p. 18).

The Northport smelter continued operation until 1921. Its smokestack today is conspicuous even from the highway. Near the stack is a small brick building screened by cottonwoods and aspens; additional stone walls line the railroad track.

At **Rossland** (17 miles from Northport), accessible via a paved loop road, mines honeycomb slopes to a vertical depth of 2,000 feet. The LeRoi Mine and an outstanding museum are open in summer. Drive the loop in a clockwise direction so as to be on the river side of the road returning south—a rare view of the untamed Columbia.

PINKNEY CITY has vanished. Drive 3 miles northeast of Colville on Aladdin Road to reach the site, now a hayfield—a classic example of how ephemeral the seemingly permanent may actually be. (A roadside sign identifies the general area of Pinkney City; the actual town stood north of Mill Creek in a long north-south valley.)

The community sprang up in the early 1860s alongside the U.S. Army's Fort Colville as a civilian supply point for miners, settlers, off-duty soldiers, and native people. Its name is that of the fort's commander, Major Pinkney Lugenbeel. Freight wagons from Wallula (near the confluence of the Snake and Columbia rivers) supplied both town and fort via the 250-mile Colville Road until 1881, when the Northern Pacific reached Spokane and shortened the distance.

The town served as the seat of a county that stretched across all of what is now northeast Washington and on to the continental divide. In bestowing that status, however, the territorial legislature changed Pinkney City's name to Fort Colville, a *third* pinpoint of white occupancy given that name: first was the Hudson's Bay Company's trading post, then the U.S. Army's fort, and finally the town. The general populace, however, continued to use the original name and to bemoan the need to travel so far to handle official business. In the book *Spokane Corona,* Jennie Bell, a teacher, is quoted regarding her journey to Pinkney City from the Spokane area to get her certificate:

I rode on horseback. There were no bridges . . . so the streams had to be forded and, when the water was high, all one could do was to crawl into the saddle, tuck in one's skirt, and let the horse swim across.

In 1883 the fort closed, and civilians moved to the present townsite of Colville.

(Also see COLVILLE, p. 38, and FORT COLVILLE, p. 40.)

ROOSEVELT LAKE stretches for 150 miles from Grand Coulee Dam almost to the Canadian border. It floods nearly 100,000 acres. To eliminate potential debris and navigation hazards, crews began clearing land for the reservoir in 1938. Nearly 3,000 men worked on the project, which included relocating small towns and rebuilding roads and bridges. At Kettle Falls, Lincoln, and Coulee City, mills cut 30 million board feet of lumber from logs floated downriver to their saws. The lake began filling in 1939. Its shores are now a recreation area administered by the National Park Service.

SAINT PAUL'S MISSION (just north of State Route 20, about 2½ miles west of the town of Kettle Falls) has been meticulously restored at its original location on a high bluff midway

Saint Paul's, one of Washington's earliest missions, opened in the 1840s.

between what was the astonishingly rich native salmon fishery at Kettle Falls and the Hudson's Bay Company fur-trading post of Fort Colvile (both now flooded by Roosevelt Lake). The chapel, built of squared logs, stands among ponderosa pines, which were not there while the mission was active; historic photographs show an open field created as people cut readily available wood for fuel. The architecture is French-Canadian "post-on-sill" style, rather than the usual log-cabin type of construction. Walls consist of horizontal logs with tongued ends, which slid into the grooves of upright posts. The posts, in turn, were joined to floor sills by mortise and tenon and secured with wooden pegs.

By the 1830s many native people in the Rocky Mountain west were seeking Christianity, which they supposed held the secret of the power so apparent among whites. They had a smattering of Catholicism picked up from devout French Canadians and converted Iroquois who trapped and traded for furs on behalf of the company. By policy, the Hudson's Bay Company officers were required to provide Christian instruction for their men, and Francis Heron, who alternated with

Archibald MacDonald in managing Fort Colville from 1829 to 1835, not only led Sunday services but also often proselytized among Indians. MacDonald, on the other hand, followed a policy toward missionaries that was cordial but filled with recommendations of other places for missions.

No Catholic mission took firm root in the Colvile district until after the region became officially American. Father Pierre Jean DeSmet picked the site of Saint Paul's in 1845, but no resident priest arrived until 1848. For the next 30 years, the mission served nearby native people, white settlers, and Irish-Catholic soldiers at the U.S. Army's Fort Colville.

In 1869 Jesuits consolidated their work in the region at a new mission in the Colville Valley. This left Saint Paul's without a resident priest, and over the next decade it gradually fell into disuse.

The **SPOKANE RESERVATION** was established in 1881 although the tribe ceded no land until 1887 and largely ignored the reservation. It now belongs to people more closely affiliated for generations than is true on several other reservations where groups were assembled largely for white convenience. Furthermore, this reservation land is part of what traditionally belonged to these particular people.

Official title to the land came after the Spokane refused to move onto the Colville Reservation, many of them objecting both to losing ancestral ties to their own territory and to the prospect of living among Catholic tribes. For the most part, the Spokane had been Christianized by Protestants. The mission at Tshimakain was Presbyterian; even prior to it, a chief known as Spokane Garry had been sent by the Hudson's Bay Company to an Anglican mission school at Red River, Canada, and upon return had preached Christianity to his people and held school classes.

Today the public is welcome on the Spokane Reservation but must stay on paved roads. Beadwork and other regalia are displayed at the tribal center in Wellpinit. The powwow grounds at the edge of town come alive each Labor Day weekend—everybody welcome.

(Also see TSHIMAKAIN MISSION, p. 21; and SPOKANE BATTLES sidebar, p. 10.)

NORTH CENTRAL Region

Homestead, west of Wauconda.

FOR SHEER, OBVIOUS *geologic shaping, few places on earth can match north central Washington. Successive floods of basalt lava two miles thick form a sagebrush plateau now conquered by agriculture. North of this realm lie the Okanogan Highlands, dotted by huge boulders that rode ice-age glaciers out of Canada, and to the west rise outliers of the Cascade Mountains. The Columbia River skirts the plateau, flowing as much as 2,000 feet below it.*

Native people felt the impending arrival of white newcomers in the mid-1700s: they acquired horses, brought to North America by Spanish conquistadors; they also began to contract diseases previously unknown. In 1811 explorer David Thompson traveled downriver and opened the fur-trade era, and half a century later the Hudson's Bay Company moved its operations out of the region and into Canada, closing that first chapter of white history. By then placer miners were washing river gravels for gold, and cattle kings were trailing herds to boomtowns and wintering them in the area around Loomis.

Unfenced land served as a great common for grazing cattle, horses, and sheep, which by the mid-1880s had eliminated the region's pristine cover of waist-high bunchgrass. Rails arrived about that same time and with them came thousands of settlers, many directly recruited by the Northern Pacific and Great Northern companies, which operated special display cars in the eastern United States and sent agents to talk with land-hungry Europeans. Wet years encouraged a belief that farming was possible. Dry years reversed the optimism.

Today orchards tuft river benches and huge irrigated fields augment a coverlet of dryland wheat. Where horses previously pulled plows, harrows, weeders, drills (for planting seeds), mowers, binders, headers, and wagons, tractors now prepare the soil and reap the harvest, and computers control the flow of irrigation, much of it from the Grand Coulee Dam project. Freight wagons, packtrains, and paddle-wheel steamers have become memory; bridges have replaced ferries; and railroads play a role secondary to highways, which even cross passes of the high Cascade Mountains with well-engineered grades and gently sweeping curves. A certain vastness nonetheless lingers in north central Washington, an unmistakable sense of place.

The Okanogan

The Okanogan includes three distinct realms: a green ribbon of orchards along the glaciated gorge of the river; grassy, farm-dotted heights that stretch as a vast tableland east of the Okanogan River; and mountainous valleys and lakes west of the Okanogan River, outliers of the Cascade Mountains. Mines abound in the back country, few of them operating, and former boomtowns continue as agricultural towns. Others have become ghost towns.

History museums are at Okanogan, Molson, and Oroville. Chesaw, now a miniature version of its mining camp glory days, hosts an annual Fourth of July rodeo. Omak is famed for its August Stampede. Tonasket holds a late-September steam threshing bee featuring equipment from before invention of the internal combustion engine. And a fall swap meet in the Aeneas Valley brings local people together to exchange everything from saddles to batches of homemade jam, craftwork to pistols.

AENEAS VALLEY (Ee′-nee-us) is named for an Okanogan chief who settled here in 1863 with his family and livestock, forsaking his ancestral lands and chiefly role in the forested region west of the Okanogan River. Aeneas could not control young men under him who wanted to kill invading white miners and settlers, yet he knew their course was futile. He moved east of the river to this grassy valley and claimed its entire 15-mile length. For a quarter of a century he raised horses, cattle, and oats here. Nobody contested his rights. Then white ranchers filed claims, and new laws reduced his holdings to 160 acres. Nonetheless, Chief Aeneas lived on at his ranch until his death in about 1905.

ARLINGTON MILL. (See "CHINA WALL," p. 55.)

BODIE was a gold boomtown. It now is a mere handful of empty buildings along the road from Wauconda to the Kettle River, but local people still speak of the Bodie Mine as "a real producer."

Henry Dewitts made a strike here before the Colville Reservation was opened for mining. As soon as mineral claims became legal, he staked several properties and sold one to his brother Ben, who hit a pocket of ore and instantly became $80,000 richer. That drew widespread attention, and the Dewittses sold to the Wrigley

Bodie now stands abandoned; it boomed sporadically from 1896 to the 1930s.

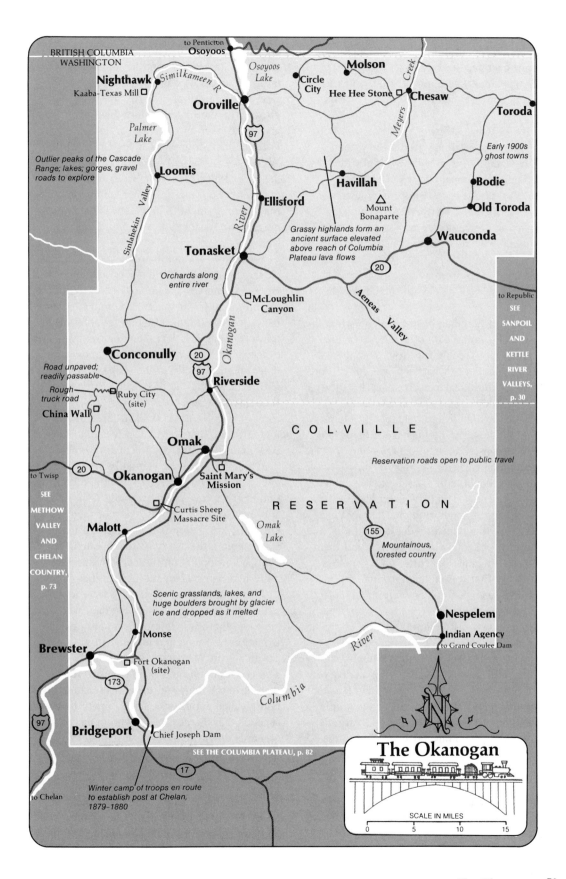

BRITISH COLUMBIA
WASHINGTON

to Penticton
Osoyoos

Nighthawk
Kaaba-Texas Mill □

Similkameen R.

Osoyoos
Lake

**Circle
City**

Molson

Hee Hee Stone □ **Chesaw**

Toroda

Oroville

97

*Palmer
Lake*

*Outlier peaks of the Cascade
Range; lakes; gorges, gravel
roads to explore*

Loomis

Ellisford

Havillah

Early 1900s
ghost towns

Bodie

Old Toroda

△
Mount
Bonaparte

*Grassy highlands form an
ancient surface elevated
above reach of Columbia
Plateau lava flows*

Wauconda

20

Sinlahekin Valley

Tonasket

*Orchards along
entire river*

□ **McLoughlin
Canyon**

Aeneas Valley

River

Okanogan

to Republic

SEE
SANPOIL
AND
KETTLE
RIVER
VALLEYS,
p. 30

Conconully

20

*Road unpaved;
readily passable*

Rough
truck road

□ **Ruby City
(site)**

97

Riverside

C O L V I L L E

China Wall □

Omak

Reservation roads open to public travel

to Twisp

20

Okanogan

□ **Saint Mary's
Mission**

R E S E R V A T I O N

SEE
METHOW
VALLEY
AND
CHELAN
COUNTRY,
p. 73

□ **Curtis Sheep
Massacre Site**

Malott

*Omak
Lake*

155

*Mountainous,
forested country*

*Scenic grasslands, lakes, and
huge boulders brought by glacier
ice and dropped as it melted*

River

Nespelem

Indian Agency
to Grand Coulee Dam

Monse

Brewster

□ **Fort Okanogan
(site)**

173

97

Bridgeport

Columbia

| **Chief Joseph Dam

SEE THE COLUMBIA PLATEAU, p. 82

17

to Chelan

*Winter camp of troops en route
to establish post at Chelan,
1879–1880*

The Okanogan

SCALE IN MILES
0   5   10   15

The Okanogan **51**

Brothers, wealthy chewing gum manufacturers with enough capital to build a reduction mill. The mill operated steadily from 1902 until 1917, then stood idle until 1934, at which time its production resumed for another six years.

BREWSTER has always been a town associated with transportation—first a ferry, then riverboats, the railroad, and now highways. Saint James Episcopal Church (123 Fifth Avenue SW; built in 1912) is constructed of rock from the Great Northern roadbed. The company agreed to donate any surplus blasted from its railway cuts during construction and, holding them to their promise, Brewster volunteers hauled rocks from as far as Chelan, then dressed it into neat blocks for the church's walls.

Settlement here had begun in 1888 when the stern-wheel steamer *City of Ellensburgh* inaugurated a twice-weekly run from Rock Island (near Wenatchee) to what then was called Port Columbia. Additional vessels soon also offered service, although somewhat unsatisfactorily. Low water created insurmountable problems. So did high water and winter ice. Rapids and rocks also caused frequent delays—and wrecks. At best, the upriver run—about 70 miles—took from before dawn until after dark. It included struggling through rapids by using cables that were threaded through ringbolts ashore, then carried back to a winch on deck. With this arrangement, paddle-wheelers could pull themselves along against the current.

Brewster first was called Virginia City in honor of "Virginia Bill" Covington, a colorful storekeeper at the steamer landing who had platted the town just before the Panic of 1893. That financial collapse delayed additional development. Furthermore, the Columbia and Okanogan Steamboat Company negotiated with Covington's homestead neighbor John Bruster for landing rights at a deepwater cove a mile north of the old landing. That ended Virginia City. Buildings and businesses moved to the favored landing. Thirty-two horses skidded even the hotel to the new location, an occasion exuberantly marked by en-route meal service and overall celebration. In 1898, the post office changed the spelling of the town's name from Bruster to Brewster.

Today **BRIDGEPORT,** just above the confluence of the Okanogan and Columbia rivers, is noticeable from the highway across the river because of its towering three-story flour mill, a symbol of earlier days. Wheat growers on the plateau, more than 2,000 feet above the river, at first took grain and other farm products to either Coulee City, Almira, Wilbur, or Mansfield—a long wagon haul. In the early 1900s men near Bridgeport joined the farmers in building a steamer landing and a road leading down to it. This was the beginning of the Bridgeport Warehouse and Milling Company.

Eventually the company operated a wheat elevator and mill at Bridgeport, a warehouse in Brewster, and two steamboats capable of carrying up to 2,600 full sacks of grain. The company flourished until trucking revolutionized transportation. Farmers then quit taking wheat to the river. They could get more money by delivering it directly to the railhead at Coulee City, eliminating the riverboats. Bridgeport's economy now rests on orchards. In season, rows of huge bins are stacked three or four high awaiting the harvest, each one holding 900 pounds of fruit. Shipment is by truck.

Chief Joseph Dam, virtually at the village doorstep, was authorized in 1946 and construction began a few years later with Congressional approval for irrigation as a part of the project. Ordinarily irrigation is a role of the Bureau of Reclamation; the Army Corps of Engineers deals with flood control; and both agencies build hydropower-generating facilities.

In this case, growers already were taking irrigation water from where the dam would be built and there was talk of eventually extending irrigation by flume and pipeline from Oroville practically to Wenatchee—enormously expensive construction (and maintenance). Rather than have the dam seal their intake, an everybody-wins solution was agreed upon: its essence is that the cost of delivering electricity to orchards downstream is far less than that of delivering water by flume and pipeline. As a result, pumps using power from the dam now lift river water fairly directly into orchards; and revenue from the sale of the power helps to pay off the cost of the dam. The matter is dull and bureaucratic sounding—except from the

When crews surveyed a railroad line to Bridgeport, settlers expecting a boom moved west from Connecticut. Actual tracks, however, were laid through Brewster (across the river).

standpoint of growers needing low-cost water and taxpayers seeking cost-effective installations.

The **CARIBOO TRAIL** (Cair′-uh-boo) constantly stayed either dusty or muddy for most of its 800 miles from Wallula and The Dalles to the mines of the upper Fraser River country. Riders drove cattle over this trail from the mid-1850s to the late 1860s, the years of the British Columbia gold boom. Huge herds grazed knee-high bunchgrass, splashed across streams, and swam the Columbia at its confluence with the Okanogan River. U.S. 97 now follows the old trail, a travel route used by native people and fur brigades long before cattle pounded it to dust. (The restored town of Barkerville, British Columbia, allows a glimpse of the delivery end of the long drives. Its 1860s population was greater than that of any other town north of San Francisco or west of Chicago, which made it a huge market for beef.)

In 1856 Ben Snipes seems to have driven the first beef-on-the-hoof to the hungry mining camps north of the Washington border. He had come to the Willamette Valley four years earlier

as a 17-year-old and from there joined a packtrain carrying apples to California gold camps. In California he prospected and also worked for a butcher who supplied miners with beef. In 1859, when word of Fraser River strikes trickled south, Snipes joined the stampede there; but on arrival he noticed a shortage of food more than an abundance of gold. He decided green grass was to create his fortune.

Beef at the mines sold for as much as a hundred times what it cost in Washington Territory. Snipes drove herds for others, borrowed money, and within five years owned more cattle than anyone else in the Northwest; estimates credit him with as many as 125,000 head of cattle and 20,000 horses at the peak of his operation. By the 1880s, when British Columbia camps had emptied, and beef was no longer in demand, he reversed direction and started driving as many as 3,000 head of cattle at a time from his Okanogan herds south to The Dalles. He paid Chief Moses a dollar a head for grazing rights in the Okanogan and sold to cattle buyers who were coming up the Columbia by steamer.

Somehow, the cattle drives of the Chisholm

In 1894 Joseph Bouska, Sr., from Austria, opened a hardware store at Bridgeport. Previously he had operated the government flour mill at Nespelem, then the Bridgeport mill.

Trail figure most prominently in Western lore, but the Cariboo Trail actually was twice as long. Furthermore, whereas the Chisholm Trail headed toward a railhead and civilization, the Cariboo led toward isolated camps that could be reached only by riding through unsettled country.

CHESAW (Chee'-saw), 21 miles east of Oroville, was once a rowdy mining center but is now a drowsy half-dozen old buildings, several new ones, and a few outlying homes. The name comes from Chee Saw, a Chinese placer miner who married a native woman, Julia Lumm, and settled down to farm her allotted land on Meyers Creek. In the 1890s, however, new regulations opened the northern half of the Colville Reservation to mining and a boomtown sprang up at Chee Saw's stream crossing, which was midway between Oroville, in Okanogan Valley, and Marcus, on the Columbia River (then a major town). Placer miners who had swarmed along Meyers Creek and Mary Ann Creek as much as 30 years earlier would scarcely have imagined the new town's splendor.

The new miners soon had surprises of their own. The reservation also opened for homesteading, and men intending to farm started selecting acreages, then brought in wives and children. Land grievances ran both ways between the two groups, logic only one. Farmers made more profit per ton on potatoes than miners made on gold.

By 1900 the town's population had grown to about 200, and it shot up to a thousand or more on Saturday nights when the two hotels held dances. Additional establishments included a bank, post office, newspaper, and emporiums of hope such as saloons, a millinery shop, and an assay office. The economy boomed, but then spiraled down. One of the hotels burned in 1906, never to rebuild. The saloon became a church by tacking on a steeple. Fire again swept town, and even buildings that escaped the flames began to collapse in upon themselves. Lumber shortages in World War I brought men to salvage wood for use elsewhere. Lumber from the two-story Chesaw school went into a Catholic church at Oroville; the Eagles Hall became an apartment house.

People still living at Chesaw remember, however, when "there was holes all over these hills" and, by staging an annual July Fourth rodeo, they recreate the old Saturday-night swelling of the town population: 20 year-round residents host 5,000 weekenders.

(Also see HEE HEE STONE, p. 60.)

The **"CHINA WALL"** is a gigantic mill foundation accessible by driving up Loup Loup Creek. (Turn off State Route 20 at Milepost 223, southwest of Okanogan, and drive 4 miles to the Rock Creek Campground; continue another 5 miles, then watch for the mill on the right, at the base of the hill. Some confusing turns; generally poor roads.)

Douglas fir and larch now screen the foundation, and all buildings—and hopes—have vanished despite the note of an 1890s government surveyor regarding shops, bunkhouses, a warehouse, and even an icehouse. Spectacular masonry accounts for the nickname China Wall. It stretches a cumulative 800 feet and rises in six courses with free-standing sections 30 feet high and three feet thick. Individual granite blocks measure as large as 4 by 2 by 1 feet, an enduring credit to the mill's builders if not to its production or promoters.

When government decrees restored the Moses–Columbia Reservation to public domain in 1886, miners staked hundreds of claims within weeks, and stages started running daily from Coulee City and Brewster to Ruby City, Conconully, and Loomis. Jonathan Bourne, a Portland lawyer infected with mining fever, bought an eventual total of 27 claims near Ruby City. Heir of a wealthy New England whaling and manufacturing family and member of Portland's genteel Arlington Club, he soon controlled more of the mining district than anyone else. No mills existed, but Bourne knew that ore would have to be concentrated before mine owners could afford to ship it to smelters at Tacoma or Helena, Montana, or even to comparatively nearby Granby, British Columbia.

He decided to remedy the situation. In 1889 he sent a mining engineer to inspect his properties. Back came reports that one so-called mine had "no vein at all," another must be "a joke," and so on. But the news might as well have been good: Bourne began a brickyard near a property named the Arlington and ordered production of 400,000 fire bricks for the furnace and steam boilers of his intended mill. He also arranged for machinery to come by ship from San Francisco to Portland, then by train to Davenport, and by wagon train the final 120 miles.

To build the mill, he hired a German stonemason named Chris Starzman who had homesteaded near Brewster. Starzman somehow organized local miners, carpenters, farmers, and ne'er-do-wells into a work force that successfully quarried granite outcrops above the mill site, skidded blocks downslope, and built massive walls, all within the summer and early fall of 1889. The superstructure never reached completion, however. Backers—mostly Bourne's fellow members at the Arlington Club—at last believed reports and withdrew support.

Bourne built a new, smaller mill on the Ruby side of the hill and actually operated it for a few months in 1892. Then the nationwide financial Panic of 1893 burst that particular bubble of hope, and he turned attention to grubstaking prospectors for the Yukon and Alaska gold rush

Bourne's mill never processed ore but its incredible "China Wall" still stands.

and to shipping Nome's first gold dredge north. A little later he served in the U.S. Senate, where he fathered the national parcel post system.

(Also see RUBY CITY, p. 69.)

The drive to **CIRCLE CITY** is best from Molson toward Oroville—downhill. West of Molson, an unpaved road follows the Great Northern grade barely inside the Washington border. About 6 miles west of town it offers a view down onto a broad flat, which geologically is the top of a kame terrace, a legacy of ice-age glaciation. The flat is the location of Circle City, now vanished except for roadbeds and memories. Railroad families and crewmen lived here from 1906 until 1932, their schedules centered on the timetable for train service between Spokane and Oroville (and eventually another 82 miles on to Princeton, British Columbia).

Trains stopped at Circle City for half an hour to cool their brakes on the downhill run, which entailed a 2,800-foot drop in elevation and required 28 miles of switchbacks. A steeply sloping spur gave runaway trains an escape track if they lost braking power, and a great U curve eased stopping for routine cooling. The downhill passenger train from Molson to Oroville took an hour. Uphill, it needed two hours, tons of coal, and three stops for water. Freight trains often barely managed the climb at all. In fact, Okanogan cattlemen as far away as Loomis delivered their herds to Molson on-the-hoof rather than send them up the grade from Oroville.

CONCONULLY (Kahn-kuh-null'-ee) today amounts to a back-roads cluster of neat buildings with businesses offering the usual services, plus the mown grass of Conconully State Park. It began in the spring of 1886 when prospectors pitched tents and started a new mining district. Congress had just sliced a strip 15 miles wide off the Moses–Columbia Reservation for the express convenience of prospectors. Placer operations had begun on the Similkameen River as early as 1859, and hardrock miners first found lode gold near Conconully in 1871. Removing land from the reservation added legality to the prospecting already going on.

During a brief heyday, the Conconully mining district produced silver, lead, and copper, along with some gold, zinc, and molybdenum. Men shipped ore to distant smelters, a huge expense that began with a 45-mile wagon haul to the Columbia at Brewster (or at Riverside whenever high water let boats churn that far up the Okanogan). From the landing, the shipments traveled downriver to the railhead at Wenatchee, then on to the smelter. High costs for such cumbersome shipping combined with the 1893 nationwide financial panic ended most mining in this area, although diehards continued annual assessment work.

Its boom over, the town nonetheless hung on. Agriculture proved an enduring form of income. As early as August 1891 a government surveyor had commented that:

. . . the entire Salmon Valley is more valuable for agricultural purposes than for mineral and although several placer claims had been taken no one pretended to work them for minerals.

The point is significant. Mining claims had to be recorded, and recording gave a legal basis for later title to the land. Cattlemen, on the other hand, could not file claims until after land had been surveyed and formally opened for homesteading. Because of this difference in procedure, farms often began as "mines."

The farming gained a boost in December 1905 when Congress authorized the **Conconully Dam** as part of an irrigation project, one of the earliest in the Northwest undertaken by the Reclamation Service (now the Bureau of Reclamation). Construction began in 1907 supervised by Lars Bergsvik, a Norwegian engineer experienced in hydraulic mining. He brought water 3½ miles by flume and used it to sluice earth from a mountainside and send it to the dam site via a second, steel-lined flume. A system of screens then dumped coarse material from this slurry onto outer slopes, and fine material and silt to the inside. Workmen puddled a watertight core held by larch pilings driven 33 feet into the ground.

The engineering of the dam was remarkable, but problems arose as soon as irrigation canals started to flow. The water supply fell short of expectations, and leaks and seepage squandered much of what there was. The newly organized irrigation district had to drop about a third of its intended acreage. This financially ruined many farmers who already had set out young orchards. Leo Klessig, who had come to the Okanogan Valley on foot in 1907 and taken up land, commented:

Everyone knew that sand would grow just as good orchards as any other soil if you got it wet. . . . We set out trees, built houses, formed a local improvement district. . . and saw a bright vision. . . .

We had heard, of course, that many privately organized and built irrigation projects had come to grief, [but] this project was different. It was backed by the government. . . . What we did not realize was that the government could not make it snow or rain. . . . There just wasn't enough water. I and many like me had a fine young orchard in the early bearing stage and dying before our eyes.

Today the Conconully reservoir nestles between mountain wall and valley flat, unobtrusively held by Bergsvik's earthfill dam, which could pass for an oversize glacial moraine. Balsamroot flowers gild surrounding slopes in April and May, and fishermen revel in myriad quiet lakes.

The name Conconully comes from a Salish word that translates as "money hole," reference to abundant beaver in the creek, their pelts usable as cash at Fort Okanogan.

The **CURTIS SHEEP MASSACRE SITE** (4 miles southwest of Okanogan on State Route 20) is on sagebrush benchland with a distant view to the Okanogan Highlands. Its ambience is peaceful, its past violent.

In 1901 a sheepman rented bottomland near Oroville and put up hay, then brought in 9,000 head of sheep. Soon after that, his hay "mysteriously" burned—700 tons of it in one night; cattle ranchers felt strongly about sheep. The cattlemen formed a protective association and warned another sheepman, A. A. Curtis, that his plans to produce wool were unwise. Curtis sold what sheep he had, then decided against intimidation and bought another band. One morning after having bedded them in portable pens, he found all 1,200 clubbed to death. Curtis salvaged what fleeces he could,

attempted prosecution, gave up, and moved away. For years, bones whitened the hillside. The site now is on the State Inventory of Historic Places as representative of the widespread enmity between cattlemen and sheepmen.

The story of **ELLISFORD** is linked with churches—and the small community is noticeable from the highway mostly because of its shrinelike bell structure. Father Urban Grassi stayed here in 1885 while building a mission chapel, but before it was done he was called to Spokane to supervise construction work at Gonzaga University. Young Father Etienne de Rouge replaced him. He finished the chapel and planted seeds sent by his mother in France, the first garden flowers many Okanogan natives and white homestead children had ever seen.

De Rouge also held services at Chief Sarsapkin's house; founded Saint Mary's Mission near Omak; and built outlying chapels at Loomis and Chopaka. In 1888 he built a larger church at Ellisford and when it burned 15 years later, he patiently began a third church. The bell preserved today is a survivor from additional fires later on. Its shelter stands behind the Brethren Church, a denomination whose people—often called Dunkards—left Germany because of prejudice in the 1700s. Many eventually settled in Pennsylvania and from there moved again during World War I. About 30 families took up farming around Ellisford.

The site of **FORT OKANOGAN** (Oh-kuh-nah'-gun) belonged sequentially to three different fur-trading companies. A state park visitor center (usually open only in summer) highlights the story and offers a sweeping view, in itself worth stopping to see.

At first, Fort Okanogan stood on a long low point edged by the Columbia and Okanogan rivers, a site now flooded by the Wells Dam reservoir. The post later moved onto higher ground, now under 20 feet of fill dirt brought in to create a broad agricultural flat.

In the fall of 1811 David Stuart and Alexander Ross, employees of the Pacific Fur Company, arrived on the east bank of the Okanogan River after a trip up the Columbia from Astoria. A mile above the Okanogan's mouth they found what they were looking for: a site suitable for a

THE FUR TRADE

In 1763 the Treaty of Paris took Canada from France and gave it to England. French fur companies withdrew and Scotsmen living in Montreal and New Englanders (who still were British subjects) rushed to fill the void. They relied on the continued brawn and wilderness knowledge of French voyageurs and employees born of French fathers and native mothers, who simply switched from working for one company to another.

Montreal provided the base of operations, a riverport roughly as far east as New York City. This position was far less advantageous than the Hudson's Bay Company's saltwater access to the western shore of Hudson Bay, a penetration of the continent to about the longitude of Minneapolis—and an exclusive right zealously guarded by the company's London directors. Freed of French rivals, the Hudson's Bay Company, already a century old, regarded the new competition as that of upstart "pedlars."

Among the newcomers were Alexander Henry of New Jersey and Peter Pond of Connecticut, who organized an amalgamation of independent wilderness traders and Montreal merchants into the North West Company. They originated two concepts crucial to fur trading in the Northwest. From native people they learned that certain rivers flowed like highways to the Pacific Ocean. Also, Pond read the account of Captain James Cook's 1778 voyage to the Northwest coast as soon as it was published and from it recognized the possibility of entering the sea-otter trade by supplying posts from the east via the rivers, then shipping furs to China.

He gained little support, but among those listening was young Alexander Mackenzie, who went on to lead an overland crossing of the continent. Mackenzie reached the Pacific at Bella Coola (northern British Columbia) in 1793, just six weeks after one of the boats from Captain George Vancouver's ship *Discovery* had explored nearby waters. Eventually he wrote a book about the expedition and in it urged that Britain should secure control of river approaches to the western edge of the continent by establishing a boundary with the United States on the south side of the Columbia River. Thomas Jefferson, newly inaugurated as President, and his secretary Meriwether Lewis read this proposal with grave concern.

Not long after the book's publication, another major player entered the growing competition for wealth through fur. This was John Jacob Astor, a German immigrant who had succeeded as a New York entrepreneur and owned a fleet of ships trading in Canton. As an American, Astor was not bound by British monopolies, such as those granted to the Hudson's Bay Company and to the East India Company (which was chartered for exclusive British trade with China).

Astor proposed to trade furs from the west coast of America in Canton and, as part of his scheme, won the cooperation of Russians in Alaska, who were barred from entering China. Astor would trade Alaskan furs for them. In exchange the Russians agreed to drop their plans for a trading post at the mouth of the Columbia, an effort that temporarily had been aborted in 1806 when one of their ships failed to cross the treacherous bar at the mouth of the river.

His ideas formulated, Astor suggested to the North West Company that they join him in giving the Hudson's Bay Company dual competition coordinated out of Montreal *and* New York. They spurned the offer, and Astor organized his own Pacific Fur Company.

The Northwest's crucial years of fur trading were about to begin.

trading post. They built a driftwood cabin for the winter, then put up outbuildings and a five-room, adobe-plastered house the following year. Not long after that, war between Britain and the infant United States caused the Pacific Fur Company, owned in New York, to sell out to the North West Company of Montreal. The acquisition intensified rivalry between the Nor'westers and the Hudson's Bay Company, an animosity that grew so ruinous that the British government in 1821 forced the two companies to merge. Fort Okanogan thereupon found itself under the Hudson's Bay Company, its third owner in just 10 years.

Operations were profitable at first. Alexander Ross, who had married an Okanogan native woman and stayed through the first winter, noted that from 1811 to 1812 he traded goods costing the company 35 pounds sterling for pelts (mostly beaver) that were worth 2,250 pounds in Canton: the equivalent of $160 ballooned into more than $10,000. Even so, six years after the Hudson's Bay Company took over, George Simpson, the dynamic governor of the company, reduced Fort Okanogan's status to little more than an interpreter's post and a repair and rest station for horse brigades traveling to and from British Columbia. He made Fort Colvile the hub of inland trade because of a central location and possibilities for a farm.

Until 1860 the company nonetheless maintained a British "presence" at Fort Okanogan. Then it moved all goods and supplies to a post at Keremeos, British Columbia. Local natives and Chinese placer miners became de facto heirs to the fort. They apparently dismantled it to salvage materials for use elsewhere.

(Also see FORT COLVILE, p. 40.)

HAVILLAH (Hah-vil′-uh) gives an excuse to sample back roads lacing the Okanogan Highlands east of Oroville and Tonasket. The world seems made of grassy hills and oats and barley fields; then a steeple appears, and there is Havillah nestled in a draw.

Physically the town amounts to an old flour mill converted to a house, a classic 1917 country church and parsonage reached by footbridge across a creek, and a handful of other buildings. Apparent along with the buildings is a tenacious local pride intact from the early 1900s. At that time many Okanogan miners became farmers, and other farmers came West on bargain-fare, one-way tickets aboard the Great Northern Railway. Among these latter were devoted German Lutherans whose descendants still center their lives on the Havillah church. "They really stick together, that whole community," neighbors say.

Martin Schweikert already had built a gristmill and store and named them Havillah before the arrival of these new settlers. The increased business opportunity they represented led him to buy a surplus engine from the railroad at Molson and hire a neighbor to haul it to Havillah by oxteam. With the boiler, Schweikert converted his mill to steam power and enlarged its capacity. Farmers from miles around brought their wheat once a year to be ground until 1915 when Schweikert moved his operation to Tonasket. The Havillah mill then became a school and, in the 1980s, a granddaughter of the original owner changed the mill/school into a home.

About the time of Schweikert's move, the Great Northern completed a branch line serving the Okanogan Valley from Wenatchee. This helped families who owned wheat farms; it also linked creameries to markets and, for many Okanogan Highlands families, that meant a way to stay financially solvent while getting irrigation, orchards, and beef herds under way. They sent their cream or butter to collection points once a week and fed the leftover skimmed milk to hogs and calves. Vern Harkness, raised near Havillah, reminisced about the period in the county historical quarterly *Okanogan County Heritage*:

Most of the cream was sour cream, but once in a while we would have a can of sweet cream, for which we would get a premium price. If Dad couldn't get to town that week, he would send the cream with the mailman and get the empty can back the same day. . . .

The [milk] separator was a hand crank machine. It took a lot of effort to get it up to full speed. . . . Twenty minutes was required to separate the milk. I think Mother needed that long to wash the separator and all the milk pails.

Cream production declined through the 1930s,

although as the *Tonasket Times* noted, "Those of us who were raised with sour cream butter on the table . . . find today's sweet cream butter flat in taste." Newly stringent health laws forbade cooling milk in well water, however, and this necessitated buying expensive refrigeration equipment, which few small farm owners could afford. Furthermore, orchards were beginning to take full-time care in the Okanogan Valley, while on the highlands beef cattle were proving more profitable than dairy herds.

Remnants of the **HEE HEE STONE** (and a county historical society sign) poignantly mark a hillside southwest of Chesaw. A Native American trail came this way and, in the 1860s, gold miners on their way to discoveries at Rock Creek, British Columbia, also used the route.

Various traditions account for the importance of the spot to native people. One is that a betrothed Spokane maiden journeying to meet her Osoyoos husband-to-be got word of his death, dropped to the ground weeping, and turned to stone. Through the years tribesmen passing her silent form left votive tokens and prayed for their own fortunes. After Jesuit priests arrived in the area, an angel appeared above nearby Bonaparte Peak and then came to the stone and told native people to plant camas and eat the roots so that they would suffer no more epidemics of white men's diseases.

In 1905 two drunken white prospectors wantonly dynamited the Hee Hee Stone, an act that inevitably caused tension between native people and newcomer white settlers. Decades later the Molson-Chesaw-Knob Hill community development club piled up the pieces and the historical society erected a heritage sign. The huge old stone had been one of the hundreds of glacial erratic boulders that rode the ice sheet

SQUATTER'S RIGHTS

All members of federal land survey crews formally swore to the honesty of their work. For example, four chainmen, having been sworn in for an 1891 Okanogan survey, promised they would

> level the chain over even and uneven ground, and plumb the tally-pins either by sticking or dropping the same [and] report the true lengths of all lines that we assist in measuring.

The surveys mattered a great deal. Until they were done, no settlers could get land titles under homestead laws. Only "squatter's rights" were available, a de facto first-come, first-served claim that was valid providing the claimant did not leave the land for more than six months at a time. Yet men often had to work away from their claims for cash; simply driving cattle to market might take three months. Claim jumpers commonly took advantage of such absences. Abuse of mining laws caused trouble, too, by letting prospectors claim any kind of land regardless of mineral value. Guy Waring, first storekeeper at Loomis, wrote that no farmer's land "unless surveyed and properly filed upon . . . is secure from depredation."

Waring himself began his holdings at Loomis with squatter's rights purchased in 1884 from a previous rancher. He wrote to the editor of *The Nation* concerning squatters' hardships:

> When [a man] has selected his claim, he cannot obtain a title to it till after it has been surveyed; and, instead of feeling secure . . . he is obliged to remain there uninterruptedly . . . till the survey has been made. I know of many instances where a residence of twenty years would go for nothing if the squatter were to absent himself for six months. . . . [Another] universal complaint is that land which has been staked out by the squatter and improved, perhaps for years, *never* coincides with the lines of the actual survey; so that half of a squatter's improved claim may be of little real value.

out of Canada onto the Okanogan Highlands.

LOOMIS, a pleasant, lived-in sort of town, can be reached either from the north via the scenic gorge of the Similkameen River (Sih-milk′-uh-meen) and Palmer Lake, or up an irrigated valley that is a tributary of the Okanogan River. Flumes cling to valley walls and snake their way, trestle by trestle, to thirsty orchards within the "rain shadow" of the Cascade Mountains.

As early as the 1870s, the Yakima cattle firm of Phelps and Wadleigh paid Chief Moses for rights to graze cattle in the area. In 1884 Harvard-educated Guy Waring took over the arrangement and began three years as an Okanogan rancher. During that time he opened a store in his house and took J. A. Loomis as a partner.

In 1886 the area opened for homesteading. Mining had begun several years earlier. Many of the prospectors who had rushed to the Fraser River and Cariboo districts in British Columbia had grown discouraged and returned south. As one man wrote to his wife:

I have been humbugged. Gold is not as plentiful as we were led to believe, and it is ten times harder work to get it than anyone could have imagined.

Some of these discouraged men found "color" along the Similkameen River and, while working these placers, also discovered nearby hard-rock silver, lead, and tungsten deposits. Okanogan native people who had started farms sold the miners meat and vegetables, and a few whites also searched for farmland—or callously preempted native farms during the owners' seasonal absences. Frontier law prevailed; there were no conventional jurisdictions, except for those long recognized by the native people but ignored by the whites.

In 1879, however, the government established the Moses–Columbia Reservation, which spread from the crest of the Cascades to the west bank of the Okanogan River, and from the mouth of the river to the British Columbia border. Whites objected. They refused to give up holdings they had come to regard as theirs and argued successfully for the removal of a 15-mile strip of land across the entire northern border of the reservation. The deletion took effect in 1883, the year before Waring arrived.

Chief Sarsapkin, who lived near Loomis, traveled to Washington, D.C.—accompanied by Chiefs Moses, Tonasket, and Lot—to negotiate compensation for the loss of land. While the four chiefs were there, government officials suggested removing all the land from reservation status and offered a twofold choice of consequences: The reservation would be restored to public domain. Natives then could accept individual allotments of land and give up all tribal rights. Or they could continue to live tribally and harvest wild resources as they always had done. If they chose this traditional pattern, however, they would have to leave ancestral lands in the Okanogan and move onto the Colville Reservation.

Sarsapkin decided to accept farming. The government agreed to allot land—from the natives' viewpoint already theirs—on the basis of one square mile per family or single adult man. From 1884 until 1886 Sarsapkin's people picked out land for farming, then the reservation ceased to exist and all remaining land opened to the public. At that point, mining and ranching south of the 15-mile strip—much of it already under way—also became legal.

Over time, various mines pocking the slopes above Loomis produced ore, and local concentration and reduction mills made periodic shipments to distant smelters for final refining. Other mines produced metal only from the pockets of investors.

Back-roads enthusiasts will enjoy exploring the **Sinlahekin Valley;** driving to **Chopaka Lake** via a steep, switchback road; or skirting the north end of Palmer Lake and paralleling the abandoned Great Northern right-of-way to **Chopaka,** once an outlying Catholic mission served by Father Griva (see REPUBLIC, p. 35.)

The silence at **McLOUGHLIN CANYON** is now broken by birdsong, not bullets. But tensions here erupted into north central Washington's only battle between natives and whites. (To reach the canyon, turn off U.S. 97 onto Janis Road 4 miles south of Tonasket.)

Treaties signed at Wallula in 1855 failed to solve land issues, and successive gold discoveries near Colville and in British Columbia exacerbated ill will by drawing thousands of miners who stampeded across the land. In late

June 1858 several small groups of miners, who first met at Fort Walla Walla, organized themselves into a single party of about 150 led by a man named James McLoughlin. These men set out for Rock Creek, British Columbia (north of Republic), with 750 pack mules. Behind them were three similar parties who even had along carpenters and blacksmiths to build a city and forge equipment.

Such wholesale trespass alarmed natives. They resented the men overall, were angered by their occasional theft of horses, and outraged by their mistreatment of native women. There already had been scattered killings.

Several Palouse led by Red Jacket followed the McLoughlin party, hoping to run off their mules. At Moses Coulee they killed one of the miners, and Chief Moses—whose territory the miners were entering at that point—warned that if the party went into the Okanogan Valley, he would kill them. Nonetheless, the miners continued. Moses had ample warriors for an attack; in fact, he had added men from the Chelan and Okanogan bands to his own. Even so, he held back, for his men had only flintlock rifles, which were no match in open country for the long-range muskets the whites were carrying. After crossing the Okanogan River, near the present town of Riverside, the Canada-bound party turned up a narrow canyon. There, as James McLoughlin years later told the *Spokesman Review:*

I noticed bushes piled against rocks, and my eyes being pretty sharp, I noticed the leaves were wilted. . . . [I] got within thirty yards when I noticed a painted buck behind a little stone fort and breastwork. . . .

The fight immediately became general and lasted from 10 a.m. until 5 p.m., when we retreated to the river, under a steady fire from the Indians. . . . We lost in the fight four killed and twenty wounded . . . also twenty-five pack animals.

As soon as Major Robert Garnett learned of the battle, he rode out from Fort Simcoe. He captured and executed eight native men as "punishment" for both the killing of miners in Yakima territory three years previously and for the recent deaths in McLoughlin Canyon. He failed to capture either Moses or Qualchin

McLoughlin Canyon figured in an 1858 battle between miners and natives.

(whom the army held accountable for the Yakima incident) but Colonel George Wright a few weeks later captured Qualchin south of Spokane Falls and hanged him, dramatically demonstrating the government's intolerance of attacks on whites. Moses had ridden to warn Qualchin, but missed him.

(Also see SPANGLE, p. 9, and SPOKANE BATTLES sidebar, p. 10.)

At **MALOTT** (Muh-lot′) a bridge spans the Okanogan River and links the secondary, westside valley road with U.S. 97 along the east side of the river. Both roads are scenic. Historic beginnings here tie Malott to the Chiliwist Trail, the main link between the Okanogan and Methow valleys until a wagon road was scratched westward from Brewster in 1891. Long a route used by native people, the Chiliwist also drew fur traders, miners, and army explorers such as Henry H. Pierce, who led a summer survey from Fort Colville to Puget Sound in 1882.

While camped south of Malott, Pierce wrote that "Lap-a-loop with four of his neighbors visited the camp, bringing melons and green corn of which we made a feast." Already elderly, Lap-a-loop had chosen farm life in preference to tribal life. On land irrigated from a spring, he raised ample oats and vegetables, although Pierce noted that "the ever-present bug [Colorado potato beetle] had made sad havoc" of his potato crop that year. The beetle was one of Washington's earliest agricultural hitchhikers. It originated on the eastern slope of the Rockies where it fed on buffalo bur (*Solanum rostratum*). As settlers passed through the region, the beetle got into their seed potatoes (*Solanum tuberosum*) and rode West. The two plants are close relatives.

Apparently not long after Pierce's sojourn, the L. C. Malott family arrived here and settled down. For years, their ranch served as a stage station. When the railroad built along the Okanogan River (1913 to 1914), a town developed as a railhead for the upper Methow Valley, which was accessible via the Chiliwist Trail.

Today's Malott is a reconstruction of buildings swept by flood in 1938 when a dam on Loup Loup Creek burst and turned the main street into watery chaos. During World War II a prisoner-of-war camp for captured German tank corpsmen, located near town, supplied men to work in the area's orchards. They filled critically short manpower needs, and at the end of the war a few of these men settled here.

MOLSON has a year-round population of about two dozen yet draws 3,000 visitors a year to its two historical museums, which consist of an outdoor collection of pioneer buildings and equipment, and also an early 1900s schoolhouse filled with displays and staffed by volunteers who lend a firsthand perspective. Harry Sherling wrote in the historical society quarterly *Okanogan County Heritage* about his arrival at Molson in the winter of 1902–1903:

We traveled by rail to Midway, B.C., then by horse sleigh stage . . . to Molson. Next day we continued in a livery barn rig to our homestead cabin. . . .

Our clothes and other finer things were kept in a trunk, which also was used to sit on. . . . Our land was broken with a one-beam plow and four walking horses.

Molson began in 1900 as a mining town developed by promoter George Meacham and financed by George Molson, member of the wealthy Montreal brewing family. The town never went through a saloons-and-shanties phase, but instead started right out with a main street 100 feet wide, augmented by 40 neatly laid out blocks. There was a 34-room, three-story hotel, a newspaper (the *Molson Magnate*), the services of an attorney, doctor, and veterinarian, and specialty stores such as a millinery and a harness shop.

Only one mine in the area ever shipped any ore, however—the Poland China on upper Mary Ann Creek—and that led the Molson family to withdraw their backing and close the bank they had opened in town. The population, which had reached 300, nose-dived but soon climbed back. Homesteaders such as the Sherlings began arriving, drawn by rumors that the northern half of the Colville Reservation would be restored to public domain. Canadian farm families living within wagon distance of Molson came regularly for supplies and to socialize. Customs officers recognized the convenience and the neighborliness of these crossings, and they ignored border formalities.

Next came an announcement that Great Northern trains between Spokane and Princeton, British Columbia, would come through Molson. That touched off "a ruckus." Meacham had squatter's rights to the town but never had filed a plat. Knowing this, John McDonald, owner of the town livery barn and a stagecoach line, took advantage of a newly completed land survey and filed a homestead that included the entire town. Angered, some of the citizenry moved a quarter mile north and established New Molson. A bank built on skids opened in Old Molson but did business for several days while being dragged from lot to lot, dramatising the land issue by supposedly seeking a clear title. A new brick school (now the museum) and a Grange hall finally brought about a compromise halfway between the two townsites. They rose from neutral ground and gave the town a third center.

The land quibble affected people in Molson and amused the surrounding community; the coming of the train affected everybody. Large crews grading the roadbed, building trestles, and laying track gave settlers on the Okanogan Highlands an instant market for farm produce. When train service began in 1906 railroad ties, lumber, cordwood, hay, grain, and livestock rode out from Molson to market, and supplies and people rode in.

In 1935 Molson lost its trains. A branch line between Wenatchee and Oroville had been completed 20 years earlier. Mines throughout the border country had shut down. And population patterns had shifted. Molson became a scenic backwater.

CHIEF JOSEPH'S RETURN FROM EXILE

In 1883 and 1884 individuals, philanthropic organizations, and missionary societies in the eastern United States directed pleas to Congress on behalf of Chief Joseph and his Nez Perce and Palouse followers, held as exiles in what now is Oklahoma. Westerners, remembering their former terror, did not join the letter campaign.

As native people understood the terms of their surrender in 1878, they were to be allowed to live on the reservation at Lapwai, Idaho, not be indefinitely treated as captives. Nonetheless, they cooperated overtly with their captors and in 1879 Joseph and Yellow Bird traveled from Indian Territory to Washington, D.C., to present their case. An interview with Joseph, published in a widely read magazine, stirred the ongoing public protest over his plight: 431 captives had been sent east; 130 had died. None were happy. Few were healthy.

Slowly the government made arrangements to return the people to the Northwest. Twenty-nine elderly men, widows, and orphans moved to the Nez Perce reservation in 1882. Two years later the remaining 268 exiles walked for a day and a night to reach the railroad and travel toward home. On May 27 their train arrived at Wallula. There a division took place. Those who professed Christianity went to Lapwai. Those who preferred to remain "blanket Indians" and continue seeking guidance through dreams and visions went to the Colville Reservation. This second group numbered 150 men, women, and children, all of them by then exhausted.

They traveled by train and wagon to Fort Spokane where Agent Sidney Waters, making no effort to conceal his displeasure, reported that the Nez Perce and Palouse had arrived "against the wishes of the people of the Territories" (i.e., Washington and Idaho). He had made no provision to care for them and supplied only one-quarter rations of food, a situation not improved for two months.

In December Joseph and his people finally crossed the mountains to Nespelem. Chief Moses, already there with his Sinkiuse (Columbia) and Methow bands, objected to their arrival. The Colville chief, Skolaskin, objected even more. Nonetheless, the move was completed, at one point with troops from Fort Spokane present to assure peace.

Few of Joseph's people ever farmed, an act of "tearing the earth," which their religion viewed as akin to tearing the breast of one's mother. Most made a living by hunting, fishing, digging roots, raising cattle, and earning cash from odd jobs. They kept up their spirits with expectations of returning to their home in the Wallowa Valley of Oregon. In December

NESPELEM (Nez-pee'-lem), headquarters for the Colville Confederated Indian Tribes, is underlain with poignancy. A business council manages logging, sawmilling, and meat packing. Schools and a health center are modern. The surrounding scenery is awesomely beautiful and almost pristine. But only a few generations have passed since this became the home not only of native people with ancestral ties here but also of others denied their own land.

Chief Moses, leader of the Sinkiuse and Wenatchee bands, lies buried near the Indian Agency, 2½ miles south of town. His tall marble headstone reads simply:

Chief Moses, Born 1829
Died March 25, 1899
Aged 70 Years

Chief Joseph, tragic Nez Perce leader, is

The grave of Joseph, tragic Nez Perce chief from Oregon, is at Nespelem.

1897 Joseph again traveled to Washington, D.C., to repeat his claim to a right to return home. The following year he was allowed to visit there, but whites—who still populated the valley only lightly—objected to the chief's proposed return. The government agent accompanying him did nothing to press the request. On the contrary, he told Joseph that white men were improving the land and "should enjoy the profit of [their] enterprise." With those words, Joseph knew his cause was lost.

buried on a hillside at the northeast edge of Nespelem. His likeness, carved into the white marble shaft marking his grave, faces southwest, toward the Wallowa Valley of Oregon, which he and his people longed to regain. They had been exiled to mosquito-infested Indian Territory (now Oklahoma) following the 1878 Nez Perce War, then in response to public outcry had been allowed to return to the West. Assigned to the Colville Reservation in 1885, Joseph's band always expected to be allowed to go home to the Wallowa Valley. It was not to be. Six years after a brief visit there, Joseph died still an exile. In 1902, two years before his death, a Spokane woman making a bas-relief of the chief from a photograph of him as a young man went to Nespelem. When she showed Joseph the picture, he murmured, "That man died long ago."

In 1935 Yellow Wolf was buried near Joseph.

(Also see COLVILLE RESERVATION, p. 31.)

NIGHTHAWK has provided enough photographs to be known as the quintessential Okanogan ghost town. Furthermore, it flanks the main road along the Similkameen River near Oroville in a "can't-miss-it" position. Thirty to 40 buildings constitute the town, some old, some recent, some occupied, some long abandoned—and all privately owned. Nighthawk is a place to enjoy through the windshield but not to investigate directly. It is best viewed from the long hill north of town, a vantage point that shows the buildings strung along the river.

Formal beginnings date to 1903 when Jim Haggerty, editor of the Oroville newspaper, platted a townsite to serve the Nighthawk Mine. His town soon boasted full amenities, including a post office and an electric plant powered by the falls of the Similkameen, which lit not only local houses and businesses but also those of Ruby City and other nearby boomtowns. When the Great Northern ran in a spur line, Nighthawk

served as a transshipping center for Loomis and Conconully. It was a prominent town. Now it symbolizes the passing of time.

South of Nighthawk, a dirt road on the west side of the river leads 1 mile south to the abandoned mill and sterile tailings of the Kaaba-Texas Mine. A producer of real wealth, this property is privately owned and posted against trespass, but even when seen only from the road it carries a feeling of a typical mine camp.

The city of **OKANOGAN** (Oh-kuh-nah'-gun) spreads along the west bank of the Okanogan River where Salmon Creek has built a broad delta. Several early buildings remain. Among them, the Methodist church (Queen Street, a block west of U.S. 97) is interestingly faced with river cobbles. The courthouse (Third Avenue) vaguely suggests Spanish Mission architecture, which was stylish in the late 1800s and early 1900s. The building opened in 1916, soon after the arrival of the Great Northern branch line from Wenatchee.

The Kaaba-Texas mill remains from Nighthawk's mining days. Riverboats and freight wagons handled the region's shipping at first; later, trains reached Nighthawk.

Old Toroda gold miners coaxed a pregnant woman to move into camp so that they could claim the birth of a white child. (Hers was the cabin at the left, now in ruins.)

Okanogan began in 1886 when "Pard" Cummings opened a store at a pinprick community called Alma. A few years later Dr. J. I. Pogue, elected a state senator, successfully spearheaded approval for the federal Okanogan Irrigation Project. Land at Alma was to be the main recipient of the water, and to show their gratitude residents considered renaming their community Pogue but in 1907 decided instead on Okanogan, the name of the project.

Today the county historical society museum is along the river at the north end of town. It offers excellent displays, plus pioneer cabins, implements, and reference material. Check for maps and back-road information at the Okanogan National Forest office at the south end of town on the main highway.

(Also see CURTIS SHEEP MASSACRE SITE, p. 57.)

OLD TORODA, at the bottom of the Bodie–Chesaw grade near Wauconda, warrants a visit. It epitomized turn-of-the-century boomtown spirit, although today it stands sagging and empty. (This Toroda is not to be confused with the present-day, loosely knit community also called Toroda, which is situated near where Toroda Creek joins the Kettle River.)

Old Toroda's population in 1898 stood at 470, a respectable showing among the dozens of mine camps dotting the eastern Okanogan. But no white child had yet been born here, a "legitimizing" mark second only to getting a post office. Potential remedy for this civic lack lay in the person of Mrs. Louisa Fries McFarlane, a Danish blonde who had arrived— pregnant—to homestead with her husband Charles near Wauconda. Charles McFarlane had ridden herd for cattle king Ben Snipes; Louisa Fries had come from Copenhagen to keep house for her brothers near Brewster. Both understood frontier priorities and, when approached with a request that their child be born in Old Toroda, they readily agreed and moved there. (The dilapidated cabin situated nearest the county road is the one they settled into.)

Soon in labor, Mrs. McFarlane could hear the swelling of pride as a celebration kept pace with her pains. When the baby came, the parents honored townsmen by naming her Toroda. To honor the baby, miners presented a gold watch with "Toroda 1898" engraved on the back.

OMAK is now a larger town than Okanogan, which virtually adjoins it. The bluff famed for the annual Omak Stampede horse race to the river shows plainly beside the bridge spanning the Okanogan River. Trampled bare by the pounding of hooves, the steep race slope is surrounded by houses.

The economy here depends on sawmills as well as orchards. As early as 1920, a major sawmill owner, J. C. Biles, moved to Omak from Peshastin where fire twice had destroyed his mills. He expanded a small apple-box manufacturing plant to produce various types of fine millwork including doors, window sashes, and coffins. That mill also burned, whereupon Biles and his partner Nat Coleman bought a mill at Disautel (17 miles to the east) and continued filling orders.

For a sample of early-day Okanogan country, drive south on the Colville Reservation to **Omak Lake,** an expanse of placid blue along the base of a bare, brown rock wall sculpted by ice-age glaciers. Beyond the south end of the lake, continue another 10 miles on the main road to the Columbia River. Benchlands there are emerald with corn and alfalfa, and a lazy current ripples the water almost as though the Columbia were still a river rather than a series of lakes backed by dams.

This portion of the Columbia is actually the upper end of the reservoir behind Chief Joseph Dam. It also is where "Wild Goose" Bill Condon (or Condit) operated a ferry as part of his Okanogan toll road. Begun in the early 1880s, it consisted of what Guy Waring, pioneering at Loomis, called "a small fleet of canoes." As use increased, the ferry improved. Omak old-timer E. J. Dorien described it as

five or six logs fastened together with log chains, grass and rawhide ropes, . . . propelled by manpower. We had to throw our lariats around the ends of the ferry, and with the other end on our saddle horns, tote it upstream quite a distance where we loaded our freight and tied our horses on behind. Condon could usually land us at the desired spot on the other side.

In the winter of 1886–1887, Condon brought in a cable and stretched it from bank to bank while the river was frozen. With the cable, he could operate a current ferry capable of carrying two teams and wagons or about 20 head of cattle. In addition to the ferry, Condon also offered his clientele a store, a livery stable, a blacksmith shop, and a saloon/hotel.

(Also see SAINT MARY'S MISSION, p. 70; and WILBUR, p. 101.)

OROVILLE lies 7 miles from the Canadian border, a modern orchard center set in the deep Okanogan trough, which divides the Cascade Mountains from the Okanogan Highlands. This geological structure gives the town spectacular views to high, glaciated rock walls and successive terraces of glacial rubble and lakes. In town, the Great Northern depot (south edge of town, west of the main street), is now a museum. It stood at the end of the line for trains laboring to and from the highlands.

A point of land jutting into Lake Osoyoos (near the airport east of Oroville) was the home of Hiram Smith, a New Englander who became the upper Okanogan's first white resident. He had joined the Fraser River gold stampede in 1858, then picked this land for a trading post and settled down with a native wife. Here, Smith planted a vineyard, vegetable garden, and the first of the Okanogan orchards. Some of his trees still bear fruit. His apples included pioneering varieties such as Waxen, Blue Pyramid, and Belle Flower.

Be sure to cross into British Columbia (5 miles north of Oroville) and drive east on B.C. 3 toward Grand Forks. The road goes through the town of Osoyoos, then climbs the valley wall to an overlook safely accessible only on the upgrade (10 miles from border to overlook). The view is of land spread below like a museum model. Smith's point protrudes into the lake, an obvious sunny expanse, gently sloped and ideal for rill irrigation. North of it, a "sandspit" (actually an intact glacial moraine) crosses the entire lake. It served as a thoroughfare for native people, fur brigades, miners, and settlers who could cross the valley here without having to cope with the raging, watery barrier of the Okanogan River.

The town of Oroville began with the swirling of gold pans, as its name implies: *oro,* Spanish for "gold." Strikes (in 1858) on the Fraser River just north of the border necessitated a final, formal establishment of the international line, and supposedly it was a British surveyor who first found gold near the mouth of the Similkameen River. By 1861 the resultant boom camp held nearly 3,000 people. Miners flowed in and out as they heard of new placer strikes, on either side of the border. This led to prospecting for lode gold and other metallics. Hard-rock mining ensued. To supply miners with beef, cattlemen drove their herds to scattered boomtowns. On the way, they discovered the relatively mild winters and rich grazing of the Okanogan benchlands. Trade and commerce picked up. Outside capital came in. Settlers arrived.

Oroville incorporated and was platted in 1892. Fifteen years later, Great Northern Railway service to Spokane began. Trains climbed onto the Okanogan Highlands—nearly 3,000 feet above the valley—then wove along the border serving mining towns and following the Kettle River Valley to the Columbia at Marcus. In 1914 a branch line reached Oroville from Wenatchee. Freight wagons and paddle-wheel steamers vanished. So did a half century of isolation.

Each step in the arrival of railway service brought outside links beyond the full understanding of people raised with rubber tires and ribbons of asphalt. When rails had first reached Coulee City in the 1890s, freight and mail for Oroville came that far by train, and stockmen shortened their drives to market by that much. In 1901 when a spur track extended to Republic, travelers to Spokane had only the highlands to cross on horseback or by buggy; they could go the rest of the way by rail. When trains from Wenatchee pulled into Oroville itself, low water in the river and winter ice conditions could no longer hold shipments or travel plans hostage. Agriculture and sawmilling could grow out of their infancy.

(Also see CIRCLE CITY, p. 56; MOLSON, p. 63.)

Turn into **RIVERSIDE** as homage to the past. Now a backwater hamlet with several buildings from the early 1900s, Riverside formerly served as trading center for the entire northern Okanogan and the Colville Reservation, a vast region equivalent in area to Connecticut or most of Massachusetts.

In 1892 growing population drew shallow-draft steamers up the Okanogan River above Brewster whenever water depth permitted. In 1903 more regular service began with the October run of the *Enterprise,* an 86-foot steamboat capable of carrying 20 tons of supplies for merchants and miners. Rapids near Republic Landing—now Riverside—marked the steamers' usual upper limit. From the landing, oxteams, packtrains, and freight wagons lumbered west, north, and east serving mine camps.

A riverboat man said of the freight accumulated:

There are acres of it, all destined for Republic, and more arriving every trip made by the steamer. . . . A train of 75 wagons could not transport the freight . . . when I left there.

In 1914 the Great Northern Railway pierced the Okanogan Valley from the south, and paddle-wheel steamers came no more. Most of the bustle drained out of the old town.

RUBY CITY pulsed as a wild-west town during its few swift years between the moment Moses–Columbia Reservation lands opened for mining in 1886 and the nationwide financial depression of 1893. Cheap whiskey, gunpowder, and rampant dishonesty characterized civic life. A mining engineer wrote of Ruby City in 1889:

The biggest liars and thieves I [have met elsewhere] are honorable, high-minded citizens compared to the beauts who abound here.

D. C. Corbin, Spokane financier and railroad builder, hoped to lay track to Ruby, mistakenly assuming its mines would have quantities of silver to ship. And for a while the town did boom and even served as county seat when the state legislature first agreed to separate Okanogan County from Stevens County (so sprawling that miners and settlers had to travel for weeks to conduct legal matters at Colville). Glass-plate photographs taken by Frank Matsura show buildings along both sides of Ruby City's single street, where now only a forested gulch and a historic marker are apparent.

Men honeycombed the hills but their main output was sweat, not wealth. At times, however, trams carried ore to concentrating mills, and heavily laden wagons lurched downslope to the Okanogan River to connect with steamboats and distant markets. Mining continues sporadically but no steady producer ever has been found. (To reach the Ruby City townsite, turn south off the Conconully road onto Salmon Creek Road. Drop down a steep canyon, cross the creek, and watch in about another mile for a pullout and a county historical society sign.)

(Also see CHINA WALL, p. 55.)

SAINT MARY'S MISSION (5 miles southeast of Omak) figured prominently in Okanogan history but today is not set up to receive sightseers. It serves as Washington's only boarding school for native students.

The Jesuit priest Etienne de Rouge built a chapel and home near Lake Omak in 1886 at the invitation of Chief Smitkin. Three years later he left to pursue ascetic studies in France, then returned and expanded the chapel into a full-fledged mission and school. He donated most of his personal fortune (a sizeable amount) and solicited additional funds from wealthy contacts in Europe who knew his family, members of the French nobility. Chief Smitkin also contributed generously to the mission. He kept gold pieces in glass jars buried around the walls of his chicken coop, wealth that reputedly amounted to two and a half rows of the jars.

TONASKET today is a modern town with the usual services. Its name commemorates Chief Tonasket who chose to give up his rights to land where the town now stands. He moved his band to the Colville Reservation on the condition that a boarding school for 100 pupils, a resident doctor, and a sawmill and gristmill be established on Bonaparte Creek. The school burned a few years after it opened and never was rebuilt.

For himself, Tonasket arranged a $100-a-year annuity as compensation for lost land rights. He then sold the farm he had developed at Lake Osoyoos to Hiram Smith and moved near Curlew, on the northern half of the Colville Reservation, which already had been opened for homesteading. The chief was born about 1820 at Osoyoos. He died at Curlew in 1891.

White settlement in the Tonasket area began across the Okanogan River from today's town. W. W. Parry opened a store there in 1888 and seven years later added a ferry for use when the river was in flood; at other times, riders and wagons simply forded. Parry controlled his growing community and also platted New Molson, near the Canadian border 40 miles to the northeast. In 1910 his finances crashed, and he lost everything.

Meanwhile, H. J. Smith had organized the Bonaparte Land Company, situated near the east ferry landing, where he also ran a store. The com-

pany optimistically advertised development of

a new town in an old-establishment, well-developed agricultural country. . . . Irrigation is coming. . . . [and there soon will be] 30,000 acres, under 3 projects.

The promotion succeeded and, when a bridge replaced the old ferry in 1912, Smith's town—called Tonasket—became the dominant settlement of the area.

The southern half of the Colville Reservation opened to homesteading in 1916 and brought on a land rush stimulated by Great Northern Railway leaflets and by a prospectus the *Wenatchee Daily World* mailed to anyone answering advertisements it placed throughout the nation. The prospectus reported that excellent, inexpensive land was available near

Omak, Colville, and Wilbur—and in Wenatchee—and that anyone with honest ambition and energy would find a welcome. So many people responded that the government land office held a drawing at Spokane for about 90,000 persons who had registered for 5,500 potential acreages. Rufus Woods, editor of the paper, was proud that his campaign had doubled the population of north central Washington at a time when growth elsewhere in the state had stagnated. Growth, per se, brought certain benefit according to the boosterism of the era.

Arrive at **WAUCONDA** (Wah-kahn′-duh) up the grade from Chesaw or Republic and the sudden openness of the 3,000-foot plateau comes as a surprise. Native people called the area by a name that meant "upper valley." At its eastern rim, the three Hedge brothers found gold in 1898 and named their strike Wauconda, for their hometown in Illinois. That first Wauconda had a log-cabin store by 1900 and a post office the following year. Today it is not so much a "town" as a focal point for scattered houses and homestead cabins.

The lone building 2 miles north of the junction of the Chesaw road with the Wauconda–Republic road is a community hall. Its origin dates to 1915 when Agnes Lorz, Wauconda schoolteacher, directed her second annual June 14 Flag Day ceremony. A cloudburst sent everyone running to the Van Brunt's barn to get under a roof, and that generated an idea. People donated money, materials, and labor and, at the Flag Day celebration two years later, they dedicated the hall. It has served ever since as a highlands focal point.

In 1908 the German John Pflug family hauled lumber to Wauconda for their home.

Methow Valley and Chelan Country

Spectacular mountains, river valleys, and orchards set the theme here. The countryside is thinly populated, the towns small, the scenery world class. Back-roads enthusiasts and hikers will find unlimited possibilities. Winthrop is popular as a "wild-west" town. Lake Chelan offers major resorts.

History museums are located in downtown Chelan and at Winthrop. Displays at the Wells Dam visitor center explain the hazards experienced by salmon eggs and young. The dam's fish passage facilities—516 miles from the Columbia River's mouth—are farther upriver than any others.

AZWELL, a pleasant Columbia River community above Wells Dam, grew out of the success of Alfred Z. Wells and his nephew Alfred Morris. Owners of a hardware store in Wenatchee, they expanded into the orchard business as a sideline, then dissolved their partnership in 1914. Wells kept the orchard business, Morris the store. Over time, Wells expanded his orchards, took a new partner, then sold out and returned to the hardware business. Finally he resumed orcharding, and Azwell became a company town with homes for about 20 resident families. Its packing plants now operate around-the-clock during harvest season, and grocery stores throughout the area feature tortillas and salsa, indication of growers' dependence on itinerant Latino labor. Rows of pickers' cottages cluster at the edges of orchards.

CAMP CHELAN. (See under CHELAN, p. 74.)

CARLTON lies 23 miles up the Methow Valley from the Columbia River, near where the valley broadens from a deep V, cut by the river, to the U shape that signifies glaciation. An unpaved road leading up Texas Creek from Carlton follows the historic stage route across the high grassy flats to Brewster (confusing turns at the Carlton end; inquire locally for directions and current conditions). Autumn ripens currants along the route and turns aspen trees golden. Forty or more settlers lived up this drainage

The Carlton stage linked the Methow Valley to the steamer landing at Brewster.

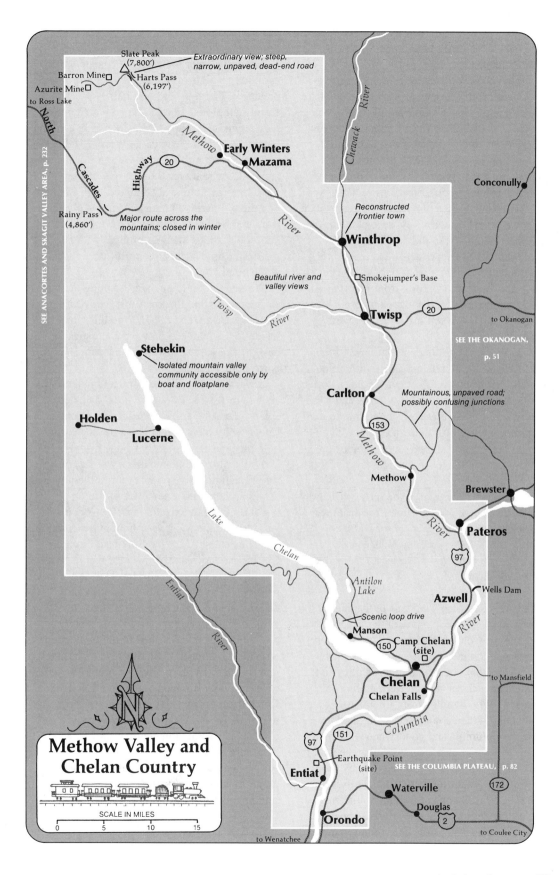

Slate Peak
(7,800')
Extraordinary view; steep,
narrow, unpaved, dead-end road

Barron Mine
Harts Pass
(6,197')

Azurite Mine

to Ross Lake

North

Cascades

Highway

Methow

Early Winters
Mazama

20

Chewack River

Conconully

Rainy Pass
(4,860')

Major route across the
mountains; closed in winter

River

Reconstructed
frontier town

Winthrop

Twisp

River

Beautiful river and
valley views

Smokejumper's Base

Twisp

20

to Okanogan

SEE THE OKANOGAN,
p. 51

SEE ANACORTES AND SKAGIT VALLEY AREA, p. 232

Stehekin

Isolated mountain valley
community accessible only by
boat and floatplane

Carlton

Mountainous, unpaved road;
possibly confusing junctions

153

Holden

Lucerne

Methow

Methow

Brewster

Lake

Chelan

River

Pateros

97

Entiat

Antilon
Lake

Wells Dam

Azwell

Scenic loop drive

River

Manson

150

Camp Chelan
(site)

River

to Mansfield

Chelan
Chelan Falls

Columbia

97   151

Earthquake Point
(site)

SEE THE COLUMBIA PLATEAU,   p. 82

172

N

**Methow Valley and
Chelan Country**

Entiat

Waterville

Douglas

2

SCALE IN MILES
0   5   10   15

Orondo

to Wenatchee

to Coulee City

until the depression years of the 1930s forced them out; occasional gingerbread Victorian homes still stand.

During the depression a Civilian Conservation Corps camp operated near Carlton (close to today's Foggy Dew Campground). At the time, one out of every four workers nationwide was unemployed, and pessimism was rampant. Within days of Franklin Delano Roosevelt's inauguration as president in 1933, Congress passed the Emergency Conservation Work Act, and the following June thousands of young men arrived at forest camps. They were clothed, fed, equipped, put to work, and paid. All were unmarried but had dependents and agreed to send home $25 of each month's $30 paycheck. Butch Hardy, sent to Carlton from Pennsylvania, reminisced, "Ten dollars a month kept the mortgage paid. It meant my folks and family had a place to live."

Work entailed building campgrounds, roads, and fire lookouts and helping with fire protection and reforestation. Most conservation corps enrollees at Carlton came from farms and were readily accepted locally. In fact community ball teams became the best in the area since, as Hardy puts it, "we had 350 guys to pick from." At other camps, the local reaction was different:

If you were an Easterner, once you spoke, right away people knew where you were from. You could see the hackles go up on the necks of some of the oldtimers. . . .[Blacks] probably had the most difficulty . . . because few of the local folks had ever met a colored man.

CHELAN (Shuh-lan´) citizens in the late 1880s expressed great discontent with the irregular schedules of Columbia River steamers. Fluctuating water conditions were part of the problem but, beyond that, the overall unreliability and cumbersomeness of service were galling. A letter sent only 70 miles from Chelan to Conconully—then county seat—first had to cross the Columbia and go to Waterville, then travel by horse-drawn stage to Wenatchee, on to Spokane by rail, back to Coulee City by train, and finally by stage again to Conconully.

Today, twin ribbons of pavement line each side of the Columbia, and Chelan has become a major resort as well as the year-round home of about 4,000 people. The large Victorian houses of early bankers, lawyers, doctors, and merchants still cluster between the Chelan River and today's highway; some now offer bed and breakfast. The four-and-one-half-story **Campbell House hotel** (Chelan and Sanders) was begun in 1900 by C. C. Campbell, a young lawyer from Iowa who came West in 1889 and picked Chelan as his home. He sent for his wife and child, who traveled to the end of the Northern Pacific line at Coulee City. Campbell met the train with a horse and buggy, plus a team and freight wagon for the boxcar load of household goods his wife brought with her from the East. Some of this fine furniture is displayed at the hotel.

Downtown, buildings worth noting include several stores and the log **Saint Andrew's Episcopal Church** (120 E. Woodin), notable inside for its stained glass and sophisticated design. The county historical museum is a block north of the church.

A Northern Pacific map given to potential settlers in 1891 shows only three towns north of Ellensburg: Chelan, Waterville, and Orondo. Chelan settlement had begun a decade earlier with the arrival of infantry troops from Fort Colville. At that time the army was responsible for protecting native people on reservations and bringing them into a new way of life.

Camp Chelan existed—briefly—because it was close to the Moses–Columbia Reservation, newly established for the Sinkiuse, Entiat, Chelan, Methow, and Wenatchee native people, and the army felt it wise to be close at hand to protect whites from attack by natives and natives from encroachment and attack by whites. The reservation lasted only a few years, however, then was returned to public domain with the agreement of Chief Moses. The Chelan post lasted even more briefly. Three companies of infantrymen camped at the mouth of Foster Creek (near present-day Bridgeport) during the winter of 1879–1880; in May, they moved to Chelan. The following October they marched back across the Columbia Plateau. Fort Spokane had been selected as the location of a new post, closer to actual reservation land and to white settlements than was either Fort Colville or Camp Chelan.

Chelan had been particularly troublesome for

quartermaster supply wagons, which had to come from Fort Walla Walla. Lieutenant Thomas Symons had picked the site for its "unlimited supply of timber and the purest water . . . available for every purpose." But in retrospect, even he remarked on the location's "terrible road," dropping down a 2,500-foot cliff to a treacherous river crossing. He wrote:

All these drawbacks so impressed [the inspector general] that he . . . recommended . . . some other point [be] selected for a post.

Nothing now remains at the site of Camp Chelan, which is near the east side of town, on private land slightly upslope from where State Route 150 begins its descent to the Columbia.

Backcountry enthusiasts should check for information at the Forest Service/National Park Service office at the western edge of Chelan (428 W. Woodin). Possible drives include the road to **Antilon Lake** above the north shore of Lake Chelan, water supply for irrigation flumes built in the 1920s; also the **25-Mile Creek** road for a spectacular view and possible continuation on to the Entiat Valley. **Manson,** 10 miles up the lake from Chelan, is an orchard town; it began as a sawmill operation. A scenic loop above the town is ideal for an evening drive—or any time.

Most popular as an excursion is the daily summer boat trip to the head of Lake Chelan at **Stehekin** (55 miles). Float plane service there is also available—and allows a view of the Cascade Mountains' vast and magnificent sea of peaks. Ideally, fly one way, take the boat the other way. Stehekin offers overnight accommodations.

(Also see HOLDEN, p. 77; STEHEKIN, p. 79.)

CHELAN FALLS is a small shipping center along the railroad and the site of a hydroelectric plant utilizing the 400-foot drop from Lake Chelan to the Columbia. The falls no longer exist except during brief periods when floodgates at the dam are open—potentially hazardous and with repeated announcements for people to stay out of the riverbed below the lake. The dam, at the lake's outlet, is a low one, which raises water level "only" 21 feet, an enormous added storage capacity considering the lake's size.

This obvious power potential led C. C. Campbell and three other Chelan men to form a company in 1893. Columbia Plateau wheat, brought by river steamer from Orondo, could be milled at Chelan Falls and the flour carried to market by train. No tracks existed yet, but everybody—in every small town—expected them "soon." In actuality, the Great Northern quietly backed acquisition of various water rights and options on the Chelan River, then held them for 20 years. Their control of a key power site blocked possible competition from other rail lines.

In 1914 the Great Northern finally finished a branch line up the Columbia and into the Okanogan Valley. Eleven years later, it sold rights to Chelan Falls to the Washington Water Power Company.

EARLY WINTERS, the site of a proposed commercial ski development on State Route 20 west of Winthrop, lies in a forested valley below the eastern end of North Cascades Highway. A U.S. Forest Service interpretive center provides information and displays.

Mining went on at a feverish pace in the mountains here from the 1890s until about 1910. By then, several homesteaders had settled the upper Methow Valley, a late pioneering perhaps owing to the possibility of unseasonal frosts even in summer and snowfall by September. Native people still came to pick berries and dry fish on racks (about a half mile downstream from where today's highway crosses Early Winters Creek). Three homesteaders dug an irrigation ditch, which has been enlarged over the years and still supplies water for local farms. Sheep provided income for several of the early settlers, who owned rather small herds compared to the thousands driven here for summer pastures by ranchers on the Columbia Plateau.

(Also see NORTH CASCADES HIGHWAY, p. 78.)

ENTIAT is a Salish word meaning "Fast Water," an apt name for one of the major rapids of the mid-Columbia River. Entiat Rapids were particularly troublesome at low water, the Methow Rapids at high water.

In the early 1900s channel improvements eliminated some of the threat at Entiat, but by then several vessels had already wrecked. The huge irrigation wheel displayed at the Cashmere county museum (west of Wenatchee) uses the steel shaft of a stern-wheeler that met disaster here, one wreck among many. One of these wrecks happened in 1902, when a boat struck a rock after taking on firewood just above the rapids, then drifted downriver and sank. Three years later a wheat boat sank in the night. The year after that, another steamer fell victim to the rapids, was beached, pumped out, patched, and started downriver under tow, but broke away and wrecked. Today the rapids have vanished beneath the reservoir backed by Rocky Reach Dam.

As early as 1868, a miner traveling north from Ellensburg found a black placer miner called Big Antoine at Entiat. He was washing gold with water brought by a ditch that Chinese miners had built earlier. Fluent in English, French, and Spanish, Antoine said he previously worked for Hudson's Bay Company at Red River, Manitoba, but had run away to San Francisco and there heard about Northwest gold strikes. Apparently he was "an Islander" (from the Caribbean), who had been educated in England and probably then employed, or indentured, as a servant. He had been at Entiat two years and was surprised to learn that the Civil War was over.

Soon after this encounter, the army commander at Camp Chelan ordered Big Antoine to leave. A native man named Silicosaska had objected to his presence. Antoine moved first to Wenatchee, then to near Peshastin, where a stream is still called Negro Creek. At Entiat, Silicosaska continued use of the ditch to irrigate a garden and peach trees left by Antoine. Settlers and steamboat crews came regularly to get fruit from the trees. About 1887 Silicosaska sold land for the Entiat townsite. At first, people in the area tried to make a living by raising and drying prunes, but the market was poor. Next they tried peaches and apricots; then found that apples grew best.

Today, a paved road beyond town leads up the scenic **Entiat Valley.** This route was proposed as a transmountain railroad route from the river at Orondo to Puget Sound.

Four miles north of Entiat on U.S. 97 is **Earthquake Point,** site of a massive landslide that dammed the Columbia in 1872. The quake came at midnight and by noon the next day the riverbed downstream from the landslide "was still destitute of water." Sam Miller, new owner of a trading post at Wenatchee, went as usual to draw water from the river and found it dry, "a most paralyzing experience." When the Columbia finally broke through, it was with a rush of water 15 feet high.

HARTS PASS offers a world-class view of mountain peaks tossed in all directions to the horizon. But the route there beyond Winthrop is via a narrow, steep road with abrupt drop-offs and no guardrail—a drive reminiscent of past travel conditions and a taste of what miners in the area experienced. The road dead-ends just below Slate Peak, highest point in the state accessible by car: 7,800 feet. A rough, rocky spur road drops west from the pass to privately owned mines and abandoned camps, which boomed in the early 1900s. Miners staked nearly 3,000 claims in the district from 1894 to 1937, gradually bringing a sense of geographic order to the welter of Cascade peaks and passes and valleys, which had puzzled earlier fur traders and military explorers.

The miners' first real producer in this area was a glory hole staked by Aleck Barron in 1892. A single shipment of its ore, packed out on seven horses, produced $35,000 in gold. A camp of tents and shacks mushroomed at the mine and soon boasted a population of more than 1,000 and amenities such as a theater and post office. A more difficult location is hard to imagine. Most Cascades ore went out to the west, but in the Harts Pass area mines were linked to the Methow Valley.

Barron convinced an entrepreneur named Thomas Hart of need for a road connection to his mine, and Hart in turn hired Charles Ballard, a civil engineer interested in mining. Ballard scratched out a track over the mountains above Mazama, then worked some of the claims in the area. He packed in a steam-powered stamp mill, an incredible feat but representative of a miner's determination. Shipments of concentrate went to the Columbia River via this "road," by then named for Hart.

After three years, Ballard left for mines in Arizona and Alaska. In 1915 he returned, staked new claims, organized a company, and began

Prospectors sought wealth even within the rugged peaks of the North Cascades.

operation of the Azurite copper property. He built a wagon trail from the Harts Pass road to the Azurite, a frail link to the world east of the mountains. Winter contact depended on radio and twice weekly dogsled from Winthrop. Freighting out ore continued to be torturous, although conditions improved in the 1930s when Civilian Conservation Corps crews brought the Harts Pass road to its present standard. The Azurite Mine closed in 1939, its deposits worked out.

To reach Hart's Pass, continue on the north side of the Methow River for 20 miles beyond the hamlet of Mazama; then follow a Forest Service road, no trailers or motor homes allowed—for good reason. From the pass (20 miles farther), be sure to drive the additional 2½ miles up Slate Peak and continue on foot to an abandoned fire lookout (a 15-minute walk, but not advised for anyone with heart trouble, owing to the high elevation). The top of Slate Peak was scraped flat during preparation for a Distant Early Warning station, which never was installed. New technology made this particular link obsolete almost as soon as its first concrete was poured.

Views to Mount Baker and the astonishing horn-peaks of the Needles and Liberty Bell above the North Cascades Highway make the Harts Pass drive one of Washington's most spectacular.

The **HOLDEN** mine in 1938 finally shipped concentrate from its mill to the smelter at Tacoma. For the next 19 years it held the state record for copper and gold production. The site now belongs to the Lutheran Church and is used as a retreat, usually also with accommodations for individual guests. (Ask at the Chelan Chamber of Commerce for current information. Holden is 11 miles above the west shore of Lake Chelan.)

J. H. Holden, discoverer of the mine, worked for Seattle's pioneering Denny family, mining their Snoqualmie Pass gold claim. While on a prospecting trip in 1896, he made the Holden strike and for the rest of his life he earned a living by promoting and developing it. He died, however—while "taking the waters" at Soap Lake—long before actual mining got under way. Low-grade ore and extreme isolation augured against major operation.

For a while the Granby, British Columbia, mining and smelting company, managed by Spokane copper king Jay P. Graves, had seemed likely to open Holden's mine. Little happened until 1930 when the Canadian Howe Sound Mining Company bought the property. They built a half-mile inclined railway to get materials and supplies up the cliff from the lake, then brought in power from Chelan Falls and built a mill. They sheathed tugboats with iron plates for breaking ice and towed specially built barges loaded with concentrate to Chelan, 45 miles. Final shipment was by rail from Chelan Falls to Tacoma.

Eventually 450 people lived at Holden. Most were single men, but there were enough families for a school. The town was a self-contained company operation replete even to tin coins for use at the commissary, the only store in town. Workers were required to buy packs of coins and have the cost deducted from their pay.

In 1957 a 50 percent drop in the price of copper proved one market fluctuation too many, and Howe Sound shut the mine. Four years later they gave the entire property to the Lutheran Church.

LAKE CHELAN. (See CHELAN, p. 74.)

LUCERNE, near the upper end of Lake Chelan, began as a jumping-off point for miners who prospected along Railroad Creek in the 1880s. It became a major shipping point for cream as settlers arrived (many of them Swiss dairymen) and as discouraged miners switched to farming. What were hayfields and pastures became orchards instead, beginning when pumps capable of lifting water onto benchlands became available in the 1940s.

MANSON. (See under CHELAN, p. 75.)

MAZAMA (Muh-zah′-muh) boomed as the departure point for mines in the rugged Harts Pass area, and it remains little more than a crossroads store, gas station, and post office. It was called Goat Creek when the post office first opened in 1900, but officials objected to two-word names. Consequently, Guy Waring, owner of the Methow Trading Company at Winthrop, suggested *Mazama,* which is often reported as the Spanish word for "mountain goat" but actually was the early scientific designation for the animal, *Mazama sericea* (now changed to *Oreamnos Americanus*).

In 1902 a gold mill operated here. In 1904 the Upper Methow Mining District had been formally organized and about 30 settlers claimed the town as home. A few years later, most mines closed and Mazama dwindled in importance.

(Also see HARTS PASS, p. 76.)

The community of **METHOW** (Met′-how) is a hamlet 11 miles west of the Columbia River in one of the state's most scenic valleys. Ideally drive the valley facing toward the mountains to see the sawtooth wall of Cascade peaks as a backdrop. The road leads along a river so clear that every stone shows. Orchards dot the lower valley. Irrigated hayfields dominate the upper valley.

Overall isolation and widely scattered houses characterized early-day life here, although neighborliness prevailed. For example, at agreed-upon times, families would "gather" by phone to share songs, instrumental solos, and poetry or other recitations—farmhouse "theater" without the benefit, or effort, of getting together physically. With equally good sense and informality the local bus service for years meant "catching the cream truck" to or from Wenatchee.

The **NORTH CASCADES HIGHWAY** opened in 1972, a climax to more than a century and a half of hopes for an easy route across Washington's northern mountain spine. In 1814 fur trader Alexander Ross crossed this way with three native companions, intending to explore "from Oakinacken due west to the Pacific on

The Methow River attracted anglers and sightseers as soon as a road was built.

foot." The party seems to have traveled from the Twisp River over Cascade Pass, or possibly over Rainy Pass, which is now part of the North Cascades Highway. Nearly 40 years later, Army Lieutenant Johnson Duncan explored the upper Methow Valley seeking a suitable pass for the proposed transcontinental railway to the coast. He reported negatively to his superior, Captain George B. McClellan.

In 1882 Lieutenant Henry H. Pierce entered the mountains to find a route for getting troops and supplies across the mountains to the Skagit River, should unrest among native people there fester into real trouble. An elderly miner at the head of Lake Chelan told Pierce about a "natural roadway" through the mountains, and the next summer two army expeditions went looking for it. One was led by Lieutenant Samuel Rodman, the other by Lieutenants George B. Backus and George W. Goethals (later famous for his work completing the Panama Canal). Neither party found anything worthy of recommendation.

Three years later, the Moses–Columbia Reservation opened to whites, and miners and homesteaders stampeded to it. Soon settlers on both sides of the mountains began urging a direct east–west travel connection, and the state authorized a wagon road from Bellingham across the mountains to Marcus. Volunteers at each end began building it. The two segments never were finished and actually would not have met, owing to miscalculation. Even so, most newspapers reported glowingly on progress, and actual bridges and sections of the road became passable—until washed out by floods.

Real chance of a road across the mountains languished until a new generation—and a new technology—took up the idea. Construction of the present highway began in 1959. Completion came 13 years later, too late for eastsiders who had dreamed of shipping butter or hay to the Coast, but in time to foster a new form of economic well-being: tourism.

ORONDO today is a riverside orchard town where U.S. 2 begins its climb onto the Columbia Plateau. Formerly an aerial wheat tramway connected Waterville warehouses—1,700 feet above the river—with the Orondo steamboat landing. Plateau farmers had been freighting their grain by team and wagon to the railhead at Coulee City. Sending it to the river by tram saved both effort and shipping costs.

The tram had a continuous cable and a series of iron buckets, each of which held four gunnysacks of wheat. On its first day of use—December 4, 1902—the tram carried down 1,600 sacks of wheat and carried up eight tons of coal. At first, operation was by gravity; later a gasoline engine was used to boost power for hauling freight up to the plateau. Today only concrete footings remain. Tram use ended in 1909 when the Great Northern's branch line onto the plateau reached Douglas.

Stern-wheelers quit plying the river after completion of the railroad along the west side of the Columbia in 1914. Mail for Orondo then was rowed across from Entiat, even through winter's floating ice. In the early 1920s motor coach service from Wenatchee to Waterville reconnected Orondo with a major transportation route. (Also see DOUGLAS, p. 87; WATERVILLE, p. 100.)

PATEROS acts as a gateway for the Methow Valley and the North Cascades Highway. It also is an orchard center. Rapids here were among the worst on this stretch of the Columbia. Aside from the rushing water, there was danger of hitting a log, for driftwood often caught against shore near the rapids—a hazard, but also useful. A 1908 issue of *The Okanogan Record* reported that for a week a horse-powered saw at Pateros had been cutting "some of the logs that were caught in the Columbia this summer." The result was a well-filled wood yard "which will no doubt be a great benefit to the town." Steamboats burned prodigious amounts of wood at the time, and supplying it contributed to the economy of many river towns.

In January 1914 crews completed rails between Oroville and Pateros; six months later they finished the line between Pateros and Wenatchee. Cliffs crowding the riverbank complicated fitting in a railway beside the automobile road, but once tracks were spiked into place, Pateros grew. Fifty-four years later, the pool rising behind Wells Dam forced most of the town—and the railroad and highway—to relocate.

STEHEKIN (Stuh-hee′-kin) nestles beneath high peaks at the head of Lake Chelan. It is reached by boat (55 miles; daily service in summer, three times a week the rest of the year) or by floatplane. The location today seems too remote to have been a reasonable choice for homesteaders, but a century ago travel throughout the Okanogan and Chelan country demanded patience and stamina, and access by boat was far easier than by horse and wagon. Furthermore, prospecting, not agriculture, lured the firstcomers, and for them the lake served as an avenue winding deep into the mountains.

Miners had combed the mountains for gold as early as the 1850s, but settlement at Stehekin did not begin until a Civil War veteran named John Horton rowed the length of the lake in the mid-1880s and started building. Soon additional settlers came in search of places where sub-sistence farming could be augmented seasonally by logging or trapping. A Swiss-style hotel with a six-story, gabled tower opened in 1905. From it, packers led fishing and hunting trips into the mountains as a source of income. Mostly, however, neighbors simply traded labor with each other and bartered goods and talents, a no-cash, self-sufficient pattern that continued until the 1950s.

Several cabins remain from the pioneer era, most notably the board-and-batten buildings of the Buckner homestead. Horses still graze the pasture there; creek water flows in irrigation ditches; pickers harvest apples each fall; and Stehekin people use the old packing shed for community square dances.

TWISP was a major fish-drying station at the junction of the Methow and Twisp rivers. The native name for it was *Twips*, "Yellow Jackets," because the pests were so numerous that women slicing salmon complained of getting stung.

Miners surged through the area in the late 1800s but soon lost hope of mineral wealth and instead settled on valley bottoms to raise livestock, try dairy farming, or raise fruit on a small scale. Most colorful among them was Scotsman Thomas Blythe, who moved to the Methow Valley in 1905 after closing a huge livestock operation on Crab Creek (near Moses Lake). Blythe organized the region's first irrigation system, aside from a few farm ditches. The company took water from the Twisp River about 4 miles above town and carried it by ditch and wooden pipe to fields on both sides of the valley.

Unfortunately, the flow proved inadequate and, after a 15-year struggle, the company cut back its services. The problems cost Blythe his savings from the Crab Creek livestock business, a financial distress that came at about the same time that he lost an annual remittance from England. Titled British families customarily sent such stipends to their sons abroad, but the practice stopped during World War I.

Old-timers remember Blythe as a refined and beloved man who wore a monocle and was chauffeured by his secretary in a Brush automobile, a conspicuous conveyance where most people still traveled by horse.

WELLS DAM (12 miles north of Chelan, completed in 1967) was built as a "hydro com-bination," an economical design incorporating powerhouse, spillway, and fish facilities in one structure. A 6,000-foot channel amounting to an artificial river was built in expectation that salmon would find it acceptable for spawning. In actuality, it has proven more practical for crews to spawn the fish, then use the channel as a conventional, human-controlled hatchery. A visitor center at the dam highlights the story.

WINTHROP has refurbished itself as a wild-west town, following Leavenworth's example of attracting tourists and stimulating the local economy by adopting a theme. The result has a wide appeal—and several of Winthrop's buildings actually do remain from the town's earlier days, albeit presently with much altered facades. The Winthrop Hotel began about 1908. After a few years, townspeople leased the building as a hospital, then restored it to use as a hotel when the lone doctor left town. Today's community building (housing the library) predates the hotel. It originated about 1895 as the Duck Brand Saloon, built by Guy Waring—a leading citizen of Winthrop—and named for his cattle brand. Waring personally harbored puritanical hatred of liquor but believed in controlling its sale as the best way to prevent intoxication.

Guy Waring was a *cum laude* graduate of Harvard and a classmate of Theodore Roosevelt (future president of the United States) and Owen

Winthrop began in 1891 as a trading post catering to cattle ranchers and miners.

Wister (author of the popular western novel *The Virginian*). Wister visited Waring in Winthrop and apparently based some of the incidents in his book on Methow characters and occurrences.

In many ways Waring is representative of Washington's early settlers. He came West in 1884 bringing his wife and three young stepchildren, and worked in Portland for the Oregon Railway and Navigation Company. He lost his job during a staff cutback, and next took over a preemption claim on Speiden Island (north of San Juan Island), intending to fatten sheep for the Victoria market. Before he really had started, however, he heard of land in the Okanogan country and moved his family to what became the town of Loomis. After three years there, they all returned to Boston for, as Waring explains in his book *My Pioneer Past,* "The social formalities of civilization die hard in a woman's mind."

The lure of the West must have died even harder in Waring's mind: he returned in 1891 and picked a site on the Methow River, where he began a trading company. Soon he had branch outlets at Twisp and Pateros as well as at the mining camps of Robinson and Barron. He promised his wife a comfortable home—the log house, which became known as The Castle. Built about 1897 with great attention to detail, it now is the Shafer Museum (named for a local businessman who bought the house and used it for his collection of pioneer implements and equipment). Waring's Methow Trading Post, incorporated in 1897, occupied the building now called Last Trading Post.

About 5 miles east of Winthrop, the **North Cascades Smokejumpers Base** usually offers tours and an introduction to fire-fighting procedures and aircraft. Operated by the U.S. Forest Service, the base is on the east side of the Methow Valley, reached by a county road (which makes a pleasant alternative to State Route 20). Jump beginnings date to 1939 when the Forest Service dropped water and chemicals onto mock fires at the Portland airport as a test. The plane really could not carry enough liquid to be effective, nor could it make accurate delivery onto a target. This led to wondering whether fire fighters could be parachuted to a blaze and contain it before it could flare out of control.

Experiments with "smokejumping" shifted from Portland to the Methow Valley and surrounding forest. At that time aerialists often parachuted as county fair attractions, but nobody knew what precautions to take for landing in rough, isolated terrain, ready to fight a fire. A Winthrop cobbler with heavy-duty sewing machines worked with Forest Service men to perfect a liberally padded, protective suit of heavy canvas. Long pockets in the pant legs let jumpers carry ropes to use in climbing down trees, should their chutes get caught. A football helmet with a special wire mask protected the head. Dummy tests succeeded. Sixty live jumps followed. And the method became standard for advance suppression of wildfire throughout the West.

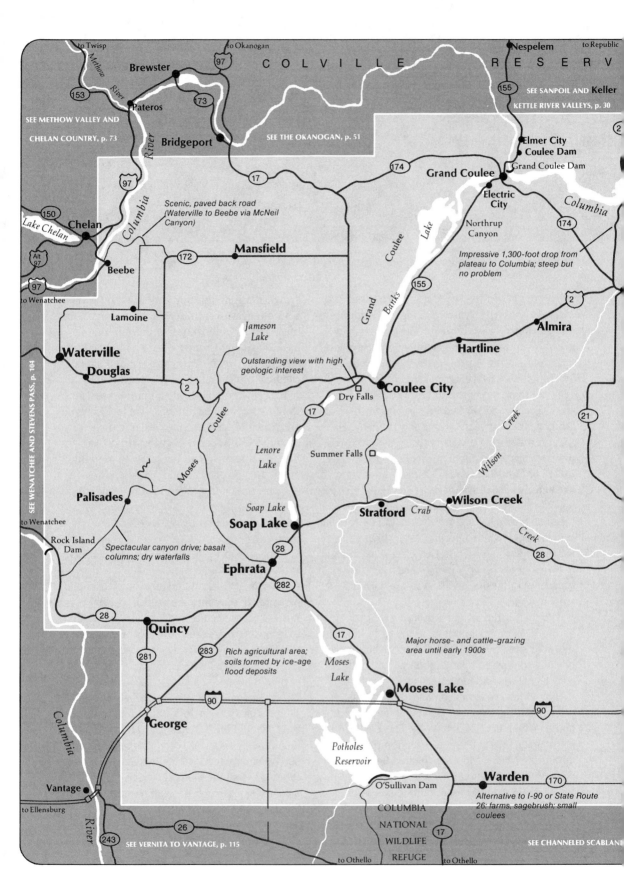

to Twisp

to Okanogan

Nespelem

to Republic

C O L V I L L E   R E S E R V

97

Brewster

153

173

155

SEE SANPOIL AND **Keller**

Pateros

KETTLE RIVER VALLEYS, p. 30

SEE METHOW VALLEY AND

CHELAN COUNTRY, p. 73

Bridgeport

17

SEE THE OKANOGAN, p. 51

Elmer City
Coulee Dam

2

97

174

Grand Coulee

Grand Coulee Dam

Columbia

150

Chelan

*Scenic, paved back road
(Waterville to Beebe via McNeil
Canyon)*

**Electric
City**

Lake Chelan

Alt
97

Beebe

172

Mansfield

*Northrup
Canyon*

174

97

to Wenatchee

Lamoine

*Jameson
Lake*

155

*Impressive 1,300-foot drop from
plateau to Columbia; steep but
no problem*

2

Almira

Waterville

Douglas

2

*Outstanding view with high
geologic interest*

□ Dry Falls

Hartline

Coulee City

21

17

to Wenatchee

*Lenore
Lake*

Summer Falls □

Wilson

Creek

Palisades

Moses

Soap Lake

Stratford

Crab

Wilson Creek

Creek

Rock Island
Dam

*Spectacular canyon drive; basalt
columns; dry waterfalls*

Soap Lake

28

28

28

Ephrata

282

281

28

Quincy

283

*Rich agricultural area;
soils formed by ice-age
flood deposits*

17

*Major horse- and cattle-grazing
area until early 1900s*

90

*Moses
Lake*

Moses Lake

90

90

George

Columbia

*Potholes
Reservoir*

Warden

170

Vantage

O'Sullivan Dam

*Alternative to I-90 or State Route
26; farms, sagebrush; small
coulees*

to Ellensburg

COLUMBIA

River

243

26

NATIONAL

17

SEE VERNITA TO VANTAGE, p. 115

WILDLIFE

SEE CHANNELED SCABLAND

REFUGE

to Othello

to Othello

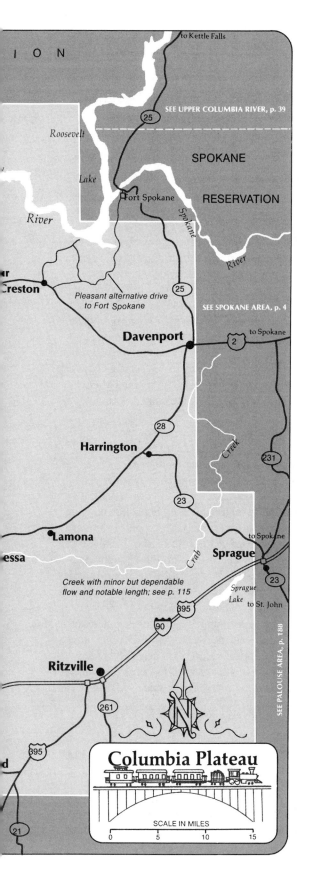

SEE UPPER COLUMBIA RIVER, p. 39

to Kettle Falls

I O N

Roosevelt

Lake

SPOKANE

Fort Spokane

River

RESERVATION

Spokane

River

Creston

Pleasant alternative drive
to Fort Spokane

SEE SPOKANE AREA, p. 4

Davenport

to Spokane

to Spokane

Harrington

Creek

Lamona

essa

Sprague

Crab

Creek with minor but dependable
flow and notable length; see p. 115

Sprague
Lake

to St. John

Ritzville

SEE PALOUSE AREA, p. 188

N

Columbia Plateau

SCALE IN MILES

0   5   10   15

The Columbia Plateau

The vast tableland of the Columbia Plateau stretches across the center of the state as rich agricultural fields, partly planted with dryland wheat, partly irrigated for fields of hay, potatoes, onions, and even some grapes. Ice-age floods sculpted the land, carving channels and filling basins with the sediments that now nourish the irrigated crops.

Points of interest range from starkly scenic basalt coulees to venerable railroad and farm centers with brick business districts and shady streets and public parks, which offer respite for cross-state drivers wearied by summer heat. Grand Coulee Dam—open for touring year-round—is a major attraction as well as a source of hydroelectricity and a gigantic irrigation project. Sun Lakes and Steamboat Rock state parks rank among the most popular in the state.

Ephrata, Ritzville, Warden, and Waterville have history museums; Moses Lake's museum spans from geologic origins to recent human events. The town of Coulee Dam has a tribal museum. Odessa holds an Oktoberfest, and the Mennonite community west of Ritzville offers crafts from wheat weavings to handmade quilts as a fall fund-raiser for the church.

ALMIRA, today a civic dot amid the wheat-lands, first blossomed in 1890. At that time the new Northern Pacific branch line known as the Washington Central was pushing west from Cheney, giving birth to towns and hopes. In part, company officials were outmaneuvering the Great Northern, which was laying track westward from North Dakota. A line across the Columbia Plateau would assure Northern Pacific control of central Washington revenue—*if* there were farmers with crops to ship and money to buy materials and goods carried to them by rail.

Brochures and discounted fares lured settlers West on special immigrant trains. Old-timers remember that by 1902 homesteader shacks dotted just about every quarter section of land. Fences went up—and open-range livestock gave way to wheat. But "a countless number" of settlers did not stay long. According to Helen

Cliffs above Banks Lake include columns that formed as the lava cooled.

Rinker, writing in *From Pioneers to Power,* many lasted:

> . . . only a few years, often just long enough to prove up, mortgage, and lose their place; the depression and drought period after the first World War depleted the area quickly. . . . A 6,600-acre ranch, mostly pasture land now, [belonged to] 21 different homesteaders.

Increased farm size was greatly strengthened through the Enlarged Homestead Act passed in 1909, federal recognition of arid land realities: claims could be 320 acres instead of 160 acres. At the time some people still were coming to homestead, but most were buying up abandoned claims rather than filing on virgin land.

Through it all, Almira endured as a trade center. When only a few months old, it had boasted in the *Spokesman* of "good, substan-tial business houses and dwellings of people full of thrift and industry," a description still applicable.

BANKS LAKE, 27 miles long, is named for the construction engineer who supervised the building of the Grand Coulee Dam. It is a confusing lake, which lies in Grand Coulee yet is not behind the dam. Roosevelt Lake, not Banks Lake, is the reservoir backed by the dam.

The explanation is partly geological. A glacier bulging out of Canada during the last ice age forced the Columbia River to find a new channel. Floodwaters raging west from Idaho and Montana joined the rerouted river. And this combined flow cut the canyon we see today. Basalt columns, which form as lava cools, fell easy prey to the water. Had the floods swept across almost any other type of bedrock, there would be no coulees. ("Coulee" is a French word meaning canyon; it came to Washington with French fur trappers from Canada.) Notches along the present canyon rim remain where waterfalls plunged into the coulee, forming lakes.

Recognizing the coulee as ready-made for a modern reservoir was not difficult. Indeed, a chain of lakes had lined its floor ever since the ice-age floods subsided. James O'Sullivan and Frank Banks explained to any group willing to listen that a high dam could generate enough power to lift water into Grand Coulee, 280 feet above the level of Roosevelt Lake. Held at each end by a low earth-fill dam, this "equalizing reservoir" could be used for irrigation. As fields turned green, farmers would pay off the cost of the land reclamation.

Today State Route 155 threads the shore of Banks Lake for nearly 30 miles. Driving along the shore means riding with head bent sideways, looking up at the sheer wall of cross-sectioned lava flows and marveling at talus spills so steep they must be at the precise angle of repose. Occasional pullouts warrant stopping, but are all on the west side of the road, potentially dangerous for northbound traffic (a reason to drive this road southbound, if possible).

At **Steamboat Rock State Park** basalt cliffs wall the coulee and watered side canyons wind down from the plateau. **Northrup Canyon** is especially enticing. (It is reached by a half-mile spur road directly across the highway from the rest area and boat launch; trails lead to the coulee rim from the end of the road. Phone state park headquarters to register before entering the area; their number is posted at the rest area.)

COULEE CITY elevators show from the head of Bank's Lake as a glare of aluminum, their high, narrow form now often joined by the broad, squat cones of modern wheat storage. The city is an "old" one: its water hole was a stop along the Cariboo Trail. Growth dates to 1890 and the anticipation of the branch railroad built by Northern Pacific to tap Columbia Plateau wheatlands. Coulee City became the end of that line, although boosters constantly hoped the tracks would continue to the Okanogan. An engineer surveying for the Great Northern described the community as "a little, miserable town" where people "think they . . . are bound to have a city hardly second to Chicago."

A stagecoach connected Coulee City to Bridgeport. Owen Wister, author of the western novel *The Virginian,* rode the stage in 1892 en route to Winthrop and wrote that the train arrived too late to make connections. In fact, the two conveyances:

. . . were scheduled to miss each other, and were invariably faithful to schedule. Had they connected, the hotel would have died. So one waited in Coulee City till next day.

At the time, cattlemen were grazing stock on the open range around Coulee City and across much of the Columbia Plateau. Settlers of the 1880s and 1890s, as George Trefry tells in *Pioneers to Power,* found:

. . . native grass so thick and tall that when it was damp your feet would become soaking wet as you rode through it on horseback. Over pasturing— mostly by horses—thinned it out and gave the sage brush more growth.

The overgrazing came as a known, last effort by stockmen to profit from a doomed way of life. They had no legal way to keep out growing numbers of farmers convinced that where bunchgrass would grow, wheat would grow even better. The farmers fenced acreages formerly the exclusive domain of ranchers; railroads solved the problem of bringing in the building materials and supplies needed for farming. Reaching market by long on-the-hoof drives no longer was necessary; crops could be shipped by rail. Furthermore, laws limiting homestead claims to a quarter section (160 acres) allowed what seemed like enough land for a homesite but could not begin to provide for raising cattle or horses. The click of train wheels rolling into Coulee City sounded a death knell for the nearby open range.

In *Pioneers to Power,* Paul Filion describes the process of claiming land and succeeding as a farmer. In 1909 his parents arrived at Coulee City in a boxcar, which also held all their household goods and livestock. Paul and his brother came a little later and:

. . . found we had to walk out to our father's place north of the Grand Coulee, about 12 miles. I took up a squatters rights . . . and later filed for a homestead. The delay of filing was because of a resurvey of the country. Cattlemen had destroyed all the markers of the first survey.

As a "cash crop," Filion drove pigs to Coulee City on foot, a three- or four-day trek, camping out at night and rounding up the pigs again each morning. Hardships included a grasshopper invasion "so devastating I hate to tell about it," when crushed grasshoppers turned wagon roads slippery and drowned grasshoppers crusted watering troughs and kept farm animals from drinking.

A trip to **Summer Falls** samples the changes begun in 1943 when workmen started building the dam for Banks Lake and the Main Canal of the Columbia Basin irrigation project. (Follow the Pinto Ridge road south from Coulee City to Summer Falls, then continue south to State Route 28; total distance 21 miles.) The road leads close to the rim of Grand Coulee and offers glimpses into the Dry Falls area. Summer Falls is named for canal water formerly released over a basalt ledge as a thunderous torrent, but the flow is now channeled through the power plant, which results in a comparatively subdued waterfall.

CRESTON, a service center between Davenport

and Wilbur, was named by railway engineers for a nearby butte that is the crest of the Columbia Plateau, 2,462 feet. Native peoples called the butte by a name meaning "The Place Where the Deer Dry Their Antlers." The area was notorious for cattlemen's feuds with home-steaders who picked streams or waterholes for their homesites and put up fences, closing land to range livestock in need of water. In frustration and vengeance, ranchers occasionally drove their herds through fields. They also pulled up surveyors' stakes to stymie homesteaders intending to file legal claims.

Two miles east of Creston an inconspicuous road turns off U.S. 2 to wind among rolling hills and along streams to **Fort Spokane.** Four miles from the highway, a spur road drops down a "break," the local term for stream drainages cutting from the plateau to the Columbia River; this road twists for 6 miles more to **Lincoln,** an abandoned sawmill site close to the river.

Good water at **DAVENPORT** made it a major campground along the White Bluffs Road, which was an important route during the Montana gold boom of the 1860s. By the 1880s the site, at first known as Cottonwood Springs, had become the service center of a growing agricultural region.

Several houses make a walk through the older residential district worthwhile. Watch for the Fry House (Ninth and Marshall), a three-story house with walls three bricks thick; the Benson House (Sinclair and Sixth) with tall white colonnades; and the towering Queen Anne–style McInnis House (1001 Morgan). The county courthouse (Fourth and Logan), built of buff-colored brick and limestone, stands on a hill across the highway from the residential part of town. The county historical museum (Seventh and Park) displays early-day photographs and farm machinery.

Settlers pioneered the Palouse in the 1870s, then spread west when the Northern Pacific main line crossed into the scablands in the 1880s. At first the route impressed train passengers for its bleak coulees more than for its rolling grasslands. One eastern skeptic commented that if farms were to succeed, the region:

. . . would need a Moses at every mile-post to smite the black, ugly rocks with his rod and make the water gush over all the parched land.

Every other section of land within 40 miles of the railroad track belonged to the Northern Pacific, a swath that embraced Davenport. The land partly subsidized the railroad company's

Combines drawn by teams of 32 (or even 40) horses or mules became available in 1891. Grain poured from a spout into sacks, sewn shut by a man riding the combine. Old-timers say mules stood heat better than horses, but horses pulled faster and tired less than mules.

enormous cost of building before towns existed to welcome the trains. Sale of that land in the 1880s raised urgently needed revenue and gave settlers an alternative to filing for government land. Terms were reasonable, including several years to complete payment at 7 percent interest.

By the end of the 1880s Northern Pacific officials began worrying about competition. The Union Pacific had gained control of the Oregon Railway and Navigation Company and was webbing the Palouse with branch lines and running a spur to Spokane Falls. They might build west onto the plateau. So might the Great Northern, then crossing Montana. Furthermore, by 1888 a small line called the Seattle, Lake Shore and Eastern was grading roadbed from Spokane Falls to Davenport, helped by local citizens' donations of land, money, and labor. This line intended to link the Inland Empire with Puget Sound via Snoqualmie Pass, a whole new orientation away from the Columbia River and Portland.

The Northern Pacific could not afford such competition. They secured right-of-way across the Grand Coulee, a crucial route westward. They also bought out the Seattle, Lake Shore and Eastern and built their own line from Cheney through Davenport, Wilbur, and Almira to Coulee City. Promoters stalked ahead of construction crews, and land seekers confident of rail access took up claims.

DOUGLAS, a hamlet 5 miles east of Waterville, shows from U.S. 2 because of its shade trees and the tall steeple of Saint Paul's Kirche. Through the 1880s Douglas rivaled Waterville in size; it later declined as small acreages proved unprofitable and original settlers moved away. Even so, the Lutheran congregation begun by a nucleus of German families (largely from Illinois) continued to grow. In 1915 they built the church with donated labor and local lumber. The result, although no longer in use, is a fine example of country craftsmanship.

For years, Douglas had the distinction of being a two-railroad town. The Mansfield branch of the Great Northern completed its track in 1909, and a year later a second, minuscule line arrived. It came from Waterville, which had been snubbed by the Great Northern although

entrepreneurs there, proud of their county courthouse and prosperous warehouses, had fully expected to also have the railroad. When it went through Douglas instead, they had little choice but to build a connecting line. Trains rattled over its tracks until 1948, when a flash flood washed out parts of the roadbed.

(Also see WATERVILLE, p. 100.)

DRY FALLS separates upper Grand Coulee, which holds Banks Lake, from the lower coulee, which ends at Soap Lake. A state park interpretive center explains the scene, and a paved road wanders from Sun Lakes State Park campground to a series of lake basins worn into bedrock as "plunge pools." The waterfall that formed them is believed greater than any other the world has ever known.

The Columbia River formerly was much larger; from an aerial perspective, its stupendous ice-age riverbed shows unmistakably. The flow in that channel dates from the period that also produced periodic floods from a vast glacial lake in western Montana. The volume and erosive force of these floodwaters swelled the river spectacularly. Soil and vegetation got stripped off, and the edge of the Columbia Plateau wore away as the torrents raced into the low country around today's Quincy. The coulee formed as the lip retreated. Before the ice age ended, the canyon had lengthened about 25 miles, from Soap Lake to Dry Falls.

Alexander Ross, traveling between Fort Okanogan and Spokane House, described the overall scene in his *Fur Hunters of the Far West.* He wrote of "subterraneous labyrinths" and "cold springs" and commented:

[We] made a short stay at a place called the Grand Coulé, one of the most romantic, picturesque, and marvelously-formed chasms of the Rocky Mountains. . . . No one traveling in these parts ought to resist paying a visit to this wonder of the West. . . . While in [one] place the solemn gloom forbids the wanderer to advance, in another the prospect is lively and inviting, the ground being thickly studded with ranges of columns, pillars, battlements, turrets, and steps upon steps, in every variety of shade and colour.

ELECTRIC CITY. (See under GRAND COULEE DAM, p. 91.)

ELMER CITY. (See under GRAND COULEE DAM, p. 91.)

EPHRATA (Eh-fray´-tuh) lies on the fertile flat of the Columbia Plateau beyond the mouth of Grand Coulee. Railway engineers for the Great Northern line bestowed the name because abundant water reminded them of Biblical references to irrigation wells at Ephrath, predecessor of Bethlehem.

The stately Grant County courthouse (First NW and C) stands west of the highway. Built in 1917, it is heated geothermally with water from a local hot spring. At the northern edge of town, the county historical society museum and pioneer village stands on the east side of State Route 28. Early-day buildings brought to the grounds and meticulously furnished range from blacksmith shop and livery to dress shop, saloon, and print shop. Farm machinery includes a steam tractor with caterpillar tread and a plethora of mowers, loaders, seeders, binders—each massive, each from an era when men needed brute strength to throw the levers that controlled machines through a system of ratchets. Even equipment that did not require strength depended nonetheless on hand manipulation. As one old-timer writing about childhood put it:

Saturday we would crank the old washing machine, turn the handle on the barrel churn, and turn the handle of the grindstone to sharpen the tools. All this turning fell to me, as I was the older [child].

Ephrata's springs served native people as a regular campsite slightly to the west. Cowhands trailing cattle north to the Okanogan, or rounding up local cattle and horses, also camped at the springs. So did settlers moving to new homestead claims and military expeditions traveling between Fort Simcoe and Fort Spokane.

The Great Northern laid its rails through Ephrata en route to Puget Sound in 1892, poor timing in view of the financial crash that began the following year. Settlers hoping to make a go of farming filed for free government homestead land newly served by Great Northern trains, but town development was slowed by the economic downturn. When Ephrata was platted as a townsite in 1901, one end of a boxcar served as post office, the other end as railway depot.

At the time, horses outnumbered cattle throughout the country from the Frenchman Hills to Moses Lake. About 25,000 ran free in Grant County alone. Although they were beautiful to see and a veritable symbol of the Old West, the situation could not continue once farms began to checkerboard the open range. Stockmen reduced herds by shipping horses out by rail. In 1906 cowboys drove literally thousands of horses to Ephrata, the last great horse roundup of central Washington.

Cattle ranchers sold most of their stock that same year. Sheepmen still departed from Ephrata each June to trail their flocks to the mountain pastures of Chelan County for summer grazing on public land, but they, too, felt the transition to a new era. Their route now lay along lanes bordered by wheatfields. Furthermore, the National Forest Service had started to charge a grazing fee on its lands, which embraced most of the summer range.

By 1909 Ephrata's population totaled 323, and the state legislature designated it county seat of newly created Grant County. "Big Bend County" had been the intended name, a reference to the great arc of the Columbia River; but legislators preferred Grant County because they had already established Lincoln, Douglas, Adams, and Franklin counties.

For a scenic backcountry drive, continue beyond the courthouse, following signs that point across Sagebrush Flats to Palisades. (See under MOSES COULEE, p. 94.)

GEORGE, an irrigation community at the western edge of the Columbia Plateau, was christened in the 1950s so as to be the only place in the nation to bear the full name of a president: George, Washington. It was a new town at the time, platted in conjunction with the arrival of Columbia Basin irrigation canals. To carry the theme further, the developers named streets Bing, Royal Anne, and other varieties of cherries—even Maraschino! Townsfolk entered into the spirit by dressing up in powdered wigs, brass-buttoned jackets, and flowing skirts on Washington's Birthday, and they baked "the world's largest" cherry pie. It now measures 8 feet across; free slices. (For summer outdoor concerts, see FRENCHMAN COULEE, p. 116.)

COLUMBIA BASIN PROJECT

Divert Columbia River water into irrigation canals and thereby turn dry sagebrush land into fields of potatoes, corn, asparagus, alfalfa, mint, and grapes. That is the story of the Columbia Basin Project, one of the most drastic landscape "face-lifts" on earth. Within three decades of the early 1950s, when the first water flowed from Banks Lake into the Main Canal, a half-million acres turned green, and plans call for another half-million acres to be brought into productivity.

Three fourths of the land in the area already belonged to private owners when the federal government first held drawings to select applicants for the precious irrigation water. Project policy nonetheless continued century-old homestead principles favoring families rather than public subsidy of corporate land development: it made water available only to holders of 160 acres, or 320 acres for a married couple. Farm size limitations now have tripled, however; success is impossible on a small acreage owing to the cost of modern equipment.

Today, 300 miles of main canals and 2,000 miles of secondary canals irrigate land stretching for 100 miles, north to south. Drains and wasteways ensure the reuse of runoff. Hydropower plants pour canal water through turbines and produce electricity. (See Summer Falls under COULEE CITY, p. 85.)

In the project's first three decades, the population of its area tripled, a figure that bears out the claim that for every 1,000 acres developed by public irrigation projects, 50 additional people find employment on farms (and more than three times that many in connection with manufacturing equipment, transporting goods, financing farm operations, shipping crops, and so on). In the 1930s, as work began on the Grand Coulee Dam, an Ephrata newspaper writer correctly predicted:

You can view the dam and be held spellbound by its magnitude; but only when you have seen the 1,200,000 acres of irrigable Columbia Basin land . . . can you understand . . . this great development.

The opening of the irrigation era amounted to the area's second birth. In the early 1900s it had been known by various names, including Fitzpatrick Springs for a waterhole tucked in a rock crevice west of the present town, reachable only by a rope and bucket until someone installed a hand pump. In 1904 scores of settlers from Minnesota arrived, among them Allouez Domberger, whose first name became the post office designation for the town.

By the following year neighbors were well enough organized to arrange for a priest to come from Spokane to say Mass. It was held outdoors with a kitchen table as the altar and pews fashioned by laying boards onto nail kegs. The sermon reportedly was given in English, German, and French, an accommodation for the varied backgrounds represented in the community.

Dryland wheat, onions, potatoes, and watermelons grew adequately as cash crops, and well drillers found ample call. Usually they succeeded in bringing in water at depths of several hundred feet. By saving bath water and kitchen rinse water for use on gardens and small orchards, families were able to raise their own vegetables and fruits. Women could exchange eggs and butter in Quincy for coffee, sugar, and flour.

GRAND COULEE DAM abounds in superlatives. It is the largest all-concrete structure on earth—nearly a mile long, a scale so huge that apparent size is hard to grasp. (Other, even larger dams have earth-filled cores.) Construction used more lumber than has gone into any other known structure. Only the Guri Dam in Brazil (dedicated in 1987) exceeds

Grand Coulee's generation of power. The third powerhouse here alone (added in the 1970s) runs more water through its turbines than the average flow of the Colorado River through the Grand Canyon.

This stupendous installation can be toured year-round; a visitor center is located on State Route 155, slightly northwest of the dam itself. (Access is easiest when traveling downhill, as though heading toward Nespelem. For guided tours, drive past the visitor center, across the bridge, and then stay straight rather than continuing on State Route 155, which forks to the north.) A Colville Confederated Tribes museum in the town of Coulee Dam (514 Birch) portrays the long tale of pre-dam days.

As early as 1918 *Wenatchee Daily World* editor Rufus Woods ran a story suggesting a dam at Grand Coulee. Congress agreed in 1930, but President Herbert Hoover would not request funds for construction; the federal budget showed a deficit, which he objected to worsening. Hoover's successor, Franklin D. Roosevelt, felt otherwise. At the time dryland farmers knew more about disaster than success, and a quarter of the families nationwide had lost their means of support. A federal power and irrigation project would turn the dry Columbia Basin green: water would generate power and irrigate fields, and farmers' purchase of irrigation rights would offset the costs of a large-scale project.

The irrigation aspect was crucial, for power demand alone did not actually amount to much in the 1930s. *Colliers* magazine even asked: "What are they going to do with the power?" Spokane interests favored a dam on the Pend Oreille River near Newport, and a network of canals to bring water by gravity to the Columbia Basin. Ephrata and Wenatchee interests, spearheaded by Woods and attorneys N. W. Washington, Billy Clapp, and James O'Sullivan, argued for a dam at Grand Coulee with a large enough power capacity to pump irrigation water and provide an excess for sale. Their plan prevailed. By the mid-1930s Germany obviously was preparing for war, which would place enormous power demands on United States production if the war expanded beyond Europe.

More immediately, a need for jobs prompted Roosevelt to go ahead with the dam. He approved funds as part of the National Recovery Act's program of putting men to work on public projects. Crews poured the first concrete at Grand Coulee on December 3, 1933. At the time, engineers had little experience with so huge a river and had to innovate as they went. When mud kept oozing from a hillside, they brought in a refrigeration unit and held the hill in place by freezing it. When a coffer dam sprang a leak, they stuffed the breach with Christmas trees and mattresses, then added bentonite clay (which expands when wet).

Visitors to Grand Coulee Dam marvel at its size and setting; others value it for the hydropower and irrigation that have revolutionized Washington's economy.

The Bureau of Reclamation was authorized to build a low dam for modest power production and navigation control. Somehow (the responsibility is unclear) they designed a foundation massive enough for a high dam. That built, the president asked Congress for additional money. Why waste the potential of such a foundation? Why not build a high dam—one that rose high enough to store water for the generation of electricity and could be used to pump irrigation water? Congress agreed.

The dam was finished in September 1941. Three months later America entered World War II. The manufacture of aluminum for planes depended on staggering amounts of electricity for a critical electrolytic process and, by the middle of the war, half the nation's aluminum came from Northwest plants. Even after peace was restored in 1945, Hanford nuclear reactors continued a high demand for power. Electricity opened a new chapter of state history.

Four towns—in three separate counties— came alive as construction began: **Coulee Dam, Grand Coulee, Electric City,** and **Elmer City.** Coulee Dam, today straddling both sides of the river, began as "Engineers Town" at the west end of the dam and "Mason City" at the east end. The government provided houses (still present but now privately owned) for engineers and project managers. Contractors and workmen lived in group housing and ate at government-run cafeterias.

Grand Coulee, Electric City, and Elmer City mushroomed as the dam became an actuality. In the winter of 1931–1932 the main street of Grand Coulee sported a restaurant, smoke shop, two saloons, and a tent where new arrivals could roll out their blankets. Soon men started putting up prefabs and "within half an hour" a newspaper would be housed or a store opened for business. Homes rose equally fast, albeit without electricity or running water. Doris Angell, wife of one of the workers, recalls in *Pioneers to Power:*

To add to the discomfort were the frequent dust storms. One could see them coming down the Coulee for miles. All doors and windows would be closed, though the temperatures were often 114 in the shade. The houses were suffocating! . . . The streets were inches thick with dust in summer and mud in winter.

(Also see BANKS LAKE, p. 84; O'SULLIVAN DAM, p. 97; and NEWPORT, p. 26.)

The **HARRINGTON** four-block, brick business district is essentially unchanged from a century ago except that upper-story windows now stare blankly, like eyes somehow blinded. The grand old Hotel Harrington (Third and Sherman) displays a decorative cornice and an arched brick entryway. Its size bears witness to the former importance of rail travel, when salesmen and businessmen would stay overnight after completing their work, then catch the morning train out of town. The two-story Bank Block built in 1904 (Third and Willis) once included an opera house. Up the street from it the two-story city hall apparently housed horse-drawn fire wagons.

The town's name comes from W. P. Harrington, a Californian who speculated in farmland here in the early 1880s. He owned 50 sections, a vast holding, and the first agribusiness in Washington. Several optimistic families moved into the area expecting that prosperity would follow in the wake of the railroad. Northern Pacific plans for Harrington evaporated, however, and hopes plunged. Those who weathered the disappointment gained their reward in 1892 when the Great Northern routed its Crab Creek line through the existing town. A bumper wheat crop five years later helped to spread word of Harrington's potential, and real growth got under way.

A post office opened in 1883 and that same year western Whitman and Spokane counties were split off into new county units. Harrington contested vigorously against Sprague and Davenport for the honor of becoming county seat. The fact that towns no more than two or three years old felt ready for an election fracas indicates the ebullient confidence of the era. Lincoln County settlement was expanding. Agricultural success seemed certain.

HARTLINE, 10 miles east of Coulee City on U.S. 2, began when the Northern Pacific's branch line across the Columbia Plateau bypassed a hamlet named Parnell. People there moved 4½ miles south to be along the railroad and renamed their town for John Hartline, the pioneer who owned the land.

Lamona stands as a lonely reminder of the former need for rural supply centers.

LAMONA has a haunting—and haunted—quality. Its empty, false-fronted 1891 general store still faces the railroad track. Two oval windows look out from the upper story and a porch runs full length across the building's front, but no one sits there in its shade. In the days of horse travel, and of slow cars on bad roads, farm communities needed such stores. But no more. Farm sizes have increased, population decreased. School buses now link families in this area to Odessa, and Lamona serves only as a railroad siding.

John Lamona bought the store in 1892 from the man who had built it the year before. A livery and upstairs "hotel" were part of the store's operation.

LIND, once on the main line, now looks bypassed. It is worth driving through, however, if for no other reason than that it is along the road to Warden, a scenic route that hugs the boundary between rich agricultural fields and rocky scablands carved by the ice-age floods. (Also see O'SULLIVAN DAM, p. 97.)

In May 1880 a Northern Pacific surveyor passing through here jotted down recommendation for a station at "Milepost 79," as counted from Wallula, the point from which the Pacific end of the transcontinental track was crawling its way east. The next year, men spiked rails into place and built a water tank and siding.

Farmers at first doubted the likelihood of success amid the sagebrush country, but with careful experimenting, they kept pushing the line of what they called "impossibly arid" farther and farther to the west. Growth came slowly although a 1903 issue of the *Lind Leader* spoke proudly of new buildings, including "several magnificent brick blocks," and urged a large turnout to fight the town's mud by "strawing all the principal roads."

(Also see RUSSIAN GERMANS sidebar, p. 96.)

MANSFIELD stands today almost as a period piece: a one-street town with unaltered brick buildings, which testify to initial prosperity and expectation. The Great Northern Railway arrived here in October 1909—or, to be precise, its tracks stopped 1½ miles northeast of the existing town and citizens moved building by building to the end of the line.

Great Northern officials had been partly spurred into adding the Mansfield branch by the impatience of Waterville financiers who threatened to lay their own track linking wheatfields to Portland markets. James J. Hill, president of the Great Northern Railway Company, often talked about such a line but his plans stayed just that, talk. Many felt that his real interest lay in Puget Sound and trade with the Orient, not in serving Inland Empire farmers.

Then came a spate of branch line construction by competing railroads, as well as announcement of Waterville's plans; Great Northern crews graded a roadbed in Moses Coulee and laid steel. The rails ended at Mansfield, not Waterville, the county seat. Historic photographs show three dozen, or more, farm and freight wagons waiting by the new tracks in Mansfield, and others loading supplies at the store. Each is drawn by at least a two-horse team, visual evidence of old-timers' memories of how many horses they needed for farming. Wheat harvesting alone depended on scores of horses to pull machinery. Teams for a single combine, especially on slopes, might run to more than 30 head, and half a dozen combines often worked together.

Farms dotted the land out from Mansfield after the railroad came, although drought and plummeting wheat prices immediately after World War I caused many families to lose their land.

Mrs. John Schweighbardt, who homesteaded just before the war began, writes in *Pioneers to Power:*

We broke the sod, fenced, and raised horses and mules. . . .[Soon] we had to move: it was first the grasshoppers, then the drought. . . . The Bridgeport Bank went broke and we lost money there. We lost more when the Mansfield Bank went broke.

John was hauling his wheat to Mansfield at the time in the winter. Twenty-seven miles with a team and sled.

Another early settler, Jennie Crider, writes:

I used to mop up the dust with water instead of trying to sweep it up, as that made another dust storm right inside the cabin.

Choking dust was routine largely owing to "dust mulching." This was a process of harrowing fallow fields up to 10 times a year. A dusty surface supposedly slowed moisture loss from the soil, and yet readily absorbed rain when the summer showers began. It was a step in experimenting with Columbia Plateau soil, although an ineffective one.

After a few years of struggling, many pioneering farmers around Mansfield gave up. They sold land and equipment to land specula-

tors or to neighbors with capital. This greatly increased the size of farms in the area, a factor crucial to success here. For a look at the home of an early-day family who succeeded, drive about 12 miles northwest of Mansfield on Deyer Road to an octagonal house with eight windows. It was designed and built in 1914 by master craftsman James Kinney as a gift for his daughter and her husband. Mr. Kinney was so pleased with results that he built a similar, smaller house for himself in Waterville.

MOSES COULEE, a magnificent, flat-bottomed gorge sculpted by water, can be entered most readily from west of Coulee City or from southeast of Wenatchee. Little developed except for occasional ranches, the coulee offers a look at "early-day" eastern Washington. Basalt layers totaling 800 feet high stack one on top of another, their joining like that of logs in a well-made cabin. Waterfalls drop as white ribbons in season and leave dark stains the rest of the year. Greasewood and sagebrush thrive— bushes typical of the Great Basin desert—yet trees line the side canyons and redwing blackbirds clutch the green reeds and burble their distinctive call.

Chief Moses and his people grew pumpkins, squash, potatoes, and corn in the coulee, which is well watered and offers protection from winds sweeping down the Columbia River and across the plateau. In 1873 the chief watched Agent R. H. Milroy ride down the rocky trail from a reconnaissance of the proposed Colville Reservation. The government was eager to establish boundaries there, withdrawing land the Northern Pacific had recently relinquished. Otherwise, they would have homesteaders' claims to contend with. Moses exchanged pleasantries with Milroy, but must have felt his heart sicken.

The government kept handing out gifts of calico and blankets, which the chief regarded as bribes. Even so, he saw the futility of a war against the whites and also the futility of predictions made by the Wanapum prophet Smohalla that a return to the old ways would drive out the newcomers. Moses sought a middle course. He talked with the agent and watched him ride on. (Also see MCLOUGHLIN CANYON, p. 61; and NESPELEM, p. 64.)

Soon stockmen began pasturing their herds in the bottomlands of the coulee Chief Moses regarded as his, and travelers rode through it, shortcutting the great bend of the Columbia River by crossing overland between Bridgeport and the Colockum Pass road to Ellensburg. The shortcut was not easy. Slopes were so steep they were called the Three Devils (north of today's settlement of Palisades) and even pious travelers came close to cursing. Men had to lighten wagons, coax teams uphill, then drive them back down for the rest of the load.

Today's roads offer three main entrances into the coulee. West of Coulee City, U.S. 2 crosses it near Milepost 172 and a spur road turns north to **Jameson Lake** (7 miles). It dips and rises like a roller coaster, a leftover from the days before roadbed engineering overwhelmed land contours. A second entry into the coulee is just west of the Jameson Lake turn. It threads the coulee floor southward, then climbs the rim and offers a sweeping view across rough scablands apparently untouched by development, except for a few faint roads.

A third entrance into Moses Coulee is from State Route 28 downriver from East Wenatchee (4 miles south of Rock Island Dam, close to where electric transmission lines cross the highway). This road leads to **Palisades** (11 miles), a small settlement set like a green oasis at the base of spectacular basalt walls. Begun in 1906, the community flourished three years later when the Great Northern Railway built its Mansfield branch line up Moses Coulee.

Beyond Palisades, the main road continues through a ranch, climbs out of the deepest part of the coulee into an upper canyon, then crosses successive terraces, and finally breaks out onto a sweeping desert landscape with grain fields far to the north; this road continues to Ephrata. Alternatively, a side road about 3 miles north of Palisades turns up **Douglas Canyon** where a cascading creek forms a verdant ribbon, huge timbers from fallen railroad trestles lie in heaps, and occasional peach trees mark former homesites. (Only experienced backcountry drivers should attempt this road. The creek must be forded; the mud can be bottomless.)

First a wagon road, then a railroad led onto the plateau via Moses Coulee.

The town of **MOSES LAKE** developed at a place known to native people as *Houaph,* "Willow." Women would wade into the shallows to gather duck eggs, then bake them in a pit layered with earth and wet grass laid above fire-heated rocks. Moses Lake also served as a traditional fishing grounds, a place to hunt sage hens and deer, and to dig biscuitroot, a major root crop. Then came whites. Thomas Blythe, a Scotsman, owned 30 sections of land and leased an additional 30 sections. He objected to the yearly "invasion" of the area by native people, bringing perhaps a thousand horses with them and, in 1898, he rode to Waterville and asked the sheriff to order the band off his land. The request was refused because of a lack of jurisdiction. "Indian problems" were the business of federal agents.

For more than a century, herds owned by native people had increased until they amounted to a major "wildlife" population. Most were cayuses, the small, agile descendants of horses brought to the Southwest by Spaniards in the 1500s and traded north as far as Washington by the mid-1700s. Columbia Plateau bunchgrass, which stayed nutritious year-round, provided ideal grazing. This characteristic attracted miners, drovers, and freighters passing through the country, and they returned to add their herds to those already on the range. By the close of the 1800s, however, farmers had staked claims to these same lands and that shunted horses and cattle away from the choice bunchgrass country into the rougher sagebrush portion of the plateau, pioneered by sheepmen. The region from Moses Lake to lower Crab Creek became the final cattle district east of the Columbia River. Settlement remained sparse.

In 1912, however, a Milwaukee German-language newspaper backed the founding of a town at Moses Lake, calling it Neppel for the wife of the publisher. Soon after the town began, brothers named McGrath built concrete walls at the shallow inlet of the lake to create holding ponds for carp. They netted the fish—which had been introduced into the lake about 1890—and held them in the ponds feeding them on corn to ready them for eastern markets. As early as the 1920s, the McGraths used a spotter plane to direct netting boats crisscrossing the lake.

Irrigation attempts in the area repeatedly failed. One try was at a Swedish settlement, which had begun in the 1920s with expectations of pumping water from the lake to irrigate alfalfa. Made into hay, the alfalfa was to be fed to dairy cows, and their milk would supply a cheese factory in Moses Lake (on Broadway). Water for the scheme probably was adequate—but that sheer abundance often led to irrigation failure. Rights to use the water were generally stymied until taken over by the vast Columbia Basin Project in the 1950s.

Economic growth turned upward, however, during the early 1940s. This came partly from planting huge potato fields, which depended on the labor of Japanese American families forcefully relocated inland by government edict at the onset of World War II. Even more, the activation of an army air force base in 1942 brought an influx of population and dollars, although the assignment was generally loathed. Most of the men had come from Glendale, California, and they sorely missed city life including Hollywood Canteen's movie-star entertainment for servicemen. One pilot-trainee described the scene at Moses Lake as:

. . . claybaked, desolate of life or vegetation. . . . Between man and horizon: Nothingness. Over the rim: Civilization. We take up where Lewis and Clark left off.

In 1945 the war ended and the air force left, then returned for a while, ostensibly to protect Grand Coulee Dam and the Hanford Atomic Works. Since 1966 the Boeing Company has used the airstrip to train crews from all over the world who fly Boeing aircraft, and Japan Airlines bases its major flight-training school here.

ODESSA presents an exceptionally tidy appearance with lawns kept green even in summer and a pleasant year-round bustle that heightens during Oktoberfest, a fall celebration of old-country origins. A white frame church (Alder and Fourth) sums up the community's background: its sign, obviously German, says "Deutsche Kongreg. St. Matthaus Kirche, Erbaut 1916." Yet the church steeple is topped by a silvery onion dome, legacy of Russia. Settlers

RUSSIAN GERMANS

Until the mid-1900s church services were held in German almost as often as in English across much of the Columbia Plateau and into the Palouse. Large families—even entire villages—of German speakers had begun arriving in Washington in the 1880s, hoping to escape problems at home and to achieve the success sketched in railroad advertisements. Hundreds came from Russia, where their ancestors had gone as pioneers a century earlier. In Washington they lived in earthen dugouts and burned cow dung and sagebrush as fuel while they successfully turned patches of desert into farms. Or families and carpenters crowded together into shanties while houses and churches rose, and wells sank to reach water. Men earned cash as railroad laborers or, after Spokane's fire in 1889, by working to help rebuild the city.

Family traditions of taming raw land had begun for these people in the 1760s when Catherine the Great, a German princess, ruled Russia. To help colonize newly acquired territory she offered free transportation, a choice of land, interest-free loans for equipment, religious freedom, village autonomy, and exemption from service in the Russian army. On the Volga steppes she wanted a buffer against the Tartars and other Asiatic tribes. In the Crimea she wanted demonstration farms as models for Russian peasants.

German families responded, eager to escape the religious and political wars and manipulations that had raged ever since Martin Luther protested Roman Catholic domination in 1517. They trekked overland to the Baltic Sea, sailed 900 miles to St. Petersburg (Leningrad), journeyed 400 miles inland to Moscow, then—escorted by Cossacks—traveled a final 400 miles to the land they were to conquer. Half a million Germans settled this new Russian frontier, managing their own schools and civic and church affairs.

The czars who succeeded Catherine, however, felt no need to continue her concessions, and religious persecution and army conscription, combined with crop failures in the 1880s and 1890s, created extreme discontent. Furthermore, the Russian practice of redividing land every 12 years caused problems. Every adult man had received 42 acres in 1798, but the per capita holdings a century later were less than a tenth that much owing to population increase. Agents sent to Russia by the Northern Pacific and Great Northern railroads had no trouble recruiting colonists.

The Russian-German pattern of geographically and psychologically isolating farm communities from their surroundings at first repeated itself in Washington. German Lutherans, Congregationalists, and Seventh Day Adventists pioneered land and built towns, or organized enclaves within existing communities. In Russia these people had turned inward for a century. Here most integrated with the mainstream in a generation or two—although the aromas of rye bread and sauerkraut continue to come from kitchens in Odessa, Ritzville, Warden, Endicott, and Farmington, and phone books carry a high percentage of German surnames.

German Mennonites and Hutterites founded isolationist settlements and zealously continue many traditional practices. For them, German remains strong. As a teacher in the Hutterite colony near Reardan puts it:

The kids need English because it's the language of the world around them. They need German because . . . it's the language of the Hutterite people. If you lose your own language, your culture is next.

here included a large group of Congregationalist and Lutheran Germans, whose parents had been invited by Catherine the Great to colonize the Volga area of Russia. Many left there for the United States in the late nineteenth century.

Other settlers came here directly from Germany, attracted by railroad promotion of the land, which was especially heavy in Germany, the Netherlands, and Scandinavia. (German financiers had backed the Northern Pacific's 1880s completion of its transcontinental line.) The railroad era really "opened" Washington, bringing with it the classic American conviction that hope and hard work were the chief ingredients needed for success. The fur-trading era had served as prelude for this later development.

O'SULLIVAN DAM, south of Moses Lake, consists of nearly 4 miles of embankment impounding Potholes Reservoir. Engineers designed the dam to fit peculiarities of the site: instead of continuous earth-fill construction, they built in sections that incorporate natural rock outcrops.

Rock from the immediate area proved too porous for use in the dam's core; instead fill had to be quarried in the Frenchmen Hills. Glacial sediments also proved porous, necessitating a concrete lining to prevent excess seepage. Despite such problems, the dam—begun in 1947—was completed in 1949. It is a major part of the Columbia Basin reclamation project. Wastewater from irrigated fields to the north is impounded here and sent on via canals to irrigate a quarter-million acres lying to the southwest. For the Columbia Basin as a whole such reuse increases the amount of water available for irrigation by a full third.

James O'Sullivan is the man honored by the dam's name. He was an Ephrata attorney who campaigned tirelessly—and effectively—for Grand Coulee Dam as a means of bringing water to the potentially productive sagebrush lands of central Washington.

The **Columbia National Wildlife Refuge** south of the dam is characterized by dramatic basalt cliffs, pothole lakes emerald with cattail, and streams and marshes. Visiting it is like stepping back 10,000 years to the end of the last ice age and seeing again the moist environment experienced by Washington's earliest-known people. Seepage from irrigation projects has raised the water table and, although the present climate remains semi-arid, water has refilled the potholes scoured by ice-age floodwaters that poured through here from the Quincy Basin.

PALISADES. (See under MOSES COULEE, p. 94.)

QUINCY plainly shows results of the Columbia Basin Project's stupendous reclamation of dry lands; simply driving past equipment sales yards is like visiting a museum of modern farm machinery. The first tractors here were hissing, puffing steam monsters that gulped firewood (usually sagebrush) at such a rate that one man's full time went into supplying the fuel. Another man was kept busy hauling water. Even so, those machines were efficient compared with horse-drawn equipment.

Quincy began life with the machine age. Developers from Ritzville laid out the town in 1901, which was shortly after the Great Northern had arrived. Professor E. E. Elliott came from the state agricultural college at Pullman to discuss setting up an experimental farm, for nobody felt sure what crops would grow in an area with a yearly precipitation of only 10 to 12 inches, more than offset by a potential evaporative loss of 14 to 16 inches. From that first test farm to the chemically fertilized, richly productive corporate farms of today represents phenomenal change.

It has not come easily. The state travel guide produced as a Works Project Administration project during the depression years of the 1930s speaks of:

. . . ghost farms, . . . a tragic residue left by settlers who, at the turn of the century, hopefully broke the land and waited for the promised irrigation to materialize.

As early as 1892, a man named G. W. Bartholomew had taken an option on 50,000 acres of Northern Pacific land on the Quincy flats, intending to pump water for irrigation. His power source was to be the hydroelectric project at Chelan Falls, but Bartholomew lost out before he even began: his financial backers withdrew owing to the widespread financial collapse of 1893.

A decade later, well drillers successfully penetrated almost 200 feet through soil and basalt to tap water. Land values soared, and by 1904 windmills were whirring and pumping at a dozen sites. Well water continues to irrigate Quincy fields today. In fact, pumping is more successful than ever, owing to better pumps and to a water table fed by irrigation seepage from the Columbia Basin Project. This leads to conflict. Who owns the rights to this water?

Southwest of Quincy, a Public Utility District dam completed in 1984 generates power by harnessing the flow of water in the Quincy West Canal. Five similar hydroelectric plants on the Columbia Basin canals are operated by Seattle City Light and Tacoma City Light; the largest of these is the Summer Falls plant on the main canal south of Coulee City.

At **RITZVILLE** turn off the freeway and drive through the newer sections of town to the old district near the railroad tracks. There, vestiges of what made the town a regional milling and wheat-shipping center still remain as if an exhibit of changing architecture and wheat technology. Structures range from round metal bins with conical roofs to tall towers of concrete or of wood sheathed with galvanized metal. In 1904 Ritzville was "the largest initial wheat-shipping point in the United States," according to the Washington State Bureau of Statistics.

The mood and pace of the era, dominated by rail travel, are reflected in the number of old hotels in town: two stand abandoned (Main and Adams); a third—the elegant Ritz Hotel—is now demolished (vacant lot at Main and Columbia). Turn-of-the-century brick and concrete commercial buildings continue to line the old road through town; note especially the buildings at all four corners of Main and Washington, including one with a sporty turret topped with a high conical roof.

Be sure to visit the county historical society museum (408 Main), which occupies the converted home of Frank Burroughs, Ritzville's doctor. Built in 1889 and remodeled three years later, the house has a free-spirited architecture in itself worthy of a look. A distinctive Carnegie library stands next door. The Leonard Mansion of salmon pink brick (Fifth and Adams), built in Queen Anne style, also warrants driving past, as

do other houses in the vicinity. Watch for one with a "widow's walk" at the peak of its roof, and for another with rounded corner windows of glass brick, a *very* 1930s Art-Deco touch. The 1930s also are represented by a mural above the door of the county courthouse (two blocks west of the railroad tracks at Broadway and Adams).

Town founder Philip Ritz was an extraordinary 1860s Walla Walla farmer and businessman who had made a fortune supplying miners in Idaho with agricultural products. When that boom collapsed, Ritz quickly shipped barrels of flour to New York City, hoping to develop demand for Washington wheat in Liverpool, England. He succeeded. Confident in the dry, gently rolling hills west of the Palouse country, he then bought 5,000 acres of Northern Pacific land near Ritzville in 1878 and began a nationwide campaign to promote settlement. The railroad company applauded this effort and gave him a contract to plant trees along its brand-new track from Ainsworth (the railroad construction camp just south of Pasco) to the infant town of Ritzville. This meant 70 miles of trees. Their presence lining the railway was intended to ease the minds of prospective immigrants: the "desert" could be made to bloom.

Ironically, the Northern Pacific's need for cash forced it to urge sheepmen to buy up their leased land at the very time that the railroad's own promotion was bringing farmers into the area and increasing potential value. In places, land purchased for $1 per acre in 1897 sold for $30 just five years later.

The town of **SOAP LAKE** stands on the shores of a lake 2 miles long, the southernmost of a chain of lakes within Grand Coulee. The native name for the lake meant "Healing Waters." The first white name was "Sanitarium Lake." Both designations came from the supposed medicinal power of the water. The name "Soap" is from the sudsy froth that formerly blew across the lake and piled on shore, but is rare now that irrigation seepage dilutes the water.

Municipal beaches give lake access, as has been true for decades. Main Street, which leads to the lake, has three commercial buildings faced with cobblestones brought here by the glacial floodwaters that repeatedly raged through

Grand Coulee; two cobblestone homes stand among others on the hill above town. A sidewalk drinking fountain downtown still provides Soap Lake water for health seekers (but drinking it is like swallowing a salty dose of sodium bicarbonate). The 1906 *Dictionary of Spokane,* however, carried this ad for the Soap Lake Remedy Company:

For Stomach Troubles, Constipation, Headache, Rheumatism, or whenever a thorough constitutional remedy is needed, take Soap Lake Capsules. Price 25 cts per box.

SPRAGUE won the Lincoln County seat when Lincoln and Douglas counties separated from Spokane County in 1883; it already had the division offices and maintenance shops of the Northern Pacific and was larger than the town of Spokane Falls. Yet today's freeway bypasses the town. Brick commercial buildings still line First Street from B to E streets, however; grain elevators stand along rail sidings; and the tall white steeple of Mary Queen of Heaven (built in 1902) points heavenward from the hill. Nineteenth-century houses face the train tracks with firewood stacked to the gingerbread of their porches and old brick chimneys erupting from new tin roofs. A pair of mirror-image red-brick houses (Second and D streets) feature squared corner turrets and arched windows. All such buildings evoke both lost optimism and determined survival.

A major "crop" shipped from Sprague in its opening days was wool—appropriate since settlement here began as a sheep camp in the late 1870s. Ranchers had shipped wool via the Snake and Columbia rivers to connect at Portland for ultimate sale in Boston. But in 1885 the Wool Growers Association won acceptable freight rates from the Northern Pacific Railroad and made Sprague their main shearing grounds. At the time, shepherds drove their flocks from low-country wintering and lambing grounds in the Snake River region to summer pastures on public land near Colville or above Chelan or Wenatchee. En route they began stopping to shear the sheep at Sprague. Fleece was then bagged and shipped east by rail.

The town was spanking new when the railroad arrived in 1881. Walla Walla farmlands had

filled. Palouse settlement was well under way. The Columbia Plateau's turn had come. People seeking land pushed west from obviously rich soils onto the slightly dubious, definitely more dry region of central Washington. Sprague townspeople harbored few doubts, however. They danced exuberantly on the railroad roundhouse floor, using the headlights of a locomotive to see by. Fifteen years later their elation sagged. Fire destroyed the town— including the roundhouse—and the Northern Pacific rebuilt at Yardley, just east of Spokane. Sprague's civic aspirations died. Davenport even captured the county seat.

Just west of Sprague, a stop at the I-90 rest area is worthwhile for its view. **Sprague Lake,** in the immediate foreground, fills a low place scoured by glacial floodwaters, and beyond it, scabland channels lead off to the south. Water more than 200 feet deep swirled here as a torrent 8 *miles* wide. The flood stripped away 100 feet of soil, which lay like the fertile hills of today's Palouse. In the water's wake stretched the present rough, starkly beautiful maze of coulees and mesas.

Turn into **STRATFORD** as an excuse to slow down. South of State Route 28, several huge grain elevators by the railroad track dominate the old part of town. Near them are a few houses, an empty store, and an abandoned hand-pump gasoline station.

Stratford's population reached 90 in 1910, based on expectations of irrigation water. People were planting orchards and waiting for additional homesteaders and large-scale development. Mail came five times daily, tossed by the sackful from passing trains. The Spokane architectural firm of Keith and Whitehouse designed a two-story school with a hip-roof at the west edge of town, symbol of community confidence. (Whitehouse is known for Saint John's Cathedral and the Hutton Settlement orphanage in Spokane; Keith designed Spokane's Riblet Mansion and Ephrata's county courthouse.)

The school, so splendidly launched, closed in the 1940s owing to a population decrease and the consolidation of rural schools. For a while the building—brick with a half-timbered upper story—became a barn. Now it has a metal roof and new life as a residence. Population again is surging as people from regional centers such as Ephrata and Ritzville seek the scale and supposed peace of a small town.

SUMMER FALLS. (See under COULEE CITY, p. 85.)

Farms near **WARDEN** could claim the nation's highest potato yield per acre by the 1970s and also successful harvests of alfalfa, feed corn, strawberries, and grapes, plus peas, carrots, radishes, and beans grown specially for seed. Circle irrigation, delivering water and fertilizer simultaneously, underlies much of the success (see COLUMBIA BASIN PROJECT sidebar, p. 89). So does the hard work of fieldhands, mostly Japanese in the early days of agribusiness here, and now Latino. The 1980 census lists Spanish speakers as more than 40 percent of the population in the Warden area. Highlights in the development of local farming are displayed at the historical society's museum (Second and Oak). The Lind Coulee archaeological site—the first early-man site known in Washington—is about a half mile northeast of Warden. It dates to 9,000 years ago. (Nothing remains visible.)

Permanent settlement began in the 1870s when stockmen drove cattle and horses onto virgin grasslands. Three decades later both the Northern Pacific and the Chicago, Milwaukee, and St. Paul arrived (1903 and 1907), making Warden the only town in the Columbia Basin Project area with two railroads. Irrigation brought today's prosperity, but the water was slow in coming. The *Seattle Post-Intelligencer* in 1946 reported the expectations of a Russian-German farmer whose experience was representative of those who settled the Warden area:

Ben O. Ostlid, who came here to homestead in 1907, . . . has been dry farming and waiting for the coming of Grand Coulee water for almost 30 years. . . . He'll make this present holding bloom when the East Low Canal reaches this far, in about another five years.

Other settlers who came at the time of the Ostlids tell of grubbing out sagebrush to use for cooking and heating fuel and of pumping water into barrels from a well and hauling it 4 miles to the house. They also tell of hand digging a well, using a windlass and bucket to lower a man with a shovel, then making bricks for a "mud house" with the clay and sand he dug from the hole.

By the end of the 1930s rural electrification brought Warden eight power poles. Unfortunately, not long afterward, World War II army air force men mistook the town's nighttime sparkle for a target and dropped two rounds of sandbag "bombs" before a civic-minded citizen could get to the powerhouse and turn off the lights. The mayor then called the sheriff, and the sheriff called the Ephrata air base saying, "I think Warden is about to surrender." The town's pattern of lights resembled that of a new bombing range near what now is Royal City (35 miles southwest of Warden).

Downtown **WATERVILLE** catches the eye: two blocks of 1890s and early 1900s brick buildings remain almost as though they belong to a movie set. Iron storefront columns and brick corbeling never have been hidden beneath modern siding; windows still are double-hung with wooden sashes.

The town began as more of a "planned city" than is usual among Washington's pioneer communities, perhaps owing to the New England upbringing of its founder, A. T. Greene. His original eight-block plat filed in 1886 reserved lots for a courthouse, schools, fraternal lodges, and a public park. Courthouse and park remain, and an imposing two-and-one-half-story hotel (now closed) stands on original parkland deeded for hotel use. Officials felt excellent accommodations should be available for anyone on business, or not wanting a night drive down the twisting canyon road to the Columbia River and on to Wenatchee, 26 miles.

In 1889 production started at Waterville's first brickyard, and the *Big Bend Empire* soon reported "talk of building brick blocks" to replace frame structures, which were considered temporary and a fire hazard. Two years later the two-story building still standing on the northeast corner of Locust and Chelan was completed, the first building to conform with the town's new standards. Owners of the three separate units— bank, lodge, and shops/offices—set the pattern responsible for Waterville's architectural charm: they agreed on style and scale.

During the next few years additional brick buildings went up; the most imposing of them was the Douglas County Bank on the northwest corner of Locust and Chelan. Gleaming white columns flank its angled entry, which is reached by a low flight of curved stairs. "Stability" radiates as a social message from such an edifice. The two-story white clapboard home of the banker (Monroe and Locust) still stands southeast of the bank. Its windows are leaded glass; its entry is angled, like that of the bank; and the roofline sweeps to the porch, emphasizing the door.

All of Waterville's downtown core is listed in the National Register as a historic district. The only early frame commercial building remaining is the false-fronted Centennial Feed Building, two doors up Chelan Avenue from the bank. The huge, boxy Nifty Theater (a half block east of the downtown center) belongs to the 1930s. The county historical society museum is housed in a new building across from the old hotel (west end of town).

Settlement at Waterville began in the mid-1880s when elimination of the Moses–Columbia Reservation brought white miners and homesteaders through the area on their way to stake claims in the Okanogan. Their route differed from that of today. The railhead was at Ellensburg. From there a wagon road crossed Colockum Pass to the Columbia near Wenatchee. It then climbed Corbaley Canyon to the Waterville Plateau, crossed it, and dropped back to the Columbia at Bridgeport. Ferry operators at the river crossings helped to pay for the road. Volunteers donated labor to maintain it.

As travel increased, Waterville grew. It never had doubted its destiny as a trade center and seat of government. The federal land office at Waterville handled a third more applicants than any other land office in the state. In fact the editor of Waterville's *Big Bend Empire* printed an "open letter" in 1904 warning that homestead and Northern Pacific land "worth taking" was all gone. The editor concluded, however, that the promise for farming appeared exceptional, and improved land could be had by lease or purchase at reasonable prices. Boosters had named Waterville well: it had more water than most of the Columbia Plateau.

For a feeling of the geographic—and historic—separation of the Waterville area from the Columbia River, drive down **McNeil Canyon**

(north of Waterville) to the Columbia River, then return to the plateau via Pine Canyon (the route of U.S. 2). Both roads change about 1,500 feet in elevation, a headache for pioneer farmers needing to get crops to the river for shipment and to bring up materials and supplies. The river flowed tantalizingly close but frustratingly hard to reach. (To find McNeil Canyon head north past Waterville's 1918 Catholic church, on Chelan Avenue, and follow the main travel route, which becomes O Street NW, then Eighth NW. A mile beyond Lemoigne turn north on F Street NW and continue another 8 miles to a road junction; from there, follow signs pointing to Chelan. The road is paved; its views are of the river backdropped by the distant Cascade Mountains.)

Beebe Orchards, at the base of McNeil Canyon, was a company town complete with its own post office in the early 1900s. The bridge piers, now standing in the river as enormous concrete sculptures, are from the one-way bridge William Beebe built in 1919 to carry an irrigation pipeline and also to link his land to the railhead across the river. The state highway bridge replacing Beebe's bridge opened in 1963.

Today's **WILBUR** began when Samuel Wilbur Condon (or Condit) settled down with a native wife about 1875. He had first come through the Big Bend region 15 years earlier, having left the burst balloon of California's mining heyday. His undertaking here was to run mule packtrains from Walla Walla to Canadian mining camps, the next outbreak of western gold fever.

At first, Condon raised horses and cattle on public land, which he claimed by squatter's rights. Then he started a ferry and built a toll road from ranch to ferry landing, and on past Omak Lake to the Okanogan. He advertised this "Pike Road and Cable Ferry" as the "Safest, Surest, Nearest and Best Route to and from Salmon River Mines, Conconully, Ruby City and Wannacut Lake." Travelers were less enthusiastic. Guy Waring said in *My Pioneer Past* that the road made his "heart sink time and again for fear [he] could not pull the hills even with four horses." Eleven days out from the railhead at Sprague, Waring and his family

approached the mighty Columbia, . . . about eighteen

hundred feet wide, and at this season running very rapidly because of melting snow in the mountains. The crossing place required a broad, even-running stretch of river, and a beach on the opposite side extending for at least a mile . . . to allow for the sweep of the current.

The town of Wilbur sprouted on Condon's ranchland and took his middle name— although for awhile settlers favored the name "Goosetown." It came from "Wild Goose Bill," a nickname that originated when Condon "mistakenly" shot a Canadian priest's tame geese. The birds had been handraised from eggs lovingly carried north from Oregon. Condon made payment but never outlived the incident.

Today's Wilbur is a farm supply center. North from it the road offers a spectacular 14-mile sample of eastern Washington physiography. Wheat fields stretch to the horizon as an endless blanket. Then comes an abrupt descent to the Columbia River flowing at the contact between the Columbia Plateau and the mountainous Okanogan Highlands, a geologically old surface never engulfed by the basalt flows that created the plateau. Successive layers of lava show clearly in canyon walls where the road drops to the river. (The road is steep, but paved and easy to drive. The ferry across the Columbia is free.)

WILSON CREEK, a mile off State Route 28 east of Ephrata, offers a vignette of the past merged with the present. Irrigation sprinklers like gigantic linear fountains turn fields green, some of the water coming from pipes connected into units as much as a half mile long and mounted on wheels to ease irrigating huge fields. In town, however, streets are quiet, and the shady city park is decidedly uncrowded. Houses range from two-story Victorians with scrollwork and spindled porches to mobile homes surrounded with marigolds and open-storage piles of wheat. Downtown the brick, 1906 Wilson Creek Bank stands on a corner lot, now forlorn and empty. Its vault once gave safekeeping to the Great Northern payroll, which covered operation of an 11-stall roundhouse and maintenance shops. Trains stopped here for water and coal, and freight trains changed engines and crews.

By the early 1900s, Wilson Creek even had electricity. A Washington State College civil engineering graduate named Charles Keller operated the Wilson Creek Light Company from sunset to midnight, brightening a few homes and providing 20 streetlights during evening hours. Needing more customers, Keller offered power Tuesday afternoons as well, "so that housewives can do their ironing." This was a real selling point. The electricity emancipated women from the old "sad irons" that had to be heated on a stove; drip-dry, no-iron fabrics, of course were not yet even a dream. When Keller sold his utility to the Washington Water Power Company in 1920, he had 150 names on his list of customers.

Immigrant trains had brought settlers to Wilson Creek aboard the Great Northern as early as 1892. Before that, sheep and cattle ranchers had utilized bottomland pastures—and before that, excellent water and natural topography had made Wilson Creek a stop along native trails and the military road from Fort Walla Walla to Camp Chelan.

Wenatchee and Stevens Pass

The drive from Stevens Pass down to the Columbia River at Wenatchee offers mountain scenery, heroic railway engineering, and picturesque orchard country. Fall color is outstanding in the Leavenworth area; spring blossoms mist apple and pear trees with pink and white from Peshastin to Wenatchee. Flumes carrying life-giving irrigation water cling to the cliffs.

Regional museums are at Cashmere, Rocky Reach Dam, and Wenatchee. A fine riverside park in downtown Wenatchee invites contemplation of the Columbia River, erstwhile scene of steamboat commerce, present source of hydropower.

BERNE. (See under STEVENS PASS, p. 109.)

Turn into **CASHMERE** to see "the past" conveniently assembled at the county historical society pioneer village and museum. Buildings, equipment, and displays from all eras intermix, all of them relevant to the local area.

Also in Cashmere, tour the Aplets Candy plant (downtown, on Mission). It was founded by two Armenian brothers-in-law who fled the horror of early 1900s Turkish massacres; landed in Seattle; drove east to escape Puget Sound drizzle; and stopped when they found high, dry country reminiscent of home. There they began Liberty Orchards, named for their new freedom. By the 1920s apple growers in the area needed a way to market their culls and fruit damaged in handling and by insects. The two men remembered a type of candy they had known in Armenia and made a batch of it to sell from a roadside stand. Next came mail orders; then commercial production in a gleaming modern plant.

Settlement by white people at Cashmere evidently began as early as 1853 when Oblate missionaries built a log hut south of present-day Cashmere; details are unclear. Twenty years later Father Urban Grassi, a Jesuit priest, is known to have rebuilt the mission just east of where the town now is. Burials at the mission cemetery include the last great leaders of the Wenatchee people, who were once rich with hunting, fishing, and grazing grounds and areas abundant with berries and roots.

Egbert Trask from Nova Scotia and his wife Annie from New Brunswick are representative of the pioneering settlers who came to Old Mission (as Cashmere was first called). As they told it:

We came into the valley to engage in sheep raising. We brought in during the fall of 1892 a band of 1,200 sheep. We laid in what we thought was an abundance of feed for them, but the winter was exceptionally severe with a heavy fall of snow which lay on the ground well into April. Our hay was running short. We bought a carload at Wilson Creek, and brought it in on the first regular train through on the Great Northern Railway to Leavenworth, March 16, 1893.

COLOCKUM PASS. (See under ELLENSBURG, p. 126.)

CRESCENT BAR is off State Route 28, between Quincy and Wenatchee. The road winds down a sandy hillside with views of old orchards and the red tile roofs and shiny RVs of a resort. A high basalt cliff stands immediately behind the developed area, its columns like the pipes of a gigantic organ. The river bar directly across the Columbia is on an equally gigantic scale. Ten-foot-high ripple marks pattern its surface, a legacy of repeated ice-age floods.

Miners thronged the area in the 1850s to work placer gold claims. Their continued intrusions even after treaties had been signed in 1855 enraged native people, and several prospectors were killed. Nonetheless, Crescent Bar remained an important river crossing, although a difficult one because of repeated changes in water level. Ferrymen had to continually shift their landing places. After dams were built, men at Rock Island would phone Grand Coulee to ask for a release of water to float the ferries.

DRYDEN is characterized by towering stacks of fruit crates, water spilling into a reservoir, and a flume clinging to the cliffs behind town. Fruit, not gold, has brought the area prosperity. Chelan County's first assessor said he would not give "four bits" for Pine Flat, as the Dryden area was called; it was too "scarred by sagebrush and thickly studded with pine trees." But men cleared the trees, floated the logs downriver to Wenatchee, and by 1908 shipped out two carloads of apples. The next year they incorporated the Dryden Fruit Growers Union, built a warehouse, and shipped 18 carloads. Heavy planting began four years later when Icicle Canal delivered its first irrigation water.

A flume supplying the Highline Canal begins at Dryden and carries water by gravity to East Wenatchee. It is a credit to superb engineering at a time when powerful pumps were unknown. Lateral ditches feed orchards west of the Columbia, and a siphon provides lift to pipe

water across the river. The Highline Canal has not changed from its 1902 design, except for repairs and replacement as sections wear out.

LAKE WENATCHEE almost became the reservoir for a Quincy irrigation system. The Northern Pacific Railroad favored development because of its vast land holdings, the Great Northern because of its need to stimulate revenue. In 1906 a Wenatchee landowner and former general agent for the Great Northern started checking the possibilities of irrigating

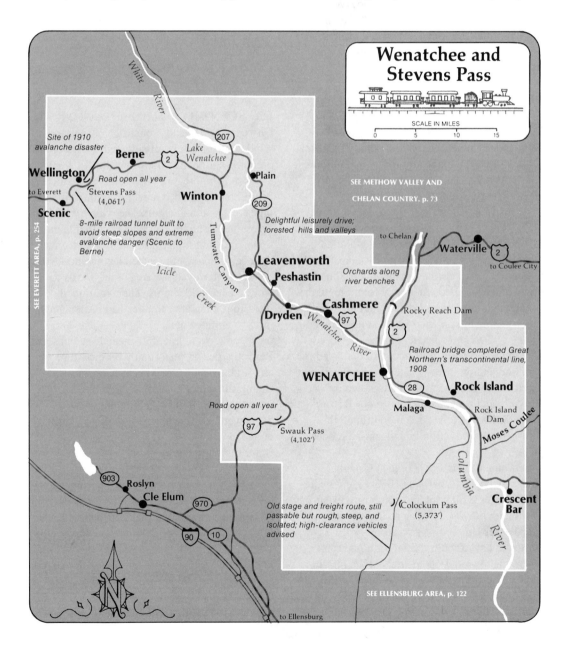

Wenatchee and Stevens Pass

SCALE IN MILES
0   5   10   15

White River

Site of 1910 avalanche disaster
Berne
Lake Wenatchee
207
Wellington
Road open all year
to Everett
Stevens Pass (4,061')
Scenic
8-mile railroad tunnel built to avoid steep slopes and extreme avalanche danger (Scenic to Berne)
Winton
2
Plain
209
Delightful leisurely drive; forested hills and valleys
SEE METHOW VALLEY AND CHELAN COUNTRY, p. 73
to Chelan
Waterville
2
to Coulee City

Tumwater Canyon
Icicle Creek
Leavenworth
Peshastin
Dryden
Cashmere
97
Orchards along river benches
Wenatchee River
Rocky Reach Dam
2

SEE EVERETT AREA, p. 254

WENATCHEE
Railroad bridge completed Great Northern's transcontinental line, 1908
28
Rock Island
Road open all year
97
Swauk Pass (4,102')
Malaga
Rock Island Dam
Moses Coulee
903
Roslyn
Cle Elum
970
Old stage and freight route, still passable but rough, steep, and isolated; high-clearance vehicles advised
Colockum Pass (5,373')
Columbia
Crescent Bar
90
10
N
SEE ELLENSBURG AREA, p. 122
to Ellensburg
River

Quincy Flats. The first idea was to use water from the Clark Fork River, which flows out of Lake Pend Oreille; the next idea was to use Lake Wenatchee water. Costs prevented action, but Quincy people formed a Water Users Association and in 1911 persuaded President William Howard Taft to issue an executive order reserving the lake for irrigation.

The federal Reclamation Service recognized central Washington as a match for central California in agricultural potential, and state officials called the Lake Wenatchee–Quincy project "the greatest . . . ever proposed for development of the State's resources." The legislature approved a bond issue to finance construction, but voters turned it down. Quincy had to wait for water from Grand Coulee.

Native people lived as far up the valley as the lake, particularly in winter. A major trail to traditional huckleberry meadows and hunting grounds near Mount David crossed the White River several miles above the lake. Settlers claimed land in that area because of huge red cedar groves, which they expected to cut and ship out by rail as soon as the Great Northern arrived. It never did.

LEAVENWORTH has had two incarnations: first as a railroad town, now as everybody's favorite North Cascades Bavarian village. Tourism provides its economic lifeblood.

Growth began along the Icicle River south of the present town. When the Great Northern announced plans to build through the valley, an investment company bought land along the right-of-way and platted a new townsite. Naming it for Charles Leavenworth, a stockholder, they offered Icicle businessmen incentives to move to the new town. In 1893 railroad machine shops and a roundhouse rose beside the new tracks; four years later work began on a railway tunnel to eliminate switchbacks at the summit of the Cascades.

A second economic spurt came with the arrival of a sawmill owned by an Iowa lumber company. They dammed the Wenatchee River to form a booming ground, opened logging camps near Lake Wenatchee, and drove logs downriver to the mill. The company founded Leavenworth's first bank and also provided light and water utility services.

In 1901 fruit orchards down the valley from Leavenworth led to organization of the Icicle Canal Company. It built a 40-mile system of flumes, wooden stave pipe, and open ditch along the south wall of the valley. Where flumes had to cross sheer rock faces, workmen tied themselves onto ropes and dangled against the cliffs to drill footings. Today irrigation ditches are lined with concrete to prevent seepage, and the rickety old flume has been replaced by a pipeline, which runs through tunnels in places. A helicopter lowered sections of the pipe to workmen who used the old flume as a catwalk.

Despite all the early irrigation work, commercial fruit growing did not succeed in the immediate area around Leavenworth. The growing season is too short and the frost too severe, although the Icicle Canal supplies water to successful orchards only a few miles down the valley. Frosts there are lighter, and damage currently is prevented by the use of tall poles topped with propellors that whirr above the trees and prevent cold air from settling to the ground.

In the 1920s the Great Northern rerouted its track up the Chumstick Valley, completely pulling out of Leavenworth. At about the same time the sawmill closed. The 1930s brought the Great Depression; whole blocks of Leavenworth's downtown business district had to be sold for unpaid taxes. Life limped along until a bootstrap movement analyzed community assets and recognized that mountain scenery dominated the list.

Inspired by how the California community of Solvang had capitalized on its Danish heritage, Leavenworth sought a unifying theme. Pioneers had included Russian Germans, as also is true throughout the Columbia Plateau; furthermore, alpine peaks are an appropriate backdrop to the town. Leavenworth decided in the 1960s to become Bavaria. Agreement within the business and civic community was far from instant, but economic persuasion won out, and the downtown district reoriented itself. Leavenworth now is a major attraction with special festivals several times a year.

Delightful drives close-by include **State Route 209,** which crosses rumpled terrain and pocket valleys from near **Lake Wenatchee to Plain;** the back road between Leavenworth and Peshastin, which threads orchards on the north side of the Wenatchee River; and **Tumwater Canyon,** where the Stevens Pass Highway follows the old railroad bed. The canyon drive, following a cascading river with views of soaring peaks, is famed for autumn color.

(Also see STEVENS PASS, p. 109.)

MALAGA lies along the west side of the Columbia River 7 miles south of Wenatchee. The name is from Malaga grapes, a Spanish variety grown by homesteader Dutch John Galler. He fled to America from Germany to escape political unrest, and in 1867 became the first permanent white settler in the Wenatchee area. Earlier, the Malaga area was called Chinaman Flat because of placer miners who diverted water from Stemilt Creek and sluiced gold along Columbia River gravel bars. Their ditch followed a gentle gradient, so expertly engineered that it later irrigated vegetables for local sale and shipment by horse and wagon to the coal mine towns of Roslyn and Cle Elum.

APPLES

Apple varieties number in the thousands, most of them the result of chance mutation, although a few are now created by genetic engineering. Formerly, various kinds of apples ripening at different times lengthened the market season. Now storage techniques slow ripening and let fruit picked in October be marketed in July with color and crunch acceptably intact. Storage has meant that by the 1970s Delicious apples—Washington's preeminent variety—could account for 90 percent of the state's crop. Similarly, it has permitted the rise of Granny Smiths during the 1980s. Washington ware-houses now store about 60 million boxes of apples annually, a figure that steadily increases. Crops from the Wenatchee, Chelan, Okanogan, and Yakima regions make apples one of the state's major industries.

The first orchards came from seeds planted at Hudson's Bay Company forts in the early 1800s. Commercial export began with the California gold rush of 1849 to 1850. During the Great Depression 80 years later, Washington apples sold on street corners in Chicago and New York seemed a token of hope: they were a tasty morsel available for an affordable nickel. Today millions of boxes reach markets as distant as Taiwan, Hong Kong, and Saudi Arabia.

Intense daytime sunshine and cool nights are ideal for growing apples, and sagebrush land converts well to orchards so long as irrigation is dependably available. The result for much of central Washington is a tufted green carpet spread along the base of dry, brown hills. Operating these orchards is a year-round job. Pruning begins in January, followed by February and March spraying to control parasitic codling moths (whose larvae are the chief source of "worms" in home-grown apples). By early April, growers rent bee hives and get ready for the onset of blossoming. At this stage the crop is still vulnerable to frost, and radio stations broadcast detailed forecasts. If temperatures drop, sensors installed in the orchards rouse men from their beds and send them out to light smudge pots or activate sprinklers or fans, which stir the air and stop the formation of frost.

Ironically, while nighttime effort goes into preventing the loss of blossoms, daytime spraying thins excess buds and flowers, leaving only the "king" (central) blossom of each cluster. In May, spraying continues for the control of insects, bacteria, and fungi. In June hand-thinning reduces the crop and ensures that the remaining fruit will grow large and uniform.

During the summer, irrigation is the crucial job. Each orchard has a fixed water

MOSES COULEE. (See p. 93.)

At **PESHASTIN** (Pe-shas′-tin), lumber-mill machinery hums around the clock, and the blossoming, fruiting, harvesting, and pruning of pear and apple orchards mark the turn of the seasons. A sign by the railroad underpass gives complete directions to the town in just five words: "Fruit Warehouse. Saw Mill. Peshastin." The business district—post office, garage, and grocery—faces the railroad embankment. Views from the surrounding hills are outstanding.

Homesteading in the Peshastin area began in 1887, and businesses grew a few years later as rail service neared reality. Leavenworth instead of Peshastin won the coveted position as Great Northern division point, but by then settlers knew that irrigated land produced well: they had supplied vegetables to railroad construction crews. Hope for increased irrigation led to meetings, and meetings to contracts for a ditch. Men eager for water agreed to clear mile-long

allotment, now usually distributed through under-tree and drip systems rather than by wasteful overhead sprinklers or open trenches and rills. August spraying hastens sugar production and evens the time of ripening (important for efficient picking). August is also the time to consult warehouse managers and decide the schedule for each block of fruit: some for the fresh market to be sold immediately after picking; some to be held in cold storage until December; some to be held longer in controlled-atmosphere storage with near-freezing temperatures and a low-oxygen, high-nitrogen environment. Growers sell on consignment to packers, which makes their year's income depend on a correct August assessment of storage potential and market likelihood.

Picking begins in mid-September with controlled-atmosphere fruit getting the first attention while its sugar content is still low; that assures safe keeping during long-term storage. A month later, all the harvesting is complete. Orchards are cleaned, baited for mice, and sprayed for weeds. In November new trees go in, and pruning for the next year begins.

A visitor center at the Washington State Apple Commission center (just north of Wenatchee at 2900 Euclid) offers a brief videotape and displays highlighting the development of Washington's apple industry. Additional displays—including

Irrigation tufts the land with orchards in a region that gets only 10 to 16 inches of rain per year. Pioneers found that trees took 10 years to provide a living; meanwhile, vegetables between the rows brought in cash.

apple box labels and early sorting/packing machinery—are at the North Central Washington Museum in Wenatchee (127 S. Mission).

segments of the proposed line—exceedingly tough work cutting trees and blasting stumps and rocks from steep slopes.

Twelve years of awesome labor and sacrifice to buy powder and small tools finally brought completion of the first phase. That meant a need to borrow money for a flume. The one bank in Wenatchee did not have enough capital for such a loan. The next stop was Ellensburg. There, an American representative of a firm incorporated in West Virginia, but doing business mostly in the Sandwich Islands (Hawaii), agreed to make a field inspection of prospects. He wrote:

[I] saw the enormous amount of work that had been done by the struggling pioneers with the scant and poor equipment at hand; realized their energy, honesty and determination; and recommended that our clients loan them a sufficient sum of money to complete the enterprise, which was done.

ROCK ISLAND, southeast of Wenatchee on State Route 28, is a railroad bridge, a low dam, and a stretch of the Columbia River with several black basalt rocks still jutting above water as a reminder of bygone navigational hazards. It also is more than all this.

Two large basalt islands divided the Columbia here into twin channels so swift that even canoes often had to portage. Nonetheless, during ideal summer water conditions and with the help of four lines to shore, Captain W. P. Gray of Pasco brought the steamer *City of Ellensburgh* up through the rapids and on to Brewster in 1888, thereby ushering in an era of riverboats.

That same year, James Keane filed land claims at Rock Island under Homestead, Pre-emption, and Desert Land Act laws. He chose a site near the Colockum Ferry landing and the Moses Coulee wagon road linking the river to the Columbia Plateau. In time he went into the real estate business and helped to sell huge blocks of Northern Pacific land for grazing. He planned a townsite at Rock Island, but it failed to boom when James J. Hill, president of the Great Northern, favored Wenatchee instead. Nonetheless, Keane's site, called Columbia Siding, endured as a supply and stopover point.

Another project of Keane's was to build a pipeline to bring wheat from the plateau to the river. Most such chutes had endless problems with clogging, or charring wheat owing to heat from friction. Keane's wheat pipe worked well and eliminated the arduous haul down Rock Island Creek by team and wagon. A warehouse at Columbia Siding stored sacked wheat for shipment by rail. (A grass fire destroyed the trestles of the Keane Wheat Pipeline in the 1940s, but lengths of deteriorating pipe still lie on the slope above the highway.)

In 1893 completion of the Great Northern gave Seattle and Spokane their first direct rail link and also for the first time tied the Columbia Plateau to a transcontinental route. Even so, trains had to be shuttled across the Columbia by ferry for three months until completion of the **Rock Island Bridge.** Building it entailed "novel and original" techniques, to quote *Engineering Record.* Most had been developed earlier by Japan's Nippon Railway. Swift current and a midchannel depth of 125 feet precluded build-ing piers or using scaffolding or falsework construction for the main span. Instead, engi-neers put the side spans in place, then kept adding blocks of rails to them as counterweight for the main truss, which was built by cantilever methods. Counterweights totaled 3,400 tons before the center span—416 feet long—was complete and the side spans could be finished.

Four miles from the bridge, **Rock Island Dam** was the first hydroelectricity project on the Columbia River. Puget Sound Power and Light Company began construction in 1929. The dam was finished in 1931. Operation today is by the Chelan County Utility District.

For a while consideration of the 1846 treaty setting the boundary between Canada and the United States delayed work on the dam. Treaty agreements included a guarantee that the Columbia River from the international boundary to the ocean would remain "free and open to the Hudson's Bay Company and to all British subjects trading with same." Ultimately, the requirement was ignored. At Grand Coulee Dam and subsequent Columbia River dams, however, engineers built in rudimentary provisions for locks—albeit less to honor the treaty than to make river navigation feasible, should demand and financing dictate such a need.

ROCKY REACH DAM, built by the Chelan County Public Utility District in the 1950s, includes an exceptionally long fish ladder where windows place viewers at eye level with migrating chinook and blueback salmon and steelhead. Films and displays highlight the area's story from prehistory to the present. A collection of early electrical equipment is of particular interest.

STEVENS PASS is named for John G. Stevens, a Great Northern survey engineer who investigated the Methow, Chelan, and Entiat approaches to the Cascade Mountains before deciding on Wenatchee Valley and Nason Creek as the best choice. Still used by trains, the route is now also an automobile highway of such high standard that yesterday's grades and curves are hard to remember.

A series of wooden trestles and benches cut into the mountains let trains switchback laboriously up one side of the pass and down the other, moving forward over a section of tracks, and pulling onto a spur track while switches were changed, then backing up the next segment of track. Thirteen miles of switchbacks connected points only 3 miles apart. To eliminate the switchbacks, workmen cut a tunnel through the mountains at an elevation 1,000 feet lower than the pass. Two and one half miles long, its construction took from 1897 to 1900. In 1929 a second tunnel, almost 8 miles long and nearly 900 feet lower still, replaced the original tunnel.

Remnants of the railroad saga are apparent while driving across Stevens Pass. In **Tumwater Canyon** U.S. 2 uses the old railroad grade and at Milepost 99 passes foundations of the hydro plant that generated electricity for the tunnels. The dam is 2 miles west of the hydroplant site. Fumes from coal-fired engines had stagnated in the first tunnel, posing a genuine threat to life. Conductors had to walk through all cars closing windows and transoms before entering the tunnel. To solve the problem, trains switched to electric power through the tunnel beginning in 1909, when the installation at Tumwater was complete.

At **Berne** (immediately west of the highway overpass at Milepost 72), a construction camp stood at the east portal of the 8-mile tunnel, the longest such tunnel in the western hemisphere and still in use. Berne's shacks formed a rollicking camp called by a New York paper "the

wickedest place in the world." Today's ventilation system needs a half hour after every train to clear the tunnel's air. A short interpretive trail (Milepost 69) highlights the story of Stevens Pass travel by rail and by road.

The mountain town of **Wellington** stood between a long snowshed and the west portal of the original 2½-mile tunnel. No buildings remain but the site (now called Tye) and its adjacent multiple avalanche runs show from a highway pullout at Milepost 61 (accessible only to westbound traffic). In 1910 the area experienced the worst-known avalanche disaster in the United States. A massive snow slide east of the pass blocked first a passenger train, then a mail train. Snowflakes "the size of soda crackers" fell but nobody expected much delay. Four thousand Great Northern trains had crossed via Stevens Pass, and the company was proud of staying nearly on schedule even during storms. Not this time.

Two days after the trains were stopped, they moved through the tunnel to Wellington, where a small railway hotel offered passengers food, if not accommodations. The timing was lucky, for fresh avalanches swept the slopes where the trains had first become marooned. Still the snow fell, coming at the rate of a foot an hour.

On March 1 the snowfall turned to rain, and an avalanche slab a mile and a half long roared into motion. It struck the stalled trains, spewed cars off the tracks, and buried passengers beneath tons of snow. Ninety-six people died; 22 survived. Others had already walked the tracks and slid down-slope to Scenic.

Partly as a result of this tragedy, railroad officials decided that snowshed protection could never be made adequate. They had built miles of sheds to shoot avalanches harmlessly across the tracks, but fires and breakage constantly plagued maintenance, and the Wellington tragedy demonstrated their basic inadequacy in any case. Work soon began on an 8-mile tunnel to avoid the highest and most hazardous slopes altogether.

This tunnel's west-side construction camp went in at **Scenic,** site of a popular hot spring hotel. The tunnel's portal is just east of Scenic; a roadside display is west of Scenic near Milepost 57. To reach a railroad interpretive trail nearby, turn north for 4 miles at Milepost 55.

WELLINGTON. (See under STEVENS PASS, p. 109.)

WENATCHEE beginnings can be traced far back in time. In 1987 workmen installing a new irrigation system at an East Wenatchee orchard uncovered a remarkable cache of Clovis points, a type of spearpoint used about 11,000 years ago by mammoth and giant-bison hunters west of the Rocky Mountains. Subsequent excavations disclosed additional stone and bone tools—a total of 120 including fragments. Preliminary tests revealed a residue of bison blood on two of the points. Archaeologists previously monitoring the realignment of a highway through another East Wenatchee orchard had also discovered evidence of prehistoric life: the remnants of two houses, which date from about 3,000 years ago.

The first permanent white residents in the area were Samuel Miller and brothers Frank and David Freer who bought a small, illicit trading post in 1871. The men had come from Walla Walla where they operated a packtrain business supplying mining camps in what now are Idaho and Montana. When mule trails developed into wagon roads and made packtrains obsolete, the threesome started looking for a new undertaking. Wenatchee seemed promising.

Seventeen years after Miller and the Freers took over the store, a town was laid out along what now is Miller Street. By then overland travel was coming via Colockum Pass from Ellensburg and down Moses Coulee from the Columbia Plateau. Stern-wheel steamboats brought passengers and freight by river, and the Great Northern Railway was soon on the way. A bank opened in Wenatchee in 1892, confident of a business boom. Its timing actually was poor, for a nationwide financial crisis the following year hit Washington hard.

As depression effects lessened, settlers resumed their search for land, and Great Northern president James J. Hill resumed his plans for a rail connection across the continent to Puget Sound. He had hoped to build across British Columbia, but that idea failed. Consequently, Hill sent civil engineer John Stevens to select an alternative route. Stevens recommended approaching the Cascade Mountains via the Wenatchee Valley, and Hill agreed. He then accepted Seattle Judge Thomas Burke's plan to develop a town on the south side of the Wenatchee River, a few miles away from the existing town. The Great Northern held title to 740 acres there.

Their announcement of a railroad depot south of Wenatchee stunned residents. Businesses and a post office were operating at the existing townsite; literary and debating societies met regularly at a public hall; Saturday night dances drew people to town from miles around. Yet the depot was to rise some distance away amid rocks and sagebrush. The railroad's development company offered equivalent size lots in the new town and agreed to pay moving costs. People and buildings flocked to the tracks. The first train arrived in 1892.

By the early 1900s industry hummed with a flour mill grinding wheat from Badger Mountain, 20 miles to the east; sawmills handling timber from the surrounding forests; and a boatyard turning out stern-wheelers for river service between Wenatchee and Brewster. Land sold well, especially as irrigation demonstrated agricultural potential.

As early as 1884 settlers in the area had tried to bring water to their fruit trees, hayfields, and vineyards by ditch or by rigging vertical wheels to lift water from the river. Some people even irrigated from tank wagons or hauled water in barrels and poured it out, a bucketful per tree. Such small-scale successes encouraged additional effort and, in 1891, Jacob Shotwell—who lived near Monitor—built the first ditch with any real possibility of irrigating a large acreage.

Settlers meeting with Shotwell soon decided to extend the ditch and even to carry water by pipeline across the Wenatchee River. Near-desert conditions, with only 12 to 16 inches of precipitation per year, existed close to the rivers, yet early pumps were unable to lift water onto benchlands that would be ideal for orchards if they could be watered. Shotwell's ditch and its ultimate extension demonstrated the feasibility of placing headworks high enough for water to flow by gravity to land miles away.

Dreams of a Highline Canal to carry water all the way to East Wenatchee revived. Tracts that previously sold for $25 per acre jumped to $400 an acre. In 1903 the new canal connected from above Cashmere to Sunnyslope, on the outskirts

Steamboat captains feuded with ferrymen, saying the small vessels were navigation hazards. The ferrymen, in turn, protested paddle-wheelers' wakes. (Notice the wood on this boat. Demand for fuel largely denuded land all along major rivers during the late 1800s and early 1900s.)

of Wenatchee, and investors were determined to carry Highline Canal water to East Wenatchee, where the Great Northern owned another large tract of land. They built a bridge, which was finished in 1908 (still in use for pedestrians and bicycles). It featured a wagon deck, two 36-inch waterpipes, and provisions for a trolley line. Wenatchee had entered its modern era.

Points of interest, keyed to the Wenatchee map:

1 The **North Central Washington Museum** (127 S. Mission) provides an outstanding look at the region's past. Displays include actual equipment for sorting apples at a packing house and an operating model of the Great Northern's Cascade line replete with switchbacks, trestles, and tunnels. (Ask to have the trains operated.) Another exhibit features Upper Columbia rock art along with a "time tunnel" that leads to a display portraying the Wenatchee people and the life of their prehistoric ancestors.

2 The **Chelan County Courthouse** (Washington at Orondo) is built of granite quarried at Index, on the Great Northern line west of

Stevens Pass. The building replaced the original courthouse in 1924.

3 The **Stone Fruit Warehouse** (southeast corner, First and Columbia) was built beside the railroad track in 1906; it became part of a lumberyard in 1952, then a Halloween haunted house, and is now a tavern and restaurant. Wenatchee's first train depot, built in 1892, stood near here.

4 The **Flour Mill** (Skagit and Wenatchee) is historically important although visually unsatisfying. Inoperative since 1960 and surrounded by industrial buildings, only its concrete elevators remain alongside the railroad. Even so, the mill is listed in the National Register of Historic Places because of its role as a farmers' cooperative beginning in 1907.

5 The 1908 **Bridge** (foot of Bridge Street) carried wagon and automobile traffic until 1951; it is now a pedestrian and bicycle crossing of the Columbia. The bridge was built primarily to carry irrigation water to East Wenatchee.

6 **Waterfront Park** (along the Columbia River, foot of Fifth) is the site of a busy boatyard where stern-wheelers were built, beginning in

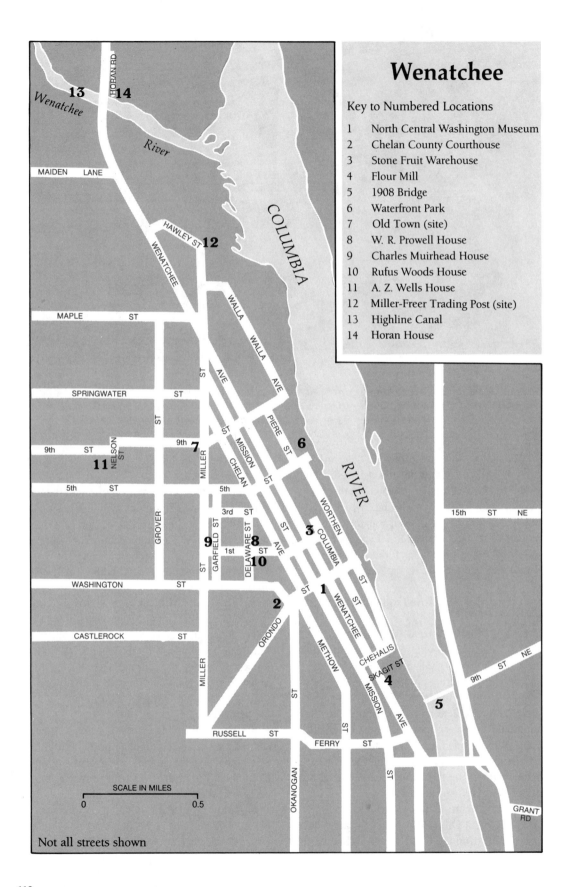

Wenatchee

Key to Numbered Locations

1   North Central Washington Museum
2   Chelan County Courthouse
3   Stone Fruit Warehouse
4   Flour Mill
5   1908 Bridge
6   Waterfront Park
7   Old Town (site)
8   W. R. Prowell House
9   Charles Muirhead House
10   Rufus Woods House
11   A. Z. Wells House
12   Miller-Freer Trading Post (site)
13   Highline Canal
14   Horan House

SCALE IN MILES

0   0.5

Not all streets shown

1892. James J. Hill brought a former Mississippi River pilot west to manage a fleet of riverboats, which linked the Okanogan country with Great Northern rails at Wenatchee. In 1914 train service was extended to Oroville, on the Canadian border, and steamboats declined in importance.

7 The site of **Old Town** (Miller Street from Fifth to Springwater) is now a modern shopping district with no indication of its 1888 beginnings.

8 The **W. R. Prowell House** (105 N. Delaware) belonged to an engineer who helped lay out the Cascade route of the Great Northern Railway in the 1890s. It is a two-story, half-timbered house with a large veranda.

9 The **Charles Muirhead House** (22 N. Garfield) was begun in the mid-1920s and styled to resemble a manor house owned by Muirhead's family in Scotland. Built of rough-cut stone with a steeply gabled roof, it is spaciously surrounded by four lots.

10 The **Rufus Woods House** (323 First; built in 1909) is a comfortable three-story, white clapboard home with arcaded porches on the first and second stories. It was built by the pioneering publisher and editor of the *Wenatchee Daily World,* a man widely influential in the development of the region, including the selection of Grand Coulee as the site for a dam.

11 The **A. Z. Wells House** (end of Nelson, behind Wenatchee Valley Community College; built in 1909) is a 10-room house built by W. T. Clark, who was instrumental in the completion of the Highline Irrigation Canal. Businessman and orchardist A. Z. Wells bought the house 10 years later. It stood surrounded by an apple orchard, and the stained glass of its entryway still carries an apple motif. Mr. and Mrs. Wells donated the property for use as a college. (The easiest approach is via Ninth Street, then a turn south onto dead-end Nelson Avenue, an obscure lane between houses at 1331 and 1335 Ninth.)

12 The **Miller-Freer Trading Post** (1600 N. Miller at the intersection with Hawley) was the first business in Wenatchee. It flourished in the 1870s. Only the site remains here; the building itself is preserved at Cashmere along with several other early-day buildings—an artificial grouping but the buildings' only hope of longevity.

13 The **Highline Canal** crossing of the Wenatchee River shows from the present highway bridge on Wenatchee Avenue, at the north end of town. The first successful large-scale irrigation in the region (completed 1903), this canal system led to increased planting of orchards.

14 The **Horan House** (Horan Road; now a restaurant; built in 1900) has a first-story veranda and second-story porch richly decorated with spindles, curved brackets, knobs, and lathe-turned posts. The Horan family, one of the 12 first families in the area, lived in a log cabin. (The original cabin has been rebuilt at the Cashmere pioneer village.) Horan managed a meat market at Roslyn; then he married and, in 1889, moved to Wenatchee where he opened a butcher shop. His was the fifth business establishment in town at the time. The others were a store, a blacksmith shop, a bakery, and a saloon.

Today **WINTON**'s one-room schoolhouse and a cluster of venerable buildings are all that catch the eye, but until about 1940 sheep by the thousands were held here in pens for sorting and shipment to Chicago. When Wenatchee National Forest was established in 1908, about 100,000 sheep grazed the uplands each summer, and their number steadily increased until the 1920s. Sheep had advantages over livestock. They could thrive on land already depleted by horses and cattle. They required less capital to start with than was true for cattle or for farming. Furthermore, they could be marketed in about two thirds the time needed for beef and offered two streams of income: wool and meat.

By the 1930s orchardists and Grange members worried that overgrazing by sheep was devastating plant cover, a situation that would affect streamflow throughout entire drainages. In response, officials drastically reduced sheep permits. Today only about 7,000 sheep graze Wenatchee National Forest lands, and they come and go by truck.

Vernita to Vantage

The role of the Columbia has changed from a river highway and a source of salmon to a barrier and a source of hydropower. Some roads in the Vernita to Vantage area allow glimpses of countryside still brightened by spring wild flowers and made rich each dawn and dusk by the play of light and shadow on rock cliffs. Other roads lace agricultural land newly made green with irrigation water. Visitor center displays at Wanapum Dam and Ginkgo State Park depict both the geological and human stories.

BEVERLY is south of Vantage. What commands attention is not the "town" but its setting and railroad bridge. The highway hugs the base of lofty basalt cliffs, in places blanketed with wind-rippled drifts of sand and patches of Mount St. Helens volcanic ash. Frequent turnouts give access to sagebrush flats by the river.

Fur trader Alexander Ross, traveling up the Columbia in 1811, wrote: ". . . we reached two lofty and conspicuous bluffs . . . directly opposite to each other, like the piers of a gigantic gate." The bluffs mark Beverly Gap, or

Sentinel Gap, a breach through the Saddle Mountains called *Wasatos,* "Spirit-power Place," by the Wanapum people. Their young men and women went to Sentinel Peak to fast and seek a lifelong spirit guardian.

The Beverly Bridge was built by the last transcontinental railway to reach the Northwest: the Chicago, Milwaukee, and St. Paul, a technologically innovative carrier that announced plans in 1905 for service from the Midwest to the Pacific. Four years and four mountain ranges later, the job was done. Expenditures were huge, timing was poor. Labor and material costs had soared, and shipping via the Panama Canal (opened in 1914) soon brought competition even more damaging than that of Milwaukee's two rivals on the route, the Great Northern and the Northern Pacific.

Undaunted, the company electrified 440 miles of track across the mountains from Montana to Idaho and 200 miles in Washington from Othello to Tacoma. By 1920 advertisements were extolling the comfort of travel free from soot and cinders. Yet just over a half century later, Milwaukee directors decided to drop their coast operation. Tracks following Crab Creek to Beverly are gone now. Only the bridge remains, its supports for the train's overhead wires still in place but the lines themselves gone.

The Beverly Bridge belonged to Washington's third transcontinental rail line.

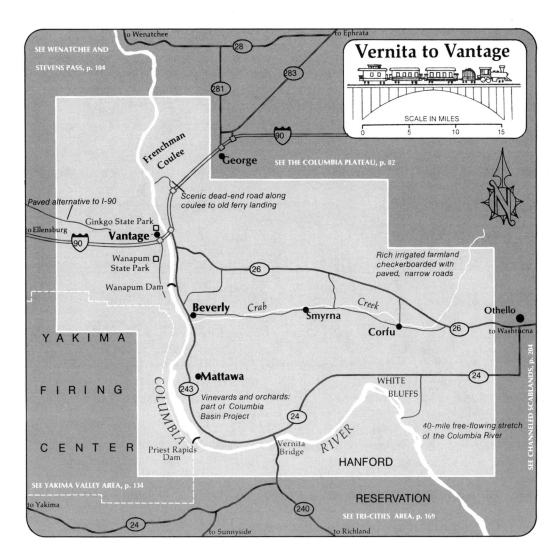

to Wenatchee

to Ephrata

28

283

281

Vernita to Vantage

SCALE IN MILES
0   5   10   15

90

Frenchman Coulee

George

SEE THE COLUMBIA PLATEAU, p. 82

Scenic dead-end road along
coulee to old ferry landing

Paved alternative to I-90

Ginkgo State Park

to Ellensburg

Vantage

90

Wanapum
State Park

Wanapum Dam

Rich irrigated farmland
checkerboarded with
paved, narrow roads

26

Beverly Crab   Creek

Smyrna

Corfu

26

Othello

to Washtucna

Y A K I M A

24

F I R I N G

●**Mattawa**

243

Vineyards and orchards:
part of Columbia
Basin Project

24

WHITE
BLUFFS

40-mile free-flowing stretch
of the Columbia River

C E N T E R

Priest Rapids
Dam

Vernita
Bridge

RIVER

HANFORD

COLUMBIA

to Yakima

24

to Sunnyside

240

RESERVATION

SEE TRI-CITIES AREA, p. 169

to Richland

SEE CHANNELED SCABLANDS, p. 204

When bridge construction began in 1907, Beverly sprang to life as a construction camp. At the same time work also was under way on what the *Wenatchee Daily World* described as "an immense irrigation scheme [backed] by a number of Seattle's leading citizens." Using power from steam plants at Priest Rapids, water was to be pumped from the Columbia and carried to farms "for a radius of 50 miles." The boom was brief: bridge construction work ended, the irrigation project failed, and by 1914 Beverly's main street buildings were collapsing.

A drive up **CRAB CREEK** will please anyone who enjoys back roads and looking at a semblance of "original" Washington. (Take the first turnoff downriver from the Beverly Bridge,

not the more prominent Beverly–Burke Road just north of the bridge. The upper end of the road is unpaved.)

Crab Creek, a major inland drainage, originates on the gentle slopes north of Reardan. Surface flow is not great but grass and small lakes characterize the entire drainage, a surprisingly green and blue landscape. The lower Crab Creek road follows the straight scarp of the Saddle Mountains, passing public fishing lakes and sand dunes open to all-terrain vehicles. Hayfields and cattle ranches alternate with wildlife refuge land and minuscule settlements such as Smyrna, established on the Milwaukee railroad line in 1910. Several county roads lead north to State Route 26.

Chief Moses wintered horses along Lower

Crab Creek while staying at what some accounts give as his birthplace near Vantage (others say he was born in Moses Coulee). His Sinkiuse band, also known as the Moses-Columbia, was the southernmost of the Inland Salish people, a huge group whose territory reached into interior British Columbia. A Sinkiuse village stood at the mouth of Crab Creek.

In 1896, when the northern half of the Colville Reservation opened to whites, the Ellensburg paper *Localizer* recommended Crab Creek as the "best and driest route to the reservation mines." The article said to cross the Columbia by ferry at Crab Creek and

from the ferry keep up Crab Creek for 25 miles to where it intersects the wagon road to Davenport and is on the direct line to Northport.

FRENCHMAN COULEE formed as water drained from Grand Coulee and the Quincy Basin toward the Columbia during successive ice-age floods. Torrents dropped to the Columbia River, 500 feet below the plateau, in a series of huge waterfalls. The coulee is now visible from I-90 but is largely ignored (although also repeatedly proposed for development). To reach it, take Exit 143 (Winery Road); turn west; and drop into the coulee. The road leads 6 miles to what was the Vantage river crossing before Wanapum Dam backed up a reservoir, necessitating a longer bridge. A natural amphitheater used for summer concerts is on a separate, well-signed road (same exit but turn onto Silica Road; check in George for tickets).

Evidently 1880s white settlers first used Frenchman Coulee to graze cattle, but soon switched to sheep. Pioneer stockmen Art Allen once commented that Frenchman Spring never was much of a water hole, but "sheep do not require as much water as cattle. As long as there is a little fog or frost, they can make out."

From the head of the coulee, **Silica Road** leads to what looks from a distance like sand dunes but is actually a bed of gleaming white diatomaceous earth, ancient lake-bottom deposits of microscopic "skeletons" from one-celled aquatic plants. Surface mines here ship to a processing plant at Quincy; the diatomite is used in industrial filters and as a mineral filler in coating agents and carriers.

MATTAWA (Mat´-uh-wah) means "Where is it?" in the Wanapum language. The settlement has been a center for pioneering farmers attempting crops on the Wahluke Slope of the Saddle Mountains and for construction workers building Priest Rapids and Wanapum dams. Growth has been sporadic: a lack of water doomed pioneer farms; Hanford Atomic Reservation took most of Wahluke Slope and closed the rest of it; construction camps folded after the dams were built. Wine production is now resurrecting local agriculture. Dry summers, mild winters, sunny slopes facing south, and irrigation water from the Columbia Basin Project make the Mattawa area ideal for grapes. The soil louse that feeds on roots elsewhere is no problem here, consequently grafting—necessary in California and Europe—is not needed here.

Fruit orchards as well as vineyards tuft the landscape, and vast corn- and hayfields spread like green—or harvest-tan—carpets. Yesterday's sagebrush and jackrabbits are gone. So far as agriculture is concerned, a new "Yakima Valley" is in the making.

PRIEST RAPIDS is dammed now, its 20-foot drop turned from a hazard for canoes and bateaux into hydroelectricity. The name comes not from a Catholic missionary but from an influential Wanapum leader. Alexander Ross wrote in 1811 that at "a strong and rocky rapid" he met a tall, middle-aged man "called Haquilaugh, which signifies. . . priest." Ross named the rapids for this man. By the late 1800s Smohalla ("teacher") was filling the same role as mystic and leader.

A dozen Wanapum villages stood along the west bank at Priest Rapids, where rocks reached almost across the river, narrowing channels and concentrating salmon runs. Villagers called the upper riffle *Iques,* "Cottontail Rabbit," because whitecaps made them think of rabbits scurrying for cover when hunted. The stretch of fast water above today's dam was *Wapixie,* "Water Drops Fast." The prime fishing station, where an abandoned 1950s powerhouse still stands, was *Wotklocht,* "Holes in Rock." Above this place was the main Wanapum village of *Pna,* "Fish Weir." Here people throughout the region came to fish and enjoy multilingual trading and gambling, and to arrange marriage ties, which would strengthen intergroup affiliations and bloodlines.

In 1884 Major J. W. MacMurray stopped at Pna while traveling to tell groups of non-reservation natives about their rights under homestead laws. He watched "a grand cere-monial service" held in a mat lodge 75 feet long. Each Sunday, Smohalla sang and led prayers and drumming in this building, while worshippers knelt in rows, chanting. Some, including Smohalla, fell into trances. A flag—triangular with a five-pointed star—waved from a pole outside the lodge. This was a Dreamer ritual. It blended a renaissance of native religion—traditionally an individual matter—with group ritual borrowed from Christianity. Several such religious movements were widespread on the Columbia Plateau and the Great Plains. They all urged rejection of white concepts of work and owning land, and of government policies. Smohalla asked:

You ask me to plow the ground? Shall I take a knife and tear my mother's bosom? Then when I die she shall not take me to her bosom to rest. You ask me to dig for stone? Shall I dig under her skin for her bones? Then when I die I cannot enter her body to be born again.

Native people should return to the old ways; live *their* lives, not white lives.

The effects of Smohalla's teachings rippled through relations between groups of native people and through their relations with whites. Natives who were Dreamers derided those who listened to missionaries or signed treaties, while government agents and army officers regarded Dreamers as a cause of "great trouble." Nez Perce Toohulhulzote, a Dreamer preacher, spoke so openly against the loss of ancestral land that General Oliver Howard arrested him and ordered all Nez Perce onto their reservation within 30 days. This began the famed saga of the Nez Perce War and the poignant flight of Chief Joseph's band almost to freedom in Canada.

The focal point of such wide-reaching influence—the site of Pna village and Smohalla's great mat lodge—has disappeared beneath slack water. Priest Rapids today has no fast water and no priest—although a semblance of the old religion continues within the Wanapum longhouse.

The last few Wanapum people live at the west end of the dam; no public access. The only "treaty" they ever signed was in 1957 when they agreed with Grant County Public Utility District to give up rights to land at Priest Rapids. Their traditional territory stretched for miles along the west bank of the Columbia—an outstanding fishing location—and also into the uplands of what now is an army firing range. The Wanapum spoke Sahaptin, related to the languages of the Yakima and Nez Perce rather than to that of the Columbia people who lived directly across the river.

In the **VANTAGE** area allow time for side trips. Each of the freeway overlooks east of the Columbia is worth seeing. (One is accessible on the upgrade, the other on the downgrade.) The river flows far below. Sagebrush, greasewood, and rabbitbrush dot dry slopes. The basalt that built the Columbia Plateau shows plainly, its layers remarkably distinct—a major sight even when considered on a world scale. The long years that elapsed between lava flows were enough for soil to develop, wildlife to fill niches, and forests to grow: the view of rock layers here is a view of time itself.

Petrified logs at Ginkgo State Park remain from just one of the ancient land surfaces. Excellent displays at the visitor center explain events; trails lead among petrified remnants of the former forest. Beyond the park, the Old Vantage Road offers a paved alternative to I-90 (about 30 miles from the park to Ellensburg). The road crosses open sagebrush and balsamroot country and fenced grazing land; irrigated fields and barns begin about halfway between the park and Ellensburg.

Another pleasant drive is along the Columbia River south from Wanapum State Park. Ideally, go in April when balsamroot, phlox, lupine, and other flowers brighten the desert hills. The road dead-ends at the boundary of the U.S. Army's Yakima Firing Range.

At Vantage itself, the first ferry service began in 1914 with a two-car barge powered by a launch. Before that, the eastside approach down the basalt wall of the plateau offered too much of an obstruction. Native people had no reason to travel that way because other, readily feasible crossings were nearby. White people living in Ellensburg, however, wanted a direct travel route to the east.

The road first built in response to their pressure followed a route so sandy and steep that horses often had to help cars up to the canyon rim on the east side. The state relocated the road twice and finally engineered one that stairsteps spectacularly along ledges (still passable; see FRENCHMAN COULEE, p. 116.) Above today's scenic overlook (upgrade between Mileposts 139 and 140), a weathered steel sculpture of 18 horses strings for 250 feet along a ridge crest. Titled *Grandfather Cuts Loose the Ponies,* it is an art project tied to the state's centennial in 1989.

Near **VERNITA,** the Columbia River winds across a broad desert flat, its last lengthy Washington stretch as a *river:* 51 miles without

Bighorn sheep—and other examples of Native American rock art—were salvaged from the rising water of reservoirs.

a dam. A ferry operated at Vernita before the bridge was built. Sheep by the thousands crossed here, which displeased the highway commission. The state had taken over ferry

operation while building the bridge, and commissioners felt that cleanup problems made sheep and cars a poor mix. They voted for herds to cross in trucks or some other form of closed vehicle, a sanitary but impractical decision since sheep—if enclosed—might trample newborn lambs. Sheepmen protested. The highway commission reversed itself. The mess remained.

At **Rattlesnake Springs** (south of Vernita near the junction of State Routes 240 and 24) a murder in 1878 sent shock waves throughout Washington Territory. Blanche and Lorenzo Perkins were riding from their ranch at White Bluffs to Yakima City (present-day Union Gap) to await the birth of their first child. As they picnicked, six Umatilla warriors approached. Full of rage over the slaughter of relatives by an army gunboat on the Columbia River, the men shot Lorenzo. Blanche, an excellent horse-woman, mounted and rode off. The men pursued her and, when her horse stumbled, they shot her.

Chief Moses sent word that he had the killers under surveillance and would turn them over to General Oliver O. Howard, whom he trusted. Instead, a posse rode after the Umatillas and, unable to find them, put Moses in leg irons and took him to Yakima City. To protect him from hotheads, the army moved the chief to Fort Simcoe. There they held him under guard until finally accepting his offer to locate the Umatilla men. One of the Umatillas killed himself before he could be captured. Two were shot while trying to escape. Three were hanged.

(Also see PLYMOUTH, p. 171, for an account of the shelling along the Columbia.)

WANAPUM DAM (Wan´-uh-pum) generates electricity that is distributed, along with power from Priest Rapids Dam, to 13 public and private utilities in the region from Spokane and Seattle to Eugene, Oregon. Viewing rooms at the powerhouse make it possible to watch salmon on their upriver migration, helped through the dam by a "ladder," a series of underwater steps. Best viewing months are April through October. Other displays highlight the long history of the area. They span from the early days of the Wanapum and Sinkiuse people through the eras of the fur trade, mining, livestock ranching, homesteading, and steam-boating. The dam was completed in 1965.

WANAPUM REMINISCENCE

Frank Buck and nephew Rex.

The late Frank Buck was the last Wanapum who could remember the days of traditional river fishing, root digging, and travel by horseback. In a 1986 interview he spoke of those days:

Vernita Bridge, where it's at now, that's where I "come-to" [first remember anything]. In those tule-mat kind of house. Lately I go into white people's house, and it's okay now but at first, when I was young, it felt like I'm not breathing right. With tules, we got this opening clear across the top and it seems like we were breathing right, this fresh air. We didn't go in for all those hamburgers and chicken eggs either. In spring we got goose eggs. One egg'd fill up a fry pan—one egg, and you cut it like a pie. Tougher than eggs now. Tasted about the same but you chew it more. . . .

Spring comes, we go root digging: Moses Lake, Soap Lake, and Waterville, too. Ellensburg. Camp with tepees. We'd get bitterroot, camas. The Indian potatoes; that grows pretty good in the sand. Gets long. Ellensburg we'd get the Indian carrots. Peel 'em, boil 'em. Looks like carrots but different: sweet. Soap Lake stay a whole week. Bake camas, dry 'em.

Then we'd fish at Horn Rapids, middle of May till maybe June. That's for salmon, good salmon [coho]. Then we fish for the eels maybe another three weeks. Then it'd be July. Then we start moving up the mountains. We already got a lotta fish, good fish. Naches Pass, that's where we used to go. It would take three days and a half with horses and buggies to get to the berry patch and we get there, put up tepees and pick berries and hunt for deer and hunt for elk and womens pick berries and same time, they're drying meat for the winter supply and drying huckleberries, too, for the winter. That's how we used to do.

When we come back from the berry picking, we'd go to Moxee. Hand pick the hops for a man my father knew from way back. We'd pick a whole month. That's for the coffee and the sugar and the lard. Bacon. For the rest, we use our own foods. Not like today. No. We'd go all winter, we don't buy anything.

When we get back from hop picking, we go up at Priest Rapids. Then we fish for fall fish. Sockeye. And we dry them up. Slice 'em in the shade, they stay cool and dry up real good. If they're in the sun they get warm; heat up too fast and get half rotten. We'd get whitefish too. . . . Mostly at White Bluffs, that was.

The old days, I like them. No worries. Plenty food; never did know how to starve even through winter. Now, everybody, why if you don't work you got nothing. Those days we were four or five families together in that tule [house] but never had quarreling mens or womens. . . . No, it's gone. It's gone forever. Now we got to live in separate homes. We still all eat together though in the longhouse, Sundays. And we have our own religion.

The **WHITE BLUFFS** area, off limits from 1943 to 1980 as part of the Hanford atomic energy reservation, is again open to the public. Northeast of the Vernita Bridge (between Mileposts 62 and 63), turn south from State Route 24 and drive to the old ferry landing, now a boat launch. Fifty-one miles of the Columbia River still flow free here, the last undammed section from the Canadian border virtually to Portland. Riverbank willows provide cover for deer and elk; beavers, muskrats, and coyotes thrive; and nearly three quarters of the remaining natural spawning grounds for Columbia River chinook salmon are here. The long closure of the area, imposed for security, prevented construction of a dam and inadvertently perpetuated the river as it was.

The name White Bluffs comes from 500-foot cliffs of layered sand, silt, and gravel along the east bank of the river. Rocks and rapids in this part of the river stopped paddle-wheelers from continuing north, although canoes and bateaux (flat-bottomed riverboats designed by French fur traders) commonly negotiated—and portaged around—the rough water. Beginning in the mid-1850s passengers and freight came to this point by steamer, then continued overland to the Colville gold camps. By the 1860s warehouses bulged with goods for shipment by packtrain to mines in British Columbia and Montana.

Portland and St. Louis merchants competed for the Montana trade. Those in St. Louis sent a special fleet of 50 to 60 shallow-draft boats struggling up the Missouri River to Fort Benton, just east of the Rocky Mountains. Portland merchants advertised that this Missouri River route was possible for only six weeks of the year, owing to water conditions, whereas they could ship up the Columbia for at least six months a year, then freight goods overland from White Bluffs to Helena, a total journey of only 17 days. In March 1866 the *Portland Oregonian* commented that a position linking river travel with overland travel assured that White Bluffs would

continue to prosper, and may become in time the Sacramento of the Columbia Valley. . . . Permanency is no longer a matter of doubt.

During the late 1800s ranchers raised livestock in the dry country surrounding White Bluffs, and by the early 1900s a series of irrigation companies started selling land to farmers. After World War I, the state legislature authorized the sale of surplus land to veterans at low prices. Along with the land, participants in this program received a well, an electric pump, a three-room plastered cottage, a barn/cowshed, a chicken house, and financial aid to pay the electric bill for two years. Even so, few succeeded at desert farming, and in 1925 the state sold out at a loss. Some settlers stayed on.

During World War II, White Bluffs residents suddenly received official notice of federal confiscation of their land, a drastic measure deemed necessary for national defense. Organized protest died as residents realized the government also had confiscated—and closed—the irrigation company. No family could fight a court case while their crops shriveled. Six hundred square miles here offered precisely what the government needed: river water for cooling; gravel for concrete; electricity from Grand Coulee and Bonneville dams; and isolation from population centers. The Hanford Reservation had begun. (See RICHLAND, p. 172.)

SOUTH CENTRAL Region

Fort Simcoe, southwest of Yakima.

*IN 1814 ALEXANDER ROSS of the North West Fur Company
entered the Kittitas Valley (near Ellensburg) hoping to buy horses
from Native Americans. He found an awesome sight:*

> *. . . a camp, of which we could see the beginning but not the end! . . .
> Councils, root-gathering, hunting, horse-racing, foot-racing, gambling,
> singing, dancing, drumming, yelling, and a thousand other things . . .
> were going on around us.*

*Forty-one years later Yakima tribal chiefs opened a three-year,
futile struggle to stop miners from crossing their lands and churning
up the Columbia River by steamer en route to gold rushes. Soon,
however, newcomers had settled to raise cattle, a "crop" that could
transport itself to market and, by the 1880s, farmers were planting
wheat on former ranchland and grinding it for livestock feed and
flour at local mills such as those still lingering at Union Gap and
Thorp. In time settlers experimented with irrigation; by the early
1900s, their trials expanded into a federal reclamation project.*

*Rail connections linked the region to markets, and mountain lakes
swollen by dams into reservoirs fed canals that turned the Kittitas
and Yakima valleys into swaths of green, a process that continues
today as Columbia Basin Project water converts sagebrush and
wild flowers into agribusiness vineyards and orchards.*

*Along the southern edge of the region the Columbia River remains
an all-season route across the state, reliable even when winter
storms close mountain passes. The river carries ever-increasing
barge, rail, and automobile traffic—and offers a timeless, dramatic
transition from Washington's dry interior to its wet west side.*

Ellensburg Area

Seen from the rim of surrounding hills, the egg-shaped basin of the Kittitas Valley is a lush checkerboard of chartreuse, gold, and emerald. It is famous for timothy hay production: racehorses from Japan to New York run on this premium fuel. North of the valley is the hundred-year-old Swauk gold mining district. Northwest is Roslyn, which once supplied half the state's coal. Ellensburg, the valley's major city and the home of Central Washington University, preserves an 1890s downtown district of great distinction.

The valley has always been a hub with routes leading east–west and north–south. Today freeways—I-90 and I-82—fill this role, but the old roads they largely replace remain paved and passable and delightful for aficionados of the bucolic. There are five of these roads. State Route 821 (Exit 109 off I-90) connects to the Yakima Valley via a scenic, twisting canyon. Another backcountry road to Yakima begins at Damman Way, climbs to 3,000 feet as a gravel road, and descends the Wenas Valley as a paved road. State Route 10 follows along the river and up the canyon to Cle Elum and Roslyn. The old road to Vantage begins as Eighth Street in Ellensburg, then runs east through the green fields of the Kittitas Valley and across open land still vegetated with sagebrush and greasewood and spring wild flowers. In addition, the old Colockum Pass stage route to Wenatchee will please all who enjoy—and are equipped for—rough, backcountry roads.

Museums are in Ellensburg, Cle Elum, and Roslyn. The Ellensburg rodeo, held on the Labor Day weekend, is the oldest in the state. It began in the 1920s. A threshing bee using antique equipment is held at the Olmstead pioneer farm near Kittitas in mid-September.

BLEWETT. (See under LIBERTY, p. 129.)

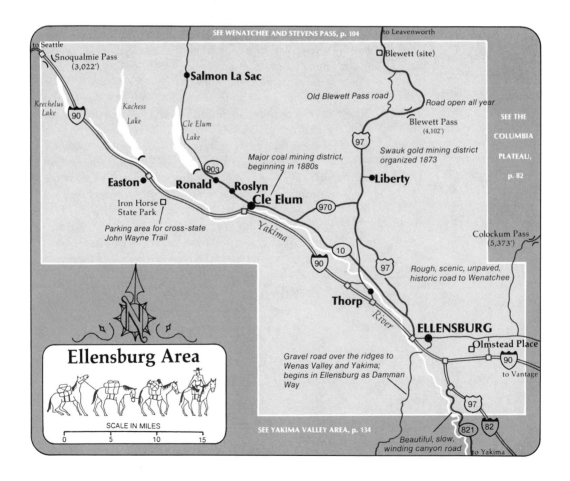

Agriculture still dominates much of the Ellensburg area. Its venerable barns seem to symbolize the hard work and self-sufficient pride that built rural Washington.

The economy of **CLE ELUM** (Klee-el´-um) has managed to keep pace with changes in railroading, coal mining, and sawmilling. It now depends primarily on logging and recreation. The former telephone building has become a museum (221 E. First). The town bakery, opened in 1906, still operates at the original location (501 E. First). Cottages built for miners and millworkers give residential streets a homogeneous, turn-of-the-century appearance.

Cle Elum has Barbara Reed to thank for its broad streets. Wife of the founder, who arrived here in 1883, she was determined that the town should have this amenity. The Reeds lobbied the approaching Northern Pacific to build a depot on their land and even offered the company half of all profit from lot sales in their newly platted townsite.

For a scenic drive follow State Route 10 from east of Cle Elum to Ellensburg (about 25 miles).

COLOCKUM PASS. (See under ELLENSBURG, p. 126.)

EASTON. (See under SNOQUALMIE PASS, p. 133.)

ELLENSBURG is a compact city graced with a university and buoyed economically by a rich farming district. The downtown core consists of brick buildings constructed in two flurries of expansion: one just after a disastrous fire in

1889, the other after the nationwide economic depression of 1893 had eased.

Ellensburg traces its roots to a trading post near the confluence of Wilson Creek and the Yakima River. In 1870, when only a smattering of white families had settled in the Kittitas Valley, Andrew Jackson Splawn and Ben Burch opened a store. They traded mostly with local native people, but also with drovers on their way over Snoqualmie Pass. The partners freighted in supplies from The Dalles, stuffing their building so full that Splawn remarked he would have to sell off the merchandise from front to back. A neighbor volunteered to paint a sign for the store, and he emblazoned the words "Robbers Roost" over the doorway. The name stuck.

In 1871 John Shoudy, brother-in-law of Seattle's pioneer banker Dexter Horton, bought Robbers Roost. Owner of a draying company, Shoudy was actively involved in improving the road over Snoqualmie Pass. He moved to the Kittitas Valley and soon platted a town in a pasture near Robbers Roost. He named it Ellensburgh for his wife (spelled with an "h" until 1894 when the Post Office Department requested a simplification). The fledgling community was well located near a river ford, and convenient to both north–south and east–west trails.

The Northern Pacific Railroad arrived in

1886. At the time 600 persons lived in the town; two years later the population had doubled. As the railroad opened distant markets, ranching gave way to farming and dairying, and Ellensburg indulged in a frenzy of expansion and optimism. According to local accounts it had everything: rich soil, rail transportation, water power, and nearby coal and iron (the deposits were later found to be of poor quality).

In 1889, the year of statehood, Washington citizens voted on the location for a permanent state capital. As one of the largest and most rapidly expanding towns in the territory, and blessed with a central location, Ellensburg considered itself a likely candidate. Olympia had been territorial capital for 36 years, yet was "still moribund," as the Ellensburg *Capital* phrased it. To the irritation of townspeople, North Yakima (present-day Yakima) also announced its candidacy. A great rivalry ensued with mudslinging by editors on both sides. The notion of centrality won; Ellensburg and Yakima together got more votes than Olympia, but in a runoff election the two cities split the votes and Olympia won handily. Undaunted, the editor proclaimed:

Capital or no capital, Ellensburgh speeds along and will get there just the same. No grass in her streets, no flies on her back, no lard on her bangs. Whoop her up again, boys!

In the midst of expansion came conflagration. More than 200 homes and nine blocks of the downtown burned to the ground on the Fourth of July, 1889. The city showed its mettle by a rapid rebuilding—in brick.

As a sort of consolation prize for losing the capital, the state legislature in 1891 chose Ellensburg as the site of a normal school. Professor Benjamin Franklin Barge, an Illinois teacher with a flair for oratory, headed the administration during the school's formative years. Part public relations expert and part lobbyist, he turned a minimally staffed, poorly equipped school into a respected institution, now Central Washington University.

Although the Panic of 1893 brought Ellensburg's post-fire building spurt to a halt, it proved less devastating here than in many other Washington towns because gold miners in the nearby Swauk District continued to rely on Ellensburg merchants for supplies. The town nonetheless came face to face with the depression in May 1894 when a thousand unemployed men passed through on their way to Washington, D.C. They belonged to "Coxey's Army," organized to pour into the national capital and petition the government for unemployment relief. Ellensburg merchants provided food and merchandise.

Ellensburg today is the center of an irrigated farming district, famous for hay and other crops. A frozen-food processing plant produces 50 million pounds of corn, 15 million pounds of carrots, and nearly 10 million pounds of peas annually.

The downtown area is replete with well-preserved examples of late nineteenth-century commercial buildings, the finest of which were built right after the 1889 fire. The historic district—listed in the National Register of Historic Places—is compact and best appreciated on foot.

Points of interest, keyed to the Ellensburg map:

1 The **Cadwell Building** (114 E. Third; built in 1889) with its dramatic horseshoe arches, now houses the Kittitas County Museum. It was built by E. P. Cadwell, a Northern Pacific attorney, who was Ellensburg's first "non-resident capitalist" with large sums invested in blocks of brick buildings.

2 The site of **Shoudy Trading Post,** or **Robbers' Roost** (Third and Main) is occupied by an 1889 building that must have been a store at the time of the Ellensburgh fire. Archaeologists excavating behind it found goods such as liquor bottles and a tombstone, apparently from the store's shelves.

3 The splendid, turreted **Davidson Building** (Pearl and Fourth) symbolizes Ellensburg's resurrection from the 1889 flames: a three-foot phoenix tops a pediment on the south facade. Notice the building's pressed-tin decorative elements. Nineteenth-century architects specified such treatments to lend three-dimensional, light-catching ornamentation to commercial buildings. Cornices and moldings were commonly prefabricated; small pieces, such as roundels and fans, were joined into large

Ellensburg

Key to Numbered Locations

1	Cadwell Building	5	Shoudy Mansion
2	Shoudy Trading Post (site)	6	Masonic Temple
3	Davidson Building	7	Barge Hall (CWU)
4	Land Title Building	8	"The Castle"

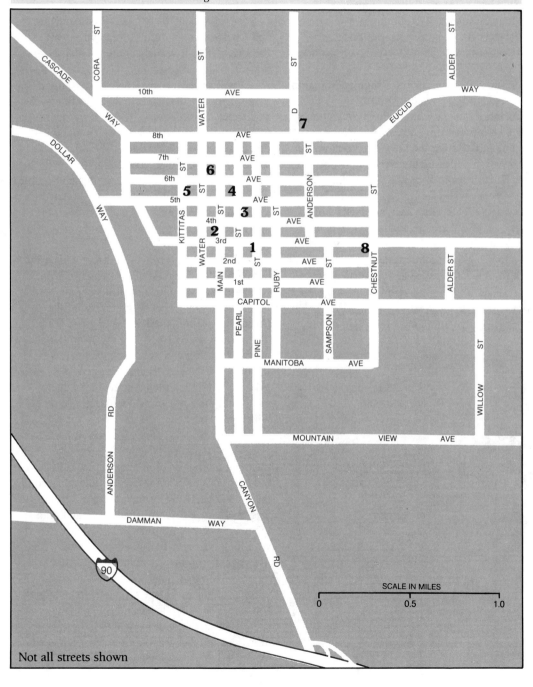

Not all streets shown

SCALE IN MILES
0   0.5   1.0

sheets. Mass production, new at the time, made the decorations readily available, although on-site workers cut and refit them to suit the dimensions of each specific building.

4 The **Land Title Building** (Fifth and Pearl; built in 1911) has decorations of sandstone chipped and sandblasted into gargoyles and sheaves of wheat. A lionlike creature stares down from the south facade, clasping in its mouth a bundle of grain that droops like an elaborate mustache. The building was originally the Farmers Bank; note its corner position and air of permanence, qualities typical of banks of that era.

5 The two-story, turreted **Shoudy Mansion** (Fifth and Kittitas) was only briefly home to Ellensburg's founding father, John Shoudy; he presented it to his son and daughter-in-law as a wedding gift. During the 1890s depression, the house passed out of family ownership.

6 The **Masonic Temple** (111 W. Sixth; built in 1890) rose when lodge members rebuilt following the 1889 fire. They needed to hold down costs and therefore solicited donations from local industries. These included brickyards and a foundry that produced decorative cast-iron work from locally milled and fabricated ore.

Ellensburg's Masonic Temple is elaborately ornamented in the Victorian manner.

(Notice the plaque saying Ellensburgh Foundry.) Small three-dimensional pieces—rosettes, fleurs-de-lis, stylized sea shells—were individually cast and bolted into place one-by-one.

7 Where campus meets town, **Barge Hall** (Eighth at the end of Anderson; built in 1894) was named to honor the first principal of the Normal School. The oldest structure on campus, the building boasts an attached tower topped by a weathervane.

8 Briton Craig built **"The Castle"** (Third and Chestnut) on a hill east of town as part of the speculative flurry surrounding Ellensburg's hope of becoming state capital. Originally it was a typical Victorian mansion—far larger than Craig, a bachelor, had need for. Sidewalk superintendents assumed, and a newspaper interview confirmed, that he was building a potential governor's mansion. The dream was short-lived. Creditors acquired the Castle during the depression of the 1890s, and it soon became a boarding house. In 1930 it was remodeled to look like a medieval castle and converted to apartments.

The old stagecoach road over **Colockum Pass** between Ellensburg and the Wenatchee area is still passable, still dirt, and still steep on both ends, rough, and exceedingly rocky in places. (From Ellensburg take Kittitas Highway east, then turn north on No. 81 Road. Turn east again on Erickson Road, and north on Colockum Road.) Experienced drivers with high-clearance vehicles will relish the commanding ridgetop views and the roadside ponderosa pines; others will not.

The road follows a major trail used by native people and demonstrates the difference between traveling by foot or on wheels. Colockum Pass requires climbing 5,000 feet, a route so steep on the Wenatchee end that men used to lower wagons by ropes, or cut small trees and drag them from rear axles to augment brakes. A ferry with long oars carried passengers, freight, and livestock across the Columbia River to the mouth of Moses Coulee. The operator rowed upriver taking advantage of eddies, then angled across the current. Because the eddies hugged each bank, the system worked in either direction. In later years a cable ferry replaced the labor-intensive sweeps.

The 1911 Land Title Building fit downtown Ellensburg's established scale.

Proposals to improve the old Colockum Road still appear from time to time. It is shorter by 20 miles than U.S. 97 between Ellensburg and Wenatchee: 70 miles via Swauk Pass, 50 miles via Colockum Pass.

At the **Olmstead Place** east of Ellensburg—operated as a heritage-area state park—an atmosphere of nineteenth-century quiet offsets the sound of nearby freeway traffic. A log cabin, a barn, outbuildings, and a restored farmhouse offer a visual tour through the decades. The house is open to the public on summer weekends; an interpretive center presents family farm displays. A mid-September threshing bee features steam tractors and other antique equipment.

In 1875 Samuel Bedient Olmstead, a Civil War veteran, arrived here with his wife Sarah to farm. He built a cabin of squared cottonwood logs, which he cut along the Yakima River. At first the Olmsteads raised beef cattle, but they later converted to dairying. During the 1890s depression, Kittitas farmers called cows "mortgage lifters," because butter shipped to the Swauk mines and to Puget Sound brought much-needed cash income. A rodent-proof granary built in 1892 was later converted to a creamery.

The **Thorp Mill,** listed in the National Register of Historic Places, stands west of Ellensburg near the quiet hamlet of Thorp. The building, which sprawls comfortably beside its

millstream, is now the focus of a preservation effort that stems from earlier community focus on the mill as a local center. (To reach the mill, turn off I-90 at Exit 101 and drive through Thorp and past the school; or follow Thorp Road for about 3 miles after turning south off State Route 10.)

For decades, farmers from throughout Kittitas County exchanged gossip and informally conducted business while delivering their grain at Thorp Mill and waiting to receive flour, bran, and livestock feed in exchange. The mill opened in 1883 powered by water that already came by canal from the Yakima River to a sawmill. The two mills became the nucleus of a town, which was augmented in 1886 by a railroad depot. In time, the horizontal waterwheel that powered both mills also provided electricity on Monday and Tuesday mornings, so that Thorp housewives could wash and iron clothes, and also each evening to supply a few hours of power for well-lit reading and school homework.

In prerailroad days, Thorp Mill was strictly a local operation. It ground grain for barter or shares, using buhrs freighted by wagon from The Dalles. Arrival of the railroad allowed hauling in more sophisticated milling machinery and hauling out flour to markets in Puget Sound and beyond. Farmers would unload grain into hoppers on the north side of the building. From there, it followed a tortuous path via bucket

The Thorp Mill—at first powered by a waterwheel—operated from 1883 to 1946.

elevators to the upper stories, then down again through many stages of cleaning, separating, and grinding. Finally, flour emerged and was sewn into cloth sacks.

The roller-mill machinery remains in functioning condition. The old waterwheel, and perhaps also the buhrstones, lie intact beneath the building. A sign now describes mill operations, which ceased in 1946.

IRON HORSE STATE PARK. (See under SNOQUALMIE PASS, p. 133.)

LIBERTY lies two miles up a valley where scattered mining machinery slowly rusts. The town—two rows of false-fronted buildings and cabins lining a single street—is listed as a National Historic District. (Note that the *town* is listed; all of the buildings are private.) At the lower end of the street is a reconstructed arrastra with an undershot, horizontal waterwheel, typical of arrastras in this mining district. (See p. 130 for a discussion of arrastra operation.)

Liberty dates to 1868 when a small party of prospectors stopped for lunch on the banks of Swauk Creek near the present junction of Liberty Road with U.S. 97. A swirl of their pans turned up a few flecks of shiny metal, which they dismissed as "fool's gold." Five

years later some of the same men returned with more experienced miners, who recognized similar shiny flecks of gold, and found nuggets as well. Within weeks hundreds of miners swarmed along Swauk Creek and its tributaries. Most made a living, not a fortune. As one expressed it, "There's a lot of gold up in that Swauk, but there's a lot of gravel mixed up with it."

In 1873 the men organized a district based on a federal mining law that Congress had passed the preceding year. That statute provided a basis for rudimentary law in frontier communities until such time as territorial, state, or county government could effectively take over. The main concern lay with guaranteeing each individual an equal chance to a mine claim. In practice, mining districts drew up their own regulations—a process with elements of pure democracy, also of vigilante expedience.

The depression that followed the Panic of 1893 set off a boom in the Swauk Mining District, partly owing to men losing jobs everywhere, partly to the national treasury's need to replenish itself with gold; printing more money had not yet become acceptable. J. A. Shoudy, founder of Ellensburg, bought a claim and laid out a town at the present site of Liberty. He sold out, and a man named T. F. Meagher jumped the claim and managed to prevail in court.

This injustice perturbed local miners, who also objected to having their town called Meaghersville. The name sounded too much like "meager," a slur on civic prospects. In 1912 the Liberty Post Office moved to Meaghersville from near the site of the original gold strike, and townspeople gladly adopted the name. Newly renamed, Liberty soon stood replete with hotel, barbershop, doctor's office, school, taxidermy shop, and gas station. It also had a railroad, a sawmill, and logging company offices—a variety of enterprises impossible to infer from the few dozen remaining structures.

In the 1920s Swauk Creek placer mining entered a new—brief—era with the use of a dredge brought in from Alaska. Mounds of gravel from this operation show plainly along U.S. 97 (just south of the Liberty Road junction). Steam shovels also scooped gravel from streams into sloping sluice boxes where flowing water carried off worthless rock and allowed gold, which is heavy, to settle against riffles. By that time, miners were tunneling along gold-bearing quartz veins and sometimes found pockets of wire gold, an unusual form highly valued by collectors.

At **Blewett** (along U.S. 2 about 23 miles north of the road to Liberty) most signs of a

Rusting equipment at Liberty remains from placer operations. Miners scooped up river gravel and washed out gold that had eroded from upper slopes and accumulated over the millennia.

Early miners crushed ore in simple dragstone mills called arrastras.

historic gold mining town have succumbed to time, fire, and highway construction, but the stone foundation of a stamp mill and an arrastra remain. To locate them watch for two roadside pullovers on the east side of the highway, about a half mile apart.

The mill remnants stand across the highway from the northern parking area, screened by vegetation. Steam-powered, this gold mill was once the largest in the state. It had 20 stamps and space for 20 more. Its foundation includes a mortarless rock wall 10 feet high, made of beautifully fitted stones that are two feet square. Guides for the stamps are still apparent, and great iron wheels remain.

The arrastra, which looks like a stone saucer with a lump in the center, nestles beside Peshastin Creek across the highway from a historic marker. No record exists of who built the arrastra, or when, but this one is unusual in that it is cut directly into bedrock. Arrastras crushed ore much as gristmills ground grain between revolving stones. Spaniards introduced the method into their New World colonies, and California miners apparently brought it north. Simplicity was the main virtue: a waterwheel, or sometimes a mule, pulled a heavy dragstone over a carefully fitted "pavement" of rocks. Once ore had been crushed, miners added mercury to the resulting slurry. This formed a mercury-gold amalgam that sank to the bottom, where it was periodically recovered and heated in a retort to vaporize the mercury. That process left only gold. The mercury was collected for reuse.

By the late 1890s at least eight arrastras operated in the Swauk and Blewett mining districts. Even though outclassed by stamp mills, most continued through the 1930s, and one until the 1950s. A replicated arrastra now stands at Liberty.

Miners returning from the Fraser River strike in British Columbia discovered the first Swauk placer gold in 1858. A special edition of the *Steilacoom Herald* carried "highly important" word of the strike—news considered valuable by Puget Sound communities that were eager to outfit gold seekers and help them spend whatever riches they managed to acquire. By the 1860s Blewett was home to 200 miners. Hard-rock mining soon followed the placer operations, and the community added a hotel, boarding-house, and store to its large cluster of shacks. Gold veins ran as wide as 16 feet, but tended to quickly pinch to nothing.

Mines still honeycomb the entire mountain west of U.S. 97. A few tunnel mouths are visible from the road, others are hidden by brush. All are potentially dangerous to enter. Placer mines included a claim on Negro Creek, which was worked by Big Antoine, a black settler who had moved here from Entiat. (See ENTIAT, p. 75.)

OLMSTEAD PLACE. (See p. 127.)

RONALD. (See under ROSLYN, p. 132.)

ROSLYN sits atop a coalfield that stretches for 7 miles from Cle Elum Lake to the town of Cle Elum. By 1898, a decade after its mines opened, Roslyn accounted for half the coal production of the state. Today the town appears remarkably unchanged: small houses dot the steep hillsides; heaps of slag mark former mine entrances; and a huge company store (built in 1889) stands at the main intersection (Pennsylvania and First). Diagonally across from the store, the Brick Tavern (built in 1899) boasts a 20-foot "gutter" spittoon with running water. During the mining heyday, workers coming off shift were automatically handed their first schooner of beer here—no charge for that first one, and no need to ask for it. A museum (a half block west of the Brick Tavern) displays photos and mementos of the mining area. Farther west a remarkable cemetery stretches along pine-clad hills with 26 separate burial plots, a reflection of Roslyn's ethnic diversity and varied fraternal orders.

Beginning in 1884 a homesteader named Nez Jensen dug coal at Roslyn with a pick and shovel and peddled it to blacksmiths in Ellensburg; his log cabin still stands (Utah and Second). Two years after that first simple mining, Northern Pacific Railroad engineers examined the deposits—and within weeks had miners digging coal, and section hands laying tracks for a spur line. By virtue of land grants, the railroad company already owned alternate sections of land in the area. Through lawsuits, they extinguished conflicting claims and established Roslyn as a company town. One Northern Pacific subsidiary operated the mines; another developed the townsite, ran the company store, and licensed saloons.

Men worked underground for 11 hours a day and, whenever the market for coal faltered, they might have as little as 12 to 14 days of work per month. Wages depended on the amount of coal each man dug, regardless of the quality of the seam he worked. Furthermore, before he was paid, the company deducted rent, utilities, health care, and charges owing at the store. Even so, two days of work gave a miner at Roslyn more than a garment worker in New York City could earn in a week.

In the fall of 1888 the Knights of Labor organized a strike in the hope of gaining an eight-hour day and more equitable wages between workers and bosses. To break that strike, the Northern Pacific contracted a black

Roslyn developed as a Northern Pacific coal-mining town. Railroads were newly crossing the continent, and thousands of European immigrants in need of work were available as miners, many of them already experienced below ground.

How much coal a man dug determined his wages, not the hours he worked—and Roslyn miners had to buy their own tools and powder, accepting pay deductions to cover the cost. Even so, they were better paid than most coal miners elsewhere.

miner from Illinois to "solicit the migration of members of his group." This brought the first large movement of black people into the state; at the time, and for years afterward, strike breaking was one of the few sources of industrial employment open to blacks. The first blacks to arrive in Roslyn were greeted with bitterness and overt hostility as "scabs." But over time, this tension eased and social discrimination focused more on language and cultural differences than on race.

Astonishing human diversity characterized Roslyn. An alphabetical listing of ethnic groups includes Austrian, Belgian, black, Chinese (who worked outlying placers), Croatian, Czechoslovakian, Dutch, English, Finnish, German, Hungarian, Irish, Italian, Lithuanian, Montenegrin (Yugoslavian), Norwegian, Polish, Russian, Scottish, Serbian, Slavonian, Swedish, Syrian, and Welsh. At its peak in the 1920s the town's population was about 4,000, most of the time with about half of the adults foreign born.

By then two million tons of coal came from Roslyn annually. Soon after that, production dwindled as oil and hydroelectric power supplied energy needs. The last mine closed in 1963. Talk of reopening has never died—and most of the coalfield remains untapped.

Ronald stands as a miniature version of neighboring Roslyn; in both, company houses have been remodeled over the years to suit individual family needs. Ronald had its own coal mine, saloon, and store, but most people traveled the 3 miles to Roslyn to shop.

In 1886, just before crews began to build the rail line across Stampede Pass, the Northern Pacific company brought in 400 Italian immigrants to open a mine simply called Number 3. Two years later, during a bitter strike, irate men attacked mine supervisor Alexander Ronald and left him bound to the tracks just outside of town. An alert brakeman pulled Ronald to safety.

At **Salmon la Sac** (up the Cle Elum River from Roslyn and Ronald) a former Forest Service guard station with steep-roofed, log architecture stands facing the Cle Elum River. Its origin stems from the investment hopes of French capitalists.

By the 1890s the Cle Elum Mining District had become famous. Prospectors had staked gold, silver, lead, iron, nickel, and cinnabar claims; and the Northern Pacific Railroad was producing enormous amounts of coal in the Roslyn area. Transporting the various ores to the railroad at Cle Elum constituted a real need and a seeming chance for profit. That attracted French investors. They formed the Kittitas Railway and Power Company in 1911 and immediately began construction of a depot at Salmon la Sac. The threat of war in Europe, however, unsettled French control at such a far-off location. The company failed.

Regardless of that bankruptcy, the Forest Service successfully sued the company for having cut trees on government land without a permit. The log building intended as a depot became a payment of the fine—and a ranger district headquarters used from 1915 until the 1980s.

Cars cross **SNOQUALMIE PASS** on a highway so broad and gently graded that little but scenery and occasional icy winter conditions remind motorists they are going over a major physiographic barrier.

Native Americans used the 3,022-foot pass regularly and as early as 1865 men from Seattle surveyed the route and raised money for a wagon road from Ranger's Prairie (North Bend) over the summit to Keechelus Lake (Ketch´-uh-lus), where a raft served as ferry. Four years after the road opened, cattlemen began to trail stock over the pass, and thereby launched Seattle's meat packing industry. Cattle, sheep, horses, swine, and even turkeys crossed under their own power in such numbers that westside homesteaders found it profitable to rent pasturage for the weary stock.

Repeated pleas to territorial legislators and to King and Kittitas county supervisors for road improvement brought little response during the 1870s, and the road deteriorated until it became impassable for wagons. Repair began in 1884, when a toll road was opened from Taneum Bridge west of Ellensburg to Ranger's Prairie. A mere four years later the Northern Pacific completed its rails over Stampede Pass, and in 1909 the Milwaukee (at this time called the Chicago, Milwaukee and Puget Sound) built its electric line across Snoqualmie Pass to Seattle. The wagon road lost importance—until the

coming of the automobile age and its conversion into a highway. (Just east of today's Snoqualmie ski lodge, watch for the large brick building that provided power for Milwaukee Road engines as they went through tunnels. East of Milepost 38, notice the huge railroad trestles that still cling to the high south wall of the pass.)

Easton developed as a sawmilling town. The arrival of the Northern Pacific in 1888 stimulated increased lumbering as opportunities for shipping expanded, and in 1909 the rails of the Chicago, Milwaukee and Puget Sound crossed the Northern Pacific rails here. (The Milwaukee line continued to Snoqualmie Pass; the Northern Pacific to Stampede Pass.) Railroad workers swelled the population; Easton was the last station where trains could be serviced before going over the mountains. In 1934 the town suffered a severe fire, but was rebuilt and now offers services for highway travelers.

Southeast of town an undeveloped parking lot gives access to **Iron Horse State Park,** which strings out along the old Milwaukee right-of-way. The park includes 25 miles of the John Wayne Pioneer Trail, open to bicyclists, equestrians, hikers, and cross-country skiers. (Take Exit 71 from I-90 at Easton and drive a half mile south of town to the trailhead. Access to the park is also available in South Cle Elum. The Department of Natural Resources issues permits for travel on the trail beyond the park boundaries.)

The trail—a wide, gravelly path with gentle slopes—utilizes 213 miles of Milwaukee roadbed between Easton and Tekoa, near the Idaho border. West of Easton, the state hopes to acquire an additional 37 miles of the roadbed to form a link with the King County trail system, thus providing a trail all the way across the state.

THORP MILL. (See under ELLENSBURG, p. 127.)

Yakima Valley Area

The Yakima Valley is actually two: the upper valley (including Yakima and Moxee) and the lower valley (below Union Gap). Before irrigation the land was a desert, although with lush vegetation along the river and an abundant salmon run. Native villages dotted the riverbank, and a major fishery was located near Selah. In the 1860s white ranchers drove herds of cattle from Oregon to take advantage of the Yakima Valley bunchgrass. Farming, in turn, began to supplant ranching a decade later as irrigation experiments demonstrated the fertility of the land. The river, the railroad (1885), and large-scale government irrigation projects (1900s) determined subsequent patterns of settlement.

Sites of particular interest include Fort Simcoe (an early military fort) and Saint Joseph's mission, which dates from the 1840s. Several homes of early settlers remain, and the pattern of irrigation development is everywhere evident.

Outstanding drives that give a feeling of the countryside include State Route 821, which twists along the river between Yakima and Ellensburg, and the drive up the Wenas Valley and over Umtanum Ridge to Ellensburg. The

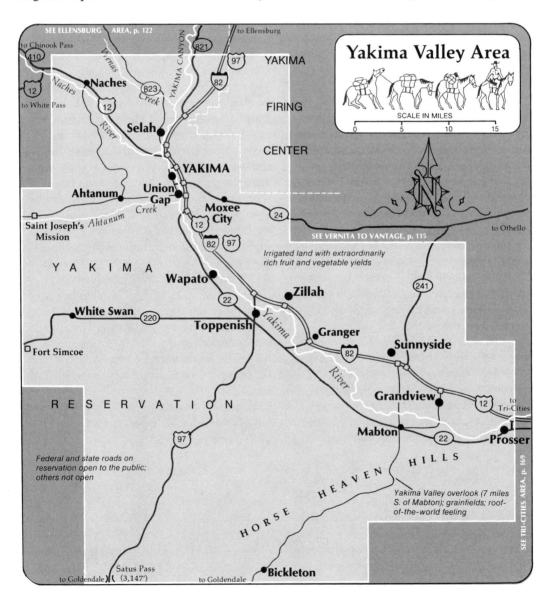

Fort Simcoe was established in 1856 to guard military roads, protect treaty lands from encroachment by whites, and impress Yakima chiefs with the army's power.

road from Mabton to Bickleton and on to Goldendale is also scenic. Museums displaying aspects of this area's human story are located at Prosser, Sunnyside, Toppenish, Union Gap, and Yakima. Long-established festivals include powwows held at White Swan during the summer and celebrations of ethnic diversity held in Wapato and Granger each spring.

AHTANUM. (See under SAINT JOSEPH'S MISSION, p. 143.)

BICKLETON. (See under MABTON, p. 138.)

The site of **FORT SIMCOE** (7 miles west of White Swan) was known to the Yakima people as *Mool-Mool,* "bubbling water." It served as a well-watered and sheltered camping place on the trail from the Yakima Valley to Celilo Falls on the Columbia River. With its oak grove and overview of the vast Toppenish flats, it remains a worthy destination. A row of country-Gothic officers' homes, a blockhouse, and a drafty, reconstructed barracks line the former army parade ground; an interpretive center offers a few exhibits; and the refurnished commandant's home is usually open to the public.

In 1855 Yakima chiefs set off a general uprising against ever-increasing numbers of whites. The army responded by constructing two inland posts in 1856: Fort Walla Walla and Fort Simcoe. Major Robert Selden Garnett, newly arrived at Fort Simcoe as its commander, first directed his energies to roughing out a wagon road from The Dalles to the fort; then he turned to constructing the buildings.

Plans for officers' quarters similar to those at Fort Walla Walla and Fort Dalles came from an architect's pattern book of country homes, and Garnett fought running skirmishes with the Quartermaster Corps over the quality of construction: stone versus brick, whitewash versus paint. The result was a row of airy, bright houses of a style that complements the light and shade of the oak trees.

A year after arriving at Fort Simcoe, Major Garnett traveled to the East Coast, married, and brought his bride Marianna to her new home, via the Panama Canal, San Francisco, and The Dalles. The journey lasted more than six weeks. Polite society at the remote fort consisted of Mrs. Garnett and three other officers' wives. According to letters, the four socialized, "with little ceremony."

In 1858 Garnett led troops into the Okanogan country as the western arm of Colonel George Wright's deadly campaign near Spokane. The men covered 500 miles in a month's marching time, and both captured and executed several native men suspected of having killed white miners. That military "justice"—typical of the era—taken care of, Garnett started home. A messenger met him one day's ride from the fort, reporting that Mrs. Garnett lay gravely ill with a "bilious fever" (typhoid). She died before the major could reach her. An infant son, Arthur, died 10 days later. Garnett accompanied their bodies to the East Coast for burial and never returned to the Northwest. A Virginian by birth, he soon resigned his U.S. Army commission and joined the Confederate forces. He died in battle at Carricks Ford, Virginia, in 1861, the first general killed in the Civil War.

Troops manned Fort Simcoe only until 1859. By then the treaty signed at Walla Walla four years earlier had been ratified. The Yakima War had ended; the Yakima Reservation had been established. The army closed Fort Simcoe and turned it over to the Indian bureau. The buildings served as agency headquarters and a boarding school for native children until 1923, when the offices moved to Toppenish, nearer to highways and population centers.

(Also see YAKIMA RESERVATION, p. 154; YAKIMA WAR sidebar, p. 148; and SPOKANE BATTLES sidebar; p. 10.)

GRANDVIEW's intact commercial and residential districts, representative of successive eras, are on the National Register of Historic Places. An unbroken wall of business buildings along Division Street has served as a retail core since 1906, and early residential streets east and west of Division still retain frame bungalows and Craftsman-style cottages. Some have been re-sided or converted to apartments, but many remain unaltered.

The Morse House (Main and Cedar; built about 1910) features a hipped roof and abundant decorative detail. The Howay-Dykstra House (Birch and Second; built about 1920) utilizes a variety of materials typical at the time of construction: tile blocks, stucco, brick, and rusticated concrete brick.

In addition to these structures, the two-story brick high school built during the 1930s as a Works Progress Administration project is highlighted by glass blocks; and at the southern edge of the town on Old Prosser Highway is a round

barn 200 feet in diameter (built about 1916), one of perhaps a dozen such barns remaining in the state. The round shape permitted a single worker to feed cows held in a fanlike array of stanchions. That efficiency was outweighed, however, by the complexity of constructing a building with no right angles. Round barns enjoyed a flurry of popularity before 1920, then faded.

In 1937, four years after the federal government repealed Prohibition, one of the state's earliest bonded wineries was built at Grandview (West Fifth and Avenue B; visitors welcome). The early winery produced fortified berry and grape wines.

About 1893 the Rocky Ford lateral from the Sunnyside Canal brought water to farms immediately south of Grandview. Even so, no town sprang up until 1906 when rail service at last helped to get crops to market. What had been a single farmhouse mushroomed in three years into a town with several neighborhoods and a distinct retail core.

With shipping assured, apple, peach, and pear orchards soon went in, although early farmers had far from an easy time. They fought "blowsand," which often carried off seeds before they could sprout and choked one canal six times in a single growing season. They also battled jackrabbits, which defied fences, poison, clubs, and guns to kill young trees by persistently nibbling the bark.

GRANGER's shady downtown streets end abruptly in plowed fields. Developed early as a fruit-packing center, the town had the sad distinction in the mid-1980s of ranking lowest in per capita income of any community in the state. Granger is headquarters for the United Farm Workers of Washington, a union that seeks improved working conditions for the largely itinerant labor force needed at harvest time. Initially these workers were mostly Native Americans, joined in the early 1900s by Japanese and Filipinos.

During World War II everyone of Japanese descent, regardless of citizenship, was interned in government camps, and growers replaced their Japanese work force with Latino laborers. Many of these people liked the area and settled permanently. Others still come seasonally. They

FARM LABOR

As World War II began, farm labor shortages led schools to dismiss classes early so that students could help with the crops. The mayor of Toppenish actually signed a resolution ordering school-children over age 12 to the fields and, during a particular crisis, the army detailed soldiers from a Yakima area gunnery range onto farms.

In 1943 the U.S. government brought in workers from towns and cities in central Mexico. These men—many of them teenagers—were regimented into forces to supply railroad or agricultural work crews on an as-needed basis. Actually, Mexican workers had already been coming seasonally—and illegally—riding the rails north and earning in a month what it would take a year to earn at home. Nor were these men the first: their fathers and uncles had been among the optimists stampeding to Northwest mine booms from the 1860s to the 1880s.

The official Bracero Program, which continued until 1964, allowed up to 50,000 Mexican workers per year to cross the border. Additionally, labor contractors traveled Texas, Colorado, and California promoting jobs in Washington's asparagus, sugar beet, and potato fields and in the orchards. Whole families joined single men riding north in the backs of trucks, or they paid out money earned from early-season Southwest crops to buy gasoline and tires for traveling to earn money from late-season Northwest crops. Joe Garcia, son of a farm labor family who became a social worker in Seattle, describes dealing with labor contractors as like "entering a network of evil and trying to negotiate with the Devil himself":

Low wages, poor conditions, unprotected, unsafe. Undocumented workers who could be manipulated. Unreported income—and so no rights to social services. Get the crops in, regardless of pesticide, poor housing. We weren't welcome except seasonally as a workforce.

I remember living at what had been the wartime relocation camp for Japanese near Wapato. The barbed wire still was up. It was awful. We had to work through the harvest, so we'd get into school late in the fall, and we never could participate in school-related activities. We were made fun of because of our clothing, skin color, language, the kind of work we did . . . Impure water. Infected dirt. Childhood diseases. Hops, vineyards, orchards, truck farms. Child labor laws? Yes, they existed. No, they didn't apply for the farm worker, not with any real effect.

Yet you knew you were an important element within the family and felt important, not for the dollar value of your little bit of work but knowing that you were helping get clothes and food for the winter so that the family could survive when there was no work. Endure. People say of Latinos, "They laugh a lot." Well, they also die young.

Now there's a buildup of urban Latinos, mostly from the Mexican-American community, the settled-out population— bilingual families that have become citizens and report their earnings, so they have some protection under the law. This urbanization happens to coincide with an in-migration of refugees from Central America. Improved agricultural technology and mechanization on the farms has brought us to the cities looking for jobs. Our kids still are born in poverty and live in poverty. Yet I'm optimistic. The road we've already traveled has been longer than the road ahead. My parents—my great grandparents—paid a higher price and sacri-ficed more than I have. I owe it to them to be positive and say that our agenda is unfinished, and that I'll keep it moving forward so long as I'm here.

work a triangle from Texas to California to Washington, following ripening crops and a chance for livelihood. Most have Mexican backgrounds—enough so that Mexican music drifts from the open doors of cafes throughout the Yakima Valley, and a Granger radio station broadcasts exclusively in Spanish. Cinco de Mayo fiestas celebrating Mexico's independence from France are as common in the Yakima Valley as Fourth of July celebrations. Granger also holds Charro Days in September, commemorating Mexican independence from Spain.

MABTON's single main street is quiet now, belying an early reputation for rowdiness. A brick high school—its windows boarded up—stands with its back to the highway, and tiny Saint Michael's Episcopal Church (Fifth and C; built in 1910) continues to serve local people.

A Northern Pacific section house and water tower formed the 1885 nucleus of the town. For a while, the Northern Pacific expected to make this a division point, but they found they needed only one, North Yakima. Regardless, Mabton grew. In 1892 S. P. Flower added a store and warehouse near the railroad tracks. Other businesses soon followed, including saloons and hotels with compliant maids who gave young Mabton a wild reputation. This spirit contrasted sharply with "holy" Sunnyside, settled by members of the Christian Cooperative Colony. A cable ferry, remembered by one pioneer as "some planks thrown on the water with a banister around it," crossed the river between the two towns and thirsty Sunnyside shoppers often found it necessary to do business in Mabton.

This early vigor notwithstanding, Mabton's development was retarded by a lack of water. The townsite company drilled an artesian well, but it produced a combination of water and gas. By 1912 government irrigation canals were in place, and fruit trees were thriving, often with interplantings of melons as an interim crop. Mabton became a shipping point for wheat and produce.

Next to a riverside dance hall called Joyland, Mabtonites staged their annual Hay Palace Fairs. From 1915 to 1924 farmers celebrating bumper crops of alfalfa built crenellated "palaces" of baled hay. Medieval-looking, tarp-roofed, and with pennants flying at the corners, the

constructs housed exhibits of agricultural products and stages for performers. Outside, cattle paraded before judges; daredevil horseback riders galloped through their paces; and overhead barnstormers flew barrel rolls.

Southwest of Mabton, a 26-mile drive to **Bickleton** crosses the Horse Heaven Hills and continues 40 miles to Goldendale. Early settlers named the hills because of their bunchgrass, which provided ideal grazing for horses. Huge herds ran wild and eventually became a pest to farmers and ranchers; they ate grass that otherwise could feed cattle and sheep, and they broke down fences enclosing grainfields. Throughout the early 1900s parties of riders combed the canyons and waterholes rounding up the cayuses. They sold some to horse traders, others to slaughterhouses.

In the mid-1960s Bickleton won the nickname "Bluebird Capital of the World" for its 2,000 birdhouses, which cap fenceposts throughout the area's rolling grainfields. One couple's hobby of building, painting, installing, and maintaining the birdhouses became a community effort several years ago. Both mountain and western bluebirds arrive each March to nest in the boxes.

The town began in 1878 when Charles Bickle and his business associate Samuel Flower opened a store here to serve arriving settlers. Six years later, when the Northern Pacific built through the Yakima Valley, Flower moved there to help establish Mabton. Bickle stayed at the store, which by then also included a livery stable and post office. Bickleton today remains a small farming community.

MOXEE CITY (Mock-see′) stands in a "forest" of hop vines strung onto wires. A two-street business section serves outlying farms. As is true of many rural communities, Moxee City finds itself so near a larger population center that it cannot support all of the services formerly essential in every hamlet.

Fielding Mortimer Thorp, the first white settler in this area, drove 250 Durham cattle into the valley in 1860 and built a house opposite the mouth of Ahtanum Creek. On the bottomlands he found ryegrass tall enough to virtually hide his livestock, and on the surrounding hills, there was lush bunchgrass ideal for grazing. No realm could be finer for cattle.

Poles, wire, and string support hop vines, which twine upward for 20 feet or more.

Farmers crowded on the heels of stockmen, however, and in less than 20 years crops largely supplanted cattle. Among the early farms was the Moxie Company, a 6,400-acre showplace owned by Gardiner Hubbard, founder of the National Geographic Society, and his son-in-law Alexander Graham Bell. The *Yakima Herald* reported that the Moxie Company owned "every patent farm implement that is of any use," and also that prospective investors and settlers with capital often dined at the manager's house "where the popping of Champagne corks created an effervescence that forced open many a tightly bound purse."

Workers set out hundreds of Johannisberg Riesling and Old Mission grape cuttings from California and experimented with peanuts, cotton, and tobacco. The *Herald* reported that Moxee Belle and Fleur de Yakima cigars met "the practical approval of constant use by the most critical smokers." Winter frost and the financial depression of 1893 ended the tobacco experiment, however, and ruined the Moxie Company. Regardless of its short life, the farm was representative of eastern capital financing development in the West and of the search for crops best suited to unknown soils and climate.

Eventually hops (used in beer) became Moxee's principal crop.

To visit the site of the Moxie Company operation, drive to the LaFramboise farm (5204 Mieras Road; turn north off State Route 24 onto Birchfield Road, then immediately east on Mieras Road). Part of the LaFramboise hop house, still in use, is said to have been built around the Moxie Company tobacco barn. The building stands below an 1885 Presbyterian church, which was converted to a blacksmith shop by Antoine LaFramboise. He arrived in 1897 under a five-year contract as a blacksmith for the Moxie Company. The Yakima Valley Museum now has the equipment from the blacksmith shop.

In the 1890s the disbanding Moxie Company successfully promoted the sale of its lands among French Canadians living in the Great Lakes region. Families moved here, and their hop production became so great that by the 1930s Moxee City billed itself as "Hop Capital of the World." Children grew up speaking only French until they started school, and Catholic services were held in French through the 1920s.

Dutch financiers, active investors in Washington's cities and farmland, advertised the

HOPS

Strung onto wires, hop vines produce flavorful two- to three-inch "cones" that are dried and shipped to breweries. In the early days wagon ramps led to the second story of hop barns, or "kilns," where the cones were spread onto burlap-covered slats and dried 24 hours with heat from a first-floor, wood-burning stove.

During this era picking hops combined tedium with an air of a picnic. Families came by the wagonload to stay in cabins provided by growers or to edge the hop yards with their tents. Merchants as distant as Ellensburg did a brisk business as Chief Moses' Sinkiuse people, Sanpoil from the upper Columbia River, and Coast Salish—some even from British Columbia villages—trailed through town to join the Yakima in the hop fields. Women and children usually traveled ahead in September to start picking. Men came in early October for a "Jubilee" of horse racing and all-night games (*lahal,* a convivial form of gambling still popular).

Margaret Thorp Hawkins, daughter of one of the earliest homesteaders in the Yakima Valley, remembered that people thought of hop picking not as "a hard and dirty job but as an opportunity for an outing." In a 1947 issue of *The Hopper* she reminisced about nightly dances in the hop houses—"mainly square dances so even the children took part"—and she described the daily routine:

How did we live? Well, we got our water from whatever ditch, creek, spring or well was handy. For food, we used what we had brought, but in addition food wagons—little traveling grocery stores—made the rounds of the hop camps. . . . We cooked everything on open campfires. We started picking about as soon as the sun came up and worked through the whole day.

Apparently Charles Carpenter, who came to the Yakima Valley via the California and British Columbia gold rushes, introduced eastern Washington's first hops in the 1870s. His root cuttings came from his father's hop farm in Constable, New York. Cultivation at that time involved planting several cuttings—usually four—at the base of 12-foot poles, which studded the fields about 900 to the acre. In spring, field hands tied new shoots to the poles. Vines lengthen an astonishing 25 feet in a season, at certain stages adding as much as six inches in a single day.

Widespread aphid infestations ruined the hops industry in western Washington beginning in 1889, but conditions east of the Cascades proved ideal. Today the Yakima area produces nearly three fourths of the entire U.S. crop (and the United States supplies about one fifth of world production; California, Oregon, and New York are the other hop-growing states). Drying now takes place in metal-sided buildings with gas burners housed in separate fireproof sheds. Picking is mechanized, but hop growing nonetheless remains labor intensive. (Also see discussion of hops on p. 437.)

Yakima Valley's superior qualities and, beginning in the 1890s, Dutch farmers moved near Moxee and added a "Holland District" to the already cosmopolitan countryside. A German Lutheran congregation also settled in the area.

Half a century later the Roza Canal expanded irrigated acreage. Originating in the Yakima Canyon north of Selah, the canal winds east through the upper Yakima Valley, cuts through the hills south of Moxee, and continues east across the lower valley to Prosser. On State Route 24 east of Moxee City "corporate pioneering" continues. Hayfields, simultaneously sprinkled and fertilized from overhead pipes, create straight lines of white mist across lush green fields, and new orchards climb the hills sheltered by windbreaks of young poplars. Meadowlarks still sing amid sagebrush, but year by year their realm shrinks.

The **NACHES** (Na-cheez´) community got its start with the introduction of irrigation, and it continues today as an orchard and fruit-packing center. Amid its warehouses, a dainty white bandstand straddles an irrigation ditch (Naches and Second). Beside the river Colonel George Wright built his "Basket Fort" (off present-day U.S. 2 near Milepost 194). It was used briefly in April 1856. (See YAKIMA WAR sidebar, p. 148.)

NACHES PASS was an established travel route in the days before automobiles. At nearly 5,000 feet, it is one of the highest of the dozen passes that cross the Cascade Mountains; it is now accessible only by trail. (Follow U.S. 410 for about 20 miles up the Naches Valley from its junction with U.S. 12; then turn up the Little Naches River on a Forest Service road. The trailhead is in another 12½ miles, at Timothy Meadows. From there to the pass is a 9½-mile hike—with an elevation gain of more than 1,700 feet. A much shorter trail approaches from the west, beyond Greenwater.) The historic trail itself no longer exists; its present ruts were cut by off-road vehicles in the 1960s and 1970s.

Native people traveling to Puget Sound used this route for generations. In 1840 Yakima chief Owhi traded horses at Fort Nisqually for cattle, which he trailed east via Naches Pass. One year later a detachment from the Wilkes Expedition crossed this way to explore the interior, guided by Pierre Charles and Peter Bercier of the Hudson's Bay Company. In 1853 Captain George McClellan, searching for a railroad route across the Cascade Mountains, considered Naches Pass but found it impassable—as he found all the passes he investigated.

McClellan's assignment included building a wagon road from Fort Walla Walla over Naches Pass, and rumor that this work was under way spread among emigrants on the Oregon Trail. Learning that funding for the work would be slow in coming, volunteers from Puget Sound settlements cleared a rough trail on their side of the mountains. McClellan paid the "road" scant heed, searching instead for a railroad pass.

At the same time the James Longmire wagon party heard rumors of the road and decided to strike out for it from the Grande Ronde Valley of northeast Oregon. Reputedly this would be 200 miles shorter from Walla Walla to Puget Sound than the usual route, which was down the Columbia and then up the Cowlitz River. Near the present Hanford reservation, native men directed the party days out of their way toward Fort Colvile, supposing that the trading settlement there must be the immigrants' destination; they could not imagine that travelers were intending to cross the mountains with 36 wagons.

The going was fairly easy west of the present-day town of Naches except for crossing and recrossing the river. That put the wagon train behind schedule. Snow covered the ground before they reached Naches Pass in October 1853. Worse, no amount of searching disclosed a road. Nothing but a treacherous trail led down a high slope so steep it seemed impassable. The men realized they had no choice but to lower the wagons by ropes and, lacking materials, they slaughtered oxen and cut the hides into strips. (Some family descendants deny this, however. Their understanding is that the pioneers had ropes with them.) In any case, the men had to wrestle the wagons down the slope with the help of ropes. They lost only two wagons, which crashed and splintered.

Next came numbing days spent felling trees and hacking brush to force a path westward through dense forest. Nearing the end of their strength, Mrs. Longmire and Mrs. Light, carrying one child and leading a three-year-old, finally stepped into a clearing where settler Andy Burge, a member of the volunteer road crew, was working. He greeted the forlorn foursome with, "My God, women, where did you come from!" and immediately emptied his saddlebags of food and left it for the wagon party while he hurried to the settlements for help. En route, Burge left signs posted on trees to mark the way.

Journey complete, the Longmire party soon separated to stake various land claims on the Puget lowlands. Their descendants number in the thousands.

At **PROSSER** the Yakima River winds past a city park to a waterfall at the east end of town, source of the town's first industry: a flour mill.

The county historical society museum (Paterson and Seventh) offers a slide show on local history, and the library (902 Seventh) includes an excellent collection of books on grape growing and wine making, indication of a current emphasis in the area's economy.

The county courthouse (Dudley and Market; built in 1926) is an imposing brick building with classical fluted columns and a central portico. Inside, terrazzo flooring, oak banisters, and molded cornices continue the monumental character of the architecture. The building—now listed in the National Register of Historic Places—was intended to symbolize Benton County's coming-of-age and to end Kennewick's rivalrous hope of luring the seat of government away from Prosser.

In 1882 Colonel William Farrand Prosser homesteaded here and opened a trading post;

Oblate missionaries at Saint Joseph's taught both farming and Catholicism.

Farrand Park on the Prosser riverfront marks the site of the family home. (An idyllic riverfront drive begins at the park and runs west for 5 miles to a junction with State Route 22.)

In 1887 former Missourian William Heinzerling built a gristmill at Prosser Falls, a traditional fishing station for Yakima native people. The mill served dryland wheat farmers from the Horse Heaven and Rattlesnake hills. It succeeded from the outset and, in 1906, a train emblazoned with an enormous banner, "Prosser Flour for the San Francisco Sufferers," rolled south to assist earthquake victims.

Early irrigation projects permitted crops, which fueled Prosser's economy—eggplant, sugar beets, strawberries, corn, apples, and other fruit. Shipping and icemaking became significant industries. With the opening of greater tracts of farmland in the Roza Project, Prosser became a major food processing and farm service center.

Thomas Hart Benton, U.S. senator from Missouri, unknowingly lent his name to the county. He was an irascible, duel-fighting young man who edited a frontier newspaper in St. Louis and won a Senate seat largely because of an intelligent analysis of western concerns. For 30 years he argued for development: federal roads and canals; free distribution of public land to those willing to develop it; and the exclusion of slavery from newly admitted western states lest the livelihood of small farmers be threatened. Under Benton's prodding, Congress in 1850 passed the Donation Land Act, which granted farmlands to settlers. In 1862 Benton also fathered the Homestead Act. Both laws greatly fostered Washington's growth.

SAINT JOSEPH'S MISSION, its dark timbers solemn against the waters of Ahtanum Creek, stands at the head of a valley rimmed with basalt bluffs and dedicated to irrigated orchards and farms. One or two sagging hop barns dot the bottomlands. (From Union Gap take Ahtanum Road west 14 miles to the mission.)

Today used only for weddings and other celebrations, the church marks the site of a Catholic mission begun in the late 1840s. Bishop F. N. Blanchet had arranged for five French Oblate missionaries to serve the

Northwest and, at the invitation of chiefs, he established several simple missions in the Yakima and Kittitas valleys.

By 1852 these included a mission at Chief Kamiakin's main summer camp on Ahtanum Creek. (At that time the mission was called Sainte Croix; later it became Saint Joseph's.) Missionary fathers Charles Pandosy and Louis d'Herbomez worked with Kamiakin's men to dig irrigation ditches, among the earliest in the region. With the water, they raised gardens of wheat, corn, melons, pumpkins, and potatoes. Although 14 whites had been killed in 1847 at the Whitman Mission near Walla Walla, the Oblates and the Yakima worked together in peace. Kamiakin brought his children for baptism; others followed suit.

The idyll was short-lived. In 1855 open hostility erupted when Yakima warriors killed white miners trespassing on their land. U.S. Army troops and Oregon volunteers sought to avenge the deaths and break the Yakima spirit. Chief Kamiakin led the native warriors. As a part of this conflict, on November 15, 1855, the mission grounds swarmed with volunteer soldiers. Ostensibly these troops served under Major Gabriel Rains, U.S. Army commander at Vancouver. Actually they often acted on their own and at odds with army policy.

In this instance, native people and missionaries had so recently fled that the soldiers found the mission fireplace still warm. Digging in the garden, they uncovered a cask of gunpowder and, using it as an excuse, decided to burn the mission. They assumed that the gunpowder "proved" the Oblates were arming the Yakima and aggravating hostilities, rather than enhancing the government's plan for reservations and the opening of the land to whites. The accusation was false but it led to the burning of all the Oblate missions in the area and government expulsion of the priests from the Yakima territory.

In addition to the gunpowder, the troops also discovered a letter "to the soldiers" that Kamiakin had dictated to Father Pandosy. In it the chief protested hangings without the army even "knowing if we are right or wrong." He also said that each tribe would "grant [whites] a piece of land" if only they would agree not to "force us to be exiled from our native country"

onto reservations. If this could not be, the Yakima people would fight. The army and the citizenry felt compelled to fight.

Kamiakin never again lived on the Ahtanum near the irrigated gardens he loved profoundly (now listed in the National Register of Historic Places, located upstream from the mission site). He moved near Spokane. (See YAKIMA WAR sidebar, p. 148, and ROCK LAKE, p. 198.)

For 12 years the mission lay in ruins. Then diocesan priests from Quebec rebuilt the church, named it Saint Joseph's, and once again offered instruction to native children. In 1870 they hewed the timbers of the current church from trees at the headwaters of Ahtanum Creek. The following year, Jesuit priests arrived. By then President Ulysses S. Grant's Indian Peace Policy was in effect, a program to consolidate tribes on existing reservations and turn over administration to church groups. The Yakima Reservation had been assigned to Reverend James Wilbur, a Methodist. His appointment came during a period of Protestant and Catholic rivalry so intense it approached mutual hatred. Wilbur—of course—preached against papist heresies and discouraged native people from visiting Saint Joseph's even though it lay beyond reservation boundaries.

As white settlers started filling the valley in the 1870s, mission priests extended their parish services to include them. Eventually the congregation built a church at the new population center of Yakima City (then called Union Gap) and, after the Northern Pacific Railroad Company started the new city of North Yakima (in 1885), the church moved there. Saint Joseph's parish continues today.

The road to the old mission goes through the town of **Ahtanum,** which along with Union Gap became a major center for pioneering settlement. A Congregational church and a Grange building still remain from the 1880s and 1890s (although altered from their original construction). A pleasant backcountry alternative to the freeway at the western edge of Yakima connects from Ahtanum north over the ridge to Naches. Most of the way is through orchards. (East of Ahtanum turn north on 64th; expect confusing jogs but continue north via Summitview and the Summitview–Cowiche Road to Naches.)

SELAH (See′-lah) occupies hills near the confluence of the Yakima River with Wenas (Ween′-ass) and Selah creeks. Pressing apple juice and packing fruit provide the current livelihood. The name means "calm and peaceful," a reference to the river's gentle flow through this area. The Yakima people had a major fishery here, catching salmon, which they dried and then stored in caves above the river.

Early settlers in the valley west of Selah ran sheep on the ridge between the Wenas and Naches drainages. Farmers took over the land and developed irrigation for such crops as hops, potatoes, alfalfa, and apples. In 1885 the Northern Pacific opened a station at Wenas, but no town coalesced until Gus Remington started a store in 1908. An immigrant from Sweden, he had changed his name from Nels Olson while working on railroad construction: there were so many Olsons that his wages kept getting misdirected. Remington chivied Selah into existence by persuading various acquaintances to open a bank, a livery stable, and a newspaper. He even donated lots for worthwhile ventures. By advertising in Swedish-language newspapers in the Midwest, he promoted his growing community. Names like Matson, Sundquist, and Larson still are common here.

The **Wenas Road** connects in 38 miles with Ellensburg. (Drive up the Wenas Valley from Selah and follow the road along the north side of the creek and onto a 3,000-foot plateau clothed with pines and aspens.) The road, which is gravel for 12 miles, passes lush creeks and crosses swelling ridges. Watch for bluebirds and deer. Near Ellensburg notice the Damman School, an example of functional beauty. In the early days a schoolhouse was on skids, pulled each year from farm to farm. In 1890 the school district erected this permanent building with a broad central hallway flanked by two classrooms on one side and a gymnasium-with-stage on the other.

Freight wagons and stage coaches rattled over Wenas Road in the 1870s bound from The Dalles to Ellensburgh (correct spelling until 1894). Some continued farther north crossing Colockum Pass, ferrying the Columbia River near Wenatchee, then climbing onto the Columbia Plateau via Moses Coulee. The route was an expedient one that conformed to the lay of the land and served the budding population centers.

For a while a settler named Jacob Durr tried operating a toll road that cut 10 miles from the Wenas–Ellensburg trip by crossing Umptanum Ridge east of the established road. But Durr's road was so harrowing that wagons had to use turntables to negotiate the switchbacks and, at a $25 annual toll, the road was no bargain. One stage driver complained that there was no hell in the hereafter: it lay between The Dalles and Ellensburg. The modern Sheep Company Road (from N. Wenas Road) follows Durr's road and provides the major access to the L. T. Murray Wildlife Recreation Area.

SUNNYSIDE, a bustling, small city, is the lower Yakima Valley's largest commercial center. Its heritage includes a pioneering livestock empire; a large-scale, private irrigation canal; and an idealistic colony.

In 1859 Ben Snipes, Washington's quintessential cowboy/self-made man, built a small log cabin near today's Sunnyside (preserved at the Sunnyside Museum, Fourth and E. Grant). That year Snipes drove his first cattle from The Dalles to the British Columbia gold fields via the Yakima Valley. Soon he and his brother-in-law H. H. Allen were running vast herds on the open range between the Okanogan and The Dalles. (See CARIBOO TRAIL, p. 53.)

In the late 1880s Thomas F. Oakes, president of the Northern Pacific Railroad, surveyed the Yakima Valley through the windows of his private car. Impressed with the fecundity of the few irrigated acres near Union Gap, he contacted Walter Granger, an engineer with irrigation experience in Montana. Oakes' offer was beguiling: an option on 90,000 acres of railroad land at a bargain price if Granger would irrigate it. Granger accepted. By 1892 he had dug the first 25 miles of the Sunnyside Canal, a 62-foot-wide man-made river that brought water to the north slope of the valley. In 1893 Granger platted the townsites of Zillah and Sunnyside.

Promotional literature published by the railroad company quoted Granger extensively, including a statement that a farmer blessed with irrigation need not:

. . . look up into the sky and wish for a downpour. . . . He merely says to the things dependent upon him for life and growth, "Thou shalt have water." And they are watered in abundance.

Granger also commented that immigrants arriving to take advantage of irrigated lands

all have been prosperous farmers where they came from and have brought with them ample means for the immediate improvement of the land.

These were the new pioneers: established citizens who lived in comfortable houses embellished with gingerbread.

Buoyed by such prospects, pioneering merchant W. H. Cline named the town Sunnyside. Lumber for his store had been thrown off the train across the river at Mabton, the nearest station. Cline had high hopes. Joined by another businessman, he built a three-story hotel and equipped it with a unique tri-level outhouse attached at the rear by walkways. Euphoria withered, however, as the Panic of 1893 sent the Northern Pacific into receivership and Granger's canal company to its creditors. A new company headed by Roland Denny, son of Seattle's Arthur Denny, took over. Through it all Granger somehow kept the water flowing, although effects of the depression caused Sunnyside's population to dwindle to just seven families.

In 1898 the town got a second start. Both seized by "colony fever" and recognizing a lucrative business opportunity, three midwesterners formed the Christian Cooperative Colony and bought Sunnyside's bankrupt townsite development company. Members of the Progressive Brethren, an offshoot of the German Baptist, or "Dunkard," denomination, announced:

We are building a community of church people who have no fear to express their convictions against saloons, Sunday desecration, dancing, horseracing, gambling, and other vices.

Every land deed included a forfeiture clause stating that pursuit of any such vices would cause the property to revert to the township company. This gave Sunnyside the nickname "Holy City," and also attracted several hundred families who welcomed life in a community of codified values.

A colony organizer acted as official greeter for newcomers. He met them with his hack at the train station in Mabton and attempted to keep up their courage as they crossed the desolate sage and sand. One prospective settler, told that all Sunnyside needed was water and a few good people, reportedly retorted, "That's all hell needs." Regardless, the combination, with its own rail link added in 1906, allowed Sunnyside to grow. Ironically, by the time the Northern Pacific got its branch line to Sunnyside, canal seepage and breaks had raised the water table so much that the town had turned soggy. Mud oozed between the planks of the wooden sidewalks and basements stood brimful of water.

At about the same time that the railroad arrived, the U.S. Reclamation Service took over irrigation responsibility by buying the Washington Irrigation Company. Small towns grew up along canals that were built, maintained, and administered by the government. Washington immigrants consistently tried to create communities that were as refined and up-to-date as those they had left. Isolated farmsteads miles from neighbors—symbol of the West—were not an ideal here, only a temporary necessity.

TOPPENISH is a town of rebuilt false fronts and tidy brick. Railroad yards, Bureau of Indian Affairs offices, and a vacant sugar factory—plus outstanding historic murals—reflect aspects of its past. South of town is the Yakima Nation Cultural Center. *Toppenish* is a Yakima word meaning "sloping and spreading land." It refers to the broad plain that sweeps eastward from the Fort Simcoe area, the flat bed of an ancient lake repeatedly filled as ice-age floodwaters were dammed at Wallula Gap.

Steel rails crept up the valley during the summer of 1884, paralleling the Yakima River from the Pasco area toward present-day Yakima. A way station at the halfway point—with section house, telegraph office, and water tower—eventually developed into Toppenish. Arrival of the Northern Pacific proved a boon to local stockmen who suddenly could ship cattle and horses to eastern markets instead of trailing them.

One of the first to make use of this advantage

was Charles Newell, horse trader par excellence. He roamed the Yakima Reservation, and his cowboys helped tribesmen round up wild horses. Newell, who was fluent in the Yakima language, picked the best animals from makeshift corrals, and offered gold on the spot. In 1885 he shipped 1,300 head to New York City; 18 years later his business peaked with an annual shipment of 6,000 horses. British agents visited Toppenish in 1899 to buy horses from Newell for the Boer War.

Shifting policies in the Bureau of Indian Affairs strongly affected Toppenish's early prospects. Virtually concurrent with the arrival of the railroad, rumors started circulating that reservation land was to come under an allotment system. No longer would it be held in common by all native people living on the reservation. Instead acreage would be parceled out to individuals, somewhat the way homesteads went to white settlers who filed claims. On the basis of these rumors members of five Yakima native families—the Bowzer, French, Olney, Robbins, and Spencer families—claimed squatter's rights on rich farmland near the Toppenish section house. In 1887, when Congress finally passed the Dawes Severalty Act, these claims became their allotments.

Little development could take place on the allotments because of government restrictions. These included 20 years of trust status intended to protect inexperienced native landowners from glib-tongued real estate developers. During that time no land could be sold in "downtown" Toppenish, although a few homes and businesses were built with private understandings between builders and allottees. A string of flimsy shops went up along the railroad right-of-way, nicknamed "Paradise Alley"; no merchant cared to invest much where he could not own the land. In 1905, when allotment holders at last were allowed to sell their land, Toppenish and neighboring Wapato quickly bloomed.

In 1918 the Utah & Idaho Sugar Company built a processing plant in Toppenish, one of three in the Yakima Valley using locally grown sugar beets. All closed after only a few seasons because of infestation by leaf hoppers. In 1931, the U.S. Department of Agriculture announced the development of a new variety of beets resistant to the blight. Aided by the Northern

Pacific, the sugar company sent farmers to Idaho to see for themselves the wonders of the new beet seed. As a result, a bigger processing plant was built at Toppenish in 1935. It operated until 1980.

Prime attraction at Toppenish today is the **Yakima Nation Cultural Center** (U.S. 97 at the southwest edge of town). The building's distinctive roofline echoes that of the large tule-mat lodges traditionally used as winter homes by the Yakima people. Inside are a restaurant, gift shop, theater, library, and thought-provoking museum. By focusing on Spilyay (Coyote, the Trickster), displays evoke Yakima attitudes toward animals, natural resources, and spiritual wholeness.

Since 1923, tribal and Indian Agency offices have been in Toppenish. (See YAKIMA RESERVATION, p. 148.)

Today's **UNION GAP** is a suburb of Yakima, but in 1870 it was the largest settlement in newly organized Yakima County. Its history is lengthy.

In 1855—before the town began—army regulars and citizen militiamen led by Major Gabriel Rains sought to offset an army defeat at Toppenish Creek. They skirmished with native warriors at Union Gap—or tried to do so. Lieutenant Philip Sheridan, of later fame as a Civil War general, wrote that the "Indians . . . marched and countermarched" in a noisy demonstration intended as "a blind to cover the escape of their women and children."

The Yakima successfully fled, and the troops moved on to Ahtanum Creek. Twin monuments, forlorn within steel mesh fences, now stand by the southbound lanes of U.S. 97 about 2½ miles south of Union Gap. They memorialize—and summarize—the opposing viewpoints represented by the clash. (Also see SAINT JOSEPH'S MISSION, p. 142; and YAKIMA WAR sidebar, p. 148.)

The engagement at Union Gap came at the onset of open hostilities between natives and newcomer whites. Headstones associated with the closing episodes of that epic struggle are in the quiet Union Gap cemetery (east end of Ahtanum Avenue). They belong to Blanche and Lorenzo Perkins, killed in 1878 by Umatilla men who were avenging a wanton gunboat attack on Columbia River fishing camps. The murder of the young couple greatly alarmed all whites in Washington Territory; the shelling of two villages distressed all native people. (See PLYMOUTH, p. 171; and VERNITA, p. 118.)

About a decade after the Yakima War ended, a white settler named Sumner Barker built a gristmill on Wide Hollow Creek at the south end of present-day Union Gap (Main Street at the entrance to U.S. 97). For decades the mill served the developing town as a commercial nucleus, and it still is operational, although remodeled and twice moved to make room for highway improvements. A turbine has replaced the original mill wheel.

In the summer of 1884 "Prosperity and Progress" drew closer to Union Gap (then called Yakima City) as Northern Pacific rails crept up the valley. However, December brought a devastating announcement: the railroad company would build a station 4 miles north of the established town in a sand and sagebrush wilderness. Yakima City merchants moved their stores to the new site. The older town, later renamed Union Gap, did not die but neither did it recover its previous eminence.

A sugar refinery built in 1917 has been converted for use by the state highway department as district offices (2809 Rudkin). It was the first of three sugar beet processing mills in Yakima Valley. (Also see TOPPENISH, p. 145.) Steam tractors, hop-picking equipment, and other early-day farm machines are displayed at the Central Washington Agricultural Museum; demonstrations each August. (Follow Main south to U.S. 97, then turn right at the Fulbright Park entrance.)

WAPATO (Wah´-puh-toh) lies in a valley between sinuous brown hills. In its outlying areas, glistening canals web a green swath of apples, cherries, mint, vegetables, grapes, hay, and hops. The town's layout, with spacious fruit warehouses close to the railroad tracks, reflects both contemporary economic life and civic beginnings. The name Wapato is the native word for a plant widely dug for its starchy roots, and a term also used for potatoes.

In the early 1900s, when clear titles to native people's land allotments became legally possible, the Wapato postmaster Alex McCredy

bought 80 acres from a Yakima Indian man named Frank Meacham. He platted the town and for his own gracious home reserved the south end of Third Street, a broad avenue with a central strip of trees. His house is gone but the site is now a city park.

White farmers bought and leased reservation land from allottees, then took advantage of government irrigation projects to turn the sagebrush desert into lush farms. They were not alone in the valley's development. It was Japanese contract laborers, brought in by the Northwest Development Company, who tended the first apple orchard on the Yakima Reservation. Their community expanded so rapidly that in 1915 at least 500 Japanese people lived in the area while the total town population was only 650. Wapato itself had a "Japanese town," which included several stores selling traditional foods and supplies.

In 1921 and 1923 the state legislature passed Alien Land acts, which prohibited Japanese farmers from directly leasing land, although they still could farm. As a result these people became sublessees, sometimes working through friendly white neighbors, sometimes with less friendly opportunists. Several Japanese immigrants had private, informal agreements with Indian landowners. On paper, these showed the Japanese as hired hands. Whatever the arrangement, the farmers constantly increased efficiency, producing tons of melons and vegetables from very small plots. With traditional respect for education, they established a Japanese Language School in the 1920s, which students attended after their regular school day ended. The first Japanese American to graduate from Wapato High School did so as the class valedictorian.

After Japanese planes attacked Pearl Harbor in 1941, causing the United States to declare war on Japan, an infamous federal Executive Order evicted 1,200 Yakima Valley residents of Japanese ancestry from their homes. Early plans called for internment southeast of Toppenish (a camp was built and fenced) but ultimately they were sent instead to Heart Mountain, Wyoming, for the duration of the war. The 10 percent who came home in 1945 found "No Japs Wanted" signs in store windows. Most never returned.

Beginning in the 1920s Filipinos also immigrated to the Yakima Valley to work on farms. These people came to the United States with special immigration status as citizens of an American territory. Many idealistically expected to pursue higher education but instead found prejudice and only menial employment. In Wapato they banded together in cooperatives for mutual economic and social advantage, buying property as they became able.

Most who came were Ilocanos from northwestern Luzon, a people known for their sturdiness and adventuresomeness. These qualities were severely tested during the 1930s Great Depression when impoverished locals vented resentment on visible "outsiders," whom they viewed as job competitors. Even earlier (1927) a gang of hooligans drove from house to house dragging Filipino farmers from their beds and beating them. Some they forced onto freight trains bound for Seattle. Such harassment continued sporadically until World War II and, more than once, Filipino families had to take refuge in the homes of white friends. Desperately distressed, yet undeterred, most Filipinos remained in the community, and names like Ibatuan, Arreola, and Tabayoyon are still common. (Also see EAST TO AMERICA sidebar, p. 194.)

One third of Wapato's population is now Latino. This began as an influx of farm workers

YAKIMA WAR

Native and white cultures clashed openly and tragically in the Yakima area during the 1850s. Neither side could control its hotheads. Neither had a unified policy or clear leadership.

The civilian territorial government considered the army lax, and the army resented the territory's volunteer troops. The white citizens feared hostile natives. Most native people welcomed guns, horses, cattle, potatoes, wool blankets, and the like; but resented whites treating them as inferiors and taking their land. Some chiefs feared white reprisal. Others so resented injustice that they favored fighting.

Treaties were a thorn. Governor Isaac Stevens virtually forced signatures without negotiating or even listening, then immediately announced that eastern Washington was open for settlement. Chief Kamiakin reacted by trying to organize a confederacy to stop invading whites. Miners, particularly, swarmed across Yakima land, often stealing horses and raping women. Native men struck back and, when agent Andrew J. Bolon went to investigate, he was murdered.

Major Granville Haller immediately marched north from The Dalles to retaliate, but met defeat at Toppenish Creek (3 miles south of where Fort Simcoe soon was built) in October 1855. Attacks also erupted in the Puget Sound country and in the Rogue River Valley. Volunteer militia units quickly formed. With 350 of these men and 350 army regulars, Major Gabriel Rains marched into Yakima territory to settle the score. At Union Gap his men skirmished with natives, then went on to Ahtanum Creek, where they burned a Catholic mission. Rains actually achieved little except to warn Chief Kamiakin that he would make "war forever, until not a Yakima breathes in the land he calls his own."

Rains' troops returned to The Dalles after this expedition, but the volunteers camped in the Walla Walla Valley and made forays, took prisoners, and demanded surrenders. Peopeo Moxmox, a Walla Walla, was among the chiefs who surrendered. To the horror of native peoples, the army, and many citizens, "while under the sacred protection of a flag of truce" Peopeo Moxmox was killed. A few volunteers even desecrated his body and kept pieces as grisly souvenirs.

Colonel George Wright, commander at Fort Vancouver, moved up the Columbia River to settle the Yakima "problem" once

when Yakima Valley farmers were desperate for help during World War II. Most American young men were in the armed services. Many wage earners had gone to defense plants on the coast. And Japanese American farmers had been expelled to "relocation centers." Remaining farmers heartily welcomed the federal government's Bracero Program, which allowed Mexican laborers to enter the United States on a temporary basis annually during harvest season. (*Bracero* comes from the Spanish "brazo," arm; used in this context it offends people who find themselves thought of as arms rather than whole persons.) Some Mexican laborers became

migrant workers, following crops annually from Texas through Colorado or California to Washington and back again. Many "settled out" in areas such as the Yakima Valley, which offered a long season of agricultural work.

Wapato's annual Cultural Unity Fair (held in the spring) celebrates this community's diverse ethnic heritage. Junior high school students perform dances from a variety of traditions, and the whole community delights in the food and music of Japanese Americans, Filipinos, Latinos, Native Americans, African Americans, and Americans with European backgrounds. (Also see FARM LABOR sidebar, p. 137.)

and for all. While he was still on the march, a large raiding party attacked Columbia River settlements near present-day North Bonneville, and troops steamed dramatically to the rescue from both Fort Vancouver and Fort Dalles. Wright returned to the river and established forts, then continued north.

He particularly wanted to talk with Kamiakin. The chief did not want war; he knew it was futile. His confederacy had never really formed. Yet he was afraid to surrender. On the Naches River (near the present-day town of Naches) Wright built an earthen breastworks topped with willow baskets of rocks, which earned the nickname "Basket Fort." He also established a base camp in the Kittitas Valley and from there pursued Yakima people who had fled into mountain valleys. At the Wenatchee River he came upon a large fishing camp and took hostages, including Chief Teias, an uncle of Kamiakin's, to insure "the good behavior" of the other tribesmen.

Wright talked with several chiefs, who all expressed a desire for peace. He gave them ultimatums (which they ignored); marched his hostages to the site that became Fort Simcoe; and proclaimed that the war was over. He felt the army had demonstrated to the chiefs that it could

control access to fisheries, root grounds, and grazing grounds; and had demonstrated to citizens, volunteer troops, and territorial government in general that it was in command.

The matter was far from that tidy, however. General John Wool, commander of the Department of the Pacific at San Francisco, ordered the establishment of Forts Simcoe and Walla Walla, and urged Congress not to ratify Stevens' treaties. This created such an uproar that Wool was replaced by General Newman Clarke, and Governor Stevens was forced to resign as superintendent of Indian affairs. Affronted, Stevens also resigned as governor and (successfully) sought election as territorial delegate to Congress.

In May 1858 prospectors near Colville petitioned for army protection, and Colonel Edward Steptoe marched north— to meet defeat and humiliation. In September, Colonel Wright again took to the field. In a series of decisive battles and brutal demonstrations of power near Spokane, he made good on his earlier proclamation that the war was over.

(Also see ROSALIA, p. 198; sidebars SPOKANE BATTLES, p. 10, ST. JOSEPH'S, p. 142, UNION GAP, p. 146, and PUGET SOUND WAR, p. 326.)

The road to **WHITE SWAN** passes redolent acres of mint and mazes of hops backdropped by Mount Adams to the west and Mount Rainier to the northwest. Originally called Stwireville, the town began near several farms that belonged to Yakima native people, among them Joe Stwire, also called White Swan. In 1868 the Yakima elected him chief to succeed Spencer, a Klickitat who had been appointed by the government when Kamiakin refused to move onto the reservation at the close of the Yakima War. Chief White Swan's brother, Stwire George Waters, had been trained for the Methodist ministry and he established a church at Stwireville. In 1908 a trading post opened, to be followed later by Joseph Miller's movie house. In his will Miller left land for the Yakima Indian Christian Mission, a boarding school where industrial arts and religious subjects were taught from 1921 to 1962. The school's brick buildings still stand south of town near the powwow grounds.

Powwows are held at White Swan in spring and summer at the traditional council grounds southeast of town. Native people come from throughout the Northwest and beyond to dance, magnificently costumed. The public is welcome; photography usually is permitted but heed any announcement to the contrary. The Tiinowit Powwow, held in early June, commemorates the signing of the 1855 treaty.

YAKIMA sits in a broad valley of orchards surrounded by velvet brown hills. The major city in south central Washington, it prides itself on agricultural preeminence. An outstanding museum warrants a visit, and many buildings from the town's early days remain to impart a sense of continuity.

In December 1884 the Northern Pacific Railroad decided to bypass Yakima City (now called Union Gap), the only town in the county. To the dismay of people there, the company placed its depot 4 miles north on an unpopulated sagebrush plain. Railroad officials claimed that a swamp prevented laying rails through the town, but more likely the lure of cheap, undeveloped land was the motive. To promote their new town, the railroad offered free lots plus moving expenses to all Yakima City businessmen who opened shop at the new location by May 1, 1885.

Economic pragmatism overcame civic outrage, and most merchants packed up and

Yakima grew as federal irrigation projects got under way in the 1900s. The valley offered good soil, a favorable climate, and river water to pump or divert into canals. (Photo taken in 1908.)

moved north. They brought their buildings with them. David Guilland's hotel was on the road for a month, laboriously pulled on rollers by mule teams. Four-inch planks placed in front of the rollers smoothed the uneven ground. Hotel business continued during the journey; patrons slept in their rooms, and the dining rooms offered full meals.

Yakima City was substantially depopulated and in 1885 voters chose North Yakima, the upstart community, as county seat. The courthouse too was rolled to the "city of the future," and the newspaper crowed:

This Christmas Day a new era flooded with joy opens on the people of the Yakima Valley, for to us is born a Messiah of Commerce.

In 1918 county seat residents complained that their "North Yakima" sounded like a suburb, and the two towns became Yakima and Union Gap respectively.

Early settlers raised livestock on the bunch-grass hills, driving both cattle and sheep to market. In the late 1870s privately built irrigation projects hastened the transition from ranching to farming. But not until 1902 when the federal government's fledgling Reclamation Service (now the U.S. Bureau of Reclamation) unified irrigation efforts did real progress begin. From 1900 to 1910 the population of the Yakima Valley tripled, and the city of Yakima established its commercial and social domination of the region. Today nearly half a million irrigated acres in the Yakima Project grow apples, hops, cherries, grapes, pears, asparagus, hay, and mint.

Points of interest, keyed to the Yakima map:

1 The **Boise Cascade Mill** (I-82 at the northeast corner of Yakima) is a direct descendant of a sawmill established in 1903 by three businessmen, including A. E. Larson, builder of the landmark Larson Building. Loggers felled trees for the mill along the Teanaway River near Cle Elum and used the spring floods to float them through Yakima Canyon. These annual river drives took five to six weeks, with a panoply of loggers in calked boots walking on floating logs to corral strays, or to break up jams with dynamite. Each season

brought lawsuits as the brimming river left logs stranded in farmers' fields. Relief came in 1917 when the company switched to rail transportation. Today the mill produces lumber and plywood, which are shipped by truck.

2 The **William Lindsey Home** (301 N. Eighth Street) was one of the houses rolled to North Yakima from Yakima City (Union Gap). It has been remodeled but vertical lines and square nails indicate its 1880s construction.

3 **Saint Michael's Episcopal Church** (Yakima and Naches) received a gift of land from the Northern Pacific Railroad, but members fretted that their building was so distant from the train depot it would forever be on the fringe of town. The church, completed in 1888, was built of basalt quarried near Painted Rocks (6 miles west of town) and hauled by horse and wagon. It was the first stone building in the new town of North Yakima. Originally only 25 feet by 48 feet, it has been expanded twice, but always using the same stone and always retaining rough-cut interior walls.

4 The **Capitol Theater** (19 S. Third Street), one of a chain that stretched from Yakima to Walla Walla, opened in 1920. Marcus Priteca, known for his Pantages theater plans, designed this Renaissance Revival–style building. Among the greats who appeared here were Madame Ernestine Schumann-Heink, Isadora Duncan, Anna Pavlova, Mischa Elman, Nelson Eddy, and Sousa's Band. A fire in 1975 caused severe damage, but the city took the opportunity to rebuild and has turned the venerable theater into a performing arts center. Tony Heinsberger, who painted the original dome murals, came out of retirement at age 83 to repaint them.

5 The **William O. Douglas Federal Building** (S. Third Street and E. Chestnut; built in 1911) was so named in 1980 to honor Yakima's most famous son, who occasionally held judicial hearings in the building. Douglas grew up and attended high school in Yakima before going on to Whitman College in Walla Walla and Columbia University Law School. He taught and practiced law for 10 years before President Franklin D. Roosevelt tapped him for the Securities and Exchange Commission. Douglas' massive reorganization of Wall Street, including more strict government supervision of corporate stock transactions, brought him

Yakima

Key to Numbered Locations

1 Boise Cascade Mill
2 William Lindsey Home
3 Saint Michael's Episcopal Church
4 Capitol Theater
5 William O. Douglas Federal Building
6 A. E. Larson Building
7 Lund Building

8 Switzer's Opera House
9 Northern Pacific Depot
10 Yakima Valley Transportation Company
11 Gilbert House
12 Yakima Valley Museum
13 Belinda Carbonneau's Home
14 Congdon Castle

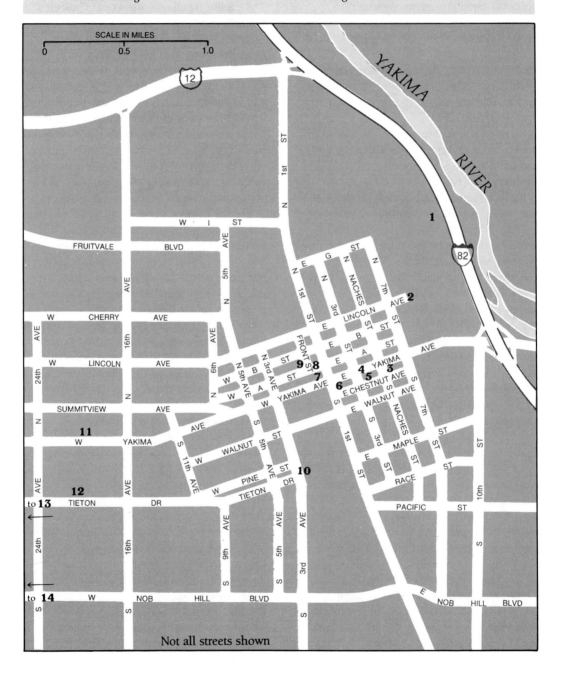

Not all streets shown

inclusion within the president's "inner circle." In 1939 Roosevelt appointed him to the Supreme Court, where he served for 36 years, longer than any other justice.

Douglas' fierce defense of the First Amendment and uncompromising stands on conservation issues alienated him from conservative compatriots in Yakima. The *Daily Herald* ran an article deploring his politics and praising the Americanism of his erstwhile high school teachers. "Yakima is not to blame," the article concluded. Nevertheless, Douglas retained many ties here, including a home on Goose Prairie in a mountain valley west of Yakima. He died in 1980, five years after he left the Supreme Court.

6 The **A. E. Larson Building** (Yakima and Second Street; built in 1931) is an Art Deco treasure. Decorative elements of the roofline seem to flow over the exterior walls' 13 shades of brick. Enter the elegant lobby to enjoy the terrazzo floors and ornamental metalwork—in particular, the bronze elevator doors.

7 The no-frills **Lund Building** (Yakima and Front; built in 1889) housed the Alfalfa Saloon. Its location at the intersection of the nascent community's two main thoroughfares guaranteed a steady trade. Rough-hewn local rock forms the walls.

8 **Switzer's Opera House** (25 N. Front) enjoyed steady patronage when it was the only theater in town. But its flat floor and stage illumined by kerosene lamps could not compete with newer, modern houses. In 1897 Switzer's was sold at sheriff's auction to the North Yakima Brewing and Malting Company. Prohibition later closed that enterprise, and new owners remodeled the interior as a warehouse for a moving and storage company. In 1982 echoes of the past filled the building when Bert Grant opened a highly acclaimed microbrewery and pub.

9 The **Northern Pacific Depot** (Front and E. A), once the city's economic heart, is again in use. It houses offices and a pub. The building went up in 1909 to replace an earlier one.

10 The **Yakima Valley Transportation Company** (Pine and Third Avenue) clanged into operation on Christmas Day 1907 with interurban trolley cars that hauled both freight and passengers. Such mass transit had an incalculable effect on the direction of Yakima's growth;

electrified line reached 43 miles west and north. The 10 miles that remain are a treasured vestige of the interurban rail systems that served western communities from early in the twentieth century until after World War II. Rides to Selah now are offered from May to October (round trip: one hour and forty minutes). Take the ride—perhaps on a warm evening—to experience yesterday's pace. The Car Barn departure point still operates as a trolley maintenance shop, now with displays added. Check there for current ride schedules and fares.

11 The **Gilbert House** (2109 W. Yakima; built in 1898), now under museum auspices, is open to the public (small fee). Horace Gilbert developed 7,000 acres in the lower valley and was instrumental in irrigation projects near Yakima. The sagebrush land where he built this Queen Anne–style home is now a neighborhood of substantial homes.

12 The **Yakima Valley Museum** (2105 Tieton) houses the William Gannon collection of 73 horse-drawn vehicles, from surreys to stagecoaches to hearses. Alcoves display typical Yakima artifacts from distinct eras. Chief Justice William O. Douglas' study is reproduced in detail, including his eccentric collection of hats.

13 **Belinda Carbonneau's House** (670 S. 48th) marks the culmination of an extraordinary career. Belinda Mulrooney, daughter of Irish immigrants, parlayed a nest egg—earned while she was a housekeeper—into $8,000 by leasing a small lot on the Chicago and Columbia Exposition Fairgrounds to a Ferris wheel operator. In the 1890s she worked as a stewardess on steamships between Seattle and Skagway and, during the Klondike gold rush, she operated various businesses including a kennel for sled dogs, and an elegant hotel in Dawson City replete with electric lights and Turkish baths. She married Charles Eugene Carbonneau, a Frenchman who claimed noble blood but actually may have been a barber from Montreal. The two honeymooned in Europe, then in 1910 settled in the Yakima Valley where they built this mansion. Polite society held the Carbonneaus at arm's length, but Yakima remained their home base. The count died in 1916 while inspecting Allied supply lines in France. Belinda continued to live in her mansion until the 1930s, when she moved to Seattle.

14 Congdon Castle (Nob Hill near 64th) was built in 1914 by absentee landlord Chester Congdon of Minnesota as a getaway home. Congdon invested in Yakima orchard land and formed the syndicate that built the Yakima Valley Canal, the second largest system in the state (after Sunnyside).

The stone construction and steep retaining walls of the house soon earned it the "castle" nickname. Surrounded by private land—and emphatically not open to the public—it can be viewed from West Washington Avenue (between 48th and 64th). Until 1987 summer trolleys of the Yakima Interurban Lines used a route that passed the Congdon orchards and house. A judge forbade that excursion, however, agreeing with the Congdon family that since the rail easement had been given for the purpose of hauling fruit from the orchards, excursionist use of the route was invalid. The trolleys ceased.

The **YAKIMA CANYON,** stark in its sere splendor, offers a 25-mile scenic alternative to the freeway route between Yakima and Ellensburg. (Follow State Route 821 between Selah and Ellensburg.) In summer the river's gentle currents attract rafters who drift in flotillas of inner tubes. Roadside pullouts allow picnicking or daydreaming.

Thirteen miles north of Yakima watch for the **Roza Dam,** which diverts water into a 1941 canal that irrigates 72,500 acres in Yakima Valley. From 1915 until the early 1930s a mill occupied this site. It supplied sugar refineries with diatomaceous earth, which was used as a filtering agent. Steam shovels strip-mined the earth along Squaw Creek; trucks hauled it to the east bank of the Yakima River; and an aerial tram carried it across the river to the mill. Japanese miners and millworkers who ran the operation lived in dormitories at the site. No buildings remain.

The **YAKIMA FIRING CENTER** is frequently audible to the public, if scarcely visible. On 263,000 acres of sagebrush land, the U.S. Army trains thousands of soldiers from the National Guard, Army Reserves, and international units from Canada and Great Britain. Highway I-82 between Yakima and Ellensburg crosses part of this land. It offers magnificent views of both the Kittitas and Yakima valleys and of dry hills, which are particularly scenic early or late in the day when shadows accentuate their contours.

The **YAKIMA RESERVATION,** at over a million acres, is the largest reservation in the state. It stretches from the forested hillsides of Mount Adams to the irrigation-lush valley of the Yakima River. Roads in the timbered back-country are not open to the general public, as posted. A handsome museum at the Yakima Nation Cultural Center in Toppenish warrants a special trip.

After the "Indian Wars" of 1855 to 1858, the Yakima clustered on this reservation—leaderless, disillusioned, and in poverty. By terms of the Treaty of Walla Walla they had ceded 90 percent of their traditional lands; with that enormous loss, their annual round of food gathering was suddenly all but destroyed. In despair, people clung to their inherent spirituality in a resurgence of traditional beliefs. Many followed Smohalla's Dreamer religion, which held out hope that adhering to traditional ways would rid the country of the white intruders. Other people became Shakers, a sect that combines elements of native belief with Christianity. (See MUD BAY, p. 354.)

In 1860 James Wilbur, a Methodist missionary, began a long tenure among the Yakima, first as a teacher and later as an Indian agent. He launched a "Bible and plow" program and worked earnestly for the "betterment" of the Yakima. He taught farming skills by personal demonstration and opened a vocational boarding school at agency headquarters, the former Fort Simcoe. He strove to enforce the law equitably for natives and settlers alike, and frequently sued whites who pastured animals illegally on Yakima land.

In 1887, five years after Wilbur's departure as agent, a change of policy in Washington, D.C., fostered legislation that threatened the reservation system. The Dawes Severalty Act of 1887 stipulated that each member of a tribe should choose up to 160 acres within the reservation. The object was to encourage personal endeavor, a "yeoman farmer" ethic dear to the hearts of Americans. Unfortunately, many

Zillah's Teapot Dome gas station exemplifies "automobile age" architecture.

allotments were soon sold out of Yakima ownership. Moreover, plots that remained in native hands were divided and redivided by heirs of the original allottees, a fragmentation of ownership that compounded the difficulties of land use. The Yakima Nation now has an ongoing commitment to buy back for tribal management any allotments that come on the market.

Additional land problems arose when a successor to Wilbur persuaded the Yakima to sell their Wenatchee fishery in exchange for an irrigation canal on the reservation. This further hastened the transfer of reservation land out of Yakima control. Early allottees, lacking expertise and expensive machinery, leased their land to white or Asian-American farmers, or sold outright. A great deal of land on the Yakima Reservation—today immensely valuable—thus passed out of native ownership.

The current Yakima Nation is governed by a council of 14 members, a recognition of the 14 "tribes and bands" that were signatories to the 1855 treaty. The council encourages education, improved housing, environmental enhancement, and economic opportunity on the reservation.

ZILLAH's orientation to the railroad tracks and

a major irrigation canal speak of its past.

William Granger, builder of the Sunnyside Canal, made his home here, and it was he who named Zillah to honor Zillah Oakes, daughter of the president of Northern Pacific Railroad. Like other communities in the lower Yakima Valley, the town thrived as an agricultural center and shipping point for local produce. From 1900 to 1910, when land sold for $55 per acre with perpetual water rights, the area attracted a sizeable influx of Dutch immigrants. A later wave of migration is reflected in the tortilla factory at the east end of town.

Also east of town (accessible from I-82 at Exit 54), the Teapot Dome Service Station spoofs the Wyoming oil-lease scandal of the same name. Headline news in the early 1920s when the station was built, the scandal sent Secretary of the Interior Albert Fall to prison for accepting money connected with the granting of government leases to private producers. The station is shaped like a fat, white teapot with a red handle and spout. Such structures—from teapots to teepees—enjoyed nationwide popularity during the 1920s and 1930s as automobiles and an expanding road network created a "highway culture."

Columbia Gorge

The Columbia River long ago carved a water passageway through the Cascade Mountains, a dramatically beautiful chasm between basalt bluffs. There, for thousands of years, villages stood at creek mouths; and there fur traders and settlers traveled between the interior and the Willamette Valley and on to Puget Sound. In time, steamboats and railroads followed the same route. Dams now subdue the Columbia, and enormous barges pushed by tugboats link eastern Washington to salt water. In 1986 Congress declared the Columbia Gorge a National Scenic Area.

Highways line both sides of the gorge: a freeway in Oregon, a two-lane highway in Washington. Both roads provide spectacular sight-seeing. Small communities, once dependent on logging and fishing, now provide amenities for travelers.

From the rolling, wheat-covered highlands near Goldendale, four volcanoes are in view: Mount Rainier, Mount Adams, Mount St. Helens, and Mount Hood. Of special interest are an eccentric millionaire's mansion-turned-museum at Maryhill, and a well-equipped public observatory at Goldendale. A small history museum at Goldendale is also worth visiting, as is an outstanding interpretive center at Stevenson.

BEACON ROCK. (See under SKAMANIA, p. 163.)

BINGEN (Bin´-jin) relies on wood products for its economy, although windsurfing, not logging, is now what catches the eye. High inland temperatures meet lower coastal temperatures within the Columbia Gorge and produce steady summer winds that blow opposite to the river's current. World-class windsurfers flit across the river as fast as 30 miles per hour. Their sport originated in southern California in the late 1960s, but aficionados claim that conditions in the Columbia Gorge are better—indeed, are nearly perfect.

The first farm in the gorge was Erastus Joslyn's, begun in 1852. Three years after he arrived, native people who were friends brought him warning of impending attack, and he and his family fled across the river. From there they watched hostile tribesmen drive off their livestock and burn their buildings and

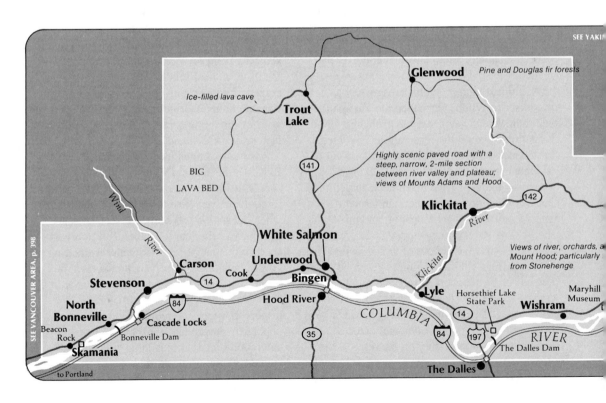

orchards. They rebuilt. Additional settlers came. And soon steamboat landings were established, and fruit orchards planted on the benches above the river.

Nobody really distinguished between the communities of Bingen on the flats and White Salmon on the bluffs until the 1874 arrival of the Suksdorf family who bought the old Joslyn homestead. Disputes over water rights and property lines then sundered the two communities, and the Suksdorfs, who were German immigrants, named the lower community after their home city on the Rhine River.

Watch along the talus slopes between Bingen and Lyle for a showy, deep rose penstemon that has gray foliage in summer, bronze in winter. The Columbia Gorge is home to many rare plant subspecies, nine of which are unknown elsewhere.

Workers built **BONNEVILLE DAM** during the Great Depression, at the same time that the Grand Coulee Dam went in upstream. The two federal projects inaugurated the large-scale harnessing of the Columbia River's hydroelectric potential. Electricity is now distributed throughout the Northwest and in California by the Bonneville Power Administration. Their visitor center, on the Oregon side of the river, includes historical exhibits and fish-viewing rooms. An Army Corps of Engineers visitors' center on the Washington side features self-guided tours that permit actually standing on top of a generator watching it spin (through Plexiglass) and stepping inside a cut-out section for a close-up view of the huge shaft and wicket gates, which control the amount of water falling onto the blades. There also are talks, audiovisual programs, and some guided tours.

CARSON, on a broad bench above the Columbia near its confluence with the Wind River, retains many of its early false-fronted buildings. A hot-springs hotel established in the 1890s still welcomes visitors. (From State Route 14 take either Wind River Road or Hot Springs Road toward Carson; the springs are about 1 mile east of town in the river canyon.) Stepping through the curtain into the old hotel's bathhouse induces a time warp: an attendant ministers to bodies that steam in rust-ringed, deep bathtubs or lie on cots swaddled in flannel sheets. River murmurs waft through the open door.

After an early career of fighting in the 1847 Cayuse War, packing freight to the Idaho mines, and steamboating on the Columbia River, Isadore St. Martin settled down here to develop the hot springs. He built the three-story, false-fronted hotel for guests who came by steamboat to take the waters. St. Martin unswervingly defended the health-giving qualities of the springs and died during a quarrel with a visitor who disputed his claims.

Since the early 1900s Government Mineral Springs (15 miles north of Carson via Wind River Road) has attracted campers who sample the sharp-tasting, cold mineral water of "Iron Mike" and other springs. Large firs and maples surround the springs.

DALLES DAM. (See THE DALLES DAM, p. 165.)

GLENWOOD. (See under WHITE SALMON, p. 166.)

GOLDENDALE, from its earliest days to the present, has been a commercial center for surrounding farm and timberland. Never

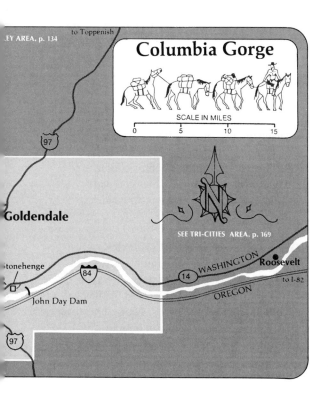

a major hub, it projects a homey, self-reliant atmosphere.

The county historical society museum, housed in the Presby Mansion (127 W. Broadway), exhibits early photographs, antique Klickitat Springs Mineral Water bottles, and a collection of regional cattle brands. Nine blocks south of the museum, the Charles Newell House (Columbus and Sentinel; built in 1891) has long been a landmark. With its tall, slender proportions and red paint, it is fondly called "The Red House." Newell made his fortune as a horse trader. (Also see TOPPENISH, p. 145.)

In 1859 eastern Washington reopened to settlement following the army's suppression of a native uprising, and the Golden family—along with a few others—trailed hundreds of cattle onto open range here. Once settled they earned cash by cutting wood for steamboats plying the Columbia. The bitter winter of 1860–1861 killed nearly all their cattle, and some families then turned to raising sheep. Wool and mutton offered a double chance at profit; also, lambs cost less than cattle for a new start. By 1888 more than 150,000 sheep were summering in Klickitat County.

Cattlemen generally hated the "woolly locusts" because of their close grazing. Their disgust is clear in this sign posted at a water hole:

NOTISE

All land in woods past
Draper Springs is for Settlers
cattle. No sheep is allowed.
Sheep men take notise.

Comitee

Nor was tension limited to ranchers. Sheepmen and cattlemen both complained that farmers plowed under the best crop Klickitat would ever produce—its grass. Regardless, a farming economy emerged by the late 1880s. When a railroad spur line connected Goldendale to the steamboat landing at Lyle in 1903, wheat became a profitable crop.

An **astronomical observatory** (1½ miles north of town via Columbus Avenue) delights amateur observers. Goldendale first got a taste of astronomy in 1918 when the Lick Observatory in California sent observers here to study a total eclipse of the sun. In the late 1960s four amateur astronomers sought a home for the 24-inch reflecting telescope they had painstakingly constructed. The town of Goldendale responded by building a public observatory, which opened in 1973. Now operated as a state park, it has two domes and several telescopes.

North of Goldendale, the **Bolon Monument** commemorates murdered government agent Andrew J. Bolon, whose death in 1855 triggered the Yakima War. (Follow Columbus Street north and continue as it becomes Bloodgood, then Pine Forest. After 5½ miles turn north on Cedar Valley Road and continue for 3 miles. The monument stands along the old trail between Celilo Falls and the Yakima Valley, 4 miles southwest of the actual site it commemorates.) Bolon, on his way to confer with Chief Kamiakin about the recent ambush of miners in Yakima territory, was himself waylaid and murdered. Su-el-lil, as a young boy, witnessed the murder and recounted the tale years later:

What I am telling you happened before the war with the soldiers. It was about the close of huckleberry time. The Indians had returned from the mountains, and our party was on its way to The Dalles to get dried salmon. . . . Soon we saw a man going on this trail, coming after us. . . . He was white. I had never seen a white person before. . . . Chief Mo-sheel was at the head of our party. He knew the white man [and he] spoke to his people: "This is the man who hanged my uncles and cousins at Wallula."

Bolon actually had not done this but, when he joined the native men around a warming fire, Mo-sheel and two others killed him. Tensions that had been building ever since the Walla Walla Treaty Council four months earlier quickly erupted into warfare between native people and whites. (See YAKIMA WAR sidebar, p. 148.)

HORSETHIEF LAKE STATE PARK, a recreational green oasis brightening a brown riverside, occupies the site of ancient Wakemap (Wah´-kuh-map), a native village at the head of the Columbia's Long Narrows. Petroglyphs and pictographs pecked and painted onto nearby rocks still overlook the site (trail closed except by appointment, owing to vandalism). A cemetery near the park entrance includes graves

Tsagaglalal *("She Who Watches")* gazes timelessly from cliffs west of Horsethief Lake. Nearby, today's fishermen pass the tip of Wakemap Mound, a village site now flooded by the lake.

moved from funerary islands and river flats flooded by water behind The Dalles Dam.

William Clark's journal describes Wakemap in 1805 as "a great emporium . . . where all the neighbouring nations assemble." Routes north-south and east-west converged in this area for, although people also crossed mountain passes, the river offered easier travel between the coast and the interior. The rapids provided rich fishing—and also terrorized white travelers. French-Canadian voyageurs bestowed the name Les Dalles (Anglicized in pronunciation as "dals"). The name, "paving stones" in French, refers to slanting, partially submerged basalt slabs.

JOHN DAY DAM—locks, hydroelectric plant, spillway, and fish ladder—stretches across the Columbia 200 miles above the river's mouth. Visitor facilities include an underwater fish-viewing room on the Oregon side. Water impounded by the dam is reserved for irrigation; locks, with an unusual vertical gate, lift vessels 113 feet into Lake Umatilla. An aluminum smelter, with its huge power needs, is the dam's immediate neighbor and a major underpinning in the area's economy.

KLICKITAT is a sawmill town with its main industry and small houses ensconced within a

narrow valley. The scenic canyon drive to the town along the rushing Klickitat River warrants a special trip (State Route 142).

The Klickitat tribe, renowned for fine basketry, lived both here and in the White Salmon river valley. They planted fruit trees, supplied by the Indian agency, on allotments of land they had accepted in preference to moving to the Yakima Reservation. (Maryhill Museum, on the Columbia River south of Goldendale, exhibits beautiful Klickitat baskets.) The Klickitat River is one of the "usual and accus-tomed" fishing places reserved by treaty; native fishermen still use dip nets to lift salmon from the foaming water.

Early-day white settlers sought crucial winter shelter in the Klickitat Valley for their stock. The Wright family found the valley especially appealing and settled here in 1889. They raised cattle and drove them to the Lyle steamboat landing for shipment to Portland. In 1903 the Columbia River and Northern Railroad, poorly ballasted and crooked-tracked, snaked down the valley from Goldendale to Lyle. Ranchers welcomed the new ease of shipment and built sheep and cattle corrals near present Klickitat. The Columbia River and Northern also purchased steamboats to continue its link to Portland. Five years later a north-bank railroad along the Columbia obviated need for the boats.

Since 1909 family-owned sawmills have formed the framework of Klickitat's economy, producing pine lumber for eastern markets and, in earlier days, box "shook" (precut fruit box pieces) for the Hood River and Yakima valleys. Today's mill, no longer a local operation, produces approximately 80 million board feet of pine lumber annually.

Tapping natural carbon dioxide seeps near the Klickitat River, a company called Gas-Ice Corporation built a plant in 1932 to produce dry ice. Its now-abandoned Mission-style building is in a shady public fishing area 1 1/2 miles east of Klickitat. The company obtained 99.6 percent pure carbon dioxide from wells 300 to 1,100 feet deep. Theirs was the first use of natural carbon dioxide for dry ice production.

At first the product was unfamiliar; Gas-Ice Corporation sold only 500 pounds throughout the Northwest. But as shippers became knowledgeable, demand increased dramatically. By 1936 the company produced 18 tons of dry ice per day. Dry ice has twice the refrigeration capacity of water ice and, instead of melting into puddles, sublimates and disperses as gas.

Railroad cars and trucks refrigerated with dry ice transported fruit, dairy products, and other perishables.

LYLE began as Klickitat Landing. Steamboats nosed into a sandbar here, and farmers and deckhands herded stock up temporary ramps. Situated at the junction of a railroad from the uplands and one along the Columbia, Lyle added sheep sheds and warehouses to its two hotels, two saloons, bank, and sawmill. The town's name commemorates James Lyle, who filed a plat in 1880 before the arrival of either railroad.

East of town the river bluffs are spectacular for their clearly separate basalt flows, formed by at least six outpourings of lava from vents in southeast Washington and northeast Oregon. The bluffs stand bare of soil to about the 1,000-foot level, the high-water mark for ice-age floods about 12,000 years ago.

Sam Hill planned the **MARYHILL MUSEUM,** a Flemish-style chateau perched on the bluffs above the Columbia, as a home. Today the

Native Americans still dipnet salmon at a traditional Klickitat River fishing station.

Financier Sam Hill dreamed of a Quaker colony at Maryhill and built a mansion as a "ranchhouse." He entertained lavishly in the house but never really moved in.

building (open March 15 to November 15) houses an eclectic art collection, from Romanian thrones to Rodin sculptures.

Hill was an enormously energetic financier who in 1888 married Mary Hill, eldest daughter of Great Northern Railway magnate James J. Hill. Three years later the couple moved to Seattle. From that home base Sam invested in companies throughout the Northwest and fell in love particularly with the area where he soon built Maryhill. He dubbed it "the land where the rain meets the sun" and soon bought property with vague plans for a Quaker agricultural community. When attempts to attract settlers failed, he decided to operate the property himself as a ranch. He brought in cattle, planted orchards, and in 1914 started to build a home overlooking the Columbia. Hill never lived in the house, though he described his intent:

I have planned it for a good, comfortable and sub-stantial farmhouse. Here I can let the world wag as it will. It is large enough to have a few friends drop in and take potluck with me. I can keep them warm in winter and cool in summer. On the roof we will have our outdoor bedrooms throughout the summer months, and we can look up and watch the wheeling constellations wing across the night sky, or look down on the sea-seeking Columbia or at Mt. Hood in all its varying moods. . . . I expect this house to be here for a thousand years after I am gone.

The "farmhouse," 60 feet wide and 400 feet long, included vehicle ramps at either end for access to the main floor. No wood was used in the building; interior walls are of steel-stud construction with plaster over metal lath. In 1917 Hill postponed additional building, and he later decided to complete the house as a museum.

In 1926 Queen Marie of Romania, a friend of Hill's, traveled from Bucharest to Maryhill under the watchful eye of every society editor in the nation. Her purpose was to dedicate the "museum." What she found was an embar-rassingly unfinished hulk in an austere landscape. Marie's regal training carried the occasion. Speaking from an improvised wooden throne, she graciously paid tribute to "vision" and "great dreams."

Sam Hill once declared that "Good roads are more than my hobby, they are my religion." He lobbied Congress for road construction, visited other countries as an ambassador of good-roads associations, and endowed a chair of highway engineering at the University of Washington. Roads on his ranch served as proving grounds for various surfacing materials. The twisting old roads, visible east of State Route 97 as it climbs the bluffs above the Columbia, remain from his experiments. In the 1950s they were used for sports car road races.

Between 1913 and 1915 Hill masterminded construction of an elegant highway along the Columbia's Oregon side. He lobbied the Oregon legislature, invested his own money, hired

Sacked wheat and crated fruit came by wagon to Grants Landing (across from Maryhill); from there, shipment was by rail to Portland. (Notice the piles of firewood for steamers to use as fuel and the stove, doubtless part of someone's freight order.)

Italian stonemasons to build retaining walls, and enlisted tree surgeons to repair damaged trees. In particular, he recommended Sam Lancaster as chief engineer for the project—a remarkably sensitive man who treated each tree and boulder as sacred and disturbed no more than necessary while threading the highway along the walls of the gorge. A modern freeway at water level now replaces Lancaster's highway, but segments of the old road can still be driven. (The most spectacular sections are near Portland: a 27-mile scenic loop stretches from Troutdale to Warrendale between Exits 17 and 37 off I-84.)

(Also see STONEHENGE, p. 164.)

NORTH BONNEVILLE began as worker housing while the dam was being built in the 1930s; it moved to this site in 1976 when a new powerhouse was added at the dam. Such newness—even that of the 1930s—belies the long history of settlement near this site.

The most violent rapids on the river, called the Cascades, churned just above here. They formed about A.D. 1250 after a landslide on the Washington side of the gorge blocked the

Columbia and backed water to about the present site of McNary Dam (135 miles). Eventually the river cut through, but its channel stayed constricted and studded with boulders and small islands; the narrowing caused the rapids. Native tradition supplies another explanation: a natural stone bridge spanned the river but was cast down because of human misbehavior.

Native people here—though so far inland— were culturally and linguistically related to the Chinook at the mouth of the Columbia. They lived in coast-style plank houses and bound their infants' heads to produce an elongated shape long regarded by the Coast Salish as attractive. Additional evidence of ties to the coast comes from Lewis and Clark's comments about finding glass beads, brass tea kettles, and blue and red cloth at this village, indication of trade with downriver people who, in turn, traded with white mariners. The Cascade people also had a thriving trade with tribes on the Columbia Plateau, probably exchanging salmon for biscuit root in addition to trading a great deal of exotica.

The rapids worked as an advantage. They

provided a rich fishing ground and also forced travelers to portage their canoes. That gave local chiefs control both of routes between coast and interior and of the flow of trade goods. When Pacific Fur Company traders began to explore upriver from their new post at Astoria in 1811, tensions quickly developed between natives and whites. Pilfering and harassment became rife as villagers helped themselves to a share of the traders' goods yet tried not to discourage them from continuing to use the river as a travel route. Worse, a virulent fever (probably malaria) wracked Columbia River villages during the 1830s, killing an appalling 80 percent of the population. The Cascade people disappeared as a distinct group; their few survivors joined other bands.

The 1840s brought an influx of thousands of American settlers traveling the Oregon Trail toward Willamette Valley or Puget Sound. The portage around the Cascades—at the end of a long, exhausting journey—was especially trying. Elizabeth Geer recorded in her journal that after five days spent reassembling wagons at the Upper Cascades (the eastern landing point above the rapids), her party began the portage:

We have 5 miles to go. I carry my babe and lead, or rather carry, another through the snow, mud, and water, almost to my knees. It is the worst road that a team could possibly travel. . . . I was so cold and numb that I could not tell by the feeling that I had any feet at all. . . . There was not one dry thread on one of us—not even my babe.

By 1850 other immigrants had built a 1½-mile, mule-powered, wood-railed portage tramway around the Cascades. It was a crude affair, but for those who could afford the rates, it eased the unrelenting toil of the portage, and it fostered a small community catering to the needs of the travelers. A competing line imported the Northwest's first steam locomotive, the "Pony," to pull cars along tracks on the Oregon side of the river. In 1869 these railways joined forces to monopolize portage business on the river.

In March 1856 a brief but dramatic battle took place at the Cascades between U.S. Army troops and plateau warriors allied with local people. A surprise attack drove settlers to shelter in a strongly built store while hostile natives torched other nearby buildings, including a sawmill. A steamer, the *Mary,* was waiting at the dock for military supplies to be loaded. The crew, seeing the attack and coming under fire themselves, got up steam, hacked their mooring lines, and cast off for The Dalles.

Simultaneously other natives attacked the settlements at the Middle and Lower Cascades, where settlers escaped to their boats and paddled to Vancouver. The siege lasted only overnight; army contingents steamed to the rescue from both east and west. A military tribunal hanged nine native men whose rifle barrels were black with powder, and the existing fort at the Middle Cascades was reinforced by blockhouses upstream and down. All three blockhouses were abandoned five years later, when troops withdrew to fight in the Civil War. A small town called Cascades developed at the lower landing; it served as the Skamania county seat until a disastrous flood in 1894 washed away most of the buildings.

The *Mary* and its companion vessel below the Cascades, the *Belle,* were among the first of a great paddle-wheel fleet on the Columbia. With the 1860 discovery of gold in Idaho, boat-builders scurried to "mine" the hordes of miners needing transportation. They produced shallow-draft, stern-wheel steamers that plied the river between rapids; portage railways carried passengers and freight to the next navigable stretch of the river. In 1896 the federal government opened the Cascade Locks to bypass Cascade Rapids. By then the construction of railroads—along the Oregon side in 1882 and along the Washington side in 1908—was preempting much of the river freight business. Cascade Locks operated until 1937 when new locks were built into Bonneville Dam.

Today the Columbia is again a major thoroughfare: tugs nudge huge barges along the subdued waterway, carrying mostly grain downriver and petroleum products upriver.

SKAMANIA is a small community tucked into a forest of cedar, alder, and big leaf maple. It is below the highway at the western gateway of the 75-mile-long Columbia Gorge. Two miles to the east, **Beacon Rock** looms as an 840-foot landmark; a switchback trail to the summit offers sweeping views up and down the gorge. The formation originated as a plug from the throat of a former volcano: it is a layered tower of olivine basalt left freestanding when the softer rock around it eroded away. At the turn of the century, concerned people bought the landmark to forestall a quarrying operation that would have reduced it to stone blocks for the jetties at the mouth of the Columbia. The group later donated the land for a state park.

At the west side of **STEVENSON** an outstanding interpretive center presents both natural and historical aspects of the Columbia River Gorge. The town became county seat in 1893, one year before a major flood swept away the town of Cascades, the former seat of government. George H. Stevenson platted the new town (named for himself) and set aside land for the county offices. He was active in state government, railroads, and, in particular, fish wheels.

The site—near the head of Cascade Rapids— was ideal for fish wheels. These massive waterwheels, 40 feet in diameter, turned by the power of the current. They had three or more mesh baskets, which relentlessly and profitably scooped salmon from the river and dumped them into receiving scows. Spawning salmon struggling upstream avoided the swift midstream current and swam close to shore. The wheels, either in fixed locations or on moveable scows,

exploited the salmon's well-traveled routes.

The first Columbia River fish wheel was built on the Washington shore in 1879, nearly 50 years after a comparable technology had been developed on East Coast rivers for shad. The Dalles and the Cascades provided optimum sites; the river as a whole had approximately 75 wheels operating by 1883. In this area fish were transported from the wheels to the canneries in an ingenious way. Attendants strung 1,000 pounds of the salmon onto manila lines, which they tied to a wooden cask. When several of these casks were ready, the men set them adrift to float to the cannery downstream. There a lookout, stationed on a balcony, used a steam whistle to guide workers in skiffs, who rowed out and snagged the buoyant loads.

Oregon finally banned the wheels in 1926; Washington passed similar legislation in 1934. Although fish wheels took a relatively small proportion of the catch, they were considered too efficient. Along with fish traps, gillnets, and seine nets, the wheels had depleted the resource for all time.

STONEHENGE overlooks the Columbia River 3 miles east of the Maryhill Museum. Begun in 1918 and completed in 1930, Sam Hill's copy, in reinforced concrete, of Britain's Stonehenge stands as a memorial to the dead of World War I. To achieve a dressed-stone texture, workers lined forms with crumpled tin. As at the real

Fish wheels, widely used throughout the West, provided an extremely efficient way to catch salmon— too efficient. In a single year (1883), Columbia River wheels took 42 million pounds of fish.

Stonehenge, they aligned pillars with the summer solstice sunrise (although the Klickitat Hills actually eclipse the dawn's first rays). A popular theory in Hill's day held that the central altar stone at the original Stonehenge had been used for human sacrifices to insure victories in war. Hill thought it ironic that the modern world still sacrificed its young to the gods of war.

Stonehenge stands on the site of yet another of Sam Hill's projects, the town of Maryhill, named for his wife. A hotel and other buildings succumbed to fire long ago, but the fountain that once adorned the hotel's entrance still stands along the approach road to Stonehenge. Sam Hill's burial marker, downhill from Stonehenge toward the river, is inscribed, "Amid Nature's great unrest, he sought rest." In addition to Stonehenge and Maryhill, Hill built a concrete Peace Arch near Blaine and a concrete home near Volunteer Park in Seattle.

Before Hill's arrival, a town called Columbus spread along the riverbank here. Steamers churned this section of the river, and pioneers cashed in on the boats' presence by cutting cordwood north of Goldendale and hauling it by wagon to a landing at Columbus. A six-ox team could haul five cords, taking two days for the round trip. Since a steamboat burned 170 cords on an average round trip, the woodcutters enjoyed a sellers' market.

Boat captains usually loaded enough wood here to carry them to Lewiston and back. The *Webfoot,* a wide stern-wheeler launched on this upper-river run in 1864, once loaded only 60 cords at Columbus. She ran out of wood at the mouth of the Tucannon River, and the captain had to buy 35 cords of inferior willow at an exorbitant price in order to puff on to Lewiston. He elected to drift with the current on the downriver journey.

THE DALLES DAM zigzags across the Columbia east of the city of The Dalles, Oregon. Exhibits at the visitor center highlight the native culture of the gorge, including petroglyphs rescued from shorelines that were inundated by dam construction. A small train carries visitors to the powerhouse and fish ladders. Like other dams on the lower Columbia and Snake rivers, this one includes massive locks to accommodate ship and barge traffic between coastal cities and inland ports.

TROUT LAKE. (See under WHITE SALMON, p. 166).

UNDERWOOD is a small community at the mouth of the White Salmon River. For more than 60 years the Broughton flume ended just west of town. It was a 9-mile, water-filled trough that carried rough-sawn boards from a lumber mill at Willard to a finishing mill on the Columbia. Representative of hundreds of such flumes operating earlier in the century, the Broughton flume was the last of its kind in Washington. It closed in 1986. Its trestles still snake along the cliffs west of Underwood.

A side trip to **Big Lava Bed,** northwest of Underwood, offers a glimpse of the volcanic origins of the landscape north of the river. (From Underwood, drive 7 miles west on State Route 14. Just west of Drano Lake, turn north on the Cook–Underwood Road; follow it 5 miles, then turn left on Willard Road. After 2 miles turn left again on S. Prairie Road. Park at the junction of Road 050 and explore on foot.) The Big Lava Bed is a 12,500-acre jumble of rock, punctured by caves and overlain with moss. Maintaining a sense of direction can be difficult here; take care to note landmarks before venturing far from the road.

WHITE SALMON lies on a gravel bench 700 feet above the Columbia River. Peach orchards (and others) fringe it on the north.

In the decade from 1905 to 1915 real estate promoters touted dryland apple orchards as the ideal crop for this area, and investors bought thousands of acres sight unseen. Local managers planted seedlings and often grew strawberries between the rows of trees as an interim crop. Insufficient rainfall and the impracticality of irrigation soon stifled success, however, and the severe winter of 1919–1920 further discouraged all but the most favorably situated growers.

White Salmon's spectacular views of the Columbia Gorge appealed to early-day vacationers, and this led several families to offer lodging to paying guests. The Jewett Farm Resort, operated by the town's founders, became nationally known. Arriving steamboat passengers could reach the hillside town via a flight of 652

The last of the lumber flumes that once were common in Washington angled down the river bluffs near Underwood. They provided efficient transport in an era with few roads.

wooden steps or a longer but gentler trail.

From the dock stage lines ran to the interior communities of Glenwood and Trout Lake, an area rich with views of fields, forests, and volcanoes. Early settlers logged the hillsides and pastured dairy cattle in the valley bottoms. Cool lava caves west of Trout Lake facilitated storing locally made cheese and butter.

Today the Forest Service maintains a picnic area at an ice cave where near-perfect natural insulation keeps winter rain seepage frozen all year. (Follow State Route 141 west from town for 5½ miles. Be careful when entering the cave; it is difficult to distinguish damp stone from slick ice or standing water.)

A Forest Service office in Trout Lake supplies maps and directions to huckleberry fields on the flanks of Mount Adams. Native people traditionally moved here in the late summer to lay in a winter's supply of berries. The practice continues among families who come from both coast and interior villages.

The railroad town of **WISHRAM** is sandwiched between river and bluffs below State Route 14 (Milepost 192). It began in 1904 when Spokane, Portland and Seattle Railroad crews arrived to tunnel through the hill east of town and to bridge the Columbia River. Ever since then, the town's economic life has depended on railroad jobs.

A mile downriver from Wishram, Celilo Falls—among the richest traditional fishing grounds on the Columbia—now lies drowned by a placid lake. For thousands of years men fished the cataract on both sides of the river, standing on precarious platforms that jutted out from the rocks. In the summer of 1811 fur traders counted 3,000 people camped on the Washington side to trade, socialize, and fish for salmon.

The Wyampam people, whose traditional home was at Celilo Falls, never moved onto the Yakima Reservation; they preferred instead to remain at their fishery. Often they fished in pairs, one man sweeping a long pole through the water, the other manipulating the dip net attached to it. By concentrating salmon runs, river constrictions provided the best locations for dip netting. Hereditary rights determined the use of specific fishing stations. Today the old-style netting continues on the Klickitat River above Lyle and on the Fraser River in British Columbia.

On March 11, 1957, native people from all over the Northwest gathered to watch and mourn as the closing gates at The Dalles Dam caused slack water to cover Celilo Falls. By 4:00 P.M. the roaring cataract had become still.

SOUTHEAST Region

Livery stable, Walla Walla.

THE SOUTHEAST corner experienced Washington's earliest missionary efforts—the Whitmans' ill-fated 1830s to 1840s establishment at Waiilatpu—and it remained a focal point with the 1855 Walla Walla treaty council and the U.S. Army's subsequent garrisoning of Fort Walla Walla. In the 1860s an Idaho mining boom made Walla Walla a supply point offering everything from gold pans and picks to flour and bacon. The town quickly burgeoned into the largest metropolis within the borders of what became Washington state.

The boom also fostered agriculture. At first farms were limited to river bottoms in the Walla Walla area, but before long they also climbed the slopes and carpeted the Palouse hills with wheat, barley, and oats. Loess—windblown soil that holds moisture and lies 100 feet deep—produced well. A fleet of steamboats, begun in 1859 by the army and expanded to transport miners, soon was carrying the grain to Portland brokers, who shipped it all over the world. Half the value of the crops went to pay transportation costs, however, for cargos had to be unloaded, portaged, and reloaded to get around rapids. In time, the siren call of profit led railroad companies to solve the problem by threading lines throughout the rich farmlands of the Palouse and into the flood-scoured Channeled Scablands.

In 1879 the Northern Pacific picked the confluence of the Snake and Columbia rivers—today's Tri-Cities area—for the beginning of its transcontinental line up the Yakima Valley and over the Cascade Mountains. The rails first provided construction payrolls, then brought the link to markets that allowed farm communities to blossom. Industry arrived during World War II when the top-secret Hanford Engineering Works drew thousands of newcomers to develop plutonium for the atomic bomb dropped on Nagasaki in 1945. At the time, less than a century had passed since Cayuse warriors had rid themselves of the pioneering missionaries at Waiilatpu: the region had passed from frontier to technological center capable of fueling holocaust.

Tri-Cities

The Tri-Cities of Richland, Pasco, and Kennewick overlook the confluence of three major rivers: the Columbia, Snake, and Yakima. Richland, the technological member of the trio, offers exhibits dealing with nuclear physics and the history of nearby Hanford Reservation atom bomb production. Pasco, the town the railroad brought to life, has a state park and a visitor center at the confluence of the Snake and Columbia rivers. Kennewick has a history museum that breathes life into the region's agricultural past.

Scenic drives include the highway along State Route 730 southwest of Wallula and State Route 221, which crosses the high, open country of the Horse Heaven Hills. At Paterson, vineyards cover 18,000 acres; across the Columbia, Echo embodies Oregon *and* Washington history.

AINSWORTH. (See PASCO, p. 170.)

ATTALIA. (See under WALLULA, p. 174.)

BENTON CITY, a cluster of homes and spacious schools, is situated on a high bench where the Yakima River bends sharply north. Founded by a railway engineer, the town got a boost in 1910 when 20 families from Bremerton arrived to settle on newly irrigated tracts. Its next great influx came during World War II when the population of 200 suddenly quadrupled, owing to the establishment of the nearby Hanford atomic energy reservation.

Smaller **Kiona,** across the Yakima River from Benton City, retains well-tended homes but no commercial enterprises. It began in 1885 with the arrival of a Northern Pacific section foreman and his family. In the early 1900s Horse Heaven Hills ranchers drove to the river near Kiona to get water for their stock. Their eight-horse teams could haul 500-gallon water tanks.

BURBANK grew into a town as early-day ferry passengers lingered to rest, or shoe their horses, or buy a meal. In 1905 a private company tried to supplement the area's meager seven inches of rainfall by developing irrigation. Hopeful farmers planted fruit trees, grapes, and alfalfa, but the boom soon faded. The irrigation company went bankrupt, and the project barely limped along until the arrival of water from the federally financed Columbia Basin Project. Burbank then stirred back to life.

Anticipating irrigation water via new canals, Pasco area farmers in 1909 cleared sagebrush.

FORT NEZ PERCE/WALLA WALLA. (See under WALLULA, p. 174.)

HANFORD RESERVATION. (See under RICHLAND, p. 172.)

ICE HARBOR DAM, the first of the four lower Snake River dams, was completed in 1962. Self-guided tours of the powerhouse and locks are available every day, year-round. A fish-viewing room and a visitor center are open in summer. Displays range from local Native American culture to Snake River navigation and computer games dealing with hydropower. Driving across the dam is permitted during daylight hours.

Ice Harbor takes its name from a nearby cove where steamboats tied up when the river was ice-bound. The Snake River flows for a thousand miles from its headwaters in Yellowstone National Park to its confluence with the Columbia at Pasco. It carries a volume greater than the combined flows of the Colorado and Sacramento rivers.

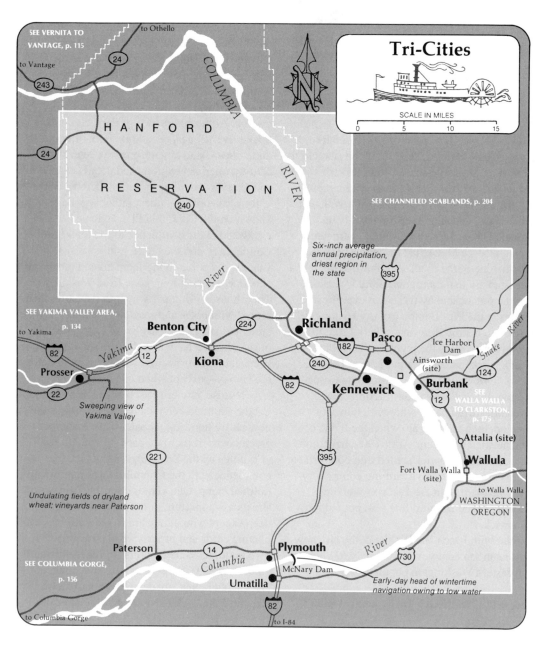

The Snake and Columbia rivers, now dammed, form a 470-mile water link to the Pacific.

At **KENNEWICK** 3 miles of riverfront are preserved as Columbia Park, ideal for picnicking and musing. A paddle-wheel from a river steamer is at the park, and a marker commemorates the 1850s "road" between Walla Walla and Naches Pass, which crossed the river here. Jefferson Davis, Secretary of War, instructed Captain George McClellan to "at least endeavor to fix the line of the road" and improve the worst places enough that immigrants could "render the route practicable by their own exertions." Exhibits at the East Benton County Historical Museum in nearby Keewaydin Park (205 Keewaydin) portray the region's development.

Kennewick came to life in the mid-1880s as the Northern Pacific began work on its Cascade Division. It faded when construction crews moved on, stirred back to life with hopes of irrigation, then faded again when the Panic of 1893 throttled optimism. After 1900, irrigation resumed and Kennewick settled into comfortable patterns as a conservative farming community—only to be overrun in the 1940s as workers streaming to the Hanford Site also poured into Kennewick.

Along with Pasco and Richland, the city now forms an urban complex second only to Spokane as an eastern Washington population center.

Water behind **McNARY DAM** floods Umatilla

Rapids, where low water from November to March stopped early-day riverboats. A community on the Oregon side of the river accommodated travelers, and a ferry crossed to Washington.

In 1945 Congress authorized McNary Dam and a series of Snake River dams to provide reservoirs and locks for slack-water navigation as far inland as Lewiston, Idaho.

PASCO is webbed by freeways and bridges, which tend to confuse travelers despite highway signs. Near the old center of town, the domed county courthouse (10161 N. 4th) epitomizes early dreams of importance, and 1906 railroad employee cottages stand as a visual reminder of the Northern Pacific's impact (A Street between First and Sixth). The houses, built by the company, were called "Red Row" for their boxcar-red paint, a uniformity no longer present. At the confluence of the Columbia and Snake rivers, Sacajawea State Park offers tree-dotted lawns and an interpretive center with Native American exhibits and details of Lewis and Clark's arrival near here in October 1805.

Remnants of the largest pithouse village known on the Columbia Plateau have been excavated at the confluence of the Snake and Columbia rivers; they date to at least 1,000 years ago. People living there hunted bison and antelope, animals long gone from Washington. Their houses—dug partway into the earth, then roofed with poles and mats—were both easy to build and snug. Students living experimentally in such houses have found that a small fire keeps the interior warm even in winter and not too smoky—except when one is standing.

In a sense, modern Pasco began as a Northern Pacific Railroad camp called Ainsworth, a site now partly flooded and partly converted into the green lawns of the state park. In 1880 the site (1½ miles up the Snake River from its confluence with the Columbia) was a brawling railroad camp. One visitor described Ainsworth streets as "a mixture of dust and sand, ankle deep except where they are paved with old playing cards and broken whiskey bottles." Two hundred white laborers, storekeepers, and gamblers, 200 Chinese laborers, and abundant "lacquered ladies" made up the population. Captain John C. Ainsworth, an official of the

Oregon Steam Navigation Company, commented that it was "anything but a compliment" to find his name given "to such a miserable place."

The Northern Pacific chose the site in 1879 as a starting point for completion of its transcontinental railroad. Funds had run out six years earlier with rails ending at Bismark, North Dakota, then resuming between Kalama and Tacoma. This left a 1,500-mile gap, even though the line to Tacoma technically met the deadline of reaching the Pacific by December 1873. The new plans called for laying track northeast from Ainsworth and also connecting to Wallula, where a paddle-wheel ferry would cross to existing tracks along the left bank of the Columbia. They in turn, would connect to Kalama.

For ties and other construction timbers, crews cut logs on the upper Yakima and Clearwater rivers and floated them to mills at Ainsworth. To lay track as fast as possible men spaced ties at four times the normal distance (and later filled in the gaps), and they bridged the Snake River at Ainsworth using stone quarried at Granite Point (near Wawawai) for the support piers and hand-hewn logs for girders. By the time the bridge's iron superstructure arrived around Cape Horn from the East Coast, the skeletal bridge was ready. It opened in April 1884—just after the collapse of the financial and organizational empire put together by railroad titan Henry Villard. The two companies he had linked—the Northern Pacific and the Oregon Railway and Navigation Company—then reverted to separate operations.

This led the Northern Pacific to resume its original plan to cross the mountains to Puget Sound rather than to continue skirting them via the Columbia River, a decision of major significance for regional development because it diverted traffic away from Portland. To start construction up the Yakima Valley, the company moved its camp from Ainsworth to Pasco. Ainsworth proprietors shifted saloons, stores, and shops to the new town, and the county seat soon followed.

Pasco became the railroad's division point with shops, roundhouse, and offices. Additional railroad construction beginning in 1906 included replacement of a temporary bridge across the Columbia built by the Northern Pacific in 1888, the first to span the river. (The replacement is still in use.) At the same time the population boomed with an influx of dryland homesteaders and a promise of irrigation. A second, even greater population explosion came in the early 1940s with the opening of the Hanford Project, an Army supply depot, and a Navy air station. From a dusty farm town of about 4,000 people, Pasco leapt in a few months to more than 10,000 with another 50,000 people living at adjacent construction sites and secret installations.

To solve the severe wartime labor shortage, companies advertised in the Deep South and sent recruiters. Previously Pasco had been the home of only a few blacks associated with the railroad, mostly porters and laborers. The sudden arrival of as many as 3,000 blacks set off intense racial discrimination, including segregated buses and authorization for the police to pick up blacks "for investigation" without any specific charge. As late as 1967 law students from Gonzaga University in Spokane and the University of Washington rallied on the steps of the Franklin County Courthouse to protest such practices.

PLYMOUTH was the site of a tragedy during the Bannock-Paiute War of 1878 (which was the last organized effort of native people to resist the white invasion of the Northwest). A government steamboat fired Gatling guns and muskets at two Columbia River fishing villages, an attack described by eyewitness Andrew Pambrun, a Hudson's Bay Company employee:

The squaws were busy washing the Salmon . . . [and] the little children happy in their innocence played along the beach . . . when suddenly the destructive missiles came screaming in like hail, laying waste to everything that came within their range, men, women, and children.

Incredibly, soon after the attack, soldiers on board the boat picked among the dead, taking curios. As retribution for the mass killing, an innocent white couple en route to Yakima City soon also met death. Their murder, in turn, sent volunteer militia reporting for duty and settlers huddling into stockades expecting an uprising that never came. Events already had forced Washington natives into accepting the new order. (Also see VERNITA, p. 118; and visit **Echo**, 4 miles south of Umatilla, site of a fort and Indian agency.)

In the hills north of Plymouth the Switzler brothers grazed as many as 15,000 head of horses, and cowboys rounded up hundreds every year for shipment east. At that time, the only railroad was on the south side of the Columbia. Consequently, the Switzlers swam herds across the river by stampeding them toward a chute that debouched into the water. A cowboy waited there in a boat to guide the lead horse across, and the rest followed, panic stricken. By the 1890s, market prices for horses had dropped and, in any case, dryland wheat farmers were claiming so much land that the herds had become a nuisance. The Switzlers held their last great roundup and sold the horses to an Oregon cannery.

RICHLAND, self-proclaimed "Atomic City" and bastion of high-technology in eastern Washington, occupies the point of land between the Yakima and Columbia rivers. Displays at the Hanford Science Center (Jadwin Avenue) are expected to be expanded into a new museum in conjunction with the Washington State Historical Society. It is to highlight not only the city's role in developing the second atomic bomb but also the entire regional story. Neighborhoods with World War II "alphabet houses," hastily built from standard blueprints, still stand: styles A and B, duplexes; E and F, cottages; etc.

Settlers made no real attempt to wrest a living from this desert land until 1863. In that year, John B. Nelson and his family built a scow at Wallula and poled upstream to the mouth of the Yakima River to raise livestock. They were joined in the 1880s by Ben and Mary Rosencrance, who opened a stage station and also raised horses, which they hired out for railroad construction. In addition Rosencrance built a 36-foot waterwheel to lift river water into a flume for irrigation, then added a fruit and vegetable business to his other enterprises. In time, developers extended a canal west of Rosencrance's irrigation system and platted the town of Richland.

The community grew only modestly until 1942 when the population jumped astronomi-cally from 200 to 17,000 as the federal government in 1943 forced farmers and the towns of Hanford and White Bluffs to abandon their land and began a "top-secret wartime project." Thousands of workers moved into trailers and barracks hastily nailed together at Hanford, 25 miles upriver, a camp totaling 51,000 people, which for a while ranked as Washington's fourth largest "city." After the war most moved away. Others settled in Richland, where the government built houses for them.

The General Electric Company became the primary peacetime contractor for the Hanford Project and also the town's landlord and city services administrator. Residents remember that they called the company even to have a fuse changed or a faucet washer replaced. The government continued its property ownership until the late 1950s, when it finally let residents buy the homes they had been living in for years and also let the city again incorporate. Population growth continued as Cold War tensions called for the stockpiling of atomic weapons.

Tours of the **Hanford Reservation** (originally 640 square miles, now reduced) can be arranged for busload groups; contact Hanford Westinghouse Company. Or travel State Route 240 for a distant view of installations. Isolated Gable Mountain (visible to the northeast) was a Wanapum vision quest site where youths fasted and meditated to make contact with spirit helpers. It also is where scientists drilled tunnels to study the feasibility of storing radioactive waste in basalt (never actually done).

About 35 miles north of Richland, where the highway nears the Columbia, atomic reactors stretched along the river for 10 to 15 miles. The first two were built in 1944 and 1945 as part of the Manhattan Project: the Hanford Site produced plutonium for the Nagasaki bomb; Oak Ridge, Tennessee, produced uranium for the Hiroshima bomb; and Los Alamos, New Mexico, did the final loading of both bombs. On Tuesday, August 14, 1945, Richland newspapers carried a headline of pride, relief, and staggering incongruity: "PEACE. Our Bomb Clinched It."

In postwar years additional reactors and chemical plants were added, and plutonium production continued. During the Cold War,

Hanford waste tanks actually held a major portion of the U.S. uranium supply. Efforts to recover it added ferrocyanide to the mix, itself now a cleanup problem. Scores of tanks with millions of gallons of hazardous waste constitute Hanford's "farms" today, bitter replacement for the pre-war orchards and fields. Solving the literal mess still involves thousands of workers, still requires security-gated operations amid the otherwise empty land where Indians hunted bison 2,000 years ago and where a last stretch of the Columbia still flows free. The cleanup is now the largest federally funded public works project in the United States. Hanford challenges adequate perception and perspective, yet is a world focal point.

WALLULA (Wah-loo´-lah) is a tiny, quiet community. It moved to this present site in 1953 to escape the water rising behind McNary Dam. It has had two other locations.

In 1816 Donald McKenzie, a trader with the North West Company, suggested abandoning the company's fur post on the Spokane River as "useless and expensive" and opening instead a new post in the Walla Walla region. Two years later a construction party of nearly 100 employees arrived at the site McKenzie had picked, a half mile north of the Walla Walla River mouth. This same general area earlier was "claimed by Great Britain [and] the N. W. Company of Merchants from Canada," according to a notice David Thompson had

The Hanford B Reactor (right center; 1945 photo) was the world's first major plutonium producer. Ironically, coal-fired steam has always supplied energy for Hanford operations.

nailed to a post at the confluence of the Snake and Columbia rivers in 1811.

McKenzie's men built a formidable stockade called Fort Nez Perces, a misnomer since it was Cayuse people, not Nez Perce, who lived in the area (and the name eventually changed to **Fort Walla Walla**). The first structure was a double-palisaded enclosure with 200-gallon reservoirs of water for use in case of fire or attack. Trade was conducted through an 18-inch-square window, as was common at most posts. Brigades outfitting here trapped as far east as Wyoming and Montana and south through Nevada and down the Colorado River to the Gulf of California. Polyglot personnel included Coast and Plateau natives, occasional white Americans, Iroquois, Hawaiians, Englishmen, Scotsmen, and French Canadians.

In 1841 the fort burned, and the Hudson's Bay Company, which had absorbed its competitor nearly 30 years previously, rebuilt with adobe bricks made of local clay and ryegrass. Despite a decline in furs, they continued to staff Fort Walla Walla until 1855 because of favorable trade with native people and because of its strategic location at the convergence of trails from the north, east, and south. Foundation stones from the fort—smooth waterworn cobbles—now lie beside a roadside marker on the west side of U.S. 12 near Wallula.

Soon after the Hudson's Bay Company abandoned the fort, its location became the first Wallula townsite. In the 1860s steamboats landed to connect with the various overland routes; most of their passengers were heading overland via Walla Walla to mines in Idaho and Montana. During a single month in 1862—the year Wallula was platted—stern-wheelers disembarked an average of 135 gold seekers each. Stagecoaches, freight wagons, and pack strings jockeyed for position along the river-bank, and the proprietors of saloons and the hotel eagerly garnered customers.

In 1874 the first railroad in eastern Washington linked Wallula to Touchet; a year later the tracks extended to Walla Walla. Farmers in the area had been selling grain to Idaho mining camps, and when that boom faded they needed desperately to reach Portland markets. Walla Walla entrepreneur Dr. Dorsey Baker saw this as an opportunity and financed,

surveyed, and built a railroad. He used wooden rails covered with half-inch strap iron and a small engine to pull passenger coaches and flatbed cars loaded with freight. The strap iron sometimes curled into "snakeheads" and slashed through floorboards, fortunately never causing serious injury.

Primitive or not, Baker's railroad served well enough that the Oregon Steam Navigation Company soon bought it. By then steamboating had dwindled. Rails were taking over. Wallula moved a mile east and became a railroad town replete with roundhouse. Its present location is another 2 miles to the northeast.

Madame Dorion Memorial Park, about a mile south of Wallula, honors a little-known Northwest heroine. This is Madame Marie Dorion, a Sioux, who according to fur traders was quietly competent and uncomplaining. The first woman after Sacajawea known to have crossed the continent on foot, she left Missouri in 1811 with her two young sons and husband, an interpreter for the Pacific Fur Company. Immediately after reaching Astoria the party turned back to the Snake River Basin with orders to establish trapping and hunting posts in the interior. Bannock warriors waylaid the party and killed the men, but Marie escaped into the Blue Mountains with her sons. She nurtured them through a bitter winter and, in spring, walked out to safety near the site of today's park.

Attalia is now marked only by a road a mile north of Wallula, but about 1900 a hamlet here epitomized many small communities clinging to existence as irrigation made its shaky debut. Attalia—like Burbank, Humorist, Hover, and a dozen other towns—began because of a private investment company. The procedure was to lay out a ditch and townsite, then advertise for farmers even though the desert actually offered chances for only marginal success.

By the 1920s all but the staunchest Attalia farmers had given up. Less and less water trickled down the Walla Walla River, where their ditch waited open mouthed. Probably overallocation upstream contributed to the scarcity, but who could hold out long enough to test the case in court? Land reverted to the county for nonpayment of taxes, and finally, as part of its preparation for McNary Dam, the federal government bought the few farms that remained.

Walla Walla to Clarkston

Fertile grainfields and prosperous towns characterize the extreme southeast corner of Washington. Walla Walla, its nineteenth-century mansions reflecting early wealth, sprang into being as a supply center for Idaho and for Montana gold mines. Smaller towns— Waitsburg, Dayton, Pomeroy, Clarkston—lie along the former Nez Perce Trail. Grain elevators and substantial homes in these towns reflect a century of service to surrounding rich agricultural districts. Whitman Mission, now a National Historic Site, lies 7 miles west of Walla Walla.

An exceptionally scenic road leads along the Snake River. Back-road enthusiasts also will enjoy the Couse Creek–Montgomery Ridge and Weissenfels Ridge roads (each about 15 miles long and with steep grades) between the Snake River and the Anatone area. Also sample the roads into the Blue Mountains beyond Cloverland. All offer views of deep, rugged canyons and high, broad grass- and wheatlands. All are passable in an ordinary car (but, if in doubt, ask locally about current conditions).

Historical museums are at Asotin, Chief Timothy State Park near Clarkston, and Fort Walla Walla Park . The Asotin County Historical Society leads a tour in June. Waitsburg hosts a Pioneer Festival in September.

ANATONE is a small dot on a windswept highland. Like many communities in southeast Washington, it was launched by the Idaho gold rush. In 1862 two partners built a sawmill here to cut lumber for the new city of Lewiston, Idaho, which was situated on land still legally part of the Nez Perce Reservation, but was booming as a supply point for Clearwater River miners. A rudimentary store sprang up near the sawmill. It amounted to an early-day convenience stop that let farmers space out their trips to Lewiston.

In 1878 threats of war came from a coalition of the Bannock and Paiute tribes, whose homelands were in Idaho and Oregon. As a precaution Anatone settlers built a stockade around a spring, setting its upright planks four feet into the ground. That summer U.S. Army troops marched past the stockade to the Grande Ronde River crossing, but no actual conflict erupted in the area. As tensions eased, a second

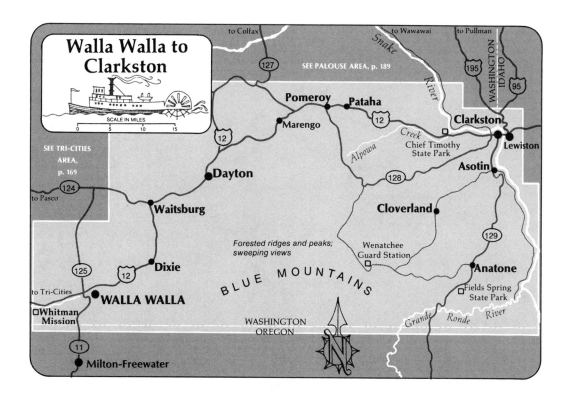

sawmill began cutting wood at Anatone and a "real" storekeeper set up shop, hauling his merchandise 80 miles by wagon from Dayton. In 1900 the community's population numbered close to 100.

South of Anatone, at the border between grasslands and the forested Blue Mountains, **Fields Spring State Park** centers on 4,450-foot Puffer Butte. The park contains a verdant "island" of trees, rich with bird song. A winding trail to the summit offers expansive views into three states.

The butte's name commemorates the A. J. Puffers who arrived here as homesteaders just in time for the Bannock War. Despite the general alarm among their neighbors, the couple built a house and began ranching operations with a herd of purebred cattle. For safety that summer of 1878, they simply camped out each night at a different place and, in the morning, climbed the butte to scan their farmyard.

Seventeen miles south of Anatone, State Route 129 crosses the **Grande Ronde River.** By native account Beaver carved the river's twisting course as he fled from the Pine Trees after stealing their closely guarded treasure—fire. Dropping from the Blue Mountains to the Grande Ronde Valley the highway twists nearly as convulsively as the river. It offers dramatic canyon views from every curve.

ASOTIN, the county seat, is a cluster of early 1900s brick buildings and comfortable homes on a sheltered flat by the Snake River. An 1899 church topped by an octagonal steeple graces the riverfront with classic Carpenter-Gothic lines, an architectural gem representative of the craftsmanship once common in small towns. An old flour mill and a 1906 powerhouse stand beside Asotin Creek Road (1 mile west of town; well worth exploring farther for a sense of countryside). The powerhouse supplied electricity for the entire region from Lapwai to Pullman at a time when homes were lit with single bulbs dangling from the ceiling. The county historical society museum (Third and Filmore) displays several pioneer buildings including a pole barn, which houses carriages and a collection of branding irons. The society conducts a historical tour each June. A riverside trail (bike, hike) leads from Clarkston to Asotin.

Native Americans camped at Asotin to fish for eels. Settlers came in the 1880s, and rival towns sprang up within shouting distance of each other—Asotin City and Asotin. By election in 1883, county seat honors fell to Asotin, which then merged with its neighbor. To win the election, Asotin had offered free rent, free office equipment, free fuel, and even free services by a treasurer and auditor. By that time, steamboats were calling to load grain from farms on

The Snake River flows from Yellowstone to Pasco; its gorge above Asotin is 2,000 feet deep.

the plateau above Asotin. By gaining status as county seat, Asotin was assured more offices and more people.

Outlying regions still display untrammeled beauty. **Snake River Road** twists south alongside the Snake River for 23 miles from Asotin to the mouth of the Grande Ronde River. Suburban neighborhoods quickly transmute to hay fields, and the paved road gives way to gravel. Intermittent sand beaches line the riverbank. Slightly upstream of Milepost 6, watch for timbers from an 1880s warehouse and grain pipe (on the side of the road away from the river). A four-inch pipe brought wheat from bluff-top fields to a riverboat landing here. Rapid descent scorched the grain; to prevent this damage, operators left the pipe full and emptied it at the bottom only as men shoveled in more wheat at the top.

The road continues past occasional ranches to Heller Bar, a small settlement and resort at the mouth of the Grande Ronde River. In the 1880s the town of Rogersburg grew up here around a Grande Ronde River ferry. South of this point the road continues up the Grande Ronde and Joseph Creek to the Wallowa Valley in Oregon.

CHIEF TIMOTHY STATE PARK is a manicured campground on an island near the confluence of Alpowa Creek and the Snake River. An interpretive center highlights the history of local Nez Perce people and of the small towns that replaced their villages.

Chiefs Red Wolf and Timothy farmed here, close to a trail that led from the confluence of the Snake and Clearwater rivers to the mouth of the Snake (near Pasco). In 1838 Red Wolf planted apple seeds supplied by missionary Henry Spalding. Irrigation ditches watered his orchard—six trees, the first in the region—and 30 acres of vegetables. When Lieutenant Colonel Edward Steptoe set out on his ill-fated "show of force" in 1858, he crossed the river here and accepted Timothy's offer of guidance. A Christian, Timothy had agreed to treaty terms with whites and may have felt some obligation to the army. The crossing lay within the Nez Perce Reservation until 1863—eight years after treaty terms had been set—when miners and settlers convinced the government to move the boundary east of Lewiston. Timothy, unwilling

to leave his homeland, broke tribal ties and filed a claim for this land. A second boundary "adjustment" came in 1895.

As early as the 1860s several white settlers moved here to offer food, lodging, and horses to Idaho-bound gold miners. John Silcott, Chief Timothy's son-in-law, established a profitable ferry, and a community called Alpowa grew up around his business. In 1882 the town was platted as Silcott. In 1975 water backed by Lower Granite Dam flooded the town.

CLARKSTON, at the confluence of the Snake and Clearwater rivers, historically has taken a back seat to its older and larger neighbor, Lewiston, Idaho, which mushroomed into existence in 1861 as a tent city. Miners bound via steamboat for claims on the Clearwater River and its tributaries arrived there by the thousands, but shallow water stopped the boats from continuing upriver.

A ferry-landing settlement, called Jawbone Flat, soon developed on the Washington side of the Snake River. There Cassius C. Van Arsdol, a survey engineer for the Northern Pacific, moved into a one-room cottage in 1896 (15th and Chestnut; later enlarged). He had lost his position when the railroad went into receivership and, looking for new opportunities, he designed an irrigation system and organized a company to build and manage it. That first undertaking failed, but the company reorganized and managed to attract financing by prominent Boston capitalists.

The investment permitted the hiring of a crew of 275 workmen, mostly Italians, who built a diversion dam on Asotin Creek and directed water into a 15-mile canal. Sagebrush tracts situated on Jawbone Flat—renamed Vineland—sold for $1,000 per acre, an exceedingly high price. The *Spokesman Review,* responding to a suggestion that an article "would be a quick lever towards . . . advertising," assured readers that Vineland had "no cyclones, no blizzards, no tornadoes, no gales . . . no sunstrokes, . . . no fogs, no pulmonary diseases, no crop failures . . ." and furthermore, that "saloons are rigidly prohibited . . . in all deeds."

In 1899 the town, called Concord after the hometown of a leading Massachusetts backer, boasted a population of 1,500. The name changed to Clarkston the following year to honor explorer William Clark.

In the 1970s the Army Corps of Engineers built the Clarkston **Greenbelt and Swallows Park,** along the river south of Clarkston, a riverside haven that offers picnicking, boating, and strolling. Its name refers to nearby Swallow Rock, a massive basalt wall dotted each spring with mud nests of cliff swallows.

On the Idaho side of the river, the 168-foot *Jean,* last of the Snake River stern-wheel steamboats, is moored at a marina. Built in 1938, her oil-fueled boilers provided power for hauling log booms.

For a scenic drive with views of towering basalt walls and modern oceangoing shipping, follow the Snake River northwest from Clarkston to Wawawai, which is now a county park, not a town. (See ALMOTA, p. 190; and WAWAWAI, p. 203.)

CLOVERLAND, on the plateau above Asotin, is no longer a place to buy gasoline or ask directions. Only a handful of early 1900s buildings remain; the sites of the others were plowed into wheat fields long ago. An attempt at orchards and irrigated fields failed, and only landowners who could buy enough acreage to raise livestock and grain were able to remain in the area. Population reached its height in 1910 with about 400 persons.

The two-story, frame Cloverland Garage is listed in the National Register of Historic Places. Originally built as a store, it became a garage in 1918, shortly after the arrival of enough automobiles to warrant such a business. Three years previously, Fred Walter, owner of the garage, had gone to San Diego, California, specifically to attend a driving school. He then took additional automotive training and opened the community's only auto dealership, repair garage, and gasoline pump. Across the road from the garage is the Barkley Hotel, now a residence. Upstairs rooms still are numbered. Cloverland was on the main road between Lewiston, Idaho, and Wallowa, Oregon, and travelers often stopped overnight.

The road beyond Cloverland climbs 14 miles to **Wenatchee Guard Station** and a lengthy, forested rim of the Blue Mountains. Make the drive if accustomed to backcountry roads; the

reward is a panorama of canyons and ridges with the Seven Devils in Idaho and the Wallowa Mountains in Oregon as a distant backdrop.

At the junction where the Cloverland road first reaches the mountain rim, a left turn leads to Anatone (16 miles with possibly confusing junctions), and a right turn leads to the guard station (a half mile). Beyond, the road follows along the rim, then back into the forest, and finally down to State Route 128 connecting between Pomeroy and Clarkston. This drive offers views across wrinkled sagebrush flats and gullies to the patterning of fields and the wall of the Snake River Canyon. (Unpaved roads lace the entire Blue Mountains area; to minimize confusion, obtain a Umatilla National Forest map, available at the district office in Pomeroy. Depending on recent weather and its effect on roads, an ordinary passenger car is usually adequate for the drives mentioned here.)

In **DAYTON** well-preserved historic buildings reflect the town's importance as an early farming and lumbering center. **Columbia County Courthouse** (Main and Third; built in 1887) bolsters the downtown district, most of its original roof decoration restored in 1991. The courthouse has two major entrances: one on the north facing the depot, one on the south facing Main Street. Above each was a bronze statue of Justice. Topping low gables on the east and west rooflines were bronze American eagles. Today the building's second-floor corridor displays historical documents and photographs, including an early view of the courthouse itself. North of the courthouse, the graceful **Dayton Depot** (Second near Main; built in 1881) sits surrounded by a tree-shaded brick courtyard. It now serves as a community center and is often open for special exhibits.

For a look at houses representative of Dayton's solid prosperity, sample the neighborhood south of Main along First, Second, and Third streets. Homes there were built between 1870 and the late 1930s. They range from small bungalows to high-style mansions. **Flour Mill Park** (Main Street and the Touchet River) is named for Dayton's first industry; the mill itself burned in the 1950s.

Settlers arriving in the late 1850s brought cattle to grassy valleys in the area, only to

Washington's oldest remaining railroad station—now a community center—is at Dayton.

experience the unusually fierce winter of 1861–1862. Margaret Gilbreath, who with her husband Samuel brought the first wagon over the Nez Perce Trail, recorded pioneering memories:

[We had wheat] intended for seed for the coming year but the hard winter of 1861 and 1862 followed when food for man and beast became so scarce that most of it was sold to the needy for food, and to keep the teams from starving. . . .

This was the most terrible winter ever experienced in the valley. The snow drifted so deep that many of the cattle were frozen standing up . . . [and] only a narrow trail could be kept open to Walla Walla by miners coming to and from the Idaho mines.

Agriculture moved from the valleys to the hills as farmers found that wheat could replace bunchgrass. At the same time, a stage route upgraded the former trail between Walla Walla and Lewiston, and this turned Dayton into a stage stop. In 1871 Jesse Day platted Dayton and offered Sylvester Wait (already prominent as the founder of Waitsburg) a free homesite and land for a flour mill. (The mill manager's home still stands at 504 N. First Street.) In 1878 Dayton became county seat and, in 1880, the town built what purportedly was the state's first public high school.

Businesses grew. A flume 18 miles long carried pine cants (squared logs) from the Blue Mountains to sawmills in town; and Jacob

Weinhard, nephew of Portland brewer Henry Weinhard, opened a brewery. Dayton felt ready for a railroad. As inducement, town fathers promised to make annual shipments of $100,000 worth of grains, fruit, wool, flour, soap, and beer. In 1880 the Oregon Railway and Navigation Company obliged with a connection to Portland; nine years later the Northern Pacific also provided service.

Well-being faltered as the Great Depression of the 1930s triggered the collapse of about one third of Dayton's businesses, including the flour mill. The town revived in 1934 when a major cannery opened to process asparagus and peas. Through it all both the population and the town's physical appearance remained remarkably stable.

DIXIE, a historic community south of Dayton, owes its name to the three Kershaw brothers—born in England—who entertained their wagon train on the trip West with nightly songs, including the Confederate anthem. A settler named Herman Actor already had a claim near the junction of Dry Creek and the Walla Walla River when the Kershaws arrived in 1861. He worked as a packer for the Idaho mines during "the open season" and stayed at his claim during the winter. The Kershaws lived with him while locating their own land. When a druggist in Walla Walla bought the Actor homestead and platted the town in 1881, he expected to call it

Baker City, but community affection for "the Dixie Boys' " singing prevailed, and the established name went unchanged.

Twenty years later community growth surged when Dorsey Baker sold his pioneering Walla Walla and Columbia River Railroad and built two new, short narrow-gauge lines, one connecting Walla Walla with Dixie, the other with Dudley (now Tracy)—about 15 miles of track altogether. The Dixie line served not only farmers but a sawmill that got logs by flume from the Blue Mountains and produced posts, bridge timbers, construction beams, railroad ties, and dimension lumber.

Orchards—peach, pear, cherry, and apple—as well as wheat characterized Dixie's early agriculture. Elizabeth Kelly, who arrived in 1890, reminisced in the Walla Walla *Union Bulletin* about women sitting in the shade (plagued by yellow jackets) to cut and seed peaches, which they dried in the sun for local sale by the gunnysackful. By that time the town had two trains a day and assorted features beyond the standard for flourishing young communities. Mrs. Kelly remembered a combination dance hall and roller skating rink (later remodeled as a Methodist church) and a quarry and rock crusher operated with convict labor from the penitentiary at Walla Walla.

She also recalled the routine of daily life including washday "in the hot summer [when] the dug wells would get so low there wasn't enough water":

Those who lived close to the creek carried water from there. [Others] went to the creek, as my mother did. We children would carry the old wooden tub, wash board and boiler. Also wood. Mother would build a fire on the bank, heat the boiler full of water, then wash on the board for a family of seven. . . . She would then carry the wet clothes home to hang on the line to dry.

FIELDS SPRING STATE PARK. (See under ANATONE, p. 176.)

GRANDE RONDE RIVER. (See under ANATONE, p. 176.)

PATAHA (Pa-tah´-hah)—except for the vacant three-story mill—nearly blends into the natural surroundings. It once had population and promise enough to serve as county seat for newly created Garfield County, but Pomeroy—a rival a few miles west—finally won that designation after fierce competition.

In 1877 John Houser purchased the Pataha Flour Mill. Its wooden machinery and elevators were powered with water that came by ditch and a 12-inch pipe from a small dam at a nearby spring. Houser shipped Pataha flour all over the world; in China his son-in-law acted as a marketing agent.

About 2 miles east of Pataha (near a roadside historical marker), travois ruts angle up the steep creek bank. They are remnants of a major trail, now partly followed by State Route 12. In general, the trail—used by generations of native people and for decades by whites—followed creek valleys from the confluence of the Walla Walla and Columbia rivers (near Wallula) to the confluence of the Snake and Clearwater rivers (near Lewiston). From there other trails fanned out, some leading to the Great Plains. Lewis and Clark used the trail in May 1806. They camped next to Pataha Creek during an unseasonal snowstorm and there ate the last of their provisions.

In **POMEROY** grain elevators and the county courthouse tell the tale of the town's development. The courthouse (Eighth and Main) boasts two towers, one of which is topped by a statue of blind Justice. The settlement began in 1864 when Joseph Pomeroy and his wife opened a stage station along the Walla Walla to Lewiston route. The owner of the coach asked Mrs. Pomeroy, a young mother with two small children, if she could cook dinner for passengers. That meant caring for two stage-loads per day, one eastbound, one westbound. Mrs. Pomeroy later reminisced:

I had told Mr. King that I had nothing to work with, no stove, table or dishes; nothing to cook and I did not see how I could accommodate him. . . .

Mr. King told me to make a list of what I needed for my house so I could feed his passengers, and finally, after much urging, I did so. He took my list to Walla Walla, had the bill filled, put on a freight team the next day and brought me a big, nice cookstove with all the things belonging to it; lots of dishes and linen, and said I could pay him when I made the money and could spare it.

The very next day I gave a dinner to ten passengers, and, oh, didn't they brag on that dinner. I never will forget all the nice things they said.

Only one other family lived along Pataha Creek at that time; several native ranchers, Chief Timothy among them, lived on Alpowa Creek.

When Garfield County was created in 1881, Pataha City (east of Pomeroy) was named temporary county seat. An election gave the seat to Pomeroy, but a judge returned the honor to Pataha City on a technicality. Each switch sent a jeering parade marching down the main street of the losing town. Then a lawsuit determined that the county had no seat at all because the temporary enabling legislation had elapsed. Next the territorial government stepped in naming Pomeroy county seat, but the clerk who copied the document left out the enabling paragraph. Finally, the U.S. Congress passed an act, which among other things, designated Pomeroy. The passion over county seats seems misplaced today, but a century ago the very existence of a community, as well as its prosperity and prestige, could be guaranteed by such a designation.

West of Pomeroy, State Route 126, in part a narrow, gravel road, provides a 17-mile, fair-weather alternative route to Walla Walla. The road drops precipitously—and scenically—into the Tucannon Valley, crossing the Tucannon River at the village of **Marengo.** East of Pomeroy, State Route 128 offers a twisting, scenic, back-road link to Clarkston.

(Also see CLOVERLAND, p. 178, for a scenic loop drive into the Blue Mountains.)

SNAKE RIVER ROAD. (See under ASOTIN, p. 177.)

A visitor to **WAITSBURG** in 1871 described it as "the most enterprising and thrifty of any town except Walla Walla in the whole valley." That description still holds, and the town still operates on the basis of its original territorial charter. The four-story, mansard-roofed grist-mill, which anchored the young town, stands next to the Touchet River (east of the Main Street bridge). The mill operated from 1865 to 1957. Its buhrstones are preserved in Coppei Park (Second and Coppei). The 1882 Bruce Mansion (Fourth and Main) has been restored and is open to the public intermittently throughout the year, and especially during the September Pioneer Festival. It was the home of an early county commissioner and school board member.

At first settlers here ran cattle and horses on the hillsides and experimented with crops. To earn cash they hauled freight for miners bound to Lewiston and beyond. In 1865, as the first large wheat crops were harvested from the fertile benchlands, a man named Sylvester M. Wait built a gristmill where mule trains loaded flour

Waitsburg's streetscape—dating from 1880 to 1930—remains remarkably intact.

for the Idaho mines. Sixteen years later, when the Oregon Railway and Navigation Company laid its tracks to Waitsburg, the town's population spurted. According to the *Waitsburg Times:*

From early morn' 'till dewy eve our thoroughfare is lined with wheat wagons and teams, our mills running day and night, and from break of day 'till midnight, a small army of men are kept busy handling grain and loading cars. At all our stores skilled clerks and salesmen are "on the jump" all day.

Waitsburg Grange, the first chapter chartered in the state of Washington, began in 1889. A 1938 Grange hall stands at the east edge of town, still in active use. The movement—originally called The National Grange of the Patrons of Husbandry—began in Washington, D.C., in 1867 as a response to agrarian discontent and the developing mechanization of traditional farming techniques. Each local Grange chapter served many needs: it was a fraternal brotherhood with secret rituals modeled on those of the Masonic Temple; it served as a gathering place for social, educational, and recreational programs; and it provided a forum for political activities that stressed agricultural justice. Grange cooperatives strove to limit the power of railroad and grain brokers' monopolies. Even today, the Grange operates an insurance program and a network of farm supply stores.

WALLA WALLA is a self-confident city where nineteenth-century mansions and ordinary cottages share shade-dappled neighborhoods. Its setting is the fertile Walla Walla Valley, near both Blue Mountains timber and Palouse wheat. Early streets (which still form the downtown core) were aligned not with compass points, as was customary, but with the ancient Nez Perce Trail. It became Main Street where it reached town.

In 1856 Lieutenant Colonel Edward J. Steptoe established Fort Walla Walla where the Nez Perce Trail crossed Mill Creek. The signing of treaties the preceding year—and the ensuing sporadic battles between whites and native warriors—led strategists to seek a greater army presence in eastern Washington. Four years later, placer miners washed gold out of streams in the Clearwater country of north central Idaho, and about 60 miners wintered over near the diggings. Their letters, published in San Francisco and Puget Sound newspapers, created a furor. By March 1861 hundreds of miners started for Idaho. By May every pick, shovel, and gold pan in Walla Walla had been sold, and pack animals were crowding the streets. A fine profit could be made on staples: coffee worth 20 cents a pound in Portland could be resold for 50 cents in Idaho; bacon, nine cents on the coast, could be sold for 40 cents near the mines. Packtrains and wagons also started north from Walla Walla on the newly completed Mullan Road to supply mines in Montana and in the Colville and Kootenai districts. As a British Columbia correspondent wrote:

To you of Walla Walla we must look for our flour, bacon, and fruit, but we can return to you gold dust worth $18 an ounce.

Camels added an exotic touch to packtrains loading in Walla Walla. Between 1865 and 1867 a freight firm regularly used camels between Walla Walla and Hell Gate (Missoula), Montana, despite the fact that the beasts spooked horses and mules. Their virtue was the load they could carry: well over a half ton per camel, a capacity that was worth "four good mules." According to old-timer Charles Canon, who remembered seeing camel packtrains:

They would be loaded with sacks of flour until you couldn't see anything of the camels except their heads. . . . They would go up and over the mountains in the roughest and steepest places and never refuse to keep moving along in their slow, deliberate way.

The U.S. Army had imported camels in the 1850s to use as pack animals in the Southwest desert but after five years they turned some loose and sold others, deciding they were just too disruptive. Packers en route to the Cariboo mines in British Columbia brought several north but, after testing them, also turned some loose and sold others. Seven went to the Montana mines; camels packed out the first gold from the fabulously rich Alder Gulch strike in 1863. A year later six of the Montana camels were sold to a Walla Walla firm. The seventh had been shot, "mistaken" for a moose.

Walla Walla's mine trade illustrates a significant aspect of Northwest development: a hunger for land and "pioneer life" was not the only incentive for settlement here. Many early arrivals were intent on living a city life as merchants or entrepreneurs. Walla Walla quickly became a commercial, banking, and—to some extent—a manufacturing center. From a total of just seven scattered houses in 1859 it mushroomed in a decade to a population of nearly 1,500, the largest city in Washington Territory. It competed on par with St. Louis and Portland for the mine trade; San Francisco merchants even offered money for repair of the Mullan Road so that goods could keep flowing up the Columbia and overland through Walla Walla rather than from Portland to the White Bluffs Road for shipment across the Columbia Plateau, or from St. Louis up the Missouri River to Fort Benton and on to the mines.

But booms end. The gold played out at the same time that agriculture was increasing. Instead of shipping inland to the mines, farmers began to depend on the Columbia River for access to markets as distant as London. Efficiency called for a better link to the river, and Dr. Dorsey Baker solved the problem in 1875 by building a narrow-gauge railroad to the steamer landing at Wallula. (See WALLULA, p. 174.)

Shipment nonetheless remained cumbersome. Sacked wheat had to be hand moved at least 10 times: from farm wagon to railroad to river steamer to portage railroad (around Celilo Falls), to another river steamer; then another portage railroad (around the Cascades), and via a third steamer to a Portland warehouse; and finally onto an oceangoing schooner. This excessive handling eased in 1882 when the Oregon Railway and Navigation Company laid tracks to Portland along the south shore of the Columbia River. Gold had triggered Walla Walla's beginnings but "golden" wheat became its mainstay.

In 1883 the transcontinental railroad was completed through Spokane, and Walla Walla lost preeminence—although not significance. It remains a regional cultural and trading center. Stately homes line several streets (for example, W. Birch and S. Palouse) and commercial districts retain dozens of fine nineteenth- and early twentieth-century buildings with proud,

decorative detail on their upper stories (E. and W. Main on each side of Mill Creek).

Points of interest, keyed to the Walla Walla *map:*

1   The 1917 **Liberty Theater** (50 E. Main; now a store) is on the site of the 1856 Steptoe Barracks (or Fort Walla Walla). It is where the historic Nez Perce Trail forded Mill Creek. In 1857 the army moved the fort to its current location southwest of town (now a Veterans Hospital).

2   The **Union Block** (N. side of Main between First and Second; built in the early 1880s) typifies Walla Walla's early commercial establishments. Its most striking building is the restored Victorian Italianate Barrett Building. The block's name apparently comes from that of an early newspaper.

3   Construction of the **Baker-Boyer Building** (Second and W. Main; dating from 1861) began as a single-story brick mercantile. In it Dr. Dorsey Baker and brother-in-law John F. Boyer had a store equipped with a safe where they stored miners' gold in sacks, each carefully marked with the owner's name. After 1869 Baker and Boyer went into the banking business full-time and founded one of the state's oldest, continuously operating banks. The present seven-story remodeling was completed in 1910: the city's first skyscraper.

4   In 1899 the **Dacres Hotel** (Fourth and W. Main) replaced an earlier hotel built by Fred Stine, a blacksmith who arrived in Walla Walla about 1872 with only 75 cents. He borrowed money, opened a blacksmith shop, succeeded, and built Stine House, a renowned hostelry. George Dacres (Deck'-ers) bought the ruins of that building after an 1892 fire destroyed it along with most of the block. He built the present three-story hotel, which features a distinctive pressed-metal frieze on the Main Street facade and corbeled brick and arched windows on the Fourth Street facade. Now refurbished, the Dacres is used for offices and shops.

5   The Classic Revival **County Courthouse** (Fifth and W. Main; built in 1916) dates from long after Walla Walla had become a county seat. That status began in 1862 when the territorial legislature established county boundaries that embraced the vast region from

Walla Walla

Key to Numbered Locations

1	Liberty Theater	6	Andrews Livery Stable	11	Small-Elliott House
2	Union Block	7	Saint Patrick's Church	12	Miles C. Moore House
3	Baker-Boyer Building	8	William Kirkman House	13	Ben Stone House
4	Dacres Hotel	9	Whitman College	14	Phillip Ritz House
5	County Courthouse	10	H. P. Isaacs House	15	Fort Walla Walla

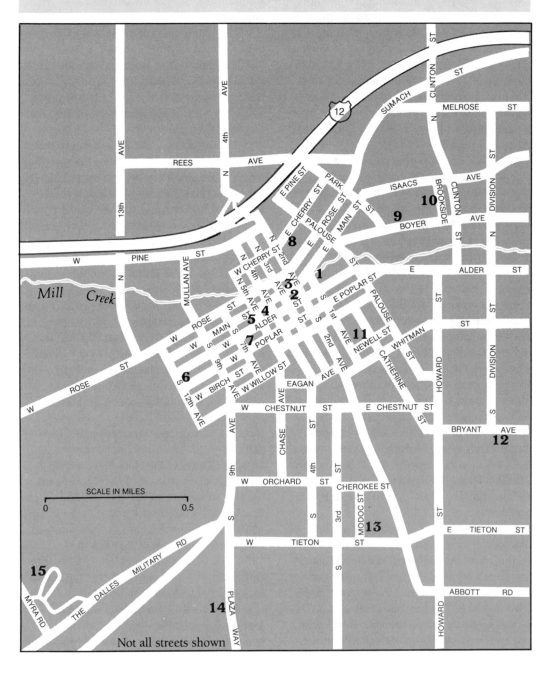

Not all streets shown

the Oregon border to the Canadian border and from the crest of the Cascade Mountains to the crest of the Rocky Mountains.

6 The **Andrews Livery Stable** (12th and W. Alder; built about 1880) lingers from the era when horsepower was a literal fact rather than a figure of speech. Such stables were common-place—although the elaborate Mission-style false front on this one is unusual. The building has been rehabilitated and is used as the starting point for an annual reenactment of the old horse-drawn mail stage crossing of the Blue Mountains to Enterprise, Oregon.

7 The interior of **Saint Patrick's Church** (Sixth and W. Alder; completed in 1881) has been modernized—including painting its woodwork—but the original marble statue of Saint Patrick remains by the altar. The exterior is red brick with sandstone trim. Its stately architecture and degree of finish indicate Walla Walla's early prosperity and sense of stability.

8 The **William Kirkman House** (Colville and Cherry; built in 1880)—a bay-windowed mansion with pressed-metal friezes and a cast-iron widow's walk—is listed in the National Register of Historic Places. Notice the sculpted faces in the keystones of the arched windows.

Kirkman came to America from England in 1852, tried gold mining in California, then headed for the Idaho boom. He made his fortune, however, in meat packing and wheat farming. He and his wife—an Irish woman whom he met in San Francisco—had 10 children, only six of whom lived to adulthood. The house has been restored by a private group, which has opened it to the public.

9 **Whitman College** buildings include the 1899 Romanesque Revival Memorial Building and clock tower (345 Boyer). Two plaques set into a boulder (southeast campus) commemorate the Walla Walla Treaty signed here in 1855. Only four years later, Cushing Eells obtained a charter to establish Whitman Seminary as a lasting tribute to his murdered colleagues Marcus and Narcissa Whitman. In 1883 Whitman changed to a four-year liberal arts college, today nationally recognized for excellence.

10 The **H. P. Isaacs House** (107 Brookside Drive; begun about 1865, rebuilt in 1886) is perhaps the oldest house remaining in Walla Walla. A former army officer, Isaacs received a large tract of land as a military warrant in 1864 and built an adobe house and flour mill. As the mill succeeded, he repeatedly altered the house. By the 1880s his flour was shipped as far as the Midwest and his shingle and clapboard house had become a cultural focal point for Walla Walla. Brookside Drive, a narrow lane now with several handsome homes, was the Isaacs driveway.

11 The **Small-Elliott House** (Newell and Catherine; built in 1879) is located on the grounds of the 1855 Walla Walla Treaty Council. David W. Small and his brother Ira worked as superintendents for Dorsey Baker during construction of the Columbia and Walla Walla Railroad. Subsequently their brother Alfred joined them in a livery business and in managing the famous 1873 hotel, the Stine House. David Small financed the steamer *Northwest* in 1878, an early vessel on the Columbia River. In 1892 he sold this house to investment banker Thompson C. Elliott, whose wife Anna was a daughter of Dorsey Baker. The Elliotts donated a parcel of their land for a Carnegie Library (S. Palouse and W. Alder) and helped raise funds for its construction. The library now serves as a community arts center.

12 The **Miles C. Moore House** (720 Bryant; built in 1883) is an elegant three-story mansion surrounded by shrubbery. It belonged to the last territorial governor, who was married to Mary Baker, daughter of Dorsey Baker. Moore's fortune came through wheat, shipping, merchandising, and—through his father-in-law—banking. The Moores' son Robert built the impressive brick Colonial house just to the east of the Moore House.

13 Plans for the **Ben Stone House** (1415 Modoc; built in 1909) were adapted by Portland architects from a Frank Lloyd Wright design published in the *Ladies Home Journal* as a "fireproof house for $5,000." Features include 10-foot cantilevered eaves that conceal ventilating grates, and an essentially flat roof that slants slightly inward so that snow melts against the chimneys. A basement cistern captures the meltwater.

14 The **Phillip Ritz House** (1869 Plaza Way; built in 1895)—complete even to an onion-domed turret—is an exact replica of a Portland house admired by Mrs. Ritz. Phillip

The Phillip Ritz home is among a score of fine mansions in Walla Walla. Begun in the 1860s, the city quickly became the most populous in Washington Territory.

died before the house was finished, but the couple's son Charles oversaw completion.

Phillip Ritz was a horticulturalist whose successes included shipping 50 barrels of wheat to Liverpool, England, as early as 1868—Walla Walla's first export of grain. A friend of Henry Villard, head of the Northern Pacific Railroad Company, he was honored by having the Columbia Plateau town of Ritzville named for him.

15 The army's **Fort Walla Walla** (The Dalles Military Road) bolstered U.S. military presence in eastern Washington and served as a base for Colonel George Wright's deadly 1858 campaign against a coalition of inland tribes. (See SPOKANE BATTLES sidebar, p. 10.) Just a year previously the fort had moved to this location from a temporary site in what now is downtown Walla Walla. In 1910 the fort closed. Several of its buildings are now used as a veterans' hospital.

At **Fort Walla Walla Park** near the fort, a historical museum includes pioneer buildings moved here for preservation. Also on display is a stagecoach that was shipped around Cape Horn in 1861 for use on the Walla Walla to Lewiston route. An adjacent agricultural museum displays a 1919 combine pulled by 33 (fiberglass) mules ingeniously harnessed so that one man could drive them. Old-timers say that it took half of the mules just to carry the harness! The park also features a farmstead that belonged to Italian immigrants who helped develop the famous Walla Walla sweet onions.

At **WHITMAN MISSION,** Marcus and Narcissa Whitman worked and died. A National Park Service visitor center portrays their effort—and era. An interpretive trail leads among outlined foundations of the adobe mission house, the "emigrant house," and a blacksmith shop. Ducks and geese swim in the reconstructed millpond and nest in the ryegrass. Water flows in the old ditch that irrigated fields to the west. And appropriate fruits and vegetables again grow in the kitchen garden. On a nearby hilltop a 27-foot monolith erected in 1897 commemorates the missionaries. A "Great Grave" at the base of the hill holds the remains of all who were killed.

The Whitmans married in February 1836 before starting mission work in Oregon; the American Board of Commissioners for Foreign Missions did not welcome unmarried candidates. On their honeymoon, the couple crossed the continent with fur traders; fellow missionaries Henry and Eliza Spalding; lay missionary William Gray; and a black helper named John

Hinds, who got sick on the way West and died soon after reaching the mission site.

The Spaldings settled at Lapwai on the Clearwater in Idaho among the Nez Perce. At first Gray worked with them; later he joined the Whitmans. Marcus and Narcissa decided on Waiilatpu, "The Place of the People of the Rye Grass." There they immediately strove to learn the Cayuse language, start a farm, and gain the confidence of the native people. Success was minimal: farm animals trampled unfenced crops; the natives' cyclic food-gathering rounds interrupted religious instruction; furthermore, they kept wanting to learn within the context of their own culture, and not be treated as inferior to whites. The men had neither precedent nor desire to labor in the fields. Perhaps worst of all, the missionaries' personalities did not fit their task. Narcissa seemed aloof and, according to a colleague, Marcus Whitman was "always at work" and "could never stop to parley." The Cayuse resented this.

The mission soon became a way station for whites arriving via the Oregon Trail. Families headed West encouraged by the Whitmans' stubborn success in getting a wagon as far west as Fort Boise and by knowing that women had endured the trip. Emigrants also sought to escape from the typhoid- and malaria-plagued Mississippi Valley—and they brought these diseases plus cholera and measles with them (although the malaria soon died out here). Whitman, a medical doctor, spent more time succoring travelers than dealing with converts. Not one Cayuse was admitted to the church during his 11-year tenure at the mission.

The beginning of the end came in 1847 when immigrants arrived with measles. Whitman worked tirelessly to treat a raging epidemic, but native people had no resistance and died despite his care. Most of the whites survived.

The Cayuse took action. On November 29, 1847, they began slaughtering mission inhabitants. Marcus and Narcissa—killed by hatchet blows and gunshots—were among the first to die. Boys under their care (but not the girls) and additional adults—mostly settlers bound for the Willamette Valley—also died that first day. Some escaped, but the murderers took 50 prisoners, mostly women and children. Peter Skene Ogden, who had succeeded John McLouglin as factor at Fort Vancouver, hurried up the Columbia River to ransom them. His prestige and his firm policy of "all released or no ransom at all," succeeded shortly before 500 Oregon volunteer militiamen arrived at Waiilatpu for revenge.

Renowned mountain man Joe Meek, upon learning his young daughter had died of measles while a captive, galloped east to tell President James Polk about the massacre. He carried a petition asking for arms and for protection under American law. Partly in response to this, the U.S. Army in 1849 established a garrison at Vancouver in Oregon Territory.

Perhaps the Cayuse struck out at the mission hoping to save their land from white invasion. If so, the hope backfired, for armed settlers soon drove native people from the Walla Walla Valley. More likely the Cayuse were eliminating Whitman as an evil shaman who was using measles to kill people. Throughout the Columbia Plateau, it was common practice to kill a person who misused his or her spirit power. In the early 1890s a Nez Perce whose brother lived at Waiilatpu at the time of the massacre told photographer Edward H. Curtis:

[A man] was crying because his wife had died of the sickness: she had taken some of the Doctor's medicine, and spots came out on her face. . . . One of the Indians made himself sick in order to test the Doctor, saying that if the Doctor's medicine killed him they would know that he was the cause of the death of the others.

He took the medicine and died. Then the headmen met in council and made an agreement that the Doctor should be killed because two hundred of the people had died after taking his medicine.

The **Whitman Sawmill Site** on Mill Creek is east of Walla Walla. (Follow Isaacs Avenue east from town about 3 miles to a right turn on Mill Creek Road. The mill stood 10 miles upstream from there.) Today's road passes substantial farmsteads and rich fields along the cobble-bottomed creek. Marcus Whitman freighted mill machinery from the East in 1843 to produce lumber for buildings and—especially—fences. Farm animals trampling and grazing crops were a constant nuisance at Waiilatpu.

Palouse Area

The undulating, sensual hills of the Palouse support wheat, wheat, and more wheat. Farmers also grow barley, dry peas, lentils, rapeseed, and grass seed; but wheat predominates. Winter is the time to see the fields green. In summer combines like huge, beneficent insects gobble the crops, and loaded trucks shuttle from fields to storage elevators. Farmsteads with equipment sheds three times the size of the houses dot the creases of the hills, and small towns with an early 1900s ambience serve local needs. Pullman—the largest community in the area—is home to the second largest university in the state, Washington State University.

Steptoe and Kamiak buttes offer panoramic views of farmlands and distant hamlets. Roads to Almota, Penawawa, and Wawawai lead dramatically from the plateau to the canyon of the Snake River, which is almost 2,000 feet deep. Remnants of wheat trams still linger (conveyances used until the 1940s to get wheat down the canyon walls to the river).

On all roads, watch for slow-moving farm equipment driving from field to field. Unpaved roads may be either dusty or muddy—and outright impossible in wet or snowy weather. Away from the highways, signs are few and optional turns many. State Route 27 connecting Pullman with Opportunity (east of Spokane) twists among the voluptuous contours of the land, edging fields and running directly through small communities (many of which have no gasoline available to the public because most farm households have their own supplies). The road is a delight for those with time to enjoy the countryside. Towns are regularly spaced 12 miles apart—indication of railroad origins. Railroad buffs will find impressive trestles at Rosalia and Tekoa.

Fairfield and Rosalia have historical society museums, and the refurbished Perkins House in Colfax is open in summer and on special occasions. Every May, Uniontown stages a German sausage dinner, prepared by the men. Colfax holds an April plowing bee and a fall harvest bee; both feature antique equipment. Oakesdale and Palouse host May festivals.

ALBION's quiet residential neighborhoods now make up a bedroom community for Pullman, 6 miles south. In 1871 Californian Levi Reynolds homesteaded here. He platted the town and named it Guy to honor his grandson Guy Whetsell, but another family began to argue that their "Guy" was the one honored. The two sides finally compromised on Albion, recalling Sir Francis Drake's name Nova Albion for California.

Albion's streets were noted in the early 1900s

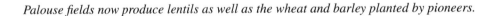

Palouse fields now produce lentils as well as the wheat and barley planted by pioneers.

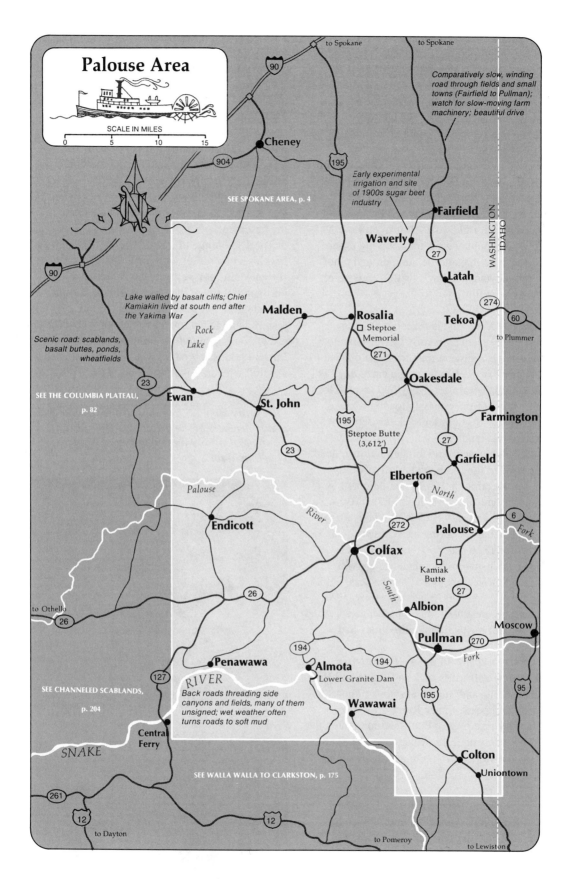

Palouse Area

SCALE IN MILES

0   5   10   15

to Spokane   **to Spokane**

Comparatively slow, winding road through fields and small towns (Fairfield to Pullman); watch for slow-moving farm machinery; beautiful drive

90

904

Cheney

195

SEE SPOKANE AREA, p. 4

Early experimental irrigation and site of 1900s sugar beet industry

Fairfield

Waverly

27

Latah

90

274

60

Lake walled by basalt cliffs; Chief Kamiakin lived at south end after the Yakima War

Malden   **Rosalia**   **Tekoa**
□ Steptoe Memorial

Rock Lake

271

to Plummer

Scenic road: scablands, basalt buttes, ponds, wheatfields

23

SEE THE COLUMBIA PLATEAU, p. 82

Ewan   **St. John**

Oakesdale

Farmington

195

Steptoe Butte (3,612') □

27

23

Garfield

Elberton

North

Palouse

River

Endicott

272

Palouse

6

Fork

Colfax

Kamiak Butte □

27

26

South

Albion

Moscow

194

Pullman   270

to Othello

26

Fork

Penawawa   **Almota**   194
Lower Granite Dam

195

95

SEE CHANNELED SCABLANDS, p. 204

127

RIVER

Back roads threading side canyons and fields, many of them unsigned; wet weather often turns roads to soft mud

Wawawai

Central Ferry

SNAKE

Colton

Uniontown

SEE WALLA WALLA TO CLARKSTON, p. 175

261

12

to Dayton

12

to Pomeroy

to Lewiston

as "peculiarly free of mud at all seasons." The town was larger than Pullman at that time and boasted its own "conservative institution of higher learning," Edwards College, which lasted until 1916. In 1910 fire destroyed Albion's commercial district. Few buildings were rebuilt, resulting in a "coreless" quality that remains to this day.

Northeast of Albion the **Rose Creek Preserve** (12 acres owned and managed by The Nature Conservancy) retains pristine bottomland unaltered by agriculture. (From Albion follow Main east for 3 miles to a left turn on Four Mile Road.) Visitors may walk trails among aspen, dogwood, rose, hawthorne, juniper, and pine; deer abound and songbirds twitter. Beware of the trailside nettles.

At **ALMOTA** the past is reflected by grain towers, the present by nearby Lower Granite Dam. A steep approach road from the plateau to the riverside is a reminder of the early-day farmers-turned-teamsters; they had to snub logs to the wheels of their heavily loaded wheat wagons as brakes in order to skid safely down to the steamboat landing.

With level ground for storage facilities, deep water close to the shore, and relatively easy grades connecting to the plateau, Almota has long flourished as a grain-loading facility. As many as seven stern-wheelers lined up side-by-side at the wharves during harvest season, and a ledger for 1876 lists 300 tons of produce shipped downstream. Merchandise arriving upstream that year included "4 threshers, 3 sulky plows, 3 reapers, 3 headers, 15 wagons, 100 tons merchandise, and 30 passengers." A year later shipments in both directions had tripled.

Irrigated orchards in relatively frost-free valleys grew soft fruits such as Elberta and Hale peaches; Stella and Superb apricots; plums, cherries, and pears. Snake River growers, shipping by riverboat to Portland, dominated the deluxe markets until the Wenatchee and Yakima districts developed irrigation and came to the fore.

COLFAX strikes the traveler as a bustling center in a lightly populated land; it even has traffic lights. At the junction of two forks of the Palouse River, it lies hemmed to the east by basalt cliffs; hills to the west are less abrupt. Vintage commercial buildings line Main Street, their brick, stucco, and granite facades augmented by locally made cast-iron columns. The 1889 Fraternity Block (N. 209 Main), a three-story red brick Victorian Gothic, particularly pleased residents at the time of construction by using only locally produced materials: lumber, bricks, and cast iron. The building housed Masons, Odd Fellows, and Knights of Pythias, and boasted an elevator powered by a horse in the basement.

The 1884 home of the town's founder, James Perkins, shares a lot with his first log cabin. (From Main turn west on Last Street near the north end of town; then turn north on Perkins Avenue. The house is the last on the left, restored and maintained by the county historical society and open to the public in summer.) James Perkins settled here in 1870 and opened a sawmill with an up-and-down saw that was slow

Fifty years after St. John beat Colfax at football, aging members of the original teams replayed the game. Colfax won and put up a "Codger Pole" on Main Street.

and inaccurate but a boon for all who were spared the trip to Walla Walla for lumber. Settlers, who urgently needed building materials, often dismantled their wagons to get planks and some lived in houses partly dug into the ground, partly built up with siding. As one Colfax citizen noted, "if the winter be a severe one, there probably will be some suffering."

Early experiments with crops proved that Colfax centered on some of the richest wheat-growing land in the nation. Consequently in 1894 the town joined other eastern Washington communities in sponsoring an immigrant bureau in Chicago, where would-be settlers were regaled with tales of rich soil and progressive communities. The Northern Pacific Railroad did its part by running special immigrant cars furnished with tables and beds, and with complete bedding available at a modest price. Curtains separated one family group from another; a kitchen with a cookstove stood at one end of the car.

Colfax soon became county seat, a position it still holds along with status as a trading center. Its population of about 3,000 has remained stable since the early 1900s.

South of Pullman, **COLTON** is a venerable community where an old-time tavern and country store/post office remain active and an exceptionally high church steeple catches the eye. It began in 1879 when a small group of Uniontown businessmen, at odds with the town-site owner there, decided to found a new community. The arrival of the Northern Pacific in 1888 boosted the new town's population to 300 and established it as a wheat-marketing center. Seven roads met at Colton, assuring commercial activity.

Both Uniontown and Colton were settled primarily by Catholic German farmers who arrived from Minnesota in 1867. The two communities—only 3 miles apart—thus shared a similar background, yet remained rivals. Each established its own school district. Colton Catholics even refused to help with the construction of Uniontown's elaborate new church and started their own parish, Saint Gall's. In 1895 Colton successfully lured a convent of German-speaking Swiss Benedictine nuns away from Uniontown to open Saint Scholastica's

Academy (demolished in 1988). The sisters stayed 10 years, then moved to Cottonwood, Idaho, where the order still teaches and has a convent and a museum. The rise of the automobile and of paved roads hastened Colton's commercial demise; Pullman and other larger trade centers became within easy reach.

For a backcountry drive near Colton turn southwest on State Route 193 (Rimrock Road) and follow it down **Steptoe Canyon** to the Snake River (about 10 miles). Lieutenant Colonel Edward Steptoe used this route on his retreat from Rosalia in May 1858. His battle-weary dragoons covered the 70 miles to the river in 24 hours. (Also see ROSALIA, p. 198.)

ELBERTON now rests quietly within its deep, pine-clad valley—a surprising ribbon of forest in this generally treeless region, and worthy of a side trip. On the main street only an empty post office and a brick church with boarded windows still remain despite hopes of developing the old town as a county park historic park. Preservation proved too costly, and a beloved—but unsafe—general store was deliberately torn down.

Once, however, Elberton seemed blessed with every advantage. In the 1870s Giles Wilbur built a sawmill here on the north fork of the Palouse River. Ten years later the Oregon Railway and Navigation Company laid tracks within yards of the mill. Sylvester Wait, a man with a penchant for town building—he was instrumental in the founding of both Waitsburg and Dayton—had bought the mill. He promptly platted a community and named it for a deceased son, Elbert. A nearby flour mill moved to Elberton, and the town began to grow.

Widespread crop losses in 1893, when drenching rains fell during the harvest, convinced Elberton-area farmers to diversify. They raised bees, cattle, and hogs. They grew broomcorn, sunflowers, beans, and potatoes. And, most successfully of all, they planted orchards—especially prunes. In 1900 a fruit dryer more than 100 feet long, "the largest in the country," stood near the town's business district. Its four furnaces could dry 66,000 pounds of fruit daily, a capacity that inspired orchardists to even greater production. More than a thousand acres in the immediate area of Elberton produced fruit, part of an agricultural diversity that was distinctive in the wheat-dominated Palouse.

The town's population reached an all-time high of 500 as the twentieth century opened. But a slow decline began when the sawmill, having exhausted nearby timber, moved to Idaho. This loss was followed by a 1908 fire and a 1910 flood. High grain prices tempted fruit growers back into wheat growing, but immediately after World War I prices fell. The huge fruit dryer declined; the flour mill, facing competition from larger mills, closed. Elberton slowly became the peaceful backwater it is today.

ENDICOTT's tidy houses and flower-filled yards *are* the town; commercial activity is practically nil. Unusually angled streets and a triangular townsite reflect the fact that railroad crews had constructed frame buildings and corrals for workhorses before the town was platted. Town surveyors simply worked around the existing structures.

In 1879 Henry Smith and his aunt opened Half Way House here, an inn halfway between Walla Walla and Spokane. Another relative opened a saloon. This western, drier section of the Palouse attracted stockmen; farmers considered its soil unproductive. When the railroad arrived in 1883, it was not grain but horses, sheep, and cattle that filled outbound freight cars.

One year earlier, eight families of Volga Germans (Germans who had lived in Russia) arrived in Endicott. Led by Philip Green, who had scouted here in 1879, they came from Kansas seeking richer farmland. These people formed a cooperative association, and the men worked on the railroad in order to finance farms.

WHEAT STORAGE: A CASE OF EVOLVING ARCHITECTURE

A century's worth of evolution in handling and storing wheat often shows at railroad sidings. The earliest structures—long and low—are "sack warehouses," also called "flathouses." Sturdy 8-by-8 posts set on 12-inch centers support the floor, which had to bear the static weight of wheat sacks piled to the ceiling. (A conveyor belt lifted the sacks, which weighed about 130 pounds apiece; at first a horse walking a treadmill powered the belt, later little one-cylinder gasoline engines provided the power.) Warehouse walls were made of 2-by-4 planks laid flat and nailed.

Farmers stacked wheat primarily because getting it to market took a lot of manhandling. Wheat was tossed by the sackful on and off farm wagons, riverboats, portage railways, and ships. Furthermore sea captains wanted sacked wheat. In the belly of a ship the sacks shifted less than bulk cargo, a crucial safety factor in rough water.

A change to bulk handling began with the completion of the Panama Canal in 1914: merchant ships no longer had to round treacherous Cape Horn en route to East Coast and European markets. Farmers started storing grain in bins rather than sacks. Next they walled clusters of bins and added a roof. That done, they increased the buildings' height. And with the height increased, they added an elevator to lift grain and shunt it into the proper bins. Walls as well as floors had to withstand pressure, and a cribbing of 2-by-10s laid flat became standard at the bottom where side pressures were greatest. For upper walls 2-by-8s and then 2-by-6s sufficed. These storage towers, called "elevators," stood 50 to 60 feet high.

As techniques for handling concrete improved, men found they could build elevators about three times as high as with wood. Round walls—inherently stronger than rectangular ones because pressures are distributed more evenly—became feasible. And grain packed better within round walls and presented less surface subject to damage from moisture or freezing.

After World War II, cost effectiveness

At first the entire group lived in a communal village and traveled out to the fields each day, as was usual in Europe. But soon they adopted the American custom of separate houses on each farm. Old-country customs nonetheless survived, and some Endicott churches conducted services in German well into the 1970s.

(Also see RUSSIAN GERMANS sidebar, p. 96.)

EWAN. (See ROCK LAKE, p. 198.)

FAIRFIELD stands at the northern edge of the Palouse grain region, close enough to Spokane to thrive as a "bedroom community." Several buildings from the early 1900s remain in use along Main Street (reached by turning off the highway). These include a large Mission-style structure, designed by Spokane architect Kirtland Cutter, with a bank at one end and a post office at the other. The former city hall (next to the library near the top of the hill) houses a history museum.

At the northern edge of town, watch for a huge white house with third-story dormer windows (west side of State Route 27, largely surrounded by trees). This was the home of Colonel Edward H. Morrison, who spent the 1890s developing sugar beet seed with capital supplied by the Chicago merchandising firm of Marshall, Field and Company. Ultimately, he combined forces with Spokane financier D. C. Corbin and opened a sugar mill at Waverly.

(Also see WAVERLY, p. 203.)

FARMINGTON lies on the eastern border of the Palouse where rolling wheat fields join forested foothills. Drive to the heights at the edge of town for an outstanding view back

Grain storage and shipping, as well as production, affect farm success or failure.

required huge farm acreages to justify the capital outlay needed for tractors, trucks, cultivators, and combines. Farmers with university degrees in business as well as agriculture could handle sales directly rather than rely exclusively on co-ops. Centralized storage lessened in importance. Rail shipment also lessened. Instead, trucks now roll along paved roads and river barges travel water highways created by damming the Snake and Columbia rivers. Metal storage bins now dot farms and, when bumper crops—or poor markets—result in more grain than elevators can hold, wheat is piled on the ground and protected with a rim of galvanized metal at the base to guard against rodents. If undisturbed, the wheat crusts over and resists moisture.

Such storage piles are temporary. If left indefinitely, they are covered with plastic sheeting and appear as huge, conical "tents" awaiting room within the elevators—part of the great torrent of food farmers must produce to feed a world population that increases by 90 million every year.

across the fields to Steptoe Butte, rising as a high, graceful pyramid. The cemetery, just south of town, includes the grave of Matilda Sager Pringle, one of the seven orphaned children who were cared for at Whitman Mission after their mother and father died while crossing the Great Plains. In later life Matilda ran a rooming house here.

Downtown Farmington—its streets not paved until 1986—has two buildings listed in the National Register of Historic Places. The Masonic Hall (now a community center) is a two-story-plus-attic, Classic Revival building with Tuscan and Ionic columns lining its porch. Designed by a lodge member who was not a professional architect, its grandeur clearly indicates the role of fraternal orders in small-town life. At the opposite end of Farmington, a bank occupies a one-story brick building with a corner entrance, which was virtually obligatory among banks at that time. Inside, the vault door is decorated with strips of stamped-metal flowers. The smallest bank in 11 western states, it is capitalized locally, offers full service, and stays financially sound through conservative investment policies—traits that characterize the farmers it serves.

This eastern section of the Palouse, with adequate rainfall and nearby timber, attracted early settlement. In 1870 stockmen began grazing cattle on the grassy hills. In 1878 George Truax laid out Farmington on his claim and named it for his hometown in Indiana. The town's first industry was a shingle mill, which shipped its finished product to Walla Walla by freight wagon. The second industry was an apple-packing plant—indication of a crop diversity now disappeared from the Palouse. After harsh winters in the 1890s killed the orchards, wheat became the favored crop along with lentils, which are rich in protein. Seventh Day Adventists, many of whom eat no meat, pioneered growing the lentils, an undertaking so successful that 90 percent of the U.S. lentil crop now comes from this part of the Palouse.

In 1886 a branch railroad reached Farmington, eliminating a long wagon haul to Almota to ship crops via the Snake River. When the Union Pacific acquired the line, Farmington found itself connected by rail to both Omaha and Portland. The town boomed. A planing mill,

brickworks, two stone quarries, and the Union Pacific regional headquarters, complete with shops and a roundhouse, provided economic security.

Farmington shrank later for a variety of reasons. The railroad moved its facilities north to Tekoa. Hard times in the 1920s and 1930s decreased the number of landholders, leaving fewer farmers who could patronize local businesses. And automobiles and highways put those businesses in competition with Spokane and Pullman.

At **GARFIELD,** gleaming grain elevators loom over Palouse hills, announcing the town's presence before the whole comes into view. The gardens of substantial two-story houses reach to the borders of wheat fields. Downtown a huge brick Grange hall (Fourth and California) looks partly like an armory, partly like a church. At the extreme north edge of town, the 1897 Robert C. McCroskey home (Fourth and Manring) commands attention. McCroskey, a banker, served as state senator and regent for the State College of Washington (now Washington State University). His spacious home, appointed with stained-glass windows, served as headquarters for a 2,000-acre wheat farm and as a social center for the regional elite.

Samuel Tant platted Garfield when the Oregon Railway and Navigation Company came through in 1882. In 1900, when 10 large ware-houses lined the tracks, both wheat and potatoes were significant crops. A decade later, Garfield began to decline. It nonetheless retains a vital retail core; State Route 27 threads directly through town; and grain begins an international journey from elevators here.

Drive to **KAMIAK BUTTE** (3,360 feet in elevation, named for Chief Kamiakin) as a refuge from summer heat and to sense the lay of the land, with the rolling Palouse hills merging into the mountains of Idaho. The road ends at a shady campground and picnic area with a fine view. For even better views, walk a half mile farther, or hike 3 miles to the summit. (Those who are car-bound will see out better from Steptoe Butte, but both peaks are worth driving up. Wild flowers are at their best in April and early May.)

In **LATAH** (Lay´-tah) early-day wooden warehouses for wheat bring to mind why settlers came—and adjacent modern elevators indicate the continuing role of farming.

The two-story, frame White Swan Hotel and several early 1900s brick commercial buildings along Market Street attest to original vitality. The Bank of Latah (founded in 1906) survived the Great Depression with no more than a brief closure during the 1933 "Bank Holiday." Preferred by many Palouse farmers to banks owned by outside interests, it now has branches in Tekoa, Oakesdale, and Palouse. William McEachern, founder of the Latah bank, lived in the grandest structure in town, an elegant Queen Anne–style home (Pine and Fifth, northwest section of Latah). Other old houses and a brick two-story school (closed) are nearby.

Mammoth bones, found in 1878 on homesteader B. F. Coplen's land and exhibited at the Chicago Museum of Natural History, helped promote awareness of the Latah area and stimulated land sales. Settlement boomed when the Oregon Railway and Navigation Company extended its rail line north from Tekoa to Spokane via Latah in 1888 to 1889.

LOWER GRANITE DAM, a half mile upstream from Almota, takes its name from a nearby granite outcropping, which protrudes into the river from both sides, unusual in an area largely covered by basalt flows. Quarries here supplied stone for various Northwest buildings. The dam operates with seven others on the lower Columbia and Snake rivers to make a seaport of Lewiston, Idaho (470 miles from the Pacific). Drive onto the dam for a view of the shipping, mostly tugs and barges carrying wheat downriver and petroleum products upriver. A visitor center includes exhibits on Native Americans, white settlement, and the steamboat era. Driving across the dam is permissible during daylight hours.

Lower Granite Dam was completed in 1975. In June of that year, the stern-wheel steamer *Portland* was the first vessel to lock through all four Snake River dams—a fitting ceremonial tribute to the late 1800s and early 1900s ancestry of modern river shipping. Even if close to a railroad, many farmers now truck their grain to the river and ship by barge.

In many ways dams now more nearly symbolize the Snake and Columbia rivers than do the salmon that formerly thronged throughout the watershed, spawning even in small tributaries. Today's dams block fish from a third of their former range, thereby eliminating unknown numbers of wild stocks with their distinctive genetic characteristics, fine-tuned over millennia. Even surviving runs are greatly affected, and no sure solution is known. The Army Corps of Engineers has tried a taxi service, barging and trucking young fish downriver to a point below Bonneville Dam where the Columbia still flows freely to the sea. Adult fish theoretically can swim back upriver to spawn, aided by fish ladders. But none of this has actually worked well. The outlook is bleak. The river's legacy now seems to be hydropower and irrigation, not fish.

MALDEN began in 1906 as a railroad town and declined in the 1920s when rail-service facilities went elsewhere. Agriculture never controlled the rhythms here—except for bringing in the railroad. With the trains now gone, tall grass and balsamroot grow at street intersections still signed as Eighth and Broadway or Ninth and Main. Nature is reclaiming the townsite. Only scattered commercial buildings and houses remain, widely separated by empty space.

Dependence on railroad jobs, economic desperation, and racial bigotry are illustrated by the summary hanging of a Chinese laborer whose sole offense was to apply for railroad work in Malden; he was unable to read the sign that announced "No Chinks Allowed." The tragedy exemplifies the distress brought by the railroads, much as they were courted and welcomed. When the national economy turned downward in the late 1880s and early 1890s, the Northwest was especially affected: transcontinental railway construction was complete and jobs vanished, but not men. White workers had come to Washington expecting their diligence would assure them a stake in the "promised land." Instead they found themselves cut off.

They reasoned that Chinese laborers were part of the problem, owing to their willingness to accept wages—as one editorial writer expressed it—"upon which a white man would starve" and to work "even on Sunday, since they are

Flour mills such as Oakesdale's are now obsolete; grain is shipped out for milling.

heathen." Furthermore, they were "apt, skillful [and] obedient." Many white workers also concluded that the problem lay with the railroad companies, which were monopolies owned by Eastern robber barons, who built mansions while workers lived in cottages. The need to "do something" appeared all the more urgent in the mid-1890s when railroad companies replaced white American workmen at first with lower-paid Chinese, then with Japanese and southern and eastern Europeans. The hanging at Malden was just one incident of widespread mob violence against the Chinese.

In **OAKESDALE** the focal point is a four-story flour mill (no longer operating but with all of its machinery—including hardwood and steel roller mills and bran sifters—still in working condition). The milling equipment came from Illinois after financial problems crippled business there. The building includes 12-inch-square timbers 40 feet long and chutes made of hand-sawed and hand-planed planks. Joseph Barron, an experienced miller, bought the mill in 1907 and had its equipment dismantled and reassembled in Oakesdale.

He produced flour until 1939, then reduced the operation to cleaning and storing grain. Faced with competition from larger-scale businesses, the mill closed in 1960. A small, adjoining mill still offers specialty flours, cornmeal, and bran. The large mill is open during Oakesdale's annual Old Mill Days (last weekend in May).

Three miles southeast of town on State Route 27 notice the **John F. Kelley Homestead Cabin.** Built in 1872, it stands as a well-preserved remnant of pioneer days.

In **PALOUSE** commercial buildings on flat land near the river bear elaborate, proud facades (and are officially listed as a Historic District); homes climb the bluff above the river. Settlers in the surrounding countryside began raising livestock in the 1870s and gradually converted to farming during the next decade. Unlike other towns in the area, Palouse got a boost from gold mining. During the 1880s and 1890s, miners from Idaho's Gold Hill and Hoodoo districts came in for supplies, and storekeepers themselves mined part-time or grubstaked those in the field. Timber on the banks of the Palouse River also fueled the economy. During spring freshets "river pigs" shepherded logs downstream, wielding peaveys to coax them along and setting dynamite to blast the jams. When payday came, it was whoop and holler on Main Street as the loggers ended months of camp isolation.

A conflict arose between the flour mill and the sawmill. City fathers effected a compromise that called for opening a dam two mornings a week to let logs through, leaving it closed the rest of the time to maintain a consistent flow for the flour mill's waterwheel. The 1893 depression derailed prosperity for a time, but the Potlatch Lumber Company, associated with the Weyerhaeuser Company, purchased the Palouse sawmill in 1904, and production soon reached a new high. The Potlatch Company built the Washington, Idaho and Montana Railroad to replace the unpredictable river as a log-delivery system. They also acquired thousands of acres of Idaho pine—and Palouse residents danced in the streets celebrating the rosy future.

They danced too soon. The lumber company decided instead to build a streamlined modern mill and company town in Idaho, closer to its logging camps. The Palouse mill cut lumber to build its rival mill and town, then, outmoded and inefficient, was itself closed. The town gently declined from its days of a booming and varied economy into simply a modest agricultural center for local farmers.

The drive to **PENAWAWA,** a major Oregon Steam Navigation Company landing, leads down one of the "breaks" connecting Palouse wheatlands with the Snake River. Such ravines harbor flowing creeks with cottonwoods and wild-rose thickets; vast grassy slopes rise as walls, in places seamed with basalt outcrops. Nothing remains at Penawawa itself—which once had a hotel, church, and warehouses—but a road leads for about 4 miles along the river now flooded by the reservoir behind Little Goose Dam. The territorial road between Walla Walla and Spokane Falls crossed the river here.

When the Nez Perce War began in 1877, settlers throughout the Palouse heard (unfounded) rumors of hostilities coming their way and were understandably terrified. At Palouse City 200 people crowded into a sturdy stockade for protection. At Colfax 60 wagons brought outlying citizens to huddle within a schoolhouse. And at Penawawa whites waiting to ship wool stacked their bales into a "fort" complete with gunports. No actual trouble developed anywhere in the region and as people learned that Chief Joseph had headed toward Montana, not toward the Palouse and Coeur d'Alene country, they returned to their farms. They found their livestock safe, watered, and fed by neighboring native people.

PULLMAN clings to five hills, its residential streets climbing up and down like roller coaster tracks. A brick commercial district, built after an 1890 fire, lines the confluence of two creeks and the south fork of the Palouse River—thus the town's first name, Three Forks. Washington State University occupies 600 hilly acres on the east side of town.

Several ranchers settled here in 1877, and one farsighted person set aside 10 acres for a town. Five years later the community was platted. In 1890 Pullman shipped one million bushels of wheat by rail. That same year a board of commissioners toured eastern Washington seeking a site for the state's land-grant college, and Pullman longed for the prestige and

The Snake River Canyon and the breaks (steep ravines) leading to it offer shelter and warmer winter temperatures than the adjoining uplands. These qualities attracted both Native Americans and pioneering farmers, who settled areas like Penawawa.

economic benefits the institution would bring. When the commissioners were due to arrive, farmers hitched their rigs and drove to town to give the community a bustling appearance. Mrs. Lulu Downen reminisced that her husband advised her to "dress up, bring the children, and keep moving around." The efforts succeeded. On a Sunday morning Pullman partisans lobbying in Olympia telegraphed the good news of a decision in Pullman's favor. Church bells pealed, and the streets filled with cheering citizens. The new institution, forerunner of today's Washington State University, opened its doors in 1892.

During this period the town drilled artesian wells with great success: the first attempt brought in a gusher of 1,000 gallons per minute. At about the same time a local farmer boosted the town's renown with a wheat harvest of 101 bushels per acre. Optimism flourished. But in 1893 a flood, crop losses owing to wet weather, and national depression dampened the outlook; two thirds of the area's farmers lost their land. College extension agents, newspapers, and chambers of commerce preached diversification, and some of the remaining farmers tried planting fruit trees and raising cattle. World War I brought tremendous demand for wheat, however, and orchards and livestock barns disappeared. Pullman grew as the college grew; today it is much the largest town in Whitman County.

At **Washington State University** the turreted 1894 **Thompson Hall** is the oldest remaining building, and the cupola from Ferry Hall (an 1899 men's dormitory demolished in 1975) stands as a midcampus gazebo.

The university, nicknamed "Wazzu" (for WSU), is a land-grant college established by the legislature soon after statehood (which came in 1889). Under the 1862 Morrill Act, the federal government gave the state 190,000 acres to finance a college promoting "liberal and practical education of the industrial classes." The 1888 Hatch Act made federal funds available for an agricultural experiment station and a statewide extension service in agriculture and home economics. The university's mandate has always been three-pronged: instruction, research, and the dissemination of scientific information, not just to farmers but to the entire citizenry.

ROCK LAKE—long and narrow and bounded with steep basalt walls—was the last home of Chief Kamiakin, who farmed here with his family until his death in 1877. (See ST. JOSEPH'S MISSION, p. 142, and YAKIMA WAR sidebar, p. 148.) After the chief's death, cattle ranchers moved into the area. The south end of the lake, with its gentle slope to the water, gave easy access for thirsty herds.

In 1903 a promoter shipped a gasoline-powered boat on the railroad as far as St. John, then hauled it overland to the lake. He offered tourist rides and soon built a hotel to accommodate his guests. The hotel became the nucleus of a small community named Rock Lake. Construction of the Chicago, Milwaukee and St. Paul Railroad brought a flurry of activity, but the completed railroad bypassed the town by way of a trestle. One mile south, the railroad built a siding and grain warehouse that became a stop for transcontinental trains.

In 1911 a developer platted the town of **Ewan** (Ee´-wahn) near the siding. Rock Lake businesses moved to the new community to take advantage of its rail service. The town now consists of grain elevators, houses, one church, and a lingering steam-railroad water tower.

At **ROSALIA** a concrete railroad trestle with multiple arches stands like a misplaced Roman aqueduct. Distinctive mansions cap each end of the main street (which is Whitman, named for an early storekeeper, not for the famous missionary). Handsome churches from the early 1900s and a brick downtown district line Whitman between the mansions. Seventh Street leads east to the **Steptoe Memorial,** a granite obelisk on a tree-shaded lawn. It honors participants in a decisive battle between the U.S. Army and warriors from the Spokane, Palouse, and Coeur d'Alene tribes. The names of seven dead are listed, all "of the First Dragoons, United States Army."

In May 1858 Lieutenant Colonel Edward J. Steptoe set out from Fort Walla Walla with 158 troops to investigate reports of depredations against miners in the Colville area. Most of the men carried only 40 rounds of ammunition and short-barreled musketoons with an effective range of about 50 yards. They also hauled two mounted howitzers. At the Snake River near

The 1903 six-bedroom Howard house at the north edge of Rosalia exemplifies architectural elegance within the Palouse. Howard was a beef rancher and shipper.

Alpowa, Chief Timothy of the Nez Perce assisted their crossing and joined as guide. On May 17 the command met 600 to 1,200 native warriors armed with superior Hudson's Bay Company muskets (which were smoothbored muzzle-loaders specifically manufactured as trade rifles). Sporadic fighting broke out and continued all day. Steptoe ordered a gradual retreat, keeping his force to ridges of defensible ground. Father Joseph Joset offered mediation, but only lesser chiefs agreed to even listen.

In the late afternoon the harassed soldiers climbed a hill near the present town of Rosalia. There Steptoe realized they could not survive another battle. He ordered men to muffle their horses' hoofs, bury the howitzers and their dead comrades, and retreat to the southwest. Twenty-four hours later the weary dragoons reached the Snake River ford. White historians have speculated about such an easy escape; most likely it was permitted. Annihilation was not part of native warfare and, up to this point, battles with the army had been skirmishes, raids, and harassments.

Steptoe's defeat triggered a retaliatory campaign by Colonel George Wright—and led to equipping the troops with better rifles. (Also see SPOKANE BATTLES sidebar, p. 10.)

ST. JOHN reveals its prosperity in tidy homes, flower-filled yards, and ubiquitous grain elevators near the railroad tracks. The tailored green of a golf course counterpoints dusty sales yards offering farm machinery, from gigantic combines to chemical fertilizer tanks.

Edward St. John settled here about 1881. Within 20 years a "Farmer's Line" telephone company was serving 134 outlying families and had an in-town rival. Barbed wire commonly did double duty at that time: farmers used it for fences and to carry phone messages.

Five miles west of St. John, the 1916 **Max Steinke Round Barn** still functions as an integral part of a modern wheat farm. The barn is actually 12-sided. Laminated planks form ribs that support the arch of the roof, and a light-weight wooden cupola tops the center. The builder favored the round design for the ease of feeding stock, mostly draft horses, and for the large stalls that simplified harnessing the teams. Today the barn stores cattle feed.

STEPTOE BUTTE (3,612 feet in elevation, the highest point in the Palouse) is listed as a National Natural Landmark because of its geological importance. It stands as a remnant mountaintop of ancient rock (Precambrian) jutting through layers of much younger basalt lava. Geologists throughout the world have adopted the term "steptoe" to designate this type of landform. Be sure to drive to the top, a 1,600-foot rise in 4½ miles. The road spirals up, making three complete 360-degree loops. The summit view is stunning. It ranges from the

BARNS

Certain contractors in the Palouse specialized in building the huge—and beautiful—barns needed on each farm in an era when 32 horses or mules were standard for pulling each combine. The golden era of construction came between the arrival of transcontinental railroads in the 1880s, which tied farms to markets and suddenly permitted expansion, and the switch to mechanization and specialization, which came in the 1940s.

"Barns are like friends," says Burt McCroskey, descendent of a prominent Palouse pioneering family who home-steaded here in the 1870s:

You can see an attitude in barns. Straight-forward. Honest, like the farmers themselves. No frills except for cupolas. A lot of cupolas came from Sears and Montgomery Ward catalogs. Others are original designs by the barn contractor.

Only the first log barns showed ethnic traces. Swedes handled logs a certain way, Germans another way. But those barns were replaced by barns built by contractors, or they were sided over. Even as late as 1910 some farmers were siding over their log barns. Churches show ethnic architecture, but barns varied depending on the individual contractor.

Some early barns were round-topped, or had gable eaves. It all depended on the contractor, on who the farmer wanted to hire. The Leonard barn on the old Pullman–Moscow road is copied from a round barn in Nebraska. Mr. Leonard remembers playing in the barn that this present one replaced; it burned down about 1911, and they decided to replace it with this barn. Round barns are an American invention. They seem to have started among the Shakers in New York. That sect made circular boxes, too, and used circular designs on their quilts. There was a symbolism.

For a round barn, the contractor just took the same basic arch of a round-top barn and spun it around. The style was popular in the 1910s; lots of farm journals discussed its merits. Believers said it took less material and was convenient for storing hay, feeding horses, and cleaning out the stalls. Critics said round barns stayed dark at the center, had less room for hay, and couldn't be enlarged later on.

When I see a barn fall nowadays, it hurts. Some things are being done to keep them—not really repairing them, but stabilizing. We've lost lots of them. We still have lots. I even found a barn I'd never seen before when I was out looking along backroads a while back. It was cruciform in outline and had a rounded top.

The Leonard barn near Pullman, like others, has been updated to serve modern needs.

jagged Bitterroot Mountains of Idaho to the more rounded, distant Blue Mountains of southeast Washington. The broad panorama makes it easy to visualize how the wheatlands formed as gigantic "dunes" of wind-deposited sediment.

From 1877 to 1883, James H. Davis—called "Cashup" Davis—operated a roadhouse at the foot of Steptoe Butte. His nickname came from insistence on cash payments, a remarkable habit in a cash-poor, barter economy. Davis loved company. He not only provided all the services a stage stop required—lodging, meals, corrals, spring-fed water troughs for the animals—he also hosted merry parties and dances that drew ranchers from all over the countryside.

In the 1880s when railroads penetrated the Palouse, stage traffic fell off. Cashup Davis, hoping to maintain the flow of visitors, built a hotel on the top of the butte in 1888. Two stories tall and festooned with wheat stalks above doorways, the building was crowned with a rooftop balcony for sight-seeing. Crowds failed to flock up the mountainside, however, and the water supply caused constant problems. Cashup was often lonely. He died in 1896. Fifteen years later the vacant hotel burned, and local newspapers reported that its flames lit the countryside like an erupting volcano.

Preservation as a park came through the generosity of Virgil T. McCroskey, a Colfax pharmacist (whose Elk Drug Store continues in business). He was raised on a 640-acre homestead at the base of the butte and retired there after leaving the drugstore; the family home, still standing on the south side of the road leading to the butte, was a local showplace with peacocks and 60 species of trees brought in from around the world. In the 1930s the town of Colfax tried to buy a road right-of-way and 40 acres at the summit of the butte, but the project failed. McCroskey then made the purchase personally and also raised money to buy the 80 acres now used as a picnic area. He donated the two land parcels to the state in 1945 and 1946, providing they be used solely as a public park, forever. (Virgil McCroskey's brother Robert was a prominent resident of Garfield.)

At **TEKOA** (Tee´-koh) a steel train trestle (north edge of town) symbolizes the com-

munity's former dependence on the railroad. The old Union Pacific depot is now a farm store, and grain elevators and warehouses reflect the current economy as do well-kept houses of various architectural eras and styles. Two streets particularly worth sampling are Broadway and Main. Note especially the large Williard House (Main and Howard) with bays and setbacks and bracketed eaves. This grand house was built by a farm couple who moved into town and achieved the wife's dream of this mansion, then curtained off the kitchen and lived only there to save heating the entire house.

In 1875 a lone settler opened a trading post at Tekoa to serve the nearby Coeur d'Alene Reservation in Idaho. He was joined by sawmill operator Daniel Truax who learned that a railroad was coming and platted a town. Rumor became reality in 1888 with the arrival of a Union Pacific branch line, at that time called the Washington and Idaho Railroad. Mrs. Truax, looking out on the construction camp, suggested the name Tekoa, a biblical term meaning "city of tents."

Though small, the town was blessed by being on the main Spokane line and on two branch lines, one to the Wallace, Idaho, mines and one into the western Palouse. A roundhouse, machine shop, coal bunker, and district administrative headquarters soon provided income for one family out of four. The Tekoa newspaper commented that it was a "gladsome sight" to see the pay car arrive in town, for it meant a "general settling up of grocery bills, etc., and, as a consequence of its arrival, everybody wears a broad smile."

After a brief lull caused by rain during harvest season and the Panic of 1893, Tekoa thrived as a grain (and in the early days, apple) shipping center. The Milwaukee Railroad laid its transcontinental rails through town in 1908, bridging the valley with a long steel trestle. As the *Tekoa Advertiser* for June 14, 1907, reported:

There is considerable trestle work to be done here and it is thought by some that the construction work in this vicinity may require two years. . . . The large steam shovel [making the cut north of town] is throwing dirt faster than it is being handled on the Panama Canal.

The Milwaukee Road further contributed to Tekoa's prosperity with one of the region's first cold-storage plants and a seed pea operation, in which about 50 women sorted and packed locally grown peas along with some that were shipped in from as far away as Lompoc, California. Trackside corrals penned thousands of bleating sheep, which traveled by train to summer pastures in Idaho and Montana.

By the 1920s increasing automobiles and trucks undercut railroad dominance, and technological advances, especially the development of diesel locomotives, reduced the number of crewmen and repair shops needed. By the 1950s the Milwaukee Road had dropped its Tekoa operations, and the Union Pacific had moved its crews to Spokane. Although trains still move grains and agricultural chemicals through Tekoa, railroad workers no longer spend their paychecks here.

In **UNIONTOWN** small homes are dwarfed by Saint Boniface Catholic Church, an impressive, twin-towered edifice topped by a seven-foot statue of the Immaculate Conception. Flanking the church (on a hill one block west of the main street) are the original parish house and convent of the Benedictine Sisters, who arrived in 1884.

In 1875 German Catholic farmers first immigrated to the Uniontown area where they built a frame church for visiting clerics. In 1887 a resident priest arrived to serve the parish. Six years later, workmen laid the foundation for a large brick church, but an economic depression interrupted construction. Saint Boniface's was not finished until 1905.

In 1889 a Northern Pacific branch railway boosted the town's economic life, previously dependent on agriculture and a brewery. Uniontown was the end of the line for passengers and freight, although there was a daily connection from there to Lewiston via horse-drawn stage. When tracks were finally extended to Lewiston, Uniontown again became a quiet agricultural trading center. (Also see COLTON, p. 191.)

South of Uniontown (5 miles) notice the **Ruddy-Collins House** at the head of Hatwai Canyon. A simple farmhouse, it was built in 1871 of hand-sawed planks. Michael Ruddy, an immigrant from eastern Canada, brought his family on the Union Pacific to San Francisco in 1869 (the railroad's first year of operation), then traveled north looking for homestead land. He and his son built this house and sent for the rest of the family. As one of the earliest residences in the region, it served as a stagecoach and mail stop, as well as a home. In 1884 Orville Collins bought the house. Primarily he grew wheat—but he also raised beef for the Klondike; owned a

By the early 1900s railroads lacing the Palouse included the Spokane and Inland electric line from Spokane to Moscow, Idaho. Here, men and horses grade its roadbed.

feed store in Lewiston, which he supplied from his own fields; manufactured bricks; served as president of a Cottonwood, Idaho, bank; and raised nine children. The house has been in the Collins family for more than a century.

Immediately south of the Ruddy-Collins House, the **Lewiston Grade** of U.S. 195 is worth driving for its sweeping view of the Snake and Clearwater confluence. Drive the old switch-back grade to understand the difficulty of early travel between the wheat fields and the river. Or follow the new route, which takes 10 minutes. This new grade descends gently but has "runaway truck" ramps at four major curves, for use in case of brake failure. Each ramp is covered with soft sand and slopes steeply uphill.

WAVERLY nestles among the productive hills of the northern Palouse, its post office still open, its few homes occupied, its grain elevators active—yet with an overall ambience of having been bypassed.

In the early 1900s, a flurry of sugar beet farming gave the town its major start. Financiers Edward H. Morrison and D. C. Corbin offered farmers free seed, hired French overseers and Japanese and Native American field hands, and built a three-story brick sugar mill at Waverly. They expected to operate during a three- or four-month harvest season with two 12-hour shifts of 70 workers each.

Sugar had been produced from beets in Europe since Napoleonic times, and California had recently begun production. An 1897 federal act requiring high duty on imported sugar set a favorable climate for the local effort and, for a while, the state offered a supportive subsidy of one cent per pound of sugar.

Bringing water from snow-fed lakes via an exquisitely engineered network of irrigation ditches, Corbin began developing beet fields both at Greenacres, east of Spokane, and at Waverly. Crops did not fare well, however. Sugar beets need "endless" thinning and weeding; are subject to blight; and require frequent crop rotation. Irrigation problems also developed, and gravel from the soil damaged knives at the sugar mill. Operations lasted only

from 1899 to 1907, then the mill closed forever. No trace remains.

(Also see FAIRFIELD, p. 193.)

WAWAWAI (Wah-wah´ -we) or "council grounds"—from the Palouse word *wa*, meaning "talk"—today consists of a richly green county park at the mouth of a Snake River side canyon. In 1877 Isaiah Metheny homesteaded here; he offered right-of-way for a road when farmers began to settle on the plateau, and investors built a warehouse on the riverbank. Metheny also platted a town, but it never developed beyond a store, warehouse, and ferry landing.

Early settlers grew fruit on the flats of Wawawai (now flooded by Lower Granite Dam). Their apples succeeded every year, and their peaches ripened five years out of six, confounding experts whose gloomy predictions overlooked the moderating effects of the canyon. Native people had recognized the situation for thousands of years, wintering along the river and harvesting roots and berries there far earlier than was possible up on the plateau.

Harvest-time orchards along the Snake hummed with a variety of languages as Chinese and Native American pickers joined local adults and children. At packing sheds workers sorted and graded the fruit and wrapped each apple or peach in tissue. Box makers sawed and hammered to keep up with the demand. Until 1908 riverboats carried the fruit 40 miles to the railroad at Riparia; after that year, a riverbank railroad stretched all the way from Lewiston to Pasco, ending the steamboat era. In the late 1930s a Wawawai orchardist pioneered the U-pick business by welcoming the public into his orchards.

Across the river and about a mile upstream watch for remnants of the Mayfield Tramway in gulches near the top of a canyon. For a closer view of wheat tram remnants, walk west from Wawawai along the railway for about a mile to the first rocky canyon (near navigational marker 5). Tram cars carried sacked wheat down 1,800-foot bluffs, from upland fields to Snake River steamer landings. The Mayfield tram operated until 1941. Fallen supports now dot the slope.

Channeled Scablands

Ice-age floods sculpted this region. They occurred repeatedly as impounded water burst through lobes of the continental ice sheet damming the Clark Fork drainage (in present-day Idaho and Montana). The most recent of these awesome floods—about 13,000 years ago—drained the entire Glacial Lake Missoula in about two weeks and sent torrents estimated at 10 times the combined flow of all the world's rivers racing southwestward. Velocities reached 45 miles per hour. The water scrubbed away soil and plucked at underlying bedrock. The channels it carved here still braid through the landscape as steep-sided canyons and gullies. Livestock graze where the remaining soil is thin; dryland wheat grows where it lies deep. Towns tend to be widely scattered dots.

Today the channeled scablands are both the wild domain of burrowing owls and badgers and of coulee-bottom hayfields and storage elevators. To sample the blend, drive from Connell to Washtucna (State Route 260) following an ancient course of the Palouse River; also drive east of Washtucna on State Route 26, which links the gouged and castellated scablands with the smooth contours of the Palouse wheat country. Several miles of the 1860s Mullan Road alignment (near Washtucna) are still passable. Palouse Falls provides a surprising torrent of water in an otherwise dry canyon. A museum in Othello highlights local irrigation and railroading history, and Snake River dams include visitor centers and displays.

At **CONNELL** (Kah-nel′) a 1905 church from the town's first pioneering period overlooks houses and stores from its second pioneering period, which came during the 1950s. The church (Adams and Third) has a distinctive corner entrance and fancy-cut shingles on its steeple. It was built just four years after the town was platted. Open-range stockmen had used the land here for cattle and horses beginning as early as the 1860s, and later sheepmen brought their flocks. But no town grew even in the 1880s, when the Northern Pacific built its main line down the coulee here and then added a branch into the Palouse wheat country.

Ordinarily the railroad chose sidings because of available water, but Connell—then called Palouse Junction for the branch line—lacked

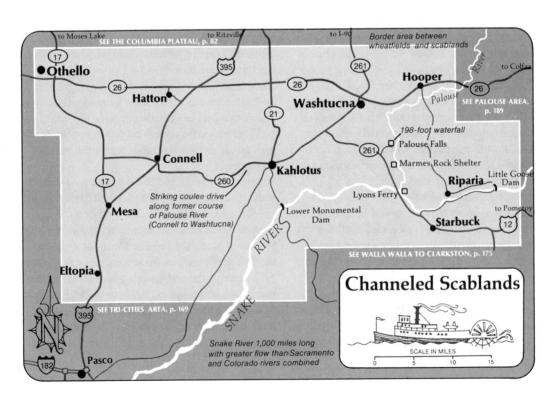

The basalt walls and mesas of Palouse Canyon typify the scenic grandeur of southeastern Washington's channeled scablands, which were sculpted by ice-age floodwaters.

even that amenity; water had to be hauled eight miles from Bluff Wells (Mesa). At Connell an 1886 magazine reported only:

. . . a sort of hotel for travelers who have to stay overnight on their way up to Colfax or Moscow [Idaho], and a saloonkeeper, on the watch for a chance to sell a glass of beer. . . . The people at the junction have a gloomy, taciturn expression.

Early 1900s land promotion brought settlers, and optimists platted Connell. Farming was extremely difficult in the area, however, and many lost their land. (See ELTOPIA, p. 206.) That pattern of toil and defeat repeated itself even in the 1950s as the Bureau of Reclamation auctioned land in the irrigated "blocks" of the Columbia Basin Project. Applicants drew lots (veterans had preference), toured the 60- to 80-acre units offered, and sat on folding chairs at the Grange Hall to hear extension agents warn of difficulties. Connell businesses restocked shelves to cope with the altered set of needs: irrigation pipe, pump parts, liquid fertilizers.

Government requirements for eligibility included having enough cash to operate a farm ($8,500 in 1958) and a "habitable residence," which had to be occupied for at least 12 months

out of the first year and a half. In his book *Years Plowed Under,* Leo Vogel tells of discovering government surplus houses "propped up on cement blocks" at Moses Lake. Some had come from the Hanford atomic-energy security zone, some from the World War II air base at Moses Lake. Vogel picked a house used by construction workers at Grand Coulee Dam and before that at Boulder Dam, to judge from Nevada automobile license plates tacked to one wall. The house cost $850, the moving job, $300.

This new pioneering era brought updated versions of many problems familiar from the earlier period. For example, navigating through dust storms called for keeping track of overhead wires. The wind also meant, according to Vogel, that:

You tasted and breathed your fertilizer if the wind was in one direction, your neighbor's if in another. . . . The water from nozzles hit the ground twenty feet beyond the pipes and most of the spray kept on going. Any pipe left lying around blew full of sand and provided me with a nice surprise and a hernia when I tried to pick it up.

Leaky irrigation ditches needed around-the-clock monitoring, yet water charges were like a lien against the farm. Those who missed a payment lost their land. When this happened it was considered a "neighborly gesture" to attend the resulting auction; besides, "You had the advantage of knowing his equipment, probably having borrowed it often enough."

Today the sheer green fecundity of the land hides the dual sagebrush-and-sweat settlement eras, and the survivors of those hardships marvel at what time and dependable water have wrought.

In **ELTOPIA** (El-toh´-pee-uh) the main street—with towering grain elevators and a lone general store—parallels the highway; curving residential streets climb the coulee wall behind this business core. The Northern Pacific needed water stops along the main line track it built across the Columbia Plateau in 1881, and Eltopia began as "20-Mile Well" (20 miles from Ainsworth, railway construction headquarters near present-day Pasco). Supposedly the name Eltopia came about when a flash flood ruined several weeks of labor, and a Cockney crewman commented there would be "hell to pay" for the loss. This became "Eltopay," then Eltopia.

By the early 1900s the Northern Pacific was selling its land. (See HATTON, p. 207.) Speculators were willing to pay $6.50 an acre in the Eltopia area, compared with a going price of $2.50 elsewhere. In 1906 one land company advertised "60,000 acres in the Great Central Washington Wheat Raising Belt" at up to $15 per acre, a tidy profit. They promised productive soil with no irrigation. Homestead land also was

WEEDS

Little native bunchgrass remains in Washington; cheatgrass *(Bromus tectorum)* has taken over. It turns lowlands green in early spring and ripens red-brown seed-heads by early summer. It "cheats" by using up winter's accumulated soil moisture and by invading farm fields. The change began in the 1890s and took only about 40 years, a remarkable altering of landscape even viewed on a world scale.

Apparently on-the-hoof delivery of beef cattle to mining camps in British Columbia and Montana prepared the way; the trampling broke the fragile crust of mosses and lichens covering the soil between clumps of sagebrush and bunch-grass. A new ecological niche opened. Ranchers increased their herds. The trampling spread, and cattle, sheep, and horses ate native grasses faster than they could replace themselves. Washington's flora had evolved with only occasional nibbling, not wholesale grazing.

By the 1880s and 1890s farmers began replacing stockmen. They set sagebrush on fire, plowed the soil, and brought in seed for crops, some of it contaminated with cheatgrass seed. Ironically, experiments at Pullman also contributed to the invasion. In 1897 state college agronomists studied cheatgrass as a possible remedy for overgrazed rangelands. They decided negatively and abandoned their experimental field, but escapees quite surely invaded additional land. Other weeds such as Russian thistle and Jim Hill mustard proved equally aggressive. These are the tumble-weeds that virtually symbolize the "Old West," but actually are newcomers. By the early 1900s both species—which tangle farm machinery—were so prevalent that in places farmers were fined for having them on their land, and as early as 1898 a professor at the state agricultural college urged funding for a horse-mounted patrol to "destroy any chance specimens of Russian thistle found." When money was not forthcoming, the professor sent a lone student to trudge the tracks. He accomplished little. By definition weeds are hardy, and Washington imports—especially cheatgrass—were already turning their toehold into domination.

available, and a genuine land rush resulted.

Mary Finkbeiner, who arrived in the area from Nebraska in 1900 with her mother, two brothers, and a sister, later wrote to relatives about traveling by wagon from the railway and cooking on a sagebrush fire with "coyotes all around us . . . howling all night." Once settled, the family lived in a house so tiny that:

. . . mornings we moved bedding out and evenings moved it in. . . . We lived in that cabin until we hauled lumber to build a four-horse barn, then moved into the barn. Two stalls. We had beds in one stall and a table and cookstove in the other one. We lived in this barn until we built a house.

Weather was generally favorable during these early years of the century, and Franklin County became known as an area that had gone from sagebrush to wheat in less than a decade. There were problems of course. Dust storms were so severe that one settler remembers getting lost on the way home from a Rebekah lodge meeting; and weeds such as yarrow, lamb's-quarter, China lettuce, and "Jim Hill" mustard invaded the overgrazed land. Cattle spurned these plants as forage, although sheep would eat them. Similarly, cheatgrass replaced native bunch-grass, fescue, and bluegrass. At first, it was considered useless for cattle although it is now recognized as palatable in early spring.

As World War I began, farm prices—and hopes—soared. After the war, prices and hopes fell, and the Dutch-owned Hypotheekbank of Spokane foreclosed on many of the mortgages it held in this area. Enough farmers managed to hang on, however, for Eltopia elevators to stay in business, and railroad employment provided a payroll. In the 1950s the Columbia Basin Project brought irrigation water and at last began to turn the land dependably green. (See CONNELL, P. 204.)

In **HATTON** wooden and concrete grain elevators along the railroad tracks announce the community's role. Originally a water stop and wheat siding called Twin Wells, Hatton up-graded to a platted townsite in 1902. The railroad even opened a land office here where prospective settlers could study maps and arrange terms for the purchase of land. The

Northern Pacific usually sold full half sections (320 acres), whereas government homestead laws allowed only quarter sections. Furthermore, the government required five years of "continu-ous" residence for land title, or an alternative six months of residence and $1.25 per acre.

Those who could afford to buy vast acreages had an advantage over small landowners, who could not justify the high cost of the machinery increasingly needed to compete even on a small scale. Finding the optimum size for farms in each area took time. Even in the 1950s, the first irrigation units offered by the government proved too small to work efficiently.

The **HOOPER** general store, now used only as an office, stands among neatly mowed lawns and huge poplar trees, which create an oasis of shade in a treeless land. If the term "town" can apply to a little more than a dozen houses, then Hooper qualifies. It is a company town built in the early 1900s by the multigeneration, family-owned McGregor Land and Livestock Company.

Hooper has a "municipal" water system; a hotel that began as a boarding house for single men and is now used for potluck dinners and quilting bees; wool, wheat, and apple ware-houses, which stand by the railroad tracks; and a still-functioning post office with its original bank of oak-fronted mail boxes. A schoolhouse was demolished several years ago when one-room schools in this part of the scab-lands consoli-dated with the Lacrosse district.

A small store across the bridge from the east end of town continues to serve the outlying community. It moved to this location from "downtown" Hooper in about 1910 when railroad construction was under way: Whitman County law forbade selling beer in an unincorporated area but, as McGregors still like to say, "Hooper is so big it straddles two counties." They simply moved the store a few hundred yards into Adams County.

The McGregors had fled Scotland during the brutal mid-1800s "clearance" when English landowners rid the Highlands of people and small croft farms so as to make room for large-scale sheep operations. The family settled in Canada and from there four of the brothers migrated to the scablands, where they became sheepherders. "Wages" then customarily

THE MULLAN ROAD

In 1853 the federal War Department ordered the exploration and survey of a route to link the Missouri River drainage with the Columbia. This would connect Fort Benton (Montana) with Fort Walla Walla, and simplify travel across the country to the Northwest. Instead of choosing between the Oregon Trail or a sea voyage involving either Cape Horn or the Isthmus of Panama, a traveler could journey in comparative ease by riverboat, then cross overland only from one river to the other. That distance—estimated by Lewis and Clark as quite short—actually proved to be 624 miles.

As surveying got under way the Walla Walla *Statesman* extolled a "most lively anticipation" of what they optimistically called "the great highway" and even assured readers that "many people in Europe" were expressing enthusiasm for this new route. Completion of the road also was expected to ease the deployment of troops and provide a freight route helpful during the possible construction of a northern transcontinental railroad.

Road construction began in 1859. Working out from Fort Walla Walla, Captain John Mullan chose a route that offered water and pasturage for livestock, and he even seeded meadows with bluegrass and timothy; his crews used thousands of mules for surveying and grading, and future travelers would also depend on animals, which would need feed. Mullan's men laid corduroy across swamps, cut trees at ground level, removed obstructing rocks, and built hundreds of river crossings (146 crossings in 100 miles along one particularly troublesome stretch). In heavily forested areas Mullan doubled the width of the road from 25 feet to 50 feet to allow more sunlight to melt the snow.

By 1862 wagons could lurch over the resulting swath from the western edge of the Great Plains, across the Rocky Mountains, to the pine country of Spokane and the sagebrush flats leading to Walla Walla. Rockslides and washouts soon changed the "road" to a mule trail, however, and wheeled travel became all but impossible. Immigrants in 1865 reported that "any other method" of reaching the Northwest would surely be better than the Mullan Road. Nonetheless heavy use prevailed, for gold strikes drew miners and mule trains shuttling between Walla Walla and a succession of gold districts to the east and north. In September 1865 the *Statesman* estimated that 1,000 mules had headed for the mines in a single two-week period, tied into packtrains averaging 50 animals each and carrying 300 pounds per mule. Farmers had a bonanza simply in supplying oats, let alone flour, beef, and pork!

Today's I-90 follows much of the original alignment through the Rocky Mountains, and in eastern Washington parts of the road itself are still in use. For a sample, east of Washtucna (near Milepost 85), turn north from State Route 26 on a dusty road with blind curves and little traffic. Still called Mullan Road, this winds for 5 miles through half-Palouse, half-scablands country, then curves to a promontory and a road tee. To stay on the Mullan Road, turn left and continue about another 6 miles to Cow Creek, where a rock foundation remains from the old way station known as Halfway House (the midpoint between Walla Walla and Plante's Ferry, near Spokane). Here the Mullan Road forked to the northeast, and the Colville Road continued north.

A 1903 photograph shows 6,000 sheep next to the McGregor shearing shed near Hooper. Expert shearers needed only four minutes to grab, position, and clip each sheep.

included a portion of the spring lambs, a system that allowed the ambitious and frugal to build up their own herds. This the McGregors did, in time owning flocks that totaled at least 15,000 ewes plus lambs.

With the keen sense of opportunity that was necessary for successful pioneering, the brothers—and their descendants—also entered other fields. They bought wheatlands and experimented with orchards, selling the fruit under their own label—a kilted Scotsman with a big red apple as his head. They ran an insurance agency and automobile dealership at the Hooper store, and developed a chemical fertilizer company that now operates throughout the Palouse and into Oregon and Idaho.

During World War II, nationwide labor shortages complicated finding sheepherders, and Congress agreed to waive the alien contract labor law and allow Basque herders to come to the United States from Spain. The McGregor company already was relying on Basques and continued to do so until the mid-1970s, when it largely closed its sheep business. Spanish was the standard language of sheep camps. The dogs even learned to respond to commands given in Spanish and could not understand commands given in English—or in poorly inflected Spanish.

(Also see WASHTUCNA, p. 214.)

The road to **KAHLOTUS** (Kah-loh´-tus) from Connell climbs through dry sagebrush and rabbitbrush country with occasional fields either green or dotted with giant rolls of cured hay, depending on the season. Then the road enters wheat and barley tablelands and becomes the main street of Kahlotus, graced with shady locust trees. The town has the pleasant quality of having been wholly bypassed by frenzy. Its high school students in the 1970s refurbished the entire three-block business district by adding a covered sidewalk and installing museum displays in the general store/tavern.

In 1883 the Northern Pacific decided to tap the fertile Palouse country by laying track up the coulee from Connell to Kahlotus and on to Colfax. This branch line was part of Henry Villard's audacious plan to control eastern Washington rail and steamboat transport through his holding company, which at the time controlled the stock of both the Northern Pacific and the Oregon Railway and Navigation companies. In January 1884, however, Villard's empire collapsed.

A perhaps apocryphal account contends that Kahlotus and Washtucna were misnamed when the railroad was built: somebody got the signs mixed up and reversed the names of the two towns. Kahlotus should have been Washtucna, and vice versa. Regardless, Kahlotus endured as a railroad town, and just before World War I enjoyed a period of burgeoning hope associated with the (abortive) Palouse Irrigation Project. (See WASHTUCNA, p. 213.)

LITTLE GOOSE DAM. (See under RIPARIA, p. 213.)

LOWER MONUMENTAL DAM takes its name from a landmark rock formation on the south side of the Snake River. William Clark described it in his journal for October 14, 1805, as "a remarkable rock verry large and resembling the hill [hull] of a Ship." The formation later became known as Monumental Rock.

Gates at the dam closed in 1969. An observation deck overlooks the generators; a small visitor center includes a fish-viewing window. A road south from Lower Monumental Dam skirts for about 5 miles along scenic basalt cliffs, which rise above the river. Driving across the dam is permitted during the daytime.

LYONS FERRY today seems little more than a bridge across the Snake River and a state park at the mouth of a canyon. Yet the history of this crossing reads like an early-day Who's Who for the state.

In October 1805 Lewis and Clark noticed fish-drying scaffolds at the mouth of the Palouse River although they saw no people. In August 1811 David Thompson, pathfinder for the North West Company, turned away from the river route up the Columbia and Snake at this point and continued east by overland trail. In 1838 missionaries Elkanah Walker and Myron Eells bought potatoes and salmon from Palouse villagers, and the following year missionaries Henry Spalding and Marcus Whitman scouted this location as a possible mission site. The Charles Wilkes expedition exploring the Northwest for the United States crossed here in 1841, as did Colonel George Wright and his troops in 1858. Wright was en route to the Spokane country and the fateful battles of 1858. (See SPOKANE BATTLES sidebar, p. 10.)

Four years later a stern-wheel steamboat under contract with the army inaugurated a military supply depot for Fort Colville. The Mullan Road crossed the Snake River here, a major route leading to the Spokane country and then east to the Missouri River drainage.

(See MULLAN ROAD sidebar, p. 208.) Ruts made by wagons struggling up the Mullan grade toward Washtucna Coulee still show at the head of the canyon. (Watch for them on the east side of State Route 261, near where the canyon tops out onto the plateau about 2 miles north of the bridge.)

By Mullan's time the territorial legislature had franchised the operation of a civilian ferry—the first on the river to replace informal service by a fleet of canoes supplied by native people. Authorized charges ranged from $5 for a wagon with two animals attached, to 40 cents for a man on foot. Loose cattle were 50 cents each, sheep or goats 10 cents. An exception was that all emigrants who had crossed the Great Plains and expressed intention of settling in Washington were accommodated at half the established rates. Ferry service continued for nearly a century, from about 1859 until 1968. (The last ferry boat is permanently displayed near the upper end of the state park's day-use area.)

Just downriver from the highway bridge is the spectacular **Joso railway bridge** (three quarters of a mile long, 280 feet above river level). It was built during the titanic struggle between railroad magnates James J. Hill, by then head of both the Northern Pacific and the Great Northern, and Edward H. Harriman, who controlled the Union Pacific, Central Pacific, Southern Pacific, and Oregon Railway and Navigation Company. For several years Harriman secretly financed costly improvements of various lines, a backing that went undetected until 1910, despite efforts to unravel the mystery. His intention was for the Union Pacific to control scores of separate local lines. The Joso Bridge was a key element in a new, superbly engineered Oregon Railway and Navigation Company alignment that cut 50 miles off the route between Spokane and Portland and improved Harriman's competitive position. The name is taken from that of Leon Jaussaud, a sheepman who lived there. Work on the bridge began in 1910 and was completed in 1914.

Construction crews included Irish, black, and Chinese workers. The Chinese—estimated at 300 to 500 men—graded the entire rail line. Black men apparently did the diving for bridge piers, built on bedrock as much as 65 feet below the river's surface, exceedingly dangerous work with many drownings. "They lost one a day," is the callous memory of a man present at the time.

Archaeological investigations preceding Snake River dam projects traced the story of native people living in the Lyons Ferry area back almost to the last ice age. Crews excavated remnants of pithouses as much as 40 feet in diameter near the present fish hatchery. These are nearly 2,000 years old. Bison bone dominated the faunal remains in the houses, indication of human diet and also of wildlife very different from that in the area today. (The nearest bison now are in Montana.)

The renowned **Marmes Rock Shelter,** a small, shallow cave, is situated about a mile up the Palouse River from the Lyons Ferry bridge. Deposits there and in the floodplain below the rock shelter held charred human bone from a cremation hearth about 10,000 years old. Artifacts included weapon points, bone needles about the size of modern embroidery needles, olivella shells strung as a necklace, and an amulet made from an owl's claw.

There are two viewpoints near the rock shelter, which is now partly flooded and inaccessible. For the best look at it follow the paved road immediately beyond the state-park resiences. The other viewpoint—reached by a short trail beyond the main parking lot at the river—offers a striking view of Palouse Canyon but not of the rock shelter.

MESA (Mee′sah), a town of trim prefab houses and several stores, lies in a coulee instead of perching on a tableland as its (locally mispronounced) Spanish name implies. A succession of moist years attracted settlers here in the early 1900s. Then rain and snowfall returned to normal—and below normal—and farmers abandoned their dusty fields. One optimistic resident, Manton Poe, who had arrived in 1886, stayed on. He bought land from departing farmers—including the entire townsite—and somehow weathered the 1920s depression in farm prices and the 1930s Great Depression. His tenacity finally paid off in the 1950s when the Columbia Basin Project resuscitated farming and breathed life into his town. Mesa is now a commercial and shipping

The Marmes site yielded human bones dating to about 10,000 years ago.

center for surrounding agricultural land.

Early come-ons invariably mentioned the availability of good water—which actually was present. But the ads failed to mention that at most places in the area, water had to be pumped from wells drilled 300 to 400 feet into basalt at great cost. With water scarce, farming was limited to hay and grain until the arrival of Columbia Basin Irrigation water. Subsistence came mostly from small herds of livestock.

Today seepage from irrigation ditches has substantially raised the water table, restoring lakes and ponds that had been dry since the close of the ice age. The original government survey maps from 1883 show only two small bodies of water in the area around Mesa. Now there are enough lakes that nesting curlews and great blue herons are not uncommon.

OTHELLO's broad main street climbs the only hill within miles of town. Conspicuous outdoor sales yards offer every imaginable form of farm machinery, and potato processing plants sprawl along the border between town and irrigated fields. Displays at the community museum (Third and Larch) highlight the roles of the local economy's dual foundation: railroads and irrigation. The museum building is Othello's first church, built by Presbyterians in 1908. During the severe nationwide flu epidemic in 1918 the building served as a hospital.

Settlement began in 1902 with the sale of land from alternate sections belonging to the Northern Pacific Railroad, part of their government land grant intended to help subsidize the cost of building a railway across empty land where revenue would be negligible. Five years after the town began, the Chicago, Milwaukee, and St. Paul Railroad built its transcontinental line directly through Othello. This seemed an assurance that settlement here would survive, but population scarcely mushroomed.

In the 1950s, however, the infusion of irrigation water from the Columbia Basin Project set off surging growth. Hammers still rang against 2-by-4s while home buyers toured sandy neighborhoods; farmers eyed arrays of shiny tractors; and schoolchildren attended double sessions. Each year from 1953 on, new tracts of land opened, and the town continued to grow. Sugar beets were a major crop until the Moses Lake processing plant closed in the late 1970s.

By then potatoes were producing a greater yield per acre than is known anywhere else in the country, and alfalfa, corn, and various seed crops were doing well. Recent years have brought the addition of cherries, peaches, pears, apricots, plums, and grapes. Diversity has been the watchword for success throughout the history of the Columbia Basin project.

PALOUSE FALLS. (See under WASHTUCNA, p. 214.)

RIPARIA today is merely a wide place in the Snake River canyon. But in the 1860s its broad flat hosted a steamboat town, which became a railroad town in the 1880s, then was razed and partly flooded by the reservoir behind Lower Monumental Dam in the 1960s.

Seventeen rapids complicated navigation on the lower Snake River; nonetheless 27 regular steamboat landings developed between Pasco and Lewiston (140 miles), an average of one every 5 or 6 miles. Mining in Idaho started the boats churning up the river and, by the time that gold fever had waned, farming was starting a new wave of migration. Stern-wheelers provided the only transportation into the region through the 1860s and 1870s. Indeed, at a time when isolation was the rule throughout eastern Washington, they gave the Snake River a rare linkage. Farmers found that wheat, barley, and

Riparia, now flooded, previously hummed with activity. Located just above a major Snake River rapids, it was the site of a native village and—later—a ferry crossing.

oats (for horse feed) grew well on the tablelands above the river, and they also began to test the possibilities of growing fruit on the protected benchlands of the river itself. The orchards succeeded, and towns sprang up to ship both wheat and fruit.

Riparia grew at the ferry crossing of the old Texas road, which connected Walla Walla with the Mullan Road to Spokane and on to Montana. As steamboat traffic grew, the settlement became a major landing for passengers and freight and a place for steamers to take on fuel at a woodyard—a major consideration in a nearly treeless land. By the 1880s it also became a railroad town.

The first line was built north from Dayton (near Walla Walla) by the Oregon Railway and Navigation Company in 1881 to link Snake River traffic with tracks down the south side of the Columbia River to Portland. This railway virtually eliminated stern-wheeler service between Portland and Riparia, but at the same time inaugurated twice-weekly upriver service between Riparia and Lewiston. As the *Lewiston Teller* reported, "Texas City [is] at the Junction of two very important steam thoroughfares and will do a fair business."

Seven years later Oregon Railway and Navigation crews built a bridge across the Snake River at Riparia and laid tracks to LaCrosse (in the Palouse country). The town bustled with perhaps a hundred year-round residents and several times that many people changing daily from train to train, or from train to steamer. This 1888 track stemmed from the breakdown of a railroad pact to divide Washington, more to please Wall Street than to serve residents of the Columbia Plateau and the Palouse. In a sense, the Oregon Railway and Navigation Company became a football tossed from the Northern Pacific to the Union Pacific after the 1884 collapse of Henry Villard's directorship.

By agreement, the Oregon Railway and Navigation Company was to continue linking the Walla Walla country with Portland but the Northern Pacific would cross directly to Puget Sound, a huge loss of potential trade that angered Portland interests. They argued for a bridge at Riparia and branch lines threading throughout the Palouse. Local people welcomed this prospect. No government regulation controlled freight rates at the time, and the only hope of lower shipping costs was through competition.

In 1908 a third railroad from Riparia—the Camas Prairie line—ran along the north bank of the Snake River, cutting the time between Clarkston/Lewiston and Portland to only 12 hours, which was half of what it had been by steamboat. This line was operated jointly by the Northern Pacific and Union Pacific, part of an uneasy truce. A few steamers nonetheless continued to ply the river. Their last regular commercial runs were made in 1940.

Little Goose Dam was completed in 1970. Displays highlight the history of hydropower. The top of the dam is open to automobile traffic during daylight hours, which facilitates driving scenic roads along each bank of the Snake River. From the south bank, notice the mammoth gravel bars across the river, a legacy of ice-age flood deposits. They show especially well from the hill directly opposite Riparia.

In **STARBUCK** an elaborate (abandoned) school and a 1904, one-story, brick bank (McNeil and Main) attest to former prosperity and expectations of permanence. In a grassy lot next to the general store, an 1893 church bell stands as a memorial to its donor, W. H. Starbuck, a renowned railroad investor.

In 1882 the Oregon Railway and Navigation Company built through this valley, and for the next 40 years railroad dollars settled here in the form of paychecks. Hotels, restaurants, and warehouses served transferring passengers and freight. A depot and telegraph office, seven-stall roundhouse, coal and oil bunkers, and maintenance shops supported large crews. Construction of a branch line to Pomeroy employed 400 Chinese and 300 white workers in 1886. Railroad income even protected Starbuck from the national financial depression of 1893.

But a mono-economy seldom guarantees security. The railroads declined and, like a movie running backwards, Starbuck's facilities were gradually dismantled. The town reverted to a quiet backwater in the wheat and hay country of the Tucannon Valley. It stirred briefly to new activity when Little Goose Dam was built in the 1960s, but now again drowses contentedly apart from mainstream frenzy.

Fort Taylor, built at the mouth of the Tucannon in the summer of 1858, served as an important forward post for Fort Walla Walla following the defeat of Colonel Edward Steptoe in May of that year. Nothing now remains. (Also see ROSALIA, p. 198; and SPOKANE BATTLES sidebar, p. 10.)

Grange City, a steamboat landing and major shipping point, was begun at the old fort site in 1872. In time it had six grain warehouses, a livery stable, blacksmith shop, hotel, and saloon.

WASHTUCNA (Wash-tuk′-nuh) lies at the junction of two major coulees, its three- or four-block business district characterized by frame buildings and its wide streets lined with trees that give summer coolness, especially when combined with a breeze. A pause at the leafy town park brings pleasant respite to a summer drive.

In 1878 George Bassett, who made a living selling horses in Montana, settled at a trio of springs—the site of Washtucna—to raise thoroughbred horses on "yard-high" bunchgrass. His nearest neighbors were cattlemen on Cow Creek a dozen miles north. In 1894 a store opened. Two years previously Tacoma business-men and "eastern capitalists" had organized The Palouse Irrigation Ditch Company. They planned to irrigate 400,000 acres between Hooper and Pasco, carrying water by flume along Washtucna Coulee for storage in Kahlotus Lake (then called Washtukna Lake). The company actually built 12 miles of ditch, only to fail financially during the Panic of 1893.

In 1902 passage of the federal Newlands Act supporting irrigation of the arid West revived consideration of the potential here, and the Reclamation Service took cores of bedrock to determine the feasibility of damming the Palouse River. The new proposal was to irrigate land only from Eltopia to Pasco, about two thirds of the original proposal. Project costs were judged too high, however, and the Reclamation Service turned its development effort to the Yakima Valley instead.

Seattle investors then decided to develop land only between Washtucna and Hooper. They organized as the Palouse Irrigation and Power Company, rebuilt existing flumes and ditches, and sold 10-acre tracts, which they promoted as suitable for everything from melons, peanuts, and walnuts to hops, tobacco, grapes, and strawberries. A population of 80,000 was expected "soon." People arrived from as far away as Florida and New York, as well as Seattle and Spokane, naively expecting to make a living from a small acreage in an area too dry to maintain even a creek from its own runoff.

The McGregor Land and Livestock Company finally took over the irrigation scheme. The only large landowner in the area, they had planted orchards—which they successfully irrigated with their own artesian water—and they had loaned money to the irrigation company for the maintenance of its system. For awhile two Dutch corporations raised money to buy out the company, and one of them started a plan to bring farmers from Holland to the Washtucna scablands. This proposal fell apart, however, and the Irrigation and Power Company went into receivership.

In 1917 the McGregor company bought the irrigation company's questionable assets. They hoped to drill more wells and abandon the flume, but this plan, too, proved disastrous. (The ditch still exists. Watch for it 4 miles east of Washtucna running parallel with the highway at the edge of the coulee bottom.)

Sixteen miles south of Washtucna, **Palouse Falls** drops as a 198-foot ribbon into a sheer-walled canyon. In spring its water is chocolate brown with topsoil from Palouse fields, an ero-sion loss slowly easing as farmers increasingly employ deliberate conservation methods. Heavy loss is probably inevitable, however. The soil is so fertile that 40-degree slopes are farmed, and spring rains wash away the surface of the bare, frozen earth. The equivalent of 160 acres of soil 80 feet deep washed over the falls in the early 1960s; the loss 20 years later had lessened by perhaps 10 percent.

About 3 miles east of Washtucna the **Mullan Road** crosses State Route 26. (See MULLAN ROAD sidebar, p. 208.)

NORTHWEST Region

Gamwell mansion, Bellingham.

THREATS OF DEPREDATIONS by warriors from native villages in northern British Columbia and southeastern Alaska spurred the U.S. Army into building a fort at Bellingham Bay in 1855, and its presence stimulated settlement already begun with the economic promise of a sawmill. Three years later the discovery of gold in the lower Fraser River region of British Columbia brought hopeful miners streaming ashore en route to the new diggings.

Some stayed to profit by supplying their erstwhile colleagues or to cut timber or dig coal; others trekked to the gold fields, then returned to carve out a living in the new towns fringing the bay. Some who had traveled through the San Juans on their way to the gold returned to claim homesteads and develop farms on the islands' beautiful shores or—eventually—to work at canneries, quarries, and lime kilns. In 1859 the islands drew international attention when a jurisdictional dispute brought the United States and Great Britain to the brink of war. The issue was settled 13 years later when binding arbitration presided over by Kaiser Wilhelm of Germany favored the United States. The ruling settled the last of the boundary questions that had begun nearly half a century earlier.

On the Skagit River delta near today's Mount Vernon and La Conner, agriculture played a dominant role after the 1870s when farmers successfully diked their fields to keep out seasonal floods and daily tides. Up the river, gold and other metals drew prospectors in the 1880s and 1890s and, at about the same time, loggers and sawmill operators tackled the awesome job of turning trees 30 feet in circumference into lumber.

Everett and its mountain hinterland became an 1890s and early 1900s speculative playground for investors as first John D. Rockefeller and then James J. Hill developed industries. Gold from the Monte Cristo Mine east of the city spurred the first wave of excitement. Timber and sawmills produced the second, longer-lasting development.

Bellingham Area

Washington's northwest corner encompasses some of the most dramatic scenery in the state: it is where Mount Baker looks down to the Strait of Georgia, and where dairy cows, berries, peas, and seed potatoes reign supreme on the rich farmlands of the Nooksack Valley. Within this setting Bellingham blends industry and academia while retaining a clear sense of the past.

Two scenic drives deserve special excursions. State Route 11 clings to shoreline bluffs overlooking Chuckanut Bay and the San Juan Islands; it is a moderately busy but peaceful road with signs at the southern end cautioning "Please drive quietly. Meadowlarks singing." State Route 142 winds toward the heart of the North Cascades and ends at the 5,000-foot level amid flower meadows, snowfields, and huge peaks. In addition to these two roads, an unspectacular but pleasant drive along the shore of Bellingham Bay gives an understanding of the city's saltwater location. Ideally, travel from the west to be on the water side of this road.

Museums are at Bellingham, Lynden, and Semiahmoo Spit. Festivals include a May celebration of Dutch ethnic origins held at Lynden with a washing of the streets, wooden-shoe races, and Klompen dancing; dugout canoe racing at the Lummi Reservation in June; and an annual tour of historic homes in Bellingham, usually in late September. Train buffs will want to check the Lake Whatcom Railroad's current schedule for a 4-mile ride into the woods, an experience complete with the nostalgic toot of a steam whistle.

BELLINGHAM, only 18 miles south of the Canadian border, lines its bay with concentric tiers of activity. Industrial mills and boatyards ring the shore. Behind them nineteenth-century brick commercial buildings intermingle with newer construction. Residential districts and the university climb the hills and form a third tier. None of this is apparent from I-5. To find it, turn off at any Bellingham exit and drive to the west—or arrive by boat.

In December 1852 Henry Roeder and Russell Peabody left California for Oregon Territory intending to start either a cannery or a sawmill, depending on what opportunities they could discover. When they found Henry Yesler's mill already supplying a settlement at the mouth of the Duwamish River, they traveled on to Port Townsend and from there paddled to Bellingham Bay. Where Whatcom Creek plunged into salt

"It is not altogether easy to clear the land from out the forest, but when a man gets started at it, it is not hard," a settler wrote at Christmas to his mother in Germany in 1879.

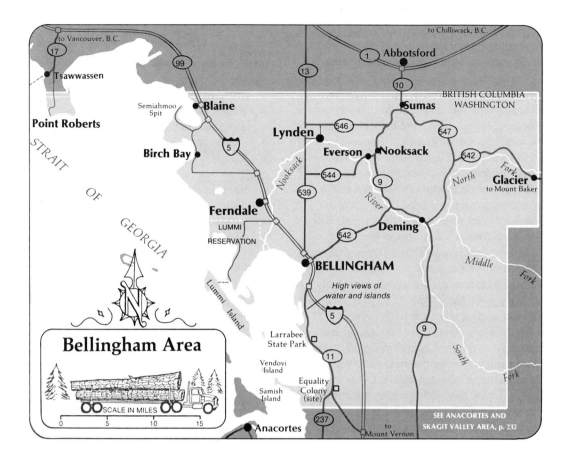

water they decided to build a mill. To get help and supplies, Roeder sailed back to San Francisco in early spring and, by summer, the men's saw was whining its way into virgin red cedar and Douglas fir.

Five years later Bellingham Bay's isolation ended when the Hudson's Bay Company shipped 800 ounces of Fraser River gold to the San Franciso mint and touched off a rush north. Miners by the thousands arrived to trudge inland by trail to Sumas and then northeast to the placers. So little cleared land existed along the shore that they set stakes on the beach to mark "lots" for their tents, then jumped each other's claims. Seven steamers and 13 square-rigged sailing ships anchored here on a single day. Pioneer Ezra Meeker and his cows even joined the melee from Puyallup; he brought the cows by barge. Their milk sold for the fabulous price of one dollar per gallon.

Bellingham's pivotal role in the gold fever was short lived, however. Miners soon could clear Canadian customs only at Victoria and,

from there, steamboat travel was the most practical way to reach the Fraser. Bypassed, Bellingham's trail fell into disuse. After the mining heyday, four communities grew up along the bay, separated from each other by dense forest: Fairhaven, Sehome, Whatcom, and Bellingham. Decades passed before these towns merged—and today's city layout still has a disjointed quality owing to this origin.

Fairhaven features an 1880s shopping district and the feel of a compact community. It began with expectations of becoming the western terminus of the Great Northern Railway. One hundred thirty-five buildings—both brick commercial blocks and fine mansions—gave a look of permanency. But bust followed boom: the Great Northern chose Seattle, and the Panic of 1893 dried up other investments in Fairhaven. The commercial district slumbered until 1973, when a private investor restored many of the remaining structures.

Sehome developed around a vein of coal that angled under the bay. Mining began in 1858 with the coal easily dumped into bunkers at the base of the hill. The son of one of the miners who moved there remembered paddling from Victoria in the "largest canoe in the Northwest . . . with all of our furniture, household goods, stoves, etc., and four goats, besides father and five boys. (Mother, sister, and baby boy went on the steamer by way of Seattle.)" The coal vein ran out about 1878. Fifteen years after that, Sehome resident and Washington poet laureate Ella Higginson persuaded officials to locate a state normal school (teachers' college) on the hill above the erstwhile mine. The school, now evolved into Western Washington University, occupies the former site of the Higginson home.

Whatcom, the earliest settlement, had a neighboring community facing it across the creek after 1880 when about 25 Kansas families signed an agreement with local promoters, bought stock in a development company, and moved West to found Washington Colony. They held no particular creed but were simply like-minded folk who migrated together. At Whatcom Creek they built a wharf, a sawmill, and a small town. In 1884 confusions over land ownership dissolved the colony in legal challenges.

Bellingham, the smallest of the bay's four settlements, began along the base of Sehome Hill at the Pattle coal claim. Although Bellingham proved to be inconsequential and transitory, the other hamlets chose its name when they decided to overcome rivalry and merge into a single town.

For a sense of the city today, sample four distinct districts: the downtown, where buildings are altered by street-level face-lifts but still show their original construction on upper stories; Fairhaven, with a commercial core and an adjoining residential section; the university area, where need for student housing saved large houses that might otherwise have been lost; and Eldridge, listed in the National Register as a Historic District because of stately mansions. (Select homes open for tours each fall, usually in September.)

Several parks also are worth visiting. Go to Whatcom Falls (1401 Electric Avenue) for its creek and forest setting, typical of the pioneer era—and of the preceding millennia. Go also to Sehome Arboretum (25th Street) for its hilltop

Bellingham

Key to Numbered Locations
1   Terminal Building
2   Waldron Block
3   Mason Block
4   Longstaff and Black House
5   "Wardner's Castle"
6   Gamwell House
7   Fairhaven Park
8   Larrabee House
9   Old Main
10 Mount Baker Theater
11 Old City Hall (Whatcom Museum of History and Art)
12 Leopold Hotel
13 Pickett House
14 Richards Building (Old County Courthouse)
15 James F. Bolster House
16 Victor Roeder House

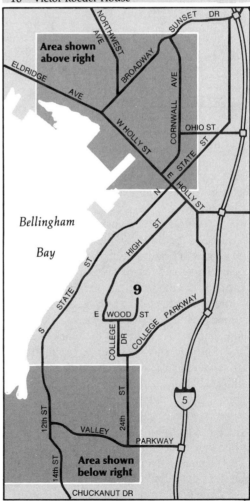

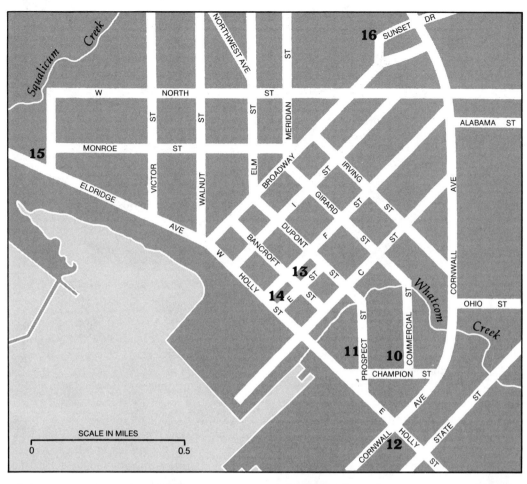

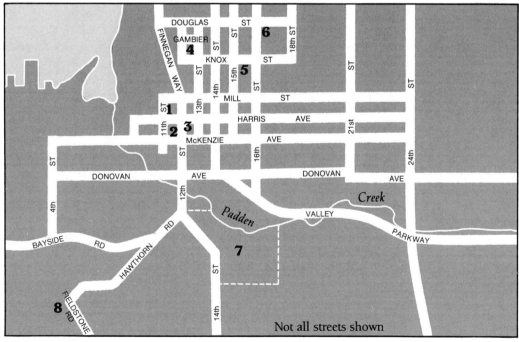

Not all streets shown

The three-story Roland Gamwell house is perhaps the finest of Bellingham's mansions.

view of Bellingham Bay and the San Juan Islands; and to Maritime Heritage Park (1600 C Street; site of Roeder and Peabody's sawmill) to watch salmon returning to the hatchery. The runs begin about Labor Day with the arrival of chinooks and reach truly spectacular proportions between Halloween and Thanksgiving with the return of chums.

Points of interest, keyed to the Bellingham map:

1 The **Terminal Building** (11th and Harris; built in 1888) reflects Fairhaven's expectation of becoming a transcontinental railroad terminus, an unfulfilled optimism although city streetcars and an interurban electric train network provided local and regional links. The Terminal Building, one of the oldest in Fairhaven, is faced with brick brought from Asia as ballast, heavy material carried in a ship's hold to make the vessel ride low in the water and thus be less likely to capsize. With sailing ships calling frequently at Bellingham Bay, ballast piled up along the shore as a ready-made supply of building material.

2 The **Waldron Block** (12th and McKenzie; built in 1890 and 1891) was still unfinished when Fairhaven's bubble of speculation burst. Brass window frames remained on its second floor, still crated, for almost a century.

3 The **Mason Block** (12th and Harris; built in 1890) is now called the Marketplace. Among

its first tenants were five real estate companies and the Great Northern Express Company. The top floor included a men's club where Mark Twain lectured in the 1890s.

4 The **Longstaff and Black House** (1210 Gambier; built in 1890) was designed to meet the needs of its bachelor owners. Shared living and dining rooms occupied the first floor, but a full wall divided the upstairs space into two apartments. Each gentleman mounted a separate staircase to his private rooms. Mr. Longstaff, a Boston architect, designed the elaborate Fairhaven Hotel (destroyed by a 1953 fire) and then, in the boom-town atmosphere of the time, found himself overwhelmed with customers. Consequently he sent for his partner, H. N. Black. Together, the men designed many of Fairhaven's signature buildings, including the Wardner and Gamwell homes.

5 **"Wardner's Castle"** (15th and Knox; built in 1890), with turrets, carved fireplaces, and stained glass, reflects Jim Wardner's personal flamboyance. One of Fairhaven's chief investors, he was a self-made man and a wizard at buying low and selling high. Wardner made his first fortune in Idaho silver, and his reputation attracted other speculators to invest in Fairhaven. He lived in this house only a year, then divested himself of all Fairhaven properties, an act of perfect timing. The boom soon collapsed. Wardner went on to invest in South African, Mexican, and Canadian mines.

6   The **Gamwell House** (16th and Douglas; built in 1892) was Roland Gamwell's gift to his bride. He built an elaborate mansion with bulging chimneys, a "turbaned" turret, and the finest possible interior finish including hardwood paneling and modern gas and electric appliances. A lover of roses, Gamwell donated several city parks for public gardens. Some of his own rose bushes still grow beside his house, and its stained-glass windows glow with floral motifs.

Gamwell had graduated from Massachusetts Institute of Technology and taken a job with an insurance company in Seattle. There he met seasoned speculators who encouraged him to invest in the Fairhaven bubble. He cleared a fortune.

7   **Fairhaven Park** (107 Chuckanut) came to the city in 1909 as a donation from Charles Larrabee's land company. The renowned Olmsted Brothers did the landscaping, a prime example of the rich legacy they gave to the Northwest. The park is especially colorful in early summer when the formal rose gardens are in bloom. When automobile travel first became common in the 1920s, the park served as a tourist camp.

8   The **Larrabee House** (405 Fieldstone Road; built in 1915) is a massive but simple family home with avant-garde touches such as a central vacuum system. Seattle architect Carl Gould drew plans for the house. Unfortunately, Charles Larrabee died before the construction was complete, but Mrs. Larrabee lived here with their four children and several servants. The family's fortune came from Montana copper, enhanced by investments in Fairhaven. In particular, Larrabee developed the Fairhaven and Southern Railroad, which was intended to connect the Canadian Pacific transcontinental line to Portland, Oregon, but was bought out by the Great Northern.

9   **Old Main** (516 High Street; begun in 1896) was the heart and soul of Washington State Normal School. A three-story, ivy-covered Georgian Revival building, it still serves as Western Washington University's administration building. The campus is noted for its abundant outdoor sculpture.

10   The **Mount Baker Theater** (106 N. Commercial; built in 1926) is a gem of a movie palace. It features an elaborate Moorish interior and the original pipe organ used to accompany silent films.

11   The **Old City Hall,** now the **Whatcom Museum of History and Art** (121 Prospect Street; built in 1892), is a massive red brick monument to civic pride. It was completed as the city hall for New Whatcom, intended by its builders as "a sure index to all newcomers,

Early Bellingham civic buildings include the Whatcom city hall, now a museum.

tourists and travelers, of our taste, thrift, enterprise, and intelligence." A self-trained local architect, Alfred Lee, produced the design. A mechanic and carriage maker from Oregon, he opened an office on arrival at Bellingham in 1890 and readily received architectural commissions. At the time of the city hall construction, high tides washed against the bluff here; subsequent landfills provide sites for many of the present buildings.

In 1962 the city hall suffered severe fire damage. A concerted community-wide effort gathered funds to rebuild and turn the beloved landmark into a professionally managed museum.

12 The **Leopold Hotel** (1224 Cornwall; built in 1899, enlarged in 1913) is the grande dame of Bellingham's historic buildings. Originally founded as the Byron House, it served as an elegant gathering place and a temporary home for newcomers. The 1899 section of the building has been razed, but many features of the 1913 building were carefully restored. Sarah Bernhardt, William Jennings Bryan, and Billy Sunday are among the famous guests who have signed the register.

In 1910 Leopold Schmidt purchased the hotel from the original owner, Captain Josiah Byron. Schmidt, founder of the Olympia Brewing Company, lived here while he established the

Bellingham branch of his brewery. The hotel now has been remodeled to provide senior housing.

13 The **Pickett House** (Bancroft and F; begun in 1856, finished in 1860) is Washington's oldest "landmark" building still in place. It began as a 15- by 20-foot cabin with walls made of upright planks held at top and bottom by wooden "collars." The planks—two inches thick—were cut at Roeder's sawmill, located in the ravine just below the house. Beneath the shingle siding, they still show marks of a waterpowered circular saw.

Captain George E. Pickett came to Bellingham to command a small blockhouse fort and separate gun emplacements intended as protection against tribal raiders who occasionally entered Washington waters from British Columbia and Alaska. (See EBEY'S LANDING, p. 268.) Pickett built his house near the blockhouse, but in 1859 was ordered to San Juan Island to defend U.S. interests during the "Pig War" boundary dispute with England. Before that issue was settled, he left to join the Confederate army and earn a hero's reputation at Gettysburg. (See AMERICAN CAMP, p. 243; and ENGLISH CAMP, p. 245.)

14 The **Richards Building** or **Old County Courthouse** (1308 E Street; built in 1858) dates from the Fraser River gold rush. Intended as a

Small canneries prevailed until the 1890s when high capitalization and improved equipment led to huge installations such as this one at Semiahmoo Spit (across the bay from Blaine).

store and a "bank," it was sturdily constructed of brick to provide safe storage for gold. The brick, made in Philadelphia, came as ballast on a ship bringing miners to the British Columbia gold rush. At the time, this part of the bay was a broad mud flat; the building is actually on pilings. In 1863 the county bought the Richards Building for use as a courthouse and jail. A later landfill raised E Street, and the original ground floor became a basement.

15 The **James F. Bolster House** (2820 Eldridge; built in 1891) stands on a broad street graced with Victorian homes. This one—replete with Queen Anne arches and fancy work—is a brick rarity in an architectural style meant to be built of wood. Construction began soon after both Seattle and Spokane had been devastated by fire, and the brick was intended to demonstrate that a fireproof home need not be inconsistent with fashionable architecture. The contractor who built the house owned a Bellingham brick factory.

16 The **Victor Roeder House** (2600 Sunset Drive; built in 1906) now belongs to the Whatcom County parks department and is open to the public. In stick-style, it has broad eaves with elaborate brackets. The interior features beautifully crafted oak woodwork. Victor Roeder founded Bellingham National Bank. His father and mother were Bellingham Bay's first white settlers.

BIRCH BAY. (See under BLAINE, this page.)

BLAINE, poised on the Canadian border, punctuates the northeastern shore of a nearly enclosed circular bay. Hundreds of commercial fishing boats make this their home port— appropriate as early residents came from Iceland, where their forebears had been fishermen for generations. At the northern edge of town a concrete gateway known as the Peace Arch celebrates the undefended character of the border between the United States and Canada: 3,000 miles without fortification or troops. The arch stands amid 40 acres of formal gardens, its bronze doors fixed permanently open. Construction was spearheaded in 1921 by Sam Hill, Washington's eccentric millionaire, pacifist, and good-roads enthusiast. (See MARYHILL, p. 160, and STONEHENGE, p. 164, for

more on Sam Hill.) Fragments from two vessels—the *Mayflower* and the *Beaver* (the Hudson's Bay Company's first steamboat on this coast)—are sealed inside the arch.

Semiahmoo Spit (Seh-mee-ah′-moo) nearly encloses Blaine's harbor. A road leading to its tip provides beach access and a sweeping view across blue—or gray—water eastward to Blaine, backdropped by the Cascades, and westward to the San Juan Islands and Olympic Mountains. In 1857, eleven years after officials set the international boundary between Canada and the United States at the 49th parallel, survey crews camped on the spit for their first season of fieldwork. The group included astronomers and surveyors to locate the line, axmen to cut clearings through the forest, and drovers to care for pack animals. A handful of merchants opened stores on the mainland to furnish supplies; these became a nucleus for Blaine.

A year after the survey began, the Fraser River gold rush swept over the spit like a high tide and resulted in a community called Semiahmoo City. Some gold seekers returned when the rush subsided, married native women, and settled along the shore. A decade later a land speculator built a street and a wharf, and a group of settlers soon arrived by chartered steamboat. Sawmilling was their first industry, followed by salting salmon.

In 1891 a cannery on Semiahmoo Spit processed 36,000 cases of sockeye salmon in a single season. That scale of productivity attracted the Alaska Packers Association, which bought the cannery and greatly enlarged it. Their docks became the supply base for a huge fleet of square-riggers that headed north each spring during the glory days of the Alaska salmon trade; Blaine was their last American port of call. In season, the association employed hundreds of white, Chinese, and Native American workers, housing each race in separate dormitories. Several of the buildings associated with the cannery remain as part of a county park, and museum exhibits depict Semiahmoo's early fishing and canning era. A resort now dots the tip of the spit.

Birch Bay, south of Blaine, offers a half-moon shoreline drive with modern condomin-iums interspersed with older vacation cottages. A state park includes beach front and, at its

CEDAR HOUSES

Several dozen cedar houses dating from the pioneer era still stand in Whatcom County, some preserved at Ferndale's Pioneer Park, others still standing where they were built originally.

Such houses can be divided into four periods. The first settlers—mostly single men—lived in rude little cabins that a single man could build from split logs. By the mid-1870s, families began arriving, and men built with cedar slabs as much as 35 feet long by 3 feet wide and 2 inches thick—massive timbers so heavy their own weight held them in place once they had been set in position. Construction depended on several men working together; the architecture developed only after there were neighbors for house-raisings and barn raisings. Available tools, however, still were limited to felling ax, broad ax, hand ax, froe, and crosscut saw.

A third era of construction began in the 1890s, when men here had fairly complete carpentry kits including tools such as draw knives, jack planes, augers, chisels, and various saws. They then began to build

Houses typical of all stages of pioneer construction remain in rural Whatcom County. Some are displayed near Ferndale; others still linger in place.

---

southern edge, offers views across a 40-acre marshland sanctuary.

The **CHUCKANUT HIGHWAY** (State Route 11) clings to cliffs above Chuckanut Bay, eminently worth driving. Each curve offers a fresh view of forested islands "floating" on a vast international sea. If possible, time the drive to be at a viewpoint when the sun makes its nightly plunge and—often—paints the sky first pink, then crimson.

At the south end of the highway, just before it climbs the flank of Chuckanut Mountain, socialism briefly reigned at a utopian colony called **Equality.** Nothing more than narrow Colony Road now remains. But in 1897 the Brotherhood of Cooperative Commonwealth, a national organization, hoped to populate sparsely settled Washington, beginning here. With one state as leaven, they then intended to slowly convert the whole country to socialism. Equality served as a beachhead but never more, although 300 members eventually lived here

supported by 3,500 "reserves" across the county. After 10 years of moderate success as a frontier community, and complete failure as a socialist leaven, Equality dissolved in a spate of lawsuits.

West of Equality's old site, a low tongue of land pushes into the bay, still called **Samish Island** although now connected to the mainland. Farmers long ago turned the island into a peninsula by diking. For centuries before that it had been the island home of the Samish. In the 1840s about 2,000 people lived here; their village included a 1,250-foot longhouse. Yet by the time of the 1855 Treaty of Point Elliott only 150 had survived the smallpox and measles epidemic that swept Puget Sound.

In 1841 Captain Wilkes of the U.S. Exploring Expedition named **Vendovi Island,** northwest of Samish Island, for a Fijian captive on board his ship. He captured and carried away the Fijian headman Vendovi, deemed responsible for the earlier murder of 10 American seamen, and the man became a celebrity along Wilkes' route despite his "criminal" status. He died shortly

two-story houses with T-, L-, or E-shaped floor plans. Some of these houses are a perfect match for those of rural Norway, the old-country home of many settlers in this area. Roofs are far steeper than necessary in western Washington, although appropriate for typical Scandinavian snowloads.

This stage of cedar-house construction merged into the final period. Homeowners decorated gable ends with fancy shingle work or sheathed their entire houses with sawn lumber and added curlicue gingerbread. Little indicates that these houses were originally built of cedar except the thickness of their windowsills.

after the expedition arrived in New York.

In the 1930s Vendovi Island sheltered a small community affiliated with evangelist Father Divine. Its seven or eight full-time residents avoided sex, liquor, and tobacco, and embraced faith healing and positive thinking. "It's wonderful!" was the catch phrase. The island provided a meditative refuge and outdoor recreation for other workers in the movement.

Near Bellingham the Chuckanut Highway reaches **Larrabee State Park,** a 2,000-acre retreat of beaches and mountain trails donated in 1915 by Mrs. Charles Larrabee, widow of a Fairhaven investor. This was the first land acquired by the newly formed State Park Commission. A 5-mile trail along the roadbed of Bellingham's former electric interurban railway joins the park to Fairhaven.

The approaches to **DEMING** (15 miles up the Nooksack River from Bellingham) are lined with strawberry, raspberry, and Christmas-tree farms but, from the outset, timber has been the

mainstay. A man named Edmund Coleman commented in 1869 that the whole upper Nooksack "never was made for anything but a lot of men from Maine with Collin's axes." Even now—using chain saws—competitors at the annual spring Logging Show demonstrate topping, falling, bucking, and other forest skills. Red galluses and unhemmed pant legs cut off above the ankle are de rigeur. (This treatment lets pants tear if they catch on something. If they held firmly, loggers might trip and be injured.)

Deming is also the location of the tribal center belonging to the Nooksack people, Salish-speakers who traditionally lived here in cedar-plank longhouses. In 1855 these people failed to attend the Point Elliott treaty council: the river had frozen, and their canoes were useless. Nevertheless, Governor Stevens treated them as signators and assigned them to the Lummi Reservation. The Nooksack never moved, however, and 15 years later most of them lay dead of smallpox. In the 1890s the government finally granted survivors part of the land where their villages had stood, and there the Nooksack continued to live communally. The tribe currently has an active program to recall, record, and teach their language.

FERNDALE is the embodiment of "middle America." Neighborhood streets are broad, houses and yards are tidy.

For a look at beginnings, drive to Hovander Homestead Park, a turn-of-the-century farm open to the public. (South of town take Exit 262 off of I-5 and drive west; just after the railroad underpass turn south on Neilsen Avenue.) A massive house with scroll woodwork exteriors and linseed oil–finished interiors is the park's centerpiece. It was built by Hokan Hovander, a self-taught architect who brought his family here from Sweden in 1898. A large barn near the house shelters antique farm equipment. Climb the interior staircase to the top of the water tower for rewarding views of the Nooksack Valley. Be sure to also walk across the fields half a mile to the Tennant Lake Natural History Interpretive Center. There a three-quarter-mile boardwalk crosses a marshy lake and offers possible glimpses of birds such as sora rails and American bitterns as well as teal and ducks.

Pioneer Park (Ferndale Road and Cherry; on the river about a mile north of Hovander Park) is a place to see the huge cedar trees that once were common in this area but were almost entirely cut as early as 1910. Also present is a collection of remarkable pioneer homes built of cedar. They have been brought in from the surrounding countryside for preservation. (See CEDAR HOUSES sidebar, p. 224.)

In the 1870s Ferndale was known to the few people who lived there as the "lower crossing" or "Jam," owing to a massive logjam blocking the Nooksack River. (Everson was the "upper crossing.") These settlers cut trees and built small sawmills as a prelude to farming. In 1884 their isolation ended with the opening of a road to Bellingham, and 10 years later the Great Northern Railway came through en route from Bellingham to Vancouver. Ferndale's economic base remained logging, fishing, and farming until the early 1900s, when raising chickens also became important. Today's farmers concentrate their efforts on dairy cattle, peas, corn, and berries.

LARRABEE STATE PARK. (See under CHUCKANUT HIGHWAY, p. 225.)

Forested **LUMMI ISLAND** is a residential island with no particular public facilities. Its south end is mountainous, its north end low-lying. A small car ferry connects to the mainland (a 10-minute trip). Near its landing, the Beach Store—a white frame building named for pioneer homesteader John Wade Beach—has served as a community meeting hall since 1901.

In the early 1900s fish traps west of the island supplied three large canneries staffed by hundreds of Chinese, Native American, and white workers. Flat-bottomed reef net boats still are stored on the beach at Legoe Bay when not in use during the Fraser River sockeye runs.

The **LUMMI RESERVATION** west of Bellingham is on a peninsula pointing toward Lummi Island like a finger. People there traditionally relied on fishing for livelihood. They still do. Lummi purse seiners and gillnetters ply the waters, and nets line the shore; aquaculture and salmon enhancement are tribal enterprises. The Stommish Festival, held each June, features 50-foot, cedar-dugout canoe races that attract teams from British Columbia and Washington villages to compete against Lummi teams.

In the mid nineteenth century, the Lummi, wracked by disease and decimated by raiding parties, abandoned villages in the San Juan Islands and moved to the mainland. They overran villages near the three mouths of the Nooksack River and there built stockades for protection. In 1855 they signed the Point Elliott Treaty, which confined them to a reservation away from the rich Nooksack delta farmlands. The treaty, however, guaranteed "the right of taking fish at usual and accustomed grounds."

For decades the Lummi people fished unmolested. But when whites industrialized the fishing/canning industry, they began struggling to maintain their treaty rights. In the 1890s the Alaska Packers Association leased land at Point Roberts and built offshore traps, which prevented Lummi fishermen from harvesting sockeye. No real resolution was reached until 1974 when Judge George Boldt interpreted Governor Stevens' treaties to mean that two *parties*—native people and whites—have equal rights to the fish. Therefore each party is entitled to half of the total catch. This decision helped to restore Lummi rights.

LYNDEN lies in the midst of a rich dairy farming area. Try timing a visit here to coincide with the annual spring draft horse plowing contest or the summer threshing bee using antique machines, demonstrations of the local ethos that "good work is good play." Year round, the Pioneer Museum (Third and Front) exhibits a fine collection of buggies, early farm equipment, and household tools arrayed in a 1910 building that originated as a blacksmith shop. A "Main Street" displays buildings.

White settlement began in 1871 when Phoebe and Holden Judson paddled here by dugout canoe and took a preemption claim. Mrs. Judson's sentimental memoir *A Pioneer's Search for an Ideal Home* recounts that the young community needed a name when other settlers arrived, and she suggested Lynden, which she remembered from "a story Eason Ebey read to us while on a visit to their home on Whidbey Island" and also from a poem beginning "On Linden, when the sun was low . . ." (changing the spelling to look "prettier").

Until 1881 logjams both at Ferndale and just below Lynden stopped stern-wheelers from navigating the Nooksack River, and supplies had to come by canoe. Overland travel was decidedly miserable owing to tangled vegetation and stretches of bottomless mud. When men finally blasted out the jams, the steamer *Willie* began service upriver, and Lynden felt connected to the outside world.

At the time, sawmills stood at every crossroad. They converted trees into shingle bolts and planks, an aid to farmers trying to create farms from virgin forest. Eventually the tedious felling and sawing succeeded, word of good land spread, and newcomers joined the original pioneers. Many came from Norway during the 1880s; from the Netherlands beginning a decade later. The Dutch arrived after Netherlands financiers had bought up a great deal of land in Washington intending to send colonists to farm. One such attempt aborted in 1893 when vigilantes hanged a supposed cattle rustler outside the hotel where Dutch families were staying while waiting to settle on Palouse farms. Frightened by this chance demonstration of the Wild West, they immediately returned home.

Netherlands investors then put their capital into Spokane real estate and banking without trying to attract their countrymen to emigrate. Word spread, however, concerning the lush

The Hovanders bought their Ferndale homestead from a widow and built this house in 1903.

green pastures of Whidbey Island and Whatcom County, and in the mid-1890s Lynden became the largest Dutch settlement in the state. Farmers found this area similar to home and introduced Holstein cows, soon making Whatcom County milk production the greatest of any county in the state. The Dutch also introduced gambrel-roofed barns, a style that allows more storage space for feed than the gable-roofed barns already in use here. (Lynden's Holland Days festival held each May celebrates the arrival of the Dutch.)

Today's farmers grow berries, corn, hay, and a regional speciality: seed potatoes. All seed crops must be grown in isolation to prevent accidental hybridization, a fact that works in Lynden's favor: the nearest major potato production is east of the mountains (near Othello), far too distant for any unwanted cross-pollination.

MOUNT BAKER, a 10,778-foot volcano, was active six times between 1843 and 1880—and today it occasionally sends up plumes of steam. State Route 542 approaches the mountain by threading a forested valley and climbing to Heather Meadows, a high mountain shoulder where it ends amid a jumble of peaks. The drive is truly spectacular even in a state well endowed with dramatic scenery.

Near Milepost 33 watch for the Glacier Ranger Station, built in 1938, with arching rockwork and heavy beams that announce Civilian Conservation Corps origins. The building—listed in the National Register of Historic Places—now houses an interpretive center. By the time the ranger station opened, the area had already passed through successive heydays of mining, logging, and recreation.

The mining came first. In the 1850s and 1860s prospectors had tested scattered creeks and ledges on their way to the British Columbia goldfields, but no particular excitement occurred until 1897 when Jack Post discovered the Lone Jack ledge east of Glacier. The richest gold lode in the district, it assayed at nearly $11 thousand per ton. In *Chechaco and Sourdough*, P. R. Jeffcoat recorded reaction to the news:

Next morning, business in Sumas was at a standstill, and groups of excited citizens were collected at usual meeting places, all discussing the news, and planning

to be off to the mines on the North Fork [Nooksack River]. [The assayer] could not be located. His wife said he had left for the mines before daylight. . . .

Post sold his interest in the mine to developers who packed in a disassembled stamp mill via a trail too narrow for wagons. The mine produced gold bullion through the 1920s and triggered over 5,000 nearby claims.

In 1909 the Bellingham Bay and British Columbia Railroad extended a spur as far as Glacier to serve the mines but, as logging moved deeper into untapped valleys, the cars actually carried out more timber than ore—and began the area's second boom. Early loggers cut valley bottoms. Later loggers reached into the steeper backcountry. Glacier acted as a logging hub for the entire drainage.

By the 1920s automobile travel brought in a third heydey: recreation. At Heather Meadows promoters built a lavish lodge with more than 100 rooms, an observation tower, and a lobby fireplace big enough to burn six-foot logs. Building materials had to come in by packtrain while the road, too, was under construction. The lodge lasted only until 1931. A fire destroyed the main building, a match for Timberline Lodge at Mount Hood or Paradise Inn at Mount Rainier. Enough structures remained, however, that Clark Gable and Loretta Young four years later filmed scenes for "Call of the Wild" there.

A madcap race from Bellingham to Mount Baker and back again—118 miles total—actually began the era of recreation even before completion of the road and lodge. Promoters organized the event in 1911 with 22 contestants signed up and 14 actually participating.

Each person could choose both route and mode of transportation for the first leg of the race. Some took a special train to Glacier, or those with automobiles rushed that far on their own; others preferred the Deming approach. All dashed up the slopes above the forested lowlands and climbed to the summit, where a fur-clad party waited to log their arrival. They then glissaded and ran down again, and a train waiting at Glacier carried off the lead contender and left the also-rans to fend for themselves. Winning time the first year was 12 hours and 28 minutes, a victory that might have been bettered had not the train derailed after hitting a cow,

At Point Roberts huge runs of Fraser River sockeye led to the development of an excessive salmon industry—and to feuds between small-boat fishermen and trap owners.

forcing the lead racer to commandeer first a horse and buggy, then a saddle horse, for the final return to Bellingham. His rival used the Deming route.

The race lasted only through 1913. Organizers then decided it was too grueling and potentially dangerous. Nonetheless that race became the inspiration for Bellingham's present Ski to Sea Race held each summer. Participants in this modern version ski, run, bike, canoe, and sail from Mount Baker to Fairhaven, Bellingham's venerable waterfront district.

NOOKSACK, a farming hamlet, is home to the Nooksack Bible Camp (Third and Harrison), which has a six-sided tabernacle shaped to suggest a tent. The Advent Christian Church built the hall in 1898 for revival meetings and regional conferences; it presently houses summer camps for children and adults.

Nooksack and its neighboring town of **Everson** first blossomed because of the Whatcom Trail, hastily built in 1858 from Bellingham to the Fraser River goldfields. This route crossed the Nooksack River near Everson, at the time known simply as the "upper crossing." Whatcom County supervisors had instructed the crew to establish a route

suitable for a pack trail not to be less than six feet in width, and not to cut fallen timber less than eight feet in width.

Overland travel was so difficult without a trail that the foreman easily recruited workers among the would-be miners camped at Bellingham Bay.

He also garnered underwriters. The trailwork fund was actually oversubscribed.

In the 1880s Nooksack grew on speculation that the Northern Pacific Railroad would establish a junction here. It never materialized, however, and the town has continued as a farming center.

POINT ROBERTS is the low-lying, sandy tip of a broad peninsula. Marinas, a Whatcom county park, and summer homes—some belonging to Americans, most to Canadians—line the shores. But Point Roberts is an anomaly of political geography. It lies separated from the rest of the United States by 25 miles of British Columbia. (Cross the border at Blaine and continue west via routes 99, 10, and 17.)

In 1861 the Joint Boundary Survey Commission erected boundary marker Number One (Marine Drive at Roosevelt Way) at the western end of the mainland boundary between Canada and the United States. The monument, a 19-foot obelisk imported from Scotland, stands near the shore in a pocket park. Watch for it facing east along the ditch that separates Roosevelt Way on the American side of the border from the kitchen gardens of homes on the Canadian side. This is the last original marker still standing.

In 1846 the United States and Canada agreed to extend the 49th parallel as the boundary between the two countries, although conflict arose over exactly how the line should thread through the archipelago offshore. This disagreement brought British and American soldiers into a 13-year standoff on San Juan

Salmon canning began along the Sacramento River in 1864 and moved to Washington three years later. Production of thousands of cans per day glutted the early-1900s market.

Island. Ironically, neither nation seemed to notice that the tip of Point Roberts had been cut from the rest of Canada.

Its settlement began early. In 1858 the steamship *Commodore* anchored off Point Roberts to set ashore 450 California miners headed for the Fraser River goldfields. A few lingered to sell supplies, mostly whiskey. For the next 25 years the federal government classified the point as a military reserve, although its actual use was by squatters who were raising cattle and operating fish traps. Fabulous numbers of sockeye salmon passed Point Roberts on their way back to the Fraser River to spawn. They drew the attention of the Alaska Packers Association, a corporation formed by Alaska and Washington cannery owners. The company installed efficient traps and canneries in the 1890s and set off a fishing frenzy. Their mechanization and heavy capitalization drove off smaller operators, in particular, Lummi fishermen. (See LUMMI RESERVATION, p. 226.)

The traps also drew raiders. In the book *River Pigs and Cayuses,* a man named Bert Jones reminisced about stealing from salmon traps on stormy nights, or any sort of night if he had bribed the watchman. He knew taking fish was "crooked" but rationalized that trap owners were equally crooked because they fished out of season. He also rationalized that traps were desirable because they provided jobs: "[Men] go into the woods and cut them big pilings a hundred feet long. . . . That cutting and pile driving puts men to work."

SAMISH ISLAND. (See under CHUCKANUT HIGHWAY, p. 224.)

SEMIAHMOO SPIT. (See under BLAINE, p. 223.)

SUMAS (Soo'-mas), snug against the Canadian border, funnels main-street traffic directly into the lineup for customs' inspection. Businesses so strongly cater to people crossing the border that a sign at the edge of town reads "Welcome to Sumas—Gateway to the Cariboo" on one side and "Gateway to the U.S.A." on the other. In residential areas, large bungalows line narrow streets. Dairies ring the edges of town, as noticeable by smell as by sight.

Sumas boomed as a way station on the Whatcom Trail during the 1858 Fraser River gold rush, and then continued as a railroad town on the Northern Pacific line joining Seattle with Canadian transcontinental railways. The Milwaukee Road also converged here.

East of Sumas, a grassy strip between twin "Boundary Roads"—one Canadian, one American—is the only physical demarcation between the nations. It acts as a reminder of the original half-mile-long, 40-foot-wide swaths that mid-1800s surveyors cleared through the forest at convenient locations. Within these, they set iron posts or rock cairns to mark the precise boundary line. Sheer physical labor necessitated only intermittent clearings; cutting a continuous line would have taken far too long.

Anacortes and Skagit Valley Area

The Skagit River dominates this area, flowing from the icy heights of the North Cascades to the rich, black delta. The river's broad, glacier-carved valley affords wide views of water, farms, forest, and peaks. Small towns—once home to miners and loggers—now cater to recreationists. Hundreds of bald eagles winter along the river, feeding on spawned-out salmon. Float trips operate year-round. The North Cascades Highway winds through spectacular alpine scenery and descends to the Methow Valley. (The highway is closed in winter for the 77 miles between Marblemount and Mazama. See NORTH CASCADES HIGHWAY, p. 78.)

Prosperous farms checkerboard the Skagit lowlands. Their crops include daffodils, tulips, and irises, which paint the fields with square miles of color in late March and April. Farm roads invite exploring and offer views of huge barns back-dropped by Mount Baker and the jagged North Cascades. Year-round ferries leave Anacortes for the San Juan Islands and Vancouver Island, British Columbia.

History museums are in La Conner and Anacortes. A North Cascades National Park visitor center is expected to open near Newhalem in the early 1990s. Tours of three dams on the upper Skagit include a boat trip on Diablo Lake.

ANACORTES lies at the northern tip of Fidalgo Island. Ferries serving the San Juan Islands and Victoria base here; oil tankers pass on their way to refineries at March Point; marinas shelter fishing boats and pleasure craft; and boatyards turn out vessels from wooden rowboats to steel-hulled purse seiners.

In the heart of town, Causland Park (Eighth and M) is surrounded by a free-flowing, cobble wall that is reminiscent of the artistry of Barcelona's Antonio Gaudi. Patterns of white quartz and red argillite swirl on a background of brown and gray sandstone. John LePage, a French-Canadian architect, designed the park in 1919 as a memorial to local men who died in World War I. It is listed in the National Register of Historic Places. Opposite the park, the town's old Carnegie Library has become a history and

Until 1981, the 163-foot W. T. Preston *(now displayed at Anacortes) served as a snag boat, retrieving drift logs, rotted pilings, and various other obstructions to navigation.*

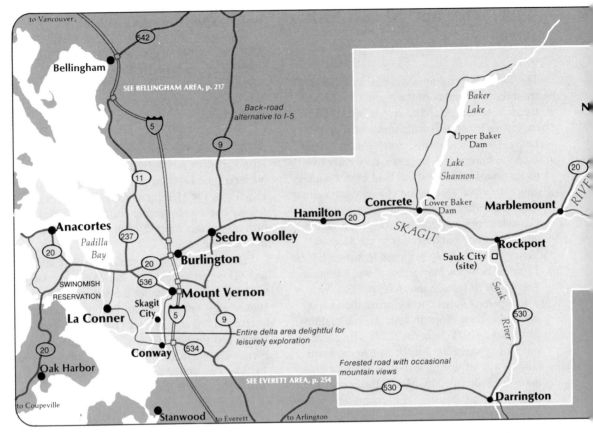

SEE BELLINGHAM AREA, p. 217

Back-road
alternative to I-5

Baker
Lake

Upper Baker
Dam

Lake
Shannon

Bellingham

Concrete
Lower Baker
Dam

Marblemount

Hamilton

Rockport

Anacortes
Padilla
Bay

Sedro Woolley

Sauk City
(site)

Burlington

SWINOMISH
RESERVATION

Skagit
City

Mount Vernon

La Conner

Entire delta area delightful for
leisurely exploration

Conway

Forested road with occasional
mountain views

Oak Harbor

SEE EVERETT AREA, p. 254

Darrington

to Coupeville

Stanwood
to Everett
to Arlington

to Vancouver

SKAGIT

Sauk
River

RIVER

N

art museum. Its entry includes a sculpted drinking fountain commissioned by the Women's Christian Temperance Union for use by horses, dogs, and humans. Museum collections include a particularly fine group of historic photographs.

The Anacortes Post Office (Sixth and Commercial) boasts a mural painted in 1936 by famed Northwest artist Kenneth Callahan, and near the business district fine nineteenth- and twentieth-century homes abound. For a sample, drive through the 1200 to 1800 blocks of Fifth through Eighth streets; the house at Eighth and M was built in 1891 by Amos Bowman, the town's founder.

Also drive the waterfront for a look at the 1919 *W. T. Preston,* the Northwest's last operating stern-wheeler (611 R Avenue), which closed the steamboat era begun in 1836 when the Hudson's Bay Company's steam vessel *Beaver* arrived. The *Preston,* commissioned in 1929, patrolled Puget Sound removing hazards to navigation until the early 1980s.

For magnificent views of waterways and mountains—Anacortes' spectacular setting—

follow Washington Park's loop road around Fidalgo Head, a high promontory jutting west (reached by driving through town on Commercial, then following Twelfth). Also drive to the top of Cap Sante, a glaciated rock outcrop with a 360-degree panoramic view. (Circle the waterfront on R Avenue, then turn up the hill on Fourth and continue.) For the highest view, go to Mount Erie (southern edge of town).

Settlement of the area began in the 1860s on March Point, east of Anacortes. Today oil storage tanks stud the point, but previously the land stretched as a bracken-covered prairie far easier to farm than the surrounding forest land. Settlers also gradually took up claims within the boundaries of the present town. Among them was Amos Bowman, a civil engineer hired by railroad interests to explore the region. On Fidalgo Island Bowman found a deep-water harbor and dense forest, ideal for logging. He bought land near the present ferry landing, built a wharf, and christened the community with a romanticized version of his wife's name: Anna Curtis.

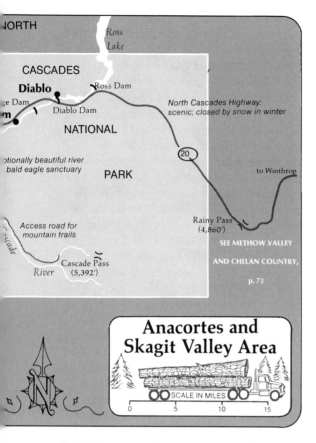

North Cascades Highway: scenic; closed by snow in winter

CASCADES

Diablo

Ross Dam

Diablo Dam

NATIONAL

...tionally beautiful river
bald eagle sanctuary

PARK

20

to Winthrop

Access road for
mountain trails

Rainy Pass
(4,860')

SEE METHOW VALLEY

AND CHELAN COUNTRY,

p. 73

Cascade Pass
(5,392')

River

Ross Lake

NORTH

Anacortes and
Skagit Valley Area

SCALE IN MILES

0   5   10   15

In 1882 steamers began stopping at Anacortes on their Seattle to Bellingham runs. That same year, Bowman earned the title "Father of Anacortes" by publishing and distributing a promotional map that touted his town's potential as a railroad terminus and seaport. He envisioned a direct rail connection up the Skagit Valley and over the mountains to Spokane. The dream seemed to materialize when Seattle and Northern Railroad agents affiliated with the Union Pacific began buying acreage in Anacortes. This set off a boom that drove up the population from 40 to 3,000 in the first few months of 1890. The town filled with merchants and workmen. Gullible investors even bought little Hat and Dot islands, represented to them as "downtown" property.

The townsite was an array of stumps, but entrepreneurs built wharves and hotels; and real estate prices soared. In November 1890 the first train arrived, and townspeople celebrated even though the track was only a connector line to the Seattle, Lake Shore and Eastern. Soon, however, the depression associated with the Panic of 1893

deflated all hope of a transcontinental link. Nonetheless, sawmills—in particular, specialty mills for boxes—soon thrived along the shore. (A 200-foot smokestack, built in 1905 for a box mill, still stands on T Avenue.) Fish processing also grew into a major industry with six large canneries and hundreds of Chinese workers manufacturing cans and filling them with salmon.

In 1905 the largest codfish plant on the West Coast opened here. The owner sent schooners to the Bering Sea, where fishermen in small dories caught cod by day, cleaned and salted them on the mothership by night. At the end of the season, they returned to Anacortes to dry and package the fish for shipment. Another fish-dependent industry was a large glue factory built about 1906 to produce carpenter's glue, wool sizing, and fertilizer.

Padilla Bay—its mud flats visible from State Route 20 on the approach to Anacortes—is a National Estuarine Sanctuary. (From the highway, turn north on Bayview-Edison Road to the interpretive center.) Black brant congregate here to feed on extensive eelgrass beds, and dabbling ducks number in the thousands.

BURLINGTON—at the modern junction of I-5 with the North Cascades Highway—developed later than most other small towns in the Skagit Valley. In 1882 it was a mere logging camp with ox-powered cars and maple-railed tracks for hauling logs to the Skagit River to be towed downstream by the steamer *Alki*. During the next decade a farming community developed on the logged-over land. North-south and east-west railroads helped the young town grow. A sawmill and shingle mills provided jobs. Today Burlington serves as an agricultural center.

The village of **CONCRETE** dots the upper Skagit Valley, worthy of a detour off the highway. Its name comes from its most important product, and its compact business district consists of concrete buildings. Most were built as a demonstration of fireproof construction following a disastrous blaze in 1921.

Amasa Everett—discoverer of coal downriver at Hamilton—found the clay and limestone that gave rise to the town here. He carried samples to New York financiers, who formed the

Washington Portland Cement Company in 1892 and built a processing plant on the east bank of the Baker River, which flows into the Skagit at this point. Six years later the Superior Portland Cement Company opened a plant on the west bank. In 1909 the two pinprick communities merged, and the companies followed suit a few years later; concrete silos at each end of town still reflect the early division. A mile-long aerial tramway from the quarry to the plant carried limestone directly over Main Street, and wayward chunks sometimes fell on pedestrians until the company installed a safety net. Workers were largely immigrants from southern Italy who at first put in 12-hour days, seven days a week. The cement plant closed in 1968.

At the east end of town a 1916 bridge, listed in the National Register of Historic Places, spans the Baker River. An engineering consultant determined that a steel bridge, not concrete, would prove the most economical, but the local company countered his recommendation by donating cement for the construction. That changed the economics, and Concrete got a concrete bridge. At the time, reinforced concrete technology was still in its infancy, and this long-span highway bridge was a trendsetter.

Puget Sound Power and Light Company built **Baker Dam** northeast of Concrete in 1924 to supply electricity for the Bellingham area. The dam can be viewed from an overlook on East Lake Shannon Road a few miles north of town. (From Concrete, cross the historic bridge and turn north on East Lake Shannon Road.) The state's largest colony of nesting osprey is at Lake Shannon.

CONWAY—now largely bypassed—began when a subsidiary of the Great Northern Railway built a line through here in the 1890s and opened a depot on the east bank of the Skagit River. An earlier town, **Fir,** already existed across the river.

Fir farmers, among them many Norwegians, organized a Lutheran congregation in 1888 and built a simple church, accessible by rowboat and footpath. That building served their needs until 1916 when they built the present Fir-Conway Lutheran Church (1 mile west of Exit 221 off I-5), its classic steeple a white beacon rising from green fields. The church stands on high ground to avoid recurrent floods, a protection also true of the lovingly refurbished farmhouses in its neighborhood.

The Fir Island Road (past the church to the west) offers an intimate view of rich delta farmlands, including fields of rapeseed, which in May are brilliant with yellow flowers. It is a road for leisurely enjoyment—and to follow as a scenic approach to La Conner. Along the way, stop for one of the state's truly spectacular—and timeless—sights and sounds: tens of thousands of wintering snow geese along with hundreds of trumpeter swans. For specific directions to the best bird-watching areas at any given time, check at the Skagit Wildlife Area office southwest of Conway. (Drive west about 1½ miles on Fir Island Road, then turn south 1¼ miles on Wylie Road and follow signs.)

Mid-January to mid-April is the best time to see migrating waterfowl; come in spring for nesting wood ducks, cinnamon teal, mallards, and others. Watch also—year round—for deer, muskrats, foxes, coyotes, hawks, songbirds, and other forms of wildlife that were common in western Washington before the arrival of farms and clearcuts and pavement. The Skagit delta and estuary constitute a particularly fine refuge.

DARRINGTON. (See under ROCKPORT, p. 241.)

South of Anacortes, **DECEPTION PASS** separates the rugged high bluffs of Whidbey and Fidalgo islands. Tidal currents as great as seven knots challenge today's outboard motors; in the sailing era, currents made the channel impassable except with careful timing and a fortunate wind. A state park now encompasses both sides of the pass; beach and forest trails well worth sampling thread the edges of the waterway. The most dramatic view of rushing water and struggling boats is from the high bridge, which was built in 1935 with Works Progress Administration funds and Civilian Conservation Corps labor. Captain George Vancouver bestowed the name Deception Pass in 1792. Until he found this passage, he had thought Whidbey Island was a peninsula.

Just east of Deception Pass is an island named for a notorious resident, Benjamin Ure. After enactment of the Chinese Exclusion Act in 1882, he used his fast sloop to smuggle Chinese workers from Canada into the United States. His wife helped by building a fire on the beach each night. If federal agents were in the area. she sat in front of the fire: otherwise she sat behind it.

DIABLO, still a Seattle City Light company town, occupies a river flat 8 miles upstream from Newhalem. Nearby, a 1927 incline lift climbs 560 feet up Sourdough Mountain. It now carries tourists, but during the construction of Diablo and Ross dams it formed the final segment of a remarkable railway carrying materials and workers. A locomotive pulled cars along the valley from Rockport to Newhalem, then crossed and recrossed the river and crept along roadbeds blasted from cliff faces. At Diablo the cars rolled one by one onto the incline lift, which hoisted them to Diablo Lake. There an electric locomotive nudged them onto a cross-lake barge, and finally they were winched ashore at the Ross Dam construction site. The railroad quit running in 1953 when a road was built to Ross Dam.

A divorcee named Lucinda Davis and her children Frank, Glee, and Idessa homesteaded near the Diablo Dam site in 1898, then accessible only by a treacherous trail from present-day Newhalem. Lucinda opened an inn where miners, forest rangers, hydroelectric engineers, and hunters found hospitality and family atmosphere. For lonely miners, the Davis Ranch was a "mecca in the wilderness." One guest wrote:

There are fruit trees, chickens, farm tools, a radio, electric lights, a comfortable farmhouse built of hand-hewn lumber . . . [and] an air of thrift and contentment everywhere.

With the passage of the Forest Homestead Act of 1906 the National Forest Service evaluated and reevaluated the validity of the Davis claim. They allowed less than half of it and, even more unfortunately for the family, final papers were not signed until 1917, just as Seattle City Light began its Gorge Dam project. Surveys and expansions of the hydro development ultimately brought legal condemnation of the Davis Ranch in favor of more electricity for Seattle. In 1929 the family moved permanently to Sedro Woolley.

A museum at Diablo highlights homemade

By marrying an underwater chieftain, the Samish Maiden of Deception Pass assured the annual return of salmon. A monumental carving of her stands on the north shore of the pass.

items from their farm, and a reconstruction of the home-built waterwheel that generated electricity for the family. Displays also include electric appliances—a vivid demonstration of how much housekeeping has changed since the 1920s—and a series of lightbulbs from 1914 argon bulbs to 1946 mercury vapor bulbs and 1952 incandescent bulbs coated blue for use while watching television. The road to Diablo edges the lake, offering views of peaks looming abruptly—and thoughts of the Davis family's choice of a homestead.

FIR. (See under CONWAY, p. 234.)

HAMILTON is now a quiet residential area just off State Route 20, but it was a bustling mining town in its younger days. In 1875 Amasa Everett found a coal seam here, and soon native canoes were hauling coal downstream to Skagit City from which it was shipped by steamer to San Francisco. Hamilton's coal potential lured settlers, and even attracted a railroad in 1891. Even so, timber became the economic mainstay. The population grew to 2,000 in the early 1900s but soon nearby trees had all been cut, loggers moved on, and the remaining residents turned to farming.

LA CONNER spreads along a steep hillside facing Swinomish Channel, a mecca for artists, writers, and tourists. Pleasure boats ply the narrow waterway bound for the San Juan Islands or Whidbey Island. False-fronted stores extend out over the water on pilings, a legacy of the steamboat era when La Conner was the region's most "stylish" town.

Of particular interest is the 1891 Gaches Mansion (Second between Douglas and Calhoun), a turreted 22-room home that is now elegantly restored and open to visitors. James

Gaches owned a store that advertised: "Everything you want kept in stock, from a needle to platform scales." Across from the mansion is the Civic Garden Club (Second and Calhoun), built in 1875 as a Grange hall. The county historical museum at the hilltop end of Fourth Street offers farmland views as well as insight into pioneer days. Down the hill, the triangular city hall (Second and Douglas) originated in 1886 as a bank. The Tillinghast Seed Company (Washington Avenue), a mail-order firm begun in 1882, has been located in La Conner since 1890.

The town began in 1867 when Alonzo Low opened a trading post on Swinomish Slough, a shallow waterway that offered protected passage for steamboats between Bellingham Bay and communities on Puget Sound. Two years later J. S. Conner bought the store and became the town's leading land developer and banker. He named the young community for his wife, L(ouisa) A(nn) Conner.

The town's location was no accident. At the time, only islands of relatively high ground like La Conner, Pleasant Ridge, Bay View Ridge, and Burlington Hill offered safety from severe flooding. The whole Skagit delta was a maze of sloughs and marshes with tidewater welling in

La Conner lies along Swinomish Channel, a partly natural, partly dredged waterway that extends 4 miles between Padilla and Skagit bays and saves rounding the point.

twice a day, and the Skagit River producing annual floods. The floods deposited rich alluvium and, in the 1860s, a few experienced farmers began diking the flats to keep out the sea and let the sediments accumulate. They worked with shovels and wheelbarrows and shoed their horses with straw sandals for support in the mud. Work was possible only at low tide, whether by daylight or moonlight. Dikes were wedge shaped in cross section—8 feet wide at the base tapering to 2½ feet at the top—and were seeded with grass for stability. Before roads, paths along the dikes provided travel routes. By 1884 they stretched for a cumulative 150 miles in the La Conner area. Ten years later severe floods struck all of western Washington, and water covered farms. Ellsworth Fulk, who lived near Pleasant Ridge, described such a flood in the county historical society publication *Skagit Settlers:*

The water kept on coming toward our house and buildings in a large rolling and tumbling wave. . . . We managed to get the barn doors open and the horses were standing in cold water about even with their backs. We shoved hay down from the mow and got them all fed. . . . The poor cows did not fare so well; we pried open the dairy barn doors and they were standing in the water with just their heads and noses sticking out above it. All we could do was herd them out and let them take their own swimming course to higher ground. We lost practically all of them from exposure and getting tangled up in the floating wire fences.

At first no one would volunteer to open a dike to let floodwater drain across his land. Some farmers even patrolled their dikes with shotguns. Soon, however, the need to let water escape brought the community together; farmers reached joint decisions, handled the problem, and then worked together to make repairs. They also began to dike the river as well as the sea.

Early farmers grew grains—especially oats—and shipped them by steamer from La Conner as early as 1875. Hops grew well, too, but statewide Prohibition in 1916 diminished the market. Today vegetable seeds, berries, and peas are common crops. And—above all—the area is renowned for tulips and daffodils grown for their bulbs and as cut flowers, a veritable

False-fronted buildings from the late 1800s characterize La Conner's downtown core. Now popular as a tourist town, the community began as a trading post.

"rainbow on the ground" during March and April and a sight worth making a special trip to enjoy. (Maps to fields currently in bloom are available in Mount Vernon and La Conner each spring.)

MARBLEMOUNT nestles at a bend in the Skagit River. Today travelers stop for a meal or to rest, much as miners did in the 1880s, and the community retains some of its early buildings and much of its wilderness charm. Tradition holds that the first business here was a tent saloon with whiskey barrels supporting a plank bar.

In 1891 William Barrett "bought" 20 acres from the local Salish people and built a hotel "for the accommodation of prospectors and mining men." He operated a cable ferry of two canoes joined by planking to assist miners on their way to Ruby Creek and the Cascade River. Such ferries continued operations until the 1960s. Hazel Tracy, who grew up across the river from Marblemount in the 1920s reminisces:

The water was shallow on the north side. The planks there didn't reach far enough, and we had to hop off the ferry onto rocks. We had wet feet all the time anyway, so we might as well have waded. From the landing, I had 2 miles to walk to school. Once the horses shied off the ferry and our load of hay went floating. All I could think about was my candy. I'd hidden a little bag of lemon drops in that hay. It stayed afloat and the next day I got them back.

MOUNT VERNON was born of one transportation corridor, the Skagit River, and today relies on another, the I-5 freeway. Skagit delta farmland forms a backdrop for the town and provides its economic mainstay. The brick buildings of the old section of town show to the west of the freeway. For a feeling of that past, attend a performance at the Lincoln Theater (on First near Kincaid). Its 1926 Wurlitzer D-Special theater organ, which once thrilled patrons of silent films, has been restored by the local organ society; its leather pneumatic connections are in place, and its lighted chimes adorn the auditorium's side walls. Concerts are given monthly with special performances during the April tulip festival.

Settlement here began in 1870 as farm families reclaimed land from the marshy riverbanks and sloughs of the Skagit River. Few ventured upstream of the huge logjams near present-day Mount Vernon. These were natural, one of them a mile in length and undisturbed for so long that tangles of uprooted trees actually hosted brush and colonies of small animals and birds. In 1876, undeterred by the territorial government's refusal of help, volunteers began removal. Five men worked for two years—two drowned in the effort—before clearing a 250-foot channel through the lower jam. That done the first steamer was able to chug upstream to the tiny settlement of Mount Vernon. In 1879 men also succeeded in cutting an opening

through an upper logjam. That final clearing enhanced Mount Vernon's development but wrought havoc downstream as loosened logs destroyed farms between the north and south forks of the lower river.

Harrison Clothier had opened a store at Mount Vernon in 1877 and, as miners came through en route to the gold excitement at Ruby Creek, other merchants joined him. The town grew but hardly became a metropolis. Even 10 years later when a man named J. M. Shields came to interview for the teaching position, he found only two hotels, neither one very satisfactory:

Those who stopped at either of these hotels on a cold night were given a room without heat. . . . The only warm room for men was the bar-room. A separate warm room was provided for the ladies. . . . In order to reach [the school] from the hotel where I was staying, I found it necessary to follow a winding trail around stumps and logs and over a rail fence.

NEWHALEM (Noo-hail'-um) today is a tidy mountain village of matching homes on a broad flat beside the Skagit River. It was built as a company town, and its houses still are occupied by Seattle City Light personnel. Several sites are worth searching out. Ladder Creek Falls (behind the powerhouse) slithers down a sinuous channel in a landscaped garden of native species. A self-guiding nature trail crosses the river on a narrow suspension bridge (end of Main Street) and leads into a riverbank forest. A steam locomotive that formerly hauled supplies and tourists from Rockport to Ross Dam is now displayed near the highway. A Seattle City Light visitor center supplies information about tours of their three dams and about features on nearby national park and forest lands.

About 3 miles down the valley from Newhalem, a National Park Service visitor center is scheduled to open in the early 1990s. Upstream, notice the oddly bare riverbed with only pools of water scattered among boulders and cobbles. This stretch of the Skagit is diverted through a tunnel and used to produce power.

The narrow canyon above Newhalem is the only constriction along the broad Skagit River from Canadian headwaters to the sea, a site obviously valuable for hydropower. Seattle City

Light eyed that potential when its Cedar River plant fell short of power demands and, in 1917, it received a federal license to develop Gorge Dam. This came as America entered World War I and was partly intended to aid the war effort. The first step in construction was to build a 24-mile private railroad from the Great Northern terminus at Rockport to the dam's staging area near Newhalem. By 1920 tents and temporary shacks sheltered 500 workers while a sawmill on Goodell Creek turned out lumber for houses and for the dam. In 1924—five years after the war had ended—work on the dam was complete, and President Calvin Coolidge threw a gold switch in Washington, D.C., to activate its generators.

Seattle City Light's superintendent John D. Ross recognized the public relations potential of the dramatic gorge and, beginning in 1928, invited ratepayers to tour the project. They rode a special train from Rockport, feasted on hearty camp meals, slept overnight in a dormitory, and walked the exotic gardens, which were lit by electricity at night, a breathtaking novelty. All this for $4.

Before the dams, activity in the area centered on mining. In 1878 five prospectors packed their gear up the Skagit Valley and over Sourdough Mountain to the mouth of Ruby Creek (at the south end of the present Ross Lake). After a profitable summer—they washed out $1,500 in two days—they returned to Mount Vernon, resisted the temptation to brag, and earned one more season on the river to themselves. But stories about gold invariably leak. The summer of 1880 found the creek banks lined with hopefuls, and another Washington gold rush was on.

Getting to the Ruby mines was a formidable undertaking. One newspaper reported:

To reach the mines from Seattle, the gold seeker must take some one of the steamers on the Skagit route for Mount Vernon. . . . [From there] a party of three can charter a canoe, manned by Indians, to ascend the river to Goodell's trading-post [Newhalem] for $30 dollars. All along the route the scenery is described as grand and picturesque in the extreme.

That was only the beginning. The hard part was the Goat Trail upstream from present Newhalem. Today's highway in this part of the gorge slips effortlessly through a series of tunnels, but yesterday's miners followed a trail clinging to the sheer north face above the rushing river. In the early years the men carried their mining supplies on their backs and scrambled across cliffs on all fours, aided in places by ladders. In the 1890s volunteers raised money to blast ledges and build hanging bridges across side canyons. At Devil's Corner, the worst part of the trail, they suspended a cedar puncheon deck from a rock overhang. One legendary pack trip via Goat Trail involved a long cable loaded in coils onto mules, with straight lengths connecting from animal to animal. The sharp bends stymied progress, and men finally had to shoulder the coils and carry them for 20 miserable miles to about where the highway now crosses Diablo Gorge at Colonial Creek.

Ruby Creek strikes failed to produce much gold, and the long haul to smelters (at Everett or Tacoma) ate up what profit there otherwise might have been. The *Puget Sound Mail* in the summer of 1880 reported, "The Skagit mines, we regret to say, have proved to be a total failure." High hopes had led 2,000 men up the valley, but they "worked down to bedrock, to find nothing of value thereon." The Ruby townsite, near the original placers, is now under Ross Lake.

NORTH CASCADES NATIONAL PARK encompasses a half million acres of forest lowlands, subalpine meadows, and austere mountain heights. Proposed in 1906 and again in 1935, the park was not established until 1968. It came about when a citizens' group, the North Cascades Conservation Council, strongly opposed the cutting of virgin timber in lowland valleys and organized public support for a park.

In designating the park, Congress stated that agencies should manage the entire North Cascades as a unit rather than arbitrarily heeding various administrative boundaries. This has led to coordinated planning for national forests, wilderness areas, recreation areas, Seattle City Light hydroelectric installations, and the national park—an unprecedented mix.

In the park, a visitor center near Newhalem is scheduled to open in the early 1990s. Trails and traverses web the rugged backcountry. Boat trips cruise the fjordlike waters of Diablo Lake and

Lake Chelan. The North Cascades Highway (closed in winter) climbs among the high peaks and crosses to the Methow Valley. The unpaved Cascade Pass road leads close to subalpine meadow country that was very nearly trampled into oblivion by visitors but has been revegetated through volunteer labor and experiments with high-elevation plants grown at a Marblemount greenhouse.

ROCKPORT is a hamlet at the confluence of the Sauk and Skagit rivers where forested foothills seem to pile against the base of icy Cascade peaks. Stop at the community's riverside park to see two early-day vessels: the Rockport ferry, in use until 1961, and a 30-foot cedar dugout canoe. Native people stood to pole their canoes, a stance that demanded perfect balance but gave a clear view of river hazards ahead. After whites arrived canoes sometimes were paired, like a catamaran, and used to transport horses or hay across the river.

Rockport represents the second attempt at a community in this area. It grew as a stop on the Seattle and Northern Railroad, built to haul ore and timber from the mountains. While Seattle City Light dams were under construction, three trains a day rolled into the depot bringing supplies, and an entrepreneur built a 21-room hotel with hot and cold running water, a dining room, and a tavern.

Rockport's forerunner, **Sauk City,** stood 2 miles downstream on the opposite bank, a way station for miners heading farther up the Skagit Valley to the Ruby Creek mines, or following the Sauk River south to the Monte Cristo mines. Steamboats brought men and supplies, a ferry operated regularly, and a hotel provided amenities for all who wearied of camp life. A shingle mill eventually gave the community greater economic stability than was possible from mines alone. But a fire burned the entire town in 1899, and a flood washed away the charred debris. Residents rebuilt on the opposite bank, and Rockport replaced Sauk City.

By the late 1880s, nearly every community

Wherever red cedar grew, men cut trees; small mills turned the logs into shingles; and metal "wigwams" burning sawdust and scrap wood glowed red at night.

along the Skagit River had a shingle mill. The first loggers simply dropped riverside trees directly into the water. Later they sawed cedar logs into four-foot sections, called "bolts," and dragged them on crude sleds to storage points along the river. Intermittently a downriver mill sent word that it was ready to buy bolts, and men branded what they had on hand, dumped them into the water, and dispatched several canoe crews to shepherd the bolts downstream. Native Americans were particularly skilled at the work, which called for maneuvering the canoes and, when necessary, wading waist-deep to free bolts that hung up on obstructions. A large canoe carried a cook, his gear, and the bolt drivers' personal belongings. Each night the crew camped along the river and tried—in vain—to dry out around a fire. In the morning they caught up again with the bolts.

The national economy also drove the movement of shingles. In 1893 and other depression years there was no work for bolt drivers and shingle weavers (sawmill workers who cut the bolts into shingles); but in periods of national expansion the demand for Washington shingles seemed insatiable, especially in the largely unforested tier of midwestern states. After World War II, cheap roll roofing and asbestos shingles largely replaced cedar shingles.

Rockport marks the western boundary of the **Skagit River Bald Eagle Sanctuary,** where 7 miles of riverfront, purchased in the 1970s by The Nature Conservancy, provide winter feeding grounds. Eagles that spend the spring and summer along the coast as far distant as southeast Alaska congregate here in late fall to feed on spawned-out chum salmon. To avoid disturbance, visitors are asked to observe only from designated roadside sites. The first of these is 1 mile east of Rockport.

Darrington, 20 miles south of Rockport, began as an overnight camp for miners bound for the Monte Cristo mines. In the early days only an unpleasantly rough trail/road linked the two communities and, after a railroad arrived, people traveling from Rockport to Darrington actually preferred the 150-mile train trip down the Skagit Valley and then up the Stillaguamish Valley, rather than the direct, 20-mile trail route. Lumber became Darrington's mainstay.

Each July the town now hosts a bluegrass

music festival, faithful to the North Carolina "Tarheel" origin of many early settlers. Their arrival here is said to have improved the quality of the area's moonshine whiskey, an economic mainstay for some families as mines and timber gave out. Local-option "dry" votes created markets even before the enactment of national Prohibition. The Carolinians brought a well-honed skill. And the Sauk and Skagit hinterlands gave them seclusion and the mountain streams needed for cooling copper coils. The resulting liquor had a reputation for purity and flavor.

(Also see MONTE CRISTO, p. 259.)

ROSS LAKE stretches into Canada surrounded by extravagant alpine scenery. It is the reservoir behind the third Seattle City Light dam on the Skagit River. In the late 1930s lumberjacks logged the valley in preparation for the flooding; when slack water later rose behind the dam, a floating camp housed men who boomed the logs and rafted them to the north end of the lake. From there, they were trucked out via the British Columbia road that now provides recreational access to the lake. At the Fraser River the logs were again boomed and floated to a sawmill at Anacortes.

Gates at the dam closed initially in 1949. Subsequent plans to increase the height of the dam were postponed indefinitely in response to opposition from the Canadian government and environmental groups.

SAUK CITY. (See under ROCKPORT, p. 240.)

SEDRO WOOLLEY, a town of venerable brick buildings, stands on the flat Skagit Valley floor surrounded by corn, raspberries, dairy cattle, and farms with large barns. In 1884 Mortimer Cook built the first shingle mill in the region and platted a town here. He threatened to name it "Bug," but his neighbors campaigned for Sedro, a misspelling of the Spanish *cedro,* "cedar." Five years later Phillip Woolley platted a neighboring town slightly to the north in anticipation of a railroad and, within a few years, his town actually had three rail lines: the Fairhaven and Southern; the Seattle, Lakeshore and Eastern; and the Seattle and Northern.

North of Woolley, a coal mine owned by

developer Charles Larrabee of Fairhaven (Bellingham) gave rise to a third town, Cokedale. Four kilns there heated coal to drive off gases and produce a clean, hot-burning fuel that sold to the Northern Pacific for use in locomotives. A spur track connected the mine to Woolley, which became the predominant community. In 1898 Sedro and Woolley merged.

A joint National Park Service/National Forest Service visitor information station is near the east side of town along State Route 20. Farther east, the former Northern State Hospital grounds are worth driving onto for a look at their Mission-style buildings and stately street plantings. Built as a state mental institution, the buildings today house federal and state social service programs.

SKAGIT CITY is now little more than a memory and a lone 1902 school building near Conway on the south fork of the Skagit. Visiting the site makes a good excuse for a pleasant delta drive. (From I-5 take Exit 221 west across the Skagit River; turn immediately north on Skagit City-Fir Road, and continue about 3½ miles to Moore Road.) Before logjams were cleared from the river near present Mount Vernon, Skagit City was the largest community—and the oldest—on the upper delta. It began in 1869 and truly flourished from 1870 to 1890. Steamboats docked at its wharves, and the military road from Fort Steilacoom to Fort Bellingham crossed the river here. After the Mount Vernon logjams were cleared in 1879, Skagit City benefited from the growth of upriver towns that were served by steamers from Port Townsend, the social and economic hub of the era.

Soon, however, railroads connected the inland towns with the outside world, and Skagit City got left behind. Furthermore, taking out the upriver logjams increased the frequency of floods on the entire delta, including at Skagit City. Erosion cut into the riverbank and left little but a deteriorated steamboat landing. The remaining Skagit City school, built in 1902, has served as a community center since 1943. Its original bell now stands by the road within a protective grill made from the iron supports of old-fashioned school desks.

The **SWINOMISH RESERVATION** faces La Conner across Swinomish Channel. The Point Elliott Treaty of 1855 reserved its 7,000 acres for the Swinomish, Samish, and Lower Skagit people. Formerly, the Swinomish had lived on northern Whidbey Island and various nearby small islands. They largely depended on fish for livelihood—an economic base that continues today with a tribally owned fish company. Logging is another modern pursuit. Samish people moved to the reservation from Fidalgo, Samish, and Guemes islands; the Lower Skagit people from central Whidbey and the Skagit delta.

During the 1870s, when all reservations were officially assigned to religious denominations for supervision, Catholic priests staffed the Swinomish Reservation. Actually their influence had already penetrated the area, beginning in the 1840s when missionary Francis Blanchet went to Whidbey Island. For his use the Swinomish built a pole-and-mat chapel with a bell, which is preserved at the present church, Saint Paul's (Reservation Road, facing Swinomish Channel; built in 1868 with the help of Father Casimir Chirouse). Also at the church is an old drawing of the Catholic Ladder, a schematic presentation of history devised by early missionaries.

San Juan Islands

The San Juan Islands form a tapestry of dark firs, rocky outcroppings, and sparkling water. Each island is distinctive, yet all are alike. Gentle south-facing slopes grow golden grass; abrupt north-facing slopes support Douglas fir and salal. Orange-barked madrona lean over thousands of pebbly coves. Curious seals inspect slow-moving boats, and bald eagles build shaggy, six-foot nests in towering snags. There are 172 true islands—including four served by ferries—and hundreds more that are barely above water. All are the tips of a mountain range that once connected the mainland with Vancouver Island. Today's watery pathways between islands are the glacier-gouged and drowned valleys of those erstwhile mountains.

From Anacortes, ferries wend among the islands with stops on Lopez, Shaw, Orcas, and San Juan; some continue to Sidney, north of Victoria on Vancouver Island, Canada. The ferry trips beguile with glimpses of winding channels and shorelines. Private planes and small airlines land on the larger islands; pleasure boats cruise to sheltered anchorages. Bicyclists and motorists should exercise caution—island roads are narrow and winding.

On San Juan Island a historic lime-manufacturing business is now a resort; the remains of British and American army camps of the 1860s "Pig War" have become a national historic park; and the county seat, Friday Harbor, offers a museum devoted to whales. The summit of Orcas Island's 2,409-foot Mount Constitution, accessible by road, presents a panorama of the islands, the Olympic Mountains, and the mainland.

Today's economy still rests on agriculture—sheep, hay, and specialty crops such as strawberries and garlic. But since the early 1900s tourists have flocked here and in recent decades their numbers have mushroomed. Businesses catering to summerfolk swell the larger communities. Some visitors become part-time residents; their cedar-and-glass "second homes" ring the shorelines.

All major islands have museums and interpretive centers.

AMERICAN CAMP (San Juan Island), now part of San Juan Island National Historic Park, consists of a small visitor contact station with displays, two stabilized buildings (a laundress' house and an officers' duplex), and a loop trail with interpretive signs, which leads among earthen redoubts and to the site of a British

Washington State Ferries serve the four main islands of the San Juan archipelago. Scheduled passenger and freight service to the islands began as early as 1873.

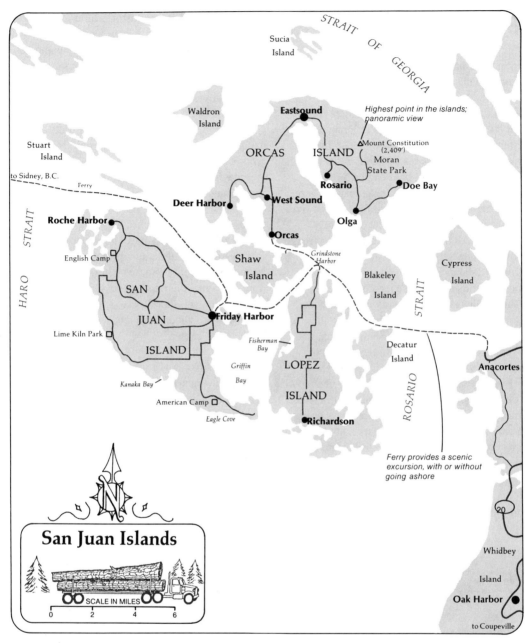

San Juan Islands

SCALE IN MILES
0   2   4   6

sheep farm. (To visit the site, drive south from Friday Harbor on Argyle Avenue and then Cattle Point Road, approximately 5 miles.) During the 1859 to 1872 boundary dispute with Great Britain, the windswept site had officers' houses, log barracks, an earthen redoubt, and gun emplacements. The fortifications commanded both the southern shipping lanes and Griffin Bay. A walk on the beach here offers views across the Strait of Juan de Fuca to the Olympics and, on clear days, Mount Rainier forms a distant white lump on the southeastern horizon.

(Also see ENGLISH CAMP, p. 245.)

DEER HARBOR (Orcas Island) today is a resort village with an ebb and flow of sailboats as constant as the ebb and flow of the tide. In 1859 four Hudson's Bay Company hunters rowed ashore here with instructions to supply Fort Victoria with venison. Though transient miners may have passed through before, these four were the earliest permanent white settlers.

EASTSOUND (Orcas Island) juxtaposes pioneer buildings with modern counterparts at the head of East Sound, a deep inlet nearly cleaving the island. The village has the usual businesses—grocery, hardware, pharmacy—and also a plethora of restaurants, boutiques, and crafts outlets, indication of the town's dependence on tourism. Orcas' airport is a mile north of town. The Outlook Inn dates to 1891, still welcoming guests. Emmanual Episcopal Church (1885), patterned after rural English churches, occupies a bluff directly above the water. A log cabin historical museum displays island artifacts, including the rowboat used by an early school superintendent to make his rounds throughout the islands.

Beginning in the 1870s Eastsound's central location recommended it as Orcas Island's main community. A single store (now incorporated into the central part of the Outlook Inn) and a nearby schoolhouse comprised the "town." In 1883, Sidney Gray, an aspiring Episcopal clergyman, arrived to organize a church. Two years later he had built a bluffside church and turned to implementing a dream. He envisioned a model village, preferably settled with English immigrants, where orchards would bloom and children would attend separate boys' and girls' schools. Gray sold lots in the "Village de Haro" (Eastsound) and solicited investors for the burgeoning fruit business. He served as superintendent of several local corporations including the Orcas Island Fruit Company and the Orcas Island Hop Company. When an 1899 bank failure brought his efforts to a halt, Gray was stricken. His personal funds were exhausted, and the neighbors who had invested at his recommendation were ruined. He quietly left for the Midwest where he confined his career to church affairs.

Eastsound remained the commercial heart of Orcas, and in the early days was a steamboat stop. When fruit growing declined, local hostelries catered to tourists who came to walk the beaches and hike Mount Constitution. Some local businessmen offered wagon rides to the summit. Nearby a lime quarry opened. Its workers, and those from rock quarries on outlying islands, spent their paychecks in Eastsound. Still, the town never experienced the rowdy, saloon-happy youth that characterized Friday Harbor.

Visit **ENGLISH CAMP** (San Juan Island), a unit of San Juan Island National Historic Park, to see museum exhibits, a miniature formal

Winding channels almost led Britain and America to war during the mid-1800s. At issue was which channel constituted the international boundary through the San Juan Islands.

The British Union Jack flew over a Royal Marines post on San Juan Island until 1872.

garden, barracks, and a shoreside blockhouse overlooking Garrison Bay. (Follow Beverton Valley Road west from Friday Harbor approximately 7 miles.) A forested trail leads around the north shore of the bay; watch for wild calypso orchids and fawn lilies in spring. Across the highway from the old military camp, a steep trail leads to a small hillside cemetery, the resting place of seven Royal Marines who died during the 13-year British occupation here. Not one died in battle; instead, the tombstones speak poignantly of drownings and other accidents. From the summit of Young Hill (above the cemetery) nearby islands dot the foreground and distant mountains and waterways stretch to the horizon in successively paler shades of blue on clear days, of gray on cloudy days.

An 1846 agreement extended the boundary between the United States and Canada along the 49th parallel to the west coast of the mainland and from there to the "middle of the channel, which separates the continent from Vancouver's Island." That phrase triggered the "Pig War." England claimed Rosario Strait was the intended channel, thus putting the San Juan Islands in British territory. The United States claimed it was Haro Strait, which put the islands under American jurisdiction. At the time, settlers were few, and the specific line made little difference. But after 1858, disappointed Fraser River gold miners, mostly Americans, drifted back to the beautiful islands they had passed through en route north. That growing white population—and a hungry pig—brought the issue to a head.

In 1855 the United States attempted to collect import duties from the Hudson's Bay Company's sheep farm on San Juan. When the company refused to pay, the county sheriff seized several purebred rams and sold them at an auction. James Douglas, governor of Vancouver Island, vigorously protested this depredation to Governor Isaac Stevens of Washington Territory, but received no satisfactory response.

Four years later a Hudson's Bay Company pig rooted in an American potato patch. The farmer shot the pig and refused to pay the demanded (excessive) compensation. British authorities threatened arrest; American settlers petitioned the U.S. Army for protection; and General William S. Harney ordered Captain George E. Pickett from Fort Bellingham to build and occupy a fort on the island. On July 27, 1859, Pickett landed with 66 troops and established Camp Pickett, now called American Camp. His mandate was to protect American settlers in their "present exposed and defenseless position" against the Hudson's Bay Company. England promptly sent warships. Pickett advised his commander that they constituted "a force so much superior to mine that it will be merely a mouthful for them."

Policy makers in Washington, D.C.—newly apprised of the situation—were appalled to find the country poised on the edge of war because of bungling local officials and a rash general. They rebuked Harney, transferred him to another post, and sought ways to defuse the situation without losing territory or face. The outcome was a joint military occupation of the island. In March 1860 Royal Marines landed at Garrison Bay and built a blockhouse, barracks, storerooms, and officers' quarters. U.S. Army troops remained at American Camp. A road joined the two camps, and the soldiers visited back and forth, each side hosting the other for holiday feasts. San Juan's equivocal status attracted outlaws from both countries who hoped to avoid police officers. Worse yet were disputed land claims, with civil and military authorities wrangling over control.

Finally Kaiser Wilhelm I of Germany acted as arbitrator and, after a year of examining old maps, treaties, ships' logs, and correspondence, issued the following proclamation:

We, William, by the grace of God, German Emperor . . . find . . . the claim of the Government of the United States . . . is most in accordance with the true interpretation of the Treaty.

The year was 1872. Both military camps quietly disbanded. And San Juan grew into a pastoral backwater despite warnings in the Victoria press that American control might threaten the safety of shipping bound for the Fraser River.

After 1872 the William Crook family homesteaded the site of English Camp. They lived in the army buildings and farmed the parade ground. In 1903 James Crook, the eldest son, built a house on the rise above the camp and there lived his long bachelor life. He was an inventor and a talented mechanic. When he wanted a wool suit, he built an immense wool carding machine, spinner, and loom to produce cloth from his own sheep's wool. The machines are now in the possession of the county historical society. His house is part of the national park property.

(Also see AMERICAN CAMP, p. 243.)

The main street of **FRIDAY HARBOR** (San Juan Island) slopes to the marina and ferry landing. A pergola decorates the shoreside intersection, and a waterfront park facilitates boat watching. Businesses cater to anglers, boaters, bicyclists, and browsers, and county government and commerce flourish. Many buildings look as they did a century ago.

The Whale Museum (First Street, 3 blocks north of the ferry dock) educates and entertains with whale lore. (Also see LIME KILN PARK, p. 248.) The internationally famous Friday Harbor Laboratories (north shore of the bay) house the University of Washington's marine biology research center. Tours are given in summer.

In 1872, at the close of joint American and British military occupation, county commissioners decided that rambunctious San Juan Town at the south end of the island was inappropriate for a seat of government. (See GRIFFIN BAY, this page.) They dispossessed Joe Friday (a Hawaiian sheep herder who had worked for the Hudson's Bay Company) and staked 160 acres overlooking a deep bay to be developed as the county seat. No merchants hastened to build at Friday Harbor, however, and the auditor's office stood forlornly alone halfway up the hill. The commissioners arranged for a post office, but the island's steamer rarely had mail to deliver there. Ten years after the town's premature "founding," a storekeeper finally opened shop, then another storekeeper came. The two added small saloons in back rooms and a wharf for landing freight; Friday Harbor was in business. Today it is the county's largest town. Official business is planned with the ferry schedule in mind.

Settlement at **GRIFFIN BAY** (San Juan Island) began with San Juan Town, a rowdy camp of international scofflaws, attracted by the presence of troops at American Camp. The major emporium was Israel Katz' store-saloon, an island branch of a Port Townsend business. It amounted to the social center of San Juan Island even after county officials made Friday Harbor the seat of government. Eventually, Katz moved his business to the new town. San Juan Town disappeared in an out-of-control brush fire in 1890.

West of Griffin Bay is **Eagle Cove,** where the island's first white settlers came ashore. They were Hudson's Bay Company employees sent from Victoria in 1850 to operate a seasonal salmon saltery. The fabulous salmon grounds just offshore supplied more fish than the men could process. Three years later the company launched a permanent enterprise that they hoped would help cement England's claim to San Juan Island. The *Beaver,* the first steamboat in the Northwest, landed Charles Griffin, his Hawaiian assistants, and 1,300 sheep at Cattle Point. Griffin built Bellevue Farm, which consisted of six log cabins.

(Also see ENGLISH CAMP, p. 245.)

LIME KILN PARK (San Juan Island) is unique: located midway along the west shore of the island, it is dedicated to whale watching. (To visit it from Friday Harbor, follow San Juan Valley road west. Turn south on Wold Road, then west again on Bailer Hill Road, which becomes Westside Road. The park is approximately 9 miles from town).

In 1983 the area became a research station equipped with underwater microphones to record whale songs. The next year it was dedicated as a park. Researchers have visually identified each individual in the three local pods of black-and-white orcas. Other pods move through the area at different seasons. Each has its own dialect, a vocalization pattern distinctive

to its group. Whale seekers often see the 25-foot mammals here, sometimes in the kelp as close as 20 feet offshore. Also nearby, but rarely seen, are shy, white-flippered minke whales.

LOPEZ ISLAND has gentle slopes, which attracted early farmers and today draw touring bicyclists. Lopez retained its agricultural focus even after the other islands became tourist meccas in the early twentieth century. Settlements are at Fisherman Bay on the west side, Richardson on the south, and a scattered commercial district in the southwest part of the island. At Lopez Center, an 1881 church stands amid tilting pioneer tombstones. At Lopez Village, a Congregational church built in 1904 features a distinctive, four-turreted tower. Nearby are the Lopez Historical Museum and a former red schoolhouse that now houses the library.

In 1852 an American logger defied the Hudson's Bay Company's claim and cut timber on Lopez Island for the San Francisco market. The company demanded he buy a license, the last one they succeeded in insisting upon, for substantial numbers of American squatters soon arrived, married native women, and settled down. In the 1870s a storekeeper began bartering with his neighbors for deerskins,

The 1904 church at Lopez Village still overlooks rolling farmland. The island is flatter than the other main islands, and this has helped it to keep an agricultural base.

garden truck, and wool. These he hauled by sloop to Victoria where he converted them to coffee, sugar, tobacco, and nails. After 1889, farmers shipped their grain, fruit, and wool from Richardson, the island's most active port. (See RICHARDSON, p. 250.)

In 1911 Thomas Gourley led a band of 150 fundamentalist Christians to Lopez. They came from Ballard (now part of Seattle) and settled into poverty and religious fervor on Lopez' southeast shore. The colonists built wood-framed tent structures for their homes, and a storehouse on stilts over the bay where a drawbridge kept out rats. They worked to maintain the colony and hired out to neighbors, accepting payment in grains, vegetables, and lumber. Members punctuated their workdays with Bible reading and prayer, and gathered twice on Sunday to hear Gourley's dramatic sermons. Colonists espoused pacifism, which stimulated their neighbors' wrath during World War I; Gourley even was tried under the Espionage Act, but the case was dismissed. In 1920, after years of economic struggle and increasing dissension, Gourley departed. A few elders kept the colony flame alive, but without a charismatic leader the members soon drifted apart.

MORAN STATE PARK. (See ROSARIO, p. 250.)

MOUNT CONSTITUTION (Orcas Island), a 2,409-foot peak, rises from the center of Orcas Island's east lobe. A road winds past two lakes to a summit observation tower built by the Civilian Conservation Corps in 1935. From here, views of the islands and the mainland unfold like a three-dimensional map with a hundred shades of green and blue. Lieutenant Charles Wilkes, head of the 1841 United States Exploring Expedition, named Mount Consti-tution for the famous ship, the *Constitution,* known as "Old Ironsides."

ORCAS ISLAND lies like a pair of drooping saddlebags, its two lobes separated by the deep bay of East Sound. Turtleback Mountain and Mount Constitution are among the highest of its many hills. Crow Valley's rich farmland stretches north–south in the west lobe. The largest community, Eastsound, occupies the narrow neck of land at the juncture of the saddlebags, while Orcas (town) at the southern tip of the west lobe is the ferry landing. The island's convoluted shape offers more coastline than that of any other island in the San Juans—and therefore more parcels of valuable water-front property. Small communites—Doe Bay, Olga, West Sound, and Deer Harbor—dot the perimeter, a legacy from days when roads were abominable and rowboats were routine conveyances.

In the 1860s, Paul Hubbs, who had been a United States customs inspector for San Juan Island during the "Pig War," opened a store near today's ferry landing. There he kept the island's only grindstone. This contribution to the early society lingers in the name Grindstone Harbor. By the 1870s Orcas' population totaled approximately 40, mostly white men married to native women. Eastsound served as the community's center. According to the lively *James Francis Tulloch Diary, 1875–1910,* among the island's early settlers was Enoch May of North Beach. He ran a swindle soliciting donations in the name of fictional missionary Lucy Bean, and he also directly hoodwinked the Postal Department by persuading at least 40 Port Townsend cronies to sign a petition claiming they lived on Waldron Island and needed mail service. May won the lucrative contract in 1878 and hired a man to row the mail daily to the island's actual dozen or so residents. The name Mail Bay on Waldron commemorates that service.

In the late 1880s Orcas boomed with enthusiasm for orchards. Farmers planted apples and prunes and prepared hopyards in the rich Crow Valley. Seven steamers a day called at island ports to load produce for Seattle markets. Profit margins were slim, but growers succeeded. So long as all Puget Sound commun-ities were served by steamboats, their farms could compete with those on the mainland. After the completion of railroads, however, they began to falter and, in the early 1900s, aggressive marketing by the newly irrigated Yakima and Wenatchee districts dealt them a death blow economically. Farmers abandoned their orchards or ripped them out, although even today some gnarled trees—untended—continue to produce fruit.

Orcas next bloomed as a resort destination. Vacationers arrived by steamer to camp out or to stay at one of the lodges that offered meals of salmon and clams bolstered with home-grown vegetables, berries, and apples. In the 1920s the automobile revolution reached the islands. Car ferries replaced passenger steamers, and ferry docks were built on Orcas and San Juan islands. The first ferry routes were similar to the present ones: from Anacortes via island stops to Sidney, on Vancouver Island.

The hamlet of **ORCAS** (Orcas Island) centers on the ferry-landing hotel built by W. E. Sutherland in 1904. By then tourists had begun to supplant produce and freight on the steamboats, which connected the islands to each other and to the mainland. The hotel now offers both meal service and lodging.

RICHARDSON (Lopez Island) today consists of a welcoming store with well-worn floorboards that yield to customers' footsteps, and a gas dock that serves pleasure boaters and fishermen.

George Richardson homesteaded here in 1874, and his name dominated 15 years later when a new owner built a wharf and store. By 1900, a cannery employing 400 workers processed over a million fish per year, making Richardson the busiest port in the islands. After 1914, salmon runs declined, but Richardson continued to serve Lopez farmers. The present store was built in 1918.

At **ROCHE HARBOR** (San Juan Island) buildings from a late 1800s lime operation ring a yacht-crowded marina. The buildings include a hotel, a restaurant (once the home of the Roche Harbor Lime Works' owner), a private Catholic chapel (open to visitors), and a store. Notice company workers' cottages (now converted to guest accommodations), and search out the broken kilns across from and beyond the present store. From the kilns an old road leads up the hill to a gaping limestone quarry and loops back past additional (abandoned) company houses. The colorful garden in front of the hotel is a delight to stroll; walkways are made of firebricks from dismantled kilns (notice the manufacturers' trademarks).

A vein of nearly pure limestone stretching across the midsection of Orcas and the tip of San Juan Island gave rise to the Roche Harbor Lime Company. Tradition holds that British soldiers burned limestone here to make mortar for use in building English Camp, and that they later manufactured lime for export by the Hudson's Bay Company. Records show that the Scurr brothers arrived in 1881, built two kilns, and shipped lime from a crude wharf. In 1886 Tacoma attorney Robert McMillin bought their operation, built kilns into the bluff, and soon had production up to 1,500 barrels per day. He employed hundreds of workers and stimulated the economy of all the islands by buying cordwood to supply the kiln fires. Stacks of undelivered wood still wait on remote beaches, and slopes—denuded to fuel the kilns—eroded so severely that harbors such as Garrison Bay (English Camp) silted in.

Lime works employees lived in company-owned cottages and received wages in scrip valid only at the company store. A steam locomotive, the only one in the county, hauled lime from the quarry to the kilns, which consumed 10 cords of wood each per shift. At a nearby "staveless barrel" factory—second of its kind in the United States—spinning knives reamed cedar logs into barrel halves. Workers packed chunks of baked or "calcined" lime into these barrels and loaded them onto company ships bound for San Francisco and Portland.

McMillin, an ardent Freemason, designed and built a family mausoleum east of the lime plant. Filled with symbolism, the shrine consists of a circle of pillars—one deliberately broken—surrounding a limestone table and chairs. The chairs hold the ashes of family members, and are inscribed with their names. McMillin planned a dome to top the pillars but, after his death, heirs decided to leave the mausoleum unfinished. A short trail leads through the forest from today's hotel complex to the shrine.

McMillin's son succeeded him at the helm of the company, but the Great Depression of the 1930s and the plant's aging machinery kept profits low. In 1956 Reuben Tarte bought Roche Harbor and converted it into a resort. It was two years before the limestone dust washed off the trees around the bay.

Today **ROSARIO** (Orcas Island) is a resort

Roche Harbor originally flourished as a lime production center. Buildings remaining from that era—including the owner's home, shown here—have now become a beautifully sited resort.

centered on a three-story white mansion with broad verandas. Robert Moran built the home in 1906 after making a fortune in shipbuilding. He was a Seattle politician who served as mayor at the time of the city's disastrous 1889 fire, and he is credited with the quick recovery from that devastation. In the 1890s he and his brothers organized Moran Brothers Company, which built riverboats for the Yukon gold rush. They expanded the company and in 1904 completed the 15,000-ton battleship *Nebraska,* the first naval ship launched from Puget Sound.

At the age of 49, exhausted from overwork, Robert Moran retired from the company and embarked—with equal energy—on his Orcas Island projects. He bought 5,000 acres and located his home at the site of a former lumbermill and barrel-manufacturing plant. He commissioned plans from an architect, but threw them out and designed the house and grounds himself, including a lagoon for canoes and a network of trails, roads, and bridges lacing the entire estate. In 1921 Moran presented 2,600 acres as the state park that today bears his name. The Moran mansion usually is open as a part of the resort operation, but usage varies; ask about the current status.

SAN JUAN ISLAND is second to Orcas in size but has long dominated commerce and government business throughout the archipelago. Particularly pleasant drives include the Westside Road along the coast south of Lime Kiln Park and the drive from Friday Harbor to American Camp. (Roads throughout the islands are narrow, however, and in summer are used by cyclists as well as cars; be cautious.)

Prime remnants from the historic past are the twin focal points of a narrowly averted war: American Camp (south end of the island; p. 243) and English Camp (northwest shore; p. 245). Several farms remain on San Juan, and descendants of pioneer settlers and Native Americans still live here; but the island has also drawn "outsiders" escaping city frenzy, and condominiums and beautifully sited homes have proliferated— some say to the limit of the island's water supply.

Because of their remote location peripheral to two nations and their endless secluded coves and passages, the San Juans' past includes a lengthy chapter as haven for smugglers. Indeed, smuggling amounted to the first industry here, beginning as early as the 1860s with fast sloops carrying contraband British wool and rum. During the next two decades so much wool came from the islands that textbooks reported impossibly extravagant yields for their sheep.

Smugglers added human cargo—Chinese

laborers hoping for work on American railroads—after passage of the Chinese Exclusion Act of 1882 and completion of the Canadian Pacific Railway in 1885 (which abruptly ended hundreds of jobs). Folklore persists that smugglers bound "Chinamen" in burlap sacks, ready to heave them overboard if immigration authorities gave chase. No documentation of this exists although at least one group of Chinese men was put ashore on an uninhabited rock; when finally rescued, by chance, they were weak from having subsisted on nothing but clams.

One noted smuggler specialized in opium and Chinese wine. The opium, legal in the United States but highly taxed, boosted his profits enviably. Liquor was the more usual contraband, with rum runners doing a lucrative business throughout the years of national Prohibition, 1919 to 1933. Perhaps the most famous of these was Ray Olmstead, a 1920s Seattle police captain, known as "the good bootlegger" because he never watered his booze. His operation, according to legend, included coded bulletins broadcast nightly to henchmen during the children's bedtime story of a Seattle radio station. Olmstead relied on knowledgeable locals to smuggle his liquor, evading both revenue boats and hijackers. A high volume—200 cases daily—allowed him to undercut competitors, yet clear as much as $200,000 a year. Finally in 1925, with evidence gained through controversial wiretaps, a judge sentenced Olmstead to four years at McNeil Island Penitentiary for conspiring to violate the federal prohibition act.

SHAW ISLAND lies in the center of the larger islands, a small enclave of private homes and farms blessed (or cursed) with a ferry dock. The island's history parallels that of its larger neighbors except that development came about a decade later. In the early 1880s only 12 men lived on Shaw, and only two of those had wives. They formed an unruly group, which included wool-smuggler Alfred Burke. His slender, dark-colored rowboat often cruised to the Canadian Gulf Islands, and returned laden with contra-band fleeces. Prices were so cheap in Canada that American ranchers gladly bought from Burke and incorporated that wool into their own stock for a tidy profit. Shaw is still a major sheep island, and hand spinning and weaving has become a "trademark" craft.

The island's combination library/historical museum includes an aged reef-net boat, which represents a method of fishing unique to the San Juans and adjacent waters. For centuries Lummi women spun willow and nettle fibers into cordage for nets, and men heeded the ritual and expertise of salmon chiefs to make enormous catches of fish bound for the Fraser River to spawn. The chief, wearing a broad-brimmed hat to shade his eyes from the water's glare, directed the operation. As the first fish arrived, he greeted them with great ceremony and honorific titles, then directed the other men in the canoes to raise the net. White fisherman adapted the practice by building towers on flat-bottomed boats from which spotters watch for the fish, a technique still in use.

By the 1890s the county-wide Farmers Cooperative Society held its meetings on Shaw because of the island's centrality. Farmers gathered to dance, discuss their mutual problems, and argue politics.

WEST SOUND (Orcas Island) hosts an idyllic community of houses whose gardens reach to the shore. A private dock stretches into the bay, and sailboats bob at their moorings. But place names tell a disquieting story. Massacre Bay and Skull Island, about half a mile west of the dock, commemorate the arrival at a Lummi camp of a Haida raiding party from British Columbia. More than a hundred native people died in the ensuing battle.

The Lummi both lived on the islands and, as one tribal elder put it, "shopped" here. The shorelines, abounding with shellfish and edible seaweeds, and the waters, rich in salmon and bottom fish, amounted to their "grocery store." In the mid nineteenth century, however, frequent attacks by natives from the north and devastating white diseases forced the Lummi to abandon their island villages in favor of the mainland.

Everett Area

Everett faces Puget Sound at the mouth of the Snohomish River—a site that favored early industrial development. Nineteenth-century lumber barons' mansions still overlook a working waterfront, and public buildings proudly assert the city's eminence. To the southeast, the old town of Snohomish has converted commercial buildings to antique shops, and residential neighborhoods retain handsome homes from the 1880s. Farther east, former gold mining and sawmilling towns dot roads leading to the mountains, and the Stevens Pass highway offers views of magnificently towering crags.

Historical museums are at Everett, Granite Falls, and Snohomish (a refurbished 1878 house). Snohomish also offers a historic homes tour in late September. Monroe hosts an October draft horse demonstration and festival.

EVERETT, self-proclaimed "city of smokestacks," manages to retain buildings and waterfront views representative of its past. To glimpse them, follow State Route 529 through the city and across Snohomish River sloughs as an alternative to I-5 between Exits 192 and 198—a route that adds no extra mileage. For a leisurely look, search out mansions, parks, and the county museum (2915 Hewitt).

The city was conceived in the early 1890s as a deepwater port, a prospect promising enough to attract first John D. Rockefeller, then other investors lured by his name. Optimism played on greed and, although various industries began, logic did not always prevail. One brochure boasted:

The expenditure of a million dollars in the building of one of the most complete smelters in the west is evidence that rich mines are located close at hand.

The frenzy of speculation and construction led Great Northern magnate James J. Hill to dangle the prospect of Everett-as-railroad-terminus before the bedazzled investors, although he ultimately decided to lay his rails past Everett to Seattle. That disappointment combined with the Panic of 1893 collapsed newly established lumber markets and several associated industries. Investors, including Rockefeller, withdrew support. Wages—when jobs could be found—dropped 60 percent, and laborers moved to other towns. Saloons closed for lack of patronage, and schools closed owing to a lack of tax revenue. Everett moldered.

In 1899 Hill took advantage of Rockefeller's financial retreat and told his Everett Improvement Company to start buying up land. To turn potential into profit by stimulating rail shipment, he had the improvement company

Tugs towed Everett's venerable Weyerhaeuser headquarters building downriver and around the point to a new location in 1984. It now houses the Chamber of Commerce.

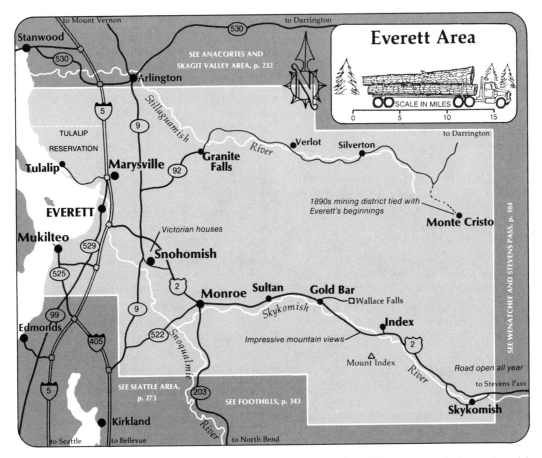

Map of Everett Area showing cities including Stanwood, Arlington, Marysville, Everett, Mukilteo, Snohomish, Monroe, Sultan, Gold Bar, Index, Monte Cristo, Skykomish, and others, with highways and rivers.

give sawmill sites to some of his Midwest friends, and he himself arranged for Frederick Weyerhaeuser, a St. Paul neighbor and associate, to buy 900,000 acres of Northern Pacific land at $6 per acre. Weyerhaeuser promptly blessed the Everett waterfront with a sawmill that within 10 years became the world's largest. Fourteen other lumber and shingle mills soon opened in the vicinity—and the city's rebirth advanced from vision to fact. Great Lakes forests had been cut; investors sought to nourish their capital in new regions.

Among those who responded was David Clough, lumberman and former governor of Minnesota. Moving to Everett, he marshalled friends, nephews, cousins, and others, including son-in-law Roland Hartley, who later served as Washington's governor. The course of development was far from smooth. As the 1900s began, longshoremen's strikes periodically rippled along the entire Pacific Coast and closed ports, including Everett. A specific crisis came in May 1916 when Everett shingle mill workers struck

for restoration of the wage scale formerly paid them but cut during a downturn. Clough, for one, had promised these wages but said that profits had not yet returned well enough. With the workers on strike, mill owners hired scabs, who attacked union pickets while police simply stood by.

The outcome was months of street-corner crusades and violence. Citizens deputized by the sheriff clashed with members of the Industrial Workers of the World (Wobblies) who came from Seattle in support of the strike demands—and also to further their own program of socialist reform. Everett citizens, appalled at the excesses of the sheriff's private army, scheduled a mass meeting on November 5. About 400 Seattle Wobblies hired a steamboat to travel to the rally. The sheriff, backed by a horde of about 500 deputies, greeted the incoming boat with an order not to land. The Wobblies answered "The hell we won't," and a shot rang out, nobody knows from which side. A gun battle left at least seven men dead, an unknown number drowned, and 51 wounded. Five months later a jury found the Wobblies innocent. The sheriff and his deputies never were charged. (Also see WASHINGTON WOBBLIES sidebar, this page; and under CENTRALIA, on p. 387.)

Owner-worker tension remained intolerably high in Everett, with the city council voting to buy 500 rifles, and deputies continuing to man the bluffs overlooking the mills. In December the Clough mill decided that it could afford a token wage increase and, although the union objected to the paltry amount, strikers without pay for months were worried about the coming winter and returned to work. The industrialists had won. Everett's smokestacks again puffed. The following year, when the federal government took steps to defuse Wobbly influence by forming the Loyal Legion of Loggers and Lumbermen, workers swore to

"give their best efforts" and owners adopted the eight-hour work day. (See SPRUCE ARMY sidebar, p. 492.)

Everett has remained an industrial city. Its base has evolved from a lumber/shingle economy into a pulp mill economy, now augmented by an aerospace installation and a navy base.

Points of interest, keyed to the Everett map:
1 The Georgian Revival **William C. Butler House** (1703 Grand; built in 1910) is representative of stately mansions in the Grand Avenue Historic District along the bluffs above the bay and river. A simple but enormous home, it belonged to a banker who invested in all of Everett's industries: logging, milling, and mining. Later it became the home of U.S. Senator Henry M. Jackson.

WASHINGTON WOBBLIES

Washington figured prominently in the labor movement of the early 1900s, as America shifted from an agrarian to a largely industrial economy. During this period, the Industrial Workers of the World—commonly called the IWW or "Wobblies"—sought to organize unskilled workers forced to endure long hours, low pay, and appalling work conditions.

The union was organized in 1905 in Chicago. Its goal was to unite the workers of individual industries—such as logging, mining, harvesting, and construction—and combine those brotherhoods into One Big Union. At that point the Wobblies expected to reshape society. They opposed capitalism. The preamble to their statement of purpose began: "The working class and the employing class have nothing in common."

In 1907 the IWW called a sawmill strike in Portland, Oregon—an unprecedented tie-up of the entire Northwest timber industry. Two years later, they won a free-speech fight with the city of Spokane, an

early demonstration of the effectiveness of civil disobedience. Their tactic was for street-corner speakers near the cheap winter hotels of itinerant workers to protest the conduct of labor agents who—for a fee—sent men to nonexistent jobs or to jobs rigged for a quick firing. The city formally banned all street meetings except those of the Salvation Army. IWW speakers continued their protest. Jails filled. The city treasury was exhausted. And after five months the ordinance was rescinded. Additional confrontations erupted in Aber-deen in 1911, Raymond in 1912, Everett in 1916, and Centralia in 1919.

During the 1920s the IWW lost strength, partly owing to divided effort at both labor reform and political reform. The American Federation of Labor (AFL) and the Congress of Industrial Organizations (CIO), previously unreceptive to unskilled workers, had become more all-inclusive. And on the political front, the newly organized Communist Party began to supersede the Wobblies.

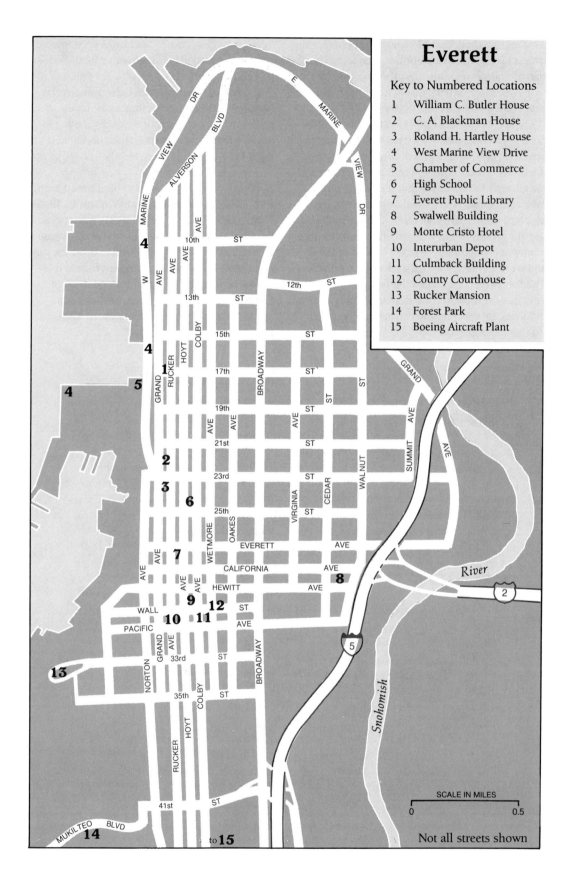

Everett

Key to Numbered Locations

1   William C. Butler House
2   C. A. Blackman House
3   Roland H. Hartley House
4   West Marine View Drive
5   Chamber of Commerce
6   High School
7   Everett Public Library
8   Swalwell Building
9   Monte Cristo Hotel
10 Interurban Depot
11 Culmback Building
12 County Courthouse
13 Rucker Mansion
14 Forest Park
15 Boeing Aircraft Plant

SCALE IN MILES

0   0.5

Not all streets shown

At the north end of Alverson Boulevard, drive into Legion Memorial Park for a view of the river mouth, Priest Point on the Tulalip Reservation, and the abortive jetty partially built of mud dredged from Port Gardiner Bay.

2   The **C. A. Blackman House** (2208 Rucker; built in 1910) belonged to the owner of Everett's first shingle mill, indeed—with his brothers—the owner of several early mills in both Everett and Snohomish. The Blackmans were known for innovative logging practices. (See under SNOHOMISH on p. 262.)

3   The **Roland H. Hartley House** (2320 Rucker; built in 1911) is part of the Grand Avenue Historic District. Hartley—industrialist and staunch Republican—served as Washington's governor during the 1920s. Graced with gleaming white columns, the house amounts to a quintessential lumber-baron mansion. It was built with profits made from supplying San Francisco with lumber following the devastating 1906 earthquake there.

4   **West Marine View Drive** follows the shore of Port Gardiner Bay, a busy port with views and amenities such as waterside restaurants pleasantly intermixed with industrial activity. Stop at the hull of the venerable ship *Equator* (west of Marine View Dr., opposite Tenth Street) to sense the varied "life" of an early-day vessel typical of the many that plied Northwest waters. This one was built near San Francisco as a two-masted schooner in 1888. She served as a trader and mail carrier in the South Pacific; was demasted and fitted with a steam engine for use by the arctic whaling fleet; served as an Alaska cannery vessel; and in 1923 ran aground near La Push (on the Olympic Peninsula) while towing a log raft. In 1956 the *Equator* was added to the Everett breakwater, then salvaged as an exhibit. Plans call for building a full-size replica of the original vessel.

5   The **Chamber of Commerce** offices (1701 W. Marine View Drive; built in 1923) are in a Tudor-style building designed to house the Weyerhaeuser offices. The architects were Bebb and Gould, a Seattle firm also responsible for several University of Washington buildings. Their intent here was to illustrate the versatility of Pacific Coast lumber for beautiful and practical construction. The building first stood at a waterfront mill, which served new markets opened up with the completion of the Panama Canal. In l984 the company gave the building to the city. Moved, it now houses the Chamber of Commerce. Eye-catching historic photographs line the interior walls; they are worth seeing (week days, during office hours).

6   Everett's **High School** (2416 Colby; built in 1910) stands as a beaux arts testimony to faith in public education as a means of bettering society. Elaborate corbeling and terra-cotta details decorate its facade—a marked contrast with the stark character of later additions.

7   The **Everett Public Library** (2702 Hoyt; built in 1934) is an Art Deco structure with curving facade and wraparound windows. Construction was financed by a private bequest and supplemented by state and federal relief programs during the Great Depression. Murals and metal sculptures adorn the interior.

8   The handsome **Swalwell Building** (2901 Hewitt; built in 1892) served as a bank during Everett's first boom; the building's Midwest commercial style implied stability and permanence. William Swalwell, one of Everett's earliest investors, built a major dock as well as this bank. The entire block is now listed in the National Register of Historical Places.

9   The **Monte Cristo Hotel** (1507 Wall; opened in 1925) resulted from an intensive public subscription campaign. The community wanted a first-class hostelry; automobile travel was in its infancy, and tourism had freed itself from the dictates of train schedules. Everett felt ready to play host—and to develop a new industry. Long closed, the Monte Cristo has reopened with apartments, offices, a restaurant, and a restored lobby used for special occasions.

10   Rail buffs will enjoy the **Interurban Depot** (3032 Colby; built in 1910), a good example of a historic building preserved by conversion to a new use—in this case office space. The dispatcher's cubicle remains on the north side of the second story. Everett's interurban trains connected with Seattle and Bellingham,

11   The **Culmback Building** (3015 Colby; built in 1924) is representative of construction during an Everett boom stimulated in 1925 when a severe earthquake hit Japan. The subsequent necessity of rebuilding Tokyo set off a business bonanza for Pacific Coast lumbermen.

12 The **County Courthouse** (Wetmore and Wall; built in 1898, rebuilt in 1910) catches the eye because of its California Mission architecture, a style briefly popular in the Northwest. Following a disastrous fire, this building rose from the ruins of a Romanesque courthouse built soon after Everett became county seat in 1897. Nearby are the city hall (3002 Wetmore; built in 1930) and the colonnaded Post Office and Customs House (3006 Colby; completed in 1917).

13 The **Rucker Mansion** (412 Laurel Drive; built in 1904) has a 180-degree view of the Everett harbor with Whidbey Island in the background. A local contractor built it, working from an architectural pattern book. He achieved a mixture of Italianate Villa, Queen Anne, and Georgian Revival styles. Handsome paneling and woodwork reflect Everett's sawmill-city reputation.

The house was a wedding gift for the bride of Bethel Rucker. He had come from Ohio with his mother and brother Wyatt, representative of scores of capitalists and entrepreneurs drawn to Washington following the arrival of the railroad. With business associate William Swalwell, the Ruckers bought most of the land now occupied by Everett. Their plan was to build a small town but, after meeting with Rockefeller's representatives, they enlarged their dream. Before relinquishing land to them, they extracted promises for construction of a sawmill, a railroad, a barge-building company, and a dry dock. The outcome launched a period of intense speculation.

14 At the southern edge of the city, **Forest Park** (accessible from 41st and Mukilteo) embraces land along the bluff and also a stretch of beach. The land was considered remote when William Swalwell donated it to the city about 1900, and landscaping waited until the 1930s.

Plantings, rubble walls, ponds, a zoo, and playfields are all typical of the era and of a Works Progress Administration style. Notice especially the huge Floral Hall, a peeled-log and shingle building listed in the National Register of Historic Places. The local gladiola society lobbied earnestly for this building; they wanted a place for annual displays and community stage presentations. A grand structure with classic rustic architecture, it still serves as a community center, now used for events from square dancing to arts festivals.

15 The **Boeing Aircraft Plant** (State Route 526 southwest of Everett) is said to be the world's largest cubic space sheltered beneath a single roof—a claim that seems believable to anyone taking the public tour and watching the assembly of 747s and other huge aircraft.

GOLD BAR, now a well-kempt town, was in 1899 a rough camp named by hopeful miners. Later it became a logging center and railroad construction camp. Anti-Chinese violence was barely avoided during the railroad era by the quick action of a construction engineer: he shipped the terrified workers out in "coffins," hastily built—with ample gaps to assure an air supply.

For a pleasant 2-mile hike, turn north at First Street and follow signs to 250-foot Wallace Falls, one of the highest in the North Cascades. Continue beyond the falls for an overview of the Skykomish Valley.

Northeast of Marysville, **GRANITE FALLS** retains early wooden buildings and brick commercial blocks with dates from 1912 to 1920 above the doors. A pleasant house with a comfortable porch has been turned into a history museum (Wabash and Union); others of similar vintage fill out the neighborhood.

The town became a railroad village along the Everett and Monte Cristo Railway, which carried lead/silver ore from the Monte Cristo mines to the smelter at Everett. Just upstream from Granite Falls, the railroad entered a 5-mile canyon through which the normally placid Stillaguamish sporadically raged. An eyewitness described the scene after an 1897 flood:

In one place a heavy steel rail is coiled like a spiral spring and stands straight up in the air. . . . Still another freak of the flood was the winding of a steel rail around a big spruce tree like a huge anaconda.

At that time Granite Falls had only a platform along the rails for the loading and unloading of freight; civic pride demanded a depot. One hundred fifty citizens signed a petition, which they presented to Everett city officials, offering to vote in favor of Everett as county seat provided they could have a depot. Everett won the election, and Granite Falls won a depot and telegraph office.

INDEX is only 500 feet above sea level, yet feels like an alpine village. It lies barely off the Stevens Pass highway, tucked beneath massive mountain walls. A small park displays a huge saw blade used for quarrying Index granite, including that used for the Capitol steps in Olympia. The Red Men's Wigwam, a 1903 fraternal lodge building, serves as a site for community social functions. The Bush House, a three-story inn built in 1898, still receives guests.

Persis and Amos Gunn homesteaded here in 1888 and built a small hotel to serve Monte Cristo miners and Great Northern railroad workers. A sawmill sprang up to serve local needs for lumber and turn out railway ties and bridge and mine timbers. When the Great Northern built an 8-mile tunnel through the Cascades in the 1920s, Index served as its western supply center. In recent years recreation has provided an economic base for the town.

At MARYSVILLE the freeway and modern shopping centers overshadow scattered remnants of the past still lingering along quiet streets. The town began in 1877 when J. P. Comeford bought 120 acres and opened a trading post to serve the neighboring Tulalip Reservation. Other businesses clustered nearby and Comeford platted a town. A corduroy road across the swampy delta connected the community to wharves and warehouses on Ebey Slough, one of the sluggish waterways at the mouth of the Snohomish River. Farmers drained and diked the river flats to create land for strawberries and dairy farms. Sawmills converted the forest into lumber and shingles. Today the town is a residential area on the edge of Everett.

Modern-day MONROE is hemmed by highways; subsistence farming and logging marked its early economic development. An autumn draft-horse "Extravaganza" now features a variety of contests and demonstrations (usually in early October).

Settlement began in 1858 at the junction of the Skykomish and Snohomish rivers. Forty

years later a nearby mill was producing 75,000 board feet of lumber and 125,000 shingles per day, all hauled by horse-drawn tramcars for shipment from Monroe via the Great Northern Railway. The mill operated until the 1930s.

In 1907 a state prison was built at Monroe to embody the Declaration of Principles of the American Prison Association: reform, not punishment. First offenders would be separated from hardened criminals, and good behavior and mastery of a job skill would earn clemency for all. Reformers hoped to tap prisoners' latent self-respect. That was the theory. In fact, the state built a physical plant with four-tiered cellblocks, 80 cells per row, identical to an 1832 prison in Ohio. The intended education program had neither facilities nor funds, and vocational training came only through working on prison maintenance and construction. Reform policies stayed on paper.

MONTE CRISTO today attracts hikers because of its mountain setting and romantic history as a major mine (although only foundations, not buildings, remain from that era). The site can be reached via the Mountain Loop Highway from either Verlot or Darrington, a road that makes a loop drive of the Stillaguamish and Sauk River valleys (mostly forested and without clear mountain views). For the mine, park at Barlow Pass and hike up the old road; or check at Verlot with the National Forest Service concerning vehicle use of the road.

In 1889 Joseph Pearsall, an adventuresome prospector, glimpsed a rock face glittering with galena ore, a mixture of silver and lead. The ore assayed as rich, but transportation from the remote site posed a problem. To solve it, men pushed a crude wagon road from Sauk City (near present Rockport) up the Sauk River in 1890. Meanwhile, tedious hand drilling opened a few short tunnels.

The Everett Land Company, which was building Everett with Rockefeller money, invested in the mines, added a smelter to their plans for the city, and built a railroad up the Stillaguamish Valley and across Barlow Pass. Monte Cristo immediately began to grow; its main street—a steep corduroy road between rough buildings—was appropriately named Dumas. Dormitories housed men near the mines, and managers, storekeepers, railroad workers, and bartenders lived in town. Tramways on the steep slopes carried buckets of ore to a concentrating mill at the edge of town. Coal smoke filled the air, and intermittent blasts of dynamite counterpointed the screech of tramway brakes. The Sauk River ran white with tailings.

Monte Cristo offered jobs at a time when most of the Northwest was reeling from the Panic of 1893. The mines shipped ore to the smelter at Everett. Even so, investors gradually lost faith and called in their loans. When the Stillaguamish flooded in 1897 and destroyed the railroad—an almost annual occurrence—the Rockefeller interests announced that they would not rebuild. Monte Cristo was cut off from the outside world and rapidly declined.

James J. Hill, head of the Great Northern Railway, bought most of Rockefeller's Everett property, including the Everett and Monte Cristo Railway. He rebuilt the line to serve sawmills, as well as to tap remaining resources at Monte Cristo and other mines in the district. Sightseers rode open excursion cars and, at Monte Cristo, picnicked and toured a mine. Small-scale operations—and schemes—continued through the 1920s. One plan even called for drilling a tunnel through the mountain from Monte Cristo to Index (about 14 miles) to avoid recurrent railroad washouts. Among miners hope dies hard.

Silverton (along the highway about 10 miles west of Barlow Pass) still has the look of a mining town, although buildings now are private houses posted with "No Trespassing" and "No Parking" signs. A second part of the old town stands across the river, accessible by bridge but equally private.

Mines in the area produced lead and silver but, as is characteristic of North Cascades mines, veins could not be followed any great distance—a matter of geology, not of mining skill. Faults (slippages within the earth) fragment ore bodies and cause them to abruptly pinch out. Continually relocating a vein is labor-intensive and costly, but often not a deterrent for miners, who typically are optimists. Silverton mines gave rise to a sizeable town. Watch for adits (mine tunnels) visible from the highway or accessible by short walks.

Remains of the **Big Four Inn** (about 5 miles up-valley from Silverton) are worth stopping to see, especially on days when the mountains soar clearly as a 4,000-foot bulwark. Bethel and Wyatt Rucker, prominent Everett investors, built the resort in 1920. It burned in 1949.

MUKILTEO (Muk-ul-tee-'-oh) today is a suburban community with a regular flow of traffic to and from the Whidbey Island ferry. Its lighthouse (915 Second Avenue; built in 1906) marks the site of the Point Elliott Treaty: on January 22, 1855, territorial governor Isaac Stevens met here with representatives of the Lummi, Skagit, Snohomish, Snoqualmie, Suquamish, and Duwamish people (including Chief Sealth, for whom Seattle is named). The natives ceded to the United States—without understanding what the word meant—all of their land from Seattle to the Canadian border and east to the crest of the Cascades. They retained only the land of the Lummi, Swinomish, Tulalip, and Port Madison reservations.

Mukilteo grew fast enough to become the Snohomish county seat in 1861. Sixteen years later it attracted Puget Sound's first salmon cannery and, four years after that, a second cannery and a brewery. The town even solicited the transcontinental railroad terminus and composed a ditty with the refrain, "To the dogs Olympia with her tide flats may go, but the railroad will help little Mukilteo."

SILVERTON. (See under MONTE CRISTO, p. 260).

SKYKOMISH is worth crossing the river to see: it still looks much like 1915 postcards that are sold at the grocery story, and the store itself is the sort that has a rush of candy and soda pop sales each afternoon when school lets out. A three-story hotel with wide verandas, built in 1904, now caters to hikers and skiers.

Soon after the Great Northern Railway surveyed a route across Stevens Pass in 1888, loggers and prospectors entered the area and communities sprouted and grew. During construction of the Cascade Tunnel in the 1920s, Skykomish's population ballooned to 8,000 with a large sawmill and two shingle mills offering jobs for men not working at the railroad roundhouse or shops. Eastbound trains stopped

During the late 1800s Snohomish townswomen living along "Soapsuds Row" did laundry for millworkers—mostly single men living at company boardinghouses.

to exchange their steam locomotives for electric engines before beginning the climb over Stevens Pass, and westbound trains similarly stopped to exchange engines before continuing down the valley. The abandoned power station that supplied electricity for the locomotives is now used to store diesel oil.

Stop in **SNOHOMISH** to enjoy old downtown buildings (First Avenue) that house scores of antique shops filled with gleaming furniture, silver, and glass; and to look at Victorian homes (Avenues A through E) gracing the neighborhood behind this original business district. The Blackman House (118 Avenue B; built in 1878) belonged to pioneer logger Hyrcanus Blackman. It is open as a museum. The Ferguson Cottage (17 Avenue A; built in 1859) was the first house in Snohomish. "Soapsuds Row" (207-215 Avenue A) was the domain of laundresses who catered to loggers and millworkers; their simple cottages are now restored as senior housing.

E. C. Ferguson—carpenter, gold prospector, and Snohomish's founding father—took a claim here at the confluence of the Snohomish and Pilchuck rivers in 1859 when the territorial legislature allocated funds for a military road between Steilacoom and Bellingham. He reasoned that a Snohomish River ferry would be needed and that a man with a claim at the right spot could make a tidy living from military traffic while a town grew. Bringing a prefabricated house and goods to stock a store, Ferguson arrived via side-wheel steamer up the Snohomish. The flaw in his plans was that the "road" never amounted to more than a blazed trail, and the army closed Forts Steilacoom and Bellingham when the Civil War began.

By then Ferguson had his store in the wilderness and knew possibilities. He had joined Ed Cady in a scheme to develop a mining service center: the men would build a trail to the new gold strike at Similkameen River, over the Cascade Mountains from Snohomish (or Cadyville as the name then was). Cady scouted a route while Ferguson solicited funds and, in the summer of 1860, they hired a crew to rough out a trail. In August the two men set out with horses and reached the Similkameen with only the usual difficulties. But the trail, too, failed to boom their town. It was a summer-only trail to a gold strike that soon played out.

Ferguson turned his energy toward politics and successfully advocated slicing Snohomish

In an extremely early photograph, dated 1865, Father Casimer Chirouse (right) poses with Tulalip mission schoolchildren. (Notice the apparent piety—except for one boy.)

County from the existing Island County and having himself appointed its principal public servant, including superintendent of schools, though his town had no children. He built the Blue Eagle saloon and conducted business there as county commissioner and auditor, justice of the peace and probate judge, as well as postmaster. (Rather than stand behind the bar all day, Ferguson left change in the till, and his neighbors bought drinks on the honor system.)

When the federal survey of the township was completed in 1867, "Old Ferg's" Snohomish at last experienced a small boom. Large lumber companies, especially the Port Gamble firm of Pope and Talbot, hired "entrymen" to claim homesteads and then transfer titles back to the companies. In the meantime, Ferguson sold these fraudulent claimants lots in Snohomish where they could build a shack and wait out the interim near the Blue Eagle.

Snohomish was also the home of legitimate pioneering loggers. The Blackman brothers— Alanson, Elhanan, and Hyrcanus—opened their first mill in Snohomish in 1882, and later expanded to Everett. They advanced logging technology with several innovations, among them a wheeled truck that carried logs on maple rails. This device could outperform eight yoke of oxen dragging logs on a skid road. It fore-shadowed the era of railroad logging. The

Blackmans also designed and built a shingle saw and were the first in the region to adopt donkey engines to haul logs to a central pile. Blackman Lake north of Snohomish was the site of the brothers' first logging camp.

Through the years Snohomish grew as a lumber center and riverboat port, and farms in the fertile valley supplied vegetable canneries. In 1888 a railroad arrived, and *The Snohomish Eye* reported arrival of "the long expected first train" of seven flatbed work cars "loaded with iron and ties." The paper also printed the words of an eight-verse song that gloats:

New sidewalks and bridges our village will have,
And all business will go with a hum;
Quick change from a village to a city we'll have
When the Lake Shore and Eastern is done.

SULTAN strings along the highway east of Monroe for a mile or two, conspicuous in an area where several "towns" shown on maps are now little more than a name at a railroad siding. In the 1850s prospectors scouring the Cascade Mountains paused here, hoping to repeat the spectacular sort of discoveries that had started the California gold rush. The Sultan River proved tantalizing—its placers were relatively rich—but no major strikes occurred. In the 1860s and 1870s Chinese miners lived in brush huts along the river, built their own equipment—including pumps of hollowed logs with plungers of hide—and worked from dawn to dusk. White miners came and went, but the patient and meticulous Chinese continued to extract gold.

In 1884 a consortium of miners and investors planned to exploit a natural bend in the Sultan River 5 miles north of town, where the river flows through a deep canyon. Men blasted a tunnel to divert the water, then washed the gravel and clay in the exposed riverbed. Early returns elated them, but the canyon's gold never repaid the cost of the tunnel. Furthermore, the river soon clogged it with rocks and mud and went back to its old course.

Sultan's population swelled to 1,000 during the early 1890s as construction crews built the Great Northern Railway across Stevens Pass, and as loggers dotted the outskirts with saw-mills and shingle mills. Native people as well as farmers supplemented their income by cutting shingle bolts and floating them down the rivers to the mills. In the 1910s and 1920s two large companies with railroads into the hinterlands employed hundreds of loggers. Then came the 1930s Depression, and men again searched for placer gold and lined the riverbanks with cabins.

At the **TULALIP RESERVATION** (Too-lay´-lip), the massive community center/bingo hall echoes the appearance of the native longhouses that stood here for generations, and an effective display inside evokes that era. Saint Anne's Catholic Church (Tulalip Road, a mile west of the community center) dates from 1903, a replacement for an 1861 church built by Father Casimer Chirouse. A statue of the Virgin Mary that Chirouse brought from France continues to offer inspiration and solace; it was rescued from the fire that destroyed the original church.

Nearby, is a Shaker church (N. Meridian) built in 1924. Johnny Steve and his wife introduced the Shaker faith to Tulalip in 1896, although agency superintendent Charles Buchanan, who was trained as a medical doctor, strongly objected to their healing practices and opposed the founding of their church on "his" reservation. (See MUD BAY, p. 354, for a discussion of the Shaker sect.)

Tulalip's history is long. In 1792 Captain George Vancouver strode ashore here on King George III's birthday (June 2) and claimed the land for England. Sixty-one years later—the year that Washington became a territory—white settlers arrived and built a water-powered sawmill (near the present salmon hatchery). Two years after that the Point Elliott Treaty established the Tulalip Reservation for the Snohomish, Stillaguamish, Snoqualmie, and Skykomish people. *Tulalip* means "Nearly Landlocked Bay" and refers to the reservation's location; it is not a tribal designation.

After missionary priest Father Chirouse was driven from the Yakima Valley in 1855, he came to Tulalip and established a school. In 1869 the federal government formally agreed to his boarding and educating native youngsters for a fixed monthly fee. This was the first such contract school in the nation; it continued until 1896. After that, the Indian Agency operated it until 1935 as a boarding school for children from tribes as distant and diverse as the Makah and Nooksack, as well as from families on the Tulalip Reservation. Parents realized that the whites were trying to "take the Indian out" of their children. They worried about illnesses; there was no "Indian doctor" to help. Yet if they hid their children, they were subject to being jailed.

Many of today's elders remember going to boarding school and being regimented by ringing bells and bugle calls "just like you was in the military—all the little kids, right down to the smallest one" and of saying "something in Indian, and then the teacher'd come along with his ruler and hit me on the hand, 'You talk English.'" Suquamish elder Woody Loughrey of Bainbridge Island attended the Tulalip school:

Mother didn't like it very well, but she said it just had to be done, that's all there is to it. . . . Along come a boat, a big motor boat . . . anchored out here and picked us up. Like little cows, we got in and away we went. We didn't even know where Tulalip was . . .

Suquamish elder Lawrence Webster also commented:

You take any nationality there is, take them away from home, put 'em with a different group altogether, stay there for quite a number of years, he's going to forget a lot that he learned at home.

Whidbey and Camano Islands

Whidbey Island (about 40 miles long) is characterized by forests at each end and sloping prairies and farmland at its center, a scene little changed for well over a century. On clear days classic Northwest Coast views of icy mountains rising beyond blue waters provide a dramatic sense of place. On cloudy days gray sky merges with gray water, and the island becomes a realm complete within itself. Historic Coupeville preserves Victorian homes, commercial buildings, and churches; a county historical society museum portrays early settlement. Four blockhouses remain on the island from the mid-1850s. Oak Harbor celebrates its Dutch heritage every spring. The county fair is held at Langley in August. Stanwood has a museum.

Two ferry routes serve Whidbey Island, and a bridge soars above treacherous Deception Pass to link the island with the Anacortes area. Camano, a forested residential island, nestles close to the mainland, connected by bridge to Stanwood.

COUPEVILLE is ideal for walking: it boasts 48 buildings officially listed as "historic." Downtown, these range from a 1901 wharf and warehouse to the false-fronted commercial buildings lining Front Street like a child's toy town set: an 1874 meat market, an 1890 hotel, an 1892 bank, a 1916 confectionery, and so on. Be sure to also visit the county historical museum (Ninth and Alexander) and its adjacent Alexander Blockhouse.

Several Victorian houses are worth noting (and town maps usually are available for the asking at the museum and from most businesses). Each house has its own tale. In 1866 Colonel Granville Haller, a military leader turned successful merchant, built his fine home (Front and Main) around a rough-hewn cabin. The Joseph Clapp House (Front and Clapp; built in 1866) features elaborate shinglework and other decorative Queen Anne details. The two-story Dutch colonial (near the waterfront east of Gould) was built in 1854 by the town's founder, Captain Thomas Coupe, using redwood brought from California. Because of shoreline erosion, it

Whidbey and Camano Islands

SCALE IN MILES

has been moved uphill; the orchard once grew directly behind the house. Coupe managed to bring a square-rigged sailing ship through Deception Pass, the only captain known to have done so.

H. B. Lovejoy, the son of a sea captain who settled here in the 1850s, designed and built the two-story Zylstra house (Seventh and Center) for himself, then sold it in 1917. Lovejoy was a craftsman and builder who constructed many of Coupeville's handsome homes and, with his brother, built steamboats for the Puget Sound trade.

The town began in the 1850s when several sea captains who traded at Puget Sound mills and towns claimed land on the south shore of Penn

Cove. Its all-weather anchorage directly opposite the Utsalady sawmill attracted them; so did the fact that several farms already existed near the cove. Seasoned gentlemen of careful taste, the captains lived in semiretirement although some also devoted part-time attention to businesses or served in local government; a few occasionally returned to the sea. All brought a cosmopolitan touch to the region. One young wife enthused, "We have more balls in this country than at home, and always have a supper."

In 1881 Coupeville became county seat, an action that clinched its role as the island's civic, commercial, and social center. That fabric remains today, a stability enriched by the fact that many descendants of pioneer settlers still live here and maintain the old houses. Coupeville forms the heart of Ebey's Landing National Historic Preserve.

Coveland, a few miles west of Coupeville at the head of Penn Cove, actually developed earlier than Coupeville. A waterwheel turned by the outgoing tide powered a mill and, in 1852, Captain Benjamin P. Barstow opened a trading post and stocked its shelves with goods from San Francisco. The first county courthouse—an 1855, two-story building now refurbished as a house—still stands just yards from the water on Madrona Way. When the commerce of the island coalesced at Coupeville, the county offices moved there from Coveland.

Before the arrival of white settlers, Native Americans had four villages at Penn Cove. According to reports of the 1841 Wilkes Expedition, one was fortified.

San de Fuca, a small cluster of buildings near the head of Penn Cove, started as a dream city, yet all that remains is a two-room schoolhouse standing alone on a slope. It is now converted to a residence. In 1889 promoters stricken by "terminus disease" visualized San de Fuca as a great port and railroad center. Ivan Doig, in *Winter Brothers,* describes the syndrome:

How strong and delusory a frontier ailment, this notion that wherever you Xed in your town on the blankness of the west, a locomotive soon would clang up to it with iron carloads of money.

Whidbey Island was not a quiet backwater. As early as the 1830s the Hudson's Bay Company had considered it for a fur post, then decided instead on Fort Nisqually (south of Tacoma). The San de Fuca partisans' proposal called for bisecting Whidbey Island with a canal so that oceangoing ships could sail directly to San de Fuca. There, they would load and unload onto trains that would connect to the island from Anacortes via Deception Pass. Developers sold lots, built hotels, and advertised tirelessly—until reality took hold. The Panic of 1893 and its

The Coupeville area abounds with well-maintained houses such as this one at Center.

The Davis Blockhouse is one of three Whidbey Island blockhouses open to the public.

ensuing financial depression closed the books on San de Fuca.

The **CROCKETT BLOCKHOUSE** (built in 1856) stands beside the county road about 2½ miles south of Coupeville (near the intersection of Engle and Fort Casey roads). The huge barn below the blockhouse and the fields sweeping down to Keystone Spit still evoke the feeling of the land during the Crocketts' era; and they are an example of the national historical reserve protecting both view and agriculture. The farm remains private; do not trespass beyond the blockhouse, which is open to the public. Walter Crockett, who built the blockhouse, was a three-time Virginia state legislator, who came West in 1854 with a few families, including the Jacob Ebeys (father of Isaac).

In the mid-1850s Whidbey Island settlers feared attack by "Indians from the North" as well as in reaction to treaties virtually forced on the tribes of Washington Territory. (See EBEY'S LANDING, this page.) As a precaution the whites helped each other build blockhouses and palisades. Four of their eight blockhouses still remain: the Crockett Blockhouse, the Alexander Blockhouse (now moved to Coupeville), the Davis Blockhouse near Ebey's Landing (open to the public), and farther west, one of four that Jacob Ebey built off each corner of his house (not open to the public).

The Crocketts built a pair of blockhouses joined by a linear stockade. In 1938 this one remaining blockhouse was restored as a Works Progress Administration project and moved alongside the road to stop people from trampling across fields to look at it. The other Crockett Blockhouse had been sold in 1909 to Ezra Meeker for use as an entrance to his restaurant at the Alaska-Yukon-Pacific Exposition in Seattle.

EBEY'S LANDING (central Whidbey Island) remains a stony beach little changed from pioneer days. Just inland from it notice the Ferry House built in 1860 as defacto tavern, hotel, and post office. From there, disembarking passengers walked or rode up the slope and across the prairie to Coupeville. At the nearby Sunnyside Cemetery (Sherman Road, half a mile south of State Route 20) search out the Davis Blockhouse, a grim reminder of anticipated attacks. (See CROCKETT BLOCKHOUSE, this page.) From the cemetery, walk out a trail for about half a mile along the bluff—a viewpoint from which to watch for orca whales—and another half a mile down to the historic beach where Isaac Ebey first stepped ashore. The main road also leads to the beach.

White farmers who moved to Whidbey Island in the 1850s considered the land an untouched wilderness, yet Salish people had lived on it for at least a thousand years and had tailored it to fit their needs far more than is generally realized. The natives burned prairies to forestall the invasion of forest (a practice that alarmed white settlers), and they regularly harvested huge quantities of bracken roots and camas bulbs. In presettlement days, a group of Klallams even paddled over from the Olympic Peninsula and invaded Skagit territory to plant potatoes on the open land that became known as Ebey's Prairie. They ringed their potato patch with a defensive palisade.

Already experts at harvesting wild root crops such as bracken roots and camas bulbs, native people had readily welcomed the addition of potatoes brought to Washington by the Spanish in the late 1700s. (See under NEAH BAY on p. 477.) The usual native system was to plant the tubers, then return for the harvest. Such cultivation was nothing new. Villagers already had been cultivating desirable "crops" by working plant refuse into the soil as a sort of compost, and by transplanting certain valued species like camas and—in places—cattail (its stems used in making mats and baskets, its seed fluff mixed in with wool from mountain goats and dogs).

The acceptance of unfamiliar foods went only one way, however. White settlers arriving on Whidbey Island tried—as Walter Crockett expressed it—"to get the land subdued and the wilde nature out of it." They fed the nutritious and time-honored camas to their pigs and cursed and discarded bracken roots, tough enough to defy plowing. Whidbey Island Salish, displaced from their land, tried to at least collect rent from white farmers, but were met with indignation or laughter. By 1853, already undermined by smallpox, malaria, syphilis, measles, and tuberculosis, the Salish resigned themselves to the usurpation. Fences snaked across fields proclaiming exclusive white ownership.

Isaac Neff Ebey, a determined and energetic man, arrived in 1850 to file a donation land claim. He delighted in his fertile land and wrote to family and friends to join him. They accepted the advice and built an enduring web of Whidbey Island settlers related by blood and friendship. Working together, they sold oak for ship planking and Douglas fir for masts and spars. They also turned prairies into farms and planted potatoes, oats, and wheat as their first crops. When ships calling for lumber began to bring in vegetables and grain from California,

EBEY'S LANDING NATIONAL HISTORIC RESERVE

Ebey's Landing National Historic Reserve is the first of its kind in the nation, although the underlying land ethic is common in Great Britain and Japan. A unit of the national park system, the reserve is neither a land bank of nature nor a program of living history. Instead, it is a blend of the two—but without any cutoff point. It fosters an ongoing relation between people and the land.

Direction comes from a local trust board that includes private landowners, business people, county and town planning boards, county and state park systems, and the National Park Service. The goals are fourfold: to make it economically feasible for farms to stay farms rather than become housing tracts; to encourage respect for the landscape by avoiding intrusive changes, particularly along ridgelines and shorelines; to augment nineteenth-century architecture with compatible modern structures using suitable materials, colors, and scale; and to find ways for public access and enjoyment without violating private ownership and interests.

These are ambitious goals. They originated when local people who were worried about losing the rural character of the island approached the National Park Service for help. In 1978 Congress designated about 13,000 acres as a national historical reserve, which permitted using federal funds to buy key parcels of land or—equally important—to buy development rights. Land with development rights consigned to the historical reserve can still be sold but will stay rural.

A sense of countryside is to remain. A madrona-log inn built in 1907 will keep on hosting city-weary guests; land first plowed with oxen will continue to be cultivated, albeit with modern machinery; waves still will lap beaches where clams squirt and shorebirds congregate and people picnic. The clock is not to be stopped, but its ticking is to be monitored.

they switched to raising sheep. Later they tried fruit, and then returned to potatoes and other vegetables.

Rebecca Ebey, Isaac's wife, wrote faithfully in the couple's diary recording passing vessels and commenting on "indians [arriving] from Vicktoria to work their potatoes," or "cannon firing from some Port or vessel . . . a great violation of the Sabbath." She also first expressed great joy at "positive news of mother starting [West]," then inutterable grief at word of her death on the plains.

An arbitrary sample of the diary (replete with quixotic punctuation) reads for August 1852;

Sunday 8th. . . . I looked for some of Mr. Crocket's people over today but they have not come they certainly do not think of me living here alone day after day or some of them would visit me I am not able to walk so far to visit them and they are provided with wagons and horses so they can ride at any time. The water is very rough this evening. . . . I always feel lonely when Mr. Ebey is gone which makes my mind meditate upon former scenes.

Wednesday 11th. Mr. Ebey arrived this morning before breakfast; I was very much rejoiced to see him it was quite unexpected for him to return at this time as I expected Legislature would continue in Session longer. . . . I do not feel so lonely now every thing assumes a different aspect.

Tuesday 24th. The rolling of the surf against the shore is very loud this evening which sounds romantic and beautiful when there is nothing else to draw the attention.

Thursday 26. Day pleasant and clear Mr Ebey & Mr Crocket are busy plowing today all very quiet no one passing today but now and then a lonely indian.

Isaac Ebey held many public posts. As U.S. Collector of Customs, he tried to collect duty from the Hudson's Bay Company on San Juan Island before the Pig War (see under ENGLISH CAMP on p. 246). In 1855 he commanded a troop of Washington volunteer militiamen. He also served as probate judge of Island County. In short, he became a leading personage—and that brought him death.

In 1856 canoeloads of Tlingit warriors from Alaska attacked a native village near Tacoma and carried off the year's potato harvest. The steamer USS *Massachusetts* pursued the Tlingits

to Port Gamble, where the captain ordered his men to open fire, killing 27 of the raiders, wounding 21, and destroying the canoes. The dead included a chief whose loss, according to Tlingit custom, demanded the death of a high-ranking white. Consequently, in August 1857 a party intent on vengeance returned and shot Isaac Ebey at his front door. The family and houseguests escaped out a back window and fled across fields to Jacob Ebey's blockhouse. The next morning neighbors found Isaac's decapitated body lying near the porch. (The Ebeys are buried at Sunnyside Cemetery, which is on Jacob Ebey's original land claim.)

(Also see PORT GAMBLE, p. 375.)

Today **FORT CASEY,** overlooking the entrance to Puget Sound, consists of a maze of concrete bunkers and parapets—with a splendid view of the Olympic Mountains forming a blue and white wall along the western horizon. Admiralty Inlet lighthouse stands nearby, moved to this position in the 1890s to make room for the fortifications. Barracks and officers' quarters now belong to Seattle Pacific University and are used for field school classes.

Fort Casey, along with Fort Worden (near Port Townsend) and Fort Flagler (on the tip of Marrowstone Island), provided a "Triangle of Fire" to prevent entry into Puget Sound and, particularly, to protect the new Bremerton naval yard. The three forts were part of an 1880s proposal for 28 steel-plated, concrete forts to be built along the nation's coasts. Their 10-inch disappearing guns raised to be fired, then swung behind a bunker for reloading. Each gun shot 600-pound projectiles with a range of nearly nine miles.

Fort Casey was completed in 1901—about the same time that improved shipboard armament began to compete favorably with stationary guns. The advent of air warfare completed the fort's transition from vanguard to anachronism, and the big guns were scrapped and melted down. Fort Casey reopened during World War II as a training center, but after the war it was sold to Washington State Parks. Two 10-inch guns used in the Philippine Islands during World War II have been placed in the proper mounts for display.

Keystone Spit and Crockett Lake, just east of

Fort Casey, are now in public ownership except for a handful of houses. The land very nearly became a real estate tract in the 1970s; the National Park Service bought it as part of the historical reserve and turned it over to the state park system—an example of the reserve functioning as intended, with public agencies and private interests cooperating for the long-range benefit of everyone. The spit is a place to walk the beach and watch ferries come and go.

FORT EBEY was built during World War II. Today it is a state park with old-growth Douglas fir and a magnificent view—and nothing left from the fort itself except the main battery bunker and two observation bunkers. The artillery here included six-inch naval barbette guns augmented by a mysterious new device: radar.

A trail leads from Partridge Point to a log-strewn beach (which all but vanishes at high tide).

Today **FREELAND,** near the south end of Whidbey Island, is a pleasant residential area with an inviting shore, a handsome beachfront park, and faint memories of having been the site of a utopian colony. The Sanford House (548 S. Freeland Avenue) remains from that era, built in 1902 on an imposing rise with views in all directions. A glass-enclosed cupola and two porches still overlook remnants of the original five-acre tract and the water.

William and Emily Sanford and their married son DeForest came from South Dakota with 24 other colonists in 1900 to help found the Free Land Association. Such groups, rather than lone settlers, characterized much of Washington's settlement pattern. In this case the people were socialists who intended to follow broad principles of cooperation and to make land available to members for a 20 percent down payment with the balance paid through dividends from an association-owned store, steamship, and other enterprises. Association members newly arrived in Washington joined others who came from Equality, the highly structured socialist community north of Mount Vernon.

"Quite a number of discontent Equalityites are now trying Freeland," the Equality newspaper reported in June 1901. Their discontent arose after a well-respected member of the Equality community affiliated himself with a Seattle land speculation company selling acreage at Holmes Harbor. The company soon went bankrupt and so did the association. In 1920 the *Whidbey Islander,* edited by DeForest Sanford and his wife, commented that "new settlers coming in now will simply have to buy land as in other places." Even so the settlement endured, perhaps because—unlike several of the state's other communal efforts—the lives of Freeland members differed little from those of people in the surrounding area. The colony described itself as "simply a settlement of socialists co-operating on semi-capitalistic principles."

(Also see EQUALITY, p. 224.)

Wooden steps at **LANGLEY** lead to a grassy strip for picnicking and sunbathing above a rocky beach. Old buildings house new businesses, and strollers set the pace on the sidewalks. Actually, catering to weekenders and vacationers began long ago here. Ferry service across Deception Pass started in 1913 and, by the 1920s, ferries also connected Whidbey Island to Mukilteo and Port Townsend. They augmented regular steamboat service from Seattle to Coupeville and Oak Harbor. In 1922 officials suggested a state park at the south end of the island, and residents in the Langley area responded favorably. The proposed land was a tract of virgin forest "not worth much for grazing." If tourists could increase business revenue, their presence would be pure gain.

Summer homes and resorts have characterized Langley for decades, and the town also has served as a hub for outlying dairymen, poultry farmers, and berry and filbert nut growers. The Island County fair has been held here every mid-August since 1924.

OAK HARBOR faces a deeply indented bay on the northeast side of Whidbey Island. Pioneer Way, the original commercial district along the water, has kept its early one-story buildings. Many other Oak Harbor buildings were lost to the rapid growth associated with the opening of the Whidbey Naval Air Station in the 1940s.

Two early houses survived that period and are worth searching out. J. P. Byrne built the town's first wharf, store, and hotel, and in 1894 moved into a gracious new home overlooking his business ventures (3010 300th Avenue, which is also called Midway Boulevard). After Byrne's death, the mansion served as a Catholic parish house. Now it is a private home again. About a half mile south of Oak Harbor the Benjamin Loers House (junction of State Route 20 with Fort Nugent Road leading to Swantown) stands on a crest of land overlooking Saratoga Passage. Loers, a retired Dutch dairy farmer, built the elaborate, onion-domed house in 1911 complete with indoor plumbing and electricity. Supposedly its floor plan is identical to that of a house in Holland, Michigan, built by the same architect.

By the 1890s many Whidbey Islanders were leasing to Chinese tenant farmers who, with diligence and careful selection of fertile plots, raised bumper crops of potatoes and provided their landlords with steady income. Even so, Oak Harbor and Coupeville townspeople resented the Chinese. Their standard of living was low. They did not shop at local stores. And "desirable" white immigrants avoided the county because good land already was taken by the Chinese. Merchants actually attempted a boycott of landowners who rented to Chinese farmers, an unsuccessful effort but indicative of the deep resentment. Tactics such as dynamiting potato storage pits forced the existing Chinese off the land, and Chinese farmers who tried to replace them were met by armed vigilantes.

Dutch farmers, on the other hand, were welcomed; they brought operating capital and money for land improvement. Experienced and innovative agriculturalists, the Dutch were attracted to Whidbey Island by reports of five-pound potatoes and dense hay crops. They drained land and established dairy farms or grew specialty crops like bulbs and seeds. Today the local Dutch heritage is celebrated in Oak Harbor's spring Holland Happenings, an annual event that includes Klompenvolk, wooden-shoe dancers.

Whidbey Naval Air Station has greatly affected Oak Harbor. The station opened in 1942 as a "re-arming base for patrol planes operating in defense of Puget Sound." This area was chosen because its light annual rainfall assured ample clear days for flight training. In the rush of wartime expansion, the first plans called for all personnel to take their meals at the naval air station in Seattle—until somebody with a sense of geography pointed out the distance involved!

Modern **STANWOOD** is divided into east and west—a reflection of its early days when the railroad ignored the existing town and opened a depot one mile east. The bypassed community laid narrow-gauge tracks and connected itself with its upstart sister community.

For a look at West Stanwood's early character, sample streets north of today's highway. Refurbished early-day homes from cottages to modest mansions line Second Avenue, among them the **D. O. Pearson House,** a three-story Victorian (next to the historical society museum; open to the public). Pearson established a general store in 1877—the first business in the area—and christened the infant town with his wife's maiden name. Stanwood served loggers from Camano Island and the Stillaguamish Valley. As farming replaced logging, the community became a food processing and packing center.

UTSALADY, at the northern tip of Camano Island, was the site of an early sawmill—and today's residents working in their gardens still uncover pieces of blue and white crockery from the mill's cookhouse. Thomas Cranney and partners began cutting spars on Camano Island in 1855, and the next year a Dutch ship loaded 100 spars, each more than 80 feet long—truly awesome timbers. Three years later Cranney built one of the largest sawmills on Puget Sound, complemented by a shipyard. The mill operated until 1890. Its machinery then was sold to mills at Port Gamble and Port Ludlow.

In 1904 Scandinavian millworkers built **Our Saviour's Lutheran Church** (850 N. Heichel, about 2 miles west of the bridge). The building has been extensively remodeled to fit changing parish needs, but the original altar and furnishings remain. They were locally carved from exotic woods brought from all over the world by ships calling at the mill.

Beyond Utsalady a loop road threads the length of **Camano Island** but passes through such dense forest that only near the state park on the southwest shore is there a view out to sea.

PUGET SOUND Region

Commercial fishing fleet.

DESCRIPTIONS OF *defensible harbors surrounded by the greatest timber in the world filled the accounts of English mariner Captain George Vancouver's 1792 exploration of Puget Sound. Fifty-three years later at Tumwater (near Olympia), settlers founded the first American community on the sound's shores, and soon a handful of sawmilling communities were dotting the waterways. Seattle's founders stepped ashore in 1852; the following year Olympia became territorial capital; and in 1854 and 1855 Isaac Stevens, the impetuous new young governor, hurried through a series of poorly conceived treaties with Native Americans. Uprisings began almost immediately.*

During the 1860s the Kitsap Peninsula dominated the regional economy as sawmills turned virgin timber into lumber that was shipped around the globe. California and New England investors supplied capital, and craftsmen built schooners to carry away the Northwest timber. In the 1870s California coal interests financed mines east of Lake Washington. Resulting payrolls and a shipping bonanza helped Seattle to grow into a major city.

About that same time Tacoma outstripped other contenders by winning selection as the western terminus of the new trans-continental Northern Pacific Railroad. Wagon roads were still relatively crude, but the water highway of Puget Sound connected bustling communities around its shores. A fleet of small steamers carried freight and passengers between flagstops and cities.

In the 1880s Seattle's population grew tenfold and other Puget Sound cities experienced similar gains. Populist politicans won votes, and utopian colonies sprang up. The region's social milieu had been set on its course. Mixed with it came a military emphasis starting with the 1890s establishment of a navy yard at Bremerton and continuing with the building of three coast artillery forts, the opening of Fort Lewis and McChord Airforce Base near Tacoma, the founding of an aircraft industry at Seattle, and—recently—the selection of Bangor as a nuclear submarine base. Vancouver's eighteenth-century recognition of defensible harbors has found an expression that dominates the twentieth-century economy.

Seattle Area

Seattle and its outlying smaller cities occupy a lowland indented with saltwater shorelines and dotted with lakes. Rolling hills provide vistas across the waters and to mountains that frame the entire scene: the Cascades to the east, the Olympics to the west. Growth has not overwhelmed the area's beauty, nor industry destroyed it. Seattle consistently ranks high in national lists of "livable cities," and many adjacent towns have distinct personalities.

Outside Seattle, there are historical museums in Auburn, Bothell, Edmonds, Redmond, and Renton. Those within the city include the Museum of History and Industry near the University of Washington and the Klondike gold rush exhibits at Pioneer Square, in addition to ethnic museums such as the Wing Luke Museum in the International District, the Nordic Heritage Museum in Ballard, and the Native American displays at the Burke Museum on the University of Washington campus.

Festivals range from the Nordic Heritage Museum's all-day outdoor Tivoli Festival in early July to the three-week SeaFair celebration in late July and early August, which includes Japanese Bon-odori street dancing and a Chinese dragon parade. In addition, the International District celebrates the New Year according to the lunar calendar, which begins the year in either January or February. May is Museum Month in King County, with various special activities, including a tour of historic sites in the White River area near Auburn.

AUBURN lies in a river valley. During pioneer times, "White River" designated the whole Auburn-Kent area, referring to the river that flowed through the region and into the Duwamish River near Seattle. In 1906 a logjam near Auburn diverted this flow southward into the Puyallup River—to the joy of flood-prone Auburn farmers and the dismay of those on the swollen river's new path. Apparently men had helped the logjam; reports of dynamite led to seven years of litigation between King and Pierce counties. A judge finally decreed that King County could maintain diversion dams and levees to keep the White River on its new course, but would have to pay for flood control measures in Pierce County. Not until 1962 when the Howard Hanson Dam was built on the Green

Ferries, operated as part of the state highway system, link outlying communities with Seattle. Their runs provide miniexursions that include views of Mount Rainier.

River was the threat of flooding in Auburn-Kent ended. That same year Boeing opened its major plant in Kent.

Long before all of this, scattered sunny prairies punctuated the dense forest of the original White River area, now dominated by manufacturing and service companies. The open prairies attracted settlers. In October 1855 native warriors led by Chief Nelson moved systematically through the valley killing settlers and burning their cabins. Several children escaped: a seven-year-old carried his baby sister and led his younger brother toward Seattle, helped by sympathetic local natives. The warriors captured another child, George King, and took him east of the mountains; later they returned him to a white family. Along with murders the previous day at Connell's Prairie near Sumner, the White River killings opened a six-month period of war in western Washington, A historical marker (30th Street NE and Auburn Way N.) memorializes the victims. (See PUGET SOUND WAR sidebar, page 326.)

A second incident occurred near Auburn in November 1855. Lieutenant William Slaughter led his troops toward White River from the U.S. Army post at Steilacoom, where he was quartermaster and commissary, and his wife, the only woman at the fort, managed the officers' mess. Slaughter halted his men near present-day Auburn while he conferred with an officer of the Washington Territorial Volunteers. As the two stood silhouetted in the doorway of an abandoned cabin, hostile warriors opened fire. Slaughter died immediately.

Word of the attack caused remaining settlers to abandon their claims and move to Seattle for safety. Even when peace returned, resettlement proceeded slowly; finally, however, a town began to grow near the sites of the killings. At first it was named Slaughter to honor the slain lieutenant, but citizens began to object when their hotel was called the Slaughter House. In 1893 they changed the name to Auburn.

During the 1880s hops became the dominant crop of the town's surrounding farmlands. Aphids brought a halt to that industry, and many farmers turned to dairying. In the early 1900s Japanese American farmers began leasing land and supplying truck crops to Seattle's Pike Place Market. Their tenancy ended in 1942 with their

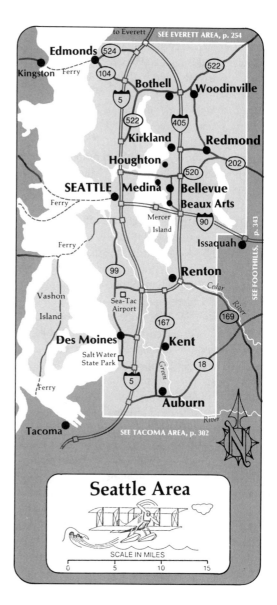

enforced "relocation" for the duration of World War II. (See under PUYALLUP on p. 321.) Defense plants soon replaced agriculture throughout the Auburn area.

East of Auburn the **Aaron Neely mansion** stands where State Route 18 crosses the Green River (12303 Auburn–Black Diamond Road, near the foot of the Auburn–Black Diamond exit from State Route 18). Neely, a second-generation Washingtonian, built the 2½-story Victorian farmhouse in 1894. Its architectural detail, including a roof portico with a round window, reflects a high degree of craftsmanship. A cabinetmaker, Neely also raised fruit trees and operated a dairy. The Neely Mansion Foundation is preserving the house and opens it for touring and for special events such as craft shows at Christmas and in the spring. Each May the association conducts tours of White River Valley historical sites, such as an 1899 salmon hatchery, other early houses, and public buildings; they also distribute a list of drive-by sites not open to visitors but visible from the road. Auburn's White River Historical Museum (918 H Street SE) chronicles the area's development.

In **BELLEVUE** glassy, high-rise office buildings jut against the sky, and a vast shopping mall topped by an art museum is the city's de facto civic center. Almost all residential neighborhoods—often elaborate homes on professionally landscaped lots—date from the 1950s and later. West of Bellevue Square, however, hints of the earlier community still linger: lilac bushes dot unfussy lawns, and houses have large screened porches. A 1929 home is open daily (Mercer Slough Nature Park).

With today's floating bridges and north-south freeways, it is difficult to imagine Bellevue as a remote hinterland. But in the 1860s most settlers preferred nearby prairies to Bellevue's wilderness of giant trees. Neither roads nor railroads penetrated the forest. Lake Washington provided access, but boats entering the lake from Seattle had to follow a roundabout route up the twisting Duwamish River and the shallow Black River. Despite the isolation, two homesteaders took up land in 1869: William Meydenbauer, a Seattle baker whose name is preserved in the bay his property fronted, and Aaron Mercer, who farmed south of the present city near Mercer Slough. Both sold out as soon as they proved up on their claims.

Speculators, such as Seattle pioneers Henry Yesler and David Denny, soon bought acreage hoping that a railroad might make the timberland profitable, and by the 1880s permanent settlers finally arrived. They logged the trees— a sawmill once operated at Wilburton near the present city hall—and began to farm. Gradually small steamers, carrying passengers and farm produce between Bellevue and Leschi Park, began to make regular crossings of Lake Washington.

The opening of the Ship Canal and Montlake Cut in 1917 gave easy access to Lake Washington (see HIRAM CHITTENDEN LOCKS, p. 297), and September 1918 brought a fleet of seven stubby vessels with harpoons mounted on their foredecks. These were whalers come for the off-season. Bellevue provided a "Scotch drydock": fresh water killed the vessels' barnacles and teredo worms. Their owner, William Schupp, head of the American Pacific Whaling Company, had recently bought a Bellevue home; for convenience he decided to move corporate headquarters here from Bay City (near Westport). Consequently crewmen spent the winter caulking decks, sharpening blades, and spinning whale stories for local children. In May the *Unimak, Kodiak, Tanginak*, and their sister ships sailed north to Alaska for summer whaling in Alaskan waters.

This pattern continued until World War II when the Coast Guard took over Schupp's dock (at the foot of 99th Avenue) and commandeered the fleet for use as patrol vessels. After the war a scarcity of whales (due to overhunting), combined with increasingly stringent government regulations, caused the company to close.

Despite such commercial use, the waterfront never was a major economic factor here. Instead Bellevue's livelihood came from premium-quality berries and vegetables produced largely by Japanese American farmers. Many moved away, however, when the 1921 and 1923 anti-alien acts prohibited them from directly leasing land. Other farmers then took over and, by the 1930s, Bellevue was famous for berries. At its annual Strawberry Festival volunteers ladled whipped cream onto thousands of shortcakes. This helped make the area an excursion destination for Seattleites, including wealthy families who began buying lakeshore property for country homes; some started commuting from here to their Seattle offices.

In 1939, construction of the first cross-lake bridge, followed by wartime industrialization of the region, ended Bellevue's countrified lifestyle. After World War II what had been a town mushroomed into an upper-middle-class adjunct to Seattle.

West of Bellevue, on Lake Washington, an enclave of estates known as **Medina** (Me-deye´-nuh) gained the nickname "Gold Coast" by the

By 1909 logging and farming gave Bellevue a population large enough to warrant modern schools.

1890s. Wealthy landowners, including timberman Marshall Blinn, publisher Leigh S. J. Hunt, and financier Bailey Gatzert, bought sizeable acreage from homesteaders who had turned logged-over land into orchards and farms. The new owners then converted the former farmland to broad lakefront lawns and built mansions to take advantage of the view. Medina's ferry terminal now serves as city hall (501 Evergreen Point Road; built in 1913). The Medina Grocery, with a corner entry and a well-used ambience, predates Medina's elegant days (800 Evergreen Point Road; built in 1908). Home delivery is still the norm.

South of Bellevue, the community of **Beaux Arts** maintains its unique identity. Founded in 1908 by a group of artists and architects involved in preparing the Alaska-Yukon-Pacific Exposition, the settlement was slated to become a garden commune for artists: only members of the Western Academy of Beaux Arts could buy lots. The art colony never blossomed, but the tranquil flavor of the 50-acre neighborhood persists.

BOTHELL, adjacent to the new high-tech I-5 corridor, clings to its rural character, although

condominiums march over the hillsides, and highways web surrounding farmland. Several pioneer buildings have been moved to Bothell Landing Park for preservation (Bothell Way and NE 180th). These include the Beckstrom Cabin, the 12- by 16-foot home of Swedish immigrants who in the 1880s rowed to their new farm on the Sammamish River; the 1890s Lytle House, which belonged to Bothell's doctor; and the Hannan House (now a historical museum), built by an 1890s storekeeper and mayor.

In 1882 George Brackett had a logging camp at the present town center, from which steamers towed rafts of logs to Lake Washington via the shallow, winding Sammamish River (earlier called the Squak River, also Sammamish Slough). In 1884 former logger David Bothell bought 80 acres and platted a town. His wife operated a boardinghouse where she fed passengers arriving on the steam scow *Squak*. As the vessel rounded the last bend before Mrs. Bothell's house, the captain blew its whistle to signal the number of dinner guests to expect. In 1887 the arrival of the Seattle, Lake Shore and Eastern Railroad opened the community's future as a freight depot. River traffic then declined. It ended altogether in 1916 when newly lowered

Lake Washington left the Sammamish River too shallow for navigation (see LAKE WASHINGTON, p. 278).

In the 1870s pioneers settled **DES MOINES** (Deh-moynz´), on the saltwater shore 15 miles south of Seattle, and promoters soon platted a townsite. They built a sawmill and tried to attract settlers, but no real growth came until 1900 when seaside property became fashionable as a refuge from city life and Seattleites came on weekend jaunts to stroll and look over the vacant lots.

Actually Des Moines residents had a choice of transportation: they could take an autostage to Seattle; catch a steamer at the town dock; or walk 4 miles to Kent and ride the interurban train that connected Seattle and Tacoma. Lumber and shingle mills provided employment; some families raised chickens or garden truck for income.

South of Des Moines is **Salt Water State Park,** a beach where native people formerly gathered shellfish. On the bluffs above the water they posted lookouts to warn of approaching raiders, particularly canoeloads of Tlingits from southeast Alaska or Haidas and Tsimshians from northern British Columbia, who came to Puget Sound to capture slaves.

EDMONDS occupies a natural amphitheater curving above Puget Sound. Flower-bedecked houses look over one another to the water and the Olympic Mountains, which line the western horizon. A ferry connects Edmonds with Kingston on the Kitsap Peninsula; the beach north of the ferry terminal is designated as a historical area—Brackett's Landing—to commemorate the town founder; and the waterfront still bustles with shops, boat-related businesses, and restaurants. Offshore a city-owned diving park fosters sea life drawn to a drydock that was sunk to calm the water near the ferry terminal. There is a museum at 118 Fifth Avenue N.

In 1870 George Brackett, a logger who supplied Ballard mills, pulled his canoe ashore to avoid storm-roiled water. He was on a trip scouting for easily accessible, plentiful timber, and he liked what he saw. Six years later he returned to buy a previous homesteader's claim. His family joined him, and Brackett became Edmonds' chief booster. He served as postmaster, built a wharf, and in 1889 started the first sawmill. Soon other mills and two brick-making plants also opened. About midway between Everett and Seattle, the town enjoyed frequent train and steamboat service, which enhanced transportation for its products. Eventually, nearby cedar was all cut, and most

A Kent Valley farmer manures his promising lettuce crop, to be marketed in Seattle.

of the mills closed. Edmonds nonetheless remained a village of about a thousand. Former city councilman Gordon Maxwell described its character right after World War II:

We just had a town marshal . . . who didn't have a car. If there was a police emergency, we'd light a red light on a pole at 5th and Main, which alerted policemen to call in. . . . When there was a fire, the telephone operator dispatched the volunteer firemen. . . . There was no need for a sewage department—we dumped the sewage into the bay in those days.

In the 1880s **JUANITA,** now a pleasant residential area at the north end of Lake Washington, was little more than a water-powered mill that shipped shingles by scow via the Black River to Seattle. Lowering the lake's water level in 1916 produced a sandy beach that became Juanita's trademark. One family opened a candy stand, then added bathhouses, shade trees, and picnic tables when Sunday visitors began coming in large numbers. King County now owns the beach as a park.

In 1931 the Catholic diocese of Seattle built Saint Edward's Seminary on a tract of land held by timber baron Marshall Blinn's descendants. The school and its later addition, Saint Thomas Seminary, stood on grounds partly reforested with second-growth trees. Until 1976 candidates for the priesthood pursued their studies here; declining enrollment caused both schools to close. Today the grounds are preserved as a state park.

KENT, 17 miles south of Seattle, lies in a broad valley bordered on the west by the I-5 freeway and bisected lengthwise by the Valley Freeway (State Route 167). Manufacturing and service companies now dominate, but previously the valley's soil attracted farmers.

In the mid-1850s several homesteaders settled in the area, then known as White River—a name no longer applicable because the river changed its course in 1906. (See AUBURN, p. 272.) The settlers left their farms during the 1855-1856 war between native people and whites, but they returned to the fertile farmland when the conflict ended.

Steamboats from Seattle soon splashed up the Duwamish to the White River. They were shallow-draft, flat-bottomed, and stern-wheeled to allow maneuvering through shoals. On their downstream runs they dragged chains to help hold the course; if the boats veered out of the channel, they grounded and remained stuck until high water freed them. At first farmers flagged the steamers whenever they had freight or needed to travel. Later, regular schedules developed, and landings grew up at Alvord's, Langston's, and Maddocksville. (Alvord's Landing was 2 miles south of Kent; the others were within the present city.) Not even the busiest landings had wharves, because water levels fluctuated too much and annual spring floods would have washed them away. The landings nevertheless became the hubs of significant communities.

The steamboat era ended as railroad construction began in the 1880s. The Northern Pacific's Columbia and Puget Sound line was the first; it extended from Renton to near Auburn. Twenty years later an electric interurban line, which greatly improved passenger service, was based in Kent to connect the valley with Seattle. Farmers shipped full milk cans each morning from small stations that dotted the line, and they picked up the empty cans in the afternoon. These depots—Orillia, O'Brien, Thomas, and Christopher—became the hubs of the communities replacing earlier steamboat landings. In 1910 the Chicago, Milwaukee and St. Paul added a third set of tracks to the valley.

That same year Elbridge A. Stuart and Herbert R. Yerxa began the Carnation Milk Company (originally called the Pacific Coast Milk Company) with a condensery housed in a former Kent hotel. Workers soldered 3,000 cans per day by hand, and horse-drawn carts delivered canned milk door-to-door as well as to grocery stores. To improve herd quality in the Northwest, Stuart also started a research dairy farm. (See under CARNATION on p. 344.)

The interurban's demise in 1928 all but ended several small communities along its line. Japanese American farmers leased former dairy farms and raised vegetables for the Seattle market. Their internment during World War II, combined with wartime industrial growth, undermined Kent's agricultural focus. The Boeing Company opened its commercial airplane division at Renton in the 1950s and its space center at Kent in the 1960s. Both plants attracted subcontractors and suppliers who contributed to the industrialization of the valley.

In **KIRKLAND,** on Lake Washington's northeast shore, fashionable restaurants and high-rise apartment buildings line the waterfront. Nearby several commercial buildings remain from the town's hope, in the 1880s, of becoming the "Pittsburgh of the West." In anticipation, architects laid out the ground floor of the Joshua Sears Building (701 Market; built in the early 1890s) as a bank slated to handle the payrolls of a steel mill. The Peter Kirk Building (620 Market; built in 1891, now an arts center) was a mercantile with the land development company offices upstairs. The Campbell Building (700 Market; built in 1890) was a large grocery with a residence above. The upstairs later became the Masonic Lodge.

In 1886 Peter Kirk, whose family owned a steelworks in England, scouted in the western United States for investment possibilities. After talking in Seattle with Leigh S. J. Hunt, publisher of the *Post-Intelligencer,* he decided to locate a steel mill on Lake Washington. Railroad expansion in the western United States, western South America, and China obviously would create a demand for steel rails; and a West Coast mill, relatively near these new markets, would have a tremendous economic advantage over East Coast mills. Furthermore, iron ore and coal were thought to abound near Snoqualmie Pass. Kirk applied for American citizenship and formed the Moss Bay Iron and Steel Works to build the steel mill, and the Kirkland Land and Improvement Company to develop a town.

In 1891 construction began on a huge mill with four blast furnaces, a steel-rolling building 320 feet long, and massive coal and ore bunkers. The Improvement Company graded the townsite, platted lots, and promoted the new town. But the Panic of 1893 soon dissipated the dream. As the economy weakened, investors refused to honor promissory notes. Railroads, upon which the mill depended for raw materials, went into receivership with a 17-mile gap still remaining between the ore and the mill. Without ore, capital, or market, the Moss Bay Iron and Steel Works failed before construction was even complete.

Even so, the town did not quite die. By the late 1890s a woolen mill was outfitting Yukon-bound gold miners, and logging and farming were supporting some families who, in turn, patronized the few local stores. Berries, fruit, bulbs, and chickens became major products. The town also was a significant eastside ferry stop with buses fanning out to neighboring communities. Beginning in 1939, with a bridge across the lake, Kirkland became a satellite of Seattle. Even so, it has managed to hold onto its own character.

At **Houghton** (neighborhood of south Kirkland) a family boatworks in 1884 produced an unlovely scow, the *Squak,* for Lake Washington passenger and freight duty. The yard built other boats, too, but was hampered by the difficulty of taking finished vessels to Puget Sound via the shallow Black and Duwamish rivers. The opening of the Lake Washington Ship Canal and the Montlake Cut in 1917 solved the problem (see LAKE WASHINGTON, p. 279), and the boatworks began to build deep-draft vessels. In the 1920s the company produced steamers for the Mosquito Fleet—small Puget Sound passenger and freight boats.

During World War II, shipyard production expanded enormously. Eight thousand workers built 29 steel tenders for the navy and repaired 500 other vessels. After the war the company dismantled the boatworks; jogging paths in a lakeside park pass the site, which is now the home of the Seattle Seahawks football team.

LAKE WASHINGTON is a shining 20-mile body of fresh water ringed by cities and crossed by two floating bridges worth driving for their spectacular views of water, city, and mountains—except during morning and afternoon rush hours when traffic overpowers all other senses. Sailboats cut across the waves, and once a year (August) hydroplanes skim the surface on an oval racecourse. East of the lake, Mount Baker and Mount Rainier punctuate the horizon.

In 1850 Isaac Ebey set out by canoe to paddle the length of the lake, the first white person to record such an exploration. He admired the water's clarity and depth, but decided against the lakeshore for a farm and eventually settled on Whidbey Island. Others claimed farms along

An historic preservation grant helped restore Kirkland's landmark Peter Kirk building.

the Duwamish and Black rivers at the south end of the lake. The Black River, the lake's outlet, was joined about a mile from the lake by the swift Cedar River, and together they flowed into the Duwamish and on to Puget Sound.

Those pioneers would marvel at the changes wrought in the landscape in the fall of 1916 as workmen dug canals linking Lake Washington, Lake Union, and Puget Sound. The lake's level lowered nine feet and, deprived of its source, the Black River dried and disappeared; the lake now drains through the canal. The Cedar River was artificially diverted to flow directly into the lake. (Also see HIRAM CHITTENDEN LOCKS, p. 297.)

Other changes occurred on the lakeshore. A sawmill at Wilburton (Bellevue), which had stood on Mercer Slough, was left high above the shoreline with no transportation for its logs, and farmers' spindly docks stood far from the water. The low plain that now holds the University of Washington stadium and sports pavilion made its appearance as dry land. The roadbed of the Seattle, Lake Shore and Eastern Railroad (now

the Burke-Gilman Trail), which had been built along the water's edge, suddenly became a barrier between newly created lakeshore property and the adjoining land.

A different story of human management of the lake concerns the water per se. Beginning in 1884 Seattle tapped Lake Washington for a water supply, but subsequent outbreaks of typhoid finally persuaded officials to seek another source. They chose the Cedar River, closing its watershed to public entry and piping the water into the city. In the early 1950s scummy masses of algae fed by septic-tank leaks, fertilizers, and phosphate detergents began accumulating on the lake surface, and swimming fell into the category of fond memory. Happily the cause of this—eastside communities were swelling with young families following World War II—also precipitated a solution. In 1958 voters passed a bond issue to finance coordinated sewer systems. Their operation led to today's clean water.

Early settlers viewed Lake Washington as an industrial asset. Sawmills, shipyards, a woolen mill at Kirkland, and a proposed steel mill all were greeted as indicators of progress. Today, little industry remains except at the south end of the lake; property values depend instead on scenic beauty.

On **MERCER ISLAND** peaceful country lanes and long driveways lead to substantial homes. Only at the island's north end does the hectic outside world intrude. There I-90 traffic flows— or creeps—hemmed by concrete walls.

Early settlers avoided the island; its heavily wooded hills daunted would-be farmers. In 1876 Vitus Schmidt, a German wagonmaker, claimed land and lived here until his cabin was crushed by a falling tree. He then left, married, and returned 13 years later with his family. He had only three or four neighboring families on the entire island, although by then loggers had skimmed the timber.

In 1889 C. C. Calkins bought acreage on the northwestern shore, which he dubbed East Seattle. He built a resort hotel topped by an elaborate turreted roof. Flower gardens with mazes and fountains surrounded the hotel, and a boathouse sheltered canoes and rowboats. Calkins even built a cable car from Seattle to Lake Washington and bought a steamboat to carry guests to the island. The resort lasted only until 1902, but it had introduced Seattle citizens to Mercer Island's beauty, and they began to build country homes here.

In 1923 a bridge connected Mercer Island with Enetai on the east side of Lake Washington. Residents delighted in driving to Seattle, even though it meant a cumbersome trip around the south end of the lake. Bridging the 1½ miles between the island and the city posed problems owing to a water depth of 200 feet. To overcome this the State Department of Highways director Lacey V. Murrow (broadcaster Edward R. Murrow's brother) advocated a concrete pontoon floating bridge. Community groups bemoaned the plan, deriding the anticipated appearance as an "ugly string of barges" and predicting that the pontoons would waterlog and sink. Murrow persisted, and in June 1940 the first car crossed the bridge (now part of I-90), at that time the longest floating bridge in the world. Its 1½-mile floating segment rests on a series of 25 anchored pontoons.

The new bridge fostered development on Mercer Island and the eastside of the lake. In the 1960s increased traffic led to construction of a second floating bridge (State Route 520), between the University of Washington and

A 1903 caption says this 22-foot stump house has "one good-size room, which is boarded up and neatly papered." Naturally hollow, old cedars offered pioneers ready-built shelter.

Evergreen Point, near Medina. In the 1980s a third span was added, close to the original bridge.

Since 1980 **REDMOND** has experienced rapid growth: housing developments spread over formerly forested hills; residents work at new high-tech companies; and, at times, bicyclists are numerous. The presence of a topnotch bicycle racetrack at Marymoor Park, one of only six in the country, accounts for the cyclists.

In 1871 Luke McRedmond, former Kitsap County sheriff, moved here with his wife Kate, and their home soon became a meeting place for territorial notables. By 1890 a store had opened and settlers were calling their town Salmonberg because of the abundant dog salmon in the Sammamish River. Loggers worked at clearing the forest, and farmers moved in to raise poultry, vegetables, and dairy cattle. Frequent steamers carried produce to Seattle; stage lines connected Redmond to the Snoqualmie Valley and Kirkland; and after 1887 the Seattle, Lake Shore and Eastern rails offered an even more convenient link with the outside.

Thirty years after the first homesteaders claimed land here, Seattle banker James Clise bought acreage intended for a duck-hunting retreat. His original modest lodge grew over the years into a 28-room Tudor-style mansion, and he turned to farming as a full-time hobby. On his estate, by then called Willowmoor Farm, he raised prize-winning Ayreshire cattle and Morgan horses. He also indulged minor fancies: on a trip to Holland he saw and admired Dutch windmills, and he commissioned one for the farm. The resultant, purely decorative structure on the banks of Sammamish River (still standing) later was modified to pump irrigation water for the estate's lawns. Today a wing of the mansion houses the Marymoor Museum (Marymoor Park, 6046 Lake Sammamish Parkway), a historical museum exhibiting artifacts and memorabilia from the Bellevue-Kirkland-Redmond area.

The **RENTON** history museum (235 Mill Ave. S.) serves as an accent for the modern industry of southern Lake Washington. A huge Boeing plant spreads near the lakeshore, built on debris from Renton's early coal mining days and on fill

dredged from the lake bottom. PACCAR, builder of sophisticated railroad refrigerator cars, is the descendant of a 1908 firm, and a clay products company founded by Seattle pioneer Arthur Denny today manufactures firebrick for aluminum smelters. Before whites took over the land, the Duwamish had a village here.

In 1853 Dr. R. H. Bigelow found coal while clearing land "near the head of navigation" (a site no longer identifiable) on the Duwamish River. Within the next two years his neighbors also were working coal in a small way and had opened a sawmill near present-day Renton's west side. Hostilities between natives and whites in the mid-1850s delayed development of coal mines, however, and frustrated native warriors burned the sawmill after their unsuccessful attack on Seattle in January 1856. When peace returned the settlers rebuilt the mill. They slowly cleared the heavily wooded land and created farms where they raised various crops for sale in Seattle or Newcastle.

Coal mining resumed, but to market the coal, miners had to load it into barges for native boatmen to pole down the shallow Black River to the winding Duwamish and finally to the Seattle waterfront. Each round trip took six days.

The 1870s brought major changes when some California investors and Captain William Renton, owner of the huge Port Blakely sawmill operation, took an interest in Renton coal. They expanded tunnels, bunkers, and other facilities, and built company housing. When determined Seattleites managed to build a railroad from Elliott Bay to Renton in 1877, production skyrocketed. The mines turned a profit, and the railroad paid for itself in coal-hauling receipts. (In 1878 the railroad continued on narrow-gauge tracks to the Newcastle mines; its backers grew wealthy. See NEWCASTLE, p. 348.)

In these years Renton was a single-industry town. The mine whistle called the tune; it blew to wake the miners in the morning, to tell them when to start for the mine, when to begin work, and when to go home. Twelve-year-old boys followed their fathers underground as "trappers" to open and close the wooden gates behind the mules that hauled coal cars to the surface. The company paid miners by piecework, and a miner with an assistant earned higher wages.

Mine production was intermittent, and between 1886 and 1895 the mines closed. Nationwide, labor disputes at the end of World War I and a switch to oil as a fuel finally ended large-scale production altogether. Other industries continued, however, and Renton's location as a transportation hub (four railroads and an electric interurban) made it the county's major manufacturing center outside Seattle.

SEATTLE enjoys a spectacular cityscape—although drivers may find its hills steep and empathize with early 1900s streetcar passengers who had to step off and push if the horse pulling a coach began to falter. Salt water washes the western doorstep. Sunrise silhouettes the icy Cascades and Mount Rainier; sunset, the jagged line of the Olympics. On downtown streets dressed-for-success executives mingle with wool-shirted outdoors folk—and on weekends both groups head for the mountains and rivers and beaches.

Seattle's story began in northern Illinois in 1851 as four covered wagons rolled out of Cherry Grove. Roberta Frye Watt wrote in *Four Wagons West* that her grandmother Mary Denny, wife of the wagon party's leader, walked a last time "through the empty, echoing rooms" of her home:

She gave one tear-blurred look about the old, familiar, homely room and then passed out into the April sunshine. The barnyard was empty; the chickens were gone; even the dog was perched up on the wagon. All that was left was her flower garden.

By fall the party arrived at Portland. Most rested there while David Denny, brother of the leader Arthur Denny, went with John Low to find a location suitable for settling. The two men traveled overland to Olympia, then continued by water. At Alki Point they noticed that a fire had already eliminated part of the forest, a blessing for anyone intending to farm. The men landed, began work on a cabin, and wrote to the main party to join them. On November 13 the steamer *Exact,* carrying mostly gold miners bound for the Queen Charlotte Islands, nosed as close as possible to shore and dropped off five families, which totaled 12 adults and 12 children.

This small group spent a blustery winter on the exposed point, christening it New York and then adding *Alki,* the Chinook Jargon word for "by and by." The name reflected pioneer expectations of future growth, an optimism that seemed justified the very next year when a brig buying piling for San Francisco stopped to load timber, the first shipment out of Elliott Bay. The shoaling beach at Alki Point made the loading difficult, however, and the settlers decided to find a place with deeper water.

By dugout canoe, they checked as far south as Dash Point (near Tacoma), then borrowed Mary Denny's clothesline, weighted it with horseshoes, and systematically sounded along the shore opposite their cabins. Eventually they decided on a place Duwamish natives called *Tzee-tzee-lal-itch,* "Little Portage," for a path leading to Lake Washington. Geography smiled on the choice. On one side lay a deep harbor with access to the Pacific, on the other (though not yet known to the Seattle settlers) lay Snoqualmie Pass and access to the vast interior.

Additional settlers soon arrived. David Maynard came north from Olympia, opened a store, and tried shipping brined salmon to San Francisco, though the fish spoiled en route. Thomas Mercer moved out from Illinois bringing the growing community its first horse and wagon, which was pressed into service for freight and milk delivery. Henry Yesler set up a steam sawmill, the first of its kind on Puget Sound, an enterprise that prompted the Olympia *Columbian* to speak admiringly of Seattle's "goaheadedness." Yesler's crew cut trees from the slopes behind what now is First Avenue and skidded the logs along what is Yesler Way; the mill's cookhouse soon took over from Maynard's store as a community center *cum* jail and church. About the same time Arthur Denny started a store, and his clerk Dexter Horton began safeguarding loggers' and sailors' money by burying individually labeled sacks in the store's coffee barrel.

The mid-1850s erupted with hostilities and expectations of hostilities between the newcomer whites and the native people on both sides of the Cascades. In October 1855 a war party under Chief Nelson killed nine settlers near their cabins in the White River Valley south of Seattle. (See under AUBURN on p. 273.) Three months later warriors attacked Seattle for a day while a

The Duwamish River mouth (top left) attracted Seattle's first white settlers. They lived through one windy winter at Alki Point, then moved to the shelter of Elliott Bay.

federal gunboat pounded the forest with shells. (See PUGET SOUND WAR sidebar, p. 326.) During this period "city" people and outlying homesteaders alike crowded into the blockhouse located at the foot of present-day Cherry Street. In 1856 the war ended west of the Cascades; in 1858 it ended east of the mountains. Clearly the white newcomers were dominant.

Seattle's second decade opened with a population of 182 (mostly bachelors). By then prospectors bound for the Fraser River gold excitement already had streamed through the area and created a flurry of business, but little except Yesler's mill anchored the economy. Furthermore, the Civil War was drawing off the nation's energy, and few immigrants were coming West. Two efforts nonetheless marked Seattle's bid for permanence.

One was that residents lobbied successfully to have the territorial university located in Seattle. They were motivated both by respect for education and by the expectation that such an institution would enhance the city's competitive standing and stimulate real estate development. In 1861 the doors of a white wooden building, dignified by four Ionic columns, swung open. The "university" sat on a knoll (at what is now Seneca Street between Fourth and Fifth), aloof from the straggling town. Asa Mercer, at age 22 the university's president and only instructor, offered to accept cordwood from prospective students as credit against tuition although it was rumored that "not one of the misses attending the University the first quarter . . . could accurately repeat the multiplication table." Regardless, the first graduate was a woman.

Thirty years later enrollment outgrew the original structure, and the university moved to its present campus on Lake Washington.

Seattle's second major 1860s effort arose when Asa Mercer, armed with a letter of introduction from Washington's governor, traveled East to bring brides to the growing city. The letter introduced him as a "Gentleman of the best standing in Society, . . . universally respected, . . . a man of honor, integrity, and moral worth." Mercer was aware of the severe gender imbalance he had been commissioned to correct and aware, too, that the situation was approximately reversed in the East where thousands of young men had died in the Civil War. He made two trips. His first, small-scale venture brought 11 ladies West to be welcomed by men who looked "like grizzlies in store clothes [with] their hair slicked down like sea otters." Cheered by success, Mercer made a second trip two years later and returned with 46 women, 10 of them widows. Descendents of these venturesome Mercer Girls now number in the thousands.

The city's third decade finally brought stability. Population hovered at over 1,000 in 1870, and that figure more than tripled by 1880. Seattle felt so sure of selection as the Northern Pacific terminus that its number of businesses doubled. Then came word that Tacoma had been blessed instead, and Seattle's reaction was two-pronged: sufficient outrage to ask Congress to nullify the land-grant subsidy intended to offset railway construction costs, and sufficient leftover ebullience to immediately organize the Seattle and Walla Walla Railroad and Construction Company with a line projected to cross Snoqualmie Pass and join the transcontinental at Spokane.

A volunteer work party turned out to grade the first mile of this rail line, enjoy a picnic, and listen to rousing speeches. Henry Yesler reportedly climbed on the wagon podium and urged, "Quit your fooling and go to work!" Words became action; four years later the rails reached Newcastle's coal mines and stopped. Coal mined there greatly improved the city's fiscal health and also attracted big-league players. Henry Villard's Northern Pacific interests bought the railroad in 1880, and coal shipments—along

In 1906 an imperial Chinese commission came to Seattle to discuss trade and strengthen relations. For decades China had provided the American West with labor but, even before 1900, rising anti-Chinese sentiment caused repeated violence.

with lumber—became a major export from Seattle to San Francisco.

Through the 1880s Seattle grew tenfold, and the area as a whole took on a cosmopolitan air as blacks and European immigrants—Italians, Welsh, Yugoslavs—began to pour in to mine the coal, and Finns bought outlying stumpland and turned it into dairy farms. At the same time Norwegian sea captains plied the coast with lumber schooners, and Swedes came to cut the forest and fish the salmon. Chinese arrived to build the railroads and perform other heavy labor.

The Chinese were almost all single men who fled a homeland rife with warfare and famine as European powers sought to force the Manchu dynasty into trade relationships. In America they fanned out over the West with little real choice but to accept menial work at low wages, usually controlled by Seattle or San Francisco labor contractors. Employers welcomed the men's diligence and low demands, but white workers came to resent the Chinese and protested that they lived on starvation wages and threatened society's best interest. Businessmen also began to complain, objecting to the Chinese habit of sending their meager earnings to families in China rather than spending them in local stores. In 1882 Congress—a year before completion of the Northern Pacific main line across the country—passed the Chinese Exclusion Act, halting legal immigration. Smugglers nonetheless kept up the supply of cheap labor simply by bringing in Chinese men from Canada.

Agitation swelled in the mid-1880s as street-corner orators and newspaper invective openly derided "Chinamen." In September 1885 whites and Native Americans joined in murdering Chinese hop pickers in Issaquah. Other whites terrorized Chinese miners at Black Diamond and Newcastle. And a mob in Tacoma drove Chinese residents from their homes on November 3, 1885. Seattle exploded two days later when the Knights of Labor held a mass meeting and announced the Chinese had "agreed" to leave Seattle. Expecting violence, army troops marched north from Fort Vancouver, and a revenue cutter entered the harbor, displaying its guns. Then matters quieted, and the troops left.

Ten weeks later—on February 7, 1886—five "committees" swarmed through the Chinese district breaking the Sunday-morning quiet by pounding on doors and leading the frightened inhabitants of homes and shops to the docks where a steamer waited. The mob loaded nearly 100 Chinese men on board the boat before a court order appeared demanding an explanation of what was going on. The committee then herded their remaining victims to a warehouse; the state governor wired a request for federal troops; the sheriff called out forerunners of the National Guard. On February 8 the guardsmen oversaw the loading of another 96 Chinese onto the steamer, which headed out to sea. They then started escorting the remaining half of the Chinese back to their homes, and thereby started a melee. Five men fell wounded, one fatally.

The next day President Grover Cleveland declared martial law and federal troops again patrolled the city. Most of the remaining Chinese "volunteered" to leave. Five ringleaders were arrested for conspiring intimidation, but were found not guilty. Within a few years, Chinese workers drifted back.

By 1890 shipyards lined Seattle's waterfront, and merchants were supplying outlying mill towns. The Great Northern Railway arrived via Everett in 1893, puffing into the city and at last providing a transcontinental link. Its route across the continent was shorter and its grades more gentle than the Northern Pacific's. Great Northern financing also was more stable; the Northern Pacific experienced repeated bankruptcy. Furthermore, the Great Northern's James Hill was unique in seeing transportation as a backbone for commerce and West Coast commerce as tied to the Orient.

Hill pushed for development of Seattle's port and sought to control its dockage rates and longshoring service. He also negotiated with a Japanese steamship company to bring silk, tea, and other goods to Puget Sound ports, then carry return cargos of lumber and steel for railroad construction. He arranged for cotton from the South to be shipped to China from Seattle and for Washington flour to go to San Francisco. Hill even built ships of his own, directly competing with Canadian companies who benefited from what he regarded as the unjust advantage of a government-subsidized railroad.

Just months after the first Great Northern train

The Moran Brothers shipyards, located at the foot of Yesler Way, built twelve paddlewheel steamers for the Yukon goldrush in the 1890s, and in 1904 completed the battleship Nebraska.

arrived at Elliott Bay, a nationwide financial panic set in. Hill's rail line and, by 1896, his trade with the Orient lessened the depression's effects in Seattle. Nonetheless, the city reeled. Lumber operations and shipping shut down, and out-of-work men joined "Coxey's Army" intending to protest their plight in Washington, D.C., although most actually disbanded when they reached Puyallup (25 miles south of Seattle). Life turned decidedly gray, at least until 1897 when the steamer *Portland* hove to with half a ton of gold from the Yukon.

That event brought Seattle national publicity as an outfitting center, some of it based on prewritten "letters home" that the Chamber of Commerce handed hopeful prospectors to mail to hometown editors. The U.S. State Department even distributed a Chamber booklet extolling Klondike riches and explaining that Seattle was *the* point of embarkation. Cash registers rang up the sale of wool trousers, pack mules, tents, and bacon as scores of ships headed north from Elliott Bay docks. The Seattle-Alaska connection forged at that time continues today; a glance at the current yellow pages of the phone directory shows dozens of Alaska firms with Seattle offices, and vice versa.

In the early 1900s, with a population of more than 80,000—double that of 1890—Seattle undertook two ambitious landscape changes. It commissioned the prestigious Olmsted Brothers firm to design a park system, which resulted in the interconnected boulevards and parks that still exist (albeit not exactly as the Olmsteds intended). Enthusiasm also grew for reshaping the heart of the city. Historic photographs show the result. Steam shovels bit into hillsides, and men used Klondike gold rush techniques to shoot jets of water from hoses and literally wash part of Denny Hill and all of the Jackson Street and Dearborn Street hills onto the tideflats, thus eliminating the nuisance of steep grades and creating acres of flat ground intended for industrial use.

An equally bold statement of civic maturity was the Alaska-Yukon-Pacific Exposition, a world's fair held in 1909 on what became part of the present campus of the University of Washington. The expo successfully trumpeted Seattle's role as a major player in Pacific Rim and Alaskan trade, set off a real estate boom, and brought nearly four million people through the city. That same year the Chicago, Milwaukee and St. Paul Railroad arrived, and the next year the Union Pacific laid tracks for a branch line to Seattle from Portland.

A decade later another side of the city persona exhibited itself as labor and populist ideals culminated in a five-day general strike, one of the first such strikes in the United States. Well-organized and nonviolent, it involved 110 unions and 60,000 workers who walked off their jobs beginning February 6, 1919. The World War I armistice had recently closed booming shipyard industries and caused lumber and agricultural markets to plummet. Wage cuts were biting into the pay envelopes of many workers; others had lost their jobs altogether. Bolsheviks had recently taken power in Russia; J. Edgar Hoover began his surveillance of radicals; and anarchy seemed to loom everywhere.

Seattle's "better element" fretted as the strike gripped the city, and unions fed strikers at labor-run cafeterias, arranged for milk delivery to babies and children, and handled citywide emergency transportation and fire protection. Shipyard workers had been the first to walk off the job; others from longshoremen and teamsters to carpenters, typographers, hotel maids, and stagehands followed suit. Banks closed. Elevators quit running. Schools did not hold classes. Restaurant and grocery store doors stayed shut. Neither streetcar bells nor taxi horns broke the silence.

Even so, the strike's goals remained vague. An editorial in the *Union Record* proclaimed that Eastern capitalists would surely notice as Seattle's workers organized

to feed the people, to care for the babies and the sick, to preserve order—*this* will move them, for this looks too much like the taking of power by the workers. . . . And this is why we say we are starting on a road that leads—No One Knows Where!

No one ever found out. The strike ended quietly although its basic confrontation continued and even intensified. Seattle's mayor, Ole Hanson, went on the lecture circuit and wrote a book, *Americanism versus Bolshevism.* The *Union Record*'s editorialist, Anna Louise Strong, moved to Moscow. Seattle had entered the industrial era.

(For the labor movement, also see under CENTRALIA on p. 387; under EVERETT on p. 254; and WASHINGTON WOBBLIES sidebar, p. 255.)

Seattle invites exploration in various forms. For an overview of the city, go high: enjoy the interplay of salt water, fresh water, and hills backdropped by mountains. For a more intimate look, go low: walk along the beach at Alki Point or the green strip of Myrtle Edwards Park north of the central waterfront; visit the locks; rent a

rowboat on Lake Union; or ride the ferry to Bremerton or the excursion boat to Blake Island.

Points of interest, keyed to the Seattle map:

1   Seattle's pioneering settlers spent their first winter at **Alki Point** but, by spring, blustery winds and poor anchorage drove them into the shelter of Elliott Bay. A plaque at the point (Harborview and 63rd) marks where they first landed in 1851. Today their sandy beach is popular, especially in summer, and a lighthouse (built in 1916) serves as a navigational aid. It now is automated; visitors are welcome on weekends.

2   **Pioneer Square** (James and Yesler at First) forms the heart of old Seattle. Here stood Yesler's mill; Yesler Way developed from its logging skid road. Here, too, were early settlers' homes and businesses. Skewed intersections along Yesler Way are reminders of the boundary quarrel between Henry Yesler and David Maynard: the two men laid out plats parallel to the beach and neither would compromise to allow streets to meet at right angles.

By the mid-1970s the area, long abandoned as a business center, had become a decrepit neighborhood of handsome, vacant buildings. Private and public restoration projects have fostered a rebirth of vitality. An iron and glass **pergola,** built in 1909 to shelter people waiting for streetcars, has been restored, and a drinking fountain originally intended for horses now serves thirsty humans. A **totem pole** carved in Alaska in 1940 replaces a pole stolen in 1899 from a supposedly abandoned Tlingit village by a Chamber of Commerce committee on a "good will visit." When that pole burned 40 years later, its charred hulk was shipped north to be copied.

An **Underground Tour** (610 First) leads to abandoned shops and streets buried by the 1890s regrading of the area. (Modest fee; wear comfortable shoes.) Two blocks south, a small, National Park Service **Klondike Gold Rush Museum** (117 S. Main) features displays and slide shows highlighting the experiences of 1890s miners who stampeded north through Seattle.

Several individual buildings in the district merit special attention. Among them are the brick and stone **Pioneer Building** (606 First; built in 1890), designed by Elmer Fisher, who

Seattle

Key to Numbered Locations

1 Alki Point
2 Pioneer Square
3 Smith Tower
4 U.S. Coast Guard Museum
5 Alaska Marine Highway Terminal
6 Public Landing
7 Colman Dock
8 Ye Olde Curiosity Shop
9 Blake Island
10 Schwabacher's Dock
11 Waterfront Park
12 Pike Place Market
13 Arctic Building
14 Rainier Club
15 Olympic Hotel
16 Seattle Tower
17 Freeway Park
18 Fifth Avenue Theater
19 Bon Marche
20 International District
21 Seattle Center
22 Maritime Heritage Center
23 Discovery Park
24 *Virginia V*
25 Ballard
26 Hiram Chittenden Locks
27 Golden Gardens Park
28 Woodland Park
29 Gas Works Park
30 Burke-Gilman Trail
31 University of Washington
32 Museum of History and Industry
33 Washington Park Arboretum
34 Lake Washington Boulevard
35 Volunteer Park
36 Museum of Flight

Not all streets shown

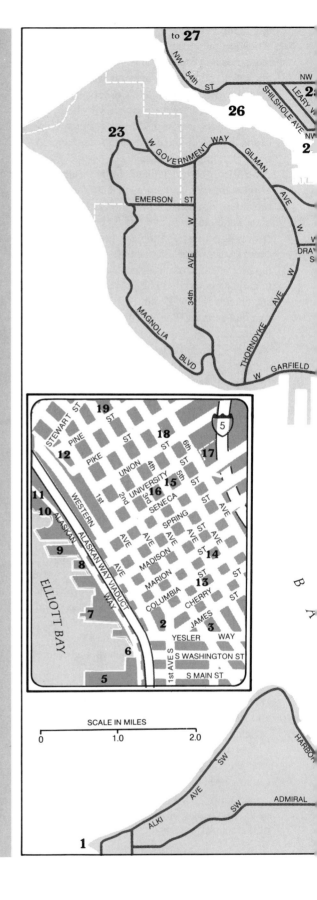

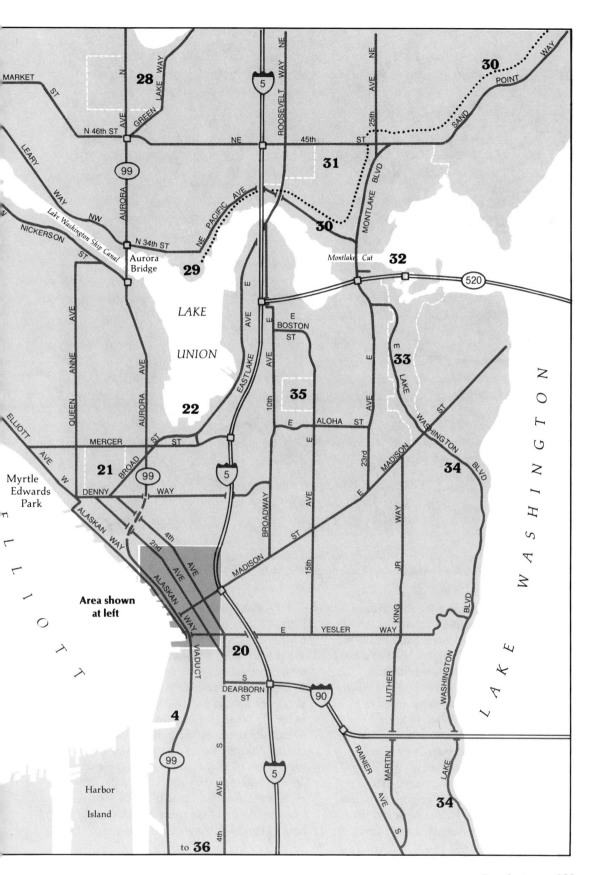

The ornate Iron Pergola at Pioneer Square was built to shelter people waiting for streetcars. (Notice the Smith Tower showing through the pergola's glass roof.)

reportedly was responsible for 50 buildings within a year after Seattle's disastrous 1889 fire; and the brick **Grand Central Building** (208 First Avenue S.; built in 1889), used as a hotel until 1968 and one of the first restoration projects in the Pioneer Square district. When the fire leveled it, Seattle was in the midst of a boom that was strong enough to finance immediate—and excellent—rebuilding with relatively fireproof materials. As business shifted uptown about the time of World War I, activity at Pioneer Square changed to warehousing and cheap housing for transients and down-and-outers. Neglect cost less than demolition, an irony that saved the district.

3 Among Seattle's most beloved landmarks is the 42-story **Smith Tower** (Yesler at Second; built in 1914). The fourth tallest building in the world when new, it dominated Seattle's skyline until construction of the Space Needle in 1962. In addition to admiring the gleaming terra-cotta facade, be sure to step into the lobby for a look at the tile floor, Mexican onyx wall paneling, beautifully rendered Indian heads (molded in plaster), and the bank of elaborate copper and brass doors closing the elevators (all elevators are still operated manually). Ask at the lobby cigar stand about access to the 35th-floor Chinese room and observation deck circling the base of the tower (small fee). Visitors are welcome when the room is not in use. Exquisite jade screens and a deeply carved ceiling are justly renowned. The Chinese room originally was used as a restaurant.

Lyman Cornelius Smith, of typewriter fame, commissioned the building partly as an investment, partly to publicize his typewriter company.

4   The **U.S. Coast Guard Museum** (a white, two-story building on the waterfront at the foot of Atlantic) displays photographs, uniforms, and models of ships, including the Revenue Service cutter *Jefferson Davis,* which patrolled Puget Sound from 1853 to 1862. Coast Guard vessels stationed here often are open to visitors on weekend afternoons.

On the fourth floor of the Coast Guard Building next to the museum, the Vessel Traffic Service directs ships in the Seattle harbor, much as air traffic control towers direct planes at an airport. Visitors are welcome to watch a slide show and view the sweeping radar screens.

5   At the **Alaska Marine Highway Terminal** (foot of S. Main), be sure to follow the painted line leading out to the end of the wharf. What appear from a distance as misplaced steamship funnels are actually giant periscopes that offer a high-angle view of the adjacent Port of Seattle container cargo docks. Reader boards describe the port's shipping history.

6   The roofed **Public Landing** (foot of Washington Street) has a small-boat tie-up and an adjoining pocket park that overlooks ferry and shipping traffic. Tlingit carvers at Haines, Alaska, carved the totem pole for the park in 1976.

7   **Colman Dock** (foot of Columbia) today serves ferries bound for Bremerton and Bainbridge Island; formerly, the dock accommodated Mosquito Fleet steamers, which interconnected communities throughout Puget Sound. Farmers brought their produce to market by steamer; mothers led children on shopping expeditions; and professionals commuted from country homes to city offices. (See also VIRGINIA V, p. 296.)

8   **Ye Olde Curiosity Shop** (foot of Spring) has become a curiosity itself by virtue of eccentricity and longevity. Since 1899 Seattleites and tourists have come to the shop to delight in mummies, stuffed mooseheads, dressed fleas, basketry, scrimshaw, souvenir postcards, and pinheads inscribed with the Lord's Prayer.

9   Excursion boats connect to **Blake Island** (foot of Seneca), a state park where Native Americans present traditional dances and salmon feasts at a cedar longhouse. The island is roadless: deer graze meadows, waves lap the shore, gulls call, and drumbeats coming from the longhouse echo the past. Camping is permitted. The return trip to Seattle offers outstanding views, especially at night with the lights shining across the water.

10   **Schwabacher's Dock** (foot of Union) is now marked by a small park and two plaques. In 1896 the *Miike Maru* arrived here from Japan, opening regularly scheduled steamship service between Seattle and Asia. The following year, the S. S. *Portland* tied up, bringing a cargo of gold. That arrival set off a gold rush to the Klondike and Alaska and eased Seattle out of financial doldrums.

11   At **Waterfront Park** (foot of Pike) observation towers, benches, and flowerpots invite pausing. Next to the park, the **Seattle Aquarium** offers an introduction to Puget Sound marine life. Its displays include a tidepool "touch tank" and glass-sided pools with sea otters and fur seals (the two species hunted during the days of the Northwest maritime fur trade of the 1780s and 1790s).

From here, the Pike Place Market is accessible on foot via flights of stairs (across from the aquarium), and Pioneer Square virtually joins the waterfront about 10 blocks to the south (at Yesler). Waterfront activity has gradually shifted southward during the last century. Large open-space wooden buildings standing on wharves—called transit sheds—formerly received cargo from the holds of sailing ships. Later focus shifted to brick, multistoried warehouses where cargoes brought by steamship awaited transshipment to trains. These buildings, now under the Alaskan Way Viaduct, have become shops and restaurants. South of them, today's giant Port of Seattle cranes lift cargo containers onto asphalt lots, where they wait in the open air until shipped to their final destinations.

12   **Pike Place Market** (First Avenue at Pike) hums with activity, as it has since 1907.

A covered arcade shelters stalls where fish, fruit, and vegetables mound in voluptuous array. Small restaurants and spice shops perfume the air. Silversmiths, potters, and artists sell their wares. Street musicians add sounds of joy.

The market began as an outlet for farmers from throughout the region; they arrived by boat, wagon, and truck. Until permanent buildings and stalls appeared in 1917, vendors displayed produce in the beds of vehicles backed to the curb. Enormous change came with World War II as Japanese American farmers, who predominated at the market, were forced off their farms and into relocation camps (see under PUYALLUP on p. 321). After the war, supermarkets and frozen foods changed the city's eating habits, and the market and its neighborhood declined. In the 1960s, urban renewal came close to turning the market into a parking lot. A grass-roots movement led by architect Victor Steinbrueck objected—and prevailed.

Ornamentation on the Arctic Building is typical of Seattle's terra-cotta legacy.

13 The richly ornamented **Arctic Building** (Third and Cherry; built in 1917) warrants a look upward: walrus heads gaze down from the third story. Their original terra-cotta tusks were removed after an earthquake in 1949 but have been replaced by lightweight fiberglass tusks that are screwed tightly into place. The architects for this building pioneered the use of terra-cotta panels over a steel and reinforced-concrete frame. Until the late 1930s terra cotta was prized because it is malleable, can be tinted, and is lighter and cheaper than stone. Furthermore, molds could be reused to make duplicates of whatever panels and motifs were needed.

The Arctic Club, an exclusive group of Seattleites who had profited from the Klondike gold rush, met in the building. In the club dining room, billiards room, and ladies' tearoom members reminisced about the North and laid plans for Seattle's future. Rooms now have been converted to offices, but many of their original appointments remain in place.

14 The **Rainier Club** (Fourth and Marion; built in 1904) was originally organized in 1888, the city's first strictly recreational and social retreat for men—meaning, of course, those with appropriate backgrounds. In their club rooms, civic and business leaders played cards and dominoes in a setting of overstuffed chairs, fireplaces, hunting trophies, and photos of balding past presidents. Camaraderie rather than specific business was the purpose of coming together. Today's membership tends to place more emphasis on business than social status, and gender and racial barriers have been eliminated. Additional clubs now augment the once-staid Rainier Club. The top two floors of the 76-story Columbia Center, Seattle's tallest building, are the sole domain of the Columbia Tower Club where members and guests banter about the justly famed ladies' room with its glorious floor-to-ceiling window and toilet stalls with glassy, high-elevation views of the city (particularly bewitching at night).

15 The **Olympic Hotel** (Fourth and Seneca; built in 1924, meticulously restored in 1982) has epitomized Seattle's elegance for three generations. Locally financed—organizers raised $2.7 million in 24 days—the hotel accommodated 2,000 top-hatted and bejewelled patrons at its opening. Its lobby boasts oak paneling and a vaulted ceiling bright with gilt; the Georgian Room has an impressive English Renaissance chandelier; the skylight Garden Court is a pleasant setting for tea and a pastry.

For the building's exterior, architects directing restoration specified glass-reinforced concrete to emulate the old terra cotta. A combination of fiberglass threads and wet concrete blown into molds, this material is even lighter than terra cotta and capable of finer modeling.

16 All who admire Art Deco architecture will want to look at the lobby of the **Seattle Tower** (Third and University; built in 1929). Its walls are marble, its ceiling gilt. Motifs are Mayan, Chinese, and Northwest Native American. Twenty-five stories high, the building stood along with the Smith Tower as a soaring beacon of Seattle's urban maturity. Before World War II buildings of such height were unusual.

17 **Freeway Park** (Seneca and I-5; built in 1976) provides a man-made oasis of green amid towering steel and glass buildings. (Walk into the park from Seneca and Sixth; or park under it by entering a lot off Spring Street.) In the spirit of the Olmsted Brothers' early 1900s plans, the park offers office workers and foot-weary city visitors a haven. A glass viewpoint beneath the flowing water of an artificial stream allows a glimpse of cars hurtling along I-5.

18 The serene facade of the **Fifth Avenue Theater** (Fifth and Union; built in 1926) belies an elaborate Chinese-style interior. The decor mimics the throne room of Beijing's Imperial Palace by featuring an elaborate, coffered ceiling and lavish gold ornamentation. A dragon coils around a dome twice the size of that in the Forbidden City. A chandelier hangs from its open jaw.

The Fifth Avenue seated 2,400 when it opened as a movie palace. Usherettes dressed in black slacks and silk tunics led the way with flashlights carefully pointed at the floor.

Over the years television replaced moviegoing and, by 1978, the Fifth Avenue Theater seldom drew a full house. It closed for two years for refurbishing, then reopened as a performing arts center.

19 The Art Deco **Bon Marché** (Fourth and Pine; built in 1930) stands at the north end of Seattle's retail district. A copper marquee above its main entrance—embellished with motifs of underwater life—protects shoppers from drizzly weather. Inside, a wavelike motif continues on the main floor ceiling. Opened in 1890, the Bon Marché represents a hometown success story. Edward Nordhoff, who began his retail career in Paris, started the company; his widow guided it through the booms associated with the Alaska gold rush and the Spanish-American War.

20 The **International District** (east of the Kingdome and north of Dearborn) is characterized by small shops, benevolent association offices, travel agencies offering special fares to Asia, family homes, and children's playgrounds. People of all ages and cultures share the sidewalks: a Chinese grandmother wearing a brocade jacket, a middle-aged Southeast Asian woman in traditional folk costume, a chic Japanese teenager with swinging hair and dark glasses.

For a sense of the district's people—Chinese, Japanese, Filipino, Korean, and Southeast Asian—visit the **Wing Luke Museum** (407 Seventh Avenue; opened in 1966 in a renovated 1930s garage). Also attend a theater performance at **Nippon Kan Theater** (622 S. Washington; built in 1909). To reach the theater, walk up the steep path from Main Street and Seventh Avenue past the family vegetable plots and flowering cherry trees of Kobe Terrace Park. The building's flexible wooden floor was designed to withstand the impact of sumo wrestlers. The stage was used primarily by local amateur groups performing Japanese drama, music, and dance. Upstairs, small rooms housed new immigrants—mostly single men—until they found jobs and moved on. (See EAST TO AMERICA sidebar, p. 294.)

21 **Seattle Center** (on Fifth from Denny Way to Mercer; built in 1962) occupies the site of the world's fair called "Century 21." Its

EAST TO AMERICA

Filipinos came as a third wave of immigrants to travel east to America. In Washington the Chinese—who came first—arrived mostly between the 1860s and the 1880s. By 1882 an Exclusion Act—to protect American workmen from the competition of cheap labor—barred legal entry for Chinese laborers. It did not, however, stop smugglers from bringing them in from Canada. Chinese merchants and scholars were unaffected by the law.

Japanese immigrants followed the Chinese and, to some extent, replaced them in the labor market. They came in the greatest numbers during the 1890s. In Seattle they formed their own neighborhood at the edge of the International District, followed their own customs, and differed markedly from their Chinese predecessors with regard to family life: Japanese custom and American law allowed them to send home for wives—the renowned picture brides, who joined their new husbands with no more acquaintance than an exchange of photographs. Chinese immigrants—almost exclusively single men—came expecting to return home, although many never could afford to do so. Japanese immigrants came to stay. Impoverishment motivated both groups to make the move.

Beginning in the 1920s, large numbers of Filipinos came to America, especially from the northern province of Iloco where poverty was rampant. Most, however (even from there), came with a different motivation: education. After the Philippines became a United States protectorate in 1902, American teachers spread throughout the islands teaching English and instilling American ideals. After 300 years of Spanish colonization the islanders were familiar with Western ways, but village people had not been educated. This changed under American rule, and the Philippine government offered stipends for students who wanted to further their education abroad.

Once in Seattle, many of them had unique experiences. For example, one newcomer stepping off the ship heard a newsboy calling out *"P-I, P-I,"* bought a newspaper and was disappointed to find that *P-I* stood for *Post-Intelligencer,* not Philippine Islands. Many other experiences here repeated those of earlier immigrants. Filipinos drew prejudice and could find only low-paying jobs, usually arranged through labor contractors, who often were abusive. Those who enrolled at the university found only menial jobs open to them, such as stewards at fraternities and sororities, houseboys for wealthy families, or dishwashers and cooks at restaurants. Juan Dionisio reminisced that he was refused a milk shake in a University District shop and that he "went to the barbershop and was told, 'We don't cut your Filipino hair; you go to Chinatown.' "

Most supported themselves as migrant seasonal laborers, traveling to California farms and Alaska canneries. Some gave up their expectations of education, others held onto the dream. Chris Mensalves, who came to study law, remembers:

Those contractors were right there on the dock. They want you to work for them. So, as newcomers, where else can you go? . . . The worst part, the contractors came and pick you up on the docks: "Okay boys, let's go." We don't even know where we were going. . . . They took us to the camps. Those camps were terrible. But where else can you go when you just come from the Philippines? You have to stay there under their conditions.

Northwest Seaport/Maritime Heritage Center is home port for the 165-foot lumber schooner Wawona, *one of two vessels remaining from a fleet of 500. Restoration is underway; open daily.*

Space Needle (modest fee) offers an observation deck and restaurants. The Pacific Science Center includes a hands-on "exploratorium" for children. A monorail, remnant of the 1962 expo, leads downtown.

In the late 1880s this land was a series of hills too steep for horse-drawn trams and therefore a barrier to development. In two muddy bursts of hydraulic activity from 1902 to 1911 and from 1929 to 1930, city engineers successfully sluiced the hill into the bay. Disgruntled property owners at first refused to sell—and found their homes isolated on pinnacles amid a sea of mud. An unquestioned engineering success, the newly flat land was not actually needed for downtown development, and it grew up in service companies, small apartment buildings, and nondescript offices.

22 The south end of Lake Union is home to the **Maritime Heritage Center,** which includes **Northwest Seaport** and the **Center for Wooden Boats.** At Northwest Seaport a nonprofit group currently owns and interprets three venerable Northwest vessels: the three-masted schooner *Wawona* (on site), which carried lumber down the coast; the 1889 tug *Arthur Foss* (moored in Kirkland), built to tow vessels across the Columbia River bar; and the 1904 lightship *Relief* (privately moored), which "relieved" the regular lightship off the Columbia River mouth. Plans call for showcasing all three vessels together.

Next to Northwest Seaport, a park overlooks the Center for Wooden Boats, which displays small, hand-built sailboats and rowboats that may be rented. The center also offers classes in boat building and, each July, sponsors the Lake Union Wooden Boat Festival.

23 **Discovery Park** (W. Government Way, reached via Gilman Avenue W.) occupies Magnolia Bluff, a peninsula northwest of the downtown district. **Daybreak Star Arts Center,** a gallery of Native American art and a performance hall, is accessible from the north parking lot via a half-mile forested trail. (If walking poses a problem, ask at the office for a vehicle permit.) An 1881 lighthouse stands at the tip of a sand-spit below the bluff. Buildings from Army days at **Fort Lawton**—plus a later radar station—overlook Puget Sound and are accessible via a footpath from the park's Emerson Street entrance.

The fort began in 1898 when loggers cleared land for a military installation. Seattle had lobbied energetically for it as a boost for the economy. The assistant quartermaster general urged approval for brick buildings, claiming that the city would be dissatisfied with wood and might feel, after their expense in donating the site, that "they should have as good a post as the government is building at San Francisco or Spokane [Fort George Wright]." His view did not prevail, however, and 12 years later wooden buildings ringed Fort Lawton's parade ground. The fort further disappointed boosters with a meager two to four companies in residence until World War II, when it became a major embarkation point for troops. Beginning in 1972 the federal government transferred large portions of the property to the city of Seattle.

24 The venerable 125-foot *Virginia V,* (901 Fairview Avenue N., south end of Lake Union, just east of the Wooden Boat Center) can be chartered for meetings and special occasions and for public cruises (modest fee); check the Seattle directory, and phone regarding current schedule. Some cruises are associated with events such as tugboat races held in Seattle in May and in Olympia in September. Others are events in themselves, such as summer jazz evenings afloat. Now a registered National Historic Landmark, the vessel is open to the public from Memorial Day to Labor Day while at its dock; other times by appointment.

Virginia V—the original owners' fifth vessel with that name—is the last of the steamships in Puget Sound's Mosquito Fleet and the last working passenger steamship on the entire Pacific Coast. Until 1939 she traveled seven days a week between Seattle and Tacoma with 13 stops along the Kitsap Peninsula en route. Web Anderson, former shipping agent, reminisced:

At Seattle's Colman Dock at 5:15 P.M. all these small vessels would pull out . . . one, two, three, four, five

. . . such congestion and activity, swarming like mosquitoes to carry commuters and supplies to the many ports of the Sound, Poulsbo, Fletcher Bay, Colby, Lisa Buela. There they would lay over, firing up early next morning to bring back to Seattle the banker who worked in the city, farmers with strawberries, women with chickens, the people and goods of regional commerce, and at 5 P.M. that day the scene was reenacted.

25 **Ballard**'s location shaped its municipal beginnings: city fathers laid out Ballard and Shilshole avenues parallel to the shore so that valuable waterfront lots could be efficiently subdivided. The result is a tangle of intersections where Old Ballard's grid meets newer, compass-oriented streets; be cautious.

Until 1907 Ballard remained distinct from Seattle—and an aura of small-town self-sufficiency still clings to Ballard Avenue. Two-story brick commercial buildings, many of them triangular or trapezoidal to fit the odd "blocks," are modestly ornamented with corbeled parapets or cast-iron medallions. They house businesses such as machine shops and hardware stores, mixed with woodcarvers' shops and art-glass studios. At the northwest end of the street, a trianglular park caps the view. It features the bell tower of the former city hall, which was demolished by an earthquake. The tower is now beautifully sited in the park, its blazing copper roof intact. The blocks near the intersection of Ballard Avenue and NW Market are lined with shops specializing in imported Scandinavian goods from kitchenware and food to furniture and wool. Voices still lilt with old-country accents.

Displays at the **Nordic Heritage Museum** (3014 NW 67th Street) portray Norwegian, Danish, Finnish, Swedish, and Icelandic immigrants' experience. Folk costumes, painted bentwood boxes, and finely crafted storage trunks bespeak the heritage they brought with them. One exhibit—with appropriately varied flooring of straw, wood, and cobbles—leads on a simulated journey of emigration: from a farm in Scandinavia, to a ship, arrival at Ellis Island in New York, a move to the Midwest, and finally to Ballard.

People came here in the late 1800s lured by knowledge that land in the United States was so plentiful the government was giving it away. Ballard, with sawmills and shingle mills and a fishing fleet, became a major haven, especially for Norwegians. A common jest was that a passport was required to cross the Ballard Bridge.

26 The **Hiram Chittenden Locks** are near Ballard (NW 54th Street and 32nd Avenue NW; begun in 1911, finished in 1917). They connect Puget Sound with Lake Union; from there, the Montlake Cut near the university connects to Lake Washington. On fine days onlookers line the railings to watch pleasure boats and small commercial vessels bob side by side as the locks gently lower or raise them. A fish ladder, seven-acre park, underwater viewing rooms, and museum enhance the site. (For the museum and the locks, drive to the Ballard side of the locks.)

The locks are named for Hiram Chittenden, district engineer for the Army Corps of Engineers, who designed them and urged congressional support. They opened on July 4, 1917, with Commodore Matthew Perry's flagship leading a boat parade through the locks and along the 8-mile ship canal to Lake Washington. Local citizens cheered from the shore and cast bouquets onto the water.

27 **Golden Gardens Park** beckons beach walkers and permits seaside views from the windshield of parked cars, ideal for brown-bag lunches on stormy days. (From the locks, follow the shoreline along NW 54th Street, then along Seaview Avenue NW, past the forest of masts at Shilshole Marina to the park entrance.)

28 **Woodland Park** (550 Phinney Avenue N.) began in the 1880s as the private estate of Guy Phinney, who kept a deer herd here. The city bought the land in 1899 and now has created a zoo ranked among the top 10 in the nation. It helped pioneer the display of compatible animal species in expansive natural settings; it also has an active rescue and release program for injured bald eagles.

Green Lake, ringed by a 2.8-mile trail, continues to draw model boat builders to test their vessels and youthful anglers to dangle lines from a special children's fishing pier—familiar activities here for generations. The land became a park in 1905.

29 At **Gas Works Park** (north shore of Lake Union, off Northlake Way N.), children clamber over the brightly painted machinery of a former gasworks; kite fliers run down the grassy slopes of a man-made hill; and lake watchers enjoy marine traffic. An interactive sundial at the top of the hill enlists the viewer's body as stylus.

In 1906 the gasworks here began turning first coal, then oil, into gas used by Seattle households for cooking and lighting. Fifty years later natural gas from Canada became a more economical source, and the city bought the 20-acre site here. It has become one of Seattle's most used parks.

30 Walkers, joggers, and bicyclists flock along the 12-mile **Burke-Gilman Trail** from Gas Works Park, along the edge of the University of Washington campus, to the north end of Lake Washington. The trail—which winds past bluffs, woods, and houses—features side-by-side paths. One is paved for bikes, the other graveled for walkers and joggers. The route follows the former roadbed of the Seattle, Lake Shore and Eastern Railroad, which was built in the early 1890s to tap Issaquah coal and the upper Snoqualmie Valley's timber.

31 On the 690-acre **University of Washington** campus (NE 45th Street between 15th Avenue NE and Lake Washington) mature landscaping and architecturally varied buildings please the eye and invite strolling. Several are of special interest. The **Burke Memorial Museum** (near the NE 45th Street entrance to the campus) presents especially fine displays of Northwest Native American material. Chateauesque **Denny Hall** (built in 1895) is the earliest building on campus. **Suzzallo Library** (built in 1927) is admired for its Gothic architecture. At **Savery Hall,** terra-cotta representations of mariners, miners, generals, and scholars crouch along the roofline; at **Smith Hall,** an ominous gas-masked face stares down from among other faces; and personifications of various academic disciplines crown the **Administration Building.** They include a bespectacled "Graduate Studies" figure above the entrance.

In preparation for the opening of the 1909 Alaska-Yukon-Pacific Exposition, landscaping by the prestigious Olmsted Brothers design firm turned virgin forest here into a park intended for use by the university after the fair. The Olmsted design can best be sensed from Rainier Vista,

The university's Drumheller Fountain, now nicknamed Frosh Pond, remains from the 1906 Expo. The buildings shown here were intended as temporary; four others were kept.

a sweeping promenade that leads the eye past circular **Drumheller Fountain** to distant Mount Rainier, a visual joining of Seattle with its unique natural setting. Appropriately, the four fluted columns of the original, downtown university building stand in a "sylvan theater" southeast of the fountain.

(A university visitor information center on the southeast corner of University Way NE and NE Campus Parkway posts notices regarding campus activities and events; in addition, traffic kiosks at campus entrances have maps available for the asking.)

32 The **Museum of History and Industry** (2700 24th Avenue E., at the lakeshore) explores Seattle's development through exhibits of pioneer days and of various industries. (From the south side of the Montlake Bridge, turn east on Lake Washington Boulevard, then quickly north on 24th Avenue, which dead-ends in the parking lot.)

A half-mile **Waterfront Trail** leaves from the museum's parking lot and winds across Foster and Marsh islands to the arboretum. Freeway traffic rushes nearby, but canoeists and muskrats paddle the waterways of the marsh, which is a haven for birds from wrens and red-winged blackbirds to bitterns and mallards. Joggers and pets are not welcome on the trail.

33 The **Washington Park Arboretum,** (threaded by Lake Washington Boulevard E.) displays both native and exotic flora and conducts botany research. Lake Washington Boulevard—one of the Olmsted Brothers' "driveways"—winds invitingly through the grounds, and paths lead strollers among the nearly 6,000 varieties of trees, shrubs, and flowers. A visitor center at the north end of Arboretum Drive E. offers maps and botany displays. A Japanese garden (southwest corner of the grounds; small fee) includes a teahouse used for tea ceremonies performed through the auspices of the Urasenke Foundation's Seattle branch. (Inquire about public tea ceremonies, usually held one Sunday afternoon a month, from April through October. Tea ceremony classes are available through the university.) An annual arboretum plant sale in April draws gardeners from throughout the Northwest.

The city acquired the arboretum's 600 acres in 1903. Thirty years later a working relationship was developed between the parks department, the university, and the private Arboretum Foundation. The Olmsted Brothers then designed the basic layout of the grounds, and armies of Works Progress Administration men hefted shovels and pushed wheelbarrows to produce the present physical configuration. According to the director during that development period:

Where Azalea Way now exists was an ugly cut-and-fill speedway for horse-racing; 10,000 or more man-hours of hand labor with wheelbarrows were used to bring back the original land contours; 500 railroad cars of cow manure and leafmold were spaded in.

34   Drive **Lake Washington Boulevard E.** between Seward Park and the arboretum to sense Seattle's delight in its watery location and for views of the Cascade Mountains. Parks dot the shore, some for swimming, some for boating, and one with hydroplane pits. Former bath-houses have been renovated as dance studios and art centers. Frequent pullouts allow pausing—and savoring the scene.

35   **Volunteer Park** (15th Avenue E. and E. Prospect) is the home of the Seattle Art Museum, famed for its Asian art collection and paintings by Northwest artists and for special programs and exhibits. Isamu Noguchi's doughnut-shaped sculpture "Black Sun" stands opposite the entry and frames the Space Needle, miniaturized by distance. A water tower (built in 1906) provides a panoramic view, and a glass conservatory (built in 1910) offers a tropical interlude any day of the year.

Seattle bought this land in 1887; 16 years later the Olmsted Brothers developed the "neat and smooth" park design still apparent. Fine houses near the park, built in the early 1900s by leading financiers and businessmen, are worth enjoying on a drive-by basis. Their architecture

Boeing's first passenger plane was a Model 40 with one open-air seat ahead of the pilot. It was built in 1927 when the government first allowed passengers to fly with the mail.

is as eclectic as the personalities who commissioned them. The houses include the blockish concrete mansion of millionaire Samuel Hill (814 E. Highland; built in 1903). Hill is particularly renowned as the builder of Maryhill, above the Columbia Gorge (see p. 160).

36 The **Museum of Flight** (I-5 Exit 158; 9404 E. Marginal Way S.) includes the Red Barn, the Boeing Company's oldest remaining building, and the 1980s Great Gallery. The Red Barn was built in 1909 as part of a shipyard along the Duwamish River, which then still flowed in its natural course. The building—of early balloon frame construction—still gives the feeling of a boat "loft." Today, historical photographs and a few splendidly restored early planes fill its space. The adjacent, ultra-modern Great Gallery displays 20 to 30 additional aircraft; some are suspended from the ceiling and can be viewed either from underneath or at eye-level from a mezzanine. Films run continuously. Aviation buffs will find pleasure in the intermittent parade of commercial aircraft taxiing on nearby runways, where they undergo final detailing and testing prior to delivery.

In 1910 William Boeing, heir to a Minnesota timber fortune, bought the Red Barn to complete construction of his yacht. When it was done, he started work on a wood-and-canvas plane for his own use, then decided to start an aircraft company. It became the gigantic Boeing Company. By 1957 nearly half of King County's paychecks came either directly from Boeing or from its suppliers. A 1970 recession curtailed aircraft orders and jolted the economy of the whole Northwest; a great number of the Boeing Company's employees lost their jobs. Diversification has now greatly strengthened the region's economy.

VASHON ISLAND presents an unpretentious face to the world. Architecture runs the gamut from 1890s farm houses to 1920s shingled cottages to 1990s cedar-and-glass view homes. Many families raise their own food: vegetable gardens are extensive and a family milk cow or a few goats are common sights. Modern occupations range from manufacturing skis to growing orchids, processing fruit juice, and making tofu. Yet many residents commute daily to Seattle or Tacoma for livelihood, and ferries connect the

northern and southern tips of the island with both cities. Maury Island is joined to Vashon by a narrow neck of land at Portage, where the view southwest across Quartermaster Harbor and northeast to Seattle is a worthy goal for an island drive.

The story of Vashon's settlement is clear only in light of the transportation realities of the day. When *no* Puget Sound settlements were linked by roads, Vashon was extraordinarily convenient. It was centrally located between Seattle and Tacoma and had a deep, protected harbor indenting its southern shoreline. Canoes, and later steamboats, plied the sound and Vashon lay on the main thoroughfare. However, as first railroads and then highways tied mainland cities to each other and to eastern Washington towns, Vashon became a backwater. Puget Sound changed from highway to moat, protecting privacy.

The earliest settler was Lars John Hansen, a Norwegian immigrant, who in the 1870s farmed with his native wife Katie where the Burton Peninsula begins its jutting into Quartermaster Harbor. Other settlers followed in the 1870s to cut timber and later to burn and blast the stumps and farm. In 1892 Miles F. Hatch, a Tacoma businessman, began a private college at **Burton,** where Hansen had pioneered. This institution inspired preparatory schools on Vashon to encourage young scholars, and it attracted students who commuted from Tacoma via Mosquito Fleet steamers. As attendance grew, the little town also flourished, but when the college buildings burned in 1910, the town languished.

On Maury Island another community grew up. **Dockton** took its name from its primary industry, a huge drydock—325 feet long, 100 feet wide, and 12 feet deep. Its owner began constructing the drydock in 1891 at Port Townsend but midway through incurred financial problems that forced him to seek other funds. Miles Hatch invested in the project and arranged for the drydock to be towed to Maury Island. Workers from Tacoma commuted by company steamer to complete the drydock and refurbish and build ships. The Panic of 1893 caused a slowdown, but four years later the Yukon gold rush gave a tremendous boost. Every vessel that could be salvaged was refitted to carry miners north. By 1910 competing businesses in larger city centers had stolen much of Dockton's business, and the drydock was moved to Seattle.

One employee, a ship designer named John Martinolich, stayed on to begin his own firm. Using the defunct drydock's ways, he opened a shipbuilding company and produced deep-draft fishing boats that became a standard design in Washington and southeast Alaska. He also built steamers for the Mosquito Fleet and during World War I completed three 235-foot schooners for the Norwegian government.

Today the false-fronted Dockton General Store (99th Avenue SW and Windmill Road) and the dilapidated Dockton Hotel (SW 260th off 99th Avenue SW), a boardinghouse for Martino-lich's workers, remain as reminders of the drydock and shipbuilding era. So does "Piano Row" (99th Avenue SW and Portage–Dockton Road; built in 1892), a group of houses built for the families of supervisors at the Puget Sound Drydock Company. Supposedly they received their nickname because only supervisors could afford pianos. Nothing remains from the shipyards.

WOODINVILLE lies on the banks of the Sammamish River where bicycle paths wind toward Lake Sammamish. Nearby a major winery occupies Hollywood, a former "gentleman's farm"; visitors are welcome to picnic on the grounds and tour the winery. (From I-405 take Exit 23, which leads to State Route 522 east. Take the Woodinville exit, turn right at the stop sign, and right again on NE 175. Cross the railroad tracks and turn left on State Route 202. Continue 2 miles to the winery.) The Hollywood School (14810 NE 146th Place; built in 1912) now houses shops.

In 1871 Ira and Susan Woodin took an 80-acre preemption claim on the Sammamish River, piled their belongings in a scow, and towed them by rowboat to the land. Their home soon became the post office/school/Sunday school for surrounding families. Ira Woodin opened a store. His wife tended the family cow and trekked to Seattle to sell butter, a journey that entailed a walk through the woods to Juanita, a

row across Lake Washington, and another walk to town.

After 1884 the Woodins enjoyed the comparative luxury of regularly scheduled stops by the steam scow *Squak,* which plied a route between Lake Washington and Lake Sammamish via the meandering Sammamish River. The *Squak* had to contend not only with shallow water but also with certain river bends—so sharp that the bow once grounded on one bank, the stern on the other.

In 1887 the Seattle, Lake Shore and Eastern Railroad improved Woodinville's transportation prospects. The town became a significant junction point, with passengers from the north changing trains here to continue their journeys to North Bend or Seattle.

In 1910 lumberman Frederick Stimson, whose family had pursued timber from the Midwest to the Northwest, bought stump-land south of Woodinville. Stimson's hobby, like that of his friend and Redmond neighbor James Clise, was an agricultural showpiece. Within four years a Craftsman-style home, a superintendent's house, and many farm buildings had replaced the stumps. Stimson also planted hundreds of holly trees, from which the farm took its name: Hollywood.

Holstein-Frisian dairy cattle lived in luxury here. Stimson bought only the best breeding stock, raised the animals and their offspring on scientifically regulated diets, and delighted in record-breaking cream and butter production. Another barn held Duroc-Jersey swine; when prices fell below the figure Stimson demanded for his prime piglets, he started a sausage business. A third division used scientific methods to raise thousands of leghorn chickens.

Mrs. Stimson's interests were horticultural. In state-of-the-art greenhouses she raised flowers for a retail florist shop she owned in Seattle. At first she shipped cut flowers to town on the daily milkwagon; later a railroad spur connected her greenhouses to the main line. Eventually Mrs. Stimson expanded into a wholesale business and shipped flowers to Alaska and Hawaii.

Tacoma Area

The Tacoma area embraces topography varying from Puget Sound islands to the summit of Mount Rainier, only 50 miles from one to the other, with winter dawns that cast the shadow of Rainier across the lowlands and onto the Olympic Mountains. Perhaps because it was the first hub of modern civilization on Puget Sound—owing to the Hudson's Bay Company post at Fort Nisqually—the area's story includes an extraordinary series of human dramas. They range from the first of the treaties with Native Americans in Washington Territory to a freedom-of-the-press issue involving a socialist colony at Home, a martial-law controversy at Steilacoom, the expulsion of Tacoma's Chinese community, and use of the Puyallup fair grounds as an assembly center for Japanese Americans during World War II.

The major historical museum of the area is the Washington State Historical Society Museum in Tacoma. Smaller museums are in DuPont, Fox Island, Mount Rainier National Park, and Steilacoom; a military museum is at Fort Lewis; and nineteenth-century homes in Puyallup and Sumner are open to the public. Festivals range from a traditional Fourth of July salmon bake at Point Defiance in Tacoma and the October apple squeeze in Steilacoom, to the Western Washington Fair in Puyallup (mid-September), one of the oldest fairs in the state.

The **ASHFORD** community forms a cluster of homes and businesses about 7 miles outside the Longmire-Paradise entrance to Mount Rainier National Park. It began with 1880s homesteads and scattered 1890s sawmills and became platted as a town in 1904 when the Tacoma Eastern Railway—a Chicago, Milwaukee, and St. Paul subsidiary—selected it as terminus. A

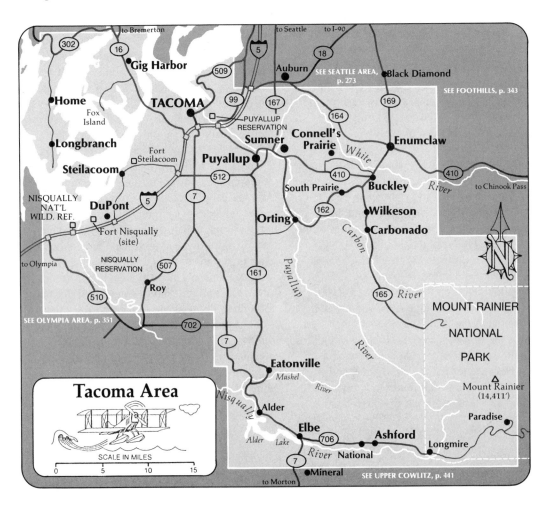

large mill at nearby National provided jobs and made Ashford a sizeable shipping center. In addition the railroad provided passenger service for tourists en route to Mount Rainier, where the company built and operated the Longmire National Park Inn.

The general route of the railroad and the earlier wagon road—and the present highway—followed a trail used by native people when traveling to the Yakima country east of the mountains.

A shingle mill at **BUCKLEY** provided employment beginning in the 1880s. Nearby coal mining also contributed to the economy, and agriculture included growing such fine peaches that the community held an annual Peacherino Festival. A Puget Sound Power and Light Company flume near Buckley diverts water from the White River into Lake Tapps, part of a hydropower project begun in 1910. A museum is on Main, southeast of River Road.

Homes at **CARBONADO** line a side road barely off the highway to the Carbon River entrance to Mount Rainier National Park. Most still show their origin as coal-company workers' housing, although individual approaches to remodeling include the addition of siding to cover the old clapboard, and porch uprights even more elaborately lathed than the original spindle uprights.

At the end of the main street (Pershing) a left turn on Railroad leads to a vault and a huge concrete foundation remaining from active mining days. A right turn on Railroad, then right again at the first road fork, leads to one of the state's most poignant cemeteries, nestled in a quiet valley. Headstones tell the story of Carbonado's people, ethnic origins, boomtime hopes, social organization, and tragedies. Ten stones in a back row carry the date, "December 9, 1899," and the words, "Killed by mine explosion." Names from Crivello and Vvotilla to McLaughlin and Llewellyn list birthplaces from Italy to Finland to Scotland and Wales.

In the 1880s coal from the Carbonado-Wilkeson field briefly made Tacoma the West Coast's major coaling station, and local investors felt pleased to have advanced financing for the rail line leading into the foothills.

Even after a geologist reported that coal at King County's Newcastle appeared more abundant and accessible than here, the mines continued production. The coal went to Tacoma, from where it was shipped to San Francisco for use by the Southern Pacific and Central Pacific railroads. The mines closed during the winter of

A photograph taken in 1891 shows the large scale of mining at Carbonado.

Grave markers evoke both Carbonado's ethnic mix and its tragic mine explosions.

1937–1938; one reopened briefly during World War II.

(Also see WILKESON, p. 341, for a discussion of coke ovens.)

CONNELL'S PRAIRIE. (See under SUMNER, p. 325.)

DUPONT—a residential area north of the Nisqually River delta—remains one of the state's most architecturally intact company towns. Its houses are now privately owned, but the community nonetheless retains a self-contained quality and an exceptionally orderly appearance (just west of I-5 at Exit 119).

Job status is reflected in the houses by size and design features, such as dormer windows and porch styles. Most workers' cottages have simple recessed porches that are like a bite out of one corner of the house (such as at 304 Louviers, 302 Barksdale, and 602 and 702 DuPont avenues). In contrast, the porches of managers' houses are protected by roof overhangs that run the length of the facade (202 and 210 Brandywine), and the assistant superintendent's house (101 Barksdale, just north of the entrance gate) has a gracious wrap-around veranda. The superintendent's house sits apart from all others, across the road from the assistant superintendent's. The former company store (Barksdale and Forcite) has been remodeled into apartments, and the butcher shop next to it now houses a historical museum.

In 1906 the E. I. du Pont de Nemours Company bought former Hudson's Bay Company land to use for the manufacture of nitroglycerine and black powder. The work began with single employees housed in railroad cars pulled onto special sidings and families living in neat tar-paper shacks. The Hudson's Bay Company house built for the chief factor at Fort Nisqually served as a community hall, and Japanese workers cutting cordwood lived in adjacent buildings at the old fort site. In 1906 the company built 56 houses and a few years later it added more.

About a mile of woodlands separated the village from the actual manufacturing, which took place in scattered, barricaded bunkers as a precaution against explosion. Oak and fir trees were kept for their value in breaking the force of possible explosions; herds of goats, cattle, and deer were maintained to control brush by browsing. Men hand-pushed rubber-tired cars on exceptionally smooth sidewalks to transport goods from one bunker to another, and employees had to wear special shoes with heels that were attached with wooden pegs rather than nails. Regulations forbade metal belt buckles. Overalls had no pockets—to guarantee that no one carried items that could rub against each other. Workers had to sign statements acknowledging that the company could search them or their possessions at any time for wooden matches. This applied even to their homes. Only safety matches were permitted.

In 1951, when commuting became feasible, the company sold the DuPont houses, mainly to employees. The plant closed in 1976, and the Weyerhaeuser Company bought the land. They have funded archaeological and historical studies. (Also see FORT NISQUALLY, p. 308.)

EATONVILLE began in 1889, when Thomas C. Van Eaton arrived via a trail long-used by the Nisqually tribe. He had come West from Minnesota three years earlier intending to start a town; the question was where. He found the "Harbor Country" (Aberdeen/Hoquiam) too rainy and decided to look at the open prairie country southeast of Tacoma. Along the Mashel River he met Henry Satulick, an aging Yakima native known as Indian Henry, who had moved

west of the mountains. He attracted other natives living off reservations to join him in forming a loosely knit village on what had been Upper Nisqually land (a sore point among people on the Nisqually Reservation, separated from their homeland). Van Eaton asked where a good place for a village would be and, in effect, got the answer "Here."

He opened a trading post and at first dealt mostly with native people, accepting furs and venison—and occasionally flecks of gold—in exchange for blankets, rifles, bacon, flour, and beans. The gold apparently came from a placer deposit Satulick and others worked as they needed it. They never revealed the location (although there are persistent tales of gold recovered from the gizzards of chickens on one particular homestead known to local people). About the only white settlers in the area when Van Eaton arrived were former Hudson's Bay Company men married to native women. Scandinavians soon came to the Ohop Valley, however, and Germans to the Alder and Elbe area. Van Eaton supplied outlying homesteaders by packtrain or let those who came to town load

Millponds, such as this one near Eatonville, were common through the 1950s; by then, improved mechanization began permitting men to handle logs on land rather than in the water.

their purchases onto one of his horses, lead it home, and then turn it loose to find its way back as far as 30 miles through the forest.

After the Tacoma Eastern Railway arrived in 1904, logging could begin. Before that there was no way to bring in machinery or to ship out lumber. The Alder area, where cedar was abundant, specialized in shingle mills including—for a while—a 10-block mill equipped with a saw that went in a circle and cut shingles from 10 separate bolts of cedar at a time. Tie mills were small operations readily moved from place to place; they produced short timbers for railroad ties and telegraph pole crossarms. The National mill (near Ashford) specialized in long timbers, once even sawing three pieces that measured three feet square by 150 feet long for the Ford Motor Company in Dearborn, Michigan.

It took a man six months just to locate suitable trees for these timbers. To get them to Dearborn the train had to be routed over tracks with as few sharp curves as possible. Three flatcars carried the timbers, which rested on the first and third cars, leaving the middle car free to accommodate to the tracks. Fire codes demanded such timbers for factory roof supports because steel beams would heat through and collapse in a fire, whereas wooden beams held until burned completely through.

By 1910 the Eatonville Lumber Company became a huge operation with 300 employees and a lumber inventory of about 10 million board feet on hand in its yard. The town had grown "really important," as remembered by old-timers in the surrounding area. "It was where the stores were—even a candy store, jewelry shop, music store, two shoemakers (one doing nothing but make boots for loggers); movies, restaurants, cars, a hospital."

Twice the mill and lumberyard burned, yet managed to resume operation—until 1954 when all the timber available to the company had been cut. The mill still stands, today used for raising chickens—somehow appropriate, for "chicken-dinner inns" were formerly a prime attraction along the approach road to Mount Rainier. The mill's "tepee" burner also stands, a monument to incalculable thousands of cords of wood considered waste.

Near Eatonville three points of interest warrant particular attention: Visitors are welcome at **Pack Forest,** a research unit of the University of Washington College of Forestry (about 3 miles from town near the junction of State Routes 7 and 161). A 7-mile drive looping through the forest is open daily except for weekends and during deer-hunting season; entry on foot is permitted even when the road is closed. Highlights include an arboretum and a grove of old-growth Douglas fir, a cascading waterfall on the Mashel River, and—from Hugo Peak or High Point, accessible by road or trail—outstanding views of Mount Rainier and even of Seattle/Tacoma and the Olympic Mountains if the day is exceptionally clear. Just inside the entrance is a walk-through model of the watershed built at a 1:100 scale. An interpretive center beyond the gatehouse explains the research under way in the forest.

The **Pioneer Farm Museum** is on Ohop Valley Road about 2 miles west of Eatonville (open daily in summer, also spring weekends; small fee). Hands-on tours let kids—or anyone—jump in the hayloft of a barn, pound horseshoes at a blacksmith's forge, churn butter, and use a spud to remove bark from a log. A Nisqually longhouse shelters demonstrations of native crafts, and a hatchery on the Mashel River presents the story of salmon, from native stories of the dream-time when people and animals were one, to the present-day need to restore the spawning runs of overfished rivers and creeks.

Northwest Trek (about 6 miles north of Eatonville, off State Route 161; small fee) is a unit of the Tacoma zoo dedicated in 1975 to display native Northwest animals in free-roaming, ecological combinations. The land was donated by Dr. David Hellyer and his wife Connie, Tacomans who bought raw, cutover stumpland here in 1937 and used it as a tree farm and cattle ranch until getting the idea for a native-species wildlife park. A 5½-mile, hour-long tour via tram now loops the park and an interpretive center houses displays and special programs.

ELBE (El'-bee) today is best known for its scenic steam train ride to Mineral (14 miles) and a tiny, but classic, Lutheran church, built in 1906 to serve German settlers. Measuring only

18 by 24 feet, the church has six rows of pews, which seat a total of 40 to 50 people, a diminutive altar rail, and an organ. Plans for the church were drawn by its pastor, Reverend Karl Killian, who rode the train from Puyallup to Elbe (40 miles) to hold services in German and attend to the parish. Local people volunteered their labor and much of the materials needed for the church. Even the iron cross on the steeple originated locally, forged by the community blacksmith Levi Engel. Before the Tacoma Eastern Railroad arrived, all public programs in the area, from religious services to community dances and elections, had been held in the Elbe town hall. With the increasing population brought by the railroad, however, people felt ready for "real" churches. Homesteader Henry Lutkens gave some of his land for the church.

A series of boardinghouses and restaurants accommodated tourists and the men who worked at various small mills in the area. Fires eventually destroyed almost all of them, including the 48-room, three-story Interbitzen Hotel owned by Lutkens. It had opened at Elbe in 1909, the same year the road up the canyon of the Nisqually River was completed.

Roads had long been an issue here, as is true in any isolated community. They had begun with a wagon road from Spanaway to Longmire, in places so steep it rose 25 feet in a hundred running feet and required three good horses to pull less than a ton of weight. Much of the surface was "corduroy," logs laid crosswise to provide a bumpy surface only slightly better than miring hub-deep in mud. The *Elbe Union* in 1896 published a 10-stanza "poem" that began:

> A great many had grown weary
> of the way so steep and dreary,
> Thinking life would be more cheery
> with an easier way to go
> To the mountain white with snow.

In 1926 the road was paved, the same year that passenger rail service to Mount Rainier stopped.

ENUMCLAW (Ee′-num-claw) today has a pleasant rural atmosphere with dairy farms and views of Mount Rainier, yet also with easy access to Tacoma and Seattle. Native American life in the area dates to at least 6,000 years ago, for archaeologists have found stone tools and fire hearths beneath the Osceola mudflow, a great outpouring of mud and rock that originated near the summit of Mount Rainier and overrode an area of about 65 square miles.

White settlement began in the mid-1850s when several bachelors claimed land following the close of the Puget Sound War. About 1870 James McClintock canoed up the Duwamish and Green rivers, then followed a trail onto the Enumclaw plateau and picked land for a farm. He returned to Scotland to marry and brought his bride here. Others also homesteaded, including Frank Stevenson and his wife, who filed in 1879 on the land that now forms the heart of town. A coal miner, Stevenson had left Cornwall, England, for Canada, then gone to the Pennsylvania mines and on to the Wilkeson mines, where he earned the cash needed to start a farm.

In 1883 as work on the Northern Pacific main line got under way in the area, the Stevensons built a hotel and started giving away lots to encourage other businesses. With a ready-built town available, they reasoned—correctly—that the railroad company would pick Enumclaw for a siding. Supposedly, an engineer grading the line asked what people were calling their town and expressed weariness with names ending in "ville." This led to "Enumclaw," the native name for a nearby mountain.

In 1889 Danish farmers began making dairy farms out of land already cleared by loggers. They operated as a cooperative patterned after farm organizations in the old country. Soon a cooperative cannery and milk condensery opened, then a Rochdale-plan store which sold everything from dry goods to automobiles according to an idealistic Socialist formula that called for members to buy shares and divide profits among them.

In the early 1900s the White River Lumber Company bought a planing mill that had burned and developed it into one of the largest and most progressive lumber operations in the state. They encouraged workers with families, who lived in their own homes and shopped at their own stores rather than relying on the company for personal arrangements as well as jobs.

Fertile land and coal-mine jobs attracted a

Stubs of Fort Nisqually's palisade were excavated as part of Weyerhaeuser Real Estate Company's archaeological and historical studies. The site is permanently protected.

cemetery turn west off the Enumclaw–Black Diamond highway on 400th Street.)

At **FORT NISQUALLY** white settlers established their first cultural hub on Puget Sound; native people were living here at least 5,000 years earlier, according to radiocarbon dating. Today the venerable site has become Northwest Landing, a modern community with homes, businesses, and infrastructure planned in advance. The village of Dupont is immediately adjoining (see p. 304).

The origins of the fort date from fall 1832, when Archibald MacDonald traveled from Fort Vancouver to Fort Langley (on the Fraser River). Chief factor John McLoughlin had instructed him to find a midway location for a station: "Your first objective is to observe if the Soil is suitable for cultivation and the raising of cattle; the next, the convenience the situation affords for Shipping."

The Nisqually area fit the requirements. MacDonald later wrote that he and his men "applied about 12 days of our time" to building a storehouse at the mouth of Sequalitchew Creek (just north of the Nisqually delta). There he left three men "in charge of a few blankets, a couple kegs of potatoes and a small amount of garden seeds." The post soon expanded, and in eight months gathered 1,800 beaver and river otter skins, "not a bad beginning," as chief trader Francis Heron wrote in a letter. Exchange rates included 16 buttons for four raccoon pelts, three buttons for seven trout, two hoes for one bear skin, and six spans of brass wire for 11 baskets.

Sequalitchew villagers changed irrevocably by virtue of this attraction at their doorstep. Trade delegations from distant tribes had to be entertained—so many that the local people could scarcely attend to getting in fish and berries and roots for the winter. Furthermore, many of them took jobs clearing land, burning brush, building fences, digging potatoes, and herding and clipping sheep: livelihood came directly into their hands without involving any chiefs, an unheard of system. Several persons already of high rank gained added status. La-halet, Sequalitchew headman, could take a fifth wife in 1838, cementing a trade and ceremonial relationship with yet another group.

colony of Slavonians (Yugoslavs) who settled north of Enumclaw at Krain. Miners' wives with farm produce to sell walked the railroad tracks carrying vegetables, fruit, eggs, and cream to towns such as Black Diamond and Franklin. Each Halloween night, Krain families still light candles and say the rosary at the community cemetery, an old-country custom. (To reach the

Such marriages were common—indeed, gaining trade advantages was an accepted reason for marriages between native women and Hudson's Bay Company men.

As early as 1829 John McLoughlin, in charge of the entire Columbia district, proposed supplementing the declining fur trade with what he called the Oragan [Oregon], Tallow and Hide Company, which would raise livestock on Puget Sound prairie land. The company's London Committee saw the possibilities of profit, changed the name to Puget's Sound Agricultural Company, and eventually gave a go-ahead. Ships might better return to England with a cargo than with stones as ballast. Furthermore, the Russians had begun to favor an offer for the Hudson's Bay Company to supply Alaska with farm products and tallow. Shipments from California had dwindled as Mexican influence waned and native workers left the formerly productive mission farms, and as the fields failed at the Russians' own outpost, Fort Ross (75 miles north of San Francisco).

The Hudson's Bay Company decided to fill the Alaskan void rather than leave it to Yankee sea captains. At Nisqually their agricultural emphasis was always on livestock, although herds were moved quarterly to "manure the land." The company continually planted wheat, oats, barley, peas, and potatoes—and continually felt disappointed with the crops. Sheep first came by sea in 1838 from Mexican ranchos and company posts in California: 160 head out of 800 died en route. Three years later the company drove livestock overland from California with comparable losses, mostly while crossing rivers and ravines. Eventually about 12,000 sheep, 3,000 cattle, and 300 horses grazed the Puget's Sound Agricultural Company land.

Farmers came to Nisqually from the Red River colony in Canada but, as at Cowlitz Farm (see p. 396), all of them left within a few years of arrival. They had been promised houses, barns, fenced land, implements, seeds, and livestock, but when the immigrants arrived at Fort Vancouver in the fall of 1841, the company told them the promise could not be kept. John Flett, the only Red River settler to eventually make his home in the Nisqually area, wrote that he even had to travel to Fort Vancouver for iron to make his own plow that first year.

Until the boundary treaty in 1846, farms leased to loyal subjects offered the British an additional frail hope of holding control of land north of the Columbia River. They turned to a concept of a yeoman-farm community, although it really was too late to stem the American tide. Among the few to attempt the life was Joseph Heath, a poignant figure from England who took over one of the farms abandoned by a Red River settler. Eldest son of a country squire, he had gambled away the family fortune. His brother, an officer on a Hudson's Bay Company ship, told him about opportunities at Nisqually and, in the summer of 1844, Heath leased 640 acres. For five years he made a lonely try at redeeming himself. At first he wrote that he was developing his farm "in splendid isolation and [with] repentant dedication." But later he wrote grimly of sitting

by the fire in the evening . . . anything but happy. Having no letters . . . constantly haunts my mind. Rain, gales, frost. . . . Can it be that I am entirely forgotten?

On March 7, 1849, Heath died, aged 44.

By then Britain no longer dominated the region north of the Columbia River. The Puget's Sound Agricultural Company still controlled land, but was plagued by American squatters who ignored trespass notices, tore down fences, drove off and even shot company livestock. An American Methodist mission had operated just outside the fort from 1839 to 1841, although the Reverend John Richmond and wife, together with assistant John Willson and wife, gained no converts and took no pleasure in frontier life.

They were still at the mission when Navy Lieutenant Charles Wilkes, leader of the U.S. Exploring Expedition, accepted the Hudson's Bay Company's offer to let him use Fort Nisqually as a base for explorations of lower Puget Sound. The company hoped to demonstrate how firmly entrenched they were—and they made their point. Wilkes' purser R. B. Robinson wrote, "I am astonished that our country should let them get such a secure footing as they already have on this land."

Perhaps to make a counter-point Wilkes decided to allow his crew "a full day's frolic and pleasure" as a Fourth of July celebration (actually held on July 5, 1841, because the fourth fell on a Sunday, inappropriate for observances other than those of the church). Wilkes describes "marching off with flags flying and music playing." At a corner of "the mission prairie," Reverend Richmond made a speech predicting that "the whole of this magnificent Country . . . is destined to become part of the American Republic." He was right; five years later the land became officially American. The Hudson's Bay Company transferred Columbia District headquarters to Fort Victoria. A reconstruction of the fort at Tacoma's Point Defiance Park follows the original architecture. (Open to the public; various living history events.)

Today the best place to sense the prairie land that attracted both the Hudson's Bay Company agricultural effort and early settlers is at Mima Mounds (see p. 353) and to some extent at Connell's Prairie (see under SUMNER, p. 325). Natural prairies actually were common when whites first came to Puget Sound. Father Francis Blanchet counted 18 such openings between Cowlitz and Nisqually in 1839, and McLoughlin reported their average size as 15 to 20 miles long by up to 15 miles wide.

Another place to view the natural landscape is the **Nisqually National Wildlife Refuge** at the mouth of the Nisqually River (I-5 Exit 114). The land has been diked and farmed, but its salt marshes, mudflats, and woodlands nonetheless convey an impression of timelessness.

At **FORT STEILACOOM** the impression today is the exact reverse of what it would have been in the mid-1800s. The fort now sits apart from traffic and bustle, but it began as a populous and regimented pinprick next to the port village of Steilacoom. The parade ground and four refurbished houses built in 1858 remain, now used for special events and exuberant historic reenactments. The larger buildings next to the parade ground belong to Western State Hospital, begun in 1870 after the army left.

The hospital—at first an insane asylum offering little treatment—replaced a private

In the 1930s the last two Fort Nisqually buildings—this square-log granary and the chief trader's house—were moved from their original site to Tacoma's Point Defiance Park.

contract system of caring for mental illness. The Sisters of Charity (later called the Sisters of Providence) were the first to work with Washington's mental patients. After a year without receiving payment, Mother Joseph (at the time still Sister Joseph) began badgering the governor for the $1,351.78 due her. It could not be paid; the territorial treasury held a balance of only $261.63. The sisters borrowed money and continued their work. When payment finally began in 1864 it was in greenbacks—paper bills, not gold—and, with the Civil War under way, the bills' value in the West was only half of their face amount. After the war two businessmen in Monticello (Longview) took over the contract but operated a disgraceful institution that was publicized nationally by crusading reformer Dorothea Dix. The territorial legislature thereupon bought the army's abandoned buildings at Fort Steilacoom and began a treatment program.

Until the 1970s, patients worked on a farm as a means of holding down costs and as a part of treatment. Half a dozen huge barns still show the scale of that operation. Near them, Waughop Lake—now a county park—retains its tranquility, also regarded by hospital directors as therapeutic for patients. (Turn east off Steilacoom onto 87th at the north end of the low cobblestone wall along the front of the fort grounds; then turn right at the first corner and follow Dresden to its end. The lake is behind the barns.)

The fort began in 1849 on land rented from the Hudson's Bay Company and previously farmed by Englishman Joseph Heath (see p. 309). A Snoqualmie raiding party had attacked the company's post at Nisqually to take retribution against Wya-ya-mooch, a native employee married to their chief's daughter. He reportedly had mistreated her. The attack failed, but in the melee an American working outside the stockade at the sawpit was fatally wounded, perhaps accidentally, by gunshot. The incident set off a call for army protection.

The importance of the fort increased as the Yakima War began in early October 1855. (See YAKIMA WAR sidebar, p. 148.) At the time, only tribes east of the Cascades were known to be hostile—specifically the Yakima and their affiliated bands. Most of the army's troops also were east of the mountains. White settlements, however, were mostly west of the mountains,

and trouble began in this region at the end of October when natives killed soldiers traveling the road north from Fort Steilacoom and attacked cabins at White River. (See AUBURN, p. 273; Connell's Prairie under SUMNER, p. 325; and PUGET SOUND WAR sidebar, p. 326.)

Word of hostilities spread throughout the Puget Sound region. People streamed to Fort Steilacoom, although its protection was more psychological than actual. It had neither stockade nor blockhouse. Furthermore, the lieutenant in charge could offer accommodations in the barracks because nearly all of his men were in the field. Ezra Meeker, Puyallup pioneer, described the situation as a "sorry mess" with women crying, men cursing, oxen bellowing, sheep bleating, dogs howling—"in a word, the utmost disorder." From a child's perspective, however, Margaret Whitesell Taylor remembered that "the sight of the marching soldiers and the sound of the drum and fife were simply miraculous to children who had spent the past year in the wilderness."

A few months later the settlers began straggling back to their land. Governor Isaac Stevens—like others—considered a Nisqually headman named Leschi primarily responsible for the recent depredations against homesteads and armed attacks on soldiers. He sent word that he wanted the necks of Leschi and his half brother Quiemuth "for the executioner." He offered a reward of 50 blankets, and on November 13, 1857, a nephew overpowered Leschi and turned him in. Leschi was held at the Fort Steilacoom guardhouse, charged with murder as a civilian rather than as a military foe. During the next 13 months, he stood trial twice, specifically accused of having killed volunteer colonel A. Benton Moses at Connell's Prairie. On November 16 his first trial ended when jurors Ezra Meeker and William Kincaid—prominent Puyallup Valley settlers—insisted that even if the charge were true, shooting an enemy soldier scarcely constituted murder. Quiemuth thereupon gave himself up and traveled under guard to the governor's office where he was held prisoner. That night someone killed him.

Leschi, still held at Fort Steilacoom, stood trial a second time on March 18, 1857, and was found guilty. Army officers and Hudson's Bay Company officials, however, considered the

MUCK CREEK FIVE

By March 1856 the war between natives and whites west of the mountains ended, although bad feelings continued, and a fundamental controversy flared between the U.S. Army and the territorial governor. General John Wool, commander of the Pacific, had come from San Francisco to Fort Vancouver the preceding November. He respected natives' rights as much as settlers' and felt that volunteer soldiers often amounted to little more than paid lynch mobs. He thought Governor Isaac Stevens should have prohibited whites from entering ceded land before treaties were ratified, and that he should have sent potentially troublesome natives to "Indian country" like Oklahoma, rather than allowing them to reserve parts of their traditional land for themselves.

Conversely, Stevens insisted that the treaties were designed "to civilize and render the conditions of the Indians happier." (He made no mention of his own happiness at acquiring 64 million acres of land.) He further recommended that "Nothing but death is a mete punishment for [the] perfidy" of any natives who resisted the terms.

After the March battle at Connell's Prairie (see under SUMNER, p. 325), the governor ordered volunteer cavalrymen to clear out "hostiles," which meant all natives not at the camps his agents had designated at Fox Island and elsewhere away from white settlements. Sweeping the country near present-day Eatonville, the troops found two elderly men and 15 women and children fishing for salmon in the Mashel River. They killed them. Next they rode to Muck Creek, where several former Hudson's Bay Company employees had settled with Nisqually wives. They rounded up five of these men on the assumption that they must have aided the enemy. Their cabins had survived the war

charge against him improper and furthermore believed that he could not have killed Moses. A time discrepancy made it impossible. From where Leschi was known to have been before the shooting, he could not have reached Connell's Prairie in time to pull the trigger. August Kautz, a lieutenant at Fort Steilacoom, and Dr. William Tolmie, in charge at Fort Nisqually, even measured distances at Connell's Prairie to prove this. No matter.

On December 18 a judge passed sentence. But a day before the scheduled execution, a U.S. marshall arrived to arrest the executioner—the sheriff—for selling whiskey illegally. This delay had been contrived by army officers and civilians still hoping for justice. Leschi remained in the guardhouse, and drunken mobs hung effigies of his chief supporters. A petition demanding death circulated and as if responding to plebiscite, the sheriff of Thurston County replaced the arrested Pierce County sheriff and rode to Fort Steilacoom with a posse. The commander refused to allow the hanging on army land. The posse led Leschi to a scaffold tree near the outlet of Steilacoom Lake. And there on February 19, 1858, they hanged Leschi.

That fall Colonel George Wright stormed through the Spokane country—and the natives' desperate effort to resist white domination went down to final defeat. (See SPOKANE BATTLES sidebar, p. 10.) A granite memorial to Leschi sits in a shopping mall parking lot on Steilacoom Boulevard (a mile north of Fort Steilacoom's main gate).

Life at Fort Steilacoom settled into a routine. Officers exchanged sociabilities with their Hudson's Bay Company landlords at Fort Nisqually, surveyed land and drew maps for territorial officials, squeezed news from visiting travelers, and took every possible opportunity to "inspect" Fort Townsend or Fort Bellingham and enjoy the adjoining towns. Officers and enlisted men continued their relationships with native wives and children who lived at a camp near the fort. And men increasingly headed AWOL to British Columbia as gold discoveries began on

unscathed. The governor asked Lieutenant Colonel Silas Casey to hold the captive farmers in the Fort Steilacoom guardhouse, as no civilian jail was available. Indeed, there was none in the entire territory.

Events then tumbled one upon another in a sequence that would read like a farce except for the grave disregard of the principles of constitutional law. The first act was for lawyers to paddle to the Whidbey Island home of a district judge to ask for a court order to release the Muck Creek Five. The judge issued the order, but the governor declared martial law and marched his prisoners to a blockhouse—actually a reinforced barn—used by the volunteer army near Spanaway. Next he packed a courtroom with armed volunteers and had the judge arrested. Stevens then appointed a tribunal of volunteer officers, who dismissed the case against the "squaw men" for lack of evidence. A civilian court then tried them, and even the prosecuting district attorney admitted he had no case. The prisoners were released.

Stevens thereupon ended martial law but refused to answer repeated summons to appear in court on charges of contempt. When a fourth order to appear came from the bench, his lawyers asked that the governor not be tried by a judge whom he had arrested. The judge refused the request and set a $50 fine. As governor, Stevens granted himself a stay of sentence and asked for a presidential review. The federal attorney general advised the president, however, that only Congress could act in such a matter, and the secretary of state wrote the governor that his case did not "meet with the favorable regard of the President." The territorial legislature thereupon censured Stevens, and he paid the fine.

The Muck Creek Five had long ago returned to their wives and farms.

the Fraser River in 1858. Their base army pay at the time was $11 a month, compared with $2 to $5 a day for skilled civilian workmen.

In 1859 troops from Fort Steilacoom went to San Juan Island for the Pig War jurisdictional standoff between England and the United States (see AMERICAN CAMP, p. 243; and ENGLISH CAMP, p. 245). When the Civil War began, many officers from southern states resigned their U.S. Army commissions and offered their services to the Confederacy. Those from northern states were ordered east. Volunteers mustered into the army at San Francisco came north to man Fort Steilacoom (soon replaced by Washington volunteers).

At the close of the Civil War army attention turned to the Southwest to "pacify" the Navajo and Apache. Fort Steilacoom's remaining 124 artillerymen and five officers left the post on April 22, 1868. The parade ground fell silent. The buildings stood empty.

A bridge crosses to **FOX ISLAND** from near Kopachuck State Park, a drive worth taking primarily because of the history museum donated in the 1980s by Mrs. Dewitt Wallace, with her husband copublisher of *The Reader's Digest*. The family vacationed on the island, and she generously sought to share the pleasure she found there. (For the public, overall sightseeing on the island is minimal because trees prevent views out, and the entire shore is privately owned and built up.)

Fox Island's first white population seems to have been Hudson's Bay Company sailors who jumped ship, perhaps plus rum runners hiding in coves. Native people had used the island for generations and, during the Puget Sound War of 1855-1856, it became a temporary reservation for Nisquallies and Puyallups ordered to either move there or be regarded as "hostiles." To officially end the war west of the mountains, Governor Isaac Stevens went to Fox Island to meet with the native people and *listen* to their concerns about the wholly inadequate lands set aside for their use by the 1854 treaty. He agreed

to larger reservations for both tribes. (See
NISQUALLY RESERVATION, p. 318; and PUYALLUP
RESERVATION, p. 322.)

In the 1860s fish packing and oyster businesses began on the island with native people hired to do the fishing and gathering. In the early 1870s a dogfish operation took huge daily catches by weirs, seines, and trawls. The industry flourished at scores of coast villages—particularly native villages—from Puget Sound to Alaska. Fins and tails from the dogfish (small shark) were shipped to France as delicacies. Heads went into making glue. And—most important—the livers gave oil used for lamps, as a base for paint, and to lubricate logging skid roads and the machinery of sawmills.

By the 1890s farmers grew huge crops of prunes on the island and a prune dryer did custom drying for the surrounding area. Huckleberries, blueberries, loganberries, and strawberries together with a cut-flower industry continued into the 1930s.

GIG HARBOR takes its name from the voyage led by Navy Lieutenant Charles Wilkes in 1841. Officers and men from the *Porpoise* explored along the shore in small boats while the ship moved from Sequalitchew (Fort Nisqually) to Commencement Bay (Tacoma). A midshipman reported a "pretty little bay . . . concealed from the Sound," and Lieutenant George Sinclair went to investigate in the gig. The village along those shores today warrants a visit for its lingering character as a self-contained maritime community—albeit backed by subdivisions and shopping malls. A waterside drive still circles the bay and on clear days offers a spectacular view of Mount Rainier.

Twenty-six years after the Wilkes expedition, three men fishing from a rowboat came into the harbor for shelter; one—a Slavonian named Samuel Jerisich—married a native woman and settled here. Additional Yugoslavian, German, and Scandinavian families soon joined the Jerisiches. Some of the men worked at a sawmill; most fished from huge rowboats, four men to a side. Often they rowed as far as the San Juan Islands, traveling with the tide and camping on shore at night; later a company boat towed them to the salmon grounds, where they worked out of a tent village and delivered each

day's catch to cannery tender boats. The pay was per fish, not per pound. By 1915 this Gig Harbor fleet numbered about 50 boats.

About that time farmers who had been rowing their products to market in Tacoma organized the Hales Pass–Wollochet Bay Navigation Company with a vessel that could carry as many as 2,400 crates of strawberries on a single trip during peak season. Berry farming, augmented by holly growing, continued through the 1930s, then fell off following World War II.

HOME. (See under LONGBRANCH, below.)

LONGBRANCH, which dots the Key Peninsula across from Steilacoom, is best known for the beautiful forest and beaches at nearby Penrose State Park. (Turn south from State Road 302 across the causeway at Purdy and follow signs to Key Center, winding for 10 miles along a green slot cut through the trees. From Key Center continue south another 6½ miles past Home and the Lakebay post office to the state park turn. From there continue another 4 miles to the Longbranch store, chowder house, and marina—plus a peaceful view across the water.)

The settlement now is quiet but in prehighway days—which here continued into the 1950s—it bustled as a resort. Its dancehall had a floor polished by kids who shaved candles and skated gleefully about in stocking feet. A ferry landing served travelers from Tacoma via Steilacoom, and a second ferry connected to Olympia from a bay on the west side of the peninsula (and there now is talk of a bridge to Johnson Point, near Olympia). In 1887 a man named William Sipple opened a carpentry shop and boat-building yard here while waiting for his prune orchard to mature. Three years later Ernest Shellgren started carrying mail to the peninsula free of charge in order to prove the need for a post office. He opened the Longbranch store in 1891 and, for people living on berry and chicken farms or on country estates, it provided a supply center and travel crossroads.

North of Longbranch is **Home,** worthy of a pause partly for the scene today and even more, for contemplation of the past. Houses three or four deep line a steep slope facing the water, many of them with clear views to the high gravel banks at Steilacoom and to Mount Rainier. Sea-walls protect against erosion, weathered pilings remain from old docks, and humble shanties mingle in egalitarian fashion with dream homes. The scene is pleasant and undistinguished; yet in the 1890s and early 1900s Home was the site of a utopian colony that gained notoriety as a den of anarchy and landed its newspaper editor in a Tacoma jail.

The founders of Home came from a short-lived socialist colony east of Tacoma and in 1896 formed the Mutual Home Association to "establish better social and moral conditions." They invited all who were willing to work hard and mind their own business to join them. Land was to be held communally; improvements would be personal property and could be sold or mortgaged. Otherwise there were no particular rules, although community spirit encouraged gathering to hear what just about anybody had to say about topics from vegetarianism and eugenics to Esperanto, the so-called "universal" language, and Koreshanity, an astonishing religion that viewed the cosmos as a hollow ball with straight up as the quickest way to reach China.

In 1901, President William McKinley was assassinated, and nationwide panic raged. The assassin was labeled an anarchist, a term similar to later use of "Wobbly" and "Communist" but more sinister. A Tacoma "vigilance committee" of Civil War veterans thought of Home, whose residents openly used the word anarchy, which they defined as freedom from a defined religion or code of behavior. The committee decided to make an armed investigation of the community and dropped the idea only after a fellow veteran who lived at Home came to talk with them.

Next someone mailed copies of the Home newspaper *Discontent, the Mother of Progress,* to federal authorities, and a U.S. marshal headed across the water from Tacoma to arrest the editors. Colonists gave him an excellent lunch and sent three prisoners back with him. All were acquitted. The charge against them was advocacy of "free love," a matter that Home resident Leila Edmonds later described as "the same thing that goes on in every community, but it is hidden."

Regardless of the acquittal, opponents of such liberalism managed to bring the 75-year-old Home postmistress to trial for mailing a monthly journal that contained an article titled, "The

Among the many idealistic group-living experiments tried in Washington, the colony at Home (north of Longbranch) was regarded as the most radical. It drew national attention.

The National Park Service built a cabin at Indian Henry's Hunting Ground in 1916. Henry (actually named Satulick) lived near Eatonville; he hunted mountain goats at Rainier.

Awful Fate of Fallen Women." She too was acquitted, although the postal inspector brought a grand jury case and succeeded in closing the Home post office on grounds that the mail had been used to "corrupt and injure . . . the body politic." The *Discontent* stopped publication, but was replaced by first the *Demonstrator,* then the *Agitator.*

This final paper was edited by Jay Fox, an active participant in the labor movement. An issue of nude bathing was what brought him before a judge. In 1911 witnesses reported seeing four Russian Dukhobors at Home enter the water "without artificial covering of any sort." A boy volunteered that he had helped his mother and sister climb a small mound for a better view of the shocking behavior. Another colonist testified to the use of field glasses and an observation of unquestionable nudity.

Nobody denied the accusation, and the defendants were ruled guilty and jailed. Editor Fox printed a commentary headlined "The Nude and the Prudes," and seven weeks later he was arrested for unlawfully advocating "disrespect for law." His sentence was two months in jail, a ruling that went all the way to the U.S. Supreme Court, where it was upheld. Fox began serving his sentence, but was pardoned when a new governor took office.

The underlying issue was freedom to report events. Behavior at Home had long worried the outside community and—perhaps inevitably as the colony grew—it also began to trouble residents. Issues of land ownership arose; the association store teetered close to bankruptcy; the communally owned seawall and meeting hall deteriorated; the dream ended.

On September 10, 1919, the Mutual Home Association disbanded. Nonconformists—some of them world renowned—had lived and lectured at Home. Ideas and practices had interacted in yeasty ferment. Questions of personal freedom, religion, economics, and social organization had undergone scrutiny. And in the end, some colonists stayed, others left.

In less than a century **MOUNT RAINIER NATIONAL PARK** has changed from a remote area accessible by train and tourist stage into a mecca that each year draws 8,000 climbers who attempt the two-day, roped expedition to the summit—so many they are issued plastic bags for human waste, to be packed down the mountain on llamas. The magnitude of so much change in so short a time emphasizes the value of the concept underlying national parks. They are to be kept natural for the enjoyment of people living now and those yet to be born— timeless samples of land bound to nature's rhythms, not those imposed by people.

Mount Rainier became America's fifth national park in 1899, made up in part of square-mile sections of land granted to the Northern Pacific as a financial incentive for building the transcontinental railroad. The company exchanged these sections for other land, an agreement that cynics say added to their wealth by trading commercially useless land for valuable timber. Yet the Northern Pacific had earlier supported establishment of Yellowstone National Park, saying, "We do not want to see the Falls of the Yellowstone driving the looms of a cotton factory, or the great geysers boiling pork for some gigantic packing house." They supported both the concept of scenery and of the tourist travel it could stimulate.

As early as 1893 awareness of Mount Rainier had rippled nationwide, sparked by a squabble

at the Chicago World's Fair where a map at the Washington State Building showed the name of the landmark peak as "Mount Tacoma or Rainier." The Nisqually name *Tahoma* ("White Mountain") was vociferously preferred by many, especially residents of the city of Tacoma, and strident argument flared until supposedly settled in 1890 with retention of the name Rainier (bestowed by British sea captain George Vancouver in 1792 to honor an English admiral).

Controversy at the fair grew so heated that the map was banished to a back room, and the renewed argument attracted public attention. Scientists noticed the slumbering volcano's extensive glacier system. Newspapers reported depredation as campers hacked trees for fire-wood and bough beds, and even set groves on fire simply for the skyrocketing brilliance of the display at night. It was time for real protection. The park was born through congressional action.

Today nearly 100 miles of road and 300 miles of trail lace the mountain's slopes; flowers paint subalpine meadows throughout a "spring" that begins in July; and 26 glaciers inch forward, fed

Huge crevasses split the surface ice of the 15 major glaciers cloaking Mount Rainier.

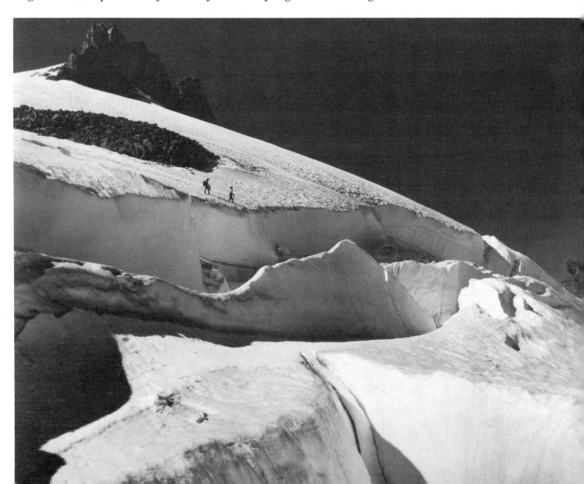

by winter snow that accumulates 30 feet deep. Visitor centers with displays, programs, and park information are at Longmire, Ohanapecosh, Paradise, and Sunrise. Roads to Paradise and Sunrise provide clear, close looks at glacier ice—which blankets about a tenth of the earth's land surface but is a rare sight in the United States outside of Alaska. Time permitting, walk as far as Glacier Vista at Paradise (3 miles round trip) or Emmons Vista at Sunrise (only a half mile). The Stevens Canyon Road from Paradise to Ohanapecosh offers one of the state's most spectacular closeup looks at mountains, perhaps most beautiful in September, when huckleberry, willow, and ash carpet the slopes with crimson and gold.

In 1988 Rainier's height was measured by signals from orbiting satellites, and the following year—the state's centennial—surveyors announced a new official height: 14,411 feet instead of 14,410 feet.

The **NISQUALLY RESERVATION** resulted from the treaty council held in 1854 at Medicine Creek (near the mouth of the Nisqually River). This was territorial Governor Isaac Stevens' first such meeting in western Washington—an enormous success from his standpoint. In just two December days, 662 assembled natives ceded two and a half million acres and were left with only three small patches. Reservations for the Nisqually and Puyallup tribes were each to be 1,280 acres. Squaxin Island was reserved for all the other native people of southern Puget Sound. Stevens' instructions had been to create as few reservations as possible. Furthermore, the federal government was to have a right to move people at any time, "if necessary." In exchange for their land, the tribes were to receive schools and instructors, a doctor, carpenter, and smithy, and were to retain exclusive fishing rights on their reserved lands as well as rights to fish and hunt "at all usual and accustomed places" off the reserved lands.

Concern over treaty terms led to war between natives and whites from 1855 to 1856. At its close both the Nisqually and Puyallup tribes received larger reservations. The Medicine Creek Treaty had granted the Nisquallies only forest land away from the river delta; the new, actual, Nisqually Reservation included river frontage for fishing and prairie land for grazing horses (which the tribe had even before the coming of whites, an unusual acquisition for saltwater natives). The new reservation land totalled 4,700 acres, nearly four times the previous stipulation. Holding more than a fragment of that land proved impossible, however. In 1917 Pierce County condemned nearly three fourths of the Nisqually Reservation for inclusion as part of the Fort Lewis military reservation. The pretext was that the tribe was not using the land. The matter has yet to be resolved legally.

Keeping fishing and hunting rights also proved difficult, although all Washington treaties include the same words: in exchange for land, natives were to fish and hunt "in common with all citizens." But as human population grew and wildlife diminished, the rights became a troublesome issue. Whites generally supposed the treaty meant equality for all, a per capita apportionment of whatever fish or game existed. Native people—and the courts—saw the meaning as part of a contract between two parties, the federal government and the tribes whose representatives signed the treaties. In 1974 U.S. District Court Judge George Boldt ruled that the state must manage salmon so that native people have an opportunity to catch "fifty percent of the runs traditionally fished by treaty tribes."

The U.S. Supreme Court—the final authority—upheld the Boldt decision. Emphasis now has switched from confrontation between natives and whites to cooperation: rebuild the overfished, woefully mistreated salmon runs and 50-50 will mean more fish for everyone.

Travelers southbound on I-5 can still see a lone, dead Douglas fir that marks Governor Stevens' first treaty grounds. Watch for it at the south side of the delta, standing by the creek (now called McAllister Creek, although previously Medicine Creek). The tree shows clearly just before the road climbs the hill above the delta. Reservation land—today only 1,650 acres—is east of the freeway. Housing projects assure homes for a large segment of the tribe and a tribal center includes a library, senior citizen facility, law enforcement building, and natural resource division to protect and improve the fish resource. The tribe works with the

Successful crops at the Boatman hop farm near Orting led to building this house in 1896. Because of large, natural prairies, the area was settled as early as the 1850s, when wagon trains first began crossing the Cascade Mountains via Naches Pass.

Pioneer Farm Museum near Eatonville to present its story to the public, especially to school children. The museum is on the traditional land of the Nisqually.

(See also PUGET SOUND WAR sidebar, p. 326.)

ORTING began with farms and continues as a farming center, although with its long-famous daffodil fields now mostly replaced by Christmas-tree farms. Strawberries, blueberries, and raspberries continue as major crops—complete with U-pick signs. In town, a huge, landmark Odd Fellows hall built in 1904 (now called the Opera House and used as an auditorium) stands by the erstwhile railroad tracks, and a church at Train and Varner displays extraordinary shinglework. Old house buffs will enjoy driving side streets for looks at late 1800s and early 1900s homes with stained-glass and etched-glass windows, comfortable porches, and an occasional carriage house. (The largest homes—predictably—are within a block or two of the old railroad right-of-way.)

The state Soldiers Home, opened in 1891, is located about 1½ miles southwest of State Route 162 (on Calistoga). Communities vied for the income and honor of having the home. Ezra Meeker offered the state 40 acres in Puyallup; San Juan County offered the use of Garrison

Bay (the English Camp during the Pig War); Tacoma offered 400 feet of waterfront on Vashon Island. Orting's offer was 85 acres of land. The home was established for "Union soldiers, sailors, marines, and members of the state militia." A Soldiers' Home Colony program allowed a veteran to bring his family to town with him. They received monthly groceries and clothing equivalent in value to his stipend. A truck made the deliveries, stopping at homes where the driver saw a white flag with a blue numeral displayed in the window.

An unusual pooling of interests brought Orting a major population influx in the 1880s. Frederick Eldredge, a New Yorker who had come to teach, filed a townsite and wanted to attract residents; farmers had planted hops and needed pickers. Thomas Lee, one of the hop growers, knew of Germans in Hawaii who had six-year labor contracts that included an offer of transportation to America upon completion of the contract.

Eldredge wrote a promotional letter dated October 25, 1887. In it he described farming opportunities, particularly growing hops but also fruit, potatoes, hay, and poultry. For those not wanting to farm, he described opportunities in logging and coal mining at nearby Carbonado and Wilkeson. "Some people have come here

A Dutch company began growing bulbs near Orting and Puyallup in the 1920s.

responded. He had left home at age 14 with his family when an agent of a sugar company came to Germany recruiting colonists for Kauai. Six years later, in 1887, Mueller read Eldredge's circular letter and decided to come to Orting, although he later reminisced that at first he "didn't like the place as there wasn't very much to it." Waiting overnight for a train out of town, however, he let residents convince him to stay. He took a job as a carpenter, then soon started raising hops.

Bulb growing—today's agricultural hallmark—began in the 1920s. A Dutch company wanting to expand its operation had bought land in South America, then decided to expand still more by buying land in North America. John and Lane Colyn, managing Van Zonnovelds' southern-hemisphere farms, tested land at Onalaska and Chehalis but found so much clay in the soil that the only way to get out bulbs was to pound the clods encasing them with wooden mallets. The brothers next tried land near Roy (east of Olympia), then leased dairy and hop land at Orting. The gravelly texture here, a legacy of origin as glacial outwash, suited bulb-growing perfectly.

As a promotional gesture in March 1929 the Van Zonnovelds' bulb farm mounted an eight-foot wooden shoe onto a truck, covered it with 11,000 daffodil blossoms, and displayed it for a week in front of Tacoma's swanky Winthrop Hotel. At least once a day they re-covered it with fresh flowers. When they started back to Orting, admirers and sightseers joined in, forming a spontaneous parade—the beginning of the annual Daffodil Parade. Usually held during the first week in April the parade still starts on Pacific Avenue in Tacoma, then breaks up and starts again an hour or two later in Puyallup, next in Sumner, and finally in Orting. The Knutson Farms (16405 Orton Road E.) still grow bulbs; turn off State Route 161 onto 78th Street E. and continue to Orton. (Also see the Van Lierop farm, under PUYALLUP, p. 321.)

In **PUYALLUP** (Pew-al´-lup) the outstanding place to visit is the 17-room **Ezra Meeker mansion** (321 E. Pioneer; built in 1875). Etched-glass windows, stained glass, a tile entry, original furnishings, Eliza Jane Meeker's clothes including an embroidered velvet gown

with families and have found work as soon as they could get their coats off," he wrote. Furthermore, "There are no poisonous snakes or spiders here; no cyclones or blizzards; few thunderstorms or hail storms." In short, people found Orting as close to ideal as reality ever allows.

Fred Mueller was typical of the Germans who

from Paris—all such items are appealing, especially in relation to one of Washington's most renowned pioneers. In 1852 Meeker came West by oxteam with his wife and baby and settled at Kalama (north of Vancouver), then moved to McNeil Island. His family opposed the isolation of island life, so the Meekers moved to Steilacoom, where he opened a store. After a ship sank with the store's order of merchandise, they moved to Puyallup, where Ezra pioneered the raising, drying, and marketing of hops. He made a fortune, and lost it.

The Meeker mansion became a home for Civil War veterans, and Ezra switched from growing hops and arranging sales in London to raising poultry. In his late 60s, he joined the Klondike gold rush to open a bank, which soon failed. In his mid-70s, he drove an oxteam back across the Great Plains and on to Washington, D.C., seeking to quicken awareness of the Oregon Trail and its role in history. In his 80s, he rode across the continent in an automobile—a pioneering venture in itself. In his 90s he flew as passenger in an open cockpit plane.

In 1928 Ezra Meeker died. He had watched scattered homesteads coalesce into a town and a virgin valley convert to hopyards, then berry and rhubarb farms, and—shortly before his death—to daffodil and tulip farms. Now the process has gone a step farther and Christmas-tree farms are replacing daffodils; the trees take less hand labor than do cut flowers and bulbs. For a look at what previously characterized the entire valley's spring display of blossoms, visit the **Van Lierop farm** and test garden. (From Meridian in downtown Puyallup, drive east on Pioneer Way for 2 miles; turn left where the road makes a sharp bend, and cross the railroad tracks. The farm is just off Pioneer at the intersection of 80th Street E. and 134th Avenue.) The Van Lierops grow about 250 varieties of daffodils and, through a 10-year process of cultivating and cross-pollinating seedlings, constantly work to develop new strains.

The **Puyallup Fair Grounds** are a place to visit, not just for events like the Western Washington Fair (early September) but also because they were the ironically named "Camp Harmony," the World War II assembly center for Japanese Americans en route to detention camps. A handsome metal sculpture commemorating the internees is inside the main gate, located—a further irony—to the right of the merry-go-round building. In 1942 families came

Families interned at Puyallup had to live in barracks not even ready to receive them.

to the assembly center ordered to evacuate the West Coast solely on the basis of having one eighth, or more, Japanese blood. No consideration was given to civil rights or individual circumstances. Citizenship did not enter in, nor did demonstrable loyalty to the United States. Tacoma's mayor Harry Cain was one of the few elected officials anywhere to oppose the evacuation.

At first ethnic Japanese were asked to move inland voluntarily. Then they were forced to do so by the War Relocation Authority. Families found themselves stripped of homes, businesses, and incomes and forced into cramped group quarters with communal eating and bathing facilities. Teachers nonetheless led school children in saluting the flag and radios played "God Bless America." Mothers behind barbed wire hung blue flags with gold stars honoring dead sons just as did other American mothers.

The **PUYALLUP RESERVATION,** now at the edge of the Tacoma tideflats, began as a 1,280-acre strip along the bluffs south of Commencement Bay (including Point Defiance). This land was impossibly small and ill suited to the tribe's needs, as Governor Isaac Stevens acknowledged in 1856 by designating instead 23,000 vaguely defined acres east and north of the bay. In 1857 President Franklin Pierce formally authorized the new reservation by invoking a treaty condition that allowed the president to assign tribes to land other than what they had originally agreed to.

In this instance, the provision worked in the tribe's favor. In general, however, it was a great source of worry, for who could predict what the government might order? Individual land speculators, the city of Tacoma, and the Northern Pacific Railroad Company all tried various technicalities and ruses to get Puyallup land and, for a while, legal status as a tribe even seemed threatened. Prolonged 1980s negotiations seem to have resolved matters, and the emphasis is now on joint city and tribe development of industrial and port facilities, together with improved fisheries and an environmental cleanup at the mouth of the Puyallup River.

A boarding school that eventually drew pupils from throughout western Washington operated on the reservation from 1864 until 1919, when the buildings briefly became a veterans' hospital, then the Cushman Indian Hospital. In 1943 the government built the present facility (2202 E. 28th Street), which it transferred to the state 16 years later. The buildings served as a reception and diagnostic center for juveniles committed by the courts into state custody. Currently, the Puyallup Tribe has its administrative offices, tribal schools, and outpatient clinics in the buildings. In time, displays open to the public may be developed. Various pressures have reduced the reservation's size to only 35 acres of trust land.

SOUTH PRAIRIE no longer has a functioning business district although old homes—several of them comfortably spacious—still face where the railroad tracks used to be, and new homes line the rim of the valley south of town to take advantage of the view.

In 1854 Paul Emery settled on this land south of Connell's and Porter's prairies (near present-day Sumner and Buckley). He joined the volunteer army the next year and never returned. Thirty-three years later when the tracks of the Northern Pacific's Cascades Division came across the prairie, hotels and a store quickly blossomed. Logging, coal mines, farms, and the railroad itself supported the area's economy. South Prairie was a division point for coal trains from Black Diamond and Wilkeson-Carbonado. It even had a roundhouse. Coke ovens left from coal-mining days remain beside the Carbon River. (Drive 3½ miles south of South Prairie and turn off State Route 162 onto 177th E.; continue for about a mile. The ovens are on the left on private property. Also see WILKESEN, p. 341, for more about coke ovens.)

STEILACOOM (Still´-uh-kum) is now a suburb along the shore south of Tacoma, but it retains a village quality. It clearly shows its early origins and can claim an impressive list of firsts: first lawyer north of the Columbia River (1851); first courthouse north of the Columbia (1853); first Protestant church north of the Columbia (1853); first incorporated town in Washington Territory (1854); first territorial jail (1858); first brewery (1858); first public library (1858).

The town's two museums are logical starting

points for a visit: the history museum is in the basement of the white, two-story town hall (corner of Lafayette and Main) and the Steilacoom Tribal Museum is housed in the former Congregational church (1515 Lafayette). Nearby, the refurbished Bair Drug and Hardware Store again offers soda fountain service (corner of Lafayette and Commercial) and behind the store (on Wilkes) is a monument with the bell of the 1853 Methodist-Episcopal church. A Catholic church built at Fort Steilacoom in 1855 and hauled here on skids is three blocks up the hill (Main and Nisqually; still in regular use).

Outstanding houses to search out include the Captain George Black and Captain Nehemiah Bartlett houses (702 and 607 Lafayette; both built in the 1860s); Nathaniel Orr house (1811 Rainier; built in 1857), which is open at times for tours; Philip Keach house (1802 Commercial; built in 1858); 17-room E. R. Rogers mansion (1702 Commercial; built in 1891), now a restaurant; and the Barber farmhouse (102 Montgomery; built in 1880).

Also be sure to drive along the waterfront north of Steilacoom to the Chambers Creek estuary, the location of an early-day gristmill and sawmills (and now a papermill). Waterfowl from buffleheads to geese rest on the water, and salmon enter the creek by leaping the spillway of a low dam at the head of the estuary. A municipal beach south of the estuary retains the timeless lap of waves and a view of shipping with the snowy Olympic Mountains as backdrop. A small ferry—reminder of preautomobile and pre–Narrows Bridge days—runs to Anderson and Ketron islands a few miles offshore. (A separate launch runs to the prison at McNeil Island.)

In 1855, when Seattle was still little but a sawmill and a cluster of cabins, and Tacoma had a sawmill, barrel factory, and fish-packing operations, Steilacoom had six stores, three hotels, three sawmills, two dance studios (one teaching waltz, the other new steps like the Portland Fancy and the Tempest), two gristmills, two blacksmith shops, a tailor shop, a four-page weekly newspaper, a wharf that accommodated ships at any stage of the tide, and a road that led over the mountains to Walla Walla via Naches Pass. Prairie land laced with creeks and lakes

had attracted the Hudson's Bay Company to the area; it also attracted settlers. Of the 985 claims filed in Washington between 1850 and 1855, almost 20 percent were for land in Pierce County. Steilacoom was *the* town for these first American settlers.

It began as an American settlement in 1851 when a Maine sea captain named Lafayette Balch dropped anchor. He assembled a precut house he had brought from New England; pried open boxes and casks of merchandise from his cargo hold; and declared a store and hotel ready for business. Soon he added a sawmill. He intended to build at Olympia, but rebuffed there, decided to start a town of his own. The entire region had been determined American, rather than British, only five years previously. That decision unleashed a backlog of settlement, and businesses at Steilacoom soon opened to cater to neighboring farmers and outlying communities.

A man named Thomas Chambers actually had arrived a year before Balch. He ignored Hudson's Bay Company demands that he leave and built a gristmill near where Chambers Creek flows into the estuary; then he waited for other Americans to settle near him. In 1852 his hope materialized, and he added a sawmill to serve the needs of the community growing up around him.

The following year Andrew Byrd and his brother Marion built a dam raising the level of Steilacoom Lake five or six feet and, near the lake's outlet into Chambers Creek, they too began to operate a sawmill. (A marker on Steilacoom Boulevard near the bridge across Chambers Creek marks the site.) In 1857 Andrew built a four-story gristmill downstream from the sawmill, and the trail blazed through the woods from Puyallup to Steilacoom became known as the Byrd's Mill Road. Chambers was not pleased. He hired Lieutenant August Kautz from Fort Steilacoom to survey the creek basin and calculate how much the dam was slowing the water flow to his mills.

Little except anger came from the feud. Furthermore, Steilacoom's role was about to change. Until the time of the Civil War and the departure of army regulars from the fort, the port town of Steilacoom enjoyed status as a major hub of Puget Sound population and activity. As was true of other towns from

Mukilteo to Seattle and Olympia, it expected to be the terminus for the transcontinental railroad. But when the Northern Pacific picked Tacoma instead, Steilacoom slipped into contented status as a suburb graced with a proud awareness of origins.

The public Apple Squeeze held each October makes a particularly pleasant occasion for enjoying remnants of that past. Owners of old-fashioned cider presses lend them to the town, which invites the public to bring apples, kids, and empty jugs—or to buy a gallon of juice already hand cranked through one of the presses. A 25-pound box of apples squeezes into two or three gallons of juice, a perfect fate for culls often otherwise left to rot.

(Also see FORT STEILACOOM, p. 310.)

Ideally go to **SUMNER** when the Ryan House Museum is open (1228 Main; built in 1875). Friends who came West with George Ryan began building a simple frame cabin for him while he worked as bookkeeper for the Port Gamble sawmill to pay for the materials. Still part of the larger house, the cabin served as post office and also as an informal court, although the only known case decided here was that of an arrest for driving a mule too fast. Several years later, when the Northern Pacific built a branch line from Tacoma to Seattle, Sumner residents felt insulted by its refusal to stop in their town. The company pointed out there was no depot and said they could not afford to build one. George Ryan remedied the situation by building a depot at his own expense and even paid the agent's salary for the first year.

The first settler at Sumner was William Kincaid, a member of the wagon train party that crossed Naches Pass with James Longmire in 1853. A widower with seven children to care for, he had extra reason to pick his donation land claim carefully: a man with a wife could claim 320 acres between them; alone, he could file on only 160 acres. What now is Sumner looked promising and Kincaid staked land along the riverbank. Other pioneers used his corners as the starting points for their own claims before official surveys were made. In writing later about the family's isolation, Kincaid's son John mentioned buying staples that came around

The original fountain at Steilacoom's 1895 drugstore still serves ice cream sodas.

Cape Horn. Flour cost $50 a barrel, salt pork $80, and potatoes—which were perishable—cost $84 a bushel. At the time wages for chopping wood were $4 per day.

By the 1870s farmers were clearing additional land to grow hops. Charles Wood, an Olympia brewer, sent to England for roots in 1865. He gave some to John Meeker, a schoolteacher at Steilacoom, who carried the roots with him when he walked to his father Jacob's preemption land claim near Sumner. He also left some at his brother Ezra's cabin at Puyallup—and within five years Ezra had large hop fields. His substantial profits—possible because an infestation destroyed most of the European crop—quickly inspired others to also plant hops. The blossoms, or hop "cones," are steeped in brewing beer to give the final product its characteristic tangy flavor.

Members of the WCTU (Women's Christian Temperance Union) felt guilty about wealth from a crop that went into beer, but Sumner bloomed with large homes financed with hops profits and graced with black Italian marble and crystal chandeliers. Housewives rejoiced at help from Chinese "house boys" and cooks—and fretted that children were learning pidgin English from the Chinese and Chinook Jargon from Native Americans who came to pick the hops. (Two hop barns from this period remain along State Route 162. One is about 3½ miles from the Main and Valley intersection in Sumner—now the landmark symbol of a Christmas-tree farm. The second hop barn shows from the road about 3 miles farther east near the Mount Rainier viewpoint pullout.)

Connell's Prairie (about 10 miles east of Sumner) remains open, rolling country dotted with Douglas fir and alder. Looking south from the cobblestone historical marker it is easy to imagine the 1850s military road that connected Fort Steilacoom with Fort Walla Walla, and to visualize the events that opened—and five months later closed—the Puget Sound War. (To reach Connell's Prairie drive east from Sumner on State Route 410 to just beyond Milepost 15 and turn north toward Lake Tapps on 214th Avenue E., also known as Vandermark Road. Continue for almost 1½ miles, then follow Connell's Prairie Road east for 1 mile to the intersection with Barkuwein Road.)

Events here began in late October 1855 when Acting Governor Charles Mason dispatched 45 volunteer cavalrymen to scour the woods and "intercept any Indians" crossing the Cascades from the Yakima country. They were also to find Leschi, a prominent Nisqually leader believed to be organizing attacks against white settlers. Supposedly he was at Connell's Prairie, and Mason wanted him brought into custody. James McAllister, a Nisqually Flats settler and a friend of Leschi's, and Michael Connell, married to a native woman, volunteered to scout the prairie. If anybody could make contact safely, they should be the ones.

The two men set out on October 27—and never returned. Comrades found their bodies lying in a swamp. None of the soldiers had seen the shooting. The assailants never were identified. On October 31 Colonel A. Benton Moses and Joseph Miles were killed as they escorted a messenger along the road to Fort Steilacoom. Leschi was blamed. The Puget Sound War had begun.

Four and a half months later, on March 10, a group of perhaps 150 native warriors attacked 100 troops crossing the prairie. Neither side emerged clearly victorious, but the battle nonetheless ended the war west of the mountains except for sporadic burning of cabins and shooting of livestock and occasionally people.

Governor Isaac Stevens directed continued attacks against isolated native camps and the arrest of Hudson's Bay Company men with native wives. Eventually—unjustly—Leschi was hanged.

For Native Americans, the entire period was one of staggering physical and social dislocation. The economic system they had followed for generations was torn apart by the introduction of agriculture and the availability of wages—or at least subsistence—in service to newcomers who were not chiefs. Mystifying diseases had emptied hereditary positions. Missionaries had talked of a form of power previously unknown. And now treaties proposed a whole new basis for daily life.

(Also see under AUBURN on p. 273 for an account of the October 28, 1855, attack at White River; under FORT STEILACOOM on p. 311; and PUGET SOUND WAR sidebar on p. 326.)

PUGET SOUND WAR

By the summer of 1855 settlers west of the Cascades feared that Chief Kamiakin would coordinate a general uprising, perhaps even drawing in British Columbia and Alaska natives. Chilcotin warriors near Bella Coola killed white surveyors running lines for a road from the coast to the Cariboo, and Haida, Tsimshian, and Tlingit chiefs continued to raid Puget Sound for slaves (see under EBEY'S LANDING on p. 268; under PORT GAMBLE, p. 375). If these northerners were to join forces with Washington tribesmen, white settlers might easily be overpowered. Native organization followed a pattern of individual tribal autonomy, not confederation, but Columbia Plateau tribes had allied to protect themselves against depredations by Blackfeet. Homesteaders feared for their lives. A clergyman at Oregon City wrote to the secretary of the American Home Mission Society that "The people of Washington Territory are farming with rifle in hand."

Most Puget Sound native people recognized that the newly signed treaties would force them onto land inadequate for their needs. Open warfare began in mid-October after Nisqually settler James McAllister sent word to acting Governor Charles Mason that Leschi (by blood half Nisqually, half Klickitat) was organizing warriors from both sides of the mountains. In response, Mason sent 19 men from the settlers' volunteer militia to the Nisqually area to bring Leschi and his brother Quiemuth into custody. Word traveled ahead, and the two families fled toward the foothills on October 24. The militia pursued them, and native warriors in hiding at Connell's Prairie killed McAllister and Michael Connell, a settler who had a land claim on the prairie, near present-day Sumner. (See p. 325.)

The next day warriors also killed eight settlers and burned cabins at White River (near present-day Auburn; see p. 273). Three days later soldiers approaching Fort Steilacoom from an encampment near Naches were attacked; Colonel A. Benton Moses and Joseph Miles fell dead from gunshot wounds.

As word of these events spread, whites streamed into at least two dozen hastily palisaded compounds. A Salem missionary wrote that people at Puget Sound

are mostly "forted up," the towns are picketed in, and the Indians are growing bolder and stronger every day, farming is stoped [sic], the cattle of many are driven off, or shot, and all are obliged to be constantly on their guard.

In November, Tumwater pioneer Michael Simmons, appointed by Stevens as Indian agent for western Washington, decided to separate "friendly" natives from "hostiles" by relocating them away from areas settled by whites. He ordered all peaceable natives to move on 24-hour notice to camps at Fox Island, Squaxin Island, Penn Cove (Whidbey Island), Bellingham Bay, and elsewhere. Most did so, although the Duwamish refused to go to Bainbridge Island; Henry Yesler encouraged them in this because he needed native labor at his sawmill, left inoperable as white volunteers marched off to be mustered, at first into the regular army, later into a volunteer militia.

Soon volunteers were camping near the foothills to cut off native attackers approaching from east of the Cascades, and the captain of the federal gunboat *Decatur* had supplied arms and a small detachment of marines to the blockhouse at Seattle. He anchored offshore until the defensive measures were complete, for, as he reported, Seattle was "the nearest point to Snowqualami pass, and the Sound to the incursions of Indians from beyond the Mountains." Settlers seeking reassurance told themselves that the Yakima and Klickitat were horsemen who would find westside forests impossible terrain for battle.

On November 7, while reconnoitering along the Puyallup River, a scouting party led by Lieutenant William Slaughter was attacked; two and a half weeks later Slaughter was killed near Auburn while conferring with volunteer captain C. C. Hewitt. A skirmish followed, leaving two other soldiers dead and five wounded. From the *Decatur,* Commander Isaac Sterrett informed the secretary of the navy that the "prowess of the Indians had been greatly underrated," and the Methodist minister at Steilacoom, John Devore, wrote to a colleague in Oregon: "We lie down at night after bidding each other farewell. . . . How intolerable [is] this state of suspense!"

Holed-up in forts, whites neglected their crops and livestock and rubbed one another's nerves raw. Crowded into the relocation camps, peaceable natives missed their winter villages and fishing. At upriver camps, native warriors and their families began to run low on food and ammunition. Elders among them felt despair and counseled patience. Youths chafed for action. Reportedly, native wives of white settlers relayed information that "Bostons" had wearied of the two-way siege and that the big chief from San Francisco—General John Wool—had moved to Fort Vancouver to take charge of campaigns.

Stevens—far from willing to renegotiate treaties and adjust wholly unacceptable terms regarding the size of reservations—on January 19, 1856, called for "war until the last hostile Indian is exterminated."

Six days after his speech, about 150 natives paddled across Lake Washington and fanned out into the forest. The commander of the *Decatur* (by then Guert Gansevoort) sent marines ashore to guard the Seattle blockhouse and brought most of the town's women and children out to the *Decatur* for protection. On January 26 he bombarded the forest with the ship's cannon and a shore howitzer, and men armed with marine rifles and carbines answered shots coming from the forest bullet for bullet.

In mid-afternoon Commander Gansevoort ordered his men back to the ship, and winter twilight settled gently on town, bay, and forest. The next morning (January 27) a test volley brought no response. The Battle of Seattle was over. Nobody now can say how many casualties there were among the native people; their custom was to carry their dead with them after a battle. Whites apparently suffered two deaths.

Occasional skirmishes and killings continued and in March 1856 a final battle took place at Connell's Prairie. With it, the fighting west of the mountains largely ended. After attempts to talk peace with the Americans were ignored, Leschi led the remnant of his warrior army and their families across Naches Pass to Yakima to await further developments. On August 5, 1858, Territorial Governor Stevens changed the location of the Nisqually and Puyallup reservation, then placed a price on Leschi's head (see under FORT STEILACOOM on p. 311).

(Also see THE YAKIMA WAR sidebar, p. 148, and SPOKANE BATTLES sidebar, p. 10.)

All of **TACOMA** can be seen at a glance from the window of a plane flying south from Sea-Tac: the buildings and streets blanket a thumb that is broad at its I-5 base, long and tapering as it juts into Puget Sound. The aerial perspective makes clear the long, protected bay with miles of useable shore and also the transformation of the Puyallup River tideflats into a broad industrial flat fingered by seven artificial waterways.

English mariner Captain George Vancouver paused with his men at the north shore entrance to this harbor and enjoyed a high-noon dinner ashore on May 26, 1792; a plaque at Brown's Point commemorates the event. Forty-nine years later U.S. Navy Lieutenant Charles Wilkes directed the crew of the 88-foot brig *Porpoise* to explore this part of Puget Sound. From below the bluff of today's Tacoma, Lieutenant George Sinclair wrote, "Called this anchorage Commencement Bay. Sent the boats out Surveying. . . ." Their results showed that although Commencement Bay offered deep water protected from storms, mudflats dominated Elliott

Bay 30 miles to the north. Wilkes penned a note describing what is now Seattle's port as "not . . . a desirable anchorage." Thus Tacoma was favored over Seattle at the start, a ranking confirmed three decades later when the Northern Pacific chose Commencement Bay as its eagerly awaited terminus.

The years between exploration and the railroad's arrival brought the beginning of Tacoma's settlement. Swedish immigrant Nicholas Delin started a sawmill in 1852 at the head of the bay (near the present intersection of Puyallup Avenue and Dock Street) and there his employees' half-dozen cabins sprouted amid the skunk cabbage. Delin built his own house of sawn lumber from his mill. He advertised in the Olympia *Pioneer and Democrat* for "SAW LOGS! SAW LOGS!" and soon rafted boards a mile and a half down the bay to load onto ships about where the Northern Pacific would later build their first depot and permanent office building. Delin's market was San Francisco, where the 1849 gold rush had created an insatiable demand for piling and lumber.

Tacoma's Old City Hall faces the Elks Temple on one side, the Northern Pacific Headquarters Building on the other; horse-drawn fire wagons were housed in the building next door.

Not far from the mill, the German Peter Judson family farmed the area that is now downtown Tacoma. In 1854 their crops included a fine stand of wheat grown where the present railroad depot stands. It threshed out to 35 bushels, and the Judsons rowed it to New Market (later Tumwater, near Olympia) to be ground at Michael Simmons' gristmill.

Ten years later Job Carr, a newly discharged Union soldier, arrived in the West to take advantage of his veteran's right to a 320-acre claim. He knew the railroad was coming; checked maps at the government land office in Olympia; looked over Budd Inlet and Steilacoom and Seattle—and chose Commencement Bay. By then Delin had sold his mill, and the Judsons had moved away. Carr lived with the government carpenter at the Puyallup Reservation and rowed daily to his claim near today's N. 30th and McCarver (in Old Town). He opened a clearing and bucked logs for a cabin. When it was habitable he based at the claim and worked part time at Byrd's Mill (between present-day Lakewood and Steilacoom). In 1866 Carr's two sons, also veterans, and his daughter joined him. All four waited for word of the railroad.

Long before its rails had made any notable progress, a town "boomer" arrived on the scene and bought most of Job Carr's land. This was Morton Matthew McCarver, a venturesome man who developed a town in Iowa; came West and developed Linntown (Oregon City) near the confluence of the Willamette and Columbia rivers; joined the gold stampedes to California and the Fraser River; and then went to the Idaho and Montana silver rush. He also served in the Oregon provisional legislature and hoped to be appointed governor of Washington Territory when Isaac Stevens resigned to serve as territorial delegate to Congress. In short, McCarver was a go-getter. He knew the Northern Pacific was en route to Puget Sound and he intended to *be* there.

In Portland he met Delin, who had moved south after selling his mill. Heeding his suggestions about land, McCarver went to the government land office on the Puyallup Reservation. There, officials commented that Delin's old site was worthless as an anchorage, but that Carr's place offered both deep water and a reasonably gentle shoreline, a marked contrast with the steep bluffs lining most of the shore. McCarver swung a deal with Carr and set about promoting the land. He wrote letters, boasted to editors about his new town and the beauties and bounty of Puget Sound, and never failed to work in mention of the Northern Pacific's plans to end their rails at Commencement Bay—a statement that caught the eye although he had no basis for it.

McCarver arrived in 1868. The next year Samuel Hadlock and John Ackerson arrived, scouting a mill location for Charles Hanson, a redwood "shingle king" in California. McCarver successfully reinforced their judgment that ships could readily load at his fledgling town; the abundance of timber was self-evident. With a sawmill thus assured, interest in town lots increased. Tacoma was on its way, and so was the railroad. In 1870 tracks finally started reaching westward from Lake Superior. Jubilation reigned.

Three years later the first work train reached Commencement Bay. It eased over the hill to the shore below the present Old City Hall—and pitched ingloriously into the mud as the tracks gave way. Nobody was seriously hurt. Nobody seems even to have cared. Tacoma had become the terminus! Its selection was based on the excellence of the harbor and on the prospect—by ignoring the townsite McCarver had laid out—of controlling development and selling real estate for income. The railroad organized the Tacoma Land Development Company, headed by Charles B. Wright. Without ever moving from his Philadelphia home, he set about fathering an entirely new town a mile or two up the bay from McCarver's plat.

The company's need for income was urgent. Rails reached Tacoma but they connected, not eastward across the continent, but only 100 miles south to Kalama. From there nearly to Bismarck, North Dakota, the Northern Pacific had no tracks whatsoever: they had built both ends of a transcontinental railroad but not the 1,500-mile midsection. Retaining their 40-million-acre federal land grant hinged on completing tracks to salt water by December 19, 1873. Rails from Kalama to Tacoma technically met the schedule.

Even that degree of compliance had been in doubt. In July 1873, with no payroll money in hand, the construction contractor J. B. Montgomery faced a crisis. He, too, was from Philadelphia, a man with enough wealth to personally back the payroll with gold. He sent his wife Mary, who lived with him at the construction camp, to get it. She traveled 10 miles by horseback to the Toutle River, then by work train to the railhead, passenger train to Kalama, and steamer to Portland. There she went to a banker's home at 6:00 P.M. He opened his safe, gave her the money, and she headed north. Thirty-six hours after starting out, Mrs. Montgomery arrived back in camp.

In September Jay Cooke and Company, the Philadelphia banking firm selling Northern Pacific bonds, had to close its door; before sundown, an additional 37 brokerage houses and banks in New York also announced failure. Depression gripped the entire nation. Work on the railroad stopped in North Dakota. It continued in Washington, however, to meet the deadline for completion and hold onto the land grant. Montgomery drew against his credit to cover costs until creditors attached his home and other property. Then he quit. At Clover Creek (in today's Lakewood)—only 10 miles short of Commencement Bay—workers went on strike for back pay and barricaded themselves behind a breastwork of ties. John Ainsworth, at the time western manager for the Northern Pacific, arrived and presented an offer for payment in part cash, part IOUs, and part iron tokens that the company store at the Hanson-Ackerson sawmill agreed to exchange for groceries.

Replenishing its purse became the Northern Pacific's top priority. Stock trades and land sales offered the only hope. Wright had a plat of standard rectangles under way when he got word that the preeminent—and unorthodox—landscape architect Frederick Law Olmsted had been asked to design a townsite irresistible to investors and businessmen. Olmsted had six weeks for the job. From his New York offices, he and his staff drew plans based on topographical maps, sketches, and information regarding water tables and runoff. Streets followed contours, intersected by diagonal boulevards that climbed gently above the bay. "Blocks" varied in size and shape to conform with the hills and had no conventional right-angle corners. Parks made use of wet sites. The result was "novel in

character"—and discarded. The Tacoma Land Development Company returned to its simple grid that ignored topography but allowed the sale of lots to begin.

By 1878 the national economy recovered, and railroad crews in North Dakota began again to grade roadbed and lay track. Five years later rails spanned the northern continent, although trains still came to Tacoma via the Columbia River/Kalama route. In 1887 Northern Pacific rails crossed the Cascade Mountains via a tunnel at Stampede Pass, and Tacoma boomed. Wealthy Easterners rode across the continent and used Tacoma as a base for searching out townsites and timberlands to develop. Some made their home here, joining the transplanted Easterners who already were producing an enclave of civility within their new, raw setting. Homes began lining the hills, and the Tacoma Hotel, just up the bay from the city hall (now the Old City Hall), offered real elegance. Gentlemen kept their private shaving mugs at the Tacoma Hotel barbershop (only working-class men shaved themselves), and a Hawaiian band played for tea dances.

The city's school population, which had totalled 964 pupils in 1886, swelled to almost 2,300 by the time the new decade opened; total population rose to 36,000. A real estate developer named Allen Mason succeeded at promoting the town that McCarver had dreamt of a decade earlier. Mason advertised everywhere—even in church bulletins—calling Tacoma the "City of Destiny" and pointing out the opportunities for jobs. He opened plats, where people built large houses to accommodate family, guests, and boarders, most of whom were single men. Jobs were easy to get at the mills or the docks. Men unloaded the tea and silk ships from Asia and loaded the wheat, hops, and refined metals to be exported. They also loaded coal from the huge bunkers lining the head of the bay, for by the 1880s Tacoma had become one of the major coaling ports of the West Coast.

From a brick city hall patterned after an Italian palazzo, elected officials handled municipal affairs including, in 1893, the purchase of a small hydropower company begun 11 years earlier at Delin's old mill site. That acquisition made Tacoma the first city in the Northwest with a publicly owned utility. Monthly rates

Rails from the mines at Wilkeson and Carbonado delivered coal to Tacoma's waterfront bunkers beginning in the 1880s. From there, most of it was shipped to San Francisco.

previously had been $10 per bulb turned off by midnight, or $14 per bulb if burned all night. Public power could offer lower rates (a situation that still distinguishes Tacoma, even among other Northwest cities).

Rudyard Kipling, at the time a journalist for British newspapers, described Tacoma as "staggering under a boom of the boomiest." Tom Ripley, who arrived fresh from Yale University in 1889 to work as secretary-treasurer at a sawmill his father had backed financially, later described his impressions:

The wooden streets were flanked by sidewalks built up on wooden stilts on the downhill side. The houses on the upside were reached by steps, so many and so steep that going home seemed hardly worth the effort. . . . Confidence in the future found expression in architecture—the more confidence, the more spindles, jigsawed brackets, and band-sawed cresting atop the roof.

Confidence aside, disaster lurked. By the spring of 1893 depression again strangled the national economy. Fourteen of Tacoma's 21 banks failed, and even those that survived found no buyers for foreclosed properties offered at bargain prices. The Northern Pacific was again in receivership; so was the Tacoma Land Company. Forty percent of all taxes in the city fell delinquent. Even the poorhouse went broke. Overcrowded, it had to close.

That same year James J. Hill's Great Northern Railway reached Seattle. In several ways it outshone the Northern Pacific. It followed a shorter route, had easier grades overall, and crossed the Cascade Mountains where steep pitches are close enough together to allow efficient use of multiple engines. The Northern Pacific had built expecting profits to come from selling land. The Great Northern concentrated on freight.

Doldrums set in. Then miners struck gold in the Klondike and, beginning in 1897, Seattle hustled a position as key supply point for Alaska and the Yukon (a relation that continues today). In Tacoma the West Coast Grocery shipped supplies to Nome merchants, and a man from Puyallup went north with a hundred goats he hoped to rent as pack animals; but otherwise Tacoma mostly watched its rival optimize a slightly more favorable location and lure the stampede through its portals. The boost Seattle gained from both the Great Northern and the Klondike settled any question of which city would dominate Puget Sound.

Tacoma had thriving shipping and milling industries, however. To encourage the use of rail, the Northern Pacific had offered the St. Paul and Tacoma Lumber Company low freight rates and, before the crash, they built an enormous mill on the tideflats. The first huge Douglas fir log had gone up its ramp in April 1888, and a band saw—the very latest in technological advancement—had bit into the wood. The following year the *Tacoma Ledger* reported that the mill was producing more lumber than any other mill in the world. Its saws kept whirring through the mid-1890s depression.

In 1900 still more capital flowed from St. Paul to Tacoma: Frederick Weyerhaeuser, a hard-working German immigrant who had become the most powerful lumberman in America, bought 900,000 acres of railroad grant land and made Tacoma his corporate headquarters. He already owned vast tracts of southeastern pinelands. For advice on whether to also buy land in the Northwest, he sent George Long to look over prospects. Long reported favorably; the deal was consummated; and Weyerhaeuser began western operations from rented offices in the Northern Pacific Building.

Additional factors in the early 1900s also helped pull the city out of the depression. In 1905 the Guggenheim brothers sent Bernard Baruch, young attorney and Wall Street speculator, hustling from one Manhattan address to another to acquire the Tacoma smelter. He succeeded; the American Smelting and Refining Company took over management, and the smelter puffed smoke and played a key role in the shipment of metal until the 1980s. Tacoma City Light continued its pioneering hydropower role by developing outlying sites from near Mount Rainier to Hood Canal. Low power rates helped attract electrochemical plants, which still process salts (now mostly from Baja California's Scammons Lagoon, the bay renowned as a breeding ground for gray whales). Ample electricity also powered improved mill equipment, including machines to peel logs and laminate plywood, and to turn wood pulp into paper, cardboard, and fiberboard.

In January 1917, an even greater economic boost for Tacoma began with a favorable county vote on a bond issue that would finance the purchase of 70,000 acres of land to give to the U.S. Army. The details of the transaction, worked out just before the United States entered World War I, included army agreement to "establish and maintain upon said reservation, a division of mobile troops." This assured civilian payrolls. The Weyerhaeuser Company provided 73 million board feet of lumber, and Camp Lewis buildings rose even faster than scheduled. Colonel D. L. Stone, in charge of construction, later reported:

We completed those barracks at a rate of one every forty minutes . . . twelve each eight-hour day. We had to provide housing for 58,000 men and we had 15,000 workers on the job.

Stone's men built 50 miles of roads, a drill field 3 miles long, 1,700 buildings, and 400 other structures. Sixteen such camps rose across the nation. After the war, the army chose seven camps to convert to permanent status and, in 1927, Camp Lewis became Fort Lewis. The *Tacoma News Tribune* had warned, "Give us a payroll or give the land back to the county."

From about 1890 until the Korean War in the 1950s, army posts were intended to physically reflect the high standards of military life, which officers considered both structured and disciplined—the very antithesis of the self-seeking civilian scramble that had developed with the industrial age. The Olmsted brothers designed Fort Lewis' overall site plan with tree-lined boulevards and a traffic circle to separate the coming and going of officers from that of enlisted men.

Tacoma still pulses with the economic lifeblood of the military. But there is also a diversification that marks a full circle: logs awaiting export line the northwestern shore of Commencement Bay (although they are smaller than the branches of the forest giants they replace); container goods arrive by sea for shipment east by rail.

Scenic roads now circle Commencement Bay, offering a sense of the city; they form a drive to share with out-of-town visitors—or to enjoy on any sunny day. There are three officially designated National Register historic districts, one at each end of Pacific Avenue and one in the Stadium High School area (from the bluff to I

Street). Houses appear as a virtual museum of residential architecture from the 1890s to the present, all comfortably maintained and relatively unaltered. Plans for the early homes had to be approved by the railroad's Tacoma Land Company; among the various stipulations was an insistence that new houses avoid blocking the view from neighboring houses. Commissions went to nationally known firms with architects trained in New York and the Beaux Arts in Paris. The legacy here—both homes and commercial buildings—will please all who enjoy architecture.

Points of interest, keyed to the Tacoma map:

1 Browns Point gives delight in several forms: easy parking, shade trees and picnic tables, a pebble beach, a small lighthouse, and views of the city and the mountains. Sailboats skim by close inshore, and tugboats come to the turning buoy to meet oceangoing ships and tow them into the harbor. (To reach the point, drive 3 miles from the 11th Street Bridge in downtown Tacoma and turn west on Marine View Drive. Continue for another 3 miles, then turn off at a small shopping center onto Le-lou-wa Place NE and follow around the water's edge.)

Beginning in 1887, a 12-foot offshore "light pole" warned mariners of the hazard of turning too sharply at this point and, in 1903, the federal government built a wooden frame lighthouse. The present lighthouse and foghorn began winking and sounding their warning in the 1930s. The installation now is automated, and the grounds surrounding it are leased as a county park. Houses—some on pilings at the water's edge, some lining the hillside—began as summer homes where families came for weeks of swimming, rowing, sailing, and singing around clambake bonfires. A road reached the point in 1925, and the community gradually changed into a year-round neighborhood.

Beyond Brown's Point is **Dash Point,** which has both a city park and a state park. The city park features a sand beach and a 200-foot pier. The state park—at the mouth of the ravine—has a long sand beach and a broad delta, exposed at low tide.

2 The **Port Industrial Area** is accessible from downtown Tacoma by crossing the 11th Street Bridge. Its arterials, which grid the tide flats and cross a series of waterways, offer an exceptional look at shipping and industry (especially enticing for passengers; traffic will command the driver's attention).

Watch for a visitor observation tower a mile and a half east of the 11th Street Bridge, adjacent to the Port of Tacoma offices. (Turn off

Houses from Tacoma's early days include a remarkable range of sizes, eras, and styles.

Tacoma

Key to Numbered Locations

1	Browns Point	11	University Union Club
2	Port Industrial Area	12	Old Town
3	Union Station/State History Museum	13	Point Defiance Park
4	Downtown District	14	Stadium High/Hist. Soc. Library
5	Medical Arts Building	15	Annie Wright Seminary
6	Pantages Theater	16	Wright Park
7	Old City Hall	17	Narrows Bridge
8	Northern Pacific Building	18	Lakewold Gardens
9	Fireman's Park	19	Java Jive
10	Elks Temple	20	Fort Lewis Military Museum

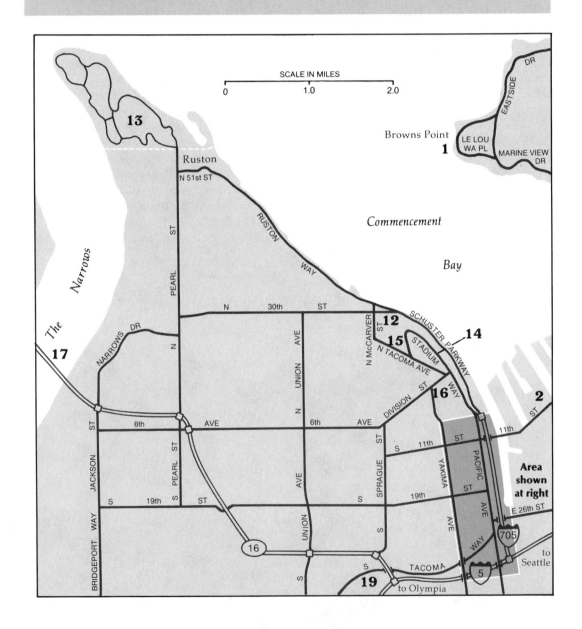

11th immediately beyond the long causeway east of the Puyallup River bridge; then follow a series of short jogs.) The tower provides a view of cranes 280 feet high unloading cargo containers for transshipment by rail. Refrigerated warehouses nearby store apples for export, and a pair of domed structures hold alumina (processed bauxite) imported from Australia for use in making aluminum. Along the waterway northeast of the tower, cars from Japan and Korea are driven off ships in colorful streams.

For those who delight in boats, the water offers an ideal vantage point for watching the ships and for sensing Tacoma's development, which proceeded from Old Town, around the bluff to where the railroad built its first terminus, and then on to the present downtown district. (Boats with outboard motors—intended for fishing—are usually available for rent at Point Defiance Park.)

3 In a sense, Tacoma did not grow, it *arrived*—by rail. The **Union Station** (Pacific at S. 19th; opened in 1911) climaxed the ebullience begun a quarter century earlier as the first train steamed down the slope to Commencement Bay a mile north of here. The new, copper-domed depot was designed by Reed and Stem, also responsible for New York City's Grand Central Station. Now restored and bedecked with glass art, it is flanked by a pair of new buildings. One houses federal courts; the other, the world-class **Washington State Historical Society Museum,** a heritage center for the entire state with extensive—and ingenious—exhibits. (Scheduled to open 1996.)

When the depot opened, the *Tacoma Ledger* assured readers, "It will be adequate for the future as well as the present." The statement proved totally true: Northern Pacific passenger travel already had peaked nationwide and soon declined precipitously as private automobiles and buses began their domination. Beginning at the end of the 1880s, the district close to the depot developed as the city's first industrial and warehouse center. Handsome brick warehouses that still face the railway depot will house a new University of Washington branch campus; original businesses ranged from a wholesale grocery and hardware outlets to a mattress factory, shoe factory, cracker factory, cabinetworks, and sash and door mills.

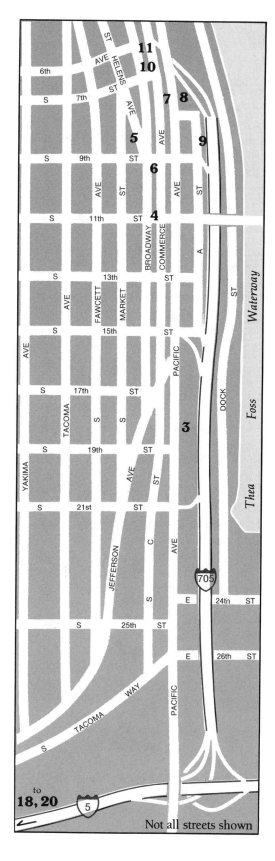

Hotels accommodated early-day travelers arriving by train and steamer ("First-class rooms for respectable people"). The six-story stone and cast-iron **Carlton Hotel** (S. 17th and Pacific; finished in 1909) opened soon after work had begun on Union Station. With rounded corner bays and elaborate roofline brackets and corbeling, it offered "The Best of Everything," including electricity, telephones, and private baths for 37 of its 120 rooms. The Carlton is at the north end of a nine-block historic district, now the Tacoma branch campus of the University of Washington. The old **Snoqualmie Falls Power building** (S. 19th and Commerce) and handsome brick **warehouses** (across from the history museum) have been—or will be—renovated for university use. The brick **Massasoit Hotel** (S. 17th and Broadway, built 1889) is just off campus.

4   A drive or walk through the **Downtown District** of Tacoma evokes a sense of changing patterns. It first existed as a string of wooden buildings along muddy streets edged with plank sidewalks. Commercial and social activity centered here, sandwiched between the industrial area to the south and the administrative center to the north. By 1883 the huge and elegant Tacoma Hotel dominated the waterfront at the foot of 10th and A streets. A wooden opera house stood up the hill on Ninth Street. Ordinances required new construction in brick and masonry after 1880s fires had destroyed individual buildings in Tacoma and raged disastrously through Seattle, Spokane, and Ellensburg.

Buildings of enduring quality and outstanding design resulted. By the 1960s, however, the nationwide popularity of shopping malls accessible by car dealt a death blow to scores of hub cities previously served by interurban trains and streetcars. In Tacoma many ornate downtown buildings were razed. Some were replaced with parking garages in hopes of encouraging the use of those that remained. Some—now shouldered by new buildings—have found adaptive uses. For example, the former **National Bank of Tacoma** building (12th and Pacific; built in 1922) now houses the Tacoma Art Museum, and the five-building **Rhodes Department Store** complex (11th and Broadway; dating from the early 1900s) has become the University of Puget Sound law school.

5   Architecture buffs will particularly admire the 10-story **Medical Arts Building** (747 St. Helens; built in 1929), which now serves as the city hall. It stands on a site that slopes both north-south and east-west, giving the building a greater architectural vitality than would be true on a flat site. Interior and exterior are rich with Art Deco ornamentation, providing an aesthetic unity. The original marble and polished-slate lobby has been faithfully restored, replete with its spectacular three-story spiral stairway and 35-foot chandelier.

At the time of construction, the building pioneered combining doctors' offices, laboratories, and hospital rooms within a single complex. It now is listed in the National Register of Historic Places.

6   The **Pantages Theater** (Ninth and Broadway; completed in 1918) exemplifies decades of continued use for its original purpose, although with an evolution from vaudeville to movies and back to live performances. It was originally designed by the master theater architect Marcus Priteca, who completed the Seattle Opera House just before his death. Tacoma's Pantages is the oldest remaining building in the famed theater chain. Its acoustics are near perfect, an effect achieved through the use of elaborate plaster ornamentation specifically designed for its effect on how sound carries.

7   The high-style Italianate architecture of the **Old City Hall** (S. Seventh and Pacific; built in 1893) reflects the exuberance Tacomans felt in building their city amid the stumps. This north end of the present downtown section developed first, its location determined by that of the first railroad depot. Wooden buildings soon were augmented—and replaced—by stone and brick structures of outstanding architectural design.

The walls of the Old City Hall are eight feet thick at the base, built of brick brought as ballast in sailing ships. The square clock tower is actually built free-standing and with walls leaning slightly inward as they rise to enhance the sense of height. Cast terra-cotta cornices further lead the eye up the facade to the crowning splendor of the tower. The building was at first intended for use by the Chamber of Commerce. In the 1970s it was renovated into boutiques and restaurants, in the 1980s into professional offices.

The renowned Pantages Theater in downtown Tacoma was renovated in 1983.

8 Directly across the street from the Old City Hall is the **Northern Pacific Building** (S. Seventh and Pacific; built in 1888, now also an office building). Trains originally stopped directly below this site at a small bay (now filled in), and the railroad commissioned the building for its western headquarters offices. Their presence here prompted the siting of the city hall: the city's two powers faced each other across its main street.

Half of the Northern Pacific Building was demolished after the railroad moved its main offices to Seattle in 1920. The area of the missing half is now a park. The remaining half still represents Tacoma's fine early architecture.

9   Fireman's Park (along the bluff, centered

at S. Ninth) is actually the lid for the Schuster Parkway and the freeway approach. Its 105-foot totem pole—raised in 1903 and allegedly dedicated by President Theodore Roosevelt—was donated by proud Tacomans who wanted a taller pole than the one in Seattle's Pioneer Square. Furthermore, they wanted it specially made for Tacoma, not stolen from a supposedly abandoned north coast village, as was true of Seattle's pole. Consequently a family of British Columbia carvers moved to Dockton (on Maury Island) and carved the pole.

10 Up the hill from the Old City Hall, the design motifs of the **Elks Temple** (565 Broadway; built in 1916) convey a sense of classicism, fashionable at the time of construction. The building boasted a swimming pool, a theater with fixed seats, and an auditorium without seats, used for cotillions. A grand stairway inspired by the famed Spanish Steps in Rome sweeps downslope beside the building.

11 The Classic Revival **University Union Club** (539 Broadway; built in 1889) retains its spectacular view out over the bay and its sense of tasteful refinement. Within paneled parlors and dining rooms, early-day city fathers met with Eastern investors. On appropriate occasions, ladies entered through a side door. The club still meets regularly.

12 **Old Town** (centered at N. 30th and Ruston Way) is the site of Job Carr's cabin and Morton McCarver's early promotion of Tacoma as a townsite. Work on **St. Peter's Episcopal Church** (2910 Starr; built in 1873) began with announcement by the Northern Pacific Railroad of Tacoma's selection as western terminus; three weeks later, on August 10, 1873, the building held its first service. The free-standing belfry was created by topping a cedar tree to a 40-foot height and hoisting up a bronze bell donated by St. Peter's in Philadelphia.

The **Slavonian Hall** in Old Town (2306 N. 30th; built in 1902) served as a fraternal lodge and social center for old-country fishermen and millworkers. Shipyards along the waterfront here specialized in building fishing boats, and members of the Slavonian American Benevolent Society contributed crucially to adapting purse-seine equipment and techniques to West Coast fishing. The society still owns the hall.

Ruston Way follows Commencement Bay for 4 miles, essentially from the wheat terminal near the Old City Hall to the smelter site (abandoned in the 1980s). It offers restaurants and a series of parks that include a bike trail, fishing shelters, a historic fireboat, and the head saw and 61-ton, two-story carriage from the huge Dickman Mill, which burned in the 1970s. The Dickman was the last of the lumber mills to line the bay.

At the north end of Ruston Way, the separately incorporated town of Ruston clustered around the smelter. It is named for William Rust who, in 1890, bought a small smelter begun two years earlier by Dennis Ryan. Rust sold to the American Smelting and Refining Corporation in 1905—and built a Classic Revival mansion of Wilkeson sandstone trimmed with wooden columns and molding. Furnishings came from Wanamakers in Philadelphia. (The house is still standing at N. 10th and I.)

13 **Point Defiance Park** (northwest tip of Tacoma) began as a military reservation set aside in 1866. Twenty-two years later, when no use had yet been made of it, the city asked for the land as a park. Real estate developer Allen Mason, who had a recent city annexation to promote, knew that a park would lead to the construction of a streetcar line, and that its only logical route lay across his property. To help assure the line, he convinced the territorial delegate to Congress to bring up the matter—and a streetcar station became the park's first structure, built even before the federal government gave the city full title to the land in 1905. A tile roof with upturned eaves suggests a vaguely Japanese design, and a Japanese garden adjoins the building. A path and stairs lead to the beach (which is also accessible by road).

At the beach a boathouse/pavilion rebuilt in the 1980s continues the function of predecessors from as early as 1902. A ferry connects to Vashon Island (p. 300). It makes a pleasant voyage on a foot passenger basis or as part of an exploratory Pugetopolis loop by car, connecting with ferries at the north end of the island.

A reconstruction of the Hudson's Bay Company's mid-1800s Fort Nisqually overlooks the Narrows. Beyond it, Camp Six (near the park's Vassault Street exit) displays buildings and steam equipment brought in from the woods as old-time logging camps began disappearing.

Essentially undisturbed forest adjoins the camp—indeed, most of Point Defiance Park has been selectively cleared but never logged. A loop drive and miles of trail wind beneath giant Douglas fir and red cedar, reminder of the environment that was home for native people and for arriving settlers. An outstanding zoo includes an introduction to local, natural environments and species, including tide pools and the rocky coast.

14   Stadium High School (N. First and N. E; begun in 1891) was designed in French chateau style by Hewitt and Hewitt, Philadelphia architects. It was to be the Tacoma Land Company's hotel, a palace that—in the words of lumberman Thomas Ripley—would

make the Frontenac in Quebec and the Canadian Pacific Railroad Hotel in Banff blush for their modest proportions. . . . [Blueprints] covered desks and the floor. We measured baseboard and casing by the mile. . . . We foresaw a jungle of carving in rare and exotic woods. It was a riot of millwork.

When walls and roofs were barely complete, the 1893 financial crash halted construction. The Northern Pacific used the building's shell as a warehouse for lumber and shingles. In 1896 the wood caught fire; the sky glowed red even in Seattle, and sympathetic citizens came by boat to help fight the blaze and to bring food. The railroad company salvaged 73,300 bricks from the facade and shipped them to Missoula, Montana, and Wallace, Idaho, for depots, then slowly prepared for demolition.

One morning in 1902 two men walking to work passed the hulk, thought of the city's need for a high school, got architect Frederick Heath to the site by noon, called a special meeting at 1:30 P.M.—and on their way home from work that evening had the satisfaction of seeing that demolition had stopped. Plans were drawn, and conversion to a high school got under way, one of the state's earliest and finest examples of the adaptive reuse of a building. The first classes opened in the erstwhile hotel/erstwhile disaster in September 1906.

Immediately north of the high school is an open-air stadium dedicated in 1910, the second such stadium in the nation. (Harvard University built one in 1908.) Beyond it is the original building of the **Washington State Historical Society** (N. Third and N. Stadium; opened in 1911 and with later additions), donated by real estate developer Allen Mason. A new museum building adjoining the restored Union Station (Pacific Avenue) is expected to open in summer 1996. The old building will continue to house the society's library, work space, and offices.

15   The **Annie Wright School** (827 Tacoma

Stadium High began as a hotel but was converted into a school after an 1896 fire.

N.; built in 1924) exemplifies the expectations of early-day families north of Tacoma's commercial and industrial heart. The school (now co-ed) began in 1884, endowed as a girls' seminary by Charles Wright, president of the Tacoma Land Company, whose young daughter Annie had died. The existence of the seminary "eased the terror of being 2,000 miles away from Eastern schools," according to one Tacoma matron with daughters to educate.

For a sense of the neighborhood surrounding Annie Wright—still a highly regarded private school—drive along C, D, and E streets between the seminary and the historical society building. Houses range in era and architecture from the elaborate Queen Anne **Vaeth House** (built about 1895) and the Classic Revival **Gower House** (built about 1905)—both at the corner of Fifth and N. E, both designed by Paris-trained Ambrose J. Russell—to the Cotswold Cottage **Hewitt House** (616 N. D; begun in 1925).

Toward Wright Park from the historical society building, notice also the **Henry Drum House** (9 St. Helens; built in 1895), which uses a variety of sheathing, siding, and shingles to express its original owners' optimism and status (now used for offices), and the **Blackwell House** (402 Broadway; built in 1900), which has been restored for use as a YWCA building.

16 Wright Park retains great charm (Sixth Avenue to Division, and I to G streets; landscaped in the 1890s). It began providing focus for north-end life at a time when Tacoma was brimming with awareness of amenities. Prominent railroad and lumber men and their wives had organized the first golf club west of the Mississippi, a lawn tennis club (men only but with the ladies campaigning to use the courts one afternoon a week), an art league, and the Northwest's first Junior League. Charles Wright donated 27 acres for the park; the city bought 3 acres.

Park development began when the treasurer of the St. Paul and Tacoma Lumber Company went to England on business, and the head of the city parks board, who had apprenticed at Kew Gardens, sent along a letter requesting a few trees for Tacoma's new park. Back came hundreds of small switches, now magnificent trees that include chestnuts, yews, mulberries, magnolias, and an exotic Empress of China. Paths wander beneath the trees, through a rose garden, and to a duck pond. An all-glass, domed conservatory (built in 1907) houses tropical species, including collections of orchids and cacti. Its seasonal displays range from chrysanthemums at Thanksgiving and poinsettias at Christmas to lilies, tulips, and azaleas at Easter.

17 Traffic first crossed the **Narrows Bridge** in July 1940. Motorists often noticed the bridge undulating and would see cars ahead of them disappear into a trough, even on days without wind. The venturesome dubbed the bridge "Galloping Gertie" or the "Roller Coaster" and enjoyed its gyrations. On November 7, however—after only four months of service and with winds of only 42 knots—the center span leapt and writhed and tilted, then collapsed into the Sound. Only one driver and one pedestrian were at risk; both managed to crawl to safety.

Most engineers thought the problem was in the construction, which was not strong enough to withstand buffeting as winds swept through the constricted Narrows. An aerodynamicist, however, argued that the trouble lay with the shape the bridge presented to the wind. Air flowing around the sidewalls formed eddies and induced vibration, somewhat as the lee edge of an improperly handled sail may flutter. Wind tunnel tests confirmed his judgment. The disastrous defect was corrected by designing open-sided plates and traffic lanes separated from each other by grates. That done, a second bridge, otherwise identical to the first one, opened in October 1950. The old bridge still rests on the bottom and serves as a home for fish.

18 Lakewold Gardens (at Gravelly Lake, in the Lakewood area; modest fee) is a private estate now open to the public on a reservation basis. The phone number is listed in the Tacoma directory; call to set a time and get directions. The Georgian-style house was built as a summer cottage in 1907 by the H. F. Alexanders, who hired the Olmsted Brothers to design their landscaping. The result, which has evolved over the decades, includes elaborate plantings and topiary, a fountain with a backdrop view of Gravelly Lake and Mount Rainier, and a lone Douglas fir deliberately kept from the original forest and now the center of a shade garden. The property is owned by a private foundation.

19 The **Java Jive** cabaret (2102 S. Tacoma Way; built in 1927) will appeal to those who enjoy the whimsical counterpoint of automobile-age architecture. Shaped like a teapot, it was built in sections at a mill on the tideflats, trucked to this site on what was U.S. 99, and bolted together. A dance floor remains, but the secret door that opened from the ladies' room into a speakeasy in back of the building is nailed shut; look for it just to the left at the entry to the powder room. Original restrooms were out-houses shaped like salt and pepper shakers.

20 At the **Fort Lewis Military Museum** (I-5 Exit 121 for southbound traffic; Exit 119 for northbound) galleries cover Northwest military history from the days of frontier posts through World War II. Outside displays include tanks and armored cars from World War I to the present—an eerie array of cumbersome monsters like updated, mobile suits of mail worn by medieval knights.

Since 1978 the museum has been housed in a striking chalet-style building that stands con-spicuously by the freeway, dramatically lit at night. It was completed in 1919 as a 150-room inn at Green Park, a rest-and-recreation area for personnel at nearby Camp Lewis. All buildings in the park had to be approved by the camp commandant.

The YMCA administered two "hostess houses" at the park; there also were ice cream and lunch parlors, a horse racetrack, and a photo studio. The inn—now listed in the National Register of Historic Places—was built by the Salvation Army. So far as is known, it is the only Salvation Army building remaining from World War I. Construction funds came entirely from public donations.

WILKESON stands as a grid of residential streets and a brick business district surrounded by forest and peaks. A handsome three-story sandstone school built in 1913 and listed in the National Register of Historic Places looms at the east end of town (turn left at the fork in the main road through town). In the center of Wilkeson, the blue "onion dome" topping the belfry of Holy Trinity Orthodox Church (built in 1910;

also in the National Register) holds a three-barred Slavic cross, indication of the back-ground of many coal miners drawn here in the 1870s. Inside the church a screen with icons separates the nave from the sanctuary.

As early as 1862 settlers spoke of finding outcroppings of coal in the Carbon River canyon, and railroad surveyors confirmed their reports. Mining began in 1873 although shipping waited another three years until the Northern Pacific extended rails to Wilkeson from Tacoma. The coal tested as suitable for coking, a process of using heat to drive off impurities and produce a fuel that burns at the high temperatures required by steel mills and smelters. In 1885 the Tacoma Coke and Coal Company began building what became a total of 160 coke ovens. Forty of them still stand in a double row on the right side of the road beyond the school. They look like 12-foot beehives of brick. A sandstone wall ran along the front of the ovens, leaving arched openings. Heat has partially melted and fused the inner surfaces of the bricks.

Men shoveled in dry, clean coal from rail cars running along the top of the ovens and built wood fires on the floors to start the coking process. From 48 to 96 hours later—depending on the quality of coke desired—they shoveled out the finished products. By 1902 at least 100 ovens were in constant use but in the late 1930s, when copper smelting switched to fur-naces fired by pulverized coal or oil, the demand for coke dropped off, and the ovens were abandoned.

Coal was not Wilkeson's only product. Until the 1970s the town was renowned for its sand-stone, first reported by Samuel Wilkeson, an assistant to Jay Cooke who helped sell bonds to finance the Northern Pacific. Wilkeson noticed the huge outcropping while reconnoitering with the chief engineer for the railroad's trans-continental route. In the 1870s the company began quarrying the stone for use as railroad ballast. In 1883 commercial contractors also started using Wilkeson stone for buildings. Best known is the capitol dome in Olympia, built of stones cut here to precise measurements and fitted without mortar by master masons.

(Also see CARBONADO, p. 303.)

Foothills

East of the Puget Sound lowlands, foothills rise gently to the Cascade Mountains, many of them still timbered and with valleys sheltering small towns that once were farming centers. Former coal mining towns, which gave King County its first major industry, still remain, some of them now bedroom communities for city workers.

History museums are at Black Diamond, Issaquah, and North Bend. Carnation is the home of a large dairy, which is open to visitors (self-guided tours). And vintage locomotives pull tourist trains from the town of Snoqualmie to a viewpoint overlooking Snoqualmie Falls and to North Bend. Train buffs will particularly enjoy historic depots at Snoqualmie, Issaquah, and Black Diamond and may want to trace the routes of the various lines that served the coal towns (and were intended to someday connect with transcontinentals).

BLACK DIAMOND is attractive in its tree-filled setting. The train station (Railroad and Baker; built in the 1880s) now houses a historical museum with the old jail moved alongside; the bakery still produces superb bread; and Mass is still said at Saint Barbara's Catholic Church, built in 1911 to serve Italian and Austrian miners.

In the 1870s the Black Diamond Coal Company, a California firm, sent representatives to scout western Washington for coal deposits. They found the valuable Black Diamond/Ravensdale/Franklin coalfield and in 1884 opened a mine, called Number 14 for its location in Section 14 of the township. Workers eventually dug two other mines—one 6,200 feet deep—and daily output reached 800 to 1,000 tons. At first the company packed out coal by trail to the Black River, and barged it to Seattle. In 1885, however, the Columbia and Puget Sound Railroad (a Northern Pacific subsidiary) laid tracks from Renton to Black Diamond to serve the new mines.

Most miners were European immigrants who lived in ethnic enclaves nicknamed Welsh Town, Swede Town, and so on. They could buy their homes but not the land beneath them; the company charged a token dollar a year rent for the land. In 1907, when Knights of Labor organizers came to Black Diamond, they had difficulty finding a place not owned by the company where they could meet. Local lore contends that a certain stump west of town in Section 15 finally served as the soapbox from which they successfully recruited members.

Men who were unable to continue heavy work in the mines instead stood at the screening tables handpicking rocks from the coal. Their jobs were noisy, dusty, and tedious.

Management—predictably—opposed the union and, during a nationwide coal strike in 1921, it ordered all striking miners to move their houses off company land. Many could not afford the cost and had to abandon their homes and start over. Tim Morgan, one of the area's earliest settlers and owner of the famous stump, offered low-cost lots; the union donated lumber. Cottages in the western section of today's Black Diamond—still called Morganville—date from this time.

With such tactics the company broke the strike, but by then Washington's coal era had ended. Effective demands for higher wages and better working conditions coincided with the decline in demand for coal as new fuels became available. Sloping coal seams made mining here particularly dangerous and expensive. They also required the use of so much machinery that generating power for underground motors, pumps, and locomotives used up much of the coal produced. The Black Diamond operation closed.

In 1890 the Leary Coal Company opened a seam at **Ravensdale** (northwest of Black Diamond) and soon had it producing so well that the mine attracted the Northwest Improvement Company, the coal-mining arm of the Northern Pacific Railroad. The company bought the property and brought in experienced Italian, Polish, and Lithuanian miners from East Coast coal towns. Mining was the one skill these men knew. In a 1961 *Seattle Times* interview, Mrs. Frank Markus, a miner's wife, described the life:

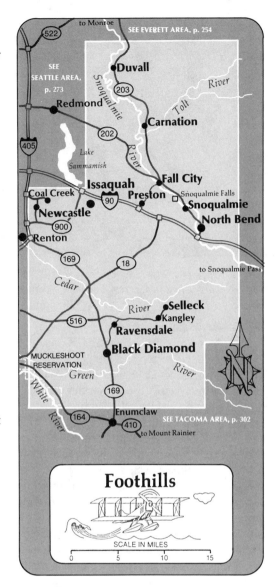

Men would walk five or six miles to work in a mine. When one closed they walked to another at Selleck or Kangley or Kanasket. . . . Pay was 20 cents an hour for a ten-hour day. . . . I knew of neighbors working in the mines from 6 A.M. to 6 P.M. for $2, and supporting seven or eight kids.

In the summer less coal was burned and the mines employed them only two or three hours a day. They worked at whatever they could get.

A 1915 explosion killed 31 Ravensdale miners, and the company abandoned the vein. Faced with declining demand, they closed the operation and moved many of the houses to Roslyn (east of Snoqualmie Pass), a coal town also operated by the Northwest Improvement Company. Eight years later another operator reopened the Ravensdale mine and continued production until 1949. Several houses remain at Ravensdale, although there are no particular indications of the mine.

Bucolic **CARNATION**—formerly called Tolt— lies in the Snoqualmie River Valley 20 miles east of Seattle. Dairies and U-pick berry farms surround the town, and a countryside drive winds back through time: Carnation is close to Pugetopolis, yet wholly apart.

The town began when James Entwistle deserted from the U.S. Army at Steilacoom in

Dairying was—and is—a major Snoqualmie Valley industry. Milk went in five-gallon cans to both creameries and groceries; bottling and home delivery came later.

1858, a fairly common occurrence at the time. Entwistle homesteaded at present-day Carnation, where he eventually became a wealthy hop farmer and respected community leader. Within a decade of his arrival, loggers working in twos and threes began chewing into the forest, and oxteams dragged logs to the Snoqualmie River. Workers boomed the logs until fall freshets raised the river, then floated the accumulation downstream to Snohomish, a cold, wet job. Pioneer Byron Bagwell remembered that they would "rough it down and hike back, often sleeping in wet clothes."

By 1876 the population had grown enough to warrant weekly mail service by packhorse from Snohomish, and river steamers sometimes came as far as Tolt during periods of high water. Steamer service was a great convenience compared to overland travel, as is evident from W. A. Templeton's description in *A History of Tolt/Carnation*. His family arrived from Seattle in 1878, having traveled for two days to cover a distance that now takes an hour to drive. First they went by stage from the Seattle waterfront to Lake Washington, where they crossed "on a little steamer (burning wood)." From there they loaded goods onto packhorses, traveled to Redmond, and stayed overnight with settlers, the Perrigo family:

The next day, Will Perrigo took his horses to take us

over the trail by Ames Lake to Tolt, since there were no roads. George Shaw met us at the top of the hill above Tolt to help carry things down to the river, where we crossed in a large Indian canoe. My mother was scared to get into the canoe and that tickled the Indians for they knew the river better than anyone else. The next day, they cut trees and made a trail so that Mr. Perrigo could get down to the river with the horses and our belongings.

Not until 1910, when the Great Northern built a line through the Snoqualmie Valley, did loggers and farmers have adequate transportation for their products. A year later the Chicago, Milwaukee and St. Paul Railroad also built through the valley.

In 1910 Elbridge Amos Stuart, owner of the Carnation Milk Company in Kent, bought 350 acres of timber and brush near Tolt. He cleared the land, diked the Snoqualmie River to control its flooding, and bought a purebred bull and 84 registered Holstein cows as the basis for a research dairy herd. Tolt thereupon changed its name to Carnation.

Stuart's farm now has grown to 1,200 acres, but its original purpose continues: to breed high-producing cows. A maternity barn, calf research barn, and milking carousel dot the grounds. A statue of "Possum Sweetheart," who in 1920 alone produced 37,381 pounds of milk—a world record—stands by the offices. In 1929 the

Carnation Company acquired Albers Milling Company and added some of its research projects to those concerning cows. The result was a complex with kennels and catteries where pet food was tested. Now Nestle is the owner and dairying is again the farm's sole purpose. It is open for self-guided tours April through October. (Drive north of Carnation on State Route 203 for about a mile and turn left on Carnation Farm Road. The farm is about 2½ miles farther.)

In **DUVALL** pleasant shops now face State Route 203, as earlier businesses once faced the Snoqualmie River. Duvall (then Cherry Valley) began in the 1870s with small outlying logging camps; a riverside mill later turned out "Rite-Grade" shingles. Farmers soon followed the loggers, and stern-wheel steamboats started bringing in freight, groceries, and supplies from Everett or Seattle. An early bridge across the Snoqualmie here was a hand-winched span that swung aside to let the steamboats pass.

In the early 1900s the Chicago, Milwaukee and St. Paul Railroad planned a line along the river to tap lumber resources. They wanted a low-level route that would put their tracks directly through the town of Cherry Valley. Negotiations ensued. The railroad offered to move buildings to higher land. Townsfolk accepted, and in 1909 Cherry Valley moved a half mile south to the present location. The name changed to Duvall in honor of an early family. Among the buildings that were moved is an 1888 farmhouse, now restored by the local historical society.

FALL CITY is named for its location 3 miles below Snoqualmie Falls. An 1880 hop shed stands in the county park a quarter mile north of town as a reminder of a once-vibrant industry. The cemetery (Lake Alice Road and SE 47th) occupies a hill overlooking the Snoqualmie Valley; it is the final resting place for pioneers Josiah Merritt, after whom Mount Si was named, and Jeremiah Borst, founder of Fall City. The pastoral views make the cemetery worth visiting. (From Fall City drive south about a half mile on Preston–Fall City Road. Turn left on Lake Alice Road.)

In February 1856 Major J. H. H. Van Bokkelen led 200 Washington Territorial Volunteers to Snoqualmie Valley to prevent native warriors from crossing Snoqualmie Pass. The soldiers hewed logs for protective forts: Fort Alden near present-day North Bend; Fort Smalley opposite it on the north bank of the Snoqualmie River; Fort Tilton, the largest, a mile below Snoqualmie Falls; and Fort Patterson at today's Fall City (none still standing). No attack parties materialized, so Van Bokkelen put his men to work exploring the countryside and building a road around Snoqualmie Falls. When conflict dissipated, some of the volunteers settled in the Snoqualmie Valley, although the isolation soon discouraged them. Most had moved on before homesteaders arrived in the 1860s.

In 1869 a trading post operated at Fall City and, four years later, a sawmill wheezed to life. Steamboats from Everett began to arrive during high water, and the town grew as a de facto commercial center for cattle ranchers and hop farmers. In 1887, aware that the railroad was coming and development would surely follow, Jeremiah Borst formally platted the town. The rails ended up bypassing his town, but

Expert sawmen began cutting shingle bolts from a cedar log 17 feet in diameter.

nonetheless contributed to overall prosperity; dependable, year-round transportation was at least close by.

ISSAQUAH today presents sprawling urban amenities to travelers arriving over Snoqualmie Pass, but those who take time to turn into the old part of town and to look at its encircling, very abruptly rising mountains will sense bygone days. Issaquah has been a milltown and dairy center, and even earlier a coal mining and hops farming town. Buildings date from as early as 1853. Notice especially the classic 1889 Seattle, Lake Shore and Eastern Railroad depot (Front and Sunset) and the false-fronted Odd Fellows Hall, now a theater (58 Front Street, also built in 1889). The new library (behind the depot) warrants a stop to contemplate the salmon-cycle sculpture with its implications of inherent and human-caused change within time's flow; a history museum (165 SE Andrews) spotlights the human tenure here. For a bucolic drive, follow the road south to Hobart.

As early as 1859 a settler discovered coal on his claim in Squak Valley, the early name for Issaquah. He formed a partnership for hauling it to Seattle via a tortuous wagon route to Lake Sammamish, then by scow down Sammamish Slough to Lake Washington, across the lake, and by wagon to the city—a 20-day round trip that rarely was profitable. Other entrepreneurs also entered the field, but until the Seattle, Lake Shore and Eastern Railroad arrived in the 1880s, Issaquah coalfields remained largely untapped.

The railroad developed during the period between the arrival of the Northern Pacific in Tacoma in 1873 and the Great Northern in Seattle 20 years later. When Daniel Gilman came West to operate his brother's Squak Valley coal mines, he recognized transportation as the immediate problem and masterminded the Seattle, Lake Shore and Eastern Railroad. Its track was to curve north around Lake Washington to the coalfields at Issaquah and the iron deposits west of Snoqualmie Pass, then cross the mountains and connect with transcontinental lines in Spokane. Seattle would benefit without tying itself to arch-rival Tacoma.

In 1888 Gilman's rails reached Issaquah, and the mine shipped its first coal. Encouraged, the Seattle, Lake Shore and Eastern continued laying track to North Bend—but stopped a few miles east of there: the touted iron deposits proved scanty, the railroad itself unprofitable. The improved transportation it brought did stimulate logging and agriculture, however, as well as serve the Issaquah mines, which produced steadily from 1888 to 1904. (Also see NEWCASTLE, p. 347.)

Norwegian brothers Lars, Peter, and Ingebright Wold left a shoe business in Seattle to pioneer hop growing here. Lars came first. In 1867 he paddled up Sammamish Slough with a native guide, seeking land and testing the soil as he went along. Issaquah seemed promising, and he bought a farm from an earlier settler. His brothers joined him, filed additional homestead papers, and built a cabin where the three claims joined: each brother had a bedroom on his own property. The next spring Lars bought hop plants from pioneer Puyallup grower Ezra Meeker and began experimenting with this new crop, although the brothers earned their living by feeding cattle driven over Snoqualmie Pass from the Kittitas Valley. They fattened the herds on rutabagas and hay, then owners drove them on to Seattle for sale.

In 1885 the Wolds contracted with a Seattle labor boss for Chinese hop pickers willing to accept low wages. Their timing proved tragic. Editorialists accused the Chinese of everything from opium addiction to "stealing" jobs from whites and saving money instead of spending it. On September 7 a mob insisted that the Wolds send their pickers back to Seattle and threatened violence when Lars refused to interrupt the harvest. That night the mob shot into tents where the 37 Chinese workers slept. They killed three men, wounded three. The alleged gunmen stood trial, but public opinion so favored them that the jury returned verdicts of "not guilty."

The Wolds, like other Issaquah growers, eventually plowed under their hops and bought dairy cows. Aphids repeatedly ruined hop vines; sprays did little good and cost a great deal. On the other hand, Seattle milk drinkers were consuming 15,000 gallons per day. Farm districts surrounding the city began to cater to this thirst.

The **MUCKLESHOOT RESERVATION** stretches along the White River valley southeast of Auburn with little to set it apart visually

In 1877 a narrow-gauge railroad crossed a ravine near Newcastle on a wooden trestle 138 feet high and 1,200 feet long; a second trestle, parallel to the first, later carried standard-gauge track. (Notice the men standing at each level in this photo.)

from the surrounding area. A building of particular interest, however, is Saint Claire's Mission (39015 172nd SE, next to the tribal center), built in 1870 with pole rafters and hand-split cedar boards. It was abandoned after windstorm damage in 1934; later it was moved to a heritage village at a Federal Way shopping center for preservation. In 1979 the Muckleshoot tribe moved it back to the reservation.

Natives who lived in the Green and White river valleys were scheduled to move to the Nisqually Reservation. In 1857, however, the federal government set aside land for them on Muckleshoot Prairie. White farmers subsequently bought or leased much of that land. The present reservation, enlarged from the original designation, forms an awkward diagonal string of sections touching only at their corners, a configuration that has caused conflicts between tribal members and their white neighbors.

NEWCASTLE today gives little hint of its industrial origins. A county park laced with hiking trails and dotted with seemingly mysterious concrete foundations encompasses the heart of the old coal district. Known mine openings, which might be dangerous, have been

sealed; a 1980s survey identified 166 such openings and land subsidences.

At a time when only small logging operations penetrated deep forest in the Bellevue area, and hopyards filled Issaquah Valley, housewives in Newcastle and Coal Creek shopped at company stores, and off-duty miners shot pool and drank beer at local saloons. The two mining towns, separated by a mile and a half of tangled, green forest, constituted King County's second largest community in the 1880s, exceeded only by Seattle. Furthermore, because Seattle had no large sawmill to foster a lumber export business, Newcastle coal amounted to a great boon. It attracted San Francisco and East Coast investors and played a major role in developing the Seattle harbor.

An 1884 *Harper's Magazine* article spoke of Newcastle straggling

in and out of the great dumps of clay and waste that extend like black spurs from the foot of the mountain, the cottages being grouped upon the rocky, stump-infested, forest-bound hillside, without an attempt at order or comeliness.

Two remnants of the coal-mining era remain at

Newcastle. The Baima house, an 1870s worker's cottage now restored to its original board-and-batten appearance, stands amid newer houses and outbuildings (7210 138th SE). About 1½ miles away is the early 1900s Ford Slope, the concrete entrance arch to a coal mine. The mine offers a destination for a short hike—pleasant on a dry day, muddy in wet weather. (The trail is accessible from the junction of Lakemont Boulevard with the Newcastle–Coal Creek Road. Use Exit 11A off I-90 to reach both house and trail; consult a detailed map to minimize confusion with jogs in the road.)

Prospectors found the Newcastle coal in 1863, a decade after Bellingham mines had started shipping coal to San Francisco. Investors formed a company and set miners to work picking and shoveling surface deposits and digging shallow tunnels. They, too, expected to supply San Francisco; Seattle in the 1860s and 1870s was still too small to offer much of a market.

At first miners sacked the coal and carted it to Lake Washington for transshipment by barge. But by 1872 profits warranted developing a more direct route. Men then dumped coal into cars that were pulled to Lake Washington by horses (and eventually by a diminutive steam locomotive). From there the cars were barged across the lake, pulled to Lake Union, barged again, then pulled to coal bunkers on Elliott Bay. In 1879 a narrow-gauge short line, the Seattle and Walla Walla Railroad, reached as far east as Newcastle—and stopped more than 200 miles short of its intended goal in Walla Walla. The improved transportation helped the mines, and the mines made the railroad profitable, a reciprocal benefit that bolstered Seattle's economy, although the line never brought the transcontinental connection that city hopefuls had expected.

Newcastle miners worked from side tunnels lit by carbide lanterns and headlamps. With explosives and handpicks they hollowed out a vast, black, underground honeycomb ventilated by air shafts. Mule-powered tram cars hauled coal to the surface, where pickers sorted out the waste rock—a step that made western Washington coal costly. The ratio of coal to dross ran about three to one. At the end of each shift, miners showered at a company washhouse—so much more convenient than home bathing that wives successfully lobbied the company for a "ladies night."

Newcastle and Coal Creek mines were uncommonly dry, which made coal dust—potentially explosive—their greatest hazard. Workers continually sprinkled entrances and tunnels with water, but even so, an October 1894 explosion killed four miners and injured five. Two months later a fire threatened to consume the hillside from the inside out. Miners escaped, some of them by climbing ropes dangling down ventilator shafts. A work party then dammed Coal Creek with baled hay and dirt and diverted the water into the mine entrance. Smoke and steam hung over the community for months as the fire slowly went out.

Production peaked in 1907 and stayed high through World War I, when the federal government took over coal production nationwide. Every Newcastle boardinghouse was filled, and some families had to live in tents. Immediately after the wartime boom, however, strikes paralyzed the coal industry, and management retaliated by locking out union miners and bringing in strikebreakers who were greeted by jeering wives and children calling them "yellow dogs" and "scabs." Newcastle started a downhill slide. The labor situation was explosive and the market poor. California oil and cheap Rocky Mountain coal offered too much competition and, when fire destroyed the bunkers where coal was washed and sorted, the company collected insurance and closed operations.

Independent "gyppo" miners leased rights and continued to mine until the 1960s, often working dangerously close to the surface at the risk of cave-ins. Indeed, the earth today occasionally collapses into a forgotten tunnel, and local people believe that some of the smoke hanging above the valley on still winter days comes from fires still smoldering underground.

NORTH BEND lies nestled at the foot of Mount Si—the mountain a westerly outpost of the Cascades, the town an easterly outpost of Pugetopolis. Picnic tables and pathways grace a park surrounding the historical museum (320 S. North Bend Avenue).

In the late 1850s Jeremiah Borst homesteaded 160 acres here on Ranger's Prairie and, as a ready-built barn, used the abandoned Fort Alden blockhouse left over from the open warfare of the mid-1850s (see PUGET SOUND WAR sidebar, p. 326). As his ranch grew Borst also appropriated the nearby Fort Smalley blockhouse. He planted an orchard, raised potatoes and onions, pastured cattle on their way from eastern Washington to Seattle packing plants, and supplemented his farm income by opening a trading post. The pattern was typical of the time and place: settlers claimed land and put it to use while exploiting other opportunities that came along.

Borst pioneered hop farming in the upper Snoqualmie Valley, then in 1882 sold his 1,000-acre ranch to the Hop Growers Association. Every fall brought the full panoply of the harvest: hundreds of native women and children moving through the rows to pick the sticky "cones"; men gambling and racing horses; and all of them enjoying around-the-clock sociability. Here, as throughout western Washington, an aphid infestation beginning in 1890 killed the hop vines and ended the industry—and the encampments.

Mount Si, near North Bend, rises as a dramatic, sheer wall. It offers a taste of the trails and scenery typical of western Washington mountains. The name "Si" is short for Josiah Merritt, a pioneer who lived alone in a cabin at the base of the mountain.

In **PRESTON** (accessible from I-5 Exit 22)

little except a 1902 church on the banks of the Raging River now sets the community apart from others, but the beginnings here have a special character. In the 1890s August Lovegren, a recent immigrant from Sweden, persuaded five friends to pool money and labor and build a shingle mill. He had picked a muddy wilderness site recommended primarily because of its position along the Seattle, Lake Shore and Eastern Railroad. One of the aspiring capitalists confided in his diary:

We saw the mill site before we came to the station and there the men were all soot and mud from clearing the land and grading for a sidetrack. When we came to the station and saw only a shanty for a depot and nothing but black stumps around us, we stood for a long time and reflected on the place we were going to make our home.

But the railroad provided transportation, and the hills held "endless" timber. In 1909 *The Coast* magazine could announce:

At Preston is a large mill operated by August Lovegren and associates who have built up in a few years a large plant, fluming from their mill in the woods the sawn timber and finishing and drying their product in Preston. The town and timber lands are owned by the company.

The festive style of the 1889 Snoqualmie train station was intended to please vacationers and excursionists to the nearby waterfall. Such pleasure travel was uncommon.

This was the American dream translated into reality. Hymns sung in Swedish merged with the sound of raindrops pounding on the church windows, and smoke wafted from the chimneys of homes where parents and grandparents remembered the old country and told the new, American generation why they had emigrated.

RAVENSDALE. (See under BLACK DIAMOND, p. 343.)

Northeast of Black Diamond, **SELLECK** has been resurrected as a bedroom community. It began life in 1909 as a company town owned by the Pacific States Lumber Company. The mill is now gone. So is Japan Town, sprawled informally alongside the mill, and the boarding-house for single men. But bungalows in the main family section of town remain, a small, orderly three-street grid built conveniently close to the mill yet discretely apart from housing for "the rougher element." A few of the family houses have been razed, others altered, but no new dwellings disrupt the sense of continuity with the past. The school, community hall, and manager's house remain.

When the company failed in 1938 most of the 700 employees left. Thirty years later an investor bought the whole town and redeveloped it. By then second-growth forest had softened the scenery and Kent and Auburn's manufacturing plants lay within commuting distance.

Interest at **SNOQUALMIE** (25 miles east of Seattle) centers on the beautifully restored 1889 train depot with its fancy-cut shingles and tower. The building symbolizes the central role that the Seattle, Lake Shore and Eastern Railroad played in the development of this area: the depot's distinctive architecture served to promote Snoqualmie as a recreation center for fishing, hunting, picnicking, and sight-seeing. A movement to preserve historic trains now uses the depot as headquarters and offers rides on restored cars pulled (sometimes) by a steam locomotive. The trip runs to North Bend and to Snoqualmie Falls.

In 1865 Snoqualmie benefited when Seattle residents raised $2,500 to build a wagon road over Snoqualmie Pass. Indeed, even before the work party had completed its efforts, a

contingent of wagons from the east clattered over the rough route. By crossing the mountains immigrants saved hundreds of miles over the alternative of following the Columbia River and then heading north.

The year 1869 marked the first cattle drives from Kittitas County to Seattle. Snoqualmie-area ranchers fattened the herds for final marketing and offered lodging to drovers. That same year violent winter storms destroyed the finally completed wagon road, although horses and cattle still could get through. (In 1884 a new toll road crossed the pass, but only four years later it lost traffic to the Northern Pacific line built over nearby Stampede Pass.)

Through the 1870s Snoqualmie and other nearby communities were economically tied to Snohomish and Everett, which could be reached by canoe or steamer, whereas getting to Seattle meant bumping over abominable wagon roads. Settlers rafted timber downriver to mills at Everett and marketed vegetables, fruit, and pork in both Everett and Seattle. Hops became a cash crop in the 1880s. In the 1890s logging and agriculture benefited from the arrival of the Seattle, Lake Shore and Eastern Railroad—supposedly en route to Spokane although it actually got no farther than a prairie east of North Bend. (See ISSAQUAH, p. 346, for details on the railroad.)

A mile north of Snoqualmie is **Snoqualmie Falls,** recognized by native people and early settlers for its power and beauty—and also as an obstacle that forced them to portage canoes. Scouts for a forerunner of the Puget Sound Power and Light Company had yet another view of the falls. They saw them as an astonishingly valuable resource. In 1898 the company hollowed a 200-foot cavern into the cliff at the base of the falls and installed five generators to supply electricity for street railways and manufacturing plants in Seattle and Tacoma. The transmission line—35 miles long—was one of Washington's pioneering long-distance systems.

The Snoqualmie hydroplant still produces power for Puget Power. A falls viewpoint (1 mile north of the town of Snoqualmie on State Route 202) offers a dramatic overlook; notice the tailrace—water discharging from the generators.

Olympia Area

Attention focused on the Olympia area even before Washington became a territory separate from Oregon. This is where the southern end of Puget Sound coincides with prairieland—ideal for settlement—and with vast forests for building materials and commerce. The mix is still apparent, and scattered pioneer and sawmill communities remain. The sprawl of Pugetopolis ends at Olympia.

Historic interest is particularly high at Tumwater (on the southern edge of Olympia), the site of Washington's first settlement by American citizens. In Olympia a tour of the impressive domed capitol building should be augmented by a look at the landscaping and statuary (mostly war memorials) and at the city that hosts the state government. Northwest of Olympia, Shelton is an example of a quasi-company town that has survived more than a century of market fluctuations in the wood products industry.

Olympia, Tumwater, Lacey, Shelton, and Tenino have historical museums; the site of Puget Sound's largest 1855 blockhouse is near Rochester. Festivals include Rochester's Swede Days in June, Olympia's Harbor Days in September (featuring the rare sight of steam tugboats racing full throttle), and Shelton's oyster-shucking contest in October. In May the four-acre rhododendron garden owned by one of Olympia's pioneer families—the Zabels—is open to the public. (Follow East Bay Drive north from State Avenue in downtown Olympia and in less than a mile turn right on San Francisco; turn left on Bethel, and continue to residence 2432. The three-acre, backyard garden has 1,000 varieties of rhododendrons and azaleas. (Open only in May; no charge.)

BUCODA (Byu-koh´-dah), northeast of Centralia, takes its name from the first letters of three pioneers, names: Buckley, Coulter, and Davis. Little is apparent while driving through the town except a cluster of houses, a railroad track, and a municipal park along the Skookumchuck River. Yet Bucoda is listed in the National Register of Historic Places: Washington's first territorial prison was here, a building with walls of 3- by 12-inch planks laid flat and spiked at five-inch intervals. Nothing remains from the prison except its site and

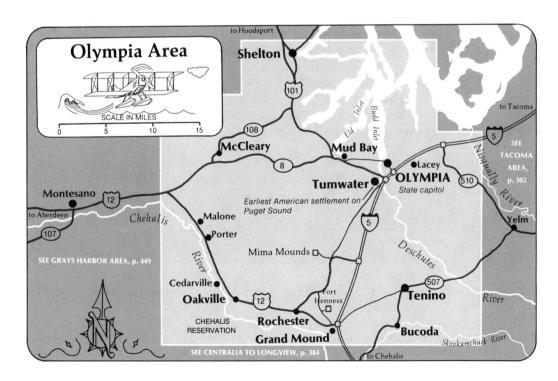

significance. The house belonging to the prison's founder (206 Main) still stands and is listed on the State Register of Historic Properties.

For years territorial legislators expected the federal government to turn over the McNeil Island Penitentiary, a transfer that had to wait another century to become reality. Meanwhile the state housed prisoners at county jails at a cost of $1 a day. In 1877 the sheriffs of Pierce and Thurston counties, together with businessman Oliver Shead, suggested instead a "strong, substantial, safe and secure" territorial prison, which they would operate on contract for 70 cents per prisoner per day.

Shead supplied land, lumber from his sawmill, and start-up capital in exchange for a share of the profits from a prison shoe shop and tailor shop and the labor of inmates at nearby coal mines and farms. The result was a living hell with men forced to constantly wear heavy leg-irons that hampered work and caused oozing sores.

South of Bucoda the open pit **Tono coal mine** gapes awesomely and the **Centralia Steam Plant** sends up a plume almost reminiscent of a Mount St. Helens eruption; huge scale makes the two worth driving past. (Follow Seventh Street past the Bucoda town park; continue south for 2½ miles to a view across the mine pit to the steam plant, on 4 miles more past the steam plant, and into Centralia via Big Hanford Road.)

The **CHEHALIS RESERVATION** offers no particular public attractions although the tribe has an active program for its own people. Material from their rich culture is displayed at the county historical society museum in Chehalis.

Two distinct groups of Chehalis spoke slightly different forms of Salish and lived in different environments. The Lower Chehalis had villages along the coast and the lower reaches of the Chehalis and Satsop rivers. The Upper Chehalis lived at creek mouths and along the middle and upper Chehalis River. Treaty negotiations for both groups began at the site of present-day Cosmopolis in February 1855 with several tribes present. Governor Isaac Stevens insisted they all move together onto a reservation of unspecified size somewhere between Grays Harbor and Cape Flattery. This would mean giving up home territory and living among people who did not

even speak Salish. The Chehalis refused.

The following year a reservation was established on Quinault land. The Chehalis still refused to move. Eventually—and without formal treaty—they agreed to accept reservations of their own at the mouth of the Black River and at Willapa Bay. As a nontreaty tribe, they never received full government assistance. Fifteen years passed before a school was built; it closed after only a year. Land was allotted, but the Chehalis had to apply for title under homestead laws rather than be given patent titles (a direct grant by the president without any need to "prove up"). Payment promised for the land the Chehalis people gave up did not come until 1962, more than a century late. Percy Youckton, tribal chairman at the time, commented:

Many of our old people spent their whole lives expecting that money [the land payment]. It was a dream they held. It glittered just ahead of them all their lives. And they died without receiving money.

FORT HENNESS. (See ROCHESTER, p. 362.)

GRAND MOUND figures prominently in the story of southwestern Washington's settlement, although today it appears as little more than a scattered community at the junction of I-5 and U.S. 12. (The name comes from an isolated hill, now covered with trees and inconspicuous.)

This was naturally open land—prairie rather than forest—and therefore attractive to American settlers as soon as the boundary dispute between England and the United States was clearly settled. The openness also made the area a logical route for the main thoroughfare between Portland and Puget Sound, and a lonely marker commemorating the Oregon Trail still stands on the east side of Old U.S. 99 just south of Grand Mound Way, an intersection that sounds more imposing than it now is.

In 1852 Samuel James arrived at Grand Mound from Cornwall, England. He wrote to his brother, "Our house is seldom a day without one, two, or three . . . strangers and neighbors calling in." Accommodating travelers and their oxen or horses constituted the family's "principal market" for farm produce. There were "persons traveling and moving with their families," James wrote, and also soldiers en route between Fort

Vancouver and Fort Steilacoom and miners stampeding for the Cariboo district in British Columbia or some other hope of quick wealth. By 1854 a stage made the trip between Cowlitz Landing and Puget Sound twice a week.

This was frontier country, yet it was far from limited to rough living in isolated log cabins. The journal kept by Mary Ann James, a daughter of Samuel James, records that in 1853 "Father hauled lumber" from a mill eight miles away and built a house with "six bedrooms, three fireplaces, a very large living room with double glass doors, and a beautiful flower garden in front." From a nursery in Cornwall he had ordered "fruit scions, flowering bulbs, and several roots [which were] duly sent, packed in moss, in a small wooden box, via Cape Horn." Included were lilacs, English gorse, tree of heaven, tulips, hyacinths, daffodils, and primroses.

Mary Ann also notes that "girls were at a premium in those days [with] twenty or thirty proposals of marriage, provided she lived to be sixteen." Donation land claim laws contributed to the urgency for marriage: a man and wife could each claim—at first—320 acres, later 160 acres each. This allowed a married farmer or townsite planner to double his holding of free land.

From the mid-1850s well into the 1900s, the Mound Prairie population continued to grow and its farms to prosper. In the 1920s the gravelly soil allowed the area to become a major producer of strawberries, complete with a processing plant that shipped 450-pound barrels of ripe berries. Rochester High School teams even were known as the "Berry Pickers." A collapse of prices during the 1930s depression and an invasion of weevils ended the berry growing, however. At about the same time, the Northern Pacific closed its Grand Mound depot, and the storekeeper went out of business. The community's social and commercial center shifted to nearby ROCHESTER (see p. 362).

In **McCLEARY**, west of Olympia, the frame Carnell House (314 Second Street) displays mementos of logging and milling days. The 1912 hotel is open for rooms; meals by arrangement (only for groups, 6 to 60). Architecture buffs should especially notice the Methodist-Episcopal Church (384 Hemlock; built in 1926), which was designed by Joseph Wohleb, Olympia's most prolific architect.

The town of McCleary began in 1898 when Henry McCleary built a small sawmill. It expanded with the addition of a plywood mill and what was described as the largest door factory in the world, a major source of employment. Angelo Pellegrini, speaking at a Northwest history conference in 1963, reminisced about his father's working there:

We were seven in the family. We came from Italy directly to McCleary . . . a pioneer lumber town in a small valley hedged in by virgin forest. Within twenty-four hours of our arrival we were wealthy; for these were our immediate assets: all the land we could till; wood fuel to last an eternity; fish in the streams and game in the hills; an abandoned fruit orchard; lumber for our building needs; an abundance of water; and immense space in which to stretch and grow. All these blessings were absolutely free. Father had a job. We were strong and willing to work. The future looked bright.

It *was* bright. But by 1941 close-by timber had been cut. McCleary considered closing his mills and town, but instead sold everything to the Simpson Logging Company of Shelton. Company-owned houses (all painted a standard gray), stores, manufacturing plants, the streets themselves—everything—became Simpson's. Jobs remained, and Simpson repaired the McCleary houses and sold them to employees for the equivalent of 18 months' rent. The new company also organized town government with an impeccable fairness that even included the mills themselves as part of the tax base.

For the next 40 years town life followed a fairly dependable course. Then in 1985 Simpson closed its old-growth logging and milling plants, including those at McCleary. The end of the original forest and of the first regrowth had truly come; the mills' machinery no longer could be supplied with the huge logs required. Such trees are gone, probably forever. The door mill still operates, and workers also now commute to jobs, many of them in Shelton.

The **MIMA MOUNDS** are a remnant of the curious natural mounds that formerly polka-dotted much of Thurston and Lewis counties. They spread 20 to 30 feet in diameter and half as high, a particularly striking example of native prairieland. (Take Exit 95 off I-5 and drive west 3½ miles to Littlerock; at the west edge of town, continue straight for 1 mile via 128th; then turn north onto Waddell Creek Road and in 1 mile watch for a sign on the left.)

A century of explaining the mounds has not resulted in overall agreement. The famous nineteenth-century naturalist Louis Agassiz thought they were made by ancient fish as places to lay their eggs. Explorers such as Navy Lieutenant Charles Wilkes assumed they were burial mounds. The eminent twentieth-century zoologist Victor Scheffer believes that generations of pocket gophers created the mounds. Geologists contend that freeze-thaw action during the last ice age is the explanation.

An ideal time to stroll among the Mima Mounds is in spring when wild flower species are in bloom, many of them rare now that most western Washington prairies have been plowed or paved. The Mima Mound area was purchased by The Nature Conservancy in the 1970s and turned over to the state for preservation as a natural area.

MONTESANO. (See p. 456.)

MUD BAY (immediately west of Olympia at the head of Eld Inlet) lies exposed to the air by a very low tide, hence the name. It is associated with the Indian Shaker religion, a blend of Christianity and traditional native belief widespread among Northwest Native Americans. The religion's beginning came in 1882 when John Slocum, a Squaxin logger who lived at Skookum Creek (near Shelton), fell sick and was thought to be dead. Friends gathered for a wake, but Slocum rose and told them he had died, but had been restored to life specifically to warn sinners to confess, learn to pray, foreswear "white-man" vices such as whiskey and horse

Natural mounds made Mima Prairie less attractive to farmers than the smoother land of other prairies; gravel from ice-age glaciers underlies all Puget Sound prairies.

The huge Bordeaux Brothers Mill near Oakville employed 400 men. They lived in damp bunkhouses that were crowded with gear and made constantly smelly by drying woolen clothing.

racing, and turn away from "Indian doctors."

After about a year Slocum again became sick. His wife Mary refused to let a shaman treat him, but his father called one anyway. Distraught, Mary prayed and fell into a trance, then ordered relatives to hold lighted candles and ring handbells while she danced, sang, repeatedly made the sign of the cross, and held out her shaking arms. Slocum opened his eyes, stood, and also began to shake.

Word of the "resurrection" spread, and people came to hear Slocum preach. Converts such as Mud Bay Louie (Louis Yowaluch) began to preach the new religion. Myron Eells, Congregationalist missionary on the Skokomish Reservation, and his brother Edwin, Indian agent for southern Puget Sound reservations, tried to prevent the meetings. Native people reacted by meeting secretly.

In 1887 the Dawes Act extended American citizenship to any native person living on allotted land or away from a reservation; two years later Washington became a state. The question then arose as to how a federal agent could tell a state citizen which church to attend. Mud Bay Louie asked James Wickersham, the defense attorney in the case, about the legality

of Shaker meetings, and Wickersham responded by drawing up a charter for Yowaluch's church. It assured Shakers their right to hold meetings and own churches—matters previously unclear—and resulted in the spreading of the religion from Mud Bay to Yakima and along the coast from northern California to British Columbia. Wickersham deserves no credit for upholding civil rights, however. He was a bigot and a land speculator who hoped to so discredit Edwin Eells that the reservation status of Puyallup land could be reversed, whereupon he and his clients would acquire it.

For a look at the Mud Bay area as it was a century ago, visit the McLane Creek Nature Trail (1 mile west of I-5 via U.S.101; then south 5 miles on Black Lake and north almost a mile on Delphi Road; watch for sign on the left.)

Southwest of Olympia, **OAKVILLE** has stayed remarkably stable while nearby towns of Cedarville, Porter, and Malone have all but vanished with logging or milling operation closures. Oakville remains the kind of community where the hardware store (built in 1889) has kept its original bulk nail bins and drawers, and the brick bank (built in 1910) has a corner entrance with a sign over the door saying simply BANK. At the time the bank opened for business, hops and logging provided livelihood throughout the area; Oakville's Northern Pacific depot received travelers and freight daily; and a new highway (U.S. 12) brought coast traffic down the main street. Of these major economic factors, only the highway remains, yet the bank and the town's wooden false-fronted stores have also survived.

Fine old Oakville homes include the three-story clapboard Jacob Van Winkle house (610 Blockhouse Street, north of U.S. 12 at the west edge of town; built in 1909). The house belonged to the area's only doctor. He had an examination room on the main floor and often used upstairs bedrooms for patients. Another house worth searching out is the Carpenter Gothic Charles Mills house (204 Harris), which belonged to the owner of the town's general store.

OLYMPIA has served as the state's capital ever since Washington Territory separated from Oregon in 1853. Its beginnings as a town predate that occasion by only a few years. In 1846 Edmund Sylvester, a Maine fisherman who had come to Portland, Oregon, heard that Michael Simmons was building a mill at Tumwater Falls. He decided to have a look, liked the area, and he and an associate, Levi Smith, each settled on a half section of land. Sylvester picked 320 acres amid virgin timber and tangled undergrowth at Chambers Prairie, away from the shore; Smith claimed a sandy point on the bay (now part of the landfill beyond the foot of Capitol Way). A few months later, en route to New Market (Tumwater), Smith fell from a canoe and drowned. Sylvester inherited his land claim and moved to the waterfront.

Fate in the form of the California gold rush played the next card. While building a mill inland from Sacramento a man named James Marshall—by chance a member of the westering Simmons-Bush party of 1844—noticed a fleck of gold "the size and shape" of a melon seed glistening in the gravel bed of the American River. Word spread, and men converged in a stampede that reverberated throughout the West. Crops went unplanted and legislative assemblies unconvened; San Francisco boomed and burned,

then repeated the cycle. Its burgeoning caused the price of Northwest lumber to jump tenfold within months.

Edmund Sylvester was among the stalwarts who rushed south with oxen, a covered wagon, and high hopes—a five-month journey. He quickly decided to return to Puget Sound, however, and with three others, including Isaac Ebey, bought the brig *Orbit* and set sail. On arrival in 1850 Ebey convinced Sylvester to develop a town instead of a farm, and he even suggested the name Olympia in honor of the ice-capped mountain range to the northwest. By 1851 the new town could boast a U.S. Customs house, if little else. In his journal an employee described clams and mussels and ducks and added:

The largest house by far in the place is now occupied by the Customs House . . . on paper designed as being near First and Main streets, though the streets, to a great extent, exist in the imagination.

The same year that Sylvester and Smith arrived, Father Pascal Ricard decided on Budd Inlet as the location for an Oblate motherhouse; tensions continuing as an aftermath of the massacre at Whitman Mission made him leery of the region east of the mountains. (See SAINT JOSEPH'S MISSION, p. 142.) A pragmatist, Father Ricard decided on land at what became known as Priest Point. He wrote:

Since in this country the colonists settle where they wish and take possession of free lands at their convenience, I would [do so] myself, nothing preventing a priest from being a colonist.

In 1852 with $60 newly received from France, Ricard also bought four lots at the edge of town and built two small buildings, which he rented for $900. Men writing up the results of the federal survey for a northern railroad route occupied one building, the newly arrived territorial governor Isaac Ingalls Stevens and his family the other. Margaret Stevens spoke French, a great joy for the aging and ill priest who disliked the "impure" language of French Canadians living nearby.

The American assumption always had been that "frontier" and "opportunity" were synonymous concepts and that self-government would progress as population grew. Olympians felt ecstatic at becoming the seat of territorial government, and were busily preparing a gala welcome for the new governor when Stevens first arrived on November 26, 1853, disheveled from days of rainy travel from Vancouver by steamer, canoe, and horse. The group readying the hotel for the event told the short, bearded stranger who dismounted at the front door to go around to the kitchen for some food. With what must have been mortification, they realized their mistake—and word quickly spread that the future had begun: the governor had arrived.

Two days later Stevens officially proclaimed Olympia as territorial capital and announced that the election of government representatives would take place on January 30, 1854, with the legislature to convene a month later. That first session met in the upper room of what later became the Gold Bar Store and Restaurant (222 N. Capitol; marked with a plaque imbedded in the sidewalk). Stevens told the assembly about prospects for a railroad, a wagon road over Naches Pass, and a dependable mail service. He also announced that he hoped to soon begin treaty negotiations with native people, whom he considered "for the most part a docile and harmless race."

Legislators at that session voted to petition Congress on behalf of George Bush, a prosperous and generous farmer south of Tumwater, listed on the 1850 census as "Negro." They urged that he be granted a land title, and Congress concurred, setting aside the terms of the Donation Land Law, which allowed only "white citizens and half breeds" to file claims. Some territorial legislators even urged that Bush be declared a citizen, but the majority refused to go that far. Bush owned his land but never could vote.

Through the 1850s, Olympia consisted of about 20 to 30 frame houses and a like number of log cabins set in a stump-studded expanse of mud. The bay held water only at high tide and drained nearly to Priest Point as it ebbed. Sea captain Samuel Percival, newly arrived from California, improved the situation by building a

Olympia has always been Washington's capital despite rivalry from other towns.

dock that at least gave boats a high tide tie-up. Soon afterward the side-wheeler *Fairy,* the first American steamer on Puget Sound, arrived from California on the deck of the bark *Sarah Warren.* At first the *Fairy* linked Olympia and Seattle; later it ran between Olympia and Steilacoom. Other steamers also began offering regular service—and cedar dugout canoes fell out of favor as the most convenient form of transportation. By 1855 Olympia's *Pioneer and Democrat* could carry advertisements that ranged from "Salt! Salt! 100 tons of Hawaiian salt [for] those engaged in the Salmon fishery" to notices such as:

Just received by the bark *Mary Melville,* a large stock of goods, consisting partly of

Bacon	Lamp Wick	Powder
Soap	Indigo	Shot
Starch	White Lead	Dried Apples

In the 1870s Olympia suffered the railroad-terminus disease characteristic of practically every settlement on Puget Sound. Lack of a deep-water port must have lowered Olympia's odds of selection, but even after Tacoma won the prize, some enthusiasts comforted—or frustrated—themselves by remembering that agents for the Northern Pacific's subsidiary Puget Sound Land Company had bought substantial acreage along Budd Inlet. To maintain secrecy and avoid a price hike, they hired Ira Bradley Thomas to act as a frontman and file for title in his own name. Unfortunately he died and, rather than wait for his estate to clear probate, the Northern Pacific acquired land at Commencement Bay and created Tacoma as the terminus. (See TENINO, p. 365, for more on Olympia's railroad struggles.)

For a sense of Olympia's setting, drive along the shore of Capitol Lake on Deschutes Parkway and also skirt the East Bay at least as far as Priest Point Park (site of Father Ricard's 1850s Saint Joseph's Mission, about 1½ miles from downtown; no buildings remaining). In addition, visit the historic district at Tumwater, listed in the National Register of Historic Places (see TUMWATER, p. 366); tour the capitol; and sample the city of Olympia, including the downtown district, the Victorian houses in "Swantown" just east of downtown, the capitol grounds and buildings, and the varied neighborhood immediately south of the capitol.

Downtown, State Avenue is one-way to the west, and Fourth is one-way to the east. Parking is difficult while legislature is in session, although curbside parking and visitor lots are available on the capitol grounds. Additional lots are served by shuttle bus while legislature is in session. All are accessible from freeway Exit 105-A.

Points of interest, keyed to the map:

1 **Capitol Lake Park** (Water and Seventh), close to the downtown core, offers parking, a lakeshore beach, semi-tame ducks, and a view of the capitol. Plans here included an elegant stairway to lead from the capitol to the lake and join an esplanade to a railroad depot and downtown Olympia. Damming the Deschutes River formed the lake in 1951, but the stairs never were built and the railroad never came.

2 A dock at **Percival's Landing** (State and Water) ushered in Olympia's era of steamboats, which lasted from the 1850s until the 1920s, when automobiles became the most convenient form of transportation. Today a boardwalk and boat moorage plus cafes and shops invite strolling, and the view up the inlet is still of a working waterfront with ships backdropped by the Olympic Mountains. Climb the observation tower at the north end of the boardwalk for a vantage point from which to watch log handling and ship loading.

Olympia is the southernmost port in Puget Sound and therefore the farthest from the Pacific, a competitive disadvantage. Furthermore, at the time Percival's Landing was built, each low tide turned the "harbor" to mud, and shipping depended on long wharves that reached across the tidal flats to the water. In the 1890s the first dredging deepened the channel, and landfills held by bulkheads of pilings and brush created sites for industries such as a knitting mill, veneer plant, shipyard, sash and door factory, sawmill, oyster-packing house, and cannery. The cannery buildings still stand across from Percival's Landing. The knitting mill, designed in 1913 by Olympia architect Joseph Wohleb, also remains (514–524 S. Jefferson).

The wooden Jefferson Apartments (114–118 N. Jefferson) are a remnant of the 1890s housing

Olympia

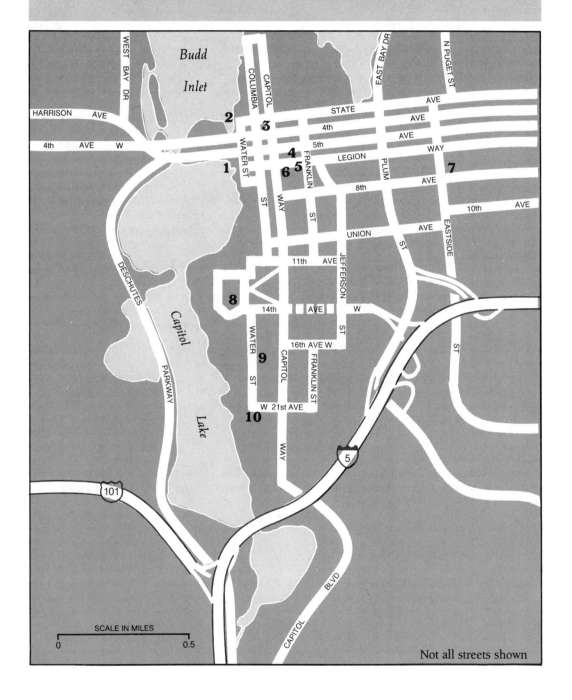

Key to Numbered Locations

1 Capitol Lake Park
2 Percival's Landing
3 Downtown Olympia
4 Hotel Olympian
5 Old Capitol

6 Sylvester Park
7 Swantown
8 State Capitol
9 South Capitol Neighborhood
10 Washington State Capital Museum

Budd

Inlet

WEST BAY DR

COLUMBIA

CAPITOL

EAST BAY DR

N PUGET ST

HARRISON AVE

STATE AVE

AVE

4th AVE W

4th

5th

AVE

WATER ST

1

LEGION WAY

4

5

6

FRANKLIN ST

WAY

8th

ST

PLUM

AVE

7

10th AVE

EASTSIDE

UNION AVE

ST

11th AVE

JEFFERSON

DESCHUTES

8

14th AVE

W

Capitol

16th AVE W

WATER ST

9

CAPITOL WAY

FRANKLIN ST

ST

Lake

PARKWAY

10

W 21st AVE

5

101

CAPITOL BLVD

SCALE IN MILES

0   0.5

Not all streets shown

Olympia's annual tugboat races recall Puget Sound's days of steam travel, which began in 1836 with the arrival of the Hudson's Bay Company vessel Beaver *at Fort Nisqually.*

that accompanied the onset of Olympia's industrial expansion.

A September Harbor Days festival (usually Labor Day weekend) brings the waterfront's past to life with steam tugboats churning down the inlet in a race that draws historic vessels from throughout Puget Sound. It is reminiscent of the old-time competition between captains: the first tug to reach a vessel needing a tow got the job.

3 Architecturally, **Downtown Olympia** presents buildings typical of towns throughout the West (the population here still hovers at only 70,000). Most of the bay windows and cornices that formerly enlivened facades had to be removed following a 1949 earthquake. Nevertheless, several buildings catch the eye. The wood-trimmed former fire station (State and N. Capitol; built in 1912) has housed various aspects of municipal government. The Cunningham Building (Fourth and Adams; built 1896) is the last wooden storefront remaining downtown; millworkers boarded upstairs. In front of it (on Adams Street) notice the sidewalk rings used for tying horses.

The Jeffers Studio (Fifth and Washington; built in 1913) is one of the first documented designs of local architect Joseph Wohleb, a remarkable self-taught man whose work ranged from commercial buildings and banks to industrial plants, schools, legislative buildings,

mansions, modest homes, and even an auto court (915 S. Capitol Way). Other Wohleb buildings at this intersection are the 1920 Martin Building, with a tile belt course separating its two floors, and the 1924 Capitol Theater Building, embellished with five stucco arches, each topped by an etched glass inset depicting one of the Muses.

4 The **Hotel Olympian** (Legion and Washington; built in 1920) catered to the specialized needs of legislators. Built directly across from the Old Capitol, it had an unusually large lobby and four dining rooms. Now, the upper floors provide senior housing, the lobby has shops—and hints of the hotel's original purpose remain. A marble stairway leads from the lobby to a mezzanine ballroom. The hotel was paid for by public subscription after complaints about a lack of acceptable accommodations.

5 The so-called **Old Capitol** (Legion and Washington; built in 1892, with a wing added in 1905) actually first served as the county's courthouse. Its architect, Willis Ritchie, also designed the towered and turreted Spokane and Port Townsend courthouses. Here, a high clock tower had to be removed following a 1928 fire, and 10 of the original 12 turrets fell victim to a 1949 earthquake. Two were restored during a 1980s renovation.

The first legislature met in 1854 above a

store/restaurant; a Masonic Lodge accommodated its next deliberations; and a two-story wooden hall finally was built in 1856. Construction of a permanent capitol began in 1893 but was curtailed by the nationwide depression and the insistence of Governor John Rogers that converting the existing courthouse to state use would cost less than completing something new. The Old Capitol housed the legislature and all state offices from 1905 until 1928. It continues to house the offices of the Superintendent of Public Instruction.

6 Sylvester Park (Washington between Legion and Seventh) began as the town square designated in Edmund Sylvester's original 1850 plat of Olympia. It has served a variety of needs from communal grazing ground to a gathering place where citizens have listened to visiting dignitaries including Presidents Theodore Roosevelt, William Taft, and Franklin D. Roosevelt. The present gazebo is a replacement of the original.

7 A slough separated **Swantown,** east of today's industrial and downtown sections, from the rest of Olympia. Several substantial Victorian homes are scattered through the present neighborhood, which overall is representative of early twentieth-century workers' housing. The William White house (Eighth and Boundary; built in 1893) belonged to a lumberman who experienced foreclosure just two years after the completion of the house. In the 1930s a new owner converted the building to apartments and salvaged lumber from the third-floor ballroom to use for outbuildings. Nearby the story-and-a-half Charles Patnude house (1239 Eighth; built in 1893) is listed in the National Register of Historic Places, not because of events but because of architectural integrity representative of its era. Patnude worked as a bricklayer and mason, incorporated his own construction company, and built his home—then lost it to foreclosure.

The C. S. Reinhart house (N. Quince and Olympia; built in 1891) belonged to a man who served as supreme court clerk and mayor. It features an ornate Queen Anne exterior and an exquisite interior with rich wood paneling and Italian tile. The earliest of the remaining Swantown homes is that of Daniel Bigelow (918 E. Glass; built in 1854). Its cottage architecture is typical of the pattern-book designs made available throughout the nation beginning in the mid-1850s. Remaining as the family home until well into the 1990s, the house still has original furnishings and memorabilia. A nonprofit group now owns it and will operate it as a place for the public to "touch history."

8 Visitors are welcome at the **State Capitol** (off Capitol Way between 12th and 16th; freeway Exit 105-A). The building is open both for individuals and for guided tours, which can be arranged weekdays, year-round, by contacting the visitor information office (just inside the main entrance to the capitol grounds at 14th and Capitol Way). Signs indicate the location of parking lots.

A nationwide competition that drew 188 entries led to the laying of the foundation for a permanent capitol in 1894. Progress then halted for two and a half decades while a depression came and went, Olympia successfully fought off efforts to move the capital, a new competition was held (37 entries), and World War I began. The colonnaded Temple of Justice (begun in 1911, finished in 1919) was the first building of the capitol group to be translated from plans to actuality. The Insurance Building came next (built in 1921), then the monumental Legislative Building (begun in 1922, finished in 1928). The 42 steps leading to its elaborate bronze doors symbolize Washington's position as the forty-second state to enter the union. Selection of bas relief designs for the doors stirred a controversy in the 1920s. The motifs finally used on the doors include grazing sheep, logging, shipping, the first territorial capitol, an early homestead, and a waterfall.

When built, the capitol's 287-foot dome was the fourth highest in the world, exceeded only by those of Saint Peter's in Rome, Saint Paul's in London, and the National Capitol in Washington, D.C. The all-masonry construction includes 1,400 stones cut to precise measurements at the Wilkeson quarry near Mount Rainier (see WILKESON, p. 341). A Tiffany chandelier—the last large commissioned work that Louis Tiffany produced—hangs from a 101-foot chain in the marble rotunda. Interior painting and the gilding of the rotunda walls and the ceiling were not undertaken until the state's centennial year, 1989.

The state reception room and the galleries of the house and senate chambers are open to the public. Grounds landscaping includes cherry trees that bloom in March or April and lilacs from the Hulda Klager garden at Woodland (see p. 411). The greenhouses on the capitol grounds are open year-round (daily in summer; weekdays only the rest of the year).

9 The **South Capitol Neighborhood** (between Capitol and Sylvester from 16th to 21st) developed in relation to the capitol. Houses include several that were moved off the grounds to make way for the construction of the legislative buildings, including a house occupied by Governor and Mrs. Albert Mead from 1905 to 1909 (NE corner of Capitol and 17th). The Meads found the official state mansion both difficult to heat and pretentious; here they kept a cow and grew a vegetable garden.

Houses at 1623 and 1624 Sylvester, built in the 1920s, are examples of the hundreds of precut houses designed by Joseph Wohleb and produced by a Tumwater mill, which advertised them as "built in a week." Wohleb built his own home on the corner of Columbia and 21st, a modest one-story house with shingle siding. Directly across from it is the brick Henry McCleary mansion (111 W. 21st; built in 1925), which Wohleb designed for the owner of the McCleary mills and company town (see MCCLEARY, p. 353). McCleary had once asked Clarence Lord, an Olympia banker, for a loan and had been refused. Consequently when he built his lavish home—replete with a copper roof—he asked Wohleb to produce an even finer house than that of the Lords, immediately to the west, also a Wohleb design. The McCleary house has been remodeled into offices and retains little of its interior splendor except for a grand staircase and a sense of spaciousness, still evident in the foyer. The Lord house is now the Capital Museum.

10 The **Washington State Capital Museum** (211 W. 21st; built in 1924) occupies the 32-room C. J. Lord mansion, designed by Wohleb in a vaguely California Mission style, landscaped by a gardener trained at Kew Gardens, London, and bequeathed for museum use in 1939. The downstairs rooms retain much of their original character; the upstairs has been remodeled for exhibit use; and the carriage house in back is used for various meetings and museum workshops and presentations. An ethnobotany garden will be added to the grounds displaying a sample of plant species used by local Indian people for food and medicines. Overall exhibit emphasis is on the distinctive nature of Washington's state government.

In **ROCHESTER,** historical interest centers on the site of **Fort Henness,** east of town (183rd SW and Apricot; drive north of U.S. 12 on Sargent Road for 2 miles, then east for 1 mile on 183rd).

The "fort" was built in 1855 when white settlers throughout the Puget Sound area feared attack by native people. (See PUGET SOUND WAR sidebar, p. 326.) Mary Ann James Shephard, daughter of a Mound Prairie settler, reminisced in 1911 about life within the stockade. She remembered corner blockhouses and "a certain number of feet [along the walls] allotted to each family" for private dwellings; "two large gates, closed at sunset"; and a "well 75 feet deep dug in one corner and walled up with rock." She also remembered moving into the fort "one cold, rainy morning" when a neighbor came to report that a settler at Chamber's Prairie and another near Tenino had been killed in what seemed to be the forerunner of organized, widespread attacks:

Father roused us up, . . . the boys yoked the oxen, and bedding, groceries, and clothing were thrown into the wagon, and I, with my pet kitten and little white dog, Cupid, cuddled in my apron, were wrapped up and lifted in.

More than 200 people lived at Fort Henness. The James family stayed about six months, then "things seemed to be quiet and Father was anxious to get back to the farm." Other families "remained there over a year." The site is now an expanse of mown grass with a memorial, a diagram of the fort's layout, and mounds of cobbles from the erstwhile chimneys and well. Across the road is the pioneer cemetery, which includes the graves of Samuel James and his wife Anna Marie.

To glimpse one of the Rochester area's substantial pioneer homes, drive to the **Mills-Brewer House** about a mile west of Fort

Henness (turn north off 183rd onto Guava Street, continue to 180th, then drive into the Scatter Creek public hunting area, near a huge old barn). The house, listed in the National Register of Historic Places, is representative of the period from the 1850s to the 1890s when fine homes characteristic of an industrialized society stood intermixed with hand-hewn log cabins, symbols of the frontier.

The Mills-Brewer house is built of inch-thick vertical planks, a mid-nineteenth-century technique popular about the same time that balloon framing developed. Plank construction lost favor because it limited a building's height more than frame construction did, and it also posed problems if a house was to be enlarged later. On the other hand, the technique allowed a builder to simply set vertical planks onto a foundation sill rather than build a framework, and this suited frontier conditions where nails were scarce, and the range of dimension lumber was extremely limited.

Another house and barn of the same era as the Mills-Brewer house are at the **Rutledge Farm** along the Black River about a mile south of Littlerock (13400 Littlerock Road SW).

Immediately south of the Rochester business district, watch for **Swede Hall,** which is repre-

sentative of the continuing community life of a rural area (185th SW and Albany; built in 1939). To build this 1½-story, gambrel-roofed hall, the Order of Runebery bought warehouses from a defunct sawmill at Malone and salvaged the lumber. Members volunteered the design and the construction work. Each June, Rochester's Swede Days still center here.

(Also see GRAND MOUND, p. 352.)

At **SHELTON** stop at the pullout off State Route 3 (on the hill just south of town) for a dioramalike view. The waterway, with its log booms and cold decks, the huge, sprawling mill, and the town's orderly houses and businesses lie directly below. Notice, too, the 11-foot wheel from a Simpson Logging Company bandsaw, which is displayed at the viewpoint. It was used to cut spruce during World War I. (See SPRUCE ARMY sidebar, p. 492.)

In town, 1920s brick buildings form the business district; the massive Tenino sandstone county courthouse dominates the intersection of Alder and Fifth; and the 1914 public library (Railroad Avenue and Fifth) has become the county historical society museum. The building was donated by the widows of Sol Simpson and Alfred Anderson, founders of the Simpson

A high steel bridge across Vance Creek was finished in 1929, part of a single-track line giving access to Forest Service land near Shelton. Wooden trestles were abandoned as timber cutting moved on; steel signified long-term expectations.

Steam donkey engines mounted on skids could be moved to new cutting sites and used to reel in logs that had been limbed. Some abandoned engines now molder; others are at parks. Their whistles, used for signaling, once rang throughout the woods.

Logging Company. They intended it to offer single men "purposeful repose" as an alternative to saloons and brothels. The building was designed by Frederick Heath, the architect also responsible for such large-scale structures as the Stadium Bowl in Tacoma and Paradise Inn at Mount Rainier. With entryway columns and decorative molding outlining a pair of arched windows, he gave the building an image of importance far beyond its actual small size.

Several houses are worth searching out. The Riley house (Cedar and First) was built in the 1880s, one of the earliest remaining buildings. In 1924 Mark Reed built an enormous colonial house on the corner where his parents-in-law's 1905 home stood (Pine and Third). To make room, their house was moved across the street (403 N. Third). It did not fit there so part was cut off and moved (302 W. Alder). Two of the Reed sons' 1928 houses still stand: Frank's at Junction and Third, Sol's on North Cliff. Tragically, an aggrieved logger shot Sol on Frank's lawn.

Early lumber mills opened along the upper reaches of Puget Sound, easier to reach from the Pacific than were mills farther down the sound. Consequently the high-quality timber of the

Shelton area at first remained untouched. In 1884, however, it attracted the attention of W. H. Kneeland, a successful Pennsylvania oil field speculator who built a sawmill near Oakland Bay and sent lumber by flume to the salt water. He also began work on a logging railroad called the Mason County Central. Two years later he gave up, unable to meet expenses.

Investors from Seattle looked at Kneeland's location, set back from the bay in the woods, and also at the farm David Shelton and his family had begun 30 years earlier at the head of the bay. They liked Shelton's land, which lay in a flat valley stretching for several miles with easy access to timber and a dependable stream to supply water for steam locomotives. The investors drew up their plans, and David Shelton filed a townsite plat and offered lots for sale. His community, terminus for the new Satsop logging railroad, quickly overshadowed the nearby county seat hamlet of Oakland.

At this point, Sol Simpson arrived on the scene. He had come to Seattle from Nevada gold camps and met William Renton, manager of the Port Blakely Mill (see p. 370). Renton sent Simpson to Mason County to build a logging railroad, which he officially incorporated as the Puget Sound and Grays Harbor Railroad although it was usually called simply "The Blakely." This line was to tap the virgin timber inland from Kamilche. Simpson contracted to operate the railroad and to supply logs for the mill, which needed 62 million board feet of logs per year. At the time milling companies bought logs from independent loggers rather than holding land and cutting their own timber, as later became characteristic.

Simpson was equal to the job Renton gave him. His men felled trees, grubbed stumps, laid tracks, and fed the hungry mill across the sound. He used horses for grading the railbed and started experimenting with horse logging, which proved faster than working with oxen. Simpson soon sold his bull teams and bought 60 head of the finest draft horses he could find, a revolutionary step. He also imported a Dolbeer donkey engine from the California redwood country. Product of John Dolbeer's ingenuity, this was a stationary steam engine with a vertical boiler. It pulled logs attached to a rope that wound around a capstan, a crude system but even faster than horses.

In 1889 the Satsop Railroad, Simpson's competitor, went bankrupt, and a Wisconsin lumberman named Alfred H. Anderson reorganized it into the Washington Central. The Shelton bank also was in trouble: Anderson reorganized it, too. Eleven years later he, Simpson, and Simpson's son-in-law Mark Reed started what became the Simpson Logging Company.

Reed headed this new operation. He had been raised in Olympia where he helped his father, the state's first auditor, and worked as a secretary to the state land commission. Literate and savvy, he was also personally experienced in the woods, having logged with oxen and gone broke during the 1893 depression, then hired on at a logging camp. A miserable bunk and sleepless nights convinced him, as he later told it, "that if I ever had charge of a real camp, I would provide decent furnishings for the men."

Under Reed, the Simpson Company became an innovator in the use of electrical machinery and diversified wood products, and it grew into the second-largest timber holder in the state (Weyerhaeuser was—and is—larger). Reed persuaded the Northern Pacific to lay a connecting rail line to Shelton, then he built his own lines to bring out hemlock from previously untouched slopes. He built a new mill for handling the hemlock, then persuaded the Zellerbachs of San Francisco to build a pulp mill that would use waste from the hemlock mill for making paper. He also convinced Henry McCleary to open an adjacent sawmill and join him in building a power station fueled by waste from all the mills.

Reed wanted a long future for both the company and the town, and to insure it he held onto logged lands to be replanted and eventually recut. In keeping with this, the company signed a unique agreement with the U.S. Forest Service in 1946, placing its lands and national forest lands under unified management and guaranteeing Simpson all sales from the reserved forests for the next 100 years.

TENINO is now a residential haven for people wanting small-town peace with access to nearby mainstream opportunities. It sits contently to the side, no longer a major railroad junction and bypassed as well by I-5. To drive along State Route 507 to Tenino is to remember why prefreeway travel was so slow.

In town several early-1900s buildings catch the eye because they are of sandstone, unusual for a community of this size. A house at 189 Wichman (completed in 1915) was intended as a model home to demonstrate the versatility of sandstone and, in the grassy town park at the end of Olympia Street (two blocks from the main street), the sandstone Northern Pacific Railroad depot is used as a history museum displaying photographs of quarrying techniques and machinery. Near the depot, which was moved to this location, is the cutting face of a quarry that operated from 1901 until 1926 and, with four other quarries, provided the state with a major portion of its building stone. The office building of the former Tenino Stone Company now serves as a community center.

In 1845 the pioneering Bush-Simmons party en route to Puget Sound came through present-day Tenino, the women driving "five or six yoke of work cattle and a number of cows" while the men "went ahead and cut the road," according to the account of A. B. Rabbeson, published in Olympia's *Washington Standard* on May 28,

1886. The party stopped here to rebuild the sleds they were using to drag their belongings through the forest. Five years later Tenino's first settler, Stephen Hodgden, claimed land and began a farm, which became a station on the 60-mile stage road between Monticello and Olympia.

In 1872 the Northern Pacific built its line north from Kalama to Hodgden's Station (Tenino) and there installed a turntable to reverse locomotive engines and start them back to Kalama. This left half a dozen Puget Sound cities continuing to hope for selection as the railroad's ultimate destination. In 1873 Tacoma won the prize—and Olympia felt doubly aggrieved. It was not the terminus. Even more insulting, the tracks to Tacoma wholly bypassed the capital, and left Olympia passengers and freight to disembark at Tenino and bounce on by wagon.

Five years later completion of a narrow-gauge railway from Olympia to Tenino at least eased this particular indignity. The service was low-key with trains stopping anywhere the engineer saw people or freight waiting to be picked up, or a cow grazing the grass between the ties. The 15-mile trip between the towns typically took two hours.

In the 1890s fine-grained, medium-hard sandstone at Tenino attracted attention and stirred the hamlet to life as more than a railway depot. Tenino stone was easy to work when first cut but hardened after exposure to the air. Even better, it lay along an existing rail line. Scottish stonecutters—among others—moved here, and by 1910 five quarries were in operation. Most stone was custom cut to size, ready for its specified use in a building. This saved paying freight on what would end up as waste material. Artisans also produced arches, columns, window frames, and even flowerpots to order. The stone was used for projects as varied as Spokane's magnificent Masonic Temple, Ellensburg's Farmers Bank, the east wing of the old state capitol, and the breakwaters at Grays Harbor.

As concrete became common, however, orders for sandstone decreased. Quarries everywhere suffered from this competition, but Tenino companies found themselves especially vulnerable since the stone here matches the gray of concrete. Understandably, the limited market remaining for cut stone preferred a lighter color.

TUMWATER, immediately south of Olympia, is worth visiting as a bridge across the eras. Freeway construction caused the razing of many historic buildings in the 1950s, but enough remain to impart a clear sense of origins. Furthermore, along the loop trail by the Deschutes River, the sound of splashing water overrides the roar of I-5 and conveys a sense of past conditions. Here by the river the first American settlement north of the Columbia River began in 1845. And here a year later industrialization got under way with the construction of a grist-mill, soon augmented by a sawmill and then by a succession of additional mills and hydropower plants, breweries, a tannery, a furniture factory, a box mill, and other industries. Today rhododendrons provide a colorful spring display, and salmon leap spectacularly each October as they enter the river to spawn—these days greeted by hatchery personnel.

Two historic houses along the river are open to the public: the Crosby house, built in 1858, and the Henderson house, built in 1905. Nearby the brewery gives tours. Next to its visitor parking lot, notice the stately Leopold Schmidt house built in 1906 by the founder of the area's first brewery (open to the public only on special occasions). Schmidt learned his art at a brewers' academy in Germany and practiced it in Butte, Montana, before coming to Tumwater. His original six-story brick brewhouse still stands by the water.

Reaching the historic district on the east side of the freeway for the first time calls for both faith and patience. The basic approach is to take Exit 103 off I-5 and immediately turn east on the Custer overpass (or to drive south from Olympia on Capitol Way and then turn west on Custer Way). From Custer, signs mark the route, which consists of turning onto Boston and driving down the hill past the present brewery, then crossing a bridge, and turning to the right.

The location of a cascading river within a mile of salt water made this an ideal site for settlement. It offered the rare combination of waterpower potential with easy access to and from the sea. Furthermore, prairie openings in the surrounding forest greatly simplified getting a start. Land did not have to be logged before it could be farmed. To see a remnant of these natural clearings, drive to Mima Mounds (see p. 353.); and to sense more of the specific setting at Tumwater—complete with a dramatic view of Mount Rainier—drive through the hilltop residential area across I-5 from the historic district. Notice the early-day clapboard church at S. Second and B (built in 1872) and the house and old apple trees at 303 S. Fourth.

A party of 32 Missourians arrived at Tumwater in 1845 led by Michael T. Simmons and George Bush. Characteristic of mid-1800s immigrants, they came seeking better opportunities, and they came en masse from the Midwest, uprooting New Market, Missouri, and replanting it as New Market, Oregon Territory. But uncharacteristically, these particular pioneers decided to settle north of the Columbia River rather than in the Willamette Valley, as they had originally intended. Bush was part black and therefore banned from owning land in Oregon. Its northern reaches—now Washington—where the British still held effective control, seemed more promising than land south of the river. Bush expected better treatment under British law than Oregon law. (Also see CAMAS, p. 400.)

Employed by the Hudson's Bay Company during the late 1820s, Bush once had traveled to the west coast of British Columbia. In 1830, at about age 40, he returned to Missouri, married a German-American woman, and settled into family life. When neighbors began talking about moving West, they naturally turned to Bush for advice and leadership: he already had *been* West. He even had heard that the Puget Sound area had a mild climate and ample flat land, although he had not gone there. When the party decided against settling in the Willamette

The old brewhouse at Tumwater was among a dozen pioneer industries lining the lower creek, a near-perfect site that offered waterpower close to oceangoing shipping.

Bing Crosby's grandfather built this house at Tumwater in 1858. It still stands.

country, Simmons and two others checked the shores of Whidbey Island and Hood Canal by canoe, then picked the Deschutes River mouth as the best place for a community.

The Hudson's Bay Company opposed the settlers' presence at Puget Sound, but nonetheless extended credit for provisions and even accepted cedar shingles as payment in lieu of (virtually nonexistent) cash. Native Americans also helped out, and William Tolmie, in charge at Fort Nisqually, insisted that the newcomers not trade for furs or compete with the Company, but pay natives the same prices he did for labor or foodstuffs. The agreed upon compensation included items such as:

3 ducks	= 1 load of powder and shot
50 chinook salmon	= 1 hickory shirt
Use of a canoe to Fort	
Nisqually and back	= 1 cotton handkerchief
Each paddler	= 1 cotton handkerchief

Within a few months of arrival at New Market (later renamed Tumwater) Michael Simmons built a water-powered gristmill. Its buhrstones came from a granitic boulder found at Mud Bay, one of thousands of such rocks that rode glacier tongues inching out of Canada during the last ice age. By early 1847 the new

settlement also had a sawmill, which was situated below the falls so that logs could be floated directly to it from salt water. The Hudson's Bay Company supplied the saw. A flume and waterwheel system powered it. And the men soon could tow a raft of lumber to Fort Nisqually to clear their debt. Settlers brought their wheat to be ground, some of them coming from as far away as Cowlitz Landing (about 35 miles to the south, near present-day Toledo), a trip that took two days each way if all went well and another two or three days waiting at the mill.

Additional settlers joined the original party as word spread concerning Tumwater's fine location and mills. Among them were several members of the Crosby family, whose descendant Harry Crosby became the beloved "Bing" of the mid-1900s. Sea captain Nathaniel Crosby (great-grandfather of Bing) sailed to the Northwest in 1846 bringing supplies sent by the U.S. government for the relief of immigrants. His assessment of prospects led him to urge his family in Maine to outfit a brig and set sail for Oregon. In 1858 young Nathaniel Crosby III built the house at the northwest end of the present historic district for his bride, Cordelia Jane Smith.

(Also see OLYMPIA, p. 356.)

Kitsap Area

The Kitsap Peninsula "fills up" the center of Puget Sound, attached at its southern end to the Olympic Peninsula. Country roads wind through second-growth timber and small-scale farms. The federal government maintains a large presence with a naval shipyard at Bremerton, a submarine base at Bangor, and an undersea weapons engineering station at Keyport. Bainbridge Island tucks into the side of the Kitsap Peninsula, connected by a bridge high above Agate Passage. Distinctive homes—hidden among towering trees—line the island's shores; roads tend to be narrow and twisting and— owing to the trees—offer fewer views than might be expected by looking at a map.

Museums at Silverdale and Winslow chronicle the area's pioneer days; one at Bremerton offers naval displays; another at Keyport highlights undersea technology; and two at Port Orchard exhibit the furnishings and accoutrements of family life at various periods. The Suquamish Museum portrays tribal transition from traditional culture to the contemporary world. And Port Gamble, still a working timber town, retains clean-lined nineteenth-century buildings and transplanted New England ambience, as though the entire town were a display. It also has a historical museum.

In May Poulsbo celebrates the Norwegian national holiday; in August, Suquamish celebrates Chief Seattle Days with salmon barbecues and canoe races.

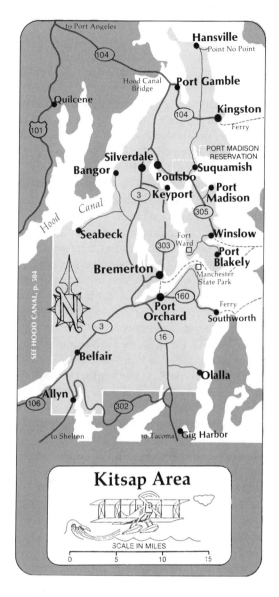

Kitsap Area

SCALE IN MILES

0   5   10   15

BAINBRIDGE ISLAND is a residential enclave near Seattle's madding crowds, yet psychologically distant. Ferries connect with the island's midsection at Winslow, and State Route 305 crosses a narrow waterway by bridge from the Kitsap Peninsula. At the north end of the island a point of interest worth searching out—and planning ahead for—is the **Bloedel Reserve,** open to the public on an advance-reservation basis. (Phone ahead for an appointment and directions; modest fee. The reserve is listed in the Bainbridge Island directory.) Paths lead through grounds exquisitely landscaped to interweave gardens and forest and demonstrate the value of varied life communities. The estate

was given for this purpose as a trust in 1984 by Prentice Bloedel and his wife Virginia. The downstairs of their home, still furnished as they left it, is now a visitor center.

South of the Winslow community, the **Bucklin house** near Eagle Harbor (7861 NE Bucklin Hill Road) was built in 1887 by Nathan Bucklin, at the time supervisor of the Port Madison Mill for 25 years. He patterned it after homes in Maine, his birthplace. The result is a simple frame house with a water tower.

At the southwest end of the island, the 1910 military reservation at **Fort Ward** today offers a forested path to beach gun emplacements;

officers' quarters are now converted to private homes. Notice especially the residence at 2099 Victorian Lane, originally built as duplex quarters for two officers' families.

In the late 1890s the army established a trio of forts guarding the entrance to Puget Sound—Forts Worden, Flagler, and Casey—and a few years later they added Fort Ward and Fort Lawton (on Magnolia Bluff in Seattle) to form a second line of defense. Fort Ward's primary defense system depended on mines—known during World War I as "torpedoes"—which were to be deployed in twisting Rich Passage, the entryway to the Bremerton Navy Yard. In addition, four-inch guns in fixed emplacements lined the beach and larger caliber guns were on the bluff (now overgrown with brush and out of sight). Shortly before World War II the navy acquired the fort and developed a state-of-the-art radio communications center with a transmitter at Battle Point, on the west side of the island, and receivers at Fort Ward. In his 1950s novel about the post-nuclear world, *On the Beach,* Nevil Shute wrote about a ghostly transmission from the Battle Point site.

During World War II, Fort Ward deployed barrier nets against submarine entry; black wooden pilings that supported the heavy cables stretched across Rich Passage still show. A double gate allowed legitimate ship traffic, including ferries, to pass. (Also see Manchester State Park under PORT ORCHARD, p. 377.) After the war, the federal government released Fort Ward, and part of it became a park.

Huge early sawmills at Port Madison, Port Blakely, Port Gamble, and Seabeck made Kitsap County for a while the wealthiest county in the nation, per capita, and from 1857 until 1864 it was the most populous (although the smallest) county in Washington Territory. It had two representatives in the legislature's lower house while King County (Seattle) had only one. Except for Port Gamble, however, the prominent ports of the past are barely identifiable today as former industrial complexes. Peaceful beach houses overlook the sites, two of them on Bainbridge Island.

In 1854 George Meigs, attracted by dense island timber, moved a sawmill to **Port Madison** on Bainbridge's north end. Lumber ships soon called from California, spurred by the gold boom there, and from Hawaii and Chile, where extensive building was also under way. In 1857 Port Madison was still the only white settlement on the island, a town with a population of 19 persons. The mill was equipped with the territory's first circular saw, so efficient it cut four million board feet per year. In 1861 the mill shipped the lumber for the territorial university to Seattle.

A blacksmith shop, machine shop, and brass and iron foundry enhanced the mill's industrial capacity. Actually the foundry operated at a deficit but it enabled the mill to make swift repairs, which was preferable to waiting for parts from San Francisco. Meigs ran a dry town and encouraged families to move in with their men. This became a distinct contrast with Port Blakely, where single workers and saloons prevailed.

When Kitsap County organized in 1857, the logical seat was Port Madison. However, economic depression in the 1890s, and embezzlement by one of Meigs' subordinates, closed its lumber mill. Shipbuilding, smoked herring, and fish oil industries that had grown up along the bay also suffered, and the resulting ghost town lost county-seat honors to Sidney (Port Orchard). Until then, people from the *town* of Seattle had come by ship to take advantage of modern stores in the *city* of Port Madison.

William Renton's **Port Blakely** mill was even larger than Meigs' Port Madison mill. It ringed the shore of Blakely Harbor on the southeast end of the island (Seaborne and Country Club roads). Evidence of the installation has been virtually obliterated by time; the area today is characterized by private homes, slow roads, and heavy local traffic.

Port Blakely is said to have been the largest lumber mill in the world, even though it twice burned disastrously. Beginning in 1864 Charles S. Holmes, a partner in the firm, oversaw marketing from San Francisco headquarters while Renton supervised mill operations, which included night shifts made possible by electric lights. During the heyday of production, from 1885 to 1895, about 1,200 workers tended the mill's giant saw, manhandled the logs, and loaded the waiting ships. Old photographs show schooners and square-riggers so crowded within the bay that their masts seem to overlap and

In the late 1800s Port Blakely (just south of today's Winslow) was a major logging, sawmilling, and shipbuilding center connected by sail to ports around the world.

their spars to blur. Renton's company owned five lumber schooners of its own, plus a tug that earned revenue custom-hauling logs around the sound. Renton also invested in Seattle-area coal mines; the city of Renton is named for him.

In the early days the Port Blakely mill—and others—bought their saw logs from independent loggers. The company advanced tools and supplies—even groceries—to men who either felled trees directly into the water or dragged them with oxteams and then floated them to the mill. The Kitsap Peninsula, with a long winding shoreline, lent itself to this style of logging particularly well: large trees could be hauled no more than a mile to reach salt water. Renton had unusual foresight, however, in realizing that waterside timber overall would soon be gone; he was in the vanguard of logging railroad construction and of acquiring land with standing timber. His company eventually held more than 80,000 acres and operated a 35-mile logging railroad from Kamilche to Montesano, at the base of the Olympic Peninsula.

In 1881 Hall Brothers Shipbuilding Company moved alongside the Port Blakely mill from Port Ludlow, attracted by beautiful, clear timber. In a cavernous molding loft, shipwrights made full-scale, precise drawings and from them cut the actual lumber. Carpenters then would lay

the keel, steam and bend the ribs, and attach the planks. Specialists caulked the seams with oakum. Other workers painted the hull and sent it down the ways to make room for the next vessel. They added decks, masts, and rudder while the ship was afloat. Hall Brothers built 77 schooners, barks, and barkentines between 1873 and 1903. (Also see WINSLOW, p. 382.)

This early industrialization fostered Bainbridge Island agriculture. As early as the 1860s, George Meigs contracted with a farmer at Island Center to supply foodstuffs for Port Madison millworkers. Later, especially in the 1880s when the timber began to be cleared from the island's interior, stump farmers developed agricultural land. The first wave of immigrants was Norwegian, but they were soon followed by Japanese farmers who transformed the economy.

Strawberries became the signature crop, although some Japanese farmers grew greenhouse specialties such as lilies, cucumbers, tomatoes, lettuce, geraniums, and chrysanthemums. The experiences of the Hayashida family are representative of the Bainbridge community. Mr. and Mrs. Hayashida sailed from Hiroshima in 1903, leaving a young son in his aunt's care. Their first destination was a Hawaiian sugarcane plantation, where they earned a stake that allowed them to move on to

Bellevue and develop a strawberry farm. In 1910 they moved to Bainbridge Island with a group of neighbors and cleared land—again. According to an account in *Kitsap County History* by their eldest son Ichiro (who as a 15-year-old rejoined his parents):

During these years, and until the 1950s, strawberries were planted by hand. The men would make holes and the women would follow planting, tightening the roots with sticks. Planting season was Festival Time; everybody helped each other, going from one field to another. Lunch and coffee would be served, and there would be a great feast.

The berry farms hired itinerant pickers during harvest season; Native Americans filled this role, as they had in hop-growing areas. During the 1920s Filipino immigrants, attracted to the thriving farms, also worked on the Japanese farms, and many settled on the island. When World War II forced Japanese families to leave their property, Filipino caretakers typically continued raising crops in the owners' absence. The Filipino Community Hall still remains from the prewar era (7260 NE High School Road; built in 1930). It served as a social center and berry shed.

BANGOR today is home port for the navy's Trident Nuclear Submarines, where signs along the perimeter fences read, "Warning: Patrolled by Military Working Dogs."

But Bangor was not always a military installation. Like other Kitsap Peninsula communities, it began as a logging site. Stump farmers then followed the loggers, and a store, schoolhouse, and dock became the community center. In 1914 owners of a floating clam cannery tied up their building to pilings in the bay and for several years provided employment for 30 workers.

Bangor's rustic solitude ended in 1944 when the U.S. Navy established a munitions depot in the town. Property owners—about 350 families—received notices to vacate their land. Patriotism overcame outrage, the landowners moved away, and construction of Bangor Naval Magazine began on schedule. Ships heading for the Alaska theater of war were supplied at the magazine. After the war, ships bound for the Naval Shipyard at Bremerton off-loaded ord-

nance there and, when repairs were complete, came back to be resupplied. The Vietnam War brought an upsurge of activity as protestors sailed small craft in the path of outbound vessels loaded with munitions. In 1973 the navy chose Bangor for its Trident Nuclear Submarine Base; the population in Kitsap County then grew by 30 percent, with more than a third of the newcomers associated with the Trident base. The station is not open to visitors.

The crossroads community of **BELFAIR** perches at the southern "hook" of Hood Canal. Not surprisingly, timber dominated its development, and most homesteaders sold their land for the value of the standing trees. As the late 1880s' trend toward company-supported loggers grew, a huge demand developed for food to put onto camp tables, and some formerly aspiring homesteaders who had sold their land to the Union Logging Company saw their former fields continue under cultivation. They had given up too soon. In 1895 a minor gold rush led hopefuls to file placer claims along Mission Creek, but little came of it.

At **BREMERTON,** battleship gray vessels line the shore, and small houses march along hilly residential streets. Passenger-only and automobile ferries operated by the state wend through picturesque Rich Passage toward Seattle (worth taking as a scenic minivoyage), and a small privately operated passenger ferry connects to Port Orchard (10 minutes; also worth taking). The Naval Shipyard Museum (120 Washington, near the ferry dock) houses exhibits related to the history of the shipyard and navy. They include actual models used in designing ships and a mock-up of a ship's bridge.

For Washingtonians, Bremerton and the navy yard are synonymous. The tie began in 1891 when William Bremer, Seattle realtor and the son of a prominent German banker, convinced the owners of waterfront land to sell it to the U.S. government. The sale greatly enhanced the value of his own property and gave an economic foundation for developing a town. Bremer died wealthy in 1910.

Government procurement agent Lieutenant Ambrose Wyckoff had argued in favor of a naval station here since 1877. He pointed to the magnificent harbor, mild climate, and access to abundant coal and timber. Congress heeded his advice and appropriated money when the United States acquired coaling stations in the Pacific—Hawaii, Samoa, and the Philippines—and therefore needed a West Coast refitting station. The Bremerton drydock—a massive 650 feet long, 130 feet wide, and 39 feet deep—was commissioned in 1896.

The waterfront land Lieutenant Wyckoff recommended had been homesteaded in 1872 but was still a "wilderness of forest and swamp." Two communities grew up on each side of the navy yard as soon as it got under way: Bremerton and Charleston (later West Bremerton), connected by a boardwalk built through the shipyard. Ironically, as navy yard construction finally got into full swing, the Klondike gold rush swept footloose workers north and a true labor shortage developed.

During World War II Bremerton's population exploded with the sudden arrival of 30,000 workers and their families. They repaired 31 battleships, including five hit at Pearl Harbor, and built ships such as the *Sacramento*, at 50,000 tons the largest ship ever constructed on the West Coast. In August 1944 President Franklin D. Roosevelt visited the shipyard aboard the cruiser *Indianapolis*. The ship was floated into the drydock, where the president thanked the workers for their invaluable contribution to the war effort.

At **HANSVILLE,** situated on the northern tip of the Kitsap Peninsula, a grocery store constitutes the entire commercial center, and the murmur of the surf is more noticeable than the hum of traffic.

A Norwegian herring fisherman was first to settle here in 1893; he and a partner sold their catch to the halibut boats. Another early arrival hired out himself and his oxteam to peninsula loggers. Other Norwegians followed, including Hans Zachariasen, for whom the town was named. In 1908 the community built the area's first road (other than skid roads) toward Point No Point. Shortly thereafter a resident imported an automobile via a fishing boat and treated his neighbors to excursions on the single mile of roadway.

About 1½ miles southeast, **Point No Point**

juts into Puget Sound. Lieutenant Charles Wilkes, commander of the U.S. Exploring Expedition, anchored here on May 8, 1841, and "found it a snug berth for the night." He nostalgically named it for a similar landform on the Hudson River he remembered from his youth.

Fourteen years after Wilkes' visit, Governor Isaac Stevens convened a treaty council at the point on a stormy January day. Three tribes attended: the Klallam, the Chimakum, and the Skokomish. Treaty provisions, modeled after those recently signed with the "Ottoe, Missouria, and Omahas," had been translated from English into Chinook Jargon for the 1,200 assembled natives. Skokomish leader Hool-hol-tan expressed the distress of most:

I don't want to sign away my right to the land. If it was myself alone that I signed for I would do it, but we have women and children. Let us keep half of it and [you] take the rest. Why should we sell all? We may become destitute. Why not let us live together with you?

But the following day chiefs and headmen, some specifically appointed by Stevens for the occasion, added their marks onto the governor's already prepared documents. With this action they ceded their lands and promised to move onto reservations.

In 1879 the government established the Point No Point light station, which winks its warning from a flat, broad beach. A sign cautions that a nearby foghorn can damage the hearing of anyone approaching too close; the horn comes on automatically when a light beam detects fog over the main shipping channel. Despite its noise, shorebirds feed and rest in adjacent wetlands, and fishermen congregate along the beach and in the tide rips to try their luck for salmon. From behind a hill to the southeast, Seattle's Columbia Tower rises like an urban phantom.

HOOD CANAL BRIDGE. (See under PORT GAMBLE, p. 377.)

At the outskirts of **KEYPORT** a sign reads, "Welcome to Keyport, Torpedo Town U.S.A." Here, a Naval Undersea Museum is open year round. It exhibits material highlighting a wide range of human association with the undersea environment from diving, exploration, and salvage to fisheries, commerce, and warfare. "If man has done it under the sea, we probably have it," is the museum staff's informal motto. (Drive through town on State Route 308 and follow signs to the naval station; at the main gate watch for a sign giving directions to the museum.)

In l910 a commission of three naval officers scouted for waterfront land where the navy could develop and test torpedoes. Requirements included a 5-mile sea range for practice and tests. In 1914 the land was condemned and former residents were required to move as soon as their crops were harvested. (One interesting farm was a holly plantation whose owner imported Mexican workers to care for the trees.) Developers platted a townsite at the entrance to the torpedo station.

World War II brought an influx of workers for whom housing was built in Poulsbo. At the station 2,000 employees worked around-the-clock shifts, seven days on, one day off. Today workers shop-test torpedoes and other weapons for the navy and for companies competing for contracts.

KINGSTON, on Appletree Cove near the northern end of the Kitsap Peninsula, features a large marina and a ferry dock with connections to Edmonds. An 1898 two-story, false-fronted hotel still stands near the ferry landing. A steam sawmill began here in 1852, but was purchased by George Meigs and moved to Port Madison two years later. By 1890 the Puget Sound Mill Company of Port Gamble owned all the land surrounding Kingston, thus blocking commercial development. When town promoters objected, the company predicted that Kingston's future lay in recreation:

Excursion parties will be run this summer, and thousands of weary mortals will cast off the cankering cares of business as they wander on the shining sands strewn with curious shells, or under the shade of great alders, willows, cottonwoods, and blossoming dogwoods that line the shore . . .

With the ferry and Hood Canal bridge, modern "excursion parties" now drive through Kingston en route to the Olympic Peninsula.

OLALLA today is marked by one grand old house, a cluster of other houses, and a general store; the store is worth entering for its display of historic photographs. The town faces Colvos Passage, a relatively narrow waterway separating Vashon Island from the mainland. Steamboats formerly plied this route between Seattle and Tacoma. A scenic drive north along the shoreline warrants exploration on a lazy afternoon.

Settlers in the 1880s chose Olalla because a creek enters the Sound here, and the shoreline dips from the bluffs to a conveniently low landing place. *Olallie* means "berries" in Chinook Jargon, and Olalla grew into its name in the early 1920s, shipping strawberries as its primary export article.

The one remaining steamboat of the "Mosquito Fleet"—the *Virginia V,* a popular cruise vessel operated out of Seattle—was built on the beach at Olalla in 1922 (see *Virginia V* under SEATTLE on p. 296). At its peak, the Olalla dock sometimes saw as many as seven vessels per day.

In 1913 Charles F. Nelson built a house with two octagonal towers and a veranda with a conical-roofed bay overlooking the waterfront. He epitomized energetic 1880s immigrants who streamed into Washington. Nelson worked on steamboats and at the Tacoma smelter, then made a few minor real estate deals, and cashed in on the gold rush by opening a store in Dawson, Yukon Territory. In 1904 he returned to Olalla and became the area's most important merchant; he ran the general store, and his wife offered food and lodging to travelers. After they built their elegant house—now listed in the National Register of Historic Places—he and his pianist wife staged musicales in their drawing room and encouraged local children to try the various instruments they kept on hand.

Remembering her childhood, Minnie Baker Hall wrote fondly in *Kitsap County, a History:*

My happy memories include invitations at Christmas time to the Nelson home. It was a treat . . . and Christmas there was a gala affair in both decor and spirit. When we left Mrs. Nelson would urge us to take a handful of hard candy.

POINT NO POINT. (See HANSVILLE, p. 373.)

PORT BLAKELY. (See under BAINBRIDGE ISLAND, p. 370.)

PORT GAMBLE appears prim and tidy, its church, houses, and cemetery straight from the nineteenth century. Visitors come in droves to enjoy the tranquility and the sense of history—and to take pictures; but shops do not cater to tourism. This is a working mill town, as it has been since its founding in the 1850s. Beautifully crafted Saint Paul's Church (built in 1870) replicates the founders' hometown church in East Machias, Maine. A professionally designed museum (in the general store's basement) chronicles the history and technology of early sawmilling. Workers' houses line the shady streets, and the cemetery offers a peaceful stroll overlooking the Sound.

Among the graves is that of Gustave Engelbrecht, who was killed in February 1856 during a battle between the steamer *Massachusetts* and a Tlingit raiding party from Kupreanof Island and the Stikine area of southeast Alaska. After harassing native villages near Steilacoom, the northerners pulled their canoes onto the beach at Port Gamble, where relatives worked at the mill. The commander of the *Massachusetts* followed and sent men ashore with an interpreter to ask them to "leave the Sound peaceably in tow of

this vessel," according to a later report of events. Defiant taunts met the request. After two more tries at a verbal request, the gunboat opened fire, and a shore party "made a very gallant charge." Twenty-seven native men were killed, and 21 were wounded, including a chief who died later. In addition, the shore party burned their "huts" and "disabled all but one of their canoes."

After 48 hours, the Tlingits sued for peace, and the *Massachusetts* carried 87 of them to Victoria. Governor James Douglas refused to let them be put ashore, pointing out that their home territory was outside his jurisdiction. The commander of the *Massachusetts* then bought canoes to replace those destroyed at Port Gamble and towed them beyond Nanaimo. There he provided the captives with 15 days worth of food for the remaining 400-mile journey to their home villages. In parting he warned them to never again venture into Puget Sound. The following summer, however, bent on vengeance for their dead chief, the Tlingits came back and killed Isaac Ebey on Whidbey Island. (See EBEY'S LANDING, p. 267.)

The town of Port Gamble originated in 1853 when the *Julius Pringle* anchored in the bay with Pope and Talbot Company directors on board. These experienced and well-capitalized Maine lumbermen had arrived to reap profit

Pope and Talbot modeled its company town at Port Gamble after a New England village.

THE LUMBER CARGO TRADE

Puget Sound lumbering began as a cargo trade in 1788 when John Meares, a British merchant-adventurer, headed west with a load of spars for China. This was the Northwest's first commercial shipment, which had to be jettisoned during a storm. A century later—as Washington gained statehood—spars, railroad ties, ships' knees, shingles, and dimension lumber were marketed in ports from California and Chile to Hawaii, Australia, and China.

All of the successful Puget Sound mills of the 1850s and 1860s had San Francisco offices to market their lumber and direct other aspects of the business; all had lumber yards in and financing from San Francisco. The mills owned sailing vessels, rather than rely on chartered carriers, and either operated company towns or at least had a company store and other basic services. All began by buying logs from independent loggers and ended up owning huge tracts of timber and running their own logging railroads and camps.

As capital invested in equipment, shipping, and operations grew, so did mill owners' sense of urgency to protect themselves from the notorious price fluctuations of the lumber market. This necessitated foreign sales. The mills at Port Gamble, Port Madison, and Seabeck were the giants of the overseas trade through the 1850s, joined in the 1860s by mills at Port Blakely and at Tacoma. Of these five, the Pope and Talbot mill at Port Gamble achieved the largest trade. Today—with a second century of milling beginning—about a quarter of Washington's lumber and wood products are marketed abroad.

---

from the Northwest forest, although their West Coast headquarters was to remain in San Francisco, the largest metropolis on the coast and an active lumber market itself. After scouting Hood Canal and Port Townsend, the party decided on *Teekalet* ("Brightness of the Noonday Sun"), a bay that Wilkes had called Port Gamble.

In September a second vessel brought mill machinery and the supervisors erected a bunkhouse, store, cookhouse, and the mill itself from timbers hewn along the shore. The millsite was a spit near the harbor entrance where sailing vessels could easily catch the strong winds after loading. Pope and Talbot, also called the Puget Mill Company, grew into a major force in Washington lumbering.

By midcentury the United States government began to view the hungry Northwest mills as disadvantageous for the country. Lumbering practices were wasteful. Loggers cut only near shorelines, only on tracts that would yield 30,000 board feet per acre, and only those trees that would yield a minimum of three logs, each 24 feet long. The rest often were burned. Even vast tracts of public land were scalped, and large companies bought huge acreages of public forest at the low prices intended to attract settlers.

In 1858 the goverment attempted to enforce laws against cutting timber on public lands. Grand juries indicted millowners from Port Madison, Port Gamble, and Seabeck, but were unable to curb the practice. A stumpage law sought to collect fees (25 cents per 1,000 feet) for trees taken from public land, and a revised timber law regulated later sales. However, delayed government surveys and limited enforcement personnel made the laws unworkable. In theory, no more than 160 acres could be sold to a single individual or "association of persons," but companies habitually evaded this stipulation by hiring "entrymen" to buy land, then sell it to the mill.

Despite obtaining logs at these low prices, Northwest mill owners often lost money. They glutted the market with lumber and watched the price sink below production costs. Profitable years regularly alternated with unprofitable ones.

Large owners built larger and larger mills to increase efficiency—and flooded the market still more. Small operators fell by the wayside.

The **Hood Canal Bridge,** west of Port Gamble, crosses 1½ miles to the Olympic Peninsula. The western half was rebuilt in 1982. Three years earlier, storm waves destroyed the original 1961 floating causeway. Winds gusted to 100 miles per hour; water poured into an open manhole and sank one section, which dragged down others. No lives were lost although bridge tenders and one courageous truck driver barely escaped. The driver backed his truck the length of the western span and reached solid ground barely before the bridge sank. Two similar bridges on Lake Washington are better sheltered against storm action.

PORT MADISON. (See under BAINBRIDGE ISLAND, p. 370.)

PORT MADISON RESERVATION. (See under SUQUAMISH, p. 382.)

PORT ORCHARD lies directly across from Bremerton on Sinclair Inlet, and a privately owned passenger ferry still connects the two towns and provides a closeup look at the mothball fleet—ships kept for possible recommissioning. (The dock is on Bay Street at the north end of Sidney.)

Time permitting, also drive along Beach Drive, which intersects with Bay at the edge of the downtown district. The road hugs the water's edge—a scenic drive, despite the lack of road shoulder, as well as blind curves, joggers, and bicyclists. A public pier is 3½ miles from downtown, and the road continues (with various names) another 6 miles to **Manchester State Park,** which occupies the site of auxiliary fortifications facing Fort Ward, on the tip of Bainbridge Island. (See p. 369.)

The two installations deployed mines, which were placed at fixed locations beneath the water and exploded by remote control. Their purpose was to sink any enemy ships approaching the Bremerton naval shipyard—a defensive system never actually needed. Today picnic tables cluster beside and within a large brick torpedo (mine) shop; nearby is the tiny building that housed the World War II control center, where a grid of electric circuits converged at a switchboard. A path leads along the shore to the battery at Point Mitchell, where the view of islands and water accented by the lone white pyramid of Mount Rainier carries the feeling of an illustration from the folios of Captain George Vancouver's voyage of discovery.

The Port Gamble Episcopal church is among buildings refurbished in the 1970s.

In town, life-size dioramas upstairs at the Sidney Gallery (202 Sidney) present vignettes of early-day Port Orchard; and the Log Cabin Museum (416 Sidney) captures a sense of how family life has changed through the decades. Its furnishings are periodically redone with great attention to details such as the magazines and board games set out on tables, the style of dishes and utensils in the kitchen, the pictures and family memorabilia decorating the house, and even the sounds coming from a windup Victrola or radio or early television set. The cabin was built in 1913 and occupied as a home until the 1970s.

Navy Lieutenant Charles Wilkes noted in his journal that "Port Orchard is one of the many fine harbors on these inland waters, and is perfectly protected from the winds," an assessment shared by his successors 50 years later when they sited the Navy Yard across the bay.

In 1884 Sidney Stevens laid out Port Orchard, the third town of that name. His teenage son suggested it be called Sidney, but later the name was changed. William Bremer, the Seattle realtor for whom Bremerton is named, helped to promote the new development. Its early industries included a four-story pottery and terra-cotta mill that produced everything from bean pots to paving tiles. Fire destroyed the plant after only four years, but the name Pottery Hill remains west of town.

POULSBO, settled by Norwegians, has transformed its heritage into a village theme. Rosemaling (painted folk art design) decorates shutters and doorways downtown. Restaurants offer Scandinavian delicacies, and costumed merchants welcome visitors during Viking Fest (held on the weekend nearest May 17, the Norwegian national holiday) and during Scandia Midsommer Fest (in late June). A marina, ringed by a park, shelters boats; a marine science center (open to the public) is adjacent. At their lodge near the waterfront, the Sons of Norway offer courses in the Norwegian language, folk dancing, rosemaling, lace making, and beading. Stroll uphill on Hostmark Street to enjoy the Victorian homes and the First Lutheran Church (built in 1908) that overlooks the town, the bay, and the Olympic Mountains.

In the 1880s and 1890s an influx of Nor-wegian loggers, fishermen, and farmers flooded the Northwest. Most had lived elsewhere in the United States before continuing their westward migration via the recently completed trans-continental railroad. By 1900 a quarter of Washington's population was foreign born and, of these, Scandinavians were by far the largest group.

Conditions on the Kitsap Peninsula paralleled Norwegians' home-country landscape: a long coastline with many harbors where they could pursue fishing; dense timber for logging; and, once the trees were cut, stumpland to transform into farms. Poulsbo in 1882 was 90 percent Norwegian, and Norwegian remained the common language until well into the 1920s.

Poulsbo's settlers brought firm Lutheran convictions with them from the old country. Children attended public school for three to five months in the winter and church school, which taught religion and Norwegian language, in the summer. In the early 1900s the community established two major charitable institutions: an orphanage that sheltered 30 children, and a home for the elderly. Norwegians from all over Puget Sound contributed to maintaining these institutions.

Liberty Bay, Poulsbo's harbor, earlier bore the name Dogfish Bay for a type of small shark with an odoriferous and viscous oil much in demand by early loggers for greasing skid roads and mill machinery. Poulsbo homesteaders caught the fish, rendered the oil, and sold it at Port Blakely or Port Madison to earn cash.

In the early 1900s Poulsbo became home port for the Pacific Coast Codfish Company. From here large schooners set sail for the Bering Sea each summer. Gideon Hermanson as a young man in the summer of 1916 joined the codfish fleet. He reminisced in the historical society's *Kitsap County, a History:*

The fishermen arose at 4 A.M., ate a hurried break-fast, got into their respective dories and rowed or sailed out from the mother ship. It amazed me how far out from the ship some would sail hoping to find a location where the cod was plentiful. Soon they were out of sight except for a small speck here and there. . . .

[One] day we dressed down 10,000 codfish and got finished at 1 A.M. The port side and the starboard

By the early 1900s Poulsbo, a Norwegian center, had become a major cod fishing port.

side dress gangs were quite evenly matched, so that meant each of us . . . headers had lifted with our left hand, cut open and headed with our right hand, 5,000 cod-fish each, some fish weighing up to 65 lbs. After a few days of this hectic work, the captain ordered the fishermen to stay aboard one day so that the dress gang could rest up, for there was no hitting the bunk at night while there was still a fish in the checkers.

In early winter the ships returned to Poulsbo and workers shoveled the catch onto the dock and wheeled the fish in carts to the processing plant. There the cod stayed in 20-ton brine tanks until retrieved for further processing. Some fish were boned and dried; some were made into lutefisk. Changing food habits and home freezers gradually diminished the dried fish market, and in 1950 the last codfish schooners returned to Poulsbo, their careers over.

During World War II Poulsbo's Norwegian purity was diluted when thousands of shipyard workers moved to the Kitsap Peninsula. The population expanded rapidly with people of varying backgrounds. Today approximately 60 percent of Kitsap County residents work for governmental agencies at the federal, state, or local level. The Trident Submarine Base on Hood Canal, Puget Sound Naval Shipyard, and Keyport Naval Undersea Warfare Engineering Station are the major employers.

SEABECK, a tiny community facing Hood Canal, today consists of a marina and a scattering of Victorian homes around a green lawn. A sign marks the site of the smokestack belonging to one of Washington's major early mills. Near it, today's lagoon is the former millpond.

In 1856 four San Francisco men formed the Washington Mill Company, a lumber marketing firm. Their first investment was a one-third interest in Henry Yesler's Seattle mill, but Yesler's output did not match their expectations. They then decided to build their own plant at Seabeck. Marshall Blinn came north to supervise operations while partner William Adams, grandfather of renowned photographer Ansel Adams, remained in San Francisco to oversee marketing.

During the 1860s and 1870s San Francisco was the company's primary market; but lumber ships also sailed from Seabeck to Valparaiso, Lima, Melbourne, Tahiti, Shanghai, and Hong Kong. Some also went to Victoria, British Columbia, to satisfy the boom associated with the Fraser River gold strike. In these years, Seabeck far surpassed Seattle in size. The Washington Mill Company owned eight sailing vessels and a tug and was building additional lumber ships at its own Seabeck shipyard. By the end of the 1870s, its prosperous future seemed assured; yet a mere five years later, the Seabeck mill was on the verge of bankruptcy. The company had doubled its capacity about the same time that other Puget Sound mills did; the resulting lumber glut drove down prices, and the Seabeck mill was unable to recover its investment in new equipment. At the same time it lost several co-owned vessels that were only partially covered by insurance.

In 1886 the mill burned. According to the diary of Jacob Hauptly, a Seabeck butcher who brought cattle to the mill town by scow:

> . . . *August 12, 1886:* FIRE FIRE FIRE. . . . While *Retriever* was discharging freight, she set the old hay barn on fire about 2:25 P.M. With strong south wind and in less than two hours, the whole, both mills, were burned down. All hands worked as hard as we could, but without success, all burned. . . . Nothing but the three chimneys standing.
>
> . . . *August 19, 1886:* W. J. Adams arrived here on the Steamer Louise about 11:30. He says that another mill will be built right away. People of Seabeck beginning to feel better. Some were pretty badly scared.

Adams' first reassurances notwithstanding, the company did not rebuild the mill. It relocated to Port Hadlock, and Jacob Hauptly, as well as many mill employees, followed to the new location. Seabeck's population of over 600 persons dwindled to almost zero. In 1914 an interdenominational group bought the 700-acre townsite for a church conference center. Religious groups still meet here.

SILVERDALE, 6 miles northwest of Bremerton, has an ambivalent downtown focus: old buildings cluster on the waterfront, as befitted a steamboat port, newer ones resolutely turn their backs to the water and depend on State Route 3. The Kitsap Historical Museum (Byron and Washington) occupies the former Silverdale State Bank (built in 1919), and a pleasant waterfront park tempts strollers. Today Silverdale serves as regional shopping center for communities like Bangor and Keyport, which have large populations of government employees.

Logging was Silverdale's primary early business. Oxteams towed logs to the bay, and a

Oxteams were practical for hauling logs along skid roads for only about a mile. Dumped in salt water, the logs were chained into rafts and towed or sailed to mills.

blacksmith shop and livery stable opened as the town's first business. In the 1880s Silverdale took its place in the Puget Sound roll call of "real towns" when regular steamer service connected it with Seattle. The boat left Silverdale at 1:00 A.M. and, after six other stops, arrived at Seattle before the markets opened for the day. Local farmers frequently raised poultry or dairy cattle because chickens or cows could coexist with the huge stumps that still dotted most farms. They banded together in a cooperative feed-buying venture, which eventually grew into the large-scale Poultry Association with a retail store and full-time manager. In 1930 Silverdale poultry farmers shipped 48,000 cases of eggs and nearly 62,000 chickens, prompting the editor of the *Silverdale Breeze* to boast, "Silverdale is the town where the eggs come from, where the cackle of the hen is heard 'round the world."

SUQUAMISH—a hamlet with a single commercial street—lies on the Kitsap Peninsula across Agate Passage from Bainbridge Island. It is known for the nearby Suquamish Museum and Tribal Center; "Old Man House"; and the grave of Chief Sealth, for whom the city of Seattle is named.

The cemetery occupies the slope behind **St. Peter's Catholic Church,** built in 1902 to replace one built in 1871 by missionary Father Francis Blanchet. Doors and windows from the original building are incorporated into the present structure. **Chief Sealth's grave,** bearing the date 1866, is marked by the uprights of a stylized longhouse with canoes on the crossbeams. Nearby are graves poignantly marked with names such as Qual-qual-blue, Kee-hop, Ha-o-dah, and Kitsap (the name of a prominent chief).

Old Man House stood along the shore about a half mile from Sealth's grave. (Walk or drive down Division to the bluff.) A small park display gives an idea of how cedar longhouses were built, but nothing of the actual house remains. The government ordered it burned in 1870, deeming it an obstacle to the "civilization" of the Suquamish people. The name Old Man is an anglicized version of *Oleman,* Chinook Jargon for "strong man" and in itself a translation of the Suquamish name *Tsu-suc-cub.*

The house stretched for 500 feet or more along the beach and varied in width from 40 to 60 feet. It was an early-day "condominium," the Suquamish people's home, fortress, and festival hall. Quite probably the house is where Chief Sealth's family held a grand potlatch to ceremonially present him with his grandfather's name. Sealth's own prowess as a raider helped him hold respect and overcome a relatively low birth: his father was a Suquamish warrior, his mother a captive from the Green River area.

As he aged, Sealth gradually allowed younger men to take over positions of war leadership while he adopted the role of elder statesman and respected headman. He befriended David Maynard and encouraged him to settle at the new community on Elliott Bay. It was Maynard who persuaded the settlers to name their town in the chief's honor—surely to the dismay of some within the tribe, and quite possibly of Sealth himself. Coast native people still regard their names as family property carrying great social and ceremonial status, not as public property.

For treaty purposes, Governor Isaac Stevens appointed Sealth chief of the Suquamish and Duwamish, a plan that outraged the Duwamish when their neighbors received a reservation but they did not. Sealth's renowned speech was addressed to the new governor when he stopped in Seattle on an 1854 whirlwind tour meeting with Puget Sound native groups. The speech's recorded style seems to reflect nineteenth-century literary embellishment—and indeed its published version came 33 years after Sealth spoke. It was printed by Dr. Henry Smith, who had come to the territory in 1853. According to the version of the speech translated by Benjamin Shaw—later Stevens' official interpreter—Sealth acknowledged that his people welcomed "Boston and King George men" for their blankets, guns, axes, clothing, and tobacco, but they wondered why whites cared to "wander so far away from their home."

Whatever the whole of Sealth's speech may have been, its underlying concept is clear. His words evoked the native people's love for their land and proved prophetic:

It matters little where we pass the remnant of our days. They will not be many. . . . At night when the streets of your cities and villages are silent and you think them deserted, they will throng with the returning hosts that once filled and still love this beautiful land. The White Man will never be alone.

Before fighting erupted in 1855, Sealth and his followers withdrew to Old Man House and, on the day before the so-called Battle of Seattle, they warned the commander of the gunboat *Decatur* that an attack could come momentarily. (See sidebar, p. 326.) Sealth had wanted Maynard to move from Olympia to the Duwamish and open a store, and he remained steadfast in his (perhaps pragmatic) friendship with white settlers even while his people sank into poverty and despair over the invasion of their lands.

Displays at the Suquamish Museum highlight the tribe's entire story from before white men came to the present day, and an unforgettable slide show blends images with elders' voices and memories. (About a half mile southeast of the Agate Passage Bridge and the road to the town of Suquamish, turn south off State Route 305 onto Sandy Hook Road and follow it to the end.)

Each August the Suquamish Tribe joins the American Legion in hosting Chief Seattle Days, a festival that includes a salmon bake, canoe races, and historical pageantry.

The **Port Madison Reservation,** mandated by the 1855 Point Elliott Treaty, is also often called the Suquamish Reservation. Its land is in two tracts: one adjoining the town of Suquamish, the other (added later) farther north near Indianola.

Treaty provisions assigned both the Suquamish, whose hereditary home was on the beach near Agate Passage, and the Duwamish, with whom they were on poor terms, to this reservation. The Duwamish stayed only as long as coerced to do so, then moved back to their own villages south of Seattle. While mills operated at Port Madison, Port Blakely, and Port Gamble, some Suquamish took jobs there. Later they became seasonal agricultural workers, picking strawberries on farms owned primarily by

Japanese. Today the tribe has an active oral history program and has begun documenting its language.

WINSLOW is the largest community on Bainbridge Island, across from Seattle; ferries link the town to the mainland. The finely crafted Eagle Harbor Congregational Church (Madison Avenue and Winslow Way; built in 1896) reflects workmanship consistent with a community that was home to many shipwrights. A restored 1908 one-room school 2 miles west of Winslow (Strawberry Hill Park, on High School Road) houses memorabilia and historic photographs, including material from the logging and ship-building heyday at Ports Blakeley and Madison.

In 1902 Hall Brothers Shipyards moved their company from Port Blakely to Winslow and enlarged their operation. Winslow Hall—for whom the town was named—was one of three brothers who learned shipbuilding in Ochasset, Massachusetts, and then came West. From San Francisco they moved to Port Ludlow, Port Blakely, and finally Winslow—always following a supply of superb timber. They built lumber schooners, stern-wheel steamers, propeller steamers—and rebuilt them years later when new owners wanted improvements. After 1916 the yard changed hands but continued through both world wars, modernizing older vessels and in 1942 and 1943 building minesweepers. Women joined the crews in the hectic 1940s. The shipyard finally ceased operations in 1959. (Also see BAINBRIDGE ISLAND, p. 371.)

Other industries ringed the harbor, including a creosote pile preserving firm.

During Bainbridge Island's strawberry heyday in the 1920s, farmers banded together to build a processing plant in Winslow. Berries were packed here and kept in cold storage for the trip to Seattle, and many were canned and sold under the name "Armour's Best." In 1937 boat service to Bainbridge centralized in Winslow, with buses fanning out to other island communities.

SOUTHWEST Region

Skamokawa, Lower Columbia River.

IN 1792 THE YANKEE seaman Captain Robert Gray crossed the bar guarding the Columbia River and entered the broad bay within its mouth, a feat that greatly furthered American claims to the land that became Washington. Late in 1805 the Lewis and Clark expedition arrived at the river mouth. Five summers later, Bostonian traders Nathaniel and Abiel Winship opened an abortive fur-trading station at Oak Point, 40 miles upriver from today's Astoria. The following year New Yorker John Jacob Astor founded the Pacific Fur Company, which he signed over to the Canadian North West Company in 1813. It, in turn, was forcefully amalgamated into the Hudson's Bay Company in 1821. Four years later Fort Vancouver opened at a new location 75 miles upriver from Astoria and on the opposite bank of the Columbia. It became the headquarters of a trading empire that reached as far north as Alaska. East of the Rockies the forty-ninth parallel had already been established as the boundary between the United States and Canada. Extending that line west, however, would bisect the Columbia River and, rather than accept that, British and American interests agreed to joint occupation of what is now Washington and British Columbia. Then in 1846, land south of the forty-ninth parallel became American.

Seven years later, settlers gained enough strength to establish Washington as a territory separate from Oregon (although few non-native people were living here at the time). A gold rush in California created insatiable San Francisco demand for Willapa Bay oysters and lumber, and subsequent rushes in northeastern Washington, Idaho, and British Columbia brought miners through the region. Some returned and settled down. Subsistence farming augmented by logging and fishing sustained the economy. By the 1880s gillnetting, seining, and fishtrap operations on the lower Columbia produced annual salmon catches of 30 to 40 million pounds, which fed the clanking machinery of 39 canneries.

By that time Portland, Oregon, had grown large enough to provide summer tourists for the 28 miles of sand beaches west of Willapa Bay, and resorts from simple camps to elaborate hotels dotted the Long Beach Peninsula. Tourism continues today; fishing and logging, incredibly productive for the first century and a half following settlement, are now much diminished. At Willapa Bay, a non-native weed threatens the mudflats: anthropogenic change.

Centralia to Longview

Rivers predominate here. They served as highways—first for native canoes and fur company bateaux, then for paddle-wheel steamers. Trains, trucks, and automobiles now follow the river corridors. Broad flats attracted pioneering farmers, beginning with the Hudson's Bay Company, which established an extensive corporate farm on Cowlitz Prairie (near Toledo).

There are several points of special historical interest in the area. At Cowlitz Landing (near Toledo) and Monticello (now Longview) settlers met in 1852 to petition Congress to separate land on the north side of the Columbia River into a territory of its own. Cowlitz Mission was the first Catholic mission in Washington. A log cabin near Mary's Corner (the Jackson House) is where the first federal court session north of the Columbia River was held. An 1856 granary blockhouse still stands at Centralia.

Paved byways parallel I-5, inviting leisurely travel. Old U.S. 99 just south of Kelso offers a high view out over the Cowlitz and Columbia rivers; it makes an excellent geographic orientation point. (Follow signs to Carrolls; the viewpoint is about a half mile farther south.) History museums are at Chehalis and Kelso. Two outstanding visitor centers near Castle Rock highlight the story of volcanism and of Mount St. Helens' eruptions. Festivals in the area include Winlock's Egg Day and Toledo's Cheese Day.

CASTLE ROCK is named for a tree-covered riverbank knob noted in the journals of Hudson's Bay Company traders as early as 1832 and used as a navigation landmark by early settlers traveling the Cowlitz River.

High dikes of volcanic debris now dominate the town's skyline. In 1980 nearby Mount St. Helens erupted and transformed the Toutle and Cowlitz rivers into a hot batter of volcanic ash and sediment that overflowed the banks and destroyed 200 houses. In a massive flood control effort the Army Corps of Engineers restored channels by dredging and then piling the spoils into dikes, now well vegetated. Eruptions and floods are nothing new here, however. Their accumulated deposits form the rich floodplain

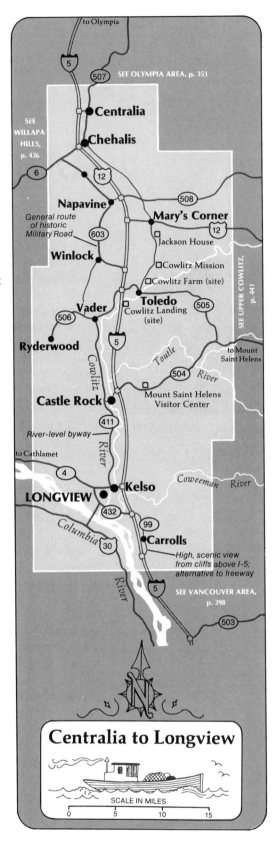

Centralia to Longview

SCALE IN MILES
0   5   10   15

Centralia's 1857 Borst house (open to the public) is finished inside with plaster laid over hand-split cedar lath; original moldings and other woodwork remain intact.

that attracted settlers beginning in the late 1840s.

Thirty-five years later the population boomed when a sawmill moved to the east side of the Cowlitz River to take advantage of the red cedar groves. The Northern Pacific Railroad left a boxcar to be loaded with shingles, which they shipped to St. Paul, Minnesota, free of charge. It was in the company's interest, as well as that of the local economy, to promote a new product—cedar shingles.

Mount St. Helens visitor centers are reached either from Castle Rock or Exit 49. One is located about 5 miles east of I-5 via State Route 504, the other 38 miles farther at Coldwater Ridge.

CENTRALIA is bisected by I-5. The main connection between its two halves is Harrison Avenue, which becomes Main Street just a few blocks east of the freeway.

Barely west of the freeway are the Borst granary blockhouse and home. (Take Exit 82 and follow Harrison west to Belmont Road, then turn south to Fort Borst Park. The blockhouse is to the left, just inside the entrance. The house is in the extreme southwest corner of the park beyond the southernmost ball field. This puts it slightly south and west of the blockhouse area—an approach harder to describe than to find.)

Joseph Borst, a young farmer, came West in

1845 and settled on the Chehalis River. During the sporadic warfare of 1855 to 1856 between native people and settlers, the Borsts lived at the Grand Mound blockhouse (called Fort Henness; see ROCHESTER on p. 362). While staying there, Borst worked with U.S. Army soldiers to build a secure storehouse next to his cabin, which was at a ferry landing. That blockhouse, intended for grain and military supplies, not for residents, has been moved about a half mile to its present position. The men built it with a second-story overhang and rifle loopholes, defensive measures never actually needed.

Apparently soon after leaving Fort Henness, the Borsts started the spacious "white house" Joseph had promised his bride. A two-and-a-half-story Greek Revival, it is open to the public on summer weekend afternoons. Beside the house is a tiny, poignant cemetery plot where five of the eight Borst children were originally buried. Three died in their first year, one at age two, another at age three.

East of the freeway, several of Centralia's old houses still stand in the 600 and 700 blocks of North Pearl (which is one-way, southbound) and of E and F streets, just west of Pearl. (Street numbers are counted from Main, potentially confusing. For example, the fine Victorian house at 715 E Street stands between First and Second streets.)

BLACK FOUNDER OF CENTRALIA

A park and library in Centralia (West Main near South Pearl) are on the donation land claim of George Washington, the black founder of Centralia, who arrived in 1852. His story exemplifies the painful status of blacks even in the West.

Washington's father was a slave; his mother was white. Friends of hers, the James Cochrans, bought the father and agreed to raise the baby to age 21. They moved with him from Virginia to Ohio, then on to Missouri. There, young Washington became a tailor, but was arrested for trying to collect money due him; he had acted illegally according to a Missouri law that denied blacks the right to bring charges against citizens. Washington then started a distillery, but the Missouri legislature passed a law forbidding blacks to produce or handle spirits or malt liquors.

Next, he moved to Illinois, only to encounter a new law requiring blacks to post a cash bond "for good behavior." Lacking the money—$1,000—and wanting to escape discrimination and the slavery issue, Washington and the Cochrans left for Oregon. They traveled by wagon and arrived to find a new law prohibiting blacks from settling in Oregon. Hoping that it would be repealed, or that he might be given a personal exemption, Washington selected land along the Chehalis River (at the time still within Oregon Territory). Ironically, the legislature granted him an exemption just two months before land north of the Columbia became a separate territory. That political change invalidated Washington's newly won right to claim land; in the new territory, the anti-black law still applied.

About this same time, two white men en route to Olympia stopped at Washington's farm, accepting the home hospitality then

A man named George Washington pioneered the land that became Centralia.

routinely accorded travelers. They admired the location and announced that they would file a claim for it. Alarmed, Washington reported the encounter to the Cochrans, who rushed ahead of the two and successfully filed in the name Cochran.

In 1857 the law barring blacks from land ownership was repealed, and the Cochrans deeded to Washington the 640 acres he had lived on and developed for the past five years. At last receiving that title symbolized the attainment of basic rights, which George Washington—and the Cochrans—had fought for through six moves in six different states and territories.

The old business district is along North Tower (one-way, northbound). Two- and three-story buildings convey a feeling of a downtown core, which is in marked contrast with today's strip development between Centralia and Chehalis. The railroad depot (Railroad at E. Pine) is a handsome brick building surrounded by brick paving, a symbol of yesterday. Near it is the Olympic Club (112 N. Tower), a landmark saloon/cardroom (plus lunch counter, tobacco counter, and barbershop). It was built in the 1890s, then remodeled after a 1908 fire destroyed most of the buildings in the block. Interior appointments include beveled-glass windows and mirrors, hexagonal Italian floor tiles, mahogany doors and wainscoting, Tiffany-style chandeliers, and stenciled ceilings. Such Art Nouveau touches set the Olympic apart from the 30 other saloons along North Tower in the early 1900s.

Seven blocks north of the Olympic Club is the site (Second and Tower) of an Armistice Day clash between members of the American Legion and the Industrial Workers of the World, or "Wobblies." It became a tragedy. That Armistice Day—November 11, 1919—was the first anniversary of the end of World War I, a period of intense patriotism and abhorrence for any interference with the war effort. In the public mind this interference included such acts as labor strikes and slowdowns orchestrated by the Wobblies, a strong union of lumberjacks, miners, and field hands. These workers were "muscles" often needed only intermittently and treated with callous disregard for their working and living conditions.

Wobblies had been driven out of Centralia following a preparedness parade in 1916, and they were threatened again as the 1919 parade approached. This time they decided to defend their union building (807 N. Tower) but did not announce the decision. When the parade halted, Centralia Legionnaires happened to be directly in front of the hall. Some rushed the door, intending a quick raid. Wobblies both inside the building and stationed at two outside locations opened fire. Three Legionnaires were fatally shot, others wounded. A fourth was killed while pursuing Wesley Everest, a fleeing assailant.

The Wobblies were jailed. That night, vigilantes broke into the jail, seized Everest, and hanged him from the Mellen Street bridge (just west of freeway Exit 81). The next morning police retrieved his corpse and stretched it out on the jail floor for his fellow Wobblies to see.

Eleven Centralia Wobblies eventually stood trial at Montesano, a change of venue intended to moderate prejudice against them. Actually Legionnaires were paid to bivouac at the City Hall and attend the trial, and army troops, requested by the prosecution to quell possible disorder, camped near the courthouse plainly in sight of the judge. The Wobblies were sentenced to the Walla Walla penitentiary. The vigilante hangmen never were prosecuted. (See MONTESANO, p. 475, and WOBBLIES sidebar, p. 255.)

CHEHALIS, squeezed between I-5 and an exceedingly steep residential bluff, often confuses drivers from out of town owing to its angled streets and one-way traffic. An ideal first destination for visitors is the county historical society museum housed in the old red brick train station (599 NW Front Street; from I-5, take Exit 79 and turn south on National Avenue for a half mile, then make a quick right turn onto West Street immediately before the depot). In 1873 the Northern Pacific did not include Chehalis as a stop along its new line from Kalama to Tacoma; it laid out a townsite at nearby Newaukum instead. Chehalis residents retaliated by daily flagging trains to a stop, a pestering that soon won them a depot. The present building was opened in 1912.

A National Register Historic District is along NW Pennsylvania. (From the museum, cross the railroad tracks and drive 4 blocks on West Street, then turn south onto NW Pennsylvania.) Sandwiched into a comfortable, unremarkable neighborhood are historic houses of diverse architecture and eras. At the south end of NW Pennsylvania, where it deadends at St. Helens Avenue, notice the octagonal house built as a carriage house. Nearby is the two-home Coffman estate with exquisite formal gardens, built about 1918.

A two-and-a-half-story house at 673 NW Pennsylvania (built in 1910) belonged originally to Osmer Palmer, the owner of a company that manufactured ready-cut houses to be sold by catalog through an Iowa firm. Palmer's

Local effort by volunteers saved the Chehalis train station as a museum. Formerly, such stations were community hubs and proud symbols of success all across the nation.

company, the largest of several Chehalis mill-work manufacturers, also provided windows, doors, and cabinets sold through the Montgomery Ward catalog.

At the other end of the spectrum from manufactured houses is the one-and-a-half-story log home erected in 1859 for the family of Judge Obadiah McFadden. Modernized about 1918 and now surrounded by a residential neighborhood, the house shows an individualistic use of logs squared on their vertical faces and chinked with mortar and wedge-shaped strips of wood. (The address is 1639 Chehalis Avenue; from the museum follow Pacific for 1 block, then turn southeast on Chehalis.) The house stood by itself at the time of construction and was reached only by trail. McFadden, newly appointed to the Superior Court, came to Washington Territory in 1853, the year of Washington's separation from Oregon Territory.

Chehalis began only a year before the McFaddens arrived. Schuyler S. Saunders, who filed the first donation land claim here, sold half of his land to Judge McFadden. American

settlers' worst fears at the time are said to have been fire, Indians, the British, wild animals, and mud. The Saunders experienced all of these except for problems with the Hudson's Bay Company. In 1855, while the family took refuge in a blockhouse at Claquato, hostile natives burned down their house and barn and drove off their cattle. The mud on their land—and throughout most of the Chehalis Valley—is described as hub deep in some places, shoe-top deep in most.

COWLITZ FARM, COWLITZ LANDING, and **COWLITZ MISSION.** (See under TOLEDO, p. 395.)

JACKSON HOUSE. (See under MARY'S CORNER, p. 393.)

Stop at **KELSO** for a look at the county historical society museum (Allen between Fourth and Fifth) and to sample the downtown district on foot. Notice the 1924 Masonic Building (Pacific between Oak and Vine); lodge symbols are set into its window arches. The 1912 train depot (First between Maple and Alder) is still in use.

A seeming excess of bridges and rivers—Coweeman, Cowlitz, and Columbia—complicates a quick grasp of Kelso's layout, yet also accounts for the town's early prominence as a shipping and service center. Peter Crawford settled here in 1847 following a suggestion by missionary Marcus Whitman that the Cowlitz Valley would be a good place to look for land. His donation land claim cabin stood between the river and the end of today's Crawford Street. An apple tree he planted now leans precariously in the garden of a house across First Avenue from the Crawford site.

The Cowlitz River served as a water highway for mail, freight, and passengers. Service began with canoes and bateaux (the flat-bottomed, double-ended boats introduced by the Hudson's Bay Company) and, as early as 1856, Cowlitz boatmen even managed to freight a Buffalo Pitts threshing machine upriver, piece by piece, from Monticello to Cowlitz Landing, about 35 miles.

As early as the mid-1850s shallow-draft steamers began operating on the Cowlitz, and in 1858 prospectors en route to gold strikes along the Fraser River in British Columbia initiated a heyday for them. Cattle, largely bound for Victoria, accounted for a major portion of the freight; the trail north was so poor that herds could not be driven overland. River traffic diminished after the railroad was built from Kalama to Tacoma in 1873, but local people continued to rely on the Cowlitz as a link to the outside world. Indeed, increasing numbers of settlers produced ever more hay, grain, and potatoes to ship to market.

A 1911 promotional booklet printed by the Kelso Commercial Club pointed out that "hill lands, originally timbered [are] ready for the next stage of their usefulness." The statement, intended to encourage farming, was based on an assumption that the soil where giant trees grew would produce equally stupendous crops—a false premise. Furthermore, as the booklet pointed out, stumps had to be cleared from the land by blasting, then dragged into piles and burned, a slow and costly process.

Most settlers farmed, but fishing also provided a livelihood. Smelt entered the Cowlitz to

Men floated cedar shingle bolts down creeks to the Cowlitz River and on to mills at Kelso. Because of stockpiling, the original logger might wait a year for his money.

spawn in such hordes that a man working alone could net a boatful in a short time. As soon as shipping by rail was possible, the fish were marketed fresh in the Midwest and in the East. They provided low-cost protein, especially valuable during World War I meat shortages.

Logging increased in importance as enough men arrived to work together. River drives filled the Coweeman and Cowlitz with floating logs and shingle bolts en route to mills, or to be made into huge rafts of piling, towed as far as San Francisco and San Diego. (Also see STELLA, p. 426.)

LONGVIEW's charms are many. Exploring the city, however, requires patience—or a Sunday morning with no traffic. The grid of streets—laid out for traffic of another era—is broken by a roundabout and diagonals that scramble mental geography and put the unwary into mandatory turn lanes. Simply driving through on either State Route 4 or 432 gives little hint of Longview's renowned "planned city" character. A former slough has been turned into a long, curving lake extending through residential districts. The main streets are wide, many of them graced with huge trees now fully mature and leafy. Street surfaces are grooved with diamond-shaped lines, which actually are the expansion-and-contraction joints for the concrete, but double as decoration. The restored Columbia Theater presents a summer season of concerts and plays.

Longview sprang to life as an industrial center created by the Long-Bell Lumber Company, one of the nation's lumber giants, but it was never a true "company town." Long-Bell selected the site because of its access to three major rail lines and Columbia River shipping. (The Longview port is now the third largest in the state.)

Supposedly "limitless" timber grew nearby. The company bought 70,000 acres and, in 1924, opened Ryderwood as a model town. (See p. 394.) At Longview, 15 miles to the south, they at first bought only a huge millsite. The valley there—at the confluence of the Cowlitz and Columbia—had to be walled off by a vast diking system, but once that was complete the resulting land was far greater than was needed for industry. Consequently R. A. Long, founder (with Victor Bell) of the company, gradually decided

to establish a whole new city, carefully planned and regulated. The result was the West's first preplanned urban center, intended to rival Portland and Seattle.

Long-Bell retained planners and landscape architects who followed City Beautiful concepts and laid out specific districts—residential, commercial, warehouse, and industrial—along with parks and a large central civic center. They also stipulated the style and height of the buildings that were expected at each stage of population growth. As one local old-timer summarized the process:

When southern pine forests gave out, R. A. Long came here. This was wilderness, but he didn't want people to live in a wild place. He planned Vision City. He was a man to look up to, one with dignity, honesty, and flair.

Points of interest, keyed to the Longview map:

1 The **Civic Center,** also called R. A. Long Park, is striking as a spacious focal point for the city. Georgian architecture sets the tone, although the post office, built a decade after the library and hotel, is 1930s Art Deco style. Note the frieze above its entry, showing a plane, train, ship, sawmill, and donkey engine. The library, donated by R. A. Long in 1926, is flanked by a rose garden. Main floor reading rooms have fireplaces and chandeliers with multiple globes. The Monticello Hotel (Mon-teh-sell´-o) lobby displays a series of 46 oil paintings portraying Northwest history. Dark paneling and carpets are faithful to the hotel's 1923 origin; upstairs floors are now used as apartments and offices. Meal and bar service continue.

Across from the hotel (18th and Olympia) is a memorial to the Cowlitz Landing and Monticello conventions. It honors the 1851 and 1852 gatherings of settlers who successfully petitioned Congress to make Washington a separate territory from Oregon. The second meeting of these men took place at Monticello, near the present Port of Longview. The memorial lists their names. They read like a litany of the pioneering claims along the old Jackson Highway—Crawford, Plamondon, Jackson, Borst, Ford, and others.

Longview

Key to Numbered Locations

1 Civic Center
2 Broadway
3 YMCA
4 Community Church
5 Lake Sacajawea

6 Kessler Boulevard
7 R.A. Long High School
8 St. Helens Auditorium
9 Long-Bell Mill
10 Monticello Convention Site
11 J.D. Tennant House

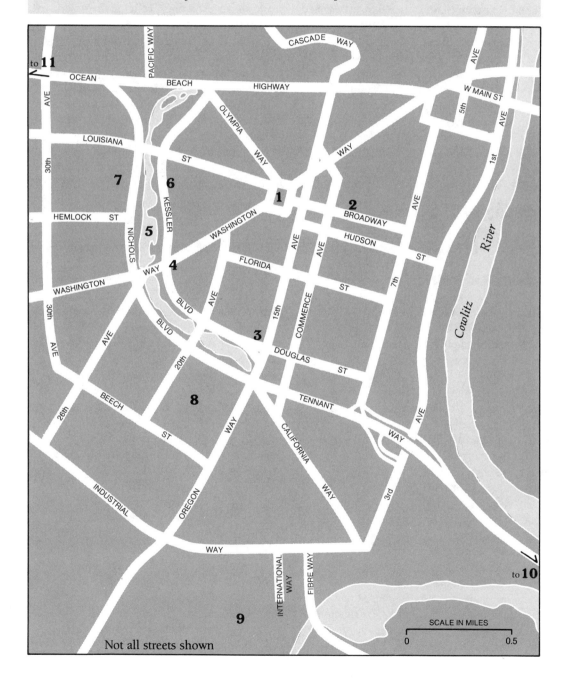

Not all streets shown

SCALE IN MILES
0   0.5

2   Broadway linked the civic square to the railway depot (now demolished) 10 blocks away. Along with the hotel and library, the depot formed the original civic grouping. Broadway was the grand arrival route, intended to convey to prospective investors the stability and promise of the town.

Walk along Broadway toward the hotel, particularly on a warm, clear evening, and a sense of what the planners hoped to achieve is apparent. The architectural style they established spread to the privately developed commercial district. Commerce Street buildings retain a sense of scale and rhythm, many of them with a mezzanine level sandwiched between the first and second stories. (Several are listed in the National Register of Historic Places, including the properties at 1166, 1208, 1226, 1233, 1239, and 1329 Commerce.) Long-Bell planned the city but did not build it all or control its growth. Gaps between buildings within the commercial core filled only slowly and with varying styles.

3   The three-story YMCA (15th and Kessler) opened in 1924 as a community building. It was financed by the Long-Bell Company but operated by the YMCA. For years social groups and churches as well as various recreation classes met in the building. Despite alteration, ancestry as a half-timbered tudor-cottage building is still apparent. The size, which was huge for a city like Longview in the 1920s, could be expected of R. A. Long. He was committed to values such as those espoused by the YMCA.

4   The Longview Community Church (Washington and Kessler) was built in 1923 of buff brick trimmed with terra-cotta. R. A. Long partially underwrote construction costs and also donated the chimes that still ring from the belfry. The church, with its Gothic Revival architecture, was intended as the ecumenical center for the city's religious life, to be augmented by smaller branches of the church in other neighborhoods.

5   Lake Sacajawea, the manmade conversion of an old river slough, curves through the heart of the original residential districts and is the focal point of a crescent-shaped park.

Native people who lived along the slough and river never signed a treaty because they did not want to lose their land and be forced onto the Yakima Reservation east of the mountains. The Bureau of Indian Affairs nonetheless still includes them among the small tribes assigned rights on the Yakima Reservation.

6   Drive Kessler Boulevard between Washington Way and Ocean Beach Highway— and adjacent streets—for a windshield tour of homes that are stately although not opulent. Combined with adjacent churches and the beauty of the park, the neighborhood's effect seems to achieve Long's belief in the orderliness of life.

7   The R. A. Long High School (2903 Nichols Road) stands by itself, reached by a tree-lined approach. The school, which faces Sacajawea Park, is of Georgian architecture with a granite entrance portico and a high clock tower reminiscent of Independence Hall in Philadelphia. R. A. Long donated the school in 1928, a time when his company had just undergone a crippling financial loss (from which it never fully recovered). To finance the high school, Long mortgaged his office building in Kansas City.

8   The St. Helens Addition (south of Nichols between 20th and Oregon Way) exemplifies the class consciousness of Longview's original plan. In contrast with the residential area west of Kessler, this was to be a workingman's district. Differences between the two are obvious, yet here, too, homes are set neatly along the street, surrounded by lawns. Longview's good life was intended for all. The modest two-story, shingle church (20th and Beech) is an example of the satellite churches intended to augment the Community Church on Kessler Boulevard; only this one actually was built. Directly opposite the church is the Community Store, a half-timbered structure architecturally similar to the YMCA building.

9   The old Long-Bell Mill sheds—now derelict—still stand near the port, difficult to reach yet spectacular because they are so enormous. (One route to them is via Industrial Way, with a turn toward the port on Columbia Boulevard.) The sheds, which are joined as doubles and triples and quadruples, are each about 600 feet long. They are built of massive timbers representative of the original, huge-scale forest of western Washington. Such buildings will never again be built.

10 Most of the **Monticello Convention Site** washed into the river in the flood of 1868; the rest is under a dike. The location was about a mile north of today's State Route 432. A city park near the west end of the bridge gives access to the dikes. (Take the Dike Road Exit.)

Monticello was a cluster of four houses, a store, hotel, and abandoned Hudson's Bay Company granary. Forty-four men met there in 1852 to request separation from Oregon. They asked that "Columbia" be the name of their new territory but, in passing the legislation, the U.S. House of Representatives decided that Columbia would be too easily confused with the District of Columbia and changed the name to Washington, apparently oblivious to the inherently greater confusion of their decision.

11 West of town, the **J. D. Tennant House,** listed in the National Register of Historic Places, opened as a restaurant in 1989. A drive to it rounds out a look at Longview. Head northwest on Industrial Way, the 5-mile rail-and-river economic lifeline of the city. Turn off on 38th Avenue, then turn toward the hill. Stone gateposts mark the driveway. Visible ahead is the imposing Colonial Revival "Rutherglen" home built by the manager of the Long-Bell mill operation.

Nearly the entire third floor is a ballroom. The walls of the library are covered with "grainart," a distinctive Long-Bell method of sandblasting a design onto wooden panels. The living room, 42 feet long, has a small fountain and pool surrounded by a low, tiled wall. Above the fireplace is an ornamental forest scene done in glazed tile. The house epitomizes "the good life." It is the ultimate expression of Longview as a structured, layered society, each segment in its proper place, with its own appropriate amenities.

At **MARY'S CORNER,** a woman named Mary Loftus opened a store in the 1920s—and the highway junction 10 miles south of Chehalis has been identified with her name ever since.

Barely south of Mary's Corner a log cabin known as the **Jackson House** stands beside old U.S. 99 (also called the Jackson Highway). The cabin was built in 1845 by John R. Jackson, one of the first settlers north of the Columbia River. Territorial governor Isaac Stevens and his family spent a night with the Jacksons on their way to Olympia in 1854. Army officers such as Ulysses S. Grant, George McClellan, and Philip Sheridan stopped here while traveling between Fort Vancouver and Fort Steilacoom. Immigrants came for advice, shelter, and supplies.

Jackson and his wife Matilda acted as impromptu innkeepers and also ran a grocery and dry goods store. The first U.S. District Court north of the Columbia River convened at their cabin in November 1850; and Jackson, who had been born in England, served as customs agent, postmaster, justice of the peace, and legislative representative.

To sense what it was like to live—and travel—in the primeval forest of this area, stop at Lewis and Clark State Park (1½ miles south of the Jackson House). A patch of old-growth hemlock and Douglas fir has survived there, a green realm padded with moss and lichens and rich with a sense of time and timelessness.

The entire Jackson Highway, between Chehalis and Toledo, makes a pleasant alternative to I-5.

MOUNT ST. HELENS is the centerpiece of a national monument administered by the National Forest Service. The present mountain, the most volcanically active in Washington, dates from less than 2,500 years ago. This extreme geologic youth accounts for the classic symmetry of the peak before its May 1980 eruption; glaciers had not yet gouged its flanks. The recent eruption blunted the perfect cone by blowing off 1,300 feet of the top. This reduced the mountain's elevation from 9,677 feet above sea level to 8,363 feet—a height that changes constantly as a new lava dome rises within the summit crater.

Hudson's Bay Company reports from Fort Vancouver in the mid-1800s several times mentioned "the atmosphere filled with ashes," and Father S. B. Z. Balduc, traveling to Cowlitz Farm in 1842, wrote:

. . . at three o'clock in the afternoon one of the sides opened and there was an eruption of smoke such as our oldest travelers here have never seen. . . . Since this volcano has broken forth, almost all the fish that are edible have died, which is attributed to the quantity of cinders with which the waters are infected.

Perhaps the primary ongoing effect of the 1980 eruption is the enormous amount of sediment washed into the rivers. Greatly increased dredging is needed to maintain shipping channels and prevent flooding.

A visitor center interpreting the history of Mount St. Helens and volcanic geology in general is located near Castle Rock (5 miles east of I-5). Displays include a walk-through model of the mountain. State Route 504 leads to the edge of the area devastated by mudflow—and quickly pioneered by returning life. Regrowth of the forest is assured. The eruption simply reset the clock.

(Also see RANDLE, p. 445, for the Windy Ridge approach to Mount St. Helens.)

At **NAPAVINE** the old business section lies just east of State Route 603. In 1872 the Northern Pacific Railway Company put up a tent store to serve crews laying track between Kalama and Tacoma. The public attitude toward Chinese workmen at the time is demonstrated by the segregation of the store's customers: clerks at a central counter served Chinese customers on one side of the tent, whites on the other. Railroad construction depended on Chinese labor, but it was the strong backs that were wanted, not the Chinese persons.

The railroad was desperately welcomed, for as one old-timer reminisced, "The military road sounds good, but it was an awful road really." Trains brought the first comfortable and reliable travel connection between the Columbia River and Puget Sound. Settlements along its route prospered. Those that were bypassed, withered. Napavine became a major depot for immigrants settling the surrounding country.

RYDERWOOD, a retirement community that began as a company logging town, nestles 12 miles west of I-5 among hills and valleys. A sign proclaims the philosophy:

> Not more years to our lives,
> But more life to our years

The entire company logging town of Ryderwood was turned into a retirement community.

State Route 506, leading to Rydenwood, curves between cutover slopes and promising tree farms interspersed with hayfields, barns, and scattered homes. In town, the old company store still stands on Morse Street, its roofed boardwalk intact. Adjoining it are other clapboard buildings from the 1920s. Houses, set within well-tended gardens, were all built as loggers' homes at about the same time.

In 1919 W. F. Ryder scouted Cowlitz County forests for the Long-Bell Lumber Company and discovered trees so big that Robert Ripley featured them in his "Believe It or Not" column, syndicated to newspapers across the nation. With a timber supply thus assured, the company built a family camp for its loggers, intending it as a decent place for decent folks. This social/industrial impulse stemmed from humanitarianism combined with a desire to protect the company against labor strife, which was rampant within the logging industry at the time.

Ryderwood loggers who were married went home each day to wife and kids. Single men lived in dormitories with hot showers and steam heat, which allowed them to dry their clothes instead of putting them on again still wet for the next day's work. Mornings began for all with the 4:30 A.M. shriek of the roundhouse whistle. An hour later, men gathered to ride by rail car to the woods. At times of peak production two log trains daily—each a mile long—headed for the company's huge mills at Longview.

(Also see LONGVIEW, p. 390, and the WASHINGTON WOBBLIES sidebar, p. 255.)

TOLEDO has roots reaching deep into the past; yet today it is a quiet hub for a rural community. The town's name is taken from the first paddlewheel steamer to provide the settlement with regular service, a feat that was achieved in 1879 amid great rejoicing. Farm families needed an efficient way to ship grain and oat hay to Portland and potatoes to California, and they yearned for a passenger connection to the outside world. Previously, they had traveled overland to Tumwater, a trip that might take a week each way if the weather turned bad, and required two days even in good weather. Men carried axes and cant hooks to handle fallen trees blocking the route. Mud regularly mired wagons. The railroad bypassed Toledo in 1873;

its nearest stop was at Winlock, 10 miles and many hours distant.

River service amounted to a lifeline. Rant Mullin, a longtime resident, remembered Toledo's ongoing welcome of steamers:

[We] always gave a dance when [the boat] docked here on Saturday. The town band showed up, and people were dancing on the boat and in the warehouse. Went on the whole night.

In the 1880s many Lewis County farmers grew hops, which were shipped to England—a valuable crop because it brought in money from the outside. The Toledo area had 68 hop "yards," which consisted of fields plus huge drying sheds where the pods were processed. (See BOISTFORT VALLEY, p. 437.) About 1900 the farmers switched to dairying as first aphids, then market fluctuations, undermined the hops industry. In 1919 a hundred farmers gathered to receive checks from their newly organized cheese cooperative; in celebration, they picnicked on cheese sandwiches. That event gave birth to the annual Toledo Cheese Day festival, still held each July.

The historic **Cowlitz Landing** for canoes was two miles downriver from Toledo. A monument on the east side of the freeway near Exit 59 (south of State Route 506) marks the landing's approximate location. No other physical indication lingers. The site is where Hudson's Bay Company men cached their canoes while traveling from Fort Vancouver to Fort Langley on the Fraser River, in British Columbia. From Cowlitz Landing they rode north on horses rented from Cowlitz Indians. Arriving at Eld Inlet, near today's Olympia, they hired Chehalis Indians to paddle them up Puget Sound.

In her diary, Margaret Stevens, wife of the first governor of Washington Territory, told of traveling to Olympia in December 1854 with her four children. She described their arrival at Cowlitz Landing thus:

As we were sitting flat on the bottom of the canoe, the position became irksome and painful. We were all day long on this Cowlitz River. At night I could not stand on my feet for some time after landing. We walked ankle-deep in the mud to a small log-house, where we had a good meal. . . . I laid down on a narrow strip of bed, not undressed, all my [children] alongside on the same bed. The Governor sat on a stool near by.

In the 1850s a settlement named Warbassport grew up at the landing. Meeting there in 1851, settlers petitioned Congress to establish what became Washington Territory. When the military road was built along ridges west of the river that same decade, Cowlitz Landing lost importance as a travel hub.

Cowlitz Mission, which became today's Saint Francis Xavier Church, stands east of Jackson Highway 3 miles north of Toledo. Father Francis Norbert Blanchet founded it in 1839 at the request of retired Hudson's Bay Company employees who had settled in the area to farm. Formerly the company had discouraged settlement north of the Columbia, but that policy changed as agriculture grew in importance and as more and more Americans kept arriving. Beginning in 1833, employees and retirees loyal to the company—most of them French Canadians—were encouraged to farm land leased from the company. The wives of these men were native women, many of them from tribes at distant trading posts. Such marriages were customary among Hudson's Bay Company employees and officers, including John McLoughlin, the chief factor at Fort Vancouver, and his assistant James Douglas, who became the first governor of British Columbia.

Apparently Simon Plamondon (Pluh-mahn'-dun), one of the Hudson's Bay Company retirees at Cowlitz, traveled to Quebec specifically to ask for a priest. Blanchet and his assistant Father Modeste Demers came in response. Blanchet devised the so-called Catholic Ladder to use in teaching the Bible to native people at Saint Francis. It consisted of small religious illustrations laid out along a Christian time line with 40 bars to represent the centuries before the birth of Christ, 33 dots for the years of his life, and 18 bars for the centuries since his death. A rendition of the ladder, painted on wood, is displayed beside the mission cemetery. Paper versions of the ladder were pasted onto white cloth and presented to native chiefs and headmen.

The present Saint Francis Xavier Church was built in 1932, the fifth church on the site. All the others burned.

Cowlitz Farm was operated by Puget's Sound Agricultural Company, a Hudson's Bay Company subsidiary formed in 1838. Fields covered about 4,000 acres, including bottomland now visible below Saint Francis Xavier Church; granaries and a warehouse stood on the Cowlitz river delta at present-day Longview.

These holdings and a second large farm at Nisqually gave the company active establishments at each end of the important overland route connecting saltwater and river travel. From the farms they shipped produce to posts throughout the Northwest and also to Russian Alaska, Spanish San Francisco, and the independent kingdom of Hawaii. By emphasizing agriculture, the Hudson's Bay Company expected to achieve several goals. The undertaking should make a profit; improve their position in Alaska, so as to overcome American trade competition along the coast; and "make provision for settlers that will be sent from England."

The agreement with the Russian American Company alone called for annual shipments to Sitka of 8,000 bushels of wheat, eight tons of flour, 15 tons of salted beef, and eight tons of butter. To meet that level of production (a goal never quite achieved by the Puget's Sound Agricultural Company), Alexander Ross and eight men supplied with implements and cattle from Fort Vancouver moved to Cowlitz Prairie in the fall of 1838. Plans called for additional, independent farmers who were to lease 1,000 acres. Agents in London were:

. . . to send a few respectable farming families . . . each family to be accompanied by two or three labouring servants under engagements, with the view of gradually forming an European Agricultural Settlement.

Somehow, this idealized immigration never happened. Its nearest approximation was the arrival of colonists from Red River, Canada. These people were displaced Scottish Highlanders who had been sent to what now is southern Manitoba during the notorious "clearances," when English landholders demolished farm cottages and whole villages to make way for large sheep enterprises. In 1841 more than a hundred Red River colonists streamed slowly southwestward, their goods loaded onto two-wheeled carts drawn by oxen. From Fort Vancouver, they were escorted to Cowlitz Prairie and shown their prospective farms. Few stayed more than a year. Why slave on leased English farms when land south of the Columbia, under American jurisdiction, could be *owned?*

The "desertion" by the Red River colonists had no real effect on Cowlitz Farm, other than to require the continual shortfall of grain production to be made up by Fort Vancouver agriculture. A missionary named T. Dwight Hunt who visited Cowlitz Farm in 1855 described it thus:

A more beautiful farming country cannot be found. Everything, houses, fences, fields, crops, cattle, people, betokened comfort & plenty. A Roman Catholic church lifted itself up pleasantly, on the road through the Farms. . . . Large barns, like great warehouses, were visible in a central place for the storing of the great crops. Still, there was about them, and about the old church, an appearance of departed glory.

By Hunt's time the agreement with the Russian American Company had lapsed, and there was growing tension regarding jurisdiction north of the Columbia River. Hunt commented on the "provoking intrusion" of American settlers, who had "impudently settled over the fairest portions of the plain." He considered these squatters as drastically—and deliberately—interfering with the long-held monopoly of the Hudson's Bay Company.

(Also see FORT NISQUALLY, p. 308, and FORT VANCOUVER, p. 40l.)

VADER, on the main line of four railroads, boomed during the 1890s and early 1900s as the most prosperous metropolis between Portland and Tacoma: population, 5,000. Sawmills, a sash and door factory, a logging and lumber company, and a brick and clay works nurtured the economy.

Today the opera house, multiple hotels, and banks are gone; but their ghosts linger, for Vader seems larger than it is. False-front buildings still line A Street (west end of town). The historic Little Falls jail, built in 1896 and used until 1950, stands near Sixth on A Street (one block

north of the highway). Next to it is an old-style telephone switchboard of the sort that required an operator who plugged in calls and also could tell you the time of day or pass along messages.

A trio of two-story homes with dormers and elaborate shingle patterns and barge boards lines B Street (north of State Route 506). The Ben Olsen House, a classic three-story Victorian with a corner turret and wraparound porch, stands on D Street (south of State Route 506). It was built in 1905 by the president of Vader's largest lumber company.

WINLOCK boasts "the world's biggest plastic egg," an appropriate symbol in view of the town's past egg and poultry production. The egg—of truly monumental scale—stands by the railroad track, which is downhill from the brick buildings of the four-block, single-street business district. Townspeople installed their first egg, made of concrete, in 1920 and replaced it 45 years later with the present one, made of wire mesh and plastic. An annual Egg Day festival draws people from throughout the region each June.

Until the 1950s Winlock shipped as much as a carload of eggs daily and two and one-half million chicks annually. Long, low poultry houses still stand between Olequa Creek and the train tracks. There, too, stands a venerable frame building belonging to the dairymen's association. A concrete elevator is a reminder that grain was a pioneer crop in western Washington as well as in the eastern part of the state.

As railroad crews started grading a right-of-way north from Kalama in the 1870s, settlers learned that the rails would bypass Toledo, the established transportation hub. That word led a man named Christopher Pagget to buy land along the new route, open a store, and plat Winlock. Three miles from the steamer landing on the Cowlitz River, the town became a new shipping and service center. Today it is along a byway alternative to I-5 between Kelso and Chehalis (about 40 miles). Scenery is pleasant rather than spectacular; local roads are inviting to explore simply to see where they go. The historic Military Road went this way, and sections of it still exist.

Vancouver Area

Possibilities for classic "country drives" abound in this area. State Route 501 winds among hayfields and dairy farms and skirts both Vancouver Lake and the Columbia River. State Route 503 twists over and around forested hills and offers views of Mount St. Helens rising as a low, broad dome above its foothill platform. (A caution, however: curves can make 10 miles of this road seem like 30 for anyone in a hurry.) North of Kalama, the pavement of Old U.S. 99 leads onto the cliffs above I-5 and offers views of the flood-prone Columbia River lowlands.

For remnants of the region's early economic life, visit the Cedar Creek Gristmill near Woodland and the Ridgefield prune dryer (private, but within view of the road). Railroad buffs will enjoy the diesel excursion train from Battle Ground to Yacolt. Gardeners—and everyone else—will admire the Hulda Klager Lilac Gardens in Woodland.

Vancouver traces its origins to a Hudson's Bay Company trading post on the north bank of the Columbia (now a unit of the National Park System) and a U.S. Army post housed in buildings rented from the fur company. These two entities—the British trading company and the American army—affected not only the immediate surrounding area but all of Washington. In addition to museum displays, Fort Vancouver offers "living history" demonstrations in its bakery and blacksmith shop; also a July Fur Brigade Encampment and an October candlelight tour that are especially effective. The county historical society museum is in the town of Vancouver, west of the

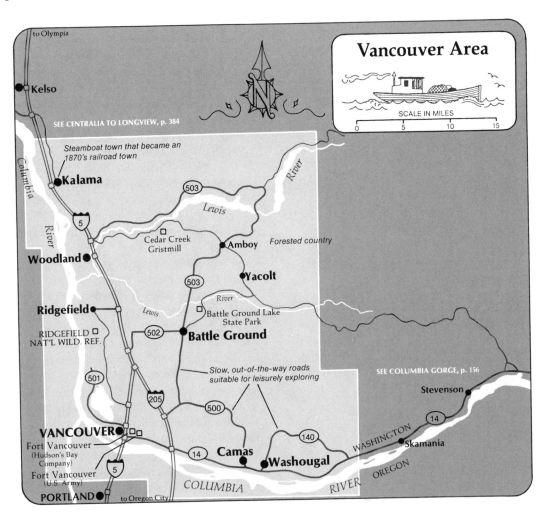

SEE CENTRALIA TO LONGVIEW, p. 384

SEE COLUMBIA GORGE, p. 156

freeway. On a clear day the upriver drive via State Route 14 is alluringly scenic.

BATTLE GROUND, a pleasant residential community northeast of Vancouver, is reached through fields and scattered stands of Douglas fir—a "generic" western Washington lowland drive. Gaps between farmhouses are now filling in with suburban architecture and mobile homes. Yet barns and white rail fences remain, and typical "for sale" signs read: "Clean Wood Chips," "U-pick Raspberries," and "Chicken Manure."

A few early-day houses remain in the Battle Ground area. They include the Henry Ward board-and-batten house (1976 Risto Road, east of the Gravel Point cemetery). When Ward built about 1860, he commented that the surrounding forest was so dense, his daylight lasted only two hours at noon. North of town, where the highway crosses the river, one house remains from the 1880s settlement of Lewisville (south of the river, west of the bridge). It belonged to Albert Green, a self-trained music teacher who traveled the county organizing vocal "schools," which would meet for six months and end with a community fund-raising concert.

In town, a much remodeled home on the southeast corner of 139th and 50th Avenue was built originally of cedar lumber from Fort Vancouver. There, the planks had been used in a cabin that served as a school and later as quarters for Catholic nuns. After the Hudson's Bay Company moved to Victoria in 1845, Nathaniel Trombly bought the lumber. Purportedly, it was sawn in England from logs sent from the fort as ballast, then returned as boards.

Four miles northeast of town is **Battle Ground Lake State Park.** Small and about 60 feet deep, a lake lies cupped within a small crater that was produced when a volcanic cone collapsed inward. English ivy grows alongside native salal and Oregon grape, sure indication of former settlement. In this case, the ivy is from a major resort that operated from the early 1900s through 1948.

In summer an excursion train complete with caboose winds from Battle Ground to Yacolt, rolling over logging railroad track, a part of which has been in continuous use since the late 1890s. (For the current schedule, check at the

Costumed as a Hudson's Bay Company employee, a Fort Vancouver baker prepares a cherry cobbler as part of the fort's "living history" program.

Lewis and Clark Railway Depot on Main Street, in Battle Ground.)

Proximity to Fort Vancouver made Battle Ground an area of early settlement. The first to pioneer here were former Hudson's Bay Company employees and soldiers from Vancouver Barracks. Over time, other settlers included disillusioned California miners, Civil War veterans seeking free land, Finns escaping conscription into the Russian army, Italian bachelors released from railroad construction gangs, and a group of Irish who named their community Dublin.

In the early 1900s additional settlers came in response to advertisements aimed at Swedish communities in Minnesota, Illinois, and Canada as well as in Sweden. With hyperbole and photographs, these come-ons portrayed easily cleared lands, shoulder-high grain, new homes, and so many springs that water sytsems were no problem. People bought land sight unseen, moved onto it, and built successful lives through sheer determination. Their one-room Venersborg school, built in 1912, still stands (209th Street and 242nd Avenue). It now serves as a community hall. The adjacent Venersborg store, also built in 1912, originally doubled as headquarters for the land development company.

Battle Ground is named for a battle that never took place, yet fanned the worries that sent western Washington settlers crowding into hastily built blockhouses. The Klickitat chief, Reverend Stwire Waters, told the tale as an eyewitness (he was an ordained Methodist minister and the brother and successor of White Swan, the chief of the Yakima tribes in the 1870s). The incident occurred in October 1855, the year of the unhappy Walla Walla treaty council and the murder of Indian agent Andrew Bolon. Following Bolon's death, troops told Klickitat people at Lewis River to come to Fort Vancouver for surveillance and for protection from hothead whites. The soldiers gave the same summons to the Titon-nap-pams, a Klickitat subgroup living in the foothills at the head of the Cowlitz River.

Both groups complied. Soon, a messenger came from White Salmon asking Klickitat warriors to join a Yakima war party east of the mountains. Chief Umtux of the Titon-nap-pams agreed, and his men left the fort at night with perhaps 300 horses. According to Stwire Waters, after two days

. . . the volunteer soldiers, 40 halfbreeds, under a captain came to us, so we stopped where we had camped. . . [and agreed], "All right. We will stay here and then go back to Fort Vancouver."

The captain was William Strong, who had arrived at Cathlamet in 1850 as the first federal judge for Oregon Territory. Strong told the Klickitats to fire into the air any loaded rifles they were carrying, and the whites to do the same. Chief Umtux rode to tell outlying scouts that there would be no fighting. A tragedy resulted. The scouts heard the volley of shots, assumed fighting had begun, and killed Umtux as he rode toward them. They mistook him for a white man, owing to his dress, which included a black coat and hat.

Strong left the Klickitats to bury their chief and to mourn. Soon afterward, they came to Fort Vancouver as promised and stayed there until June 1856, when overall tensions eased. The government then sent them back to White Salmon by steamboat.

CAMAS, a modern riverside mill town, was one of Lewis and Clark's camps in 1806. From here, Clark crossed the Columbia to reconnoiter the Willamette Valley while Lewis oversaw the hunting and drying of meat for the return trip to St. Louis.

The party of prospective settlers led by Michael T. Simmons, who ultimately settled near Olympia (see pp. 356 and 367), spent the winter of 1844 near present-day Camas. They had expected to settle in the Willamette Valley but, on arrival at The Dalles, learned that the provisional government had decided "all Negros and mulattos" in Oregon would be flogged "once every six months until he or she shall quit the territory." George Bush, a member of the party who was half black, had come West to escape such persecutions. Bush had chosen the Oregon country partly because it was not totally under American control. He expected British protection from color prejudice. If that did not prove true, he planned to see what protection the Mexican government gave to blacks in California (which was part of Mexico until 1848).

The Oregon law was intended to sidestep the entire issue of slavery, then threatening major trouble between northern and southern states. *No* blacks would be allowed, free or slave. Simmons, Bush, and the others worked for the Hudson's Bay Company that winter, making shingles, then moved on to Puget Sound, which the British still hoped to control.

In 1883 Portland investors bought land embracing LaCamas Lake and both sides of its outlet stream. This gave them exclusive riparian rights, needed to develop waterpower for mills. At the mouth of the creek they planned to develop what promoters called a "manufacturing village" with a paper mill, flour mill, sawmill, furniture factory, and other manufacturing plants. By the summer of 1884 Chinese laborers were clearing land and digging a tunnel for the first mill's water system. This was a paper mill. In May 1885 the Vancouver *Independent* reported that its first paper, "manufactured from the pulp of the cottonwood tree," was strong and uniform and with "an even texture and surface." Fir and straw, as well as cottonwood, went into the paper. Camas paper production today includes shopping bags, paper towels, tissue wraps for fruit, card stock, facial tissue, and napkins.

FORT VANCOUVER

FORT VANCOUVER (a Hudson's Bay Company trading post) has been partially reconstructed and is now administered by the National Park Service, complete with a living history program and a visitor center.

The fort began officially on March 19, 1825, when Governor George Simpson, in his words, "baptized [a new trading post] by breaking a bottle of Rum on the Flag Staff." Four years earlier the Honourable Company had merged with its rival the North West Company. Four *months* earlier Simpson had completed a journey down the Columbia River with John McLoughlin, whom he had picked to head the new post.

The two men had inspected Spokan House, Fort Okanogan, and Fort Nez Perces (Walla Walla); they also had decided to abandon Fort George (Astoria). As replacement, McLoughlin picked the new location on the north bank of the Columbia. The name—Fort Vancouver—was intended as a pointed reminder that Britain's Vancouver expedition had been the first to explore beyond the Columbia River mouth.

Hudson's Bay Company directors were unsure how much trade would come from the Columbia district (roughly southern British Columbia, Washington, Oregon, and Idaho, although defined by wherever McLoughlin had fur brigades and trading ships rather than by geography). They felt the region in general would make a buffer for their rich lands farther north however, and might serve additional purposes. McLoughlin's instructions were to outcompete Yankee sea captains and drive them off; open trade with Russian Alaska; send fur brigades toward California; strip fur from the approaches to the Columbia, to deter American trappers; build Fort Langley on the Fraser River; and start a farm. Gathering furs for shipment to London, of course, was fundamental. So was holding down expenses.

Since 1818 England and the United States theoretically had shared equal rights within the domain McLoughlin now in effect ruled; there seemed no urgency to complete the boundary between the United States and Canada. It followed the 49th parallel from Lake of the Woods (Winnipeg) to the Rocky Mountains, which, after the Louisiana Purchase in 1803, formed the western boundary of the United States. That parallel made sense as far as the Rocky Mountains: it divided two great river drainages, the Saskatchewan and the Missouri. West of there, however, the Fraser and Columbia rivers ran north–south and created a problem. Rather than decide on that final 600 miles of the border, the two nations agreed to temporarily share "free and open access" to the entire region.

Several boundaries were in flux at the time.

John McLoughlin and James Douglas—later the governor of British Columbia—shared the factor's house at Fort Vancouver. (To see McLoughlin's last home, visit Oregon City.)

HAWAIIANS IN THE NORTHWEST

Hawaiians came to Washington as early as the 1700s. On return to Boston from his first Pacific voyage, Captain Robert Gray carried 17-year-old Attoo on board the *Columbia* and then brought him along as personal servant on his 1792 voyage of discovery. Captain George Vancouver had Toweroo with him when he left London for the Pacific, and at Nootka Sound (on what is now British Columbia's Vancouver Island) he picked up two teenage girls who had been on board Captain James Baker's *Jenny* and were ready to return home. Vancouver obliged, leaving all three off as he passed through the islands.

Hawaiians eagerly asked to sail on board the ships. A superb seafaring people, they must have wondered about the new, pale mariners and their winged vessels. High-class nobles came to the Northwest; so did commoners, who eventually were selected by local chiefs and the Hawaiian government to work for the Hudson's Bay Company, often on three-year contracts with an assurance of being returned home at the end of the term. As early as 1811 a group of 24 Hawaiians came with North West Company fur traders en route to Astoria. David Thompson took one of these men named Coxe to Fort William (Lake Superior). The son of a Kona Coast chief, the man was amazed by the cold weather, strange landforms, and unfamiliar customs. Indeed, he is reported as sorely puzzled as to why snow, in itself novel, turned to water when it landed on his arm.

By the 1830s the Hudson's Bay Company apparently had 300 to 400 Hawaiians employed as sailors, gardeners, cooks, servants, laborers, sawyers, millers, and even informants who mingled with Native Americans and reported to the Honourable Company regarding trade opportunities and tribal moods. They served in fur brigades and at most of the company's forts. At Fort Vancouver they lived outside the palisade with English, Scottish, French Canadians, Iroquois, and Northwest Coast natives who worked for the company.

Expanding trade with the islands assured passage back and forth across the Pacific, for Hawaii became a major station where Northwest Coast sea traders outfitted and routinely augmented their crews. Hawaiians were considered good workers—with part of their merit lying in a willingness to accept low pay, or at least a resignation to that treatment. They were called *kanakas,* the Hawaiian word for themselves in contrast with *haole,* for everybody else. The Hudson's Bay Company used *kanaka* as a respectful term, but American whalers later gave it a derogatory meaning.

The Russian czar had announced in 1821 that his Alaskan domain reached south as far as the 51st parallel (about the north tip of Vancouver Island). Three years later he yielded to British and American pressure and accepted 54° 40´ as the southern boundary. About this same time, Spain gave up its claims north of the 42nd parallel (the present California-Oregon border), and Britain and America made their joint occupancy agreement.

This was the international stage upon which Fort Vancouver began its 21-year lead role. Narcissa Whitman, accepting McLoughlin's hospitality while her husband set about establishing their mission site near Walla Walla, described Fort Vancouver as "the New York of the Pacific Ocean." Certainly it was a focal point economically, politically, and socially. McLoughlin followed the Hudson's Bay Company's policy of "profits and peace," providing protection for *all* whites within his domain—even rivals—and dealing fairly with native peoples while leaving tribal affairs other than trade in the hands of chiefs and headmen. Romantic frontier tales of outlaws and Dodge Cities—characteristic in most of the American

West—simply do not exist for the Hudson's Bay Company era in the Northwest.

Fort Vancouver farms occupied the plains for 25 miles along the river and 10 miles inland. Its mills produced a surplus of lumber and flour, which the company shipped to Hawaii, along with salmon, receiving in exchange coffee, sugar, rice, molasses, and salt. Dairy herds— about 700 head in all—produced milk for butter and cheese. And the fur network provided furs for shipment to London.

Employees—from Métis boatmen to Iroquois hunters and Anglo clerks and carpenters—lived a rough life with little expectation of improvement even for their children. Officers, of course, fared much better. Records show 1,800 gallons of French sherry in one ship's cargo and archaeological excavation of the chief factor's house included recovery of fine Spode and Copeland china and a variety of spice bottles and snuff containers (snuff was the tobacco of the upper class).

The beginning of the end came in 1846 when the international boundary issue finally was settled at the 49th parallel rather than along the north bank of the Columbia River, as the Hudson's Bay Company had hoped. Major company responsibilities were transferred to Fort Victoria, although the Vancouver operation continued as a merchandising enterprise and farm before finally closing its gates forever in 1860. By then the U.S. Army already was occupying trading post land.

FORT VANCOUVER (U.S. Army), now listed as a National Historic District, has retained its 1800s ambience, including the officers' row, parade ground, bandshell—and view of Mount Hood. (For particulars, see Officers' Row under VANCOUVER, p. 407. For the Hudson's Bay Company's FORT VANCOUVER, see p. 401.)

American immigration to Oregon leapt nearly 50-fold from 1841 to 1845: the figures went from 65 new arrivals a year to 3,000. To protect the immigrants, Congress in 1846 authorized the establishment of military posts along the Oregon Trail. Almost immediately, however, Congress also declared war on Mexico, an action that drew all available troops south. It was May 1849 before two companies of artillerymen stepped from the steamer USS *Massachusetts* onto the Hudson's Bay Company dock at Fort Vancouver. In October, 561 additional men and officers arrived overland, exhausted by a four-month journey from Fort Leavenworth, Kansas. They had lost 70 men, 300 horses and mules, and 45 wagons en route.

Captain Rufus Ingalls, quartermaster, was already at work constructing officers' quarters and mess halls and he also had rented buildings from the Hudson's Bay Company and also in nearby Oregon City—virtually deserted as men headed for the California gold fields. The arrival of the U.S. Army gave the company a sudden new market for its merchandise and farm produce. Chief factor Peter Skene Ogden, McLoughlin's successor, even loaned the army money to pay teamsters who had accompanied Mounted Riflemen overland, and he provided company horses and boats at a reasonable cost.

At first the military installation was called Camp Vancouver, then Columbia Barracks, followed by Fort Vancouver, and finally (after 1879) Vancouver Barracks. The fort served as military headquarters for the Department of the Columbia. Officers and high-status civilians were all American-born, but more than half of the enlisted men were European immigrants, mostly from Germany and Ireland. Desertion was rampant. About half of the riflemen housed at Oregon City deserted; indeed, a common reason to enlist was to get transportation west, then head for the gold fields.

Through the years, many of the nation's military greats served at Vancouver. Ulysses S. Grant, later president of the United States, was quartermaster here while a brevet captain; to supplement income and pay off debts, he grew potatoes and oats on leased land (immediately west of today's I-5, between Fifth and Sixth), managed a wood-cutting business, once tried shipping chickens to San Francisco (they died en route), and once tried shipping ice (it melted). George B. McClellan conducted his 1850s railroad surveys from this post. Nelson A. Miles and Oliver O. Howard, famed as "Indian fighters," had their headquarters here. William T. Sherman, renowned for his Civil War march through Georgia, served here early in his career, as did Philip Sheridan, Union cavalry ace. So did George W. Goethals, renowned for completion of the Panama Canal, and George C.

Marshall and Omar Bradley, heroes of World War II.

Two characteristics of **KALAMA** draw attention. The Catholic church, high spired and white, stands like a beacon on the hill behind town. And I-5 slices through the heart of town and separates the riverfront and port from the business district. Potential flooding necessitated lifting the freeway 20 feet above street level, but the result overwhelms the town.

The drive up the hill to Saint Joseph's Church (Elm and Fourth) offers a sweeping view. Oblates built the first church in 1876; the present building dates from 1909. Stations of the cross are from the original church. A matching pair of side altars came around Cape Horn from Italy for the 1909 church.

For additional views of town and river, drive east of the church at least as far as the school, which provides an easy place to turn around. (Follow Fourth, then turn on China Garden.) During the railroad boom, this hill was the Chinese section of town. A single paddle-wheel steamer is said to have unloaded a thousand Chinese laborers at the town wharf in the 1870s. Many lived here as an enclave. No particular evidence remains today.

West of the freeway, a surprisingly large port includes a public park, a chemical plant, grain elevators, a marina, and enormous "cold decks" of logs for export. (To reach the port, cross the dredge spoils of Mount St. Helens ash piled onto the river flats.) Kalama has a long history as a hub for cargoes and travelers passing through en route elsewhere. The role began with John Kalama, a Hudson's Bay Company agent stationed here to collect fur from nearby Indian villages. Kalama was one of the many Hawaiian men who worked under contract for the company. His wife was a daughter of Chief Martin, a leader of the Nisqually people.

In the 1850s steamboating gave birth to the town because of the naturally deep water along the riverbank. Two decades later, the Northern Pacific started laying track from Kalama toward Puget Sound. This was part of its transcontinental line, a monumental undertaking that did not actually begin in the East and proceed steadily across the prairies to the West. Quite the contrary. Financial problems and corporate restructuring resulted in multiple starts and stops.

Congress had offered land grants as an incentive for linking the continent with rails but, to receive title to the land, the Northern Pacific had to reach salt water by December 31, 1873. Nothing said the tracks had to span from coast to coast, only that they must reach the Pacific. The company's ultimate strategy called for crossing the mountains but, to meet the deadline, they picked Kalama as a point from which to lay new tracks toward Puget Sound.

Various considerations went into the decision. Construction machinery and material had to come around Cape Horn by ship, and unloading at Kalama would save 42 miles over sending the ships on upriver to Portland, an established port. Kalama also would shorten shipping distances to coastal ports and the Orient. And a railroad north from Kalama would give a useable connection between the Columbia and Puget Sound, whereas the only existing link was over a road so muddy that six horses were needed to pull a stage through the mire even if the passengers got out and walked.

In 1871 crews supervised by James B. Montgomery began laying track. Montgomery was a Pennsylvania newspaperman to whom President Grant had once offered the governorship of Washington Territory. (Mrs. Montgomery objected because she did not want a life of politics.) Montgomery hired 750 Chinese men through San Francisco labor agents and also signed on about 250 immigrant Scots, Irish, Swedes, Germans, and Americans. Mary Montgomery and their three children lived with him in the field, housed in a suite of large tents.

The Northern Pacific let contracts for one section of track at a time—and made no announcement of where the line would end. By the time the rails reached Tenino, only 40 miles south of Tacoma, speculation regarding the terminal had reached fever pitch. Describing that period, Montgomery wrote:

It was there that the railroad company proposed a little strategy on the cities, towns and holders of real estate on Puget Sound. They gave me a contract for 100 miles, which indicated that they were going to run about 60 miles beyond Tacoma. Everyone from Budd's Inlet to Bellingham Bay thought they had the proper site for the "terminal." And it was to put people off the track that the "100-mile contract" was given to me. . . . [A] saving clause . . . permitted [stopping] after 40 miles had been constructed. . . .

In July 1873 the company announced Tacoma as its final destination. On December 16 they drove a last spike and rolled a train to the shores of Commencement Bay. This first "transcontinental" track in Washington then waited another decade before it linked with any other rails. The Northern Pacific actually went bankrupt several weeks before reaching Tacoma. Work on their line west from Lake Superior had stopped in North Dakota, and a 1,500-mile gap separated that track from Kalama, where it was to continue. (Also see under TACOMA on p. 329.)

In late 1878 rail construction resumed, thanks to an infusion of money raised by bond sales in Germany. Three years later dignitaries and cheering citizens gathered for another "last" spike celebration in Montana. By the following year, trains from the east could reach Kalama, aided by a side-wheeler ferry to carry them across the Columbia from tracks on the Oregon side of the Columbia from Portland to Goble. The ferry was 338 feet long and had three tracks on its deck. It hauled two engines and 23 freight cars at a time. The Northern Pacific had built it in Delaware, then knocked it into 57,159 pieces, which were sent around Cape Horn for reassembly.

Kalama boomed from the arrival of the first railroad surveyors until the late 1880s, when rails across the Cascade Mountains to Tacoma captured traffic away from the original Columbia route. Automobiles, cars, and trucks later displaced trains, and the population shrank more. Ironically, however, the automobiles are bringing people back: the freeway overwhelms the town, but also permits commuters to live here and work elsewhere.

RIDGEFIELD was called Union Ridge by its first settlers, Civil War veterans who came West only a few years after the Union had defeated the Confederacy.

Ridgefield (located 13 miles west of I-5) is set amid handsome barns, hayfields, and a few remnant prune orchards. To sample this countryside, drive both north and south of town. To the north, search out the Lancaster House, built in 1850 by Judge Columbia Lancaster, the first Washington Territory delegate to Congress.

The Arndt prune drier represents the period from the 1890s to the 1930s, when orchards carpeted hills all around Ridgefield. This one is the last of its kind in the area.

(Turn north on Main, past a charming 1883 church. Continue as Main becomes 71st Avenue, then Lancaster Road. The house—not open to the public—is at the end of the road.) Lancaster, born in Connecticut in 1803, was christened Thomas but, when Lewis and Clark returned to the East with a description of the legendary Great River of the West, his parents renamed him Columbia.

South of Ridgefield, follow the road that runs along a narrow ridge with views of Mount St. Helens to the east and the Columbia River to the west. (To reach this road, turn south on Ninth Street, at the eastern edge of town. After about a half mile, watch for the Henry Shobert House on the west side of the road, shortly before a wild-life refuge sign.) The house dates from 1905, built by the son of pioneer settler Frederick Shobert, who came West from Illinois with his wife and bachelor brother Napoleon Bonapart following an unsuccessful stint in the California gold fields. Frederick and Henry worked as builders and operated a boat landing on Lake River. Another son, Stephen, opened the first general store in the area. Napoleon served as constable.

About 2 miles out of town, watch for a small orchard on the eastern skyline. Among the trees is a modest drying shed for prunes, a type of structure and enterprise typical throughout the area from the 1880s until the 1930s. When production was at its peak around 1900, and dried prunes were shipped as far as Germany, Clark County had perhaps 200 such dryers. This last remaining dryer, operated by Fred Arndt, was built in 1898. Its heat comes from a wood fire maintained for 30 to 40 hours per "batch" of prunes. The fruit is momentarily dipped into a lye solution to crack its skin, then placed on wooden trays above the firebox.

During the 1880s and 1890s, a paddle-wheel steamboat called regularly at Ridgefield to load products that ranged from wheat and butter to blocks of basalt quarried north of town for use in paving Portland streets. The northern unit of **Ridgefield National Wildlife Refuge** includes the old quarry and land that belonged to the Carty family, pioneering farmers. Refuge land is partly left wild, partly farmed, a situation that permits seeing the broad Columbia River flood-plain much as it was in pioneer days. A quarter

million waterfowl spend the winter here, and sandhill cranes stop to rest and feed while migrating. (The northern unit is just beyond the edge of town, reached via Main Street. The southern unit is about a mile south of town via Ninth.)

A large Chinook village called Quathlpotl stood at Ridgefield when Lewis and Clark came through in March 1806. The villagers gave the explorers food, which included smelt, sturgeon, and wapato, a nutritious root. Clark wrote that the women collected the wapato:

. . . by getting into the water, sometimes to their necks holding by a small canoe, and with their feet loosen the . . . root from the bottom of the water. They collect and throw them into the canoe, [and] those deep roots are the largest and the best.

Archaeological evidence suggests that people lived at this village for at least 2,000 years. Yet only three decades after their hospitality to Lewis and Clark, all seem to have died of epidemic smallpox, venereal disease, and "intermittent fever" (probably malaria or influenza), diseases introduced by whites.

The city of **VANCOUVER** grew up around the army's Fort Vancouver, which, in a sense, replaced the Hudson's Bay Company trading post, also named Fort Vancouver. Indeed, early settlers suffered through decades of uncertain land title, owing to conflicting American and British claims and also to claims by the Catholic mission, Saint James. Official surveys were not made until the 1860s, the time that the Hudson's Bay Company finally withdrew. During World War I, shipyards lined the riverbank west of today's I-5 bridge, and the army's "Spruce Division" operated a specialized mill for cutting dimension lumber too large for other mills to handle. (Also see SPRUCE ARMY sidebar, p. 492.)

During World War II shipyards owned by industrialist Henry Kaiser built more than 140 ships and operated two dry docks upstream from the I-5 bridge; the huge wooden ways remain. Production included Liberty ships, troop transports, LSTs (Landing Ship, Tanks), aircraft carrier escorts, and merchant marine cargo ships—an extraordinary variety from one shipyard. Employment peaked at 38,000 with

Ulysses S. Grant visited in this house, now named for him, but did not live in it while stationed at what became the army's Fort Vancouver. He arrived in 1852, three years after establishment of the post (then called Columbia Barracks).

a quarter of the workers women, a new situation. Today, riverside restaurants and a delightful walkway west of I-5 offer views of sailboats and barges.

(Also see both the Hudson's Bay Company and the U.S. Army FORT VANCOUVER entries, pp. 401–4.)

Points of interest, keyed to the Vancouver map:

1 At **Officers' Row,** 10 houses and 11 duplexes dating from 1849 to 1906 face the old army parade around, many of them made into apartments and offices. The two-story **Grant House** (built in 1849) originally served as the post commander's house. Constructed of hand-hewn logs, long-since concealed beneath clapboard siding, the house is now open as a restaurant—particularly appropriate because when first built it served as an officers' club as well as a home (also see p. 403).

The **Howard House** (completed in 1879) was built for General Oliver Otis Howard who came to Fort Vancouver fresh from serving as president of Howard University. It will house an interpretive center for the entire heritage area.

The **Marshall House** (built in 1886) accommodated still another new post commander. It dates from when frontier conditions had eased enough that married officers customarily had their families with them. The first floor has been restored to an 1800s appearance; the second has

become offices for public officials. Expect to find some downstairs rooms closed to the public at times owing to conferences and receptions.

2   Fort Vancouver National Historic Site (east of Exit 1-C) has been administered by the National Park Service since 1949. Reconstructed buildings and "living history" demonstrations give a feeling of 1800s life within the fort's palisade. Special programs are held at Christmas and on Queen Victoria's birthday (third weekend in May); a costumed Encampment (mid-July) recreates the arrival of a fur brigade; and during a mid-October candlelight tour, visitors are encouraged to walk silently through buildings and across the grounds, watching costumed employees and volunteers go about routine evening tasks and pastimes.

Fort Vancouver was the Hudson's Bay Company headquarters for 23 forts and five lesser trading stations. Its first buildings stood a mile from the final site, selected in 1829 to be closer to this river. The original site is at Grand Boulevard and E. Sixth (now occupied by the School for the Deaf). The site of the fort's sawmill—the first lumber operation in present-day Washington—is 6 miles east of Vancouver (identified by a marker along State Route 14). A second sawmill was at Willamette Falls, now Oregon City (15 miles south of Vancouver, worth visiting for its historic buildings including the house that chief factor John McLoughlin retired to after leaving Fort Vancouver). (Also see p. 401.)

Vancouver

Key to Numbered Locations

1 Officer's Row
2 Fort Vancouver National Historic Site
3 Pearson Airpark
4 Old Apple Tree
5 Providence Academy

6 Slocum House
7 Downtown Vancouver
8 Saint James Church
9 Hidden House
10 County Historical Museum
11 Covington Cabin

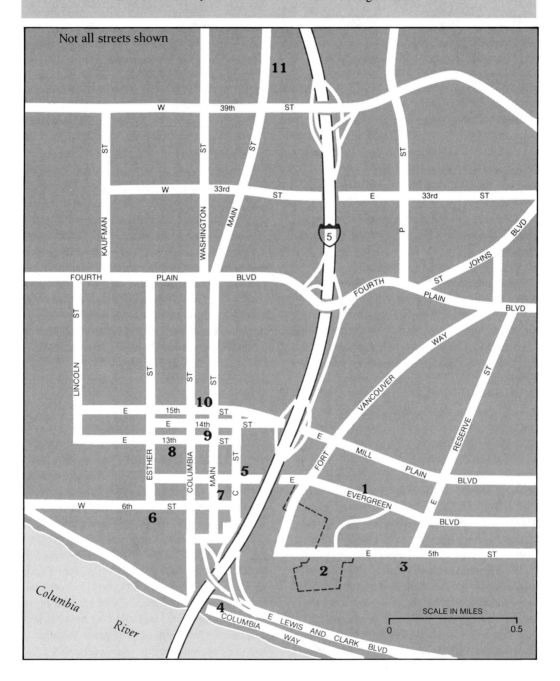

Not all streets shown

Columbia River

SCALE IN MILES
0   0.5

3 Pearson Airpark is to become a major aeronautical attraction highlighted by the M. J. Murdock Aviation Center, an interpretive museum and conference center (accessible by car off State Route 14 via Grand Blvd., or via E. Fifth, or on foot from Fort Vancouver). Restored hangars will display historic aircraft, interactive exhibits, and a children's hands-on activity center. One will also provide a workshop for the repair of historic aircraft, with the process of working with wood and fabric visible to public view.

Originally the polo grounds for Vancouver Barracks, the field first served aviation purposes in 1905 when a dirigible hopped across the Columbia River from Portland and landed here. Six years later the field began its involvement with heavier-than-air flight and went on to serve as an Army Air Corps field. During World War I an army spruce mill stood here, part of the effort to supply wood for military planes (see p. 492).

4 The **Old Apple Tree,** a beloved Vancouver landmark, evidently remains from the trees planted by the Hudson's Bay Company. (It is east of I-5, at the north end of Waterfront Park; use the Columbia Way parking lot and walk under the railroad overpass.) The tree—tucked in a quiet corner, yet close to the freeway and to modern bustle—provides a living bridge between Washington beginnings and present.

5 Providence Academy (400 E. Evergreen) stands alongside the freeway as a reminder of the past. The building housed the Providence School for Young Ladies and an orphanage from 1874 until 1966. It was considered the largest structure north of San Francisco at the time it opened. Barely saved from wrecking, the academy now houses offices and a restaurant.

The building's architect was Mother Joseph, a remarkable self-taught French-Canadian nun who learned design and carpentry from her father, a Montreal carriage maker. A colleague described her as striding about "with saw and hammer at her girth . . . praying aloud while she worked." That work began in Washington Territory in 1856, when Mother Joseph arrived at Vancouver with four other Sisters of Providence in response to a call from Father Blanchet. To finance her projects—which included 11 hospitals, seven academies, five schools, and two orphanages—Mother Joseph led begging

Providence Academy (above); Sisters of Providence begging tour (below).

expeditions throughout the Northwest, visiting even remote logging and mining camps.

6 The **Slocum House** (W. Sixth and Esther) is a solitary 1860s survivor. It belonged to a prosperous neighborhood by the river, partially cleared in 1908 to make room for a railroad and further demolished in the 1960s during an urban renewal project. Built with a wraparound porch, central cupola, and widow's walk, the house is said to have been Vancouver's first fine mansion. Moved to Esther Short Park, it now serves as a theater and houses other programs.

Charles Slocum arrived in Vancouver in 1857 and worked as an army carpenter. In 1860 he opened a general merchandise store and soon had branches in Walla Walla, Lewiston, and Boise. He supplied these outlying stores by steamer up the Columbia, then by mule pack-trains over the Blue Mountains to Boise, or by oxteam via the Nez Perce Trail to Lewiston.

The park is named for the wife of Amos Short, who set aside the land in his 1850 town-site plat. The Short family arrived in 1846 and jumped the claim of a man who was away at the time, a situation further complicated because the Hudson's Bay Company regarded the land as theirs—and treated the family in what Mr. Short described as a "rough, rude, insolent and angry manner."

7   Downtown Vancouver (lower Main Street from about Fifth to Eighth; accessible via Exit 1-B) retains the scale and appearance of early twentieth-century business blocks. Architecture buffs will enjoy several buildings including the 1930s Classic Revival bank (Main and Eighth), the renovated 1912 Heritage Building (Main and Sixth), and the Evergreen Hotel (Main and Fifth; listed in the National Register of Historic Places). The hotel is now a retirement home. It opened with great ceremony in 1928. City lights were turned off for a few minutes just before the president of the Hudson's Bay Company, in London, pressed a telegraph lever and turned on a new lighting system surrounding the hotel, a symbol of the link between Vancouver's historic past and fashionable present. Two hundred and fifty invited guests marveled at the effect, then moved into a banquet hall.

8   Saint James Church (218 W. 12th), like Providence Academy, is built of brick from Vancouver's pioneering Hidden Brickyard. The parish traces its origin to the Northwest's first Catholic priests, Fathers Francis Blanchet and Modeste Demers, who arrived at Fort Vancouver from Montreal in 1838; the present church, a stately neo-Gothic building set on a slight rise above surrounding terrain, opened in 1884. Inside, the pews were designed by Mother Joseph of Providence Academy; the wooden altarpiece was shipped around Cape Horn for installation here; and the religious paintings were brought from Mexico by Bishop Augustine Blanchet.

9   The brick Hidden House (Main and 13th; built 1885) was the home of a prominent Vancouver family that arrived from New England about 1864. Danish craftsmen lived in the house while fashioning its ash and black walnut woodwork.

Lowell Hidden, who built the house, opened a brick factory in 1871 (at Main and 15th); he also operated a flour mill and a farm (which the Kaiser Company rented for its shipyard during World War II). Lowell's brother Arthur planted the county's first prune orchard (Main and 26th). Lowell's grandson, Robert Hidden, the third generation to manage the brickyard, bought Providence Academy in 1969 to save it from destruction. In 1976 he renovated the old family home.

10   The County Historical Museum (1511 Main) occupies a 1909 Carnegie Library building. Lowell Hidden donated land for the library, which was somewhat reluctantly accepted by the city council because it was "way out of town." Exhibits include extensive railroad memorabilia, a country store, and a pioneer kitchen as well as artifacts from native villages along the river and at Vancouver Lake.

11   The Covington Cabin (4208 Main) is well north of the downtown area. It was built about 5 miles east of the present location by Richard and Anne Covington, who came from London in 1846 to teach the children of Hudson's Bay Company employees. Two years later they moved to the Orchards area and operated a boarding school, which included this building. The cabin is usually open part time in summer; check the current schedule.

The **WASHOUGAL** (Wah-shoo'-gal) area was explored in 1792 by Lieutenant William Broughton who sailed the brig *Chatham* upriver as far as the Columbia Gorge, exploring for England as a part of the Vancouver Expedition. About 4 miles upriver from today's town,

Broughton planted the flag and claimed the land for England. Fourteen years later Lewis and Clark noticed adult seals and pups feeding on migrating salmon at the mouth of the Washougal River, which they called Seal River. *Washougal* is a Chinook word meaning "land of plenty, and pleasant." Archaeological evidence suggests that villages here date back to about 3,000 years ago.

The first white settler seems to have been Richard Howe (pronounced, Cockney fashion, "Ow," and sometimes spelled Ough). A Hudson's Bay Company employee, Howe stood over six feet tall and weighed 240 pounds. His wife was White Wing, the daughter of Sly Horse (Slahuts). Howe first noticed her during a meeting between her father and company officials, and he married her on the riverbank near Fort Vancouver in 1838 with John McLoughlin officiating.

Six years after Howe and White Wing built their cabin, David Parker arrived from Missouri with his wife and four small children and settled on land at the river mouth near the Howes. To receive supplies and accommodate riverboats, he built a dock, which became the nucleus of a community called Parkersville (located at the end of what is now SE Ninth). In the 1870s a property dispute developed among early settlers, and a man named Fritz Braun moved his hotel and saloon from Parkersville to the present location in Washougal. Other businessmen followed, and Parkersville declined. Washougal had begun after a man named Joe Durgan bought Howe's land and opened a combination butcher shop and post office as an adjunct for his cattle operation east of town.

In 1912 a Vancouver man named Clarence Bishop bought the mortgage of a woolen mill that had recently opened at Washougal. Three years earlier his family had taken over the Pendleton Mill (Pendleton, Oregon), and he expected the two operations to dovetail. Soon the Washougal mill had a reputation for excellent cassimere (a thin twilled wool), flannel, and other types of suiting. During World War I the mill produced blankets for the U.S. Army. In 1918 Bishop opened a division in Vancouver, hoping to capitalize on the company's reputation for quality woolen fabric by manufacturing plaid shirts of equally fine design and crafts-

manship. Not long afterward, an additional specialty—from the Washougal mill—became woolen "smelter bags" used as smokestack filters to recover sulphur otherwise lost in fumes. (The mill is on 17th Street.)

The local historical society museum is in the basement of the Washougal library building (Fifth and Franklin).

WOODLAND's main street is lined with several old buildings that stand like sentinels from a more bustling past. The town lies along the Lewis River, a tributary of the Columbia—although this position is scarcely apparent today except from a road looping Horseshoe Lake, an old river bend.

A 50-foot side-wheeler named *Fashion* began calling here in 1854. No rails linked Woodland to Puget Sound until 1903. Their arrival gave a better means of reaching markets. Dairymen's main product was cheese and, even shipped by rail, it had to be of top quality to keep; refrigerated cars had not yet been invented. The newly available transportation, plus cheap stumpland and seasonal logging work, attracted subsistence farmers to the area. Many were Finns. A marker 4 miles east of Woodland on State Route 503 commemorates the Old Finn Hall.

The **Hulda Klager Lilac Gardens,** listed in the National Register of Historic Places, grace the southwest edge of Woodland. (From I-5, drive through the old business district by following first Goerig, then Davidson. Turn left on Fifth, and in a tenth of a mile watch on the right for a circular driveway and a small sign saying "Gardens." A token entry fee helps volunteers keep the gardens open.)

The story here is appealing. In 1903 friends gave a book about Luther Burbank's methods of horticulture to Hulda Klager, who was recovering from an illness. Reading it, she decided to try hybridizing apple trees, for, as she put it,

I was pretty busy then, what with children to rear, and canning and preserving galore to do. It was too provoking to have to stop and peel dozens of apples for a couple pies. So I started out to get a better big apple.

That achieved, Mrs. Klager spent the next 55 years experimenting in her garden, particularly with lilacs, her favorite flower. On spring mornings she would use a fine brush and magnifying glass to apply flourlike pollen to tiny individual blossoms, then cover each spray with a paper bag to shield it from bees or other pollinators. Four years later she could see results; lilacs take that long to develop from seed to blossoming plant.

In a 1928 interview for *Better Homes and Gardens,* Hulda Klager confessed that at first she was disappointed if the blossoms fell short of expectation. "But now if I get one out of 400 worth saving, I rejoice."

The Woodland "lilac lady" earned an international reputation—although even today hometown people remember her neighborliness more than her acclaim. Beginning about 1915, the Klagers opened their garden each May for Lilac Day, and visitors came by horse and buggy, bouncing over country roads. They still come, arriving now via the freeway. The four-acre garden is open all year, but continues the traditional emphasis on lilac time. Sale of seedlings and slips of various flowers and ornamental shrubs provides money for upkeep of the garden and its original Victorian farmhouse, carriage house, water tower, windmill, and lilac nursery. Mrs. Klager used to say:

It's no fun for me to raise lilacs in quantities and ship them off to town. It *is* fun to have people come here. . . . You see, I do all the work, so why shouldn't I have all the fun I can get from my garden?

The **Cedar Creek Gristmill,** 10 miles east of Woodland, is a local landmark saved through volunteer effort. (From Exit 21 off the freeway, turn east toward LaCenter and Amboy. Immedi-

The Cedar Creek Gristmill—now isolated—long served as a community focal point.

ately after crossing the Lewis River, turn left on County Road 16, and in about 8 miles, turn left on unpaved Gristmill Road and follow it for a half mile.) The drive leads along the river past farms and scattered rural homes, then winds among forested slopes. In places, Mount St. Helens looms above the horizon.

The mill—small and out of the way—formerly acted as a magnet. Families brought their grain and exchanged gossip while they waited for it to be ground. The mill's 1870s craftsmanship has been carefully restored. Hand-hewn posts and beams are joined and pegged rather than nailed. A flume diverts creek water to a turbine.

When the mill first opened in the summer of 1876, customers came by boat along the Lewis River, but a few months later men finished building a road across Chelatchie Prairie, and people could also reach the mill by team and wagon. During the depression years of the 1890s, far-flung neighbors gathered every Saturday night for a dance. Children slept in the grain bins while night slipped into dawn: the dance had to last long enough to justify the long trip.

In the early 1900s a new owner converted the gristmill into a machine shop by using its turbine for electricity, which he also supplied to neighbors. After World War II, the mill stood unused and neglected. Restoration began in the 1980s.

YACOLT is accessible via State Route 503, or—in summer—on board the diesel excursion train from Battle Ground. A typical rural community today, the town is best known for the disastrous fire of 1902, which cost 38 lives and the loss of 238,000 acres of forest. At the time of the fire a man named Frank Barnes noticed its effects from a hundred miles away. He wrote:

The [Yacolt] smoke so darkened the sun that . . . we had to use lights to run our mill and the chickens went to roost in the daytime. All day, leaves would come floating through the air and light on the lake. When they touched, they dissolved into ashes.

Grace Stearns, a new teacher at Yacolt, dismissed school because at midafternoon her 12 pupils could no longer see to read. People loaded wagons and evacuated the town during the night as paint began to blister on the buildings. Miss Stearns wrote:

We planned, if necessary, to get into the creek, if the fire came too close. We had buckets and blankets, the buckets to throw water, and the blankets to put over our heads if we had to get into the creek. . . . The fire was creating a ground draft that was bitterly cold. [It] bent the tops of young trees almost to the ground.

After the fire, the Yacolt community of a dozen families swelled to accommodate 500 loggers who worked for two decades to salvage fire-damaged trees, some of them seven feet in diameter. Austrians and Slavonians laid track extending a Northern Pacific spur line to carry blackened logs to a booming ground on Lake River, just below Ridgefield. Finns, Swedes, and Russians worked as fallers and buckers, wielding crosscut saws and producing 40-foot logs, which fit onto the railroad cars.

How the Yacolt Burn started is still uncertain. At the time, some said that it had blown over the mountains from the sheep country to the east. Some thought that the crew of a steamboat on the Columbia had gone ashore to cut wood for fuel and, while there, set fire to a wasp's nest, then watched as flames raged through the dry underbrush. The public accepted wildfires as inevitable. Sparks from logging trains and donkey engines started them every summer and fall; residents simply fled when they had to. An aftermath of the Yacolt Burn, however, was a beginning of fire prevention through a forest lookout system and a coordinated effort at extinguishing small fires before they blazed out of control. The Yacolt Burn accounted for a full third of the 35 billion board feet of timber that was destroyed in 1902 by 110 Washington and Oregon fires. It probably sprang from multiple origins. Furthermore, the area burned repeatedly, in places destroying biological carryover and resulting in land that seemingly cannot be reforested.

Lower Columbia River

The area around the Columbia River mouth is geographically small but historically large. Events of national and statewide significance focused here, including explorations by land and sea. Pioneering settlement was well under way by the 1830s and 1840s, which is earlier than in most of Washington. In addition, this is a scenically unique location; its high headlands, immensely wide river (4 miles), and forest could not be confused with any other place on earth.

Museums are at Cathlamet, Skamokawa, Forts Canby and Columbia, Ilwaco—and also across the bridge at Astoria, where the Maritime Museum warrants a special trip. Spectacular lighthouses are at Cape Disappointment and North Head.

The trip to **ALTOONA** and on to Pillar Rock is through trees and along the river with not so much as a cafe or a gas station along the way. Yet in the early 1900s six fish-buying stations and canneries operated within a six-mile stretch of river here, and Altoona was a major stop for steamers traveling between Portland and Astoria. Today only a few houses remain nestled against the river bluff at Altoona, and the cannery

stands empty at the end of its dock, its red paint chipping, its roof now of shiny metal. The many windows gave light and ventilation; they date the building as from a time before fluorescent tubes and air conditioning.

Millers Sands, the shallows offshore from Altoona, provided such a rich salmon seining ground that in the early 1890s pioneering cannery operator William Hume opened a new fish-receiving station here. Among the fishermen soon working for him was Hans Peterson, who owned land at the station. In 1902 Peterson saw possibilities of adding a cannery to the existing boardinghouse, hotel, and buyer's dock. He contracted to have 830 acres of his timber cut, and he checked into getting a post office established.

He decided on "Altoona" as the name, a slight misspelling of his home village of Altona in Germany and the name of the fish-buying launch he operated.

The cannery opened in 1904. By the end of the decade its production ranked fourth among Columbia River canneries: 18,000 cases of salmon in a single year. A fleet of 25-foot, sail-rigged gillnet boats operated out of Altoona fishing at night, when nets were invisible to salmon. In 1935 a road of sorts reached Altoona. Twelve years later the cannery processed its last salmon and drastically reduced the

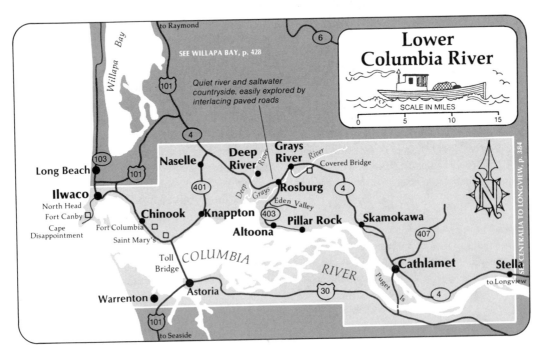

Altoona was a major river port in the early 1900s, but it now exists as little more than a handful of houses and a long, picturesque cannery still perched on rotting pilings.

operation, which eliminated jobs for scores of people from Chinese workers to suppliers of tin cans and printers of salmon labels.

The loss of the salmon came largely as a result of Grand Coulee Dam, completed in 1941. The dam blocked summer Chinook salmon from reaching their spawning grounds and thereby virtually destroyed that particular run of salmon, the one Altoona had staked its reputation on. With its premium pack gone, the cannery lost its place in the market and, although it tried canning tuna, it failed and had to close.

(Also see PILLAR ROCK, p. 423.)

BAKER BAY lies within the curving hook of Cape Disappointment and Sand Island. The river road between Fort Canby State Park and Ilwaco skirts its shore (and is highly scenic, especially driven from west to east so as to be traveling along the water side of the road). The bay retains a sense of the pristine, with dense vegetation ashore and wide views out across the river.

Before the days of jetties and channel dredging, ships entering the Columbia hugged the north bank as they crossed the bar, and Baker Bay offered the first anchorage with water deep enough to prevent possible grounding at low tide. The bay's name commemorates

Captain James Baker, who quite possibly brought his merchant schooner *Jenny* into the Columbia a few weeks before Captain Robert Gray's arrival on May 11, 1792. Gray was American, Baker was British—significant in an era when simply arriving first gave "possession" of lands actually already long inhabited by native people. The *Jenny* had a reputation as an African slave ship and, with growing British condemnation of slavery, her owners decided to switch to the Northwest Coast fur trade. They ordered Baker not to talk about his activities or to keep a log, consequently little is known about him.

In October 1792 the great British navigator Captain George Vancouver arrived at the Columbia River to investigate what he had learned from Gray concerning a major river. He stood by on HMS *Discovery* while Lieutenant William Broughton sailed the smaller *Chatham* across the bar. Safely inside, Broughton fired a signal to indicate arrival, then another to let Vancouver know he had sighted a vessel: Baker's *Jenny*. Baker mentioned that he had been inside the river mouth earlier, but gave no details. If his first entry predated Gray's, it might have affected the ultimate sovereignty of the "Oregon country." American rights to the Columbia were based largely on Gray's discovery of it.

Less than two decades after Broughton's surprise sighting of the *Jenny,* the Pacific Fur Company very nearly selected Baker Bay instead of the south bank of the river for its trading post. In 1811 Jonathon Thorn, captain of the company's vessel *Tonquin,* unloaded 50 hogs just inside the shelter of Cape Disappointment. He started to set ashore the rest of the cargo, but head traders Duncan McDougall and David Stuart objected and insisted that he cross the river. Their reason apparently had more to do with mistrust of whatever the captain decided than with any real awareness of advantages on the other side of the river. The two men had tried to reconnoiter that shore, but capsized. They would have drowned had not Chinook Chief Comcomly seen what they were attempting and ordered his men to follow them.

(Also see GRAYS BAY, p. 420.)

CAPE DISAPPOINTMENT is the opposite of its name: it delights anyone interested in landscape and history. **Fort Canby State Park** near Ilwaco embraces both the cape and the new flatlands accreting at its base (owing to the jetties' effects on river currents and the deposition of sediment). The drive along the north jetty is particularly dramatic. Waves crash. The lighthouse winks. And ships glide slowly by. On the cape itself, outstanding state park interpretive center exhibits tell the story of the Lewis and Clark Expedition's approach to the Columbia in 1805 and of the evolution of the old Lifesaving Service into the U.S. Coast Guard. A short trail leads to the lighthouse. (Also see FORT CANBY, p. 419.)

The name Cape Disappointment dates from 1788 when English trader John Meares failed to find the "great river" that had been noted thirteen years earlier by the Spaniard Bruno Heceta. Meares saw a large opening with waves breaking on a shoal but disregarded it and wrote that "no such river exists . . . as [that] laid down in the Spanish charts."

Even after the river mouth was charted, seamen dreaded the actual crossing. Well over 200 ships have wrecked here. Some stood off the bar for a month or more, awaiting proper conditions; occasionally their supplies of food and water ran short while they waited. All of the difficulties led to a conclusion that the hazards of the river bar would "forever" preclude settlement along the Columbia. Lieutenant Charles Wilkes, commander of a U.S. Navy expedition in 1841, lost his ship *Peacock* on the bar and wrote:

[The Columbia] can never be entered at night and only at particular times of the tide and direction of the

Extreme navigational hazards near the Columbia River mouth prompted the addition of a second lighthouse, built at North Head in 1898. Due to contrary winds and shifting sandbars, ships sometimes took two weeks to sail up the river to Fort Vancouver.

wind. . . . Mere description can give little idea of the terrors of the bar. All who have seen it have spoken of the wildness of the scene and the incessant roar of the waters, representing it as one of the most fearful sights that can possibly meet the eye.

Official recommendation for **Cape Disappointment Lighthouse** was submitted in 1848 just two years after Britain and America had agreed on the 49th parallel as the boundary between the Oregon country and British Columbia. Ironically, in 1853, a ship bringing construction materials for the lighthouse wrecked while crossing the river bar. The captain had waited offshore a week for favorable conditions, but he struck a shoal when he finally tried to make the entry. He lost the entire cargo. Three more years passed before a beacon at this cape gleamed through the dark and fog. That first light came from five oil wicks, each eight inches wide.

North Head Lighthouse and the Cape Disappointment Lighthouse stand closer together than any other lights on the Pacific Coast, indication of extraordinary circumstances here: poor visibility can cause confusion as to which headland marks the river entrance. To aid mariners, the North Head light began service in 1898 (nearly 40 years after the Cape Disappointment light). It beams only white light, whereas Cape Disappointment's light is red alternated with white.

CATHLAMET is a river town to turn into and also to view from Puget Island, where its position along the high palisades of the Columbia shows clearly. Today's highway totally bypasses the old section of Cathlamet.

Venerable downtown buildings and homes have no frozen-in-time, stage-set quality, but there are several of individual interest. Samples include the Pioneer Church (Second and Angle streets; built in 1895) now used as a senior center; the Bradley House (across from the courthouse on Main Street; built in 1907); and the home of longtime Congresswoman Julia Butler Hansen (Butler and Main), built in 1857 by James Birnie, founder of the town. The timeworn hotel in the center of town stirred major excitement when it opened in 1927. Cathlamet couples hired baby-sitters, took

rooms, and "spent most of the night calling each other up on the phones."

Displays at the county historical society museum (65 River Street) include an astonishing array of heavy, rusting logging equipment and a photograph collection that shows individuals living it up at a tavern, or cooking at a logging camp, or showing off a record-size sturgeon— small glimpses of everyday life. The museum stands on the site of a Chinook tribal village apparently begun in the early 1800s when scattered survivors of a series of epidemics decided to form a new, amalgamated village. There, James Birnie paddled ashore from Astoria in 1846 after retiring from the Hudson's Bay Company. He filed a donation land claim and opened his own trading post.

Birnie immediately encouraged others to join him, and among those who came was William Strong. Newly appointed as the territorial judge, Strong left New York by sea with his wife and two small sons in December 1849. The family arrived at Astoria eight months later and en route to Oregon City stopped at Birnie's wharf. While there, they decided to take an adjoining land claim. From that home, Judge Strong presided over a district that reached from the mouth of the Columbia River to the crest of the Rocky Mountains, perhaps the largest district ever assigned to one judge. In a book titled *Cathlamet on the Columbia,* the judge's son Thomas tells of the isolated life, which was particularly odd for his mother, "a refined and cultivated young woman, thoroughly educated and accustomed to the best social circles of the Eastern States."

In 1866 George and William Hume opened a salmon cannery at Eagle Cliff, about 8 miles east of Cathlamet, the first of an eventual 39 canneries on the lower Columbia. Success came immediately. During their second year the Humes packed 4,000 cases and shipped most of them to Australia. In 1869 the Warren Cannery opened at Cathlamet. Its huge riverfront sheds still serve as a net loft and boat storage.

Logging began here almost as early as canning. The pattern typical throughout western Washington prevailed—settlers cleared land by either burning the trees they felled or rolling them into water. Sawmill owners sold lumber for the canneries and the workers' housing proliferating locally. The owners also developed export markets first in Hawaii and San Francisco, then later in Chile, Australia, Japan, and China. When timber close to rivers all had been cut, loggers used five or six yokes of oxen and pulled logs to water.

Steam donkeys appeared about 1890; high-lead logging about 1918. Flumes shot logs to the Columbia. Logging railroads snaked up drainages and across chasms. In time, gravel roads and logging trucks replaced rails. Through the technological changes, lumberjacks bunked at camps scattered throughout the hinterlands. The last logging camp in Wahkiakum County, a Crown Zellerbach camp, closed in 1959. The virgin forest had lasted for about a century. Today's logging is on a much smaller scale.

CHINOOK is a town with a 1906, two-story, false-fronted general store and beautifully restored 1890s and 1900s fishermen's houses—buildings easily overlooked because the highway traffic seldom permits pleasant windshield viewing. The west end of the frontage road off State Route 4 offers a fine river view, and there the Chinook Packing Company, founded in 1915, still processes salmon and also tuna, crab, and shrimp.

Washington's first state-run salmon hatchery began on the headwaters of the Chinook River in 1895. It was headed by Alfred Houchen who had been experimenting with hatcheries at his tideland farm on the Bear River and at a friend's farm on the Chinook River. At the time nearly every family in the area operated some sort of fish trap and, to supply the new hatchery, they took turns donating a day's catch. Fish from the traps were put into crates and towed up the Chinook River to Houchen. A nonprofit corporation today continues the hatchery operation. (It is open for tours; the rearing ponds are most active September through May.)

Fishing grounds at Chinook were productive, so much so that by the late 1880s about 125 fish traps stood in the bay as a maze of pilings and nets. Chinook claimed to be the wealthiest town per capita of any in the United States. Remnant pilings standing barely above the water's surface remain. They were driven into the shallow river bottom like fenceposts to form a V. Attached nets funneled salmon toward a narrow opening where they were caught in a "pot." One trap owner collected 12,000 pounds of fish in a single day. Individual salmon weighing 80 pounds were not uncommon. (The traps were declared illegal in 1935.)

DEEP RIVER actually is a slough fed by meandering tidal creeks. Spruce boughs reach over the water, their trimline the result of high tides; beaver dams block channels and maintain ponds where low tides otherwise would produce mud flats twice daily. Wooden gillnet boats ply the river. Modern, metal barns replace huge, old, sagging pioneer barns. At the head of the slough (1½ miles inland from the highway) a few buildings sag forlornly. In the 1910s, a 20-room hotel, tailor shop, barbershop, pool hall, sauna, community hall, and school also stood here at the head of the slough.

A Civil War veteran from England, an Irish family, a Canadian Scotsman, an English shipwreck survivor, a German family, Swedish and Norwegian loggers, and Finnish seamen all migrated to Deep River. A Swedish settler who came about 1900 claimed his arrival was like crossing an international line: all he heard was Finnish. The Finns—already used to patient work and hardship in the old country—moved farther into the forest than most of their neighbors were willing to do. The firstcomers took timber claims and cleared enough land to farm. Later arrivals worked for the Deep River Logging Company, which set up family camps as well as bachelor bunkhouses and mess halls.

To sense the pioneer isolation of this drainage, turn up Wirkkala Road (off East Deep River Road near the head of the slough) and follow it for a mile to the Holy Trinity Evangelical Lutheran Church, completed in 1902. One family gave land for the church, another the bell. A carpenter styled the pulpit after his memory of the pulpit in his childhood church "back home." Services were in Finnish. Eventually the Naselle Finnish Lutheran congregation grew, while this one declined. The two merged and now the Deep River church is used only on special occasions such as Easter or weddings.

Outlying homes in the Deep River area stood along a logging railroad where anyone with a "speeder" had free use of the tracks. These conveyances were small open cars propelled by a hand pump. People without speeders walked the tracks worrying at each trestle whether a milk train or log train might come hurtling around a curve. A precaution was to put an ear to the rail: an oncoming train could be heard for a mile or more, which gave enough time to cross even the longest trestle.

Away from the railroad tracks, overland travel was difficult. Grays River is only 3 miles from Deep River; but most people preferred to ride the passenger boat to Astoria and then catch the Grays River boat back to the north side of the Columbia rather than walk the trail. Rowing down Deep River, across the bay, and up Grays River was impractical; it meant pulling against the tide part of the way, which is difficult even for a strong man. Walking was even worse; the forest was a tangle of fallen trees and dense brush plus mud.

EDEN VALLEY. (See under ROSBURG, p. 424.)

FORT CANBY began with the 1852 establishment of a federal military reservation at a wild townsite speculation called Pacific City. When the Civil War began a few years later, the army installed muzzle-loader cannons close to the Cape Disappointment Lighthouse—in fact, so close that they shattered its windows when fired. Worry that Confederate gunboats might enter the Columbia River had prompted placement of the cannons here. Land for a fort across the river had been "purchased" from the Clatsop tribe, but the 4-mile width of the river combined with the limited firing range of guns at that time necessitated forts on both sides.

The fort here was first called Fort Cape Disappointment, but was renamed Fort Canby about 1875. Officers' quarters, barracks, shops, and stables were added to the dock below the Cape Disappointment gun batteries, and a bulkhead held fill dirt to create a parade ground. No shot other than for practice ever was fired from Fort Canby, although during World War II a Japanese submarine shelled Fort Stevens, this fort's Oregon counterpart. After World War II, the army closed Fort Canby. Part of its land went to the Coast Guard, part to the state park, part to the Army Corps of Engineers, which needed rock for jetty repairs and extensions.

(Also see CAPE DISAPPOINTMENT, p. 416; and FORT COLUMBIA, this page.)

FORT CANBY STATE PARK. (See under CAPE DISAPPOINTMENT, p. 416.)

Construction at **FORT COLUMBIA** began in 1898 with the outbreak of the Spanish-American War in Cuba, but no troops arrived until five years later. The fort, a classic of its time, remained active until the close of World War II. Land and buildings then came under state park jurisdiction. The trim wooden barracks and officers' houses as well as the grim cement gun batteries and bunkers remain today as though a full-scale diorama representing the past. Displays in one of the barracks buildings interpret the fort. The interior of the commander's house has been restored.

Before the federal government established its military reservation at Chinook Point, the land belonged to English sea captain James Scarborough, who served as boatswain and later skipper on Hudson's Bay Company trading ships. Scarborough settled on this site in the mid-1840s and filed a claim to it soon after the Donation Land Claim Act was passed in 1850. He raised cattle driven north from California and from time to time served as impromptu pilot for ships crossing the river bar. In 1857 Rocque DuCheney, a Hudson's Bay Company store manager, bought the Scarborough claim and started a salmon-packing business.

DuCheney married a granddaughter of Chief Comcomly, whose family had lived at the point for countless generations. Lewis and Clark reported finding 36 longhouses there in 1805, a large population because each house sheltered several individual families. Comcomly was a high-ranking Chinook chief who welcomed the new forms of wealth brought by early white traders; his own people were skillful traders well known along the coast as far as British Columbia and up the Columbia River into the Yakima territory. Comcomly married two of his daughters to head traders at Astoria: Duncan McDougall of the Pacific Fur Company and Archibald MacDonald of the Hudson's Bay Company. (Also see RANALD MACDONALD sidebar, p. 36.)

The Hudson's Bay Company appointed

Comcomly its head river pilot. When a ship approached the bar, the chief's slaves paddled him out to it. He then guided the vessel upriver. His knowledge of landmarks, currents, and shifting shoals was far superior to that of any newcomer white man.

GRAYS BAY is the broad notch in the shoreline where the Grays and Deep rivers empty into the Columbia. It offers a view of ridges and points fading into the distance, each a successively lighter shade of blue on clear days, of gray on overcast days. On May 14, 1792, Captain Robert Gray, a Boston fur trader already two years at sea, anchored on a sandbar here. Three days earlier he had brought his three-masted, square-rigged brig *Columbia Rediviva* into the river.

On May 19, after finishing with his local explorations, Gray named the river for his ship. His exploration of the river mouth gave the United States a basis for territorial claims disputed by England.

(Also see BAKER BAY, p. 415.)

The **GRAYS RIVER** community is best seen from the side road looping off State Route 4.

Huge, vulnerable barns stand on soggy bottomlands along the river; they convey a "look-now" urgency, for as these fall replacement will not be in kind. The barns testify to pioneering hardihood and pride—and available timber. Washington's last public covered bridge is accessible from this side road. The Grays River cooperative creamery building—a landmark of united farm endeavor—stands on State Route 4 near the western end of the side road.

The bridge was built in 1905, a blessing for farm families on the south side of the Grays River who needed to get cream to market. In 1908 men added a corrugated iron roof to protect bridge timbers from snow and rain. Later they enclosed the entire bridge to increase its longevity. Flood damage in the mid-1980s forced temporary closure, but community determination assured reopening. The bridge is listed in the National Register of Historic Places.

Community betterment grew out of Grange meetings as soon as a Grays River chapter was organized in the early 1900s. From the outset its membership included fishermen and loggers as well as farmers. Early Grange efforts went into improving roads in the area. Waterways gave

Grays River boasts Washington's last covered bridge still in public use.

valley dwellers access to the Columbia, and steamers linked the river to the world; but water travel was slow, depended on tides, and often was hazardous owing to storms, ice, or shifting sandbars. Men willingly signed up to build roads and also to provide teams of horses. At first their labor counted toward payment of county taxes, but by the 1920s and 1930s the work seems to have been more nearly an act of civic desperation without any tax benefit. Farmers worked together on Sundays to build one segment of road at a time.

ILWACO is a modern town yet with a sense of place: local people still own knee-high rubber boots; heed the daily tide schedule; and drive fearlessly across riverbank mud to cut drift logs into firewood. Regional highways converge in Ilwaco and create a tendency for travelers to drive through town without stopping—a mistake.

Fine old commercial buildings line the downtown streets, their facades bright with murals that depict local history, and highways and side streets lead among two-story fishermen's homes with decorative corner windows, fish-scale shingles, and ample scrollwork. The Colbert House (Quaker and Lake) is listed in the National Register of Historic Places. It was begun in the 1870s by one of the early fish trap owners here.

Be sure to stop at the Ilwaco Heritage Museum (115 SE Lake, near the center of town). Exhibits portray the life of the Chinook people, who perhaps were more totally devastated by white diseases than any other native group in Washington. Additional exhibits highlight local industries such as cranberry growing, fishing, and logging. The old Ilwaco Railroad Depot has been restored and is part of the museum complex. It served the "Clamshell Railway," which linked the Long Beach Peninsula with steamer service from Astoria. The depot now houses a 50-foot model of the peninsula as it was in the 1920s. It includes an operating scale model of the railroad. (Also see KLIPSAN BEACH, p. 429, for more on the railroad.)

Settlement at Ilwaco began in the 1840s with a mix of individuals from varied backgrounds. For example, John Pickernell—an American—came from Champoeg, Oregon, where French-Canadian and American settlers had disagreed over political organization and whether to raise a local militia. Pickernell voted with the minority, then moved here seeking a new start. James DeSaule arrived here in 1841 as a cook for the Charles Wilkes U.S. Naval Expedition. He deserted from the navy when the vessel he was on board—the *Peacock*—ran aground and broke up. DeSaule was a Peruvian black man recruited at Callao. Supposedly, Jim Crow Point and Creek (5 miles west of Skamokawa) are named for him; he lived there when he first jumped ship. He later moved to Ilwaco, from which he ran a freight service between Astoria and Cathlamet.

Much of Ilwaco's early development came from its role as a transportation hub. In 1873 the county levied a special assessment against three saloons and used the money to build a plank road to the ocean beach (called the "weather beach" because of storms blowing in off the Pacific). Hard-packed sand served as a low-tide roadway on up the peninsula. In 1874 soldiers at Fort Canby built a road along the shore of Baker Bay to Ilwaco; and that same year a sheep farmer who lived about midway along the peninsula raised money and built a wharf. At this time the minuscule community was known as Unity, a celebratory name marking the end of the Civil War. Regardless, most people called it Ilwaco, for Elowahka Jim, a son-in-law of Chief Comcomly. The plat filed in 1876 used the name Ilwaco.

Population burgeoned to about 300 people with the 1882 introduction of a Great Lakes method of catching salmon. This involved traps made of rope webs strung on pilings. Installation called for a considerable outlay of cash and a permanent location. As the *South Bend Journal*'s special Pacific County edition of 1900 reported, the traps "attracted a settled, home-seeking population." Their success proved so phenomenal that word of it spread, attracting a number of midwestern fishermen. Gillnetters found their best fishing grounds preempted by the huge webs and organized efforts to get rid of them. They terrorized watchmen holding lonely night vigil at each trap, set pile drivers adrift, and burned the well-tarred nets spread on shore to dry. The violence continued into the 1900s,

Pilings mark the huge 1870s sawmill town of Knappton but little else remains.

aggravated further by cannery strikes, which at times even brought federal troops. (Also see under CHINOOK, p. 418, for discussion of traps.)

Nonetheless, although the *Journal*'s special edition described fishing as Ilwaco's mainstay, it (rightly) added that with the popularity of the ocean beach "the city has a bright future before it in this direction alone."

KNAPPTON's abandoned pilings (10 miles east of Chinook) draw attention even along a riverbank well studded with pilings. These number a phenomenal 1,000 or more arrayed in rows and blocks, and now bisected by State Route 4.

Jabez Burrell Knapp came to the Northwest by wagon in 1852, losing his wife and a daughter to cholera en route. While exploring the banks of the Columbia, he found a ledge of rock that he felt sure could be used to make high-quality cement. He bought the land and in 1867 started a town called Cementville. Unfortunately, the ledge of raw material soon gave out and operations ceased.

Undaunted, Knapp next opened a sawmill and began supplying lumber and piles for the canneries and workers' housing then expanding along the Columbia. The census for 1870 lists a community of "76 males and 36 females" at Cementville, nearly a third of them foreign born. A hotel, or boardinghouse, provided lodging for single men who ate at a mess hall staffed by Chinese cooks. The company barged millworkers' row housing across the river from an Astoria shipyard and added other houses on the hills and flats near the mill. A great many Finns came to work at the sawmill.

A federal quarantine station stood on a long wharf a mile downriver from the sawmill. From 1900 until 1938 it amounted to a Columbia River "Ellis Island" for ships bringing in European or Asian immigrants. Communicable diseases—especially smallpox, influenza, and measles—had earlier tragically decimated lower Columbia native people, who had little immunity. Whites, too, fell victim to epidemics, and by the 1890s people in Portland and Astoria clamored noisily about the danger of ships bringing in cholera, yellow fever, malaria, bubonic plague, and smallpox.

An inspector at Astoria checked arrivals and, when he found disease on board, sent the ship to Diamond Point, near Port Townsend, for quarantine. Columbia River people wanted a disinfecting station and hospital of their own—although not on the populous south side of the river. As a result, Congress approved purchase of the abandoned Eureka and Epicure Packing Company buildings at Knappton (formerly Cementville) for conversion into a quarantine station. Ships moored at the wharf to disembark passengers, who showered while their clothing and baggage were treated in huge retorts, and the ship itself was fumigated with burning sulphur. A decommissioned ship from the Spanish-American War provided quarters during the fumigation, which took 48 hours. A lazaretto (a small hospital) on shore cared for the ill.

NASELLE is a major crossroads community and a stronghold of Finnish tradition celebrated with a major July festival every other year (check current plans). Smorgasbords and oyster feeds, popular since pioneering times, still draw far-flung neighbors; housewives get out family recipes from the old country; musicians dust off their *kanteles* (Finnish stringed instruments similar to dulcimers).

Settlement began in the Naselle area in the 1850s and swelled during the 1880s and 1890s with the arrival of people from Finland. An 1897 "immigrants' manual" *(Suomalaiset Amerikassa)* written in Finnish included photographs of homes and healthy families and made no mention of isolation, constant dampness, and mammoth trees to clear before farms could be made productive. Regardless, conditions at that time were worse in Finland.

Arriving here, families came up the Naselle River with the rising tide, bringing their household goods and farming equipment; on the outgoing tide, they shipped furs and farm produce to market. Homes faced the river, which was lined with family docks, or "tie-ups." Reminiscenses of the time mention "big fish flopping on the frosty river bank, and always the huge trees, falling, falling, falling" and also tell of "walking with mother through the narrow winding trails, over the stiles and swinging

cable bridges, to the nearest neighbors."

The 1890s era of dreams and schemes included promotion of Naselle—then called Stanley—as "the Seattle of Shoalwater Bay." This swindle even included a railroad on paper—which was called the Stanley, Cascade and Eastern. A hotel, wharf, and several houses actually were built.

Gold discoveries in the Klondike drew men stampeding north and interrupted development here, but as that craze ended many returned. Others continued to arrive, particularly from Finland. The Naselle phone book still shows a leaning toward names such as Paavola, Wiitala, and Wirkkala.

NORTH HEAD LIGHTHOUSE. (See under CAPE DISAPPOINTMENT, p. 417.)

To reach **PILLAR ROCK,** continue 4 miles past the end of State Route 403 at Altoona. A narrow road winds up a steep hill where school bus hours are posted as a warning of when to expect oncoming traffic. High views of the Columbia are striking in winter, nearly non-existent in summer owing to the green screen of alder and maple leaves.

A mile before the end of the road, a row of modern houses faces the river, and a fine three-story Victorian house with fish-scale shingles and scrollwork stands alone on a hill. This is the Chris Henry house built in 1887, when lower Columbia River salmon fishing and canning were at their height. The Pillar Rock Cannery packed salmon from 1877 to 1947, other kinds of fish and crab after that.

As early as the 1830s the Hudson's Bay Company began a fish-receiving station and saltery at Pillar Rock and shipped the output to the Sandwich Islands (Hawaii). Ten years before that the company had tried shipping salted salmon to London from their Astoria trading post, but had little success. Then an American trader sailing the brig *Owyhee* started brine packing salmon on the south side of the river below Fort Vancouver, and the Boston businessman Nathaniel Wyeth also attempted a salmon fishery on the lower Columbia. The Hudson's Bay Company had no intention of idly watching competitors, and opened the Pillar Rock saltery. At that time, salting was the only known means of preservation, other than the native people's method of drying and smoking salmon, which produced a result that did not appeal to whites.

Perhaps of more lasting effect than the salmon sales, was a demonstration at Pillar Rock of white "justice." For some reason, in 1840 two slaves belonging to Chinook headmen murdered Kenneth McKay, the manager of the Pillar Rock saltery, and his native helper. Perhaps the men were escaping and had tried to get supplies from McKay. Regardless, an Iroquois employee of the Hudson's Bay Company shot the principal offender, a slave from Vancouver Island. Chief Skamokawa captured an apparent accomplice, a Quinault slave (or, some accounts say, a Hoh slave) and turned him over to Hudson's Bay Company factor John McLoughlin, who came by barge from Fort Vancouver to Pillar Rock.

Native people and whites gathered to see what would happen. McLoughlin held a trial; a jury of settlers from the Willamette Valley found the accused guilty. McLoughlin ordered a gallows and with the help of the assembled witnesses hoisted the man ineptly and let him strangulate. Native observers took note of white vengeance.

Thirty-five years previously the Lewis and Clark party of 31 men plus Sacajawea and her baby had camped at Pillar Rock. That day they broke out of fog a few miles upriver and saw the water ahead open out with a high rock offshore. In camp, Clark wrote:

Great joy in camp. We are in view of the ocian [sic], the great Pacific Ocian which we have been so long anxious to see, and the roreing or noise made by the waves brakeing on the rockey shores may be heard distinctly.

The wind and waves—and rain—were altogether real, but the "ocian" actually lay another 10 days ahead of Lewis and Clark. Nonetheless, their Pillar Rock camp was triumphant.

The bridge to **PUGET ISLAND** was dedicated in August 1939 with President Franklin D. Roosevelt officially cutting the ribbon from the White House "through the power of electricity." A drive around the island today is bucolic; bicycling is ideal.

Mailboxes bear Swedish and Norwegian names, and local people gossip from pickup trucks stopped side by side in the road. Dikes and ditches drain fields where farmers pasture dairy and beef cattle. The diking is necessary. Originally the land was so soggy that the island had to have several schools so that children would not have far to walk. School House Road led to the first consolidated school.

The only remaining ferry of the many that once served the lower Columbia makes a 15-minute crossing from Puget Island to Westport (a village on the Oregon side near Wauna). On foggy days cars ride with their headlights turned on as a navigational precaution to help the skippers of other vessels see the ferry.

Settlers began coming to Puget Island in the 1880s. The Ostervolds were first. The Meiier family came not long afterward. Mrs. Meiier reminisced in the *Wahkiakum County Eagle* about piling bucketsful of earth around spruce stumps to build up enough dry soil to grow potatoes and about housing the pig in a shed built on a log "raft":

When the tide rose, the pig floated contently rocking on his own barge until the ebb allowed it to settle on land again. Some chickens were next but . . . these scatter-brained creatures could not be convinced to stay put when the tide rose.

ROSBURG today is essentially a store, post office, consolidated school, 1885 cemetery, and an official, enameled sign at the head of State Route 403 warning, "Water Over Roadway at High Tide."

The post office opened in the 1880s after outlying neighbors had tired of the long row to Grays River for mail and appointed representatives to sail to Astoria and request a post office of their own. The mission succeeded, but finding a centrally located postmaster proved difficult. A man named Peter Nelson refused the job, even when bribed by offers to name the post office for him. Finally German immigrant Christian Rosburg agreed, although he had to have the job description translated into German before he understood what was expected.

The 1890s population was large enough to warrant a community hall at Rosburg, and its Saturday night dances became famous. People living along logging railroad tracks started for

Rosburg by handcar, then rowed and walked—dress shoes tucked into coat pockets as protection from the mud that is inevitable where rainfall reaches 110 inches a year. Other dancers came as far as they could by fishing boat, then rode by wagon or walked with a lantern "listening to see if we could hear a cougar or a bear, scared to death."

Turn up **Eden Valley** to find countryside that is little changed since pioneer days, except for roads. (The turn is off State Route 403 about 2½ miles toward Altoona from Rosburg.) Until the mid-1930s, when a road finally arrived, daily tides dictated the timing of all contact with the world beyond Eden Valley, except for the mail, which came from the cannery at Brookfield. Settlers took turns walking there: the trek was only about 4 or 5 miles but was through such a jungle of forest and swamp that it took a full day to get there and another to return.

For entertainment the 30 families of Eden Valley organized an orchestra. Carrying lanterns, they met at the schoolhouse to fill the night with the music of seven violins, two saxophones, two clarinets, two trombones, three guitars, a piano, and either a flute or an accordion (both played by the same man and therefore selected according to the particular piece of music). Lanterns gave the only light until electricity arrived in the late 1940s.

SAINT MARY'S CHURCH stands alone on the north side of State Route 4 about 2 miles downriver from the Astoria bridge. For generations native people seined salmon at this site. They used long nets—probably made of spruce root—which were weighted at the bottom with stone sinkers and held vertical by wooden floats attached along the top edge. Men positioned the nets from canoes and drew them in from shore by hauling on ropes, essentially the same system later used by whites.

In November 1805 Lewis and Clark camped near the present church. Fifty years after that, an Irish clothing merchant named Patrick James McGowan arrived from New York via the California gold rush. He started a salmon saltery at the old seining ground and filled the market void left by the Hudson's Bay Company's declining dominance. He also watched while others, particularly the Hume brothers, experimented with canning equipment and methods. When the system worked well, McGowan built a cannery at the town already named in his honor. In 1904 he donated land for Saint Mary's Church and financed its construction.

Father Joseph Louis Lionnet had claimed the site of McGowan's town for a mission half a century earlier, but he stayed only from 1848 to 1852. Of his mission, Stella Maris, Lionnet wrote sadly that only one result remained among the natives: "the various names with which I had baptized them."

Lionnet's mission was located about where Saint Mary's stands; no sign of it remains. At Saint Mary's a visiting priest still says Mass during summer months (most years).

The country store at **SKAMOKAWA** (Ska-mock´-a-way), built in 1908, stands on pilings with water lapping at the back. Its plank floor has an old-fashioned unevenness and is pocked by decades of loggers walking into the store in their spike-soled boots. Redmen Hall, on the hill above the store, was built in 1894 as the Central School; when schools were consolidated in 1926 it became the meeting hall for the Fraternal Order of Redmen. It now belongs to the Friends of Skamokawa, who have refurbished it.

Homes from the 1880s and 1890s line Skamokawa Creek, their backs to the road. Town founders platted the community in relation to creeks and sloughs, and waterways are still highways for fishermen. No roads existed in the area until about the time of World War I.

Be sure to stop at Skamokawa Vista Park along the riverfront—and heed the sign that warns against standing close to the water's edge when a ship passes. A freighter's wake sends waves sweeping along the shore, dramatic to see but potentially disastrous. Also drive along the dike road of the national wildlife refuge (a loop off State Route 4 with Skamokawa at the west and Steamboat Slough Road at the east). Watch for white-tailed deer and elk, flocks of widgeon and wild swans. And notice the overall wetness of the land, a great hardship for pioneering farmers throughout this area.

Settlement at Skamokawa dates to 1844 when Portland pioneer Captain John Couch opened a short-lived trading post next to a Chinook longhouse. In the 1860s people of Anglo-Saxon background came to fish and farm, cut cordwood for steamers and timber bolts for barrel factories at Portland. The 1870s brought Scandinavian immigrants who settled the three valleys fingering into the hills from Skamokawa. With sheer tenacity and industry these pioneering families turned wilderness into subsistence farms so productive in cream and butter that a teacher boarding with one family later wrote that she gained 22 pounds during the school term. By 1899 a typical monthly shipment from Skamokawa included 91 ten-gallon cans of cream and 74 boxes of butter as well as sacks of potatoes, boxes of fish, crates of live poultry and hogs, and also quarters of dressed pork and beef.

The Bayview Cannery, built slightly downriver by Robert Hume, operated under various auspices from 1873 until about 1920. Fishermen seined with horses to drag their nets ashore. Men and beasts lived in-season on huge scows that were towed to fishing grounds such as Millers Sands and Grassy Island. Gillnetters and fish trap owners also sold catches to the cannery.

In the 1870s a sawmill on Skamokawa Creek supplied ties and construction timber for the Northern Pacific Railroad, then under construction from Kalama (south of Kelso) to Tacoma. From that beginning, the toot of steam whistles and the thud of trees hitting the ground became commonplace throughout the forests surrounding Skamokawa. Logging camps accommodated up to 100 men and often also included family homes and schools. Loggers were mostly Scandinavian and Anglo-Saxon. Italian crews built and repaired rail lines. For all, working conditions generally called for 60 hours a week, and if a man was injured he sat by a stump until the end of the day, then often waited again for a boat to the hospital at Astoria. Nothing could be allowed to slow production— except downturns in the market. By 1920 Skamokawa had three sawmills.

At **STELLA** the highway from Longview, which has been following a narrow slough of the Columbia, suddenly comes upon the full width of the river. Little remains of the old river town today except for a post office building and a 1907 blacksmith shop, which houses a museum. The local historical society plans, however, to bring several outlying buildings to the town-

Salmon fishermen near the Columbia River mouth used horses for pulling seine nets.

Tugs towed Stella's mammoth oceangoing log rafts as far as San Diego.

site. At the western edge of Stella, a road up Germany Creek Valley leads past huge wooden barns. The largest of them—120 feet long—was built in 1932 using planks from a flume that had carried timber to the Columbia.

John Guizendorfer filed a donation land claim here in the 1850s, and 20 years later the Weist family and other German immigrants came to homestead. They started logging both to supply local needs for timber and to provide cordwood for Columbia River steamboats, which landed at Stella to take on fuel.

Sometime before 1895, Coal Creek Slough's quiet water became the booming ground for cigar-shaped rafts that were towed as far as San Francisco and San Diego. Hugh Robertson, a native of Nova Scotia, pioneered the technique. Men laid pilings and spars into a cradle similar to a shipway and secured them end to end with what the *Portland Oregonian* described as an "immense iron chain, the single links of which are enough to task the strength of a man lifting [them]" and also with an "endless number of smaller chains crossing over and under" to prevent the timber from shifting. In addition to

their heavy timbers, the rafts carried deckloads of shingles, sawn lumber, lath, or cedar poles.

Several companies soon produced this style of oceangoing raft, and Robertson himself also had such operations in West Seattle and Westport, Oregon. Around 1900 he even made a trip to East Asia and announced plans for rafts 1,000 feet long to be towed to Japan and China, 60-day trips. Actual rafts by then were up to 800 feet long and 50 feet wide. A decided problem was that when they broke apart, their timber "scattered over the water for miles around," a great hazard to navigation. Congress considered banning the rafts—whereupon Robertson announced he would transfer his operations to British Columbia.

By the early 1900s Stella had two hotels and ferry service linking several communities to Mayger, Oregon, for train connection to Portland. Fire destroyed most of the town in 1907. Bigger buildings rose from the ashes. Twenty-six years later fire again swept town and this time rebuilding was on a lesser scale. By 1929 a road linked Stella to Longview, and the town lost its self-sufficiency.

Willapa Bay

Attractions on the Long Beach Peninsula include oceanside resorts active for more than a century and 25 miles of sandy ocean beaches. The bay side of the peninsula is characterized by tideflats, studded with the stakes of oystermen, and the town of Oysterville, a quiet residential community visually little changed from a century ago. Between Raymond and Tokeland, the highway traverses flat land with panoramic views of Willapa Bay and of tidal pastures laced by winding creeks.

A county historical society museum is in South Bend. Raymond holds a Loggers Day celebration each August.

BAY CENTER, an early oyster-harvesting settlement on Willapa Bay, is now a quiet fishing village reached by a spur road off U.S. 101. A few old homes still stand, and the view from the county park on Goose Point (which is right in town) has changed little since the 1850s when Bay Center was established. The community's name identifies it as midway along the bay, not as a "center" of human activity.

Most of **BRUCEPORT**'s site eroded into Willapa Bay before 1900. Today's historic marker and the view across the bay are about 3 miles south of the settlement's actual location. Oysters dominate the area's present economy and account for the scores of willowy stakes out in the bay. These markers are placed at low tide for two purposes: they guide vessels "seeding" young oysters during high tides, and they also mark where boats should anchor at harvest time.

Apparently even before actual settlement here, white men had occasionally come by schooner to harvest oysters and cut piling for San Francisco, which was booming because of California's newly won separation from Mexico and the discovery of gold at Sutters Mill. But no one stayed along Willapa Bay until 1851 when the small schooner *Robert Bruce* arrived after a four-day sail from the Golden Gate. For reasons that are unclear, the boat's cook drugged the four or five men on board (or some accounts say there were as many as eight men). He also set the boat on fire, which stranded the "Bruce

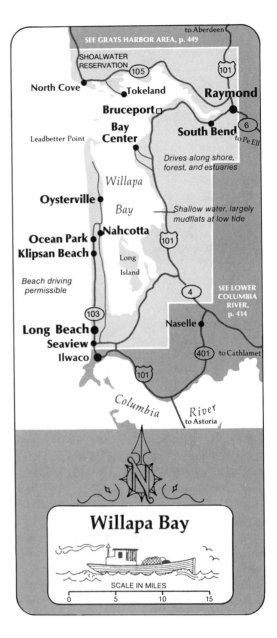

Boys." That had no particular consequence, however, for the men had come as partners to start an oyster business. The fire simply determined its location. In 1853 additional oystermen settled across the bay at Oysterville.

In his 1857 book *The Northwest Coast,* James G. Swan evokes this period of life at Shoalwater Bay (the name of Willapa Bay at that time). While working in San Francisco, Swan met one of the Bruceport oystermen and accepted his invitation to go north because he wanted to see "the great Columbia, and to learn something of the habits and customs of the tribes of the Northwest." He arrived in December 1852 and the next year filed on 320 acres at the mouth of the Bone River, near Milepost 42 (about 4 miles south of the Bruceport marker).

There, Swan attempted an oyster business, which did rather poorly, but he also got himself appointed as a U.S. Customs inspector and was one of the whites who helped Governor Stevens with the (inconclusive) treaty council near modern Cosmopolis. Swan lived at Shoalwater Bay for only three years, then moved to Neah Bay and later to Port Townsend.

ILWACO. (See p. 421.)

At **KLIPSAN BEACH** turn onto the beach access road for a look at the old lifesaving station, which is listed in the National Register of Historic Places. Buildings have been converted into private homes but the boathouse still clearly shows its origin. Its entire front consists of the wide doors that accommodated the surfboats used to rescue shipwreck victims.

The station began in 1891, midway between other stations at the mouth of the Columbia River and the north end of Willapa Bay. Duty at Klipsan Beach included nighttime patrols along the shore and daytime watching the ocean for signs of vessels in distress. When a foundering vessel was spotted, specially trained horses pulled surfboats directly into the breakers, and men rowed to the scene of the disaster. The horses' willingness to walk into the water eased the launching and retrieval of the boats. In summer "Clamshell Railway" trains bouncing along the poorly ballasted tracks between Ilwaco and Nahcotta stopped one day a week to let passengers watch lifeboat drills. In an emergency the trains would pick up the lifeboat and its crew and carry them as close as possible to a stricken vessel.

The Klipsan Beach station closed in 1947. By

By 1888 the federal Lifesaving Service operated a rescue station at Klipsan Beach. The service had been established 40 years earlier as a forerunner of today's U.S. Coast Guard.

then ships had engines—a modernization that lessened the likelihood of running aground. Furthermore, radar permitted "seeing" the shore and other vessels even on foggy nights; and air patrol and radio contact had revolutionized rescue techniques. Today's only remaining rescue station is at the mouth of the Columbia River.

The town of **LONG BEACH** triples in population each July and August, as do the other towns strung along State Route 103. The Long Beach area is where William Clark carved his name into the trunk of a small pine while scouting north from Baker Bay on November 19, 1805. The event is commemorated by a small city park (east side of the highway at Third Street).

Washington's cranberry industry developed from pioneering beginnings on Cranberry Road (just north of Long Beach). A San Franciscan named Anthony Chabot owned several hundred acres of marshland and, having noticed native cranberries growing there, decided to try commercial production. He founded a company and sent his nephew Robert Chabot to Long Beach as an agent. In 1881 the company planted its first cranberries, brought here from Cape Cod. Two years later they hired local white women and children, Chinese, and Native Americans to handpick the crop. Matt Koski, who was raised in Ilwaco, reminisced about the harvest for the county historical society quarterly *Sou'wester*. He described "picking those tiny berries" and the big wooden boxes "that took forever to fill" and added that, "The most rewarding part of this child slavery was when the word came to pack up and go home. And boy, did I work then."

After a decade, the cranberry company went out of business. The cost of shipping was too high, as was preparing the land for planting. Furthermore, imported vines arrived with mildew and pests and were genetically unsuited to the Northwest climate. Speculators considered pressing peat from the cranberry bogs into briquettes for fuel, but abandoned the idea when they realized how much firewood already was available within a reasonable marketing area.

In 1923 the State College of Washington (now Washington State University) opened an experi-

ment station on Pioneer Road, near the former Chabot Bog. There specialist D. J. Crowley worked out sprays to control pests and overhead sprinkling as protection from winter frost and summer scald. (His system is now used not only by cranberry growers but also in orchards, from Washington apples to California oranges.) During the nationwide depression of the 1930s, cranberry growers here had little capital to invest but, after World War II, improving finances let them expand their farms.

(Also see CRANBERRIES sidebar, p. 452.)

LONG ISLAND, part of the Willapa Bay National Wildlife Refuge, lies close to shore at the southern end of the bay. It harbors an ancient grove of red cedars with individual trees as much as 1,000 years old. The grove itself is a self-perpetuating community that has survived for an astonishing 3,000 to 4,000 years. (This dates to about the time that the present climate developed; it had been first substantially colder than now, then warmer, following the close of the last ice age.) The Long Island forest is unmatched anywhere else.

The only access to the island is by private boat; and it has no services or settlements. In the 1870s a community called Diamond City flourished there briefly. Before that native people fished, clammed, gathered oysters, and hunted on the island for centuries—or perhaps millennia. To find the cedars, walk along the main road from the boat landing for about 2½ miles to a loop trail. (Sometimes certain sections are closed for the protection of nesting birds or for scientific studies. Check at the refuge headquarters for current information.)

At **NAHCOTTA** today docks are lined with small boats, including the double-ended gill-netters that are traditional in this area. (The hull design protects against swamping even in rough water, and the open cockpit gives fishermen easy access to nets on either side of the boat.) Gulls perch on huge piles of oyster shells, and men working on the sand flats fork oysters into wire baskets at low tide. Their rain garb stands out as a bright yellow accent against gray waters and sky.

Nahcotta began in 1888 as terminus for a railroad from Ilwaco. It was favored over the already-established Oysterville because of deeper water close to shore. Actually for several years two towns graced this northern end of the train tracks. The community named Nahcotta was platted by the founder of an oyster company capitalized with San Francisco money. Its twin—and for years more successful rival—was Sealand, platted by an Ilwaco canneryman.

The railroad serving the two towns replaced a horse-drawn stage that ran the length of the peninsula—20 miles—on the hard-packed sand of the low-tide beach. This timing by tide was second nature for local people and an appro-priate background for the new train service. Steamers docking at Ilwaco needed a high tide, so the train set its arrival and departure times according to the tide. This basic adaptability gave birth to an extraordinarily flexible schedule. The train might stop to deliver gro-ceries, to unload the crew so it could help catch a runaway horse, or to allow passengers to look at shipwrecks or stranded whales. And if the engineer saw a family with tired children walking toward the depot, he stopped and gathered them on board wherever the train happened to meet them.

The first locomotive burned wood as fuel, a boon for families who earned cash by cutting wood and stacking it along the tracks. Tourist fares provided revenue for the train in summer. The rest of the year the train— officially part of the Ilwaco Railway and Navigation Company, but better known as the Clamshell Line—carried oysters, cranberries, and spruce logs rafted across the bay to be shipped to market from Ilwaco.

In 1900 the Clamshell Line became a branch of the Union Pacific. The new management regularized the schedule, built a tunnel under the hill at Fort Columbia, and connected the rails to deep water at Megler. Today's highway uses the tunnel and also the old railroad grade between Ilwaco and Nahcotta.

A modern State Fisheries laboratory at Nahcotta (Sandridge Road) researches shellfish management. It is not open to the public, but a bulletin board display and taped message describe the life cycle of oysters and the story of the industry at Willapa Bay.

NASELLE. (See p. 423.)

OCEAN PARK strings along the beach with old homes nestled into the protection of pines, and new houses and condominiums defiantly facing the sea—shielded from storms by improved building materials and techniques. Drive or stroll side streets to glimpse the character of the community. Many of the older houses are still owned by descendants of the original builders. Many are still identified by name.

The Wreckage (Cambridge Avenue; built in 1912) is a one-and-a-half story house constructed from logs salvaged when a raft under tow to San Francisco split apart at the river bar. The S. A. Matthews House (Bay and Broadway; built about 1891) is nicknamed the Whalebone House because of bones brought from the beach to the front lawn. The board-and-batten Clam Cottage (Melrose Avenue; built in the 1890s) served as a parsonage. All of the walls of the "Door House" (Wabash and Melrose) are built entirely of paneled cedar doors salvaged from one of the pavilions at the 1905 Lewis and Clark Exposition in Portland.

The community began in the summer of 1883 when a group of Methodists from Portland met here for the sermons, singing, and picnicking typical of camp meetings (similar to those organized about the same time at Pacific Grove in California and Ocean Grove in New Jersey). After 10 years of these meetings the group decided to expand their camp into a summer resort. They offered members land leases and deeds with restrictions against liquor and gambling, a written stipulation many deemed unnecessary since "the class of people who patronize this place is such that nothing of this kind would be tolerated." A summer at Ocean Park was free of vice. It also was thrifty, as noted in a 1906 special Pacific County edition of the South Bend *Journal:*

One feature of Ocean Beach life which commends it to many an overworked paterfamilias is the fact that the pleasure-seeker lives so economically that his enjoyment is not disturbed by fear that he is going beyond his means.

Cottages multiplied as Portland women and children moved to the beach for the summer, joined on weekends by their men. Year-round

The house Tom Crellin built at Oysterville in 1869 faced the bay, as did the others in town at that time; travel was by boat more than by land. Today's houses open to the road.

residents also moved in. Taverns in Ocean Park are still restricted to south of Bay Avenue, a legacy of Methodist beginnings. Today's Taylor Hotel dates from 1887, one of the early resort boarding houses.

OYSTERVILLE, listed in the National Register as a Historic District, is one of the oldest towns in the state—and one of the most beloved by all who have admired its double row of gracefully aging wooden houses and picket fences. Yards are ample, porches comfortably inviting, eaves and gables rich with eye-catching gingerbread and scrollwork and fish-scale shingles.

Oldest of the town's 15 or so original houses is the 1863 Red Cottage (just south of the church), the home of Willard Espy, who wrote the book *Oysterville* as his family's biography. The 1892 Baptist church, no longer used for regular Sunday services, is often open during the travel season and is available for special occasions. A 1904 one-room school is near the northwest end of town, close to where the county courthouse stood beginning in 1855. "South Bend raiders" made off with the court-house records in 1893, ending what many considered the nuisance of having to travel to isolated Oysterville simply to transact a few minutes of business. Oysterville's last cannery, built about 1940, stands abandoned on the waterfront at the north end of town.

Other than a small store and post office at the north end of town, there are no public services or businesses in present-day Oysterville. (The post office, however, is the oldest in the state operated under one name.)

Before the coming of white oystermen, Native Americans harvested and dried Willapa Bay oysters, and even used them as a standardized trade item that amounted to a form of currency. In 1854 Chief Nahcati (Nah'-kah-tee) invited R. H. Espy and I. A. Clark to what became Oysterville in response to their question about where to start an oyster business. The two men arrived by canoe in a fog. Nahcati heard the splash of their paddles and beat on a hollow log to guide them to shore.

Espy had been in the area cutting timber to ship to San Francisco as wharf piling. Clark, a tailor from New York, had newly arrived after modest success in the California gold fields. Both men filed donation land claims and started shuttling canoeloads of oysters across the bay to Bruceport for shipment south. Not long after-ward, San Francisco ships began to call at Oysterville. A store, saloons, and hotels as well as houses quickly mushroomed—and in time there was even a jail so that Espy, the county sheriff, no longer had to board prisoners at his cabin. A "stage"—actually a buckboard with five seats and spaces to stand clinging to the outside—ran up the low-tide beach from Ilwaco.

Passengers from Grays Harbor rode a similar stage to North Cove and then crossed by steamer to Oysterville.

By the 1880s overharvesting had decimated the native oysters, and Oysterville lapsed into genteel decline. East Coast oysters transplanted to San Francisco Bay supplied the market there. Japanese oysters had not yet been tested at Willapa Bay; they were believed too large to sell well.

Windswept **Leadbetter Point** forms the tip of the Long Beach Peninsula and stands guard at the entrance to Willapa Bay. (Drive 3 miles north of Oysterville, first via Oysterville Beach Road, then Stackpole Road. Walk north on the Leadbetter State Park trail, then along the beach. During nesting season the beach may be closed.) The extreme tip of the point is 2 or 3 miles from the parking lot. Spring and fall migrations bring thousands of shorebirds and waterfowl; awesome winter storms batter the beach.

In 1778 the English explorer/merchant John Meares tried unsuccessfully to work through breakers off the point into the quiet, shallow water visible from the ship's mast. He named the bay he could see but not enter "Shoalwater," then coasted on south—and failed to find the Columbia River, previously reported by the Spaniard Bruno Heceta but not yet discovered by Robert Gray.

RAYMOND has a settled-in look. Houses sit in carefully tended yards with well-established plantings. Historic orientation to the water is still apparent. The annual August Loggers Day festival indicates the town's origins.

The public library (Fifth and Duryea) was built in 1929 in a vaguely Tudor-cottage style. Stained-glass windows in the children's area sparkle with *Mother Goose* and *Wizard of Oz* characters, those in the adult section with early English bookplates. The fireplace mantel is inscribed with the words "Great minds live again through books."

Raymond began in 1904 and during the next few years a land company attracted nearly 20 mills and manufacturing plants to tideflats here by offering "free" waterfront sites. Developers filled the piling beneath the retail core with sediment pumped from the waterfront, "thus with one operation deepening and widening

[the] harbor and improving [the] business district," according to newspaper reports. German, Polish, Greek, and Finnish immigrants arrived to work at the proliferating mills.

Shipyards opened during World War I, causing a housing shortage. Old-timer C. S. Beall reminisced about the period in a 1937 issue of the *Raymond Herald:*

We found a house—finally. . . . It had piling underneath, not just spindly uprights. Those pilings gave a great feeling of security as the logs floated about, bumping under the building on high tides. . . . It took a little learning, but ultimately the roar and rumble of cars over planked streets . . . became a soothing lullaby.

SEAVIEW began as a beach resort town in 1881 augmented economically by adjacent cranberry bogs and, briefly, by a commercial clamming enterprise that shipped 8,000 to 9,000 boxes of razor clams a year in the early 1900s.

A 1909 promotional booklet for the entire peninsula singles out the "palatial summer homes" of Seaview and the hotel managers who took "personal interest in their guests and [were] forever organizing parties and expeditions." The Shelburne Hotel (in the heart of town on the beach side of the highway; listed in the National Register of Historic Places) is the last of these early hotels. It actually is two separate buildings linked together in 1911. One is modestly ornate, the other simple. Guests en route here generally came by steamer down the Columbia from Portland, bringing their bags and pets and perhaps even their cow. At Seaview they settled in for two or three months of swimming, clamming, crabbing, and fishing—a vacation pattern fundamentally unchanged except for modern transportation and shorter stays.

At the **SHOALWATER RESERVATION** development consists of a cluster of houses and a store. Beginnings as reserved land date from 1866 when President Andrew Johnson signed an executive order designating 355 acres for the Lower Chehalis and Chinook people. Fifteen years earlier the tribes had signed a treaty presented by Indian Agent Anson Dart, but its terms never were implemented. The Senate withheld ratification, a formality that repeatedly confused native groups. They had no experience with deliberations conducted at great distances by men who were not directly involved with the matters at issue.

Four years after the Dart treaty council, Governor Isaac Stevens urged native agreement to the principal of moving onto reservations, although he declined to specify exact locations. Understandably, the chiefs refused. Eventually the land was specified and 30 to 40 families moved onto the reservation.

SOUTH BEND's character is immediately apparent. Huge piles of oyster shells, docks, fishing boats, and crab processing plants line the shore. False-fronted buildings stand like snap-shots from a 1900s album, and one of Washington's most stately county courthouses sits on a hill in back of town (Memorial and Cowlitz; begun in 1910). If possible, visit the courthouse during business hours to admire the colorful art-glass dome above the rotunda and the scenes of Willapa Bay history, which were painted in the 1940s by a county jail inmate. Stop also at the county historical society museum downtown (1008 W. Robert Bush Drive/U.S. 101); and search out various old

houses in the auspiciously named residential districts of Nob Hill, Quality Hill, and Alta Vista—high gound never subject to the flooding that repeatedly troubled the householders and businessmen in nearby Raymond.

Boom and bust tells much of South Bend's tale. It was founded in 1869 and soon had a large, busy sawmill and a constant line of lumber schooners tied to the docks. In 1889—the year Washington became a state—a group of men associated with the Northern Pacific Rail-road Company bought land at South Bend. The excellent natural harbor attracted them, and they envisioned a seaport linked by rail to the Yakima Valley. The mere word "railroad" triggered a population explosion—from 150 to 3,500 in only five years.

A quick succession of new industries included sawmills, a planing mill, a sash and door factory, a salmon cannery, and a tannin extract factory (using hemlock). That was the boom. The bust that followed was caused by overinvest-ment, speculation, the 1893 national financial crisis, and a railroad line that went only to Chehalis, not to Yakima. Fishing and farming continued nonetheless. So did logging and shipping.

The Tokeland Hotel became popular with beachgoers in the 1890s. Built as a private home, it at first simply accommodated occasional guests, later expanded into a business.

Tokeland Hotel guests sat at long tables and were served a family-style, set menu.

TOKELAND dots the sandy cape at the north end of Willapa Bay. The pavement leading here from Raymond seems as much a road through time as a geographic link. It threads the shore with views of the waves that form a white line as they crash against the shoal at the bay's entrance. There are pilings from abandoned boat docks and log booms, and stakes that mark present-day oyster beds. Trees are shaggy with chartreuse lichen. Emerald pastures stay sodden with rain and a naturally high water table. Sloughs and creeks link bay and land, alternately draining and flooding with every change of the tide.

In Tokeland, houses huddle within the protection of a jetty, and the venerable two-story Tokeland Hotel (listed in the National Register of Historic Places) remains from a time when steamers brought as many as 500 people a day from South Bend and Nahcotta. A small mooring basin for fishing boats and pleasure craft now replaces that former hub of activity, and an abandoned Coast Guard station built in 1920 lingers as a symbol of marine peril and shore vigil.

North Cove, a former resort town and a curving, 3-mile point of beach a few miles west of Tokeland, washed into the bay; only its pioneer cemetery and relocated houses remain. The erosion resulted from drastic changes at the Willapa Bay entrance. Before 1930 the channel alternated first north, then south on a 12-year cycle. But since the completion of jetties at Grays Harbor and the mouth of the Columbia River, this movement has been steadily northward. Fifteen hundred acres where homes and hotels and a lighthouse previously stood are now covered with salt water. The jetties, which affect where sand is deposited, contribute to this change, yet they probably do not wholly account for it. As early as 1869 the *U.S. Coast Pilot,* published regularly as an aid to mariners, noted for Shoalwater Bay (the old name for Willapa Bay):

This bay, as its name implies, is so full of shoals that at low tides about one half of its area is laid bare. Good narrow channels are found throughout its extent, but no direction can be given for running them.

Ironically, pride in the natural excellence of Willapa Bay as a harbor contributed to the present problem at the entrance. Although never a major port, the bay attracted lumber and oyster schooners beginning in the 1850s. Soon after 1900, when federal Rivers and Harbors acts started making development funding available, there seemed to be no urgency for development here. Ships already were coming. And by the 1940s, when a need for harbor improvement arose, public spending priorities had changed.

WILLIE KEIL'S GRAVE. (See under MENLO, p. 439.)

Willapa Hills

State Route 6 threads gently across both landscape and time, conforming to slopes and swales as it winds along the upper Chehalis and Willapa rivers. It offers no spectacle, but is a pleasantly scenic drive through broad, flat farmland edged by wooded hills. There are old barns and new and old farmhouses. Near the Chehalis/Centralia end of the road, modern houses line a ridge: view property has become a resource where once there were only timber and good soil.

The town of Frances holds a Schwingfest each July; Menlo has hosted the county fair every August since 1896.

ADNA grew at Goff Landing, the uppermost point that steamboats could reach on the Chehalis River. Today a side road leads to the old landing, which is unmarked and bypassed by the highway. All river freight and passengers between Grays Harbor and Claquato, a major village, used this landing. Upstream from Adna, only the meager drainage of the Willapa Hills flows into the Chehalis; the river never had deep enough water for navigation except by canoe. Below Adna, snow-fed creeks and rivers draining the Cascade Mountains join the Chehalis and greatly increase its flow.

Adna began in the 1850s. Its early land deeds included a clause prohibiting the sale of liquor and, as a result, the town has never had taverns or saloons.

The **BOISTFORT VALLEY** (Boyst´-fort) provides a bucolic side trip off an already bucolic highway. Pierre Charles, an employee of the Hudson's Bay Company, named the valley when he made it his final home in the 1850s and declared intention to become an American citizen. Boistfort (French for "dense forest," although with a "t" added to *bois*) was the name of a Canadian rendezvous point used by the North West Company before its absorption into the Hudson's Bay Company. That merging brought with it many Nor'westers, Pierre Charles among them.

Settlers began farming the Boistfort Valley in 1851, and within three years their population had increased enough that they organized a public school district, the first in Washington Territory. That emphasis on education did not go unrecognized: in 1855 the Olympia *Pioneer and Democrat* announced: "The University of Washington is proposed to be built in Seattle with a branch at Boistfort Prairie."

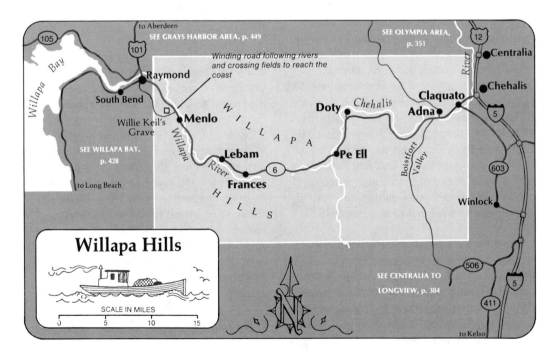

By the 1900s Boistfort Valley hopyards operated huge kilns that included wagon ramps to well-ventilated, second-story drying floors. The large number of workers posed here asssured the itinerant photographer a good sale of this picture.

The valley's first farmers grew wheat, oats, barley, and timothy hay on land that had been thick with camas, a "crop" harvested by native people for its nutritious bulb. From the 1880s to about 1920 hops became the mainstay of agriculture despite the lack of a nearby market: the cones were sold to breweries in England and Germany. Herman Klaber of Boistfort Valley owned what was touted as the largest hopyard and drying kiln in the United States. About 2,000 men, women, and children came each September to pick and dry the crop.

To accommodate them, Klaber provided 400 simple huts, each with a wooden floor, a woodburning stove, and a nearby water spigot. Tents augmented this housing. Whites, Asians, Native Americans, and—in later years—blacks formed their own camps. They worked hard and socialized festively. Schools delayed opening until after the harvest. Stores advertised "Hop Pickers" sales of gloves, straw hats, and children's wool dresses, "just the thing for cold mornings and evenings during hop picking." Merchants accepted hop tickets in place of currency, which was in short supply. The tickets were slips that a foreman punched for each box filled with 125 pounds of hops. This system made early morning the favored time for picking: cones covered with morning dew weighed more than those picked in midafternoon. (An experienced adult needed about three morning hours to pick the 125 pounds.)

World War I closed the German market for Washington hops and imperiled shipments to England. In 1912 Herman Klaber drowned while returning from a hop-selling trip in Europe. He was aboard the *Titanic*. (Also see HOPS sidebar, p. 140.)

Before the arrival of whites, the Boistfort Valley had been the home of the Kwalhioqua people, an isolated pocket of Athapaskans (the natives of interior Alaska and British Columbia). Migrating widely, this language group reached as far south as the American Southwest by the early sixteenth century and there became the present Navajo and Apache tribes. In Washington the forested uplands and open prairies at the headwaters of the Willapa River were their only homeland; it was country similar to what they knew in the northern interior. Surrounding the Kwalhioqua were people who spoke languages totally different from theirs and followed different customs. They regarded the Kwalhioqua as "fierce mountain people."

Evidently the ancestors of the final group of Athapaskans in the Boistfort Valley arrived at least 3,000 years ago. By the mid-1800s they vanished through venereal disease and intermarriage. Their isolated location spared them some of the ravaging epidemics that devastated the surrounding Chehalis and Chinook people beginning in the 1830s, but they lost their separate identity within the "melting pot" of the Chehalis Reservation where people from several (formerly distinct) villages eventually settled.

To reach **CLAQUATO** (Cla-kwah´-toh) turn off I-5 onto State Route 6 just south of Chehalis. (From the historic marker 2 miles after the turn, drive up the hill, then turn left onto Water Street.) The most striking of the town's buildings is a white frame church completed in 1858, the oldest remaining church in Washington. Neighbors in nearby Boistfort Valley presented the original congregation with the pews and pulpit, which are still in use. A bronze bell that came around Cape Horn from Boston hangs in the distinctive belfry, which is designed to symbolize Christ's crown of thorns. Regular worship services still are held here in summer, and the church also is used for weddings, christenings, and other special occasions.

Lewis H. Davis, the town's founder, brought his family West by wagon in 1853, the same year that Washington separated from Oregon Territory. He took a donation land claim on a ridge known as Claquato Hill (*claquato* means "high ground" in Salish). This slight elevation soon made the land desirable for part of a mud-free route from the Columbia River landing at Monticello (now Longview) to the tiny port towns of Olympia and Steilacoom. Davis donated land at Claquato for the road, and the national and territorial governments supplied funds. Settlers volunteered their labor.

The church at Claquato dates from 1858.

A concern for the difficulties of travel had figured in the first requests for funds presented to Congress by territorial representatives. Settlers wanted military roads in case of raids by native people, and Jefferson Davis, the Secretary of War (and president of the Confederacy during the Civil War), personally studied maps and recommended a route along the Columbia and Cowlitz rivers. Specifications for the road required at least a 12-foot width, with stumps left no more than 10 inches high. Swampy places were to be filled with puncheons (split logs laid crosswise) of no greater than 10 inches in diameter—all in all, a decidedly rude roadway across a densely forested land.

In 1855 settlers fled along the road terrified by rumors that the Yakima War might spread to southwest Washington. (See PUGET SOUND WAR sidebar, p. 326.) At Claquato, "half a dozen families, and as many bachelors" took shelter in a hastily built blockhouse. Phoebe Goodell Judson recalled the experience years later:

The quartermaster general of the Claquato Stockade was good Esq. Davis, who did not object to "women's rights" in times of danger. He gave me a musket to carry and I practiced loading and firing at a mark, and, had it become necessary, would have used it in defense of my home and country.

No shots actually were fired, and in time the settlers went home to their crops and livestock.

Stage service along Military Road brought civilian travelers through Claquato, as well as army personnel en route between Fort Vancouver and Fort Steilacoom. In addition, paddle-wheel steamers came up the Chehalis River from Grays Harbor to the Claquato landing at Adna— although shallow water often made it necessary for passengers and freight to come part way by canoe rather than steamer. In 1862 Claquato became county seat. A decade later the Northern Pacific built north from Kalama to Tacoma bypassing the high ground in favor of flats slightly east of town. Chehalis then took over as county seat and Claquato changed from metropolis to backwater.

DOTY (along the Chehalis River just north of today's highway) flourished as a mill town from the 1890s until the onset of the Great Depression.

Its largest lumber mill closed in 1929, and what kept Doty alive was the simple fact that its houses already existed. With automobiles, men began commuting to jobs elsewhere, a pattern that still prevails.

FRANCES today consists of a charming Catholic church, a few scattered houses, and Elk Prairie Road, which loops the site of what was a sizeable town. The plat was filed by a San Francisco lumber company in 1893, when the Northern Pacific Railroad laid tracks through the valley. By then, German and Swiss pioneers were already well settled, and heartache and litigation arose once official surveys were made: many of their claims—held only by squatter's rights—turned out to be on railroad land. The Northern Pacific sold these landholders the acreages they already were living on, a situation that engendered outright hatred of the company regardless of the convenience of having its rails.

A 1909 promotional booklet for Pacific County speaks of two shingle mills at Frances and a sawmill specializing in the production of porch columns. One of the shingle mills, owned by Paul Christen, provided electric lights for the town "when the mill was running." An additional amenity was an all-men community band that played at dances and marched in parades throughout the area, resplendently uniformed. The band leader, Ferdinand Calouri, commuted by train from Chehalis to South Bend to give piano lessons. A Frances optometrist also served a wide area, and Louis Christen, brother of Paul, acted as unofficial doctor/dentist. His "office" was the Christen Brothers Columbia Saloon, where he dispensed home remedies and pulled teeth after first offering a shot of whiskey.

Catholic families walked to Pe Ell to attend Mass, a long, muddy hike. In 1888 a priest from Mount Angel, Oregon, said Mass at one of the pioneer's homesteads and, after train service became available, priests came to Frances fairly often. The present Church of the Holy Family was built in 1892 and enlarged in about 1908 by local craftsmen, who worked without an architect or a contractor. A parishioner's brother, who lived in California, made the stained-glass windows (or, some say, they came from Germany). Altar paintings are from Switzerland, created by the brother of another parishioner.

Each July, Frances celebrates its Swiss ancestry with a Schwingfest, which features Swiss wrestling, yodeling, and—some years—the playing of a 13-foot alpenhorn. The festival is held at the Swiss Society Hall on Elk Prairie Road.

LEBAM (Luh-bam´) is a three-building town plus a school, outlying rural homes, the nearby Willapa State Salmon Hatchery (established in 1899), and evocative road names like Oxbow, Maude's Landing, and Trap Creek.

A fine stand of red cedar attracted the earliest donkey-engine logging in the county; stump ranchers planted fruit trees and hops on cutover land, then turned to dairying. After the Northern Pacific arrived in 1893, Lebam prospered. The town withstood repeated fires but finally, following a fire in the early 1920s, began to dwindle. By then the largest mill had shrunk from a major employer to a small operation producing only piano legs, and the town's bank, barbershop, ice cream parlor—even the saloons—simply did not rebuild after the fire.

Lebam's name is Mabel, spelled backwards. The first name was Half Moon Prairie, but the postal department insisted on something shorter. Complying, the postmaster reversed the letters of his daughter's name.

MENLO—today with a general store and the 1880s Fern Hill Cemetery—began as a dairying center. Cheese factories operated here for 40 years, beginning about 1914 when a local train stopped daily at farms to trade empty milk cans for full ones. Reportedly, farmers tolerated crews dipping out a bit of cream before loading cans on board the train—perhaps minor graft, but far preferable to farmers hauling the milk themselves via muddy roads.

Willie Keil's Grave is just northwest of Menlo, commemorated by a roadside marker (south side of the highway). The Keil story—which has elements suitable for grand opera—begins in Bethel, Missouri. About a thousand idealistic followers of self-styled "Dr." William Keil decided in 1855 to move their communal colony to the Northwest in order to escape the prying of neighbors. Scouts picked Willapa Valley as isolated enough to provide a shield against outside influence, large enough to allow for growth, and forested enough to supply ample building materials. Livelihood would come from farming.

Dr. Keil promised his teenage son Willie that he could ride in the lead wagon heading for "the Willapa Country," but the boy died shortly before the time came for departure. The grieving father filled a zinc-lined casket with alcohol, placed the body in it, and ordered the procession to toil West behind a hearse. Two thousand miles later—with German hymns counterpointing the vast stillness—Dr. Keil buried Willie on a hill above the Willapa River.

Most of the colonists had waited in Portland, Oregon, while Keil decided on a final destination. Only about 10 families went with him to Willapa and, although most of them settled there, Keil himself returned to Portland and selected new land south of Salem for the colony (today's Aurora; worth visiting). He disliked the Willapa land his scouts had picked. Keil said that when the rains had set in his shoes rotted from his feet. The area offered the ample building materials he had asked for, but the forest impressed him as so tangled with undergrowth and fallen trees that it was "absolutely impossible for a man and livestock to penetrate."

The families who chose to live at Willapa stayed in touch with the main colony at Aurora and regularly exchanged visits back and forth.

PE ELL, the largest community between Chehalis/Centralia and Raymond/South Bend spreads comfortably across its natural prairie, a contrast to lumber towns hunkered within manmade clearings. Several houses and a few other buildings remain from earlier days. Outstanding among these are the Masonic Lodge (north side of Main Street, near Sixth), a two-story clapboard building that provided its members with a social center and a sense of fraternal unity, and a Polish National Catholic church (Third and Queen, on the south side of town). Distinctive square towers with octagonal spires rise from the front corners of the church.

Polish and Swiss settlers in the Pe Ell area organized a Roman Catholic parish in 1892. It first was served by Polish priests who came from Tacoma, later by priests from Enumclaw.

When parishioners requested a resident priest, the Seattle diocese assigned a man who was not Polish. Disappointed, Polish speakers decided to separate from English speakers and from Roman Catholicism. They affiliated instead with the Polish National Catholic Church, which let congregations own their buildings, direct parish affairs themselves, and follow a liturgy in Polish rather than Latin. Membership at Pe Ell was open to anyone of Polish or Lithuanian ancestry, or married to a Polish or Lithuanian person. Families worked together to build Holy Cross Church from local materials. They dedicated it in 1916.

Just two years previously, the Northern Pacific had completed its line through the area, linking farmers with markets. A fruit cannery opened in Pe Ell to take advantage of this new, improved means of shipping, and the *Centralia Chronicle-Examiner* ran a story headlined "Southwest Washington Needs Farmers." The report spoke of European demand ready to absorb "every bushel of wheat and barley" that local growers could supply. It also mentioned the new railroad, calling it "another tie to the outside world."

Logging and milling provided major payrolls throughout the area, including the communities of **McCormick** and **Walville,** just west of Pe Ell. The Walville mill was operated by an almost entirely Japanese crew during the labor unrest of the 1910s and 1920s. Owners hired the Japanese because they would work for lower wages than whites and were not unionized. (Unions at that time were for whites only.) Companies shut down during the 1930s Great Depression, and workers drifted away to look for jobs elsewhere.

The explanation of the name Pe Ell has several slightly varying versions. All agree that it stands for "P. L.," the initials of the Hudson's Bay Company employee Pierre Louis Charles. He pastured horses on the prairie that became the townsite, and his son—also Pierre Louis— owned one of the early land claims here.

RAYMOND. (See p. 433.)

SOUTH BEND. (See p. 434.)

WILLIE KEIL'S GRAVE. (See under MENLO, pp. 439-40.)

Upper Cowlitz

U.S. 12 threads the length of the broad and flat Cowlitz River bottom. Just to the north, State Route 508 twists through commercial forestlands. Sheep, cattle, Christmas tree farms, sawmills, barns, occasional two-story farmhouses, and a mix of modern homes characterize both roads. Pavement lies gently and seems to belong to the landscape rather than to overpower it.

Tacoma Public Utilities' dams and hatcheries are along the Cowlitz River. Access to the most spectacular view of effects from the 1980 Mount St. Helens eruption is via the town of Randle. White Pass offers outstanding mountain scenery. Morton has a small history museum. Each August, a Loggers Jubilee is held in Morton.

The **COWLITZ SALMON HATCHERY** (built in 1968) is perhaps the most spectacular fish hatchery in the state. (It is about 6 miles east of Ethel; turn south off State Route 12 on Fuller Road, then east on Spencer; total distance, less than 2 miles.) A glassed-in mezzanine offers an eerie view of the effort of one species (man) to perpetuate others (coho and chinook salmon). A conveyor belt lifts anesthetized fish from a holding tank onto a spawning table. There,

hatchery personnel squeeze the underbellies of males to "milk" their sperm, and hold females by the tail to strip eggs into buckets for hand mixing with the sperm.

Outside, an operator sits in a booth above a series of flumes and shunts unspawned fish into separate concrete ponds according to sex, size, and species. Huge salmon, newly arriving upriver, hurl themselves against the wooden grates.

ETHEL, about 6 miles east of I-5, is a farming community spread comfortably upon broad, flat land where sheep and cattle graze and dahlias brighten the yards of modest homes. It is notable today for the Paul Lindeman house. Two-story, built of hand-hewn cedar timbers taken from a grove on the property, the house was put together without nails in 1886. Wall planks are two feet wide and six inches thick.

Lindeman filed under the Homestead Act after moving north from San Francisco. His wife and family stayed in California for two years until the house was ready. Today it remains one of the least-altered pre-statehood houses in Washington. Watch for it on the north side of the road at Milepost 73, just west of Ethel.

MINERAL takes its name from deposits of

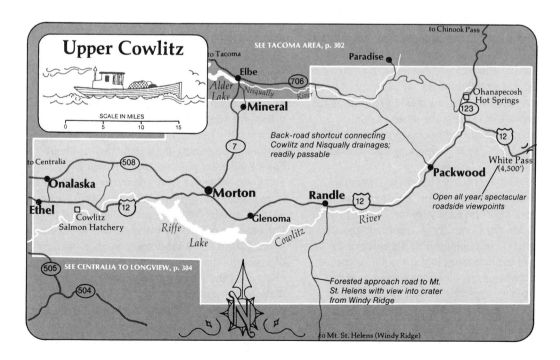

Mineral remains a logging town—now with an excursion train rather than log trains.

cinnabar, an ore rich with mercury, which can be recovered simply by heating in a retort. Indeed, home fireplaces made of local rock ooze spots of mercury.

Mineral spreads along the shores of a mountain lake, reached in summer by excursion steam train from Elbe (14 miles), as well as by road. It has been—and is—a forest products town, known also for a two-and-a-half-story log inn built in 1906. The original owners, a man named Gilfellin, hired Scandinavian craftsmen in the area to build the inn. His hope was to attract wealthy urbanites seeking relaxation. When they failed to come in substantial numbers, Gilfellin added liquor, gambling, and "other vices." These led to repeated raids and closures.

For a while a self-styled doctor operated the inn as a sanitorium for "the alcoholic, the epileptic, and the mildly insane." Later the L. T. Murray Company (a Tacoma logging firm) bought it as a lodge for officials and guests. Present use continues to fluctuate. Even seen from the road, the building is an outstanding example of log architecture.

MORTON is situated in a classic glacier-carved valley with a broad, flat bottom and steep

sidewalls. A small museum in the city park at the west end of town (on State Route 508) displays historic photographs and artifacts. A skid house next door is representative of the distinctive architecture that facilitated moving a logging camp en masse from one site to another as timber was cut. A few remnant skid houses still serve as homes in this area; watch for them near Ashford (State Route 706, approaching Mount Rainier National Park) and Glenoma (U.S. 12, about 7 miles east of Morton). Each August since the 1930s, Morton has hosted a spectacular Loggers Jubilee with woods skills turned into contests.

Four trails intersected at Morton, reason for settlement beginning in the late 1800s. About half of the early pioneers were Scotch Irish and German people from the dirt-poor hill farms of the southern Appalachians. Most came by rail to the Chehalis Valley, then set out on foot or horseback—or later by wagon—for the isolated upper Cowlitz, similar to the mountain "hollers" of home. With "rolling bees," they helped each other clear the land by cutting trees and levering them into heaps for burning. But crops posed a problem. Corn, sweet potatoes, and tobacco brought to the West in seed form did not grow in this climate; instead the newcomers accepted the advice of native people and settlers from northern climates, who recommended growing potatoes and dairying.

Despite this initial farming uncertainty, however, the move was as if to paradise. One ex-Kentuckian living near Morton told his neighbor Woodrow Clevenger about it in the 1930s. He had come here from the South because:

The land thar was gittin' corned-out and settled-up. 'Twas so a man couldn't rustle a livin' anymore— shootin' deer, bear, and turkey. . . . My kin who'd gone West afore me [wrote] how they were makin' good wages at public works [road building,] in the mills, and at trappin', and how easy it was to git a piece o' land and rustle your own meat such as deer, bear, and salmon.

In 1912 the Tacoma Eastern Railroad reached Morton to tap the forests for sawlogs needed by Puget Sound mills. That ended Morton's long isolation and led to rapid growth. By 1929 an automobile road connected between Packwood and Chehalis. It was built almost entirely by hand labor augmented with teams of horses.

ONALASKA is notable for its exceedingly tall smokestack, remnant of a lumber mill and now the focus of a town park. The owner of the Carlyle Mill at Onalaska, Wisconsin, obtained land here as part of his wife's dowry when he married. Cutover land was about all that remained of Wisconsin's once-great forests; consequently in 1914 the company moved its operations to the West. Workers' houses— company owned—stood in two rows along the main street where a wooden sidewalk saved pedestrians from a quagmire of mud.

In 1942 the mill closed, and the company tried to topple the 225-foot stack, intending to cut it into lengths suitable for sale as silos but, as local people today say, "It just was built to stay." The stack is now regarded as a landmark.

PACKWOOD remains a jumping-off point for the surrounding mountains. A National Forest Service district office is at the east end of town (maps and backcountry information available). A frame hotel, continually operated since its opening in 1911, stands alongside the highway in midtown. Across from it is a two-story log library.

In 1907 an enterprise called the Valley Development Company stirred excitement with

Loggers' skid houses rank among the Northwest's indigenous architecture. When an area was too cut over for fallers to continue working, the houses were moved to a new camp.

an ambitious hydroelectric project. They planned to build a dam and enlarge Packwood Lake by bringing water from surrounding creeks by flume. Discharge from the lake would then flow through a tunnel to a penstock and power plant on the outskirts of town (at a point across the river from the present La Wis Wis Campground). The plan was for electricity—or perhaps the whole installation—to be sold to the city of Tacoma.

By 1910 more than a hundred men were at work gauging water flow, building a road, packing in machinery, grading a narrow-gauge railway bed, and surveying flume routes. For a while, the North Coast Railroad Company investigated the project's potential, on the chance they might need to electrify a railway across the Cascades—if they built one. But they never did. Nor did Tacoma follow through on its early expressions of interest in Packwood power. The development company first started stalling its operation, then eventually dismantled the power plant, pipeline, and rails and shipped them all to Portland for sale.

In the 1920s outfitters based in Packwood guided vacationers to Ohanapecosh Hot Springs (now in Mount Rainier National Park) and to Packwood Lake for fishing and hunting. They also worked for the Forest Service and supplied sheepherders who grazed huge flocks in the mountains. Hitching rails lined the road through Packwood, and farmers rented out pastures and sold all the hay they could grow.

The name Packwood honors a member of the wagon train that crossed Naches Pass with James Longmire in 1853. The summer after that harrowing wagon journey, William Packwood joined Longmire in looking for a more sane connection from the Oregon Trail to Puget Sound. He found Cowlitz pass (north of White Pass) and cut a trail over it to the east side of the mountains. He also discovered a coal vein and filed on it, claiming mineral rights. To legally maintain his claim, he returned to Packwood each summer from his home on the Nisqually Flats.

The Ohanapecosh/Stevens Canyon entrance to **Mount Rainier National Park** begins 10 miles east of Packwood. A forested, summer-only back road leading near the Nisqually/

By the 1920s outfits based at Packwood were supplying summer sheep camps, freighting for the National Forest Service, and packing tourists into the mountains on vacation.

Paradise entrance to the park begins just at the east edge of town. (See MOUNT RAINIER, p. 316.)

RANDLE, a small crossroads supply and service center, began in 1866 as the site of a sawmill. Its surrounding area is called the Big Bottom, borrowing a southern Appalachian term for pockets of level land surrounded by mountains. This bottom stretches for 30 miles, the bed of an ancient lake long since filled with glacial and river sediments.

The first outsiders to penetrate the area were Simon Plamondon and two companions, North West Company employees who came from Fort George (Astoria) in the spring of 1820 to investigate trade possibilities with the Upper Cowlitz tribe. They were taken captive when they beached their canoe about where today's freeway crosses the Cowlitz River. Two years earlier Iroquois hunters and trappers working for that same fur-trade company had raped Cowlitz women and in an ensuing skirmish a Cowlitz chief had been killed. Further killing took place when the company sent more Iroquois men to investigate the first attack.

The Iroquois—who caused a great deal of trouble—had been brought in by the North West Company during its final, bitter period of rivalry with the Hudson's Bay Company when their usual voyageurs and hunters were needed east of the Rocky Mountains. Because of the Iroquois, the Upper Cowlitz wanted nothing to do with fur companies. They captured the Plamondon party and held them captive. But after several weeks trust replaced suspicion and Chief Schanewah not only allowed them to continue exploring, he brought them upriver as far as the Big Bottom. The following year, Plamondon returned with blankets and tobacco as gifts. The chief was so pleased that he offered Plamondon his choice among three daughters as a wife; he could see the advantages of a trade alliance with a man such as this. But only a decade later almost all the Upper Cowlitz people were dead. They had no immunity to the "ague" and "intermittent fever" brought by white people, and in 1830 Plamondon wrote:

Those left living fled in terror to the sea coast. . . . The green woods, the music of the birds, the busy humming of the insect tribes, the bright summer sky, spoke of life and happiness, while the abode of men was silent as the grave, and like it, filled with putrid, festering carcasses.

Only two native families were left in the Randle area when the first white settler arrived in 1883. This newcomer was August W. Joerk, a German immigrant who heard of the fertile Big Bottom country and walked up from Chehalis to establish a land claim. The same year that Joerk arrived, an Irishman, a Canadian, and steadily increasing numbers of Tennesseans, Kentuckians, and other southern hill folk also arrived.

Most of the southerners came in twos and threes to join "kin," although in 1906 a man named Colly hired a train coach and, for a fee, brought a contingent of Virginia highlanders to Chehalis. From there, most made their way to the Big Bottom country. Some lived off by themselves, hunting and trapping as they had done in the southern Appalachians. Some cut shingle bolts and floated them downriver to Kelso in early spring "drives." The work required wading the river to keep the bolts afloat, a chilling task that lasted for two to four weeks with no chance to really dry out or warm up.

Another source of cash for settlers was to drive "walking crops" of pigs, cattle, and even turkeys to markets as distant as Chehalis, Kelso, and Puget Sound. The turkeys ran wild feeding on grasshoppers, berries, and whatever they could find, then were fed grain and boiled potatoes as market time approached. Owners clipped wing feathers and hung small bells around toms' necks to assure finding flocks that wandered off into the forest en route to town. Some drives included several hundred turkeys. Young boys welcomed the chance to go along as a way to "get out of the woods and see the sights."

Windy Ridge, the automobile road most closely approaching Mount St. Helens, is accessible from Randle. (Turn south on the Cispus Road, which becomes Forest Road 25; in another 20 miles, turn right on Forest Road 99.) The drive crosses areas of trees knocked over by the 1980 eruption and now lying splayed like bristles on a worn hairbrush. At road's end there are spectacular views into the Mount St. Helens crater and to debris-choked Spirit Lake and the

Fallen trees near Windy Ridge show the force of the Mount St. Helens' 1980 eruption. Plant regrowth began quickly, however, part of a cycle that nature has repeated over and over.

vast tongue of mud that overwhelmed the once-lovely Toutle River valley. Climb the stairway (361 steps) for an even more striking look into the crater and for views of Mount Rainier and Mount Adams.

The **WHITE PASS** highway opened in 1951, linking the logging and farming areas east of the Cascade crest with the sawmills and markets of western Washington. Its completion was the realization of a dream long held by residents of the upper Cowlitz—and of decades of appeals both through the Good Roads Association and to the state legislature.

At first, plans had been to build over Carlton Pass (north of White Pass) and connect with a road to Bumping Lake. Actual work began in 1922 when the National Forest Service started from Randle, building one section of road per year. As their crew neared the summit, the federal Bureau of Public Roads checked the proposed route and decided that White Pass was preferable.

The present highway follows an easy grade notched spectacularly into a cliff and threaded across forested slopes. Drive the route in October to see the golden torches of larch and the crimson of vine maple brightening avalanche runs. Two outstanding viewpoints are the Palisades (2 miles east of the junction of U.S. 12 with State Route 123) and Clear Creek Falls (2 miles east of the summit). Each is accessible via a pull-through loop. The Palisades are a wall of dacite lava columns 500 feet high; they stand like gigantic gray organ pipes brightened with chartreuse lichen. The falls leap as a 300-foot bridal veil of water. The summit of White Pass—4,500 feet above sea level—is high enough for a long season of skiing.

East of the pass, the highway parallels the shore of Rimrock Lake, an irrigation reservoir, then follows the rushing Tieton River. Pines, oaks, and bitterbrush line the road; balsamroot and cheatgrass grow on south-facing slopes; and an irrigation flume strings along north-facing cliffs.

OLYMPIC PENINSULA

Cedar dugout canoe, Hoh River.

LIKE AN INCREDIBLE thumb of forests, wild beaches, deep river valleys, and icy mountains, the Olympic Peninsula holds onto the sense of isolation that made it one of the last regions in the nation to be homesteaded. No road linked the communities of its lowland perimeter until completion of U.S. 101 in 1932, and no electricity reached places like the Hoh Valley until the late 1960s.

In 1792, while exploring for England, George Vancouver wrote: "To describe the beauties of this region will, on some future occasion, be a very grateful task to the pen of a skilled panegyrist." By his time, Spanish mariners had already raised the cross of possession on peninsula beaches and built a short-lived fort at Neah Bay. Sixteen years after Vancouver, a Russian expedition sailed from Silka, Alaska, looking for a suitable place to establish a colony on the Washington coast, but their ship wrecked near La Push and their plan was never implemented.

On today's peninsula Native American villages still resound with the rhythms of ages-old drumbeats and songs as well as with the blare of compact disc players and the throb of diesel fishing-boat engines and outboard motors. Gigantic half-burned stumps—and modern clearcuts—stand as monuments to the conquering of the forest in favor of farms and profits, and fish runs are regulated by a host of interacting agencies and tribes. Even so, logging and fishing still provide the region's economic lifeblood, now augmented by recreation.

Olympic National Park is listed as both a World Heritage Site and an International Biosphere Reserve, and a 5-mile floating bridge across Hood Canal turns yesterday's remoteness into today's respite from city pressures.

Grays Harbor Area

The Grays Harbor area offers a look at logging country, river valleys, a huge bay covering 95 square miles, and smooth sand beaches that have attracted vacationers and clam diggers for more than a century.

The recent story here has evolved from dugout canoes and stern-wheel steamers traveling the Chehalis River in the 1860s to real estate promoters flying prospective buyers to a glitzy strip development at Ocean Shores in the 1960s. Agriculture has progressed from homesteaders peeling and chopping rutabagas for winter cattle fodder to cranberry growers and oyster farmers tending domesticated versions of what their predecessors harvested without need for cultivation.

History-oriented museums are at Aberdeen, Hoquiam, Montesano, Ocean Shores, Taholah, and Westport. Celebrations related to the land and human story include Grayland's March driftwood fair and June cranberry festival, and the Quinault Nation's Taholah Days, held on the Fourth of July weekend. Local artists have painted historical murals on buildings throughout the area. They include "The Story of Aberdeen," painted by school children (Morrison Riverfront Park on the banks of the Chehalis River).

Today **ABERDEEN** and Hoquiam blend together with no obvious separation, but when the towns were new they stood 3 miles apart, each at a river mouth.

To sense Aberdeen's early 1900s sawmilling and shipping heyday, drive along the industrial waterfront (Port Industrial Drive) or sample Wishkah and Heron streets, where concrete, stone, and brick construction was required by city code following a 1903 fire that destroyed 22 blocks. The five-story Finch Building (219 E. Heron; built in 1910) was the first large reinforced-concrete building in the area, reported as a "skyscraper" by the *Aberdeen World*. It stands on 1,200 wooden pilings, now derelict yet a symbol of Aberdeen's transition from a mill town to a city with a merchant and professional class. The architect was Seattle's A. W. Gould.

Workers' bungalows on narrow lots characterize residential neighborhoods built close to waterfront mills. Notice their huge rhododendrons and other mature plantings. By 1900 a "Nob Hill" district developed, with fine homes designed by eastern architects who favored Colonial Revival, Tudor Revival, Mission Revival, and Prairie Style houses. For a look at them, turn off Wishkah or Heron onto North Broadway and continue toward the hill in the vicinity of Benn Memorial Park.

The Aberdeen Museum (111 E. Third, in the old Armory) offers an excellent narrated slide show of historical photographs and a range of exhibits. Craftsmen of the Grays Harbor

A 1903 fire in Aberdeen started in a wooden Hume Street hotel used by loggers and sailors.

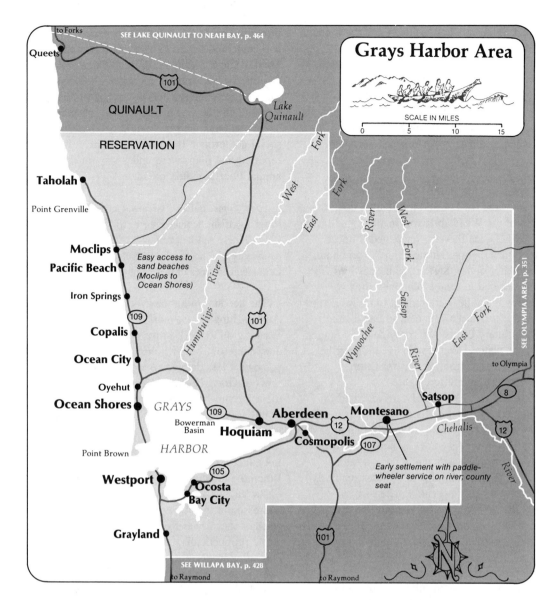

SEE LAKE QUINAULT TO NEAH BAY, p. 464

Grays Harbor Area

SCALE IN MILES
0   5   10   15

to Forks

Queets

101

QUINAULT

RESERVATION

Lake
Quinault

West Fork

East Fork

West Fork

River

Taholah

Point Grenville

Moclips

Pacific Beach

Easy access to
sand beaches
(Moclips to
Ocean Shores)

Iron Springs

109

Copalis

Ocean City

Oyehut

Ocean Shores

GRAYS

Bowerman
Basin

Hoquiam

109

Aberdeen

12

Montesano

Satsop

SEE OLYMPIA AREA, p. 351

to Olympia

8

Satsop River

Wynoochee River

East Fork

Chehalis

12

Point Brown

HARBOR

Cosmopolis

107

Early settlement with paddle-
wheeler service on river; county
seat

Humptulips River

101

Westport

105

Ocosta

Bay City

River

Grayland

SEE WILLAPA BAY, p. 428

101

N

to Raymond

to Raymond

Historical Seaport (east entrance to town) built a full-scale, operating replica of Captain Robert Gray's 105-foot brig *Lady Washington as* part of the 1989 state centennial celebration and next will replicate Gray's other ship, the *Columbia Rediviva.* The two vessels were used on his 1792 fur-trading expedition, which resulted in the discovery of Grays Harbor.

William O'Leary, an Irishman probably deserted from a British ship, settled along the south shore of the harbor in 1848, and was soon joined by others. The 1860 census listed 285 "free inhabitants" in the county, 29 of them foreign born (Canada, Britain, and Norway).

Samuel Benn, another Irishman and the founder of Aberdeen, was among these pioneers. He arrived in 1859 from New York via the Isthmus of Panama and the California gold fields. He staked a claim at the mouth of the Wynoochee River, then hiked to Olympia, built a wagon, hauled his goods (including a 30-foot flat-bottomed sailboat) to the Black River, and floated to the Chehalis River and on to his claim.

After marrying in 1862, Benn traded land with his father-in-law and thus ended up at the mouth of the Wishkah River. In 1877 a neighbor, James Stewart, happened to meet canneryman George Hume in an Astoria hotel lobby. After plying Stewart with questions, Hume decided to send a schooner already loaded with cannery equipment to Grays Harbor instead of to Alaska. Benn, who had a small salmon saltery of his own, provided free land. When he platted Aberdeen six years later, he set aside other waterfront parcels for future industrial use, a rare foresight.

In 1884 A. J. West, newly arrived, laid foundation timbers for Aberdeen's first sawmill (and the third on Grays Harbor, coming after mills at Cosmopolis and Hoquiam). Aberdeen then had only half a dozen buildings, all so close to the riverbank that flood tides regularly sent water seeping beneath kitchen stoves and bedsteads. Woodpiles and outbuildings floated away so often that one family solved the problem by building their chicken house on a raft. The population totalled 17 whites and 13 Chinese cannery workers.

By 1910 a total of 34 lumber mills and shingle mills lined the harbor and tidal portion of the rivers, and Aberdeen's population alone had burgeoned to 17,000. Beyond town, the woods reverberated with the toot of whistle-punks' signals, the crash of falling Douglas firs and hemlocks, and the chugging of steam engines. In town, plumes of steam and cinders rose from the mills, saws whined and rasped, and conveyor chains clanked and groaned as they hauled logs from the holding ponds and through the mills. New men tending the saws and the planers noticed that it was a rare veteran who had all eight fingers and two thumbs.

Unmarried men who worked as mill hands, loggers, stevedores, and sailors roistered through Aberdeen's saloons and bawdy houses and cemented the city's reputation as wide open. Most of those filling the insatiable demand for unskilled labor were immigrants. They banded together in separate enclaves, living in boarding-houses with their own countrymen, patronizing "their" saloons, and building lodge halls for social gatherings. In 1914 the *Aberdeen World* reported that plans were under way for the annual Fourth of July parade:

Swedes, Finns, Italians, Greeks, Germans, English, Russians, Irish, Scotch, French, Swiss, and possibly Chinese and Japanese will take part . . . each nationality . . . headed by men clad in the old-fashioned costumes of the country.

The account might have added Poles and Austro-Hungarians, most of whom had come to Washington to work in the coal mines of Roslyn and Wilkeson, but switched to the cleaner, somewhat less dangerous work in the woods and mills of Grays Harbor; Canadians, the predominant foreign-born group, who had the advantage of culture and language and therefore gravitated toward management and professions; and even a few men from Mexico, Jamaica, Turkey, Lebanon, Afghanistan, India, and Australia. When the old city hall was torn down in 1965 to make way for a new building, a 1905 letter addressed to the city council was found in the cornerstone. It was from Aberdeen Finns who wrote prophetically, "National self-assurance is beginning to disappear. We will be absorbed, not only into Americanization, but into the global society and therein lies the nation's fortune and future."

Through World War I, Grays Harbor boomed with mills, salmon and clam canneries, and shipbuilding yards. In 1920 the last sailing ship to load Aberdeen lumber filled its cargo holds, and the leisurely era of a single winch and half a dozen longshoremen stowing lumber gave way to steamships that tied up for only two or three days while multiple winches hoisted lumber aboard and gangs of stevedores hastily positioned it. Lumber had become a commodity within a world market, subject to price swings which, in turn, caused mill owners to abruptly cut back on production and employment. Aberdeen labor agitation led by the Industrial

For millennia Copalis was a Native American village site; it is now a resort center.

Workers of the World from 1911 through 1917 had achieved little except to entrench owners, determination to manage mills as they saw fit. Wages fluctuated according to mill orders and, when necessary, families relied a bit more heavily on their gardens and clam digging and fishing.

Gradually, however, genuinely hard times set in. National Prohibition had closed the saloons, and technological improvements reduced manpower needs. By the 1930s, the nationwide depression idled nine major Grays Harbor mills. When there were strikes, owners imported Filipino and Hindu workers and paid them at half the rate of their regular workers.

As the economy recovered, diversification into plywood plants, furniture mills, paper mills, door factories, pulp mills, and chemical companies softened Aberdeen's stagnation, but the city never regained its early vigor.

(Also see HOQUIAM, p. 454.)

BAY CITY. (See under WESTPORT, p. 461.)

COPALIS (Co-pay´-lis) is a beachside supply and resort center. Digging for razor clams at low tide has drawn vacationers here for generations, and during the 1930s Great Depression the clams provided livelihood for itinerant diggers and families. Nighttime low tides turned the velvet black beach into an oddly choreographed ballet of bobbing lanterns as diggers filled five-gallon kerosene cans with clams and emptied them into big-wheeled carts, which they pushed

along the beach. Small canneries at Copalis and Oyehut (near Ocean Shores) bought the catch for two cents per pound.

Driving on the firm, smooth sand still is permitted under a 1901 law that established beaches as part of the state highway system. For safety, use moderate speed and drive the beach only on an outgoing tide; the high number of tow trucks in the area have a reason for being here. Driving on the clam beds (extreme low tide zone) is illegal.

In early settlement days the beach linked homesteaders living up the creek valleys with Grays Harbor. They would walk to Oyehut, then go by boat to Hoquiam. Old-timers described this natural highway as "quite satisfactory for most of its length except when the tides were full." A man named Ben Grigsby operated a freight business along the beach from Taholah to Oyehut (with rudimentary wagon roads scratched out over the headlands). About 2 miles north of Copalis he built a halfway house that served as post office and rendezvous point and offered limited supplies.

About 4 miles north of Copalis, Dr. O. G. Chase opened the area's first resort at **Iron Springs.** By 1900 he was promising cures "by the use of Professor Beckwith's ozone battery and the rare mineral waters cropping out of the rocks at the sanitarium." The reddish iron stain is still apparent at the creek, and the resort is still popular—although with no therapy other than scenic beauty and the endless rhythm of the surf and tides.

CRANBERRIES

Cranberries have grown wild on peat bogs near Grayland since the end of the last ice age. Native Americans here called them *pil-olallies* and used them for food, poultices, and red dye. As early as 1851, the schooner *Sea Serpent* carried 20 barrels of the berries to San Francisco along with its primary cargo of Willapa Bay oysters.

In 1912 Aberdeen pioneer Sam Benn prepared several bogs for commercial production. He imported bushes from the cranberry-producing areas of Massachusetts and sold developed plots to Finnish immigrants, who found cultivating cranberries not unlike tending lingonberries in the old country. Small cranberry farms of 10 to 15 acres produced enough fruit to support a family—and they still do. The process is almost like gardening. It begins with clearing a peat bog, then sanding and ditching it, and digging an irrigation pond. Sprinklers jutting a few inches above the bushes now provide spray to protect blossoms against frost and ripening berries against summer scald, as well as to keep the underlying bog constantly damp.

These preliminary steps are expensive, but a properly established cranberry bog will produce for generations. The first full harvest, after about six years, yields five to 10 tons of berries per acre—and four times that amount for some new varieties. The production is astonishing when visualized in terms of grocery-store packages per acre.

Winter fields appear as lumpy mats of reddish vegetation. Spring bushes begin to bloom—and to need human vigilance against frost damage. In summer, the main chore is to guard against weeds, fungi, and insects. October is harvest time: four or five pickers are enough for a typical farm today—a contrast to the old days of hand picking when scores of workers crept through the bogs on their knees gathering cranberries in wooden scoops shaped like dustpans with projecting fingers. Erstwhile bunkhouses for these harvest hands now serve as storage sheds for tools and supplies.

On the Long Beach Peninsula south of here, most cranberries are "wet harvested": workers flood bogs; knock off berries with mechanical beaters; and float them onto conveyor belts that run to bogside trucks. Such harvesting is suitable only for berries to be processed into sauce or juice. At Grassland, most cranberries are for the fresh market, which requires dry harvesting. This method depends on a mechanical harvester like an oversized lawnmower, which simultaneously crops the berries and prunes the bushes. An expert operator learns to "feel" the appropriate cutting depth. Carts pushed along rails carry the berries and twigs to the warehouse where a blower separates them. Trucks then cycle repeatedly between Grayland and a processing plant at Markham on the south shore of Grays Harbor about 10 miles distant.

(Also see under LONG BEACH, p. 430.)

COSMOPOLIS, the oldest town on Grays Harbor, gives few clues to its varied past, but on a hill above the waterfront the Neil Cooney mansion dates from boom days (802 E. Fifth; built in 1910, now used as a bed-and-breakfast inn). Cooney built the house to display his company's products: every room features Sitka spruce paneling, wainscoting, and beams.

In 1852 James Pilkington filed on a donation land claim at the site of the present town. Three years later Quinault, Quileute, Chehalis, and Chinook native people met in his clearing with territorial governor Isaac Stevens, who failed to secure the treaty agreement he sought despite a week of exchange. In 1851—before Washington became a separate territory from Oregon—Anson Dart, Superintendent of Indian Affairs, had also tried to negotiate a treaty. He first suggested that coast people move east of the Cascade Mountains, which they of course refused to do. Eventually Dart obtained "signatures," but when none of the promised payments arrived, chiefs expressed contempt for the newcomer whites.

Stevens, too, suggested consolidating coast tribes' territory on a single reservation. The natives refused, although some spokesmen were willing to sell part of their land if they could also keep some. The following year a treaty was signed establishing the Quinault Reservation, but several groups neither agreed to the terms nor moved to the reservation.

Not long after the treaty council on his land, Pilkington abandoned his claim. Others homesteaded in the area and tried to make a success of various industries. A brickyard failed for lack of suitable clay. A tannery, which used hemlock bark, had ample tanning materials but few hides. A waterpowered gristmill failed for a lack of grain, although the defeat turned to success in 1878 when a new owner converted the machinery to a sawmill. Trees, after all, *were* abundant. Furthermore, settlers were beginning to need lumber.

In 1882 the giant lumber firm of Pope and Talbot bought the mill, enlarged it, and created a subsidiary called Grays Harbor Commercial Company. (For Pope and Talbot, see PORT GAMBLE, p. 375.) Unlike other Grays Harbor communities, Cosmopolis became a company town with bunkhouses, a huge messhall where Chinese cooks served 1,200 men per meal, and a company store.

Lumberman Neil Cooney arrived in town as a shipwright and worked up through the ranks until he became owner of the Grays Harbor Commercial Company in 1920. Cooney ruled with a hot temper that made "his name among the workers as infamous as Satan's." He paid lower wages than those at other mills, and workers who objected to the pay, the mill conditions, or the town could simply move on. It was all the same to Cooney. He had a standing order with a Seattle labor contractor for new mill hands. One recruit remembered that "it took three crews to run the mill, one coming, one going, and one working."

The Grays Harbor Commercial Company closed in 1929, a victim of the Depression. Eventually, the Weyerhaeuser Company bought the property and built a pulp mill.

At **GRAYLAND** (about 6 miles south of Westport) cranberry bogs provide the main interest, especially attractive in spring when pinkish white flowers crown the low bushes. Drive the side roads east of the highway to see the fields; in October—the harvest time—be alert for large trucks on the narrow roads.

Each March Grayland hosts a driftwood show

Today cranberry picking is partly mechanized, but total production remains extraordinarily labor intensive. Commercial bogs in Washington cover about a thousand acres.

Gigantic log jams resulted from the use of splash dams, which provided a way to float logs downstream by opening sluice gates and releasing immense rushes of ponded water. Logging companies operated scores of such dams in the Grays Harbor area.

at the community hall, which draws participants from throughout the Northwest. Beach-gleaned entries vary from elegant, natural "sculptures" to mere "found objects," still slightly sandy.

Three miles north of Grayland, walk the Shifting Sands Nature Trail at Twin Harbors State Park to sense the distinctive character of the coast here. The trail winds through coastal pine and Sitka spruce and across sand dunes to a broad beach. Ten to 15 waves roll in at any given moment, their leaping bands of foam fading into white mist that stretches for miles both north and south.

(Also see CRANBERRIES sidebar, p. 452.)

In **HOQUIAM** a prime attraction is the Robert Lytle mansion, "Hoquiam's Castle," listed in the National Register of Historic Places (515 Chenault; built in 1897). Lytle and his brother Joseph, who built the Queen Anne–style house next door to the castle, operated one of Hoquiam's most successful lumbering operations. Robert Lytle's house was designed by Watson Vernon, the architect also responsible for the county courthouse in Montesano. Additional homes in the neighborhood warrant a drive-by look for insight into Hoquiam's social stratification during its lumber and shipbuilding heyday. Sample especially Bluff Avenue and other streets with expansive outlooks.

The Polson Museum (1611 Riverside Avenue, which is U.S. 101 through town) is the former F. Arnold Polson home built in 1923. Notice its knot-free hemlock floorboards, which run the length of each room, an indication of the premium lumber available here at the time. The museum exhibits logging equipment and Grays Harbor memorabilia.

Early settlers began grazing cattle on the Hoquiam tideflats in the 1850s. To market the beef, they shipped cattle by scow up the Chehalis River, then herded them to Olympia, or sometimes as far as the British Columbia mines. Women milked dairy cows and churned butter, which they stored in barrels of brine. During the rainy season the normally shallow Black River ran deep enough that Native American canoe men could freight the butter to Olympia.

In 1882 Grays Harbor's vaunted timber attracted California lumberman Captain Asa M. Simpson. He bought 300 acres at the mouth of the Hoquiam River and built the North Western Mill, one link in his 900-mile chain of logging operations that stretched from Washington to California.

A few years later Simpson bankrolled a shipyard adjacent to the mill and began building a schooner to carry lumber and a tugboat to bring ships across the Grays Harbor bar. About that same time the Polson brothers arrived from

Nova Scotia and gradually developed a logging operation that included two tidewater sawmills, a shingle mill, 12 logging camps, and 100 miles of logging railroad. In a single year, from 1889 to 1890, Hoquiam's population rose from 400 to 1,600 as workers streamed in to man saws and load ships.

Ironically, the town was isolated although connected by its exports to capitals around the Pacific rim. Local travel entailed rowing across the Hoquiam River and slogging a muddy 3-mile path to Aberdeen. A plank road built in 1890 improved the situation, but not much. Indeed, local wit Charlie Gant wrote:

Did you ever try to ride it on a buggy or a bike,
A lumber cart or stage-coach for all are just alike—
And bump against the knotty boards with mammoth
    cracks between?
It's a regular "liver turner" is the road to Aberdeen.

In 1892 the Northern Pacific Railroad built a line from Chehalis to Grays Harbor, but instead of ending at one of the established mill towns, it skimmed through Cosmopolis and continued west to Ocosta-by-the-Sea (see under WESTPORT, p. 462). Hoquiam and Aberdeen citizens yearned for a railroad connection and banded together to build a spur. Mill owner J. M. Weatherwax donated rails salvaged from a wrecked British ship (and so pitted from six years on the sea bottom off Oyehut that old-timers say the tracks never gave a smooth ride). A. J. West donated ties cut in his Aberdeen mill. And Aberdeen booster Sam Benn gave a free lot to every volunteer who put in 10 days of work on the roadbed.

In 1895 this homegrown line connected the Northern Pacific tracks to Aberdeen and four years later it reached Hoquiam. Aberdeen's head start gave it an advantage that Hoquiam never overtook. Even today Aberdeen remains the commercial hub of Grays Harbor and Hoquiam settles for being the town next door.

Park along its docks by the Hoquiam River to sense the town's character, with gulls by the hundreds and small fishing boats by the score. The bustle of the sawmilling glory days is long gone, and the human pace flows at the same easy rate as that of the winding river. Boom boats and men with caulked boots and peaveys no longer shove floating logs, and pilings rise as useless derelicts steaming silently as their wood slowly rots. What few raised log scaling platforms remain now sit by the highway, not by the river. (Also see ABERDEEN, p. 448.)

Immediately west of Hoquiam, **Bowerman Basin** provides a vantage point for seeing how big Grays Harbor is. Twelve miles wide, it reaches inland for 17 miles, one of only eight

The 1859–1860 legislature voted to maintain the Chehalis as a navigable river. As a result, river steamers joined oceangoing ships along Hoquiam's waterfront. The 110-foot Montesano *was launched at Cosmopolis in 1889 as the era of sail gave way to steam.*

natural harbors along the West Coast between Mexico and Canada. In spring and fall the basin's wetlands furnish resting and feeding grounds for as many as 50,000 shorebirds at a time. The last week in April is the best time to see them—ideally, at high tide when they are concentrated. At low tide they spread across the mud flats to feed. (Follow State Route 109 west from Hoquiam. Turn left on Paulson Road and continue for about a half mile to the airport. Park near the hangars and walk to the end of a nearby sandspit.)

About 22 miles north of Hoquiam, U.S. 101 crosses the **Humptulips River,** which drains the famous Township 21, Range 9, known in logging circles for its stupendous yield of virgin Douglas fir. To handle the output, Al Stockwell of Aberdeen formed the Humptulips Boom and Driving Company. It operated 27 splash dams on the east and west forks of the upper river, floating logs to Stockwell's booming ground on the lower river, where they were sorted and rafted for delivery to the mills. The dams were sturdy, cribbed log structures as much as 45 feet high and with up to eight sluice gates that could be opened to release a sudden burst of water. Its force swept logs that had been rolled into the riverbed toward tidewater. The water and the wildly churning logs utterly devastated riverbank vegetation and fish spawning grounds.

Splashing began as early as 1884 in Grays Harbor and lasted into the 1930s. State regulations required fish ladders with dams, but none were built here, and the dams effectively blocked more than half of the area's salmon-spawning potential. In the 1950s the state ordered scores of abandoned dams removed, and the fish responded almost immediately, reclaiming waters that were again accessible.

A Northern Pacific spur to **MOCLIPS** served two purposes beginning in 1903: it connected a score of shingle mills with Grays Harbor, and it brought tourists to the resorts along North Beach, as the coast between Grays Harbor and Point Grenville is called. Moclips was the end of the line and therefore a major supply point and destination. Its 300-room hotel stood on pilings only a few steps from the depot until 1911 when storm waves destroyed about half of the buildings in town, including the hotel. An exceptionally high tide coincided with flooding at the mouth of the Moclips River, and the combination formed an eddy that swirled around pilings. A *Seattle Times* reporter wrote that the hotel

which had been swaying and teetering in the wind since midnight went down with a crash that could be heard above the roar of the storm. Fifteen minutes

The three Schafer brothers, sons of a Satsop Valley pioneer family, developed an oxteam operation into one of the largest and most successful logging companies in the county.

after it hit the beach, the wood was ground to match-wood and scattered along the coast.

As cedar has become increasingly scarce, mills at Moclips have closed, and the population has declined although the beauty of the beach continues to draw tourists.

Turn into **MONTESANO** (Mon-teh-say´-no) about 10 miles east of Aberdeen for a look at regional history impossible to attain at highway speed. The town is small in size but large in importance. It has been county seat since 1886. Montesano's newspaper, the *Vidette,* has been published continuously since 1863 when increasing timber claims, each requiring publication of legal notice, led to its establishment. Steamboats began churning this far up the Chehalis River as early as 1859. Twenty years later the *Vidette* reported that "vessels drawing 15 feet of water can be loaded as well on the upper river as on the harbor" and that Montesano offered regular steamer connections with San Francisco.

By 1885 a Union Pacific subsidiary line reached Montesano, and the *Vidette* reported that the "Northern Pacific [is also] in the race to the ocean." Traffic was so heavy that the Montesano city council in 1889 funded construction of a "pest house" west of town, reasoning that "constant travel to and from the Sound, and other places where [smallpox] exists, is liable to bring it to the city." Such local quarantine centers were common at the time.

The Grays Harbor county courthouse (Broadway W. at First; opened in 1912) dominates the town with its soaring clock tower and pillared entrance. Inside, a marble stairway rises between facing murals of Captain Robert Gray discovering Grays Harbor in 1792 and Governor Isaac Stevens conducting a treaty council at Cosmopolis in 1855 (this painting is a fanciful rendition with teepees and feathered head-dresses, which were never actually a part of Native American life here).

At the top of the stairs and to the left is the oak-paneled courtroom where 11 "Wobbly" defendants stood trial for the 1919 shooting of American Legionnaires during an Armistice Day parade in Centralia. (See CENTRALIA, p. 387; also see WASHINGTON WOBBLIES sidebar, p. 255.) "Several hundred witnesses and additional hundreds of spectators" flooded into town for the trial, according to a 1920 American Legion booklet:

Hotels being overcrowded, the large rooms of the City Hall were pressed into service, private citizens opened their homes for visitors and, for the ex-servicemen in attendance, the upper floors of garages were fitted into barracks. . . . Legionnaires came from every corner of the state, in uniform, to prevent any intimidation of the trial by the I.W.W.

Ideally, approach the courthouse up First Street from Pioneer Avenue to see the setting and the comfortable homes backdropped by forested hills. The city hall (Broadway and Main; built in 1914) stands a block to the east, readily identifiable by its Mission-style architecture. Also drive—or walk—the neighborhood around the courthouse (especially behind it) for a look at 1890s and early 1900s houses. The Charles N. Byles house (121 Broadway W.; now used as a funeral home) was built by a man who came West as a nine-year-old, traveling with the 1853 wagon train across Naches Pass. He platted part of his farm west of Montesano's present Main Street and donated a site for the original courthouse. The huge, half-timbered Schafer house (207 N. Main), built by one of the county's most successful loggers, featured a walnut-paneled library with curved, leaded windows, a tearoom with birds painted on the ceiling, and a sunroom with an Italian tile floor and gold-leaf decoration. Montesano was a busy center of government, commerce, and social grace, *not* a small town bypassed by travelers hurrying between Olympia and Aberdeen.

Isaiah Scammon and his wife Lorinda settled here in 1852, claiming land opposite the mouth of the Wynoochee River. Their home became a de facto hotel offering accommodations and stern house rules. Travelers who once brought a keg of whiskey onto the porch to enjoy through a long evening watched Lorinda roll it into the river. Others who cleared a Bible from a table in order to play cards were ordered to put the Bible back and leave the house. Scammon, "a man of tireless industry," according to those who knew him, served as postmaster and judge for the surrounding area and operated a ferry with rates set by the territorial legislature at 50 cents for a man and horse, 75 cents for a horse and carriage, and $1 for two horses or oxen with a wagon.

In 1860 the county's 74 voters—all of them white men, since women, Native Americans, blacks, and Asians were not yet allowed to vote—picked the "Scammon Place" as county seat. The home/hotel/post office then became also the courthouse, a role it filled until 1886 when the records were taken across the river to Montesano. A pioneer museum is housed in a 1906 church building at the west side of town (703 W. Pioneer).

For a side trip, drive along the **Satsop Valley,** settled in the 1860s and 1870s by French Canadians and Germans, including the John Schafer family, who moved here from Wisconsin. The three Schafer brothers formed one of the area's biggest logging companies, which grew from an oxteam operation to a timber ownership served by miles of logging railroad.

The valley today is characterized by green fields, huge barns, cutover hills, and two atomic towers atop a ridge south of the towns of Satsop and Elma. At 500 feet high, the towers are among the Northwest's tallest skyscrapers. Begun in 1968 and never completed, the installations—along with three others at Hanford—are also the region's greatest financial embarrassment, a $24-billion fiasco that generated scandal rather than electricity and earned the Washington Public Power Supply System an acronym mispronounced as "whoops." Owing to staggering cost overruns, strikes, and contracting mismanagement as well as public concern about nuclear safety, work here halted on one plant (only 17 percent complete) in 1982 and on the other (nearly finished) in 1983. The towers' future remains uncertain.

The **Wynoochee Valley** draining from the Olympic Mountains to Montesano offers a pleasant drive through farmland into the fabled timber country of Grisdale. A readily passable road leads southwest from there to connect with U.S. 101 between Hoquiam and Lake Quinault.

Today **OCEAN CITY** is a community of private summer cottages and trailer resorts plus a state park about 3 miles south of town. As early as 1890, when homesteading the ocean-front and creek valleys here became particularly active, a land developer named John Banta commented: "The beach is all taken up by parties who think it will be a great summer resort some day."

From the 1870s until 1903 towers used by sea otter hunters stood in the surf along the entire beach between Point Grenville and Point Brown (south of today's Ocean Shores). Twenty to 60 feet high and topped with a shelter just big enough for one man, the towers gave a vantage point for shooting sea otters, which came close to shore to feed on clams. Private Harry Fisher, who crossed the southern Olympics from Hood Canal to Grays Harbor as part of an 1889 army exploration, described the scene:

Derricks were constructed near the low tide line. Once the hunter gained his cache there was no escape from it until the tide receded. . . . A rule is established that each man is allowed but one lookout [tower] and that no closer than half a mile to his neighbor's. Each hunter has his own private mark upon his bullets, and when an otter is supposed to have been wounded the beach is walked in that vicinity three or four times per day until the sea gives up its dead.

The hunters told Fisher that otters had become so scarce they considered themselves lucky to get three or four in a season (from May to October). In 1903 hunting sea otters became illegal; no pelts were openly marketed from then until 1968 when Aleutian sea otter furs were auctioned in Seattle for $1,000 each.

Of **OCEAN SHORES** a 1970s *Seattle Times* columnist remarked that "10 years makes a pioneer." The community strings along the sand dunes and swales of the 6-mile peninsula at the north entrance to Grays Harbor. It is the product of mid-twentieth-century real estate "booming," as surely as Ocosta-by-the-Sea was the product of 1890s dreams, although Ocosta at least expected a railroad, whereas Ocean Shores always knew it was not on the road to anywhere else. (See **Ocosta** under WESTPORT, p. 462.) Another difference is that Ocosta essentially vanished before it really appeared. Ocean Shores residents, however, managed to wrest control of their community away from the development

During the 1930s depression, razor clams gave subsistence income to squatters who lived along the beach; the clams now are dug for sport.

hype and Hollywood celebrity investors that began it.

Ten years of real estate deals and trumped-up glitter left a legacy of "city" streets crossing mostly empty land and a four-lane, limited-access entry boulevard with complicated intersections but little traffic. Beyond that historical—however recent—origin, the town offers a range of accommodations and a long, broad sand beach. At times a ferry connects from Point Brown, at the mouth of Grays Harbor, across to Point Chehalis. A historical society museum highlights the sequence of local events.

Before Ocean Shores developers arrived, Ralph Minard owned land homesteaded by his grandfather A. O. Damon in 1878, plus additional acreage he had purchased. His cattle ranged the entire peninsula south of Oyehut on land otherwise little used except by occasional duck hunters and squatters who subsisted by digging clams. In 1956 Minard bought the new land accreted along the oceanfront as Grays Harbor jetties (completed in 1916) changed natural currents and caused sand to accumulate. A 1928 law granting adjacent property owners rights to "new land" formed the basis of the purchase. An earlier law, however, reserved new land for public ownership, and the matter was settled only by a State Supreme Court ruling in Minard's favor.

In 1959 developers bought 6,000 acres of uplands, beach, swamps, ponds, and beaches—including the accreted land—from Minard. They laid out drainage ditches and suburban lots on cul-de-sac streets, built a restaurant nightclub and motels, flew in prospective buyers, and cycled themselves through promises and bankruptcies until 1970, when Ocean Shores residents voted to take control of Shangri-La themselves. Since then, churches, medical facilities, a library, and other amenities of daily living have developed and, although the town is tourist and vacation oriented, it also has a core of year-round residents. The North Beach high school, built in 1989, replaced the previous consolidated school at Moclips, an action that typically affects the destiny of small towns. What began in the 1960s as Las Vegas north has become a hometown complete with high school.

OCOSTA. (See under WESTPORT, p. 462.)

PACIFIC BEACH, 32 miles north of Hoquiam, became one of the larger communities along this stretch of the coast when the navy opened a research station in 1958. Almost a century earlier the land had been part of a claim staked by a sea otter hunter named Henry Blodgett. He gave one acre to a fellow otter hunter, who sold it for the development of a beach hotel. During World War II, the navy took over the hotel as billet for an anti-aircraft gun-nery school and, in 1958, they converted the installation to high security research generally thought to deal with underwater devices for submarine detection. In 1987 the navy closed the research operation and converted facilities back to recreational use. Nothing of the original resort hotel remains, nor is the present one open to the public.

In the 1920s a plank road "improved" the old system of using the low-tide beach as a natural highway. A road seemed necessary with towns platted, resort hotels drawing tourists (who came by train), shingle mills providing wages, and automobiles becoming increasingly common. Construction, however, involved little more than laying 12-inch planks lengthwise and lining their inner edges with 4 by 4s to keep wheels from slipping off into the swamp. Cars passed each other only at turnouts spaced sporadically along the way. Even so, the road here was better than its counterpart from Grays Harbor to Westport. There, in the words of one old-timer, "when the tide was high the whole thing would be floating."

State Route 109 crosses **POINT GRENVILLE** slightly inland—without an ocean view—but crashing waves, jagged rocks, and a sand beach make the southern base of the bluff scenic. (All beaches on the Quinault Reservation—including this one—are subject to tribal regulation. Non-Quinaults must obtain passes from the tribal office in Taholah before going onto them. New satellite aids to navigation have rendered the former Loran station at Point Grenville obsolete, a modern effect at a historic headland.

On July 14, 1775, the Spanish explorer Bruno Heceta rowed ashore here with his chaplain Fray Benito Sierra, three ship's officers, and 20 armed seamen. Their purpose: to plant the cross of possession and formally claim this land for King Carlos III. The men lingered only briefly—not even long enough for Sierra to say Mass—because the *Santiago* was not well anchored. Meanwhile its accompanying ship, the *Sonora,* commanded by Juan Francisco Bodega y Quadra, had paused at the river mouth near the village of Taholah and traded some strips of metal for salmon, whale meat, and other food.

In the evening Bodega y Quadra sent a seven-man party ashore to replenish water and firewood supplies. Native men attacked them and killed five of the seamen; the other two

drowned while trying to escape. Village chiefs owned their beaches and must have regarded the shore party as both stealing and showing disrespect. Furthermore, the natives had tried earlier to trade for the fittings of the shore boat, which they still wanted. When canoes approached, the Spaniards opened fire, killing six or seven men and wounding others. They then raised sail and departed. Heceta turned back toward San Blas, Mexico. Bodega y Quadra continued north.

At the time Spain claimed the land north of Mexico but had little idea of its extent or nature. By the late 1700s, however, the Russians were expanding down the coast from Alaska; the British outfitted Captain James Cook for his voyage of discovery; the French—reading Cook's reports—sent Comte I. F. G. de la Pérouse to the coast; and American sea captains had joined the growing commerce and exploration. This international rivalry prompted the Spanish viceroy in Mexico to send ships north. In 1789 Spaniards opened a fort at Nootka Sound (on the outer coast of Vancouver Island). Six years later they closed it and withdrew their interests from the Northwest.

QUINAULT RESERVATION. (See under TAHOLAH, this page .)

SATSOP. (See under MONTESANO, p. 458.)

TAHOLAH, at the mouth of the river draining from Lake Quinault, and Queets, on the next major river to the north, are the only two villages on the Quinault Reservation. The Quinault History Foundation maintains a small exhibit center with historic photographs in Taholah (122 W. Quinault, immediately behind the tribal office). Passes for reservation beaches may be obtained during business hours at the tribal office. Also, arrangements can usually be made for a fishing guide (salmon and steelhead) or a trip on the river; often these arrangements need to be made in advance. Taholah Days, held over the Fourth of July weekend, is open to the public. As its highlight, cedar dugout canoes fitted with outboard motors race from the ocean 32 miles up the river to Lake Quinault.

In 1855 Governor Stevens held a treaty council at Cosmopolis, intending to establish a reservation for coastal tribes somewhere between the Quinault River and Cape Flattery. The council ended without agreement, but later that year Indian agent Michael Simmons met with Quinault and Queets chiefs and concluded a treaty with them. On January 25, 1856, the governor signed papers establishing the reservation, and three years later its ratification came from Washington, D.C. In 1873 the reservation was enlarged to 190,000 acres, giving it the size apparent on a map—actually a misleading impression because the land is divided by ownership and uses which leave little for the Quinault Nation as a whole. The chaos has come about as a result of various court rulings.

Quileute and Hoh people were originally assigned here along with the Quinault and Queets. Their territories lay close by to the north, yet these people spoke a language entirely different from Quinault. In 1907 the government began allotting 80-acre parcels of reservation land to individuals of the four groups, each acreage carrying legal title and the right to sell it at any time to any person. In 1932 the U.S. Supreme Court ruled that members of the Chinook, Chehalis, and Cowlitz tribes—also entirely separate groups—were also to be allotted land on the reservation.

By 1933 the Quinaults owned no land as a tribe. It all had been allotted and much of it had been sold to timber companies, which stripped the cedar and spruce forest and damaged the salmon waters without regard for the destruction. About a third of the reservation is still in timber ownership, although the tribe is actively trying to buy up these interests. Individuals—some of them whites—own the rest of the land except for about 5 percent, which is tribal. With this small base, today's Quinault Nation manages a fisheries program complete with a salmon hatchery and fish-processing plant and a commercial razor clam business. A tribal forestry division seeks to correct past abuses.

WESTPORT has been a commercial fishing and sportsfishing port—and it still is, although now with more worry than ebullience owing to the scarcity of fish. Even so, the town remains a mecca. Stroll its half-mile-long fishing dock at the north end of town. West of town, watch surfers or walk the dunes-crest trail at Westhaven

State Park; also notice the old Westport Lighthouse, now far from the water's edge owing to land accreted since the construction of jetties (which cause major changes in nearshore currents and deposition of sand). Gray whales still migrate close by on their long journeys between Mexican breeding grounds and Arctic feeding grounds, and charter boats now cater to whale watchers as readily as to fishermen.

The old Coast Guard station (2201 Westhaven Drive) houses a history museum. Climb the tower for its view of the Grays Harbor bar and jetties.

In 1860 the army arrived at Westport in the form of Captain Maurice Maloney, Mrs. Maloney, and 60 troopers from Fort Steilacoom. Ostensibly they came to Point Chehalis to protect settlers from local natives, although tribal resistance to white encroachment actually had ended four years earlier in western Washington and two years earlier east of the mountains. Some speculated that the "danger" was concocted by Captain Thomas Wright, owner of a steamboat, who wanted to enhance his business. Wright brought the Chehalis River its first stern-wheeler in 1859, the 115-foot, open-hulled *Enterprise*. The previous year he had plied it to great advantage on British Columbia's Fraser River during the gold rush there. On the Chehalis River, however, he hit snags and shoals and, before the first season was out, tied the vessel to a tree and went out on foot to Olympia.

Few actual functions were performed at Fort Chehalis (at the sandy point just inside today's Westport harbor) other than Captain Maloney's attempts to enforce laws against selling liquor to native people. In June 1861 troops were ordered East to fight in the Civil War, and the fort fell silent. Settlers bought most of the buildings and moved them to various sites around the harbor. Nothing now remains.

In the 1880s Elijah Wade and his wife Martha began a farm near present-day Westport. From there, Elijah—ever busy "argufying and carrying on in politics," according to his wife—established a campground for reunions of Union soldiers. Appropriately, he chose land near that of erstwhile Fort Chehalis (about a half mile south of today's lighthouse). As Grand Army of the Republic veterans lessened in number, the campground recruited those from the Spanish American War and then opened to the general public. Encampments lasted throughout July and August—and put Westport on the map as a vacation destination.

A whaling station established in 1911 by the American Pacific Whaling Company stood at nearby **Bay City,** now a sprinkling of houses along three carefully laid out streets just east of the Elk River bridge. Until 1925 the station processed 200 to 300 whales each year. One of three stations owned by the company, this one was equipped with steam-powered rendering machinery and huge storage vats. Crews on the four 87-foot steam vessels equipped with explosive harpoons hunted humpbacks, finbacks, and sperm whales. A local butcher marketed some whale meat, but the primary products were oil and fertilizer. (Also see BELLEVUE, p. 274.)

Near Bay City oyster beds today cover the tidelands. At a special facility where holding tanks keep a precise temperature, workers grow spat (young oysters) on old shells. They attach these nurse shells at six-inch intervals to nylon rope by forcing the shells between the plies. The ropes are suspended between poles where tidal action leaves them exposed to the air part of the time. Oysters thrive particularly well where fresh water mixes with salt, such as here at the estuary. They mature in three to four years. Workers then pull the ropes and harvest the oysters.

The site of **Ocosta** across South Bay from Westport, is marked by Scotch broom and scattered mobile homes plus several barns and a handful of old homes topping knobs and ridges. A century ago the community expected to eclipse Aberdeen and Hoquiam as the focal point of Grays Harbor. The Northern Pacific Railroad had platted Ocosta-by-the-Sea and sold 300 lots in a single day to speculators. The new dream town was to be the Northern Pacific's Grays Harbor terminus, a cost saving, the company claimed, over establishing a depot at the actual towns of Aberdeen or Hoquiam.

Ocosta had two advantages: it was near the harbor's mouth—convenient for shipping—and it lay along the relatively deep, southern entry channel across the bar. Developers touting similar paper towns like Laidlaw, Drummond, and West Aberdeen printed a special chart of the harbor showing factual deep readings but omitting all of the shallow readings. At the time ships coming into the harbor drew an average of 16 to 17 feet of water. The entrance bar offered 18 to 21 feet at high tide but dropped to as little as 10 feet at low tide. A location on the deepest channel was an asset potentially measurable in dollars. In 1890 members of the army's O'Neill Expedition, who had crossed the southern Olympic Mountains, stayed in town overnight en route back to Puget Sound. One wrote:

We remained here all day and night and had ample opportunity to talk the few inhabitants all to sleep had they been of ordinary materials. . . . There were ten houses, nine real estate offices, and one drug store. . . . Ocosta is scarcely above the tide and a salt marsh.

Unfortunately for town boomers, severe storms in the winter of 1892–1893 buried the newly laid Northern Pacific tracks under landslides and drift logs. Howling winds made the wharf nearly impossible to approach. And, most significant of all, the Panic of 1893 undercut investment. The railroad company went into receivership. Aberdeen citizens built their own spur line, and the company never bothered to resuscitate Ocosta as terminus. Its chief distinguishing feature today is a 90-degree bend in State Route 105.

Lake Quinault to Neah Bay

Drive the west side of the Olympic Peninsula to enjoy dramatic, islet-studded ocean beaches and a virgin rain forest inside Olympic National Park, with more gigantic trees of more different species than are known anywhere else in the world. Sitka spruce and western hemlock predominate; sword ferns grow waist high; and mosses and clubmosses pad branches and trunks, producing layer upon layer of life. Towns are few and widely spaced. Those towns belonging to Native Americans trace their origins to the dreamtime when Changers were creating the world as we now know it. Modern towns began in the 1880s, based on the assumption that logging and fishing could last forever. Market swings have characterized their economies from the outset.

A museum at Forks portrays the history of logging; a National Park Service visitor center at the end of the road in the Hoh Rain Forest high-lights the natural cycle, and short nature trails lead through the forest. At Neah Bay the Makah tribal museum displays material recovered archaeologically from Ozette and, if plans materialize, also from the Hoko River site. A Fourth of July celebration at Forks features logging skills. Neah Bay hosts Makah Days in late August; events include 11-man dugout canoe races, traditional dancing, and a salmon bake.

Native Americans lived at **CLALLAM BAY** from time immemorial. When the Hudson's Bay Company built Fort Victoria on Vancouver Island in 1843, they took Klallam people with them to grow potatoes at the new post, and James Douglas, chief factor of the fur-trade post and later the first governor of British Columbia, reserved treaty land for them at Esquimalt (near today's downtown Victoria).

The modern community of Clallam Bay is a supply center for residents, tourists, and a state prison—welcomed in the 1980s as a possible economic mainstay. Town beginnings date to the 1880s as a stop for steamboats. At first white men in rowboats and native men and women in

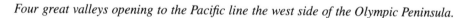

Four great valleys opening to the Pacific line the west side of the Olympic Peninsula.

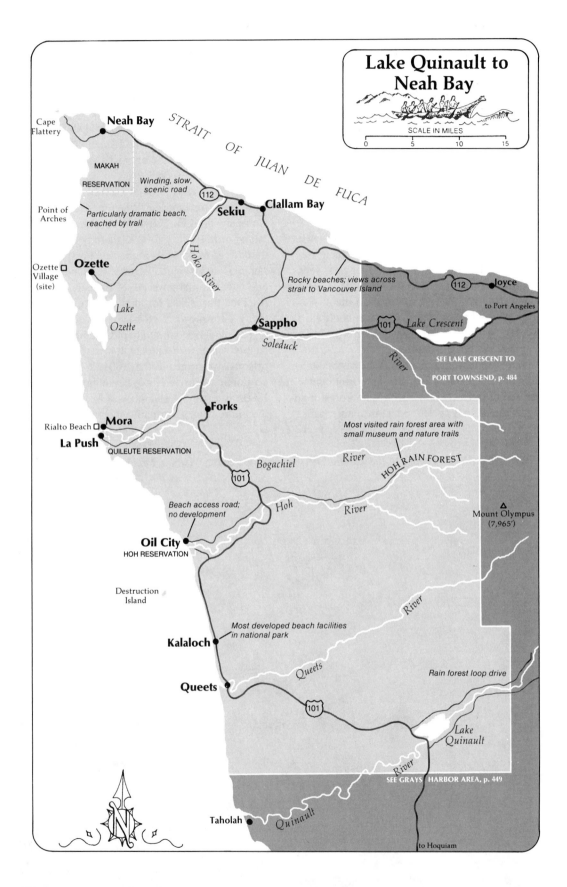

Lake Quinault to
Neah Bay

SCALE IN MILES

0   5   10   15

Cape
Flattery

Neah Bay

STRAIT OF JUAN DE FUCA

MAKAH
RESERVATION

*Winding, slow,
scenic road*

(112)

Sekiu   **Clallam Bay**

Point of
Arches

*Particularly dramatic beach,
reached by trail*

Hoko River

Ozette
Village
(site)

Ozette

*Rocky beaches; views across
strait to Vancouver Island*

(112) **Joyce**

to Port Angeles

(101) *Lake Crescent*

*Lake
Ozette*

Sappho

Soleduck

River

SEE LAKE CRESCENT TO
PORT TOWNSEND, p. 484

Forks

Rialto Beach   **Mora**

*Most visited rain forest area with
small museum and nature trails*

La Push

QUILEUTE RESERVATION

Bogachiel   River

HOH RAIN FOREST

(101)

Hoh   River

*Beach access road;
no development*

△
Mount Olympus
(7,965')

Oil City

HOH RESERVATION

Destruction
Island

River

*Most developed beach facilities
in national park*

Kalaloch

Rain forest loop drive

Queets

Queets

(101)

*Lake
Quinault*

River

SEE GRAYS HARBOR AREA, p. 449

N

Taholah   *Quinault*

to Hoquiam

cedar dugout canoes met the boats to onload and offload passengers, freight, and mail. Captains simply came as close to shore as they dared—indeed, Jessie Ayers, daughter of the Tatoosh Island assistant lighthouse keeper from 1884 to 1889 wrote:

To strangers it was startling to feel the little ship's keel grating on a sandbar or rocks, and have to wait hours until she was righted by an incoming tide.

By 1890 a long dock fingered into the bay, and a sawmill—which burned and closed two years later—offered seasonal employment to men needing cash while "proving up" on their homestead and timber claims. Clallam Bay became a hub for the entire west side of the Olympic Peninsula: the erstwhile sawmill company store continued in business; an annual drive brought marketable beef cattle from Quillayute Prairie (near La Push) and Forks for hoisting by derrick off the dock into the hold of a ship; and a two-horse buckboard bounced on regular schedule from Clallam Bay over Burnt Mountain to Forks, a 20-mile, 10-hour trip.

For years an official weather station maintained contact by telegraph with Tatoosh Island, allowing captains to row ashore here for information on what sea conditions to expect. As many as 12 to 15 ships waiting out a storm often dotted Clallam Bay, the first moderately sheltered port inside the Strait of Juan de Fuca. They came from nations as distant as Sweden, England, France, Germany, Spain, Chile, and Peru. The telegraph also served to alert tugboat owners and pilots that sailing ships were on the horizon off Cape Flattery. That word would set off a full-throttle race up the strait to garner business. The telegraph office later moved to Port Crescent and then—by 1914—to Port Angeles.

DESTRUCTION ISLAND. (See under KALALOCH, p. 468.)

From its beginning **FORKS** has been a logging center. A Seattle branch bank here has special drive-in lanes for logging trucks and crew buses. A logging museum built by the Forks High School carpentry class is along U.S. 101 on the south side of town. And the Fourth of July

celebration centers on logging skills.

Yet fur trappers and farmers arrived here before loggers. A few bachelors lived on Forks Prairie at least part time while running traplines in the 1870s, and the Luther Ford family arrived to homestead in 1878 having heard that railroad construction was soon to begin on the Olympic Peninsula. They traveled from San Francisco to Seattle, where they turned down an offer of 40 acres in what is now the heart of the city: the peninsula seemed to hold a greater potential. In Port Townsend the Fords waited out a storm, then took a schooner to Neah Bay and waited out another storm. Finally, they went by dugout canoe to La Push, a 14-hour trip in the rain. Supplies and mail continued to reach Forks by this route for years and, when Ford started a dairy herd in 1879, he brought the cows to Neah Bay by schooner, then drove them south, partly along the beach, partly following rough trails.

Forks served as the community center for outlying settlers. Minnie Nelson Peterson, raised on the Hoko River, used to tell of riding 22 miles to Forks with her brother and sisters to attend dances. They would carry party clothes in their saddlebags and "dance all night so it would be daylight when we started home and we could see where we were going." What had been a hop-drying barn became a dance hall; the little freight boat that called at river mouths arrived on such a decidedly uncertain schedule that hops often got damp and spoiled while awaiting shipment. Beef cattle proved the most practical farm product, although they had to be driven around the entire north tip of the peninsula to Port Townsend where lumber ships needing provisions provided a good market.

In January 1921 disaster struck the Forks area in the form of a "blowdown," a wholesale toppling of trees by wind. William Taylor, in town when the storm struck, remembered that "sudden gusts bellied in the back of the store . . . [and] a terrifying roar told of the falling of great trees all around." Up the Hoh Valley, homesteader John Huelsdonk was out on his trapline near the present rain forest visitor center. He would stand near a tree, feel its roots start to lift beneath his feet, and move to another tree. The wind toppled 1,700 "full size trees" onto the road between Sappho and the west end of Lake Crescent, according to the *Port Angeles*

Evening News. Settlers who had claimed land in order to sell it to timber companies simply left the area. Their land was worthless.

Thirty years later another disaster struck. The summer of 1951 brought 108 days with no rain and, on September 20, a fire roared west along the Soleduck River driven by high wind and the force of its own updraft. It traveled 18 miles in six hours; destroyed more than 30,000 acres of timber; and smothered Forks in such dense smoke and cinders that automatic streetlights switched on at noon and drivers evacuating town could hardly see the road or avoid hitting panic-stricken deer that were fleeing the holocaust. In Forks 28 houses, four garages, three barns, and a mill stood in ruins before a light rain fell and put out the fire. Men worked for three years salvaging timber damaged by the flames and heat.

Drive into the **HOH RAIN FOREST** (reached by an 18-mile spur road off U.S. 101 south of Forks) for a look at virgin forest and at the difference between nature's time and human, economic time. Occasional gigantic stumps, usually blackened by fire, stand as monarchs from the past; denuded hillsides testify to recent logging; and close-set trees of identical age and of a single species characterize regrowth. Forest products rank as the state's second most important industry, following only aerospace. This is the economic reality of recent decades.

At the end of the road, inside the national park, time—and reality—follow a different beat. Spruce and hemlock soar 200 feet and are as much as 10 feet in diameter. Alders and cottonwoods line the riverbanks; vine maples create green arches and tangles; big-leaf maples support a living upholstery of mosses and ferns. Elk act as "landscape gardeners" by browsing selectively, and salmon and steelhead spawn where river gravels are free of sediment and water temperatures are right. Fallen trees act as nurse logs for seedlings, their huge decaying masses a reservoir of moisture and nutrients. Time is measured not in years but in centuries and millennia.

A visitor center highlights aspects of the forest cycle, and short interpretive trails sample its actuality of rippling creeks, roaring river, dripping skies, scampering squirrels, twittering birds, browsing elk, and one green layer growing on top another. The forest is a community of intertwined lives. Their full implications for commercial timberlands are only beginning to be understood: harvesting second-growth and third-growth trees has succeeded so far, but such a rapid cutting cycle may not be indefinitely sustainable. *Economy* may have to acknowledge *ecology*. The national park is a laboratory of nature's system as well as an outdoor cathedral.

The Hoh Valley, like the other valleys along the west side of the Olympic Peninsula, hosted heroic efforts at homesteading. The pattern stemmed from an American conviction that life at the periphery held opportunity for all who could endure until development overtook pioneering. It was a conviction bolstered by U.S. laws granting free land to those who settled the frontier. Dora Huelsdonk Richmond, born at a Hoh River homestead, once mused about the process:

Those years when most of the settlers came, from 1893 to about 1898, there was no work to be had. It was depression time. A chance at a homestead looked very good, as having a piece of land of their own to live on was almost the only way out of a bad situation. . . . Many found clearing very difficult, especially in the heavier timbered areas or cedar swamps, which required draining as well as clearing. Good land extended far upriver from the last settlements . . . but it was so very far from the source of supply that the latecomers chose more difficult land closer to the river mouth.

Homesteading meant cutting brush by day and burning it by night, so as to have room to cut more the next day. Those who shortcut the process by picking natural clearings close to the river often watched their fields—and cabins—wash away as fluctuating snowmelt and glacier runoff shunted the Hoh from one channel to another. Creating farmland meant felling trees to clear fields and also to eliminate the danger of their falling on a cabin or barn during a windstorm. Stumps remained as obstacles to plant and mow around. Blasting them out was expensive and difficult. Burning took time and patience. It involved drilling intersecting holes at the top and sides and then "putting in a panful

Turning virgin forest into farms called for cutting trees and ridding the land of mammoth stumps, a laborious process of pulling, blasting, and burning—wearisome and costly work. Even so, cutover land was touted as ideal for farming.

of charcoal or bark chips and fanning the stump by hand or with bellows."

The first settlers came to the rain forest to create niches without really affecting the entirety. The second wave of settlers came to use the forest, not to live within it. "Spruce stands heavy along the Hoh River and is very large. Logging will be cheap," reads a government survey published in 1902. Today logging efficiency has escalated, and the size of the trees trucked out of the forest has shriveled to about that of those burned as slash through the 1960s, while old-growth timber seemed abundant. The national park boundary forms a line dividing people's hurry from nature's patience.

The **HOH RESERVATION** at the mouth of the Hoh River is one of the smallest in Washington (just over 400 acres). It was established by executive order in 1893 to assure people living there the use of a traditional fishing station and a patch of their own land. In addition, the Hohs (who speak Quileute), together with the people at La Push were "assigned" to the Quinault Reservation.

By the late 1960s, the population on the Hoh Reservation had dropped to only a dozen households. Now, however, families have moved back, and the population is growing. The people depend on salmon for their living and have multiple programs to protect and improve the spawning runs. No particular tourist facilities have been developed at the reservation. An informal campground is available at the opposite side of the river mouth (within Olympic National Park; also see OIL CITY, p. 478).

HOKO RIVER. (See under SEKIU, p. 483.)

The long, straight beach at **KALALOCH** (Clay′-lock) warrants its popularity. There are magnificent views and a range of accommodations from a national park campground to a lodge and cabins. Waves crash close to the bluff at high tide; a wide sand beach is exposed at ebb tide. It is a ceaseless rhythm that somehow counters the stress of present-day frenzy.

The first whites to settle here seem to have come north from Grays Harbor about 1890 to open a cannery, which attracted a population of 15 to 20 workers. During this same period placer gold mining began along the Olympic Peninsula beaches. Sluice boxes dotted the banks wherever creeks flowed into the surf. Some produced well enough that during the depression years of the 1930s prospectors again moved to the beaches and—outside the national park—a few operations continued into the 1960s.

A resort opened at Kalaloch in the late 1920s, shortly before completion of the highway looping the peninsula. During World War II, the Coast Guard used the property and buildings as part of the Coast Lookout System. Similar patrol units operated out of La Push and Lake Ozette. Their task was to constantly patrol the beach to watch for—and prevent—enemy landings and to prevent communication between someone on shore and a vessel at sea. Shelters were built on headlands and at creeks every 5 to 10 miles along the entire Olympic coast with four men assigned to each. An official report completed at the close of the war commented that "no other area in the country offered more disadvantages for patrols." It described the "walls of rock which projected out to sea" but had to be climbed and the vegetation that was "practically impenetrable" but had to be traveled through. Anyone who has backpacked along the wilderness coast of the park will know the truth of the statements.

Offshore from Kalaloch, the lighthouse at **Destruction Island** flashes its warning in a pattern of 10 seconds on, then 2½ seconds off. When completed in 1891, the light's five wicks each burned two gallons of lard oil per night, all of it carried up a 115-step spiral staircase by the keeper. A Fresnel lens, eight feet high and ground with 1,152 prisms and 24 bull's-eyes, magnified the wavering flicker of the lamps into an effective warning beacon. That same lens now magnifies the gleam of an automated light, visible for 24 miles out to sea. The energy source will soon be switched from diesel to solar.

The island's name results from two separate eighteenth-century incidents when shore parties were attacked—and killed—by native warriors. The first attack came in 1775 at Point Grenville, south of the Quinault River, when Spaniards went ashore for wood and water. All were killed (see p. 460), and the Spanish captain, Juan Francisco de la Bodega y Quadra, entered the name *Punta de los Martires,* "Point of the Martyrs," on his chart, and named the island *Isla de los Dolores,* "Island of Sorrows." Twelve years later British trader Charles William Barkley sent a party of six ashore for water at the Hoh River, where they were killed by natives who wanted the boat's metal fittings. Barkley entered "Destruction River" on his chart, but successors somehow transferred the name to the

During World War II, soldiers stationed along the Olympic coast constantly patrolled the beaches, including Point of Arches (now part of Olympic National Park).

island and restored a semblance of the native name to the river.

The road to **LAKE OZETTE** (a 20-mile spur off State Route 112) crosses through logging country to one of the last areas in the nation to be homesteaded by using little except energy, ingenuity, and hand tools. The lake itself—almost 10 miles long—now lies within Olympic National Park, protected in its natural state and with no development at the road's end, other than a ranger station and small campground.

Two trails to the beach lead through the forest (about 3 miles), offering a chance to see the type of landscape pioneers entered. Indeed, the Indian Village Trail crosses a prairie where homesteader Lars Ahlstrom lived alone from 1902 until 1958. "I'm too busy to get lonesome," he used to say. "And if I do, I put a good polka on the phonograph and dance a whirl with myself."

Settlement began in the Lake Ozette area about 1890, stimulated by rumors of a railroad and by county promises of a road, which actually was not completed until 1935. "Locators" helped newcomers find unclaimed land, some of it previously taken but abandoned. Reaching the area—and bringing in supplies and

livestock—was difficult. One way was to walk 28 miles from the steamer landing at Clallam Bay. Another was to walk up the beach from La Push, then inland to the lake and either continue walking along its shore or cross by boat. The third way was to hire Makahs and travel by canoe from Neah Bay around Cape Flattery to the mouth of the Ozette River or to the Ozette whaling and sealing village on the beach south of the river, then inland by trail. Logjams usually blocked travel on the river.

In 1897 the Ozette area was included within the newly established Olympic Forest Reserve, and many settlers left. In 1907 the boundaries changed, and a second influx of settlers arrived although without real intention of staying. They filed on homestead and timber claims, built whatever they needed to gain title, then sold to timber companies. The cabins of this era included some that were windowless hovels with only a trapdoor in the roof for entry. Technically these counted as improvements. So did a crop of winter onions or potatoes, which grow and produce without tending.

At its height, the community of true settlers numbered about 130 families, many in two-story homes with hand-fashioned scrollwork along the eaves and parlors decorated with wallpaper ordered from Sears Roebuck mail-order catalogs. These settlers were mostly Scandinavians, accustomed to hardship in the old country and here filled with hope. Men earned cash by "working out" at sawmills and logging camps. Women took in travelers, surveyors, timber cruisers, and schoolteachers as boarders and occasionally cooked at camps and mills. From their farms, the settlers earned a little cash by shipping out cream in five-gallon cans slung on each side of a saddle, or clipping the wool from sheep kept on Tivoli Island.

Ole Boe, who came in 1891, wrote of the early years as a "budding time" for the settlement. "Land was free, and a road had been promised, many new homes were being built, and it looked promising indeed!" But, in the end, the isolation proved overwhelming. Neighbors left and Boe wrote:

It soon became depressing to walk along the narrow trails. Often in the ruins we find books, old country trunks, and implements so needed here, but too hard

Ozette settlers used sledges for hauling; wheels would catch in the tangled vegetation.

to pack out again by those who had fled this hopeless land. All the clearings very soon were reclaimed by the relentless forest. Often one sees a big evergreen tree, where 30 years ago we remember a cradle had stood. . . . Here now in January 1925 there are only twenty-two grown people and six children in the whole Ozette country.

K. O. Erickson began a small store at the north end of Lake Ozette as a branch of his operation at Mora (near La Push) and, in 1935, homesteaders opened a small resort there. Soon after the Japanese attack on Pearl Harbor in December 1941, "soldiers from Panama with about a hundred mules" took over the Ozette resort and nearby abandoned homestead houses. The men belonged to a hastily concocted West Coast defense system. In September 1942, Coast Guardsmen took over from the army. They built barracks and other buildings at the lake, including kennels for 40 dogs, which were used on beach patrols. (Also see KALALOCH, p. 467.)

The **Ozette Village** site at Cape Alava, now a detached unit of the Makah Reservation, dates archaeologically as at least 2,000 years old and is remembered fondly as a childhood home by Makah elders. Families left only after the newcomer white government demanded that children be in school, yet provided none at Ozette. Parents then moved to Neah Bay.

In the winter of 1969-1970 storm waves cutting into the bank at the edge of the village washed out cedar house-planks, a canoe paddle, a whaling harpoon shaft, and wooden halibut hooks. The Makah Tribal Council asked

Washington State University archaeologists to resume an excavation they had started three years earlier. This led to a decade-long investigation of what is regarded as one of the world's foremost archaeological sites, a virtual "Pompeii in mud."

Artifacts recovered from wet layers beneath mud slides provide a detailed look at the wooden implements and carved artwork of people who lived at the village as early as the 1400s. A deeper layer, dated to about the 1100s, has been located but not excavated. The Makah Cultural and Research Center at Neah Bay includes displays of the Ozette material. (See page 469.) The archaeological site is marked by a plaque and small-scale cedar longhouse (accessible only by 3½-mile trail; no current excavation).

A turn off U.S. 101 to **LAKE QUINAULT** (Kwi-nalt´) and beyond it for 10 to 15 miles into the rain forest fills the senses with *greenness*. In maple groves the air itself seems crème-de-menthe green, an effect especially beguiling in the soft, even light of cloudy or rainy days.

Roads on each side of the river penetrate farther up-valley here than in the Hoh or Queets valleys, thus giving visitors a distinct advantage for windshield viewing of the rain forest. A short nature trail about a quarter mile west of Lake Quinault Lodge threads among huge trees and ferns, representative of the forest that formerly carpeted almost the entire peninsula. Inside Olympic National Park that green and padded realm still prevails. Outside, such forest is mostly memory. Roads often still lead through green corridors, but many are just that— corridors. The logging of commercial timberlands has outstripped regrowth.

Settlement of the lower Quinault Valley began in the 1880s and increased in the 1890s. By coincidence, three father-and-son combinations figured prominently in the pioneering process. Alfred Higley, a widower and Civil War veteran who had marched through Georgia with General William Sherman, came to Seattle with his 19-year-old son Orte, heard about the Quinault Valley, and, in August 1890, traveled by stern-wheeler to Hoodsport (on Hood Canal). There the two set off on foot up the Skokomish River, crossed the mountains, and selected land near Lake Quinault.

Byron Loomis and his son Bud came two years later, starting out from Montesano and finally arriving via a cedar dugout canoe, which they attempted to maneuver upriver by themselves, but turned sideways to the current and upset. Only their frying pan remained. Undaunted, the men located a claim, then returned for the rest of the family. In the book *Trails and Trials of the Pioneers,* Bud reminisces about starting out from Grays Harbor:

We had about a thousand or fifteen hundred pounds of stuff . . . to be taken in to our place eight miles above the end of Lake Quinault. Had a horse and a Jersey cow and a two-year-old heifer, and a yearling. The road was all mud—no puncheon on it then. . . . Mother rode on the wagon on top of the load. We upset three times the first day. . . . When we reached the Humptulips River . . . we stayed a day or two and rested. Then we borrowed a pack saddle and packed some necessities on the Jersey cow [but] the cow got slow and laid down pretty often. . . . Mother carried a broom in her hand all the way. When she walked

she used it for a cane, and when she rode the horse she used it for a whip. She thought a broom was a very necessary thing.

In 1891 the *Seattle Post-Intelligencer* reported the conclusions of Charles Gilman and his son Samuel concerning the Olympic Peninsula. They had traveled the length of the Quinault Valley and into mountains of "frightening grandeur" two years earlier. Hired by a railroad company to check on the feasibility of laying track the length of the peninsula, they had immediately set out from the mouth of the Pysht River (on the Strait of Juan de Fuca) and walked to Grays Harbor. The men commented on the rich bottomlands they found, "well adapted to the production of vegetables," and on the "abundant rainfall which renders failure of crops an impossibility"—an accurate choice of an adjective, with an average precipitation of 134 inches per year. The Gilmans also concluded that within five years the "unknown country of the Olympic Peninsula" would be well

The notoriously rainy Quinault Valley attracted settlers beginning in the 1880s.

populated, productive, and easily accessible.

For Lake Quinault, the accessibility came in 1915 with the opening of an automobile road from Hoquiam; work on the road continued until a final ribbon cutting for the Olympic Loop Highway (U.S. 101) in 1931. By then the lake— 4½ miles long—was well established as a recreation area.

Automobiles brought a democratization of travel and a heightened appreciation of outdoor vacations. To cater to this interest, a well-financed Grays Harbor company applied to the Forest Service for permits to build wilderness chalets, and by 1929 Portland's *Sunday Oregonian* carried word that the "heretofore aloof Olympic Mountains" would soon be "a summer playground." The next year a log chalet stood at the head of the North Fork of the Quinault, accessible only by trail, and a shelter offered simpler accommodations at the midway point beyond road's end.

As early as 1929 the Olympic Chalet Company, owners of the developments, proposed a landing field for planes at Low Divide, beside the chalet, and also considered damming an alpine lake to create a big enough body of water for seaplanes to land. The 1930s Great Depression bankrupted the company. An avalanche destroyed the chalet.

In 1931 the five Olson brothers, members of a Quinault homestead family, opened a competing backcountry chalet at Enchanted Valley, 13 miles by trail up the east fork of the Quinault Valley. The Olsons packed in milled lumber for the interior and bricks and mortar for the chimney by horse. They even rigged a sled and dragged in a bathtub. A Forest Service brochure described a 13-day trail ride through the Olympics with a stop at the chalet for "cooks, ashless food, a bath, good beds. How welcome the sight!" A separate promotional piece spoke of Enchanted Valley's "imposing precipices and

In 1931 homesteaders built a tourist chalet at Enchanted Valley. It still stands.

Until the mid-1960s, fishermen at La Push regularly used cedar dugout canoes.

ridged escarpments" and of waterfalls which, "in [the] moister season shoot, trickle, cascade or otherwise pour over these cliffs." In the early 1980s volunteers from the Olympians, a Hoquiam hiking club, worked with the National Park Service to stabilize the 2½-story log chalet, which continues in use as a shelter (although not as a hotel).

LA PUSH (14 miles west of Forks) boasts one of the peninsula's most spectacular views. Waves line a sand beach, small islands stand just offshore, and the Quillayute River flows behind a long sandspit and pours into the ocean. Gray whales often swim close to shore. Motel accommodations are available in the village (although usually booked well in advance). Second and Third beaches, part of Olympic National Park, are accessible by half-mile trails through the forest; watch for their parking areas shortly before descending the final hill into La Push. The beaches, studded with sea stacks and rich with tidepools, are among the most beautiful on the entire Washington coast.

For unknown generations the river mouth at La Push has been the home of the Quileute people, who also had fishing villages inland along the rivers. The reservation was not set aside until 1889. Quileute territory was so isolated that the tribe somehow was overlooked when a treaty council was held at Cosmopolis in 1855.

White settlers had already arrived by the time the Quileute Reservation was designated. Dan Pullen came as early as the 1860s to work as a logger and oxen driver, and in the 1870s to manage a fur trading company, which, at its peak, shipped 8,000 seal skins to Seattle in a single year. By the 1880s Pullen claimed 1,500 acres of land at the mouth of the Quillayute River. Much of it, along with Pullen's two-story Victorian home and his trading post, lay within the one square mile reserved by executive order for the Quileutes.

Fury at the threat to his land title surged within Pullen and, when villagers left for Puyallup to pick hops in the fall of 1889, he burned their houses and surrounded his house with barbed wire. The Quileutes rebuilt in a slightly different, less desirable location, and the feud escalated. Pullen based his sense of rights on a stipulation that said the withdrawal of reservation land was not to "affect any existing, valid property right of any party." Ultimately he lost in court, but not before several additional years of profitable business as settlers increasingly arrived in the area. Maps of the 1890s show them living at creek mouths along the coast and up the major river valleys wherever bottomland offered possibilities for farms. Daffodils still bloom at several of these locations as yearly reminders of bygone expectations.

As late as 1907 Walter Newbert and two other men surveying for the Union Pacific Railroad on the cliff above Third Beach (south of La Push) discovered a half township that was unrecorded on state maps. They filed homestead claims, although only after difficulties persuading officials that the land actually existed. Using lumber from buildings at an abandoned oil well, they built houses. (Machinery left from the well, which never actually produced, still stands along the trail to Third Beach.) No roads gave access. Materials, supplies, and amenities—which included a piano—had to be brought by canoe and hoisted up the 200-foot cliff by cable. Persistence, ingenuity, and hope overcame such drawbacks. Three families lived at the point high above the sea, but only for a few years. They proved up—and left, discouraged by the isolation, disillusioned by the failure of the railroad to arrive.

Across the river from La Push is **Mora,** begun as "Boston" in the 1870s. It originated as a commercial venture supplying settlers with staples brought by schooner to the river mouth or—under the ownership of K. O. Erickson— brought by open boat from Seattle. Erickson salvaged copper from the hull of a shipwreck 3 miles up the beach and used it to repair the lifeboat that was his only form of transportation. In 1901 he opened a post office and changed the name Boston to Mora, commemorating his birthplace in Sweden. He started a hotel over his store, which later was built as a separate struc- ture. (It stood where the campfire circle of Olympic National Park's Mora Campground has now been built. English ivy growing along the north side of the road near Rialto Beach marks additional erstwhile development.)

MAKAH RESERVATION. (See NEAH BAY, this page.)

MORA. (See under LA PUSH, this page.)

The **NEAH BAY** village now climbs the hills yet still faces the beach, still reverberates with timeless drumbeats and songs—which sometimes come from tape recorders as Makah people practice the rhythms and words that are family birthrights. (Songs are associated with ceremonial rank and considered family property.)

For an understanding of the long continuity here, stop first at the Makah museum (eastern edge of the village, south side of the road). Displays include wooden implements 500 years old that were recovered archaeologically at Ozette, one of the five main Makah villages at the time white people arrived on the coast. (Also see p. 470.) In addition, Makah artists have replicated canoes, whaling and sealing equip- ment, storage baskets, and hats that are displayed with an invitation to touch them and sense the character of the equipment used in the past.

Walking reservation beaches is permitted, but not gathering shells or digging clams, which are reserved for use by Makahs. Ocean charter fishing is available; ask at the tribal center regarding stream fishing (often permissible with a license). The 4-mile trail to Shi Shi Beach and Point of Arches, the most spectacular of Olympic National Park's beaches—begins at Mukkaw Bay, southwest of Neah Bay. Cape Flattery, the westernmost point in the forty-eight states, is accessible by an unpaved road. Ideally walk the additional ¾-mile trail for a look at Tatoosh Island and at magnificent cliffs tunneled by waves.

The Makah Reservation was established by treaty in January 1855, a culmination to a century and a half of contact between native people and pale-skinned newcomers. Dealing with outsiders was not a new experience for Makahs, or any Northwest Coast people. Potlatching (ceremonial displays of wealth and reiteration of claims to ceremonial rank) drew distant tribes and involved dealing with people who spoke different languages and followed different customs. Trading and raiding also put villagers in touch with "others." Occasionally so did the ocean currents: bamboo and pieces of steel, probably from Japan, lay within the buried houses excavated at Ozette; and Makah families have stories of Asian people drifting to their shores. Such occurrences are recorded historically; in fact, as recently as 1988 a

MAKAH MEMORIES

In 1962 Ada Markishtum, a Makah elder, reminisced about her life:

We used to wait for evening when the tide was in, then all go down and pull the whale in with ropes. One time I had been out picking berries and I was really tired, but I told my grandmother to wake me up early because I wanted to see that whale we had pulled in. Well, she didn't and it was 9:00 when I got down to the beach. They had the blubber already off, and the meat. Just the ribs left, sticking up. They had to cut it while the tide was low. But you should see the beach! Covered with that whale—blubber and meat. And those teeth [baleen]! They were for fish gear. And the sinew. It was as big around as your thumb. You cut and dried it for thread; then you pounded it and wet it and sewed. Or used it to fasten a harpoon on the shaft. *Klukutup* we called it. Just like thread in the house when you had that. Oh, the whale . . . You could use it for everything.

I remember when we were at fish camp out on Tatoosh Island, too. The first halibut my grandfather would catch—in June, I think it was—we would eat the meat and then we would put the bones in a bucket and I would take them out to the edge and toss them in the water. "Here you are. Be sure to come back next year, Mr. Halibuuuuut," I would say. You hold onto the end of the word that way with your voice: "Halibuuuuut." Little girls had that job to do. All families did it.

Everybody was all the time going places in canoes then. They were big. Some were 60 feet long and eight feet wide and they could carry three families at once. We used to go to Victoria after the last of the halibut was dried—six or seven canoes of us. We children

Ada Markishtum, a skilled basket maker, coils cedar bark newly pulled from a tree. Her next step is to dry the bark, then split it into strips.

were different then. We knew how to sit still. We would leave about 9:00 in the morning and get to Victoria at 5:00 that same day. Grandmother and the other ladies took big bags with the baskets they had made and they went to Hudson's Bay and traded for cloth and shawls. Then we went to the Fraser River and worked in the cannery; and then we went to Seattle by canoe and from there to Puyallup in a wagon to work in the hop fields. Then it was time to come home for the fall salmon fishing. After that was the time for dances and singing. That's how it was every year, every year.

Taiwanese fishing boat drifted as a derelict for eight months and ended up off Cape Flattery.

What was new about eighteenth-century Europeans and Americans was their feeling of superiority and their determination to dominate

the coast. Juan Pérez came first, in 1774, sailing along the Washington shore without dropping anchor. The weather was clear enough that he saw Mount Olympus and named it Santa Rosalía; yet he somehow failed to enter the

The modern Makah village of Neah Bay lines the beach near Cape Flattery.

legendary strait apparently located by Juan de Fuca, a Greek seaman who sailed under the Spanish flag in 1592. Pérez sailed on a highly secret mission, instructed to explore the territory north of Mexico, which Spain claimed but knew nothing about. In 1778 Captain James Cook also sailed along the coast, exploring for England. He, too, failed to enter the strait (although, in his case, the weather was foggy).

In 1790 Manuel Quimper came south from the Spanish outpost at Nootka (on the outer coast of Vancouver Island), instructed to sound and chart all possible harbors. He entered Neah Bay; named it Nuñez Gaona for a high-ranking naval official; traded sheet copper for sea otter pelts; and erected a cross of possession. He strode about whacking brush with his sword and scuffling stones, and at the base of the cross buried a stoppered bottle holding written notice that the land belonged to King Carlos IV. Two years later a Spanish colonizing expedition headed by Lieutenant Salvador Fidalgo sailed to Neah Bay from San Blas, Mexico (the Spanish naval headquarters south of Mazatlan). By then

it was clear that England, too, claimed the Northwest Coast, and the Mexican viceroy thought abandoning Nootka and opening a post at Neah Bay instead might be prudent.

Native people were not consulted, although Maquinna, the chief at Nootka, found the presence of foreign ships greatly to his advantage because of the wealth they made possible through trade. Furthermore, unlike their *conquistador* predecessors, the Spaniards of the 1700s came with instructions from the viceroy that their voyages were to be "carried out without offending in the slightest degree those unhappy beings who in their ignorance clamor for my humanity and compassion."

Neah Bay was selected as a location commanding entry into the strait, which recent exploration established as a strategic waterway. The new post also would be in a more open, accessible position than Nootka. It was intended as a permanent settlement with families to be sent from Mexico. Their farm produce and bakery goods would be used to provision Spanish ships.

At the west end of Neah Bay—where a little stream still flows onto the beach—Fidalgo's men built a barracks and, in June 1792, mounted four cannons on its roof. They fired these at dawn and dusk to impress Makahs and any visiting natives with Spanish power. They also raised a log palisade at the mouth of the stream, assuring a water supply in case of attack; and they rigged corrals and pens for sheep, goats, pigs, and cows they had brought with them. In addition, the men planted seedlings they had carefully nurtured on board ship so as to give their vegetable garden a head start. Apparently among these starts was what Makahs today call *cawicz,* a small yellowish potato of a primitive variety. Neah Bay families regard these potatoes as of superior flavor and grow them in home gardens.

The Spaniards stayed at Neah Bay only four months. While Fidalgo had been busy building the new outpost, the Spanish naval commandant Juan Francisco de la Bodega y Quadra had been negotiating with the British envoy Captain George Vancouver at Nootka. Bodega y Quadra concluded that the British might interpret a Spanish withdrawal to Neah Bay as admission of an uncertain claim to the coast, and this might jeopardize Spanish sovereignty everywhere north of San Francisco. Consequently, he decided to abandon plans for Neah Bay, and he sent word to Fidalgo to dismantle his structures and bring all personnel, animals, and useful items to Nootka. On September 29, 1792, Fidalgo set sail for the north.

Just over a half century later, whites arrived to stay. In 1850 Samuel Hancock opened a trading post at Neah Bay. Three years later a brig from San Francisco arrived with smallpox on board, and an epidemic broke out. Hancock wrote:

In a few weeks from the introduction of the disease, hundreds of natives became victims of it. The beach

Makahs traditionally cook salmon by an alder fire with the fish held in split cedar sticks. Archaeologists found sticks identical to these in the houses buried at Ozette.

for a distance of eight miles was literally strewn with the dead bodies. . . . I could scarcely walk about round my house, and was obliged to have holes dug where I deposited fifteen or twenty bodies in each. . . . Still they continued . . . to die in such numbers that I finally hauled them down the beach at a time of low tide, so they would drift away.

In 1855—just two years after the social, economic, and psychological devastation of the epidemic—Governor Isaac Stevens arrived to negotiate a treaty.

THE WRECK OF THE *SV NIKOLAI*

In 1808 a shipwreck at Rialto Beach (just north of La Push) played a role in discouraging Russian settlement south of Alaska. At the time, world powers viewed the territory from San Francisco to Sitka as largely available for the taking. Britain and France were preoccupied with fighting each other in Europe. Spain had withdrawn from the Northwest to California. The United States dominated the maritime fur trade but had not yet formulated interest in the land beyond sending Lewis and Clark on their journey to the Pacific. Recognizing opportunity, the Russian American Company was considering expansion. By hurrying, they hoped to occupy the Columbia River mouth and other points outside of Spanish California (and from 1812 to 1842 they did operate a trading fort and farm near Cape Mendocino, California).

Aleksandr Baranov, company manager at Sitka, dispatched two vessels south to trade for furs and explore. They were to rendezvous at Grays Harbor, but on November 1, winds drove the schooner *SV Nikolai* onto shore. Twelve Russians were on board, including the commander, Nikolai Isaakovich Bulygin, and his wife, Anna Petrovna; an Englishman who worked for the Russian American Company; two Aleut women from Kodiak Island; and five Aleut men. Nobody was injured. Indeed, they salvaged muskets, ammunition, and provisions from the vessel and huddled in tents made from the sails.

For a day or two the forlorn group stood off attacks by Quileutes, then they crossed the Quillayute River in a skiff rescued from the *Nikolai* and struck out overland for Grays Harbor. At the next river mouth—the Hoh—natives captured four of the party, including Anna Petrovna. The others barely escaped, some of them critically wounded. The skies turned gray, rain added discomfort to distress, and the castaways decided to retreat upriver. By November 12, they had "not even a speck of food," according to supercargo Timofei Tarakanov's report published serially in Russia 14 years later. During the next several weeks, however, they occasionally traded for salmon and berries, and at other times stole them from fishing camps, conscientiously leaving beads and "fake pearls" as payment. At one point they tried to ransom Anna Petrovna, but her captors wanted muskets, which Tarakanov—now the leader in place of the psychologically devastated Bulygin—felt it necessary to refuse.

On December 10, snow fell and the party decided to build a cabin "with sentry boxes at the corners for the guards." They planned to live in it for the winter and resume their march in spring. Through trade and coercion, they acquired a canoe from natives, and also built a vessel of their own, which is described in Quileute oral tradition as an "unwieldy, crazy boat." In February the Russians and Aleuts set out in these craft.

At the mouth of the Hoh River they learned that their captured comrades "had fallen by lot to another tribe." A week later Makahs led by "an elderly man dressed in European jacket, trousers, and a beaver hat" appeared on the south side

OIL CITY (at the mouth of the Hoh, on the north side) began, and ended, in the 1930s with expectations of a major pumping operation, which was actually a repeat of earlier drilling about 3 miles north near Hoh Head. The "city" today is a patch of sword ferns and access to the southern end of the Olympic National Park's wilderness beach, but nearby settlers remember that during World War II, when rationing severely limited supplies of gasoline and oil, Coast Guardsmen stationed at the drill site sometimes used oil from the abandoned well in

of the Hoh and with them was Anna Petrovna. Her words struck "like a clap of thunder," for she advised surrender, saying "It is better for me to die than to wander about with you in the forest, where we might fall into the hands of a cruel and barbarous people." She insisted that the chief who held her treated her well and promised deliverance to a sailing ship when one appeared.

After deliberation Tarakanov, Bulygin, and three others surrendered and were taken north. The others tried to escape by boat, capsized, and were captured. Over time, all of them were shifted from village to village as their chiefs moved or chose to get rid of captives, "sometimes by selling, sometimes by exchanging us, or—because of kinship or friendship—giving us as gifts."

In August 1809, Anna Petrovna Bulygin died. Six months later her grief-stricken husband also died. As slaves, the two had been together at times, apart at other times. On May 6, 1810, a "double masted vessel came into view," the *Lydia*, commanded by Captain T. Brown, who sailed for the Russian American Company. The chief who held Tarakanov—and had held Anna—made good on his promise. The chief holding the Englishman John William finally released him for a payment of "five patterned blankets, 35 feet of woolen cloth, one locksmith's file, two steel knives, one mirror, five packets of gunpowder, and the same quantity of small shot." With similar payments, Captain Brown ransomed 13 survivors of the *Nikolai* and on June 9, 1810, returned them to Sitka. Seven others had died. Two

had been sold to "distant people."

Baranov, learning at last the particulars of the *Nikolai* party's fate, decided to forgo his plans for the Northwest Coast. He had lost strategic advantage for, during the last two years, the Canadian North West Company had established trading posts on the upper Columbia, and the American Pacific Fur Company had begun trade at the mouth of the Columbia. Instead, Baranov turned attention to California and immediately sent Tarakanov there.

A petroglyph of a sailing ship—not necessarily the Nikolai—*is pecked into the rock of a point between traditional Quileute and Makah territories.*

their jeeps. "It worked—very smokily." In the 1970s an additional search for commercially profitable oil proved unsuccessful at the homestead about a mile inland from the road's end.

OZETTE. (See LAKE OZETTE, p. 469.).

QUEETS today is the name of a tribal village that is part of the Quinault Reservation (no tourist facilities) and of a rain forest valley accessible by a 10-mile spur road. In 1890 the valley was the site of a hopeful colony of homesteaders professionally "located" on 160-acre claims by John J. Banta, who was paid a fee for his services. Banta, age 26, had come to Tacoma and formed a partnership with S. Price

Sharp. The two thought about opening a rooming house but decided instead to look for land. They investigated Bellingham, the San Juan Islands, and Port Townsend, then traveled to Crescent Bay (12 miles west of Port Angeles) and on to Sappho, where they happened to fall in with Charles Gilman and his son Samuel who were making a railroad reconnaisance along the west side of the peninsula. The four traveled together.

At the Hoh River they hired a native man as guide. He took them to his longhouse up the Queets River, and Banta wrote in his diary, "Here is where I think I want to take my homestead." That was on December 23, 1889. On Christmas Day, with snow on the ground and

The upper Queets is one of Olympic National Park's rain forest valleys.

heavy packs to carry, he wrote, "I would rather be in Tacoma." Two weeks later, he and Sharp were back in the city,

making arrangements to organize a Colony to settle on the Queets River. We charge $50 for our services. They pay us nothing until they see the land and are satisfied.

In February 1890 the men traveled to Queets with their first 10 prospective settlers, eight of whom staked claims. In March word came that the Portland–Port Angeles and Victoria Railroad had incorporated and Banta wrote in his diary, "Our country will Boom!" During the next year the partners conducted more than 40 prospective homesteaders to the Queets, traveling from Tacoma to Kamilche by steamer, then by train to Montesano, stern-wheeler to Oyehut, north along the beach by stage to Grisby's "halfway house" near Copalis, on by foot to the mouth of the Queets River, and up the valley in a dugout canoe.

Twice Banta and Sharp made special trips taking in nearly two tons of supplies for their colonists, once freighting the goods up the beach from Hoquiam and Oyehut, once shipping by ocean canoe from Dan Pullen's store at La Push. During this time Lieutenant Joseph O'Neil came down the Queets Valley having completed his exploration of the inner Olympics. He wrote of 30 to 40 homesteaders from Tacoma who had built "very good cabins" along the Queets River and planted gardens. They were all eager to be connected to the trail the O'Neil party had scouted, for they wanted to bring in merchandise from Lake Quinault rather than continuing the cumbersome route up the beach from Grays Harbor.

During the next year Banta and Sharp took another 56 settlers to the Queets, this time traveling by chartered schooner around Cape Flattery to the river mouth. Colonists found that gardens flourished—especially potatoes—and, "to brighten things up," a newcomer brought in rose cuttings and gave one to every woman in the valley. Fish came from the rivers; razor clams from the beach; elk, deer, wild pigeons, and grouse from the forest. In 1895 Banta himself moved to the Queets with a new wife and stepson, then decided to go to California and start a lumber business.

His colony—called Evergreen on the Queets—continued to thrive, even served by mail backpacked from Quinault. The carrier, Orte Higley, found sacks going into Queets particularly heavy because settlers subscribed to the San Francisco *Call Bulletin,* which they read and then used to paper their walls for warmth. Most Queets families were recent immigrants from Germany, Sweden, Scotland, and Ireland. Most, according to an 1894 surveyor, "experienced some discouragement at the task of clearing the land of its dense vegetation."

Many left. A few stayed, making a subsistence living by farming and coping with their isolation until 1931, when the Olympic Loop Highway was completed. In 1953 the entire Queets Valley was included in Olympic National Park. About 40 clearings remain, as do decaying fence posts, two barns, one cabin, and scattered garden shrubs and flowers. Even today some of these are reached only by wading the river and walking up-valley beneath giant spruce and hemlock and across grassy maple glades browsed by elk.

RIALTO BEACH. (See under LA PUSH, p. 474.)

SAPPHO today is little but the junction of the Burnt Mountain Road to Clallam Bay with U.S. 101, a minuscule community updated from its longstanding position as a trailside way station. Sappho also has been a homestead (beginning in 1895) and a logging camp (until 1972). For a time, developers had high hopes. In 1895 the *Beaver Leader,* voice of the community at Lake Pleasant (2 miles west of today's Sappho), carried word of "The New Town," Sapho— which they spelled with one "p":

Those interested in the undertaking are not laboring under the impression that Sapho will be a Second Chicago, but expect to make it the trading point for the settlement of the upper Quillayute valley—make it to the interest of everyone to do their trading in here instead of sending out to up-sound points and paying enormous freight and package charges.

The scheme never really materialized although a hotel and store were built. By 1916 a road connected Sappho to the county ferry that crossed 10-mile-long Lake Crescent, and the route from the steamer landing at Clallam Bay to Forks continued to pass through Sappho. In the 1970s that route—begun as a trail used by native people—became a modern highway.

Just east of Sappho (at Milepost 211) a side road turns off U.S. 101 to **Snider Work Center,** begun as a Civilian Conservation Corps camp in the 1930s and now used by the National Forest Service. Beyond it a road suitable for high-clearance vehicles and experienced drivers climbs 8 miles to the ridge and the nostalgically rebuilt (but unmanned) fire lookout at North Point. (The road is steep and narrow with sharp curves and abrupt dropoffs. Another approach road—somewhat easier but 12 miles longer—branches from E. Twin Road, off State Road

112.) The lookout has views of the forest and mountains. A branch road leads to an overlook above the Strait of Juan de Fuca: Mount Baker punctuates the eastern horizon; Vancouver Island stretches to the north; the open Pacific shimmers in the west.

Kloshe Nanich, built in 1915, was one of the first two lookouts on the Olympic Peninsula. (The other was Finley, near Lake Quinault.) During World War II both served as part of the Aircraft Warning Service, an army operation begun in 1941 when enemy air attack was widely feared.

SEKIU (See´-kew) changes drastically with the seasons. Sport fishing creates a summer city of recreational vehicles and sprinkles the water

Through the 1960s, steam trains brought logs to the booming grounds at Sekiu.

with kicker boats so closely packed they look like a migrating flock of oversized seabirds. Winter empties the waterfront—and closes several of its businesses for the season. The view across the Strait of Juan de Fuca is equally changeable. On clear days ships bound to and from Puget Sound and British Columbia waters sail a sea more blue than the sky. On gray days, the world closes in upon itself, limited to the dripping trees and the twisting road; the strait and British Columbia simply vanish.

Commercial activity here began with salmon fishing in the late 1870s when a Seattle company built a cannery. In 1887 a California-owned leather company opened a tanbark operation, which employed large crews to fell virgin hemlocks—then worthless for lumber—and peel the bark from them. The wood was left to rot. The bark was crushed, then steam heated in huge vats to produce a liquor rich with tannic acid. This infusion was distilled, barreled, and shipped to tanneries, mostly in Victoria but also in Seattle. At the time, leather still played a major role in commerce. Harnessing steam power on ships and in factories depended on leather belts, which connected one drive wheel to another; leather also prevented the chafing of ships' masts and spars, hitched as many as 30 to 40 horses and mules into effective teams, shod the feet of humans, and furnished upholstery for ships and trains.

The demand for tanning liquor could scarcely be met. Even the hemlock waste left in the processing vats was sold as "sawdust" in circus rings. Then the market collapsed, and the plant at Sekiu closed. By the mid-1890s new chemicals greatly simplified the old tanning methods and, at the same time, substitutes for leather began to gain popularity. Meanwhile, the cost of production rose as the distance between sources of hemlock bark and processing vats lengthened.

The plant closed. Men turned to fishing. They sold salmon for 25 cents each—regardless of size—to a fish-buying barge anchored in the bay. Large-scale logging opened in 1907 and lasted until the 1970s; timber cruisers found 650,000 board feet of Douglas fir on a single acre along the Hoko River. By the 1980s, both old-growth forest and salmon were depleted. The process took only a century.

At the mouth of the **Hoko River** (about 5 miles west of Sekiu) archaeologists working throughout the 1980s excavated deposits from a fishing village nearly 3,000 years old. Constantly wet layers along the riverbank have yielded parts of 300 baskets, more than 400 wooden fishhooks, a quartz crystal knife still hafted in its cedar handle, and even a gill net of split cedar root. Dry deposits in a nearby rock shelter (a small cave) lay 12 feet thick. They held discarded shell and bone—and also carefully stored implements such as harpoons probably used for catching seals and salmon, and spindle whorls of whalebone used to spin yarn— probably of dog wool—to use in weaving blankets. The materials belong to the Makah tribe and eventually will be displayed at the Neah Bay museum.

Lake Crescent to Port Townsend

Communities on the northern Olympic Peninsula are doubly blessed with scenery: snowy mountains rise behind them, the Strait of Juan de Fuca lies before them. Forest products fuel the economy although farming was—and to some extent still is—significant in the Sequim–Dungeness area, and Port Angeles harbors a fishing fleet. Port Townsend's commercial buildings and homes convey a sense of the vigorous economic optimism of the 1890s; they are said to be the finest collection of Victorian architecture north of San Francisco. An alcohol distillery in Hadlock, now converted to a restaurant and hotel, speaks of industrial hopes.

Historical society museums are in Port Angeles, Port Townsend, and Sequim. An Olympic National Park information center with modest displays is at the base of the Hurricane Ridge Road in Port Angeles. Sequim holds an Irrigation Festival in May, one of the oldest community celebrations in the state. Port Townsend hosts events tied to local history, including a September wooden boat festival and spring and fall historic homes tours.

Today **CHIMACUM** is a crossroads community at the junction of bucolic Center and Beaver valleys. South of town sheep, cattle, and horses stand in pastures; ducks paddle on ponds; and old barns complement new metal sheds.

In 1853 William Bishop and William Eldridge, together with five crewmates from a British man-of-war, jumped ship in Victoria and rowed to the Olympic Peninsula. The two men claimed land in Center Valley, started a series of business ventures, and raised large families whose members eventually intermarried. In the 1920s author Betty MacDonald came as a young bride to Beaver Valley to raise chickens. Her biting memoir *The Egg and I* included the characters Ma and Pa Kettle, portrayals that local people still resent.

In 1945 a 35-foot incendiary balloon landed—harmlessly—at Chimacum. It was one of more

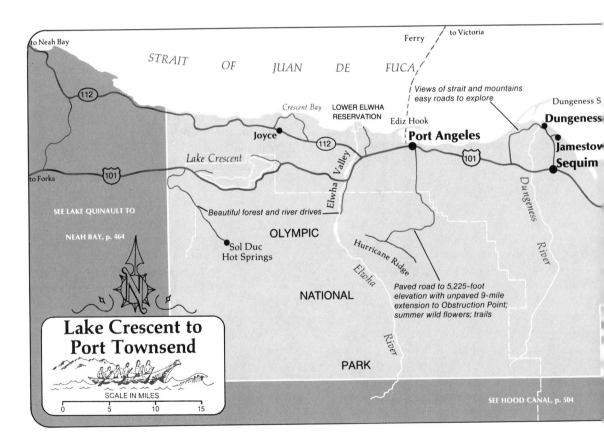

than 9,000 balloons released in Japan beginning in November 1944 to set American forests on fire and cause panic. Twenty-five landed in Washington; one drifted as far east as Michigan. The United States kept strict secrecy about all sightings, lest the Japanese know their system was working and release more balloons. What few fires actually ignited were quickly located and put out.

The pristine sweep of **CRESCENT BAY** now gives little clue of the town that once lined its shore; only a few persistent roses mark former cabin sites. Salt Creek Recreation Area offers beach access, camping, flaming summer sunsets, and agates mixed with wave-washed beach gravel.

In the 1860s several men—purportedly working for the Hudson's Bay Company—tended traplines and hunted on the north shore of the Olympic Peninsula, selling their furs and meat in Victoria. One lived in a cedar stump at Pysht (west of Crescent Bay). Others filed claims at Crescent Bay. Gradually loggers came

to cut coastal timber, and homesteaders along Salt Creek harvested marsh hay to sell as feed for the loggers' bull teams. In the late 1880s three Port Townsend investors foresaw great promise at Crescent Bay and platted a 166-block town, which they called Port Crescent. Their plans included a massive breakwater to protect oceangoing steamers and transcontinental rail connections plus a ferry to Victoria. They courted the Northern Pacific with tales of timber and gained incorporation of the Victoria, Port Crescent, and Chehalis Railroad Company. Crews surveyed a line to Grays Harbor and cleared the first 6 miles of right-of-way.

By 1888 about 600 people—mostly loggers—had moved to Port Crescent. A luxurious hotel faced the bay; stores opened; and, in 1891, a mill started sawing lumber and shingles. Meanwhile, the townsite company set to work on the breakwater. It proved too costly, however. The Northern Pacific therefore cancelled its interest. The townsite company went bankrupt. The bustling town—which had almost won the county seat—regressed into a quiet backwater.

In 1898 entrepreneur Michael Earles bought the vast timberland between Crescent Bay and the Elwha River and started bringing logs by rail to be boomed at Crescent Bay and towed to his brother's mill at Bellingham. The work sustained a camp of about 300 during the logging season, from April to October. In 1914 the Milwaukee Railroad built westward from Port Angeles, but stopped its tracks at Joyce, not at Crescent Bay. Logs then rolled by flatcar to Earles' huge new mill in Port Angeles. Stumpland and mud dotted with farms remained as testimony to successful logging and payrolls, but Port Crescent's day was over. Owners dismantled their buildings and moved them. The Joyce store, still in use, once stood at Crescent Bay.

During World War II, the federal government bought Port Crescent, razed the few remaining buildings, and built Camp Hayden. (Gun emplacements still remain in the county park.) Strategists feared invasion by Japanese forces and hastily fortified Puget Sound. The existing forts—Worden, Casey, and Flagler—were out of date, yet the Boeing aircraft plant and Bremerton naval shipyard were obvious targets. Defensive preparations included mining bridges,

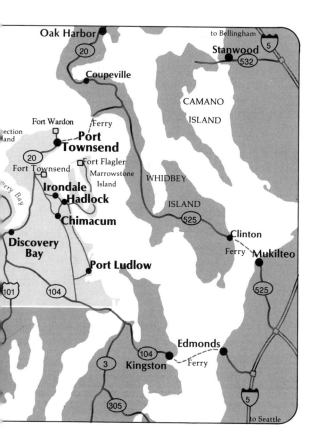

An octopus, crab, and oyster fishery formed at Dungeness. Octopus there (the world's largest species) weigh up to 80 pounds.

training civilians to watch for aircraft, installing submarine nets, and placing powerful guns at Camp Hayden. West of here, brush now hides fortifications at Cape Flattery and Portage Head (north of Point of Arches); supply problems thwarted actually installing guns. East of here, wooden gun barrels at Discovery Bay were intended to mislead the enemy.

Camp Hayden's 500 acres included barracks along Salt Creek and a powerful searchlight on Striped Peak (just east of Crescent Bay), where personnel logged the names of passing ships. Concrete bunkers held an underground mess hall and kitchen and two 45-foot rifled guns, the largest ever produced in the United States. Cots lined corridors so that soldiers could rest during alerts. The guns were fired only once—for practice. At the end of the war they were scrapped. (The bunkers now are included in Civilian Defense plans and used to store emergency supplies.)

DISCOVERY BAY forms a deep scallop southwest of Port Townsend: the highway follows the east shore; Diamond Point Road leads to the west shore. In 1792 the British naval officer Captain George Vancouver dropped anchor and sent his men ashore here to cut a new spar for his flagship, the sloop *Discovery*. Vancouver noted that the shore offered "thousands of the finest spars the world produces"—the first written mention of Washington's rich forest resources.

About 1848 William Brotchie also cut spars at Discovery Bay. He had served on the Hudson's Bay Company side-wheeler *Beaver* and on return to London convinced investors to send a ship for spars. Brotchie's men laboriously felled and limbed trees and dragged them to the water with help from local natives. Working for four months, they loaded 17 spars—each 70 to 90 feet long—into the hold of their vessel, the *Albion,* and were at work on an eighteenth when the U.S. customs collector traveling from Astoria to Steilacoom seized both spars and ship for unpaid duty. The United States and England only two years earlier had agreed on the 49th parallel as international boundary, and Brotchie (probably honestly) claimed not to know a customs office even existed. No matter. The customs collector ordered the *Albion* towed to Steilacoom and sold at auction. It sank (in San Francisco Bay) before its British owners could pay a fine and arrange redemption.

From 1858 to 1892 the S. B. Mastick Company of San Francisco operated a Discovery Bay sawmill that spawned a company town of about 300 residents including a "Chinamen's Gulch" where Chinese workers lived. Mastick's sloop, the *War Hawk,* loaded lumber at the end of a long wharf and made regular 16-day round-trip voyages between Discovery Bay and San

Francisco. Nearby settlers worked at the mill in spring, summer, and fall, then spent the winter cutting timber on their own homesteads for sale to the company. This was an ideal arrangement. It provided cash for clearing land, which the men would do anyway as a preparation for farming.

Today **Protection Island** (at the head of Discovery Bay) is a national wildlife refuge set aside especially for nesting rhinoceros auklets, pigeon guillemots, black oystercatchers, and glaucous-winged gulls. Over the years various settlers attempted to make homes on the island, but were defeated by a lack of water. In 1914 the superintendent of the quarantine station at Diamond Point (at the western entrance to Discovery Bay) proposed using the island as a leper colony. In the 1920s and 1930s a private gun club raised—and hunted—pheasants. In the 1950s promoters attempted a real estate development, which failed for a familiar reason: lack of water. The island has largely reverted to the wild. It is not open to the public.

Little remains of venerable **DUNGENESS** except the bare, worn pilings of a dock, several proud old houses, a two-story school building now used as a community hall, and the timeless view across the water to a long sandspit and the broad strait beyond. Victoria lies to the northwest, the San Juan Islands and Mount Baker to the northeast.

Marine Drive hugs the bluff west of the old town center. One and a half miles from the old school, a road drops to the beach at Cline Spit. Another 3 miles west, a short path leads to the base of Dungeness Spit from Dungeness Recreation Area (a county park occupying land that formerly was a Voice of America broadcast site, although never successfully used). Enjoy as much of the possible 5-mile beach walk as is appealing or perch on a drift log to gaze at passing ships and listen to the lap of waves. Anyone with a canoe or a kayak will find it worthwhile to paddle the broad, quiet waters of Dungeness Bay, protected by the spit and backdropped by the Olympics. Winter is especially beguiling with the mountains white and the bay speckled with great numbers of waterbirds.

In the early 1850s—about the same time that communities were beginning at Seattle and Port Townsend—a few settlers came to New Dungeness, among them Captain Elijah McAlmond who filed a donation land claim. He farmed the salt marsh here, traded along the coast, and built sailing ships. In the early 1860s McAlmond set his ship's carpenters to work building a house of sawn lumber brought from the mill at Discovery Bay. The result still stands on the bluff just west of the Dungeness River (Twin View Drive). A speaker addressing the local historical society in 1892 described the boost the house gave the community when new:

Houses were mostly built of logs with clapboard roofs and clay fireplaces. When Captain McAlmond built one of real lumber throughout, actually lathed and

Women at Dungeness worked together to save the school as a community center.

plastered inside, with real boughten doors and a cornice around the roof, there was a general feeling that the county had taken a long stride toward the opulence and luxury of the old world. The captain was elected justice of the peace out of pure deference for his superior attainments.

In 1891 a new townsite company built a long dock east of the river (end of Sequim–Dungeness Road), and businesses gradually clustered there, forming a second beach-level community 2 miles from New Dungeness, perched on the bluff. The dock was a marvel. It stretched for 4,300 feet with turnouts to let wagons pass each other and had racks of fire-wood hanging from its rails to service steam-boats. Farmers short on cash but long on trees filled the racks in return for credit on account.

Manifests for 1902 show primary incoming cargoes of whiskey, glass windows, seed wheat, and milk cows. Outgoing products were cream, butter, eggs, and potatoes.

Dungeness Spit—a narrow, 5½-mile fingerling of sand, drift logs, and beach grass stretching into the Strait of Juan de Fuca—is said to be the longest natural sandspit in the world. Black brant depend on the eelgrass that fringes its inner shore; loons, Canada geese, and shorebirds also frequent the protected waters, and seals haul out along the shore. The spit has been a wildlife refuge since 1915.

A lighthouse has occupied the tip of the spit since 1857. Its first keeper fed the lamp with lard oil and every few hours, day and night, wound the weights of a fog bell. The falling weights powered a gear mechanism—like that of a grandfather clock—which rang the bell automatically. The keeper rowed to Victoria for supplies. In an era of great isolation this was a convenience that ranked duty at the Dungeness lighthouse as highly desirable.

The **ELWHA VALLEY** (8 miles west of Port Angeles) penetrates deep into the Olympic Mountains. A road threads beside the river for 4 miles to campgrounds. An easy half-mile trail—paved and accessible by wheelchair—begins just inside the park boundary and leads for a half mile past homestead and mine sites to Madison Falls. From the road's end at Whiskey Bend, another trail leads up-valley into the heart of the Olympics. Sample it for a feeling of the Elwha; watch for elk in late fall when leaves have fallen from the alder and maple, permitting maximum visibility onto riverside meadows. At 2½ miles the trail reaches Humes Ranch, an 1890s homestead where a cabin of dovetailed logs still stands. Humes once mused:

Everybody in the city is saving for money—more money; always more. Yet they can only buy trash with it—not health, not youth, and all too often not contentment. The life they lead has no attraction for me and I am glad to get back to the cool, green woods and the peace and quiet and beauty to be enjoyed there.

Pioneers began settling the flat rim of the Olympic Peninsula in the mid-1850s, but the mountainous interior remained mysterious. Washington's Governor Eugene Semple spoke of that hinterland as "wonder-making in its unknown expanse of canyon and ridge." Many speculated that a great valley—or a plateau—filled the interior like a Shangri-la, albeit a Shangri-la with cannibals. In 1885 a sudden burst of exploration began. Lieutenant Joseph O'Neil led an army exploration into the moun-tains of the northern peninsula, and Charles and Samuel Gilman (father and son) crossed the mountains from Hood Canal to the Quinault Valley and also journeyed the length of the western lowlands. In the summer of 1890 O'Neil entered the mountains again, and a party of five would-be miners prospected the northeast Olympics. The real exploration sweepstakes that year, however, were won by the *Press* Exploring Expedition sponsored by a Seattle newspaper. Its young stalwarts started up the Elwha Valley in December 1889 "in order to be over the first ranges and into the central valleys ready for work when spring should open."

The *Seattle Press* had editorialized that a "fine opportunity for . . . fame" awaited whoever would "unveil the mystery" of the inner Olympics, and the writer called for someone to venture there and report his discoveries to the paper. On November 6—by chance, five days before Washington gained statehood—James Christie responded from North Yakima. He was a 35-year-old Scotsman who had spent three years exploring northwestern Canada. In less than a month six men, led by Christie, assembled for the expedition. They met at the ranch of Edmond Meany, a noted historian who was also a member of the *Press* staff. (His land was on what is now Roosevelt Way south of 45th, in Seattle's University District; at the time it was well out of the city.) Five expedition members were in their 30s; one—a cowboy from the Yakima Valley—was in his 20s. Two men were English, two Canadian, two American. One soon withdrew owing to the illness of his wife.

No map existed but, as any passenger steaming along the Strait of Juan de Fuca could clearly see, the Elwha Valley gashed deep into the mountains and offered a promising point of entry. The *Press* wrote of the party's "abundance of grit and manly vim." The men themselves demonstrated the vim by buying two mules and, with "splashing and plunging . . . shouting and braying" starting up the wintry Elwha with food, survey instruments, camera equipment, and 50 pounds of "colored fire" to use for lighting up, "if possible, some peak visible from Seattle."

In late December they worked with frozen fingers and frozen lumber to build a 30-foot, flat-bottomed boat—the *Gertie*—intended to carry them upstream "like Lewis and Clark." Unfortunately, however, they watched *Gertie* "leak like a thirsty fish" on completion. They upended her over a fire, dried the planks, recaulked, and relaunched—although their success included repeated episodes with "all hands overboard in water to the waist" to save the cargo from the "swirling and boiling" of the river.

By the end of January deep snow stymied the mules, and the party built sleds for hauling their supplies and gear. Each man followed his own design. Charles Barnes, expedition cartographer, wrote of one sled, "It is its glory that it did not fail—it never started." Three months of ebullience and stubborn effort had netted the party only 20 miles.

A month and a half later the men clawed up what they supposed was a divide separating the Elwha from the Quinault, but they had misjudged and dropped back. "Such is the fate of explorers," Barnes wrote. "We are here to find these things out."

On May 4 they again scaled rock walls, using a rope to haul up packs and the three dogs that

had accompanied them. The prize was finally theirs. The party descended into the Quinault Valley; met a settler ("God help his plug of tobacco!"); and in another few days had hired a team of horses and were "bowling down the beach" from the mouth of the Quinault River to Oyehut. There they sailed to Aberdeen and the luxury of hotel beds. Christie telegraphed Meany that the journey was done—and to please send money by return wire.

"With pardonable pride," the *Seattle Press* on July 16, 1890, published the men's accounts, which established for the first time that the Olympics were not an ordinary range but a welter of peaks totally lacking a vast central valley or a plateau and without cannibals.

In 1910 Thomas T. Aldwell, manager of the *Port Angeles Tribune-Times* and an effective entrepreneur, began building a hydroelectric dam at an Elwha River site he had bought in the mid-1890s. Potential profits were backed by industrial beginnings at Port Angeles plus agreements from Port Townsend and from a steel mill at Irondale to purchase power. Aldwell also had tentative agreement from the Bremerton Naval Yard and Forts Worden and Flagler. Unfortunately, contractors hung the dam from canyon sidewalls rather than footing it against bedrock, disastrously poor judgment. During an October 1912 downpour, deep glacier gravels beneath the dam blew out. The entire impoundment of 12,000 acre-feet drained down-valley in less than two hours, a roaring, swirling torrent that destroyed property but took no lives. Aldwell rebuilt, and in 1926 a second dam was added at Glines Canyon.

The dams continue to provide power—and controversy. They were built without passage-ways for salmon and steelhead, despite state requirements. Today volunteers and hatchery-men have restored runs to the lower Elwha well enough that watching fish enter from salt water into the river makes an impressive fall sight. (From the east side of the Elwha River bridge, turn north off State Route 112 and follow signs to The Place, a row of residences at the beach along the strait. Turn east and park near the river mouth.) The dams also affected the flow of sediment into the Strait of Juan de Fuca and the loss of this material, carried east by the current, has caused Ediz Hook to erode. Maintenance requires rock riprap, a costly Army Corps of Engineers project. (For a look, drive to the harbor at Port Angeles and follow around the water to the Coast Guard base at the tip of the sandspit.)

HADLOCK forms the commercial core of the three-community area of Hadlock, Irondale, and Chimacum. Modern stores line today's crossroads, and along Hadlock's waterfront wooden buildings of the old "downtown" section still remain, used as restaurants and shops (Water Street at the foot of Lower Hadlock Road). Across the bay from them is an enormous former alcohol distillery, now converted to a hotel and restaurant.

The alcohol plant belonged to the Washington Mill Company of San Francisco, which first operated a sawmill here in 1886 after its Seabeck mill burned (see p. 380). The Port Hadlock wharf could accommodate the multiple schooners needed for that company's scale of business. From the Hadlock dock, lumber went to build Forts Worden, Flagler, and Casey and the naval depot on Indian Island. It also moved to world markets.

In 1907, however, the company closed the mill, owing to a severe drop in prices. Company president William J. Adams (grandfather of renowned photographer Ansel Adams) then decided to try a new method of turning softwood sawdust into alcohol. He bought patent rights, secured technical assistance from the parent firm in France—the Classen Chemical Company—and began plans for a distillery at Hadlock. In 1911, after a delay caused by Adams' death, the plant opened. In theory, alcohol production was an ideal Puget Sound industry. Sawdust was both cheap and abundant; the market for fuel alcohol was growing; and distillery byproducts, mixed with molasses, could be sold as an animal feed called bastol.

Difficulties arose immediately, however. The first batch of alcohol was returned to Hadlock as substandard, and the first hundred sacks of bastol mildewed in a San Francisco warehouse. Company managers switched their process to making alcohol from Hawaiian molasses instead of from sawdust, and more difficulties set in. Historians generally say that Eastern manufacturers, who used sawdust from hardwood,

resented a new, softwood product appearing in "their" alcohol market and colluded to shut out Hadlock. In his autobiography recounting family history, however, Ansel Adams comments that Hawaiian sugarcane growers, who produced alcohol directly from cane, reacted negatively to the competition. According to Adams:

The Hawaii Sugar Trust put the company out of business by buying up the stock, discharging the directors and executives, and operating the plant in a thoroughly destructive way.

Hadlock production never got beyond the experimental batches of bastol and alcohol. In 1913 the plant closed. It stood derelict for 65 years until its present innovative remodeling.

Today **IRONDALE** is a residential area: row upon row of large lots, large trees, and scattered houses characterize its neighborhoods. Nearby Hadlock provides commercial and professional services; Chimacum has a huge consolidated school complex. Irondale now has no particular center, but Moore Street (which dead-ends at the waterfront) once led to an iron smelter.

The smelter began in 1879 when Samuel Hadlock, who already had platted the Hadlock townsite, joined with other local businessmen to incorporate the Puget Sound Iron Company. They planned to use bog iron from the Bishop family's farm at Chimacum as ore. To process it workmen built a 38-foot conical furnace from beach cobbles. They heated the ore with charcoal and added limestone from Roche Harbor (on San Juan Island) to draw out impurities. Every eight hours they tapped the furnace and poured molten iron into molds hollowed in sand.

In 1881 the company began mixing the bog iron with ore from Texada Island, British Columbia (offshore from Powell River). They built 20 kilns to turn nearly a thousand cords of wood per day into charcoal, and employed 400 men to mine and smelt the ore. The resulting high-quality iron readily found a market in San Francisco, but the plant closed in 1889. Crude machinery, inept management, high import duty on Canadian ore, labor costs, and the indifference of San Francisco stockholders all contributed.

Twelve years later the company reorganized

to produce steel. Seattle's *Post-Intelligencer* speculated that a steel mill on Puget Sound would "mean more to Seattle and the state of Washington than even the discovery of gold in Alaska." In December of that year black smoke "shot out of the big flue, followed by a red blaze," and foundries from Alaska to California started using Irondale's output.

In 1909 the *Port Townsend Weekly Leader* leaked information that Seattle's Moran Brothers might move their shipyards to Irondale and that the Western Steel Company was looking forward to the building of the Milwaukee railroad. By the following year Irondale had steam heat, electric lights, a newspaper, six stores, a contract for a hospital, and a signed agreement to import ore from Hankow, China. The plant was producing nearly 700 tons of finished steel per week. Crews worked around the clock. But as 1911 opened, word came that the East Coast's Carnegie Trust had suspended operations. Bankruptcies ensued. Irondale collapsed. After a brief reopening during World War I to use up stockpiled raw materials, workers dismantled the machinery and smokestack and surrendered the rubble to wild blackberries.

JAMESTOWN stretches along the beach north of Sequim, a narrow enclave of flower-bedecked houses. Its origins represent Native Americans' remarkable ability to bridge cultures without losing heart.

From the 1850s through the early 1870s, white settlers at Dungeness displaced native Klallam people, and additional displacement came with the opening of a sawmill at Port Discovery (Discovery Bay). Under terms of the 1856 Point No Point treaty all Hood Canal natives had been "assigned" to the Skokomish Reservation—a small, infertile tract at the base of Hood Canal—but few moved there. Instead, they shifted from camp to camp as incoming whites increasingly dominated their territory. (Also see HANSVILLE, p. 373.)

In 1874 tribal leader James Balch spearheaded the purchase of about 250 acres of land that had been logged. By accepting white men's rules, he hoped to guarantee his people a home no one could preempt. All contributors received parcels according to how much they had paid in—and those who could not pay anything also received lots. A total of about 130 Klallam moved to Jamestown, named for Balch.

They continued making individual spirit quests and gave potlatches (although Balch, who was not a hereditary chief, opposed the custom). They also fished from dugout canoes, and some men added oarlocks to the gunwales. Many worked for wages at the cannery and sawmill operating in their traditional territory; they also raised pigs, planted orchards among the cedar stumps on the land, and raised oats for their horses. Elders who had once watched the ships of Spanish and British explorers sail along their shore now lived in houses with glass windows and watched the oncoming generations play baseball and dance waltzes.

In 1980, after decades of negotiations, the federal government finally recognized the Jamestown Klallam as an entity entitled to relations on a government-to-government basis.

Ten-mile-long **LAKE CRESCENT** almost poses a dilemma for drivers: the curving road and the scenic beauty both demand full attention. The water—deep blue on clear days, dove gray on overcast days—laps against rocky ballast at one side of the road; forested slopes meet the other side. In April vine maple tips glow wine red and alder tassels hang like diminutive bursting sausages. In October bigleaf maple leaves the size of dinner plates carpet the earth with gold.

An Olympic National Park information station housed in the historic Morgenroth cabin is situated about 2½ miles from the east end of the lake. Chris Morgenroth served as ranger in the Olympic Forest Reserve, predecessor of both Olympic National Park and Olympic National Forest. He gained renown for planting trees after the 1907 Soleduck fire—the National Forest Service's first attempt at reforestation—and for advocating the protection of representative stands of old-growth forest rather than logging every readily merchantable tree. In 1905 Morgenroth built this finely crafted cabin as a guard station and home, the first such structure in the reserve. Nearby, the Marymere Falls trail (2 miles round trip) leads away from the sounds of road traffic into well-padded forest, which is graced with the trill of winter wrens and the splashing of the falls.

SPRUCE ARMY

By the time the United States entered World War I in 1917, the Allies desperately needed aircraft. At first armies used "aeroplanes" only for observation; then a French ace mounted a machine gun on his plane, and soon weapons manufacturers perfected timing so that a gun could fire between the blades of a whirling propeller. Aerial warfare had arrived.

Airplanes were fragile constructs. Spruce framed the fuselage and wings; linen sheathed that frame. Aircraft manufacturers specified spruce because of its light weight, strength, and resilience. Moreover, its long, tough fibers tended not to shatter when hit by gunfire.

Northwest forests abounded in spruce, but the summer of 1917 brought a bitter loggers' strike and the virtual shutdown of the Northwest's woods. In September the army sent Colonel Brice Disque, a former prison warden and an adroit manager, to rectify the situation. Disque formed the unique Spruce Production Division, an army corps dedicated to supplying top-quality spruce for combat planes. Disque's soldiers—some experienced loggers, some draftees—cut trees, laid track, manned existing sawmills, and built new ones. Eventually 30,000 soldier-loggers were in the Spruce Division, about a third of them detailed to railroad construction. The men lived under military discipline but received civilian wages, which were standardized from camp to camp.

The influx of military personnel affected Northwest logging. Clean bedding—an amenity the Industrial Workers of the World had demanded vainly for years—became accepted throughout the industry. After brief refusal, management also instituted an eight-hour workday, another previously proposed reform. In part, these changes came about through the Loyal Legion of Lumbermen and Loggers, organized by Disque. The 4-L, as they were dubbed, served as a "union" for both management and workers. Through it, grievances could be hammered out. The main function was patriotic. Members adopted eight objectives, including determination

. . . to aid this country in every way possible . . . particularly by speeding up the production of spruce and fir for airplanes and ships.

To render first aid to the boys who are fighting in France, by giving them aircraft that outclasses anything the Kaiser can produce.

The Spruce Division proved expensive, but efficient. In one year soldier-loggers cut 150 million board feet of spruce, graded and laid 130 miles of railroad track, and began building one of the world's largest sawmills in Port Angeles. On November 11, 1918, the war ended, and on November 12 the Spruce Division stopped cutting trees. The division's longest railroad (from Lake Pleasant to Joyce, about 50 miles) never carried a single log, and the Port Angeles mill stood only 70 percent complete. But the Armistice spared more than human lives. Had the war continued, today's rain forest in Olympic National Park would certainly have fallen to the saws of the "Spruce Army."

Rosemary Inn, a rustic resort that opened about 1916, now provides quarters for summer field seminars open to the public; ask about them at any Olympic National Park information station (and, to attend, make an advance reservation). Lake Crescent Lodge, a refurbished early-day resort (opened in 1915 as Singer's Tavern) is just west of Rosemary Inn.

Spur roads reach the north shore of Lake Crescent connected by a 4-mile trail along the roadbed of the 1918 Spruce Division Railroad. (From the west end of the lake at Fairholm, follow Camp David Jr. Road to its end; or from the lake's east end, follow East Beach Road 4

The army's Spruce Division built a logging railroad along Lake Crescent's shore.

miles to a trailhead parking lot.) Another hike leads 3½ steep miles up Pyramid Peak to an aircraft warning station that was built during World War II. (The trailhead is 3½ miles off U.S. 101 on the Camp David Jr. Road.)

The first of several families to homestead the shores of Lake Crescent arrived in 1890. They found themselves almost immediately catering to the needs of fishermen, hikers, and nature enthusiasts and, within a year, Paul Barnes (brother of Charles Barnes, a member of the *Press* Exploring Expedition) added an excursion boat to the amenities he offered. He built it at Crescent Bay and hauled it by team and sled over the rough 7-mile trail to the lake. The county later added auto ferries, which operated until a road along Lake Crescent was completed in 1922.

Beginning in 1912 lakeside resorts included a "health and biological institution" called Qui Si Sana, somewhat ungrammatical Latin for "Here Get Well." In many ways Qui Si Sana was representative of the health resorts of the era, including nearby Olympic Hot Springs in the Elwha Valley (now closed, although the springs remain in their natural state) and Sol Duc Hot Springs (Soleduck Valley, still operated as a resort). In other ways Qui Si Sana was unusual.

Its owner and director was a German-born naturopathic physician named Louis Dechmann who provided guests with 60-degree baths, vinegar "wraps," open-air cabins, and assurance that good health could be guaranteed through diet and exercise augmented by hydrotherapy and radium treatments. His operation closed in 1918 apparently in part owing to World War I accusations that Dechmann was "pro-German" and had raised the German flag above the American flag at Lake Crescent. Buildings and grounds eventually were converted for use as a county youth camp (Camp David Jr.). Original structures have been replaced and little remains of Qui Si Sana's once elaborate landscaping and statuary.

The **LOWER ELWHA RESERVATION,** 9 miles west of Port Angeles, is one of three small enclaves inhabited by descendants of Klallams who signed the 1855 Treaty of Point No Point. That document arranged for all Klallam bands to move to the Skokomish Reservation on Hood Canal, but most refused because the reservation had few resources and lay in the territory of traditional enemies. Instead they remained on their ancestral land: one band bought land at Jamestown; another settled near Port Gamble;

and a third band settled at the mouth of the Elwha River. In the 1930s the federal government purchased land for this third band, creating the Lower Elwha Reservation.

(Also see JAMESTOWN, p. 491.)

MARROWSTONE ISLAND and adjacent Indian Island (now a naval ordnance depot) lie southwest of Port Townsend, connected to the mainland by a bridge. Marrowstone's road leads past the 1890s bayside village of Nordland and on to Fort Flagler, once a major component of Puget Sound coastal defense and now a state park with abandoned gun placements, weathered barracks, and a windswept beach. Each summer members of the Seattle Youth Symphony use the barracks for intensive music training and offer public performances.

When the Puget Sound Naval Shipyard at Bremerton opened in 1896, the 50-year-old forts at Steilacoom, Bellingham, and Port Townsend suddenly seemed woefully inadequate. Reviewing coastal defenses, Secretary of War William C. Endicott had submitted a revolutionary plan for camouflaged forts of reinforced concrete armed with rifled cannons on disappearing carriages. Some East Coast forts were refitted to meet these specifications, and Congress authorized three new, "pure" Endicott forts for Puget Sound: Fort Worden at the northeast corner of the Olympic Peninsula, Fort Casey on the protruding west shore of Whidbey Island, and Fort Flagler on the northern tip of Marrowstone Island. The three served as training facilities during both world wars, and were eventually sold to the state for use as parks.

OLYMPIC NATIONAL PARK offers a greater variety of nature's magnificence than characterizes other parks outside of Alaska. It has been designated a UNESCO World Heritage Site (one of only 112) and an International Biosphere Reserve.

The Olympic Mountains stand less than 8,000 feet high yet host about 50 glaciers that have sculpted deep valleys. Wild-flower meadows carpet mile-high slopes free of snow for only about 10 fleeting weeks per year. Forty miles of wilderness beaches line the western edge of the park. And between the peaks and coast, magnificent virgin forest spreads like a shag rug of green. The park is a choice, lingering sample of primeval western Washington.

Its land was first set aside in 1897 as a forest reserve, then nine years later as Mount Olympus National Monument. The monument was intended to preserve elk, which were being hunted to the point of possible extermination simply for their teeth, popular as watch fobs and worth a considerable sum. Boundary changes later removed the elk's winter range from protection—and thereby restored huge stands of cedar and spruce for possible logging. Beginning in 1936 Congress considered bills for a national park and finally approved one in 1938, after President Franklin D. Roosevelt had visited the peninsula and expressed support. The ocean strip was added in 1953.

Questions concerning park boundaries—and adjustments and attempted adjustments—have repeatedly focused on lowland forests, owing to their commercial value. Timber interests have testified to the dollar value of *single trees* that each would yield 40,000 board feet of lumber, an astonishing size compared with trees in Eastern forests—and now in western Washington forests—where production *per acre* is less than a third of that. The argument has been that even these last huge trees should be "harvested." At the initial hearings for the park, however, Chris Morgenroth, the first ranger for the forest reserve, urged the opposite:

Those tremendous trees . . . They say they are ripe, overripe. They are overripe, yes; and some of them will fall down. Some of them have fallen down a hundred years ago, and some of them will keep on falling down and others will take their place in the process which has gone on for a thousand years, and will keep on going, just like the human race, exactly.

Advocates argued that the national park belongs to the ongoing process; within it, people are to observe—and enjoy—but not dominate or consume. Nature is to be viewed as a community rather than a commodity.

PORT ANGELES edges a sheltered harbor created by **Ediz Hook,** a 4-mile sandspit. Welcoming its protection in 1791, Spanish explorer Francisco de Eliza named the harbor Puerto de Nuestra Senora de Los Angeles, "Port of Our Lady of the Angels."

Snow covers Hurricane Ridge from October to July. The inner Olympic Mountains—almost 8,000 feet high—host about 50 glaciers (snow packed to ice by its own weight).

The town now sits like a stage set walled by snowy, mile-high Hurricane Ridge in Olympic National Park (reached by a paved 18-mile road) and with 6,000-foot Blue Mountain just to the east (also accessible by an 18-mile road that is mostly unpaved, narrow, and winding; ask about current conditions). A Park Service visitor center is at the base of the Hurricane Ridge Road (at the southern edge of town, reached by driving toward the mountains on Race Street). Victoria, British Columbia, lies 23 miles across the Strait of Juan de Fuca from Port Angeles, served by ferry. (It is a 1½-hour crossing worth taking as a scenic excursion; downtown Victoria is readily accessible from the ferry dock without an automobile, and tour buses connect with all major sightseeing attractions.) A road leads along Ediz Hook, ideal for its view across the harbor to the town and mountains. For an introduction to local history, visit the county historical society museum (Lincoln and 4th, moving after 1998 to 8th and C).

Port Angeles' basic tale involves two Smiths: promoter Victor Smith, who dreamed of a "National City" in the 1860s, and George Venable Smith, who founded a utopian colony in the 1890s. Victor Smith, U.S. customs collector, arrived in Washington Territory with his family in 1861. Although based at Port Townsend, he nonetheless actively promoted Port Angeles as a better port of entry. Port Townsend, he said, was a "rotten borough" with only a "roadstead" and no safe harbor. Far from coincidentally, he also invested in a Port Angeles real estate development and repeatedly wrote officials in Washington, D.C., pointing out the relative merits of Port Angeles versus Port Townsend. In 1862 Secretary of the Treasury Samuel Chase sent a note to the Senate Commerce Committee siding with Smith. Port Angeles was superior because of its location

nearer the ocean and commanding the Straits of Fuca, and the shipping to and from Victoria, and also on account of its better harbor, there being no good and safe accommodation for vessels at Port Townsend.

Smith's lobbying had succeeded. Not only did Congress authorize moving the official port of entry to Port Angeles, but President Abraham Lincoln signed an order reserving Ediz Hook and the land within its protective arm for federal purposes. These included a lighthouse at the tip of the sandspit, a "Navy and Military Reservation" at the base, and about 3,000 acres as a townsite reserve. Its lots would be sold. The treasury, depleted by the Civil War, needed revenue.

Since the mid-1800s, Olympic Peninsula logs have supplied local mills and have been shipped abroad. Here, Port Angeles longshoremen load hemlock on board ships from Japan.

When Smith returned after three months in the nation's capital, however, he found that the customs collector serving in his absence—Lieutenant James Merryman—had discovered discrepancies and refused to turn over the customs records. Smith got them, but only by such tactics as first threatening to bombard Port Townsend with the guns of the *Shubrick,* a lighthouse tender, and subsequently churning the water to a frenzy with the ship's paddle wheel so that a marshal rowing out to deliver an indictment was forced to turn back.

Port Angeles became the port of entry, but not for long. In 1865 Victor Smith drowned in a shipwreck off the California coast and, the following year, Port Townsend regained its prize. Most of the few residents who had tied their dreams to Smith's moved away from Port Angeles. With him gone, all that was left of his development scheme was choice land rendered inaccessible for settling by its status as a federal reserve.

For 20 years Port Angeles moldered. Then attorney George Venable Smith, a leader in Seattle's anti-Chinese riots, set about founding a cooperative colony. He selected land just east of the federal reserve at the mouth of Ennis Creek. A declaration of 26 principles included a statement that "everyone shall act as a civilized being, shall avoid all excesses, be just and undeceiving to all." With this as a foundation, a brochure published in 1887 promised that at the Puget Sound Cooperative Colony:

Want and Misery, and their supposed antidote, Charity, will be unknown, as there will be no poor. . . . Women will receive equal pay with men, for equal work. . . . Doctors will be employed on salary . . . and as sickness would only increase their work without a corresponding increase of income, it would be to their interest to aid everyone to keep in perfect health. . . . Lawyers will be scarce, as no litigation can occur under our proposed system.

The colony founded a newspaper, cleared land, built a sawmill and shipyard, opened a school, and issued its own scrip as payment for labor. As with many other colonies, the experiment succeeded, then frayed. The adjoining town of Port Angeles had grown, and young people from town and colony married one another and charted a new destiny.

The decade of the 1880s created a boom; the Northern Pacific brought both investors and immigrants seeking land. The federal reserve restricted expansion at Port Angeles but, on July 4, 1890, squatters marched onto it, surveyed lots, and settled down. They had "jumped" the reserve. They won. After three years Congress acquiesced, and the land became public domain. Squatter's rights prevailed.

A creamery opened, also a brewery and various mills—even a sequence of offices representing railroads, including the Union Pacific and the Northern Pacific. In 1914 the Milwaukee line finally arrived via a railroad ferry across Puget Sound to Port Townsend and—soon—on to Port Angeles. That same year a hydroelectric project on the Elwha River west of town began supplying power, and a huge sawmill opened on the land that had been settled by the cooperative colony. Timber resources became the town's economic lifeblood, with an emphasis also on commercial fishing.

At **PORT LUDLOW** gleaming condominiums climb the hillside and individual homes are tastefully sited amid hemlock and spruce. Their view is across a deeply indented harbor where pleasure boats tie to docks and ride at anchor. The scene contrasts strongly with Port Ludlow's past as a Victorian sawmill town, its bay bristling with the masts of lumber ships.

That original town began in 1853 when San Francisco investors sent W. F. Sayward here to build a sawmill. His was a small-scale operation, not really efficient or reliable but located on a magnificent site: Port Ludlow lay near the eastern end of the Strait of Juan de Fuca, surrounded by timber. In 1879 Pope and Talbot bought Sayward's property and rebuilt the mill.

Cyrus Walker, manager of the company's mill at nearby Port Gamble, added overseeing the Port Ludlow mill to his responsibilities. His stern and conservative policies shaped both communities. When sales were slow, he had employees work at improving facilities and equipment, and he never hesitated to roll up his own sleeves and join them. Through his guidance, Pope and Talbot became a leader in systematically buying forest land—not just stumpage. These purchases included 15,000 acres of former federal land that had been released in 1861 to finance construction of a territorial university. Purchases also included 17,000 acres paid for with scrip issued to veterans of the 1846 to 1848 Mexican War; the scrip was good only for buying land, and men who had no interest in acreage readily sold their scrip at a discount to Pope and Talbot.

The company also bought private holdings. After 1878 it used—and abused—the Timber and Stone Act to acquire still more. That law allowed individuals to file for title to 160 acres of land unsuitable for agriculture as a timber claim, providing they did not do so on a speculative basis. In actuality, even ship's crews came ashore and filed under the act, then sold to timber companies.

In 1885—at age 58—Walker cemented ties to Pope and Talbot by marrying Emily Talbot. The couple lived in the manager's house at Port Gamble; it burned, and they moved to a new mansion at Port Ludlow, for which Walker hand-picked every piece of lumber. Admiralty Hall's front doors slid open like those of a ship's cabin, and a massive stairway rose right and left leading to a dozen second-story bedrooms. Chinese houseboys tended to guests; a 38-star flag fluttered above a third-story square cupola; and a ceremonial cannon beside the porch roared salutes welcoming lumber ships from South Africa, Argentina, Australia, the South Sea Islands, California, Mexico, and Peru.

The opulence had a short life. Through the 1890s market gluts and poor prices repeatedly closed the Port Ludlow mill, as all Pope and Talbot business was concentrated at Port Gamble. The Klondike gold rush boosted Puget Sound's economy in 1897 and temporarily revived production, but Port Ludlow's era really had ended. Rail lines were replacing sailing

The manager of the huge, late-1800s sawmill at Port Ludlow entertained guests from all over the world at Admiralty Hall, his mansion. No indication of the house remains today.

ships, and docks stood quiet most of the time. The Walkers moved to San Francisco. The port became a ferry terminus; by 1914, travelers slept at Admiralty Hall and dined with the silver and crystal left from its days of past glory.

The mill limped along until 1935, operated for its last 10 years by a Delaware firm rather than by Pope and Talbot. In 1940 wreckers demolished the mansion and, to help fill World War II housing shortages, other company homes left Port Ludlow by barge for use elsewhere. The mill, which had been dismantled, burned.

In the late 1960s Pope and Talbot repurchased their former land and developed today's residential and resort complex. Gulls still roost on log booms at night, but the masts rising and falling with the tide are made of aluminum and carry radar dishes in their rigging.

(Also see PORT GAMBLE, p. 375.)

To fully appreciate **PORT TOWNSEND,** view it from the Whidbey Island ferry or a private boat. The town extends along the shore where the Strait of Juan de Fuca turns into Admiralty Inlet; every vessel in and out of Puget Sound passes by. Two neat rows of masonry buildings fill the narrow flat between the waterfront and the bluff, and fine homes and churches occupy the uplands—a scene little changed in a century.

To explore the town—much of it designated as a National Historic District—drive or walk along Water Street with its rhythmic facades of the late 1880s and early 1890s. Many of the buildings now house galleries, craft outlets, and specialty shops. The **Mount Baker Block** (Water and Taylor; built in 1890) was first planned as a five-story hotel but changed to a commercial and office building. It ended up with only four stories, the top two of them framed in but left unfinished. Diagonally across the street the three-story **Hastings Building** (Water and Taylor; built in 1889) was designed by Elmer Fisher, one of Seattle's most prominent architects after that city's disastrous 1889 fire. A Port Townsend foundry fabricated the Hastings Building's cast-iron facade; the ceiling is "fireproof" embossed metal molded to look like decorative plaster. The 1904 **Rose Theater** (on Taylor near Washington) has been restored. It began with vaudeville and switched to silent movies. Original murals remain. The county historical society **museum** in the 1891 city hall building (Water and Madison) displays memorabilia from sailing-ship heydays.

Public buildings worth seeking out include the county courthouse and the combined customs house and post office, on the hill above the waterfront at the southwest side of town. The **courthouse** (Jefferson and Cass; built in 1892) radiates a sense of eminence and stability. Willis Ritchie was the architect; his other remaining county courthouses are in Bellingham, Olympia, and Spokane.

The three-story federal **customs house and post office** (Washington and Harrison; built in 1893) was completed just as Port Townsend's boom ended. The building is brick veneered with stone. Notice the capitals decorating columns at the southern entrance (intended as the main entrance but relegated to side-door status, then closed, because of prevailing winds). The stone faces represent Klallam headman Chetzemoka, his two wives, and his brother. They were nicknamed the Duke of York, Queen Victoria, Jenny Lind, and King George by whites, who probably did not think of the names as condescending or of dominating Klallam land as anything other than inevitable.

Chetzemoka had visited San Francisco aboard a lumber ship in 1850 and been impressed by the "Bostons'" power. Five years later, following the Point No Point Treaty, he had watched 50 loaded canoes paddle out from the native village at Port Townsend and tie on behind a steamer, which towed them to the Skokomish Reservation at the base of Hood Canal. Fire set by whites leapt from the natives' beachside houses even before the canoes were out of sight. (A city park— famed for its view across Admiralty Inlet and its 1905 gazebo—is named for Chetzemoka; the park is located on the bluff at the foot of Blaine Street.)

Buffs of Victorian architecture will find gems on almost every residential street in Port Townsend; local contractors used pattern books to assure frontier clients the fashions and comforts available in more established regions. Several houses now offer bed-and-breakfast accommodations; some are open for touring year-round; and May and September historic homes tours provide entrée to others.

Two houses in particular bracket the 20-year period of expansion here. The simple **David Rothschild house** (Jefferson and Taylor; built in 1868) is the clean-lined, Classic Revival home of a successful merchant whose varied enterprises included warehouses and oil tanks as well as outlets for ships' stores and wholesale merchandise supplied to Seattle retailers. (The State Parks System now manages the house, which still holds original furnishings including clothing worn by household members. The house was occupied until 1959 by a spinster daughter, who kept things as they always had been.) In contrast, the **Starrett house** (Adams and Clay; built in 1889) radiates tasteful flamboyance. A free-standing spiral staircase climbs a round corner tower with ceiling murals of maidens representing the Four Seasons (one of whom—Winter—impressed society matrons as lewd because of her wind-tossed draperies). Starrett, in his 20s, worked as a carpenter and contractor; in 1889 he told the Port Townsend Leader that he had built dozens of houses in town and was now building his own. Its craftsmanship and design represent Starrett well.

The "uptown" (Lawrence Street) shopping district in the midst of the residential neighborhood was developed to offer respectable matrons an alternative to the coarse waterfront of the 1880s. Nearby, **Saint Paul's Episcopal Church** (Jefferson and Tyler; built in 1865) has a bell donated by the captain of a revenue cutter. He had been saved from running aground in foggy conditions by the sound of a hand bell calling students to class. In appreciation, he brought the church bell on his next trip to Port Townsend, asking that it be rung during foggy weather. Two blocks away, the **Presbyterian church** (Franklin and Polk; built in 1890) features an organ with 692 pipes. A fire bell tower stands on the bluff (end of Tyler Street).

West of the main historic district is turreted **Manresa "Castle"** (Sheridan and 7th; built in 1892). Charles Eisenbeis arrived in 1858 to open a bakery supplying ships with pilot biscuit (hard, dry crackers that keep well). He also owned a brewery, grocery, brickyard, and clothing store and was instrumental in nearly bringing the Union Pacific to town. He built a colossal three-story home doubtless intended as a reminder of Prussia, his childhood home. In 1925 the house was purchased by Jesuits, who named it Manresa Hall, added a wing, and faced the entire building with stucco. Eisenbeis had built with the warm texture of brick.

Port Townsend began with homestead claims filed in April 1851, six months before Seattle's pioneering Denny party landed at Alki Point.

Alfred Plummer and Charles Bachelder came here by canoe from Steilacoom (near Tacoma) to farm and supply salted salmon and timber for Captain Lafayette Balch, who traded between San Francisco and Steilacoom. A few months later the Francis Pettygrove and Loren Hastings families joined them, having moved north from Portland (co-founded by Pettygrove and named for his home, Portland, Maine).

In 1854 the U.S. Customs office moved here. It had been in Olympia, which forced sea captains to sail the length of Puget Sound before legally going ashore. Isaac Ebey had been appointed customs collector in 1853, and he campaigned for Port Townsend to be designated as the official port of entry. From his home on the west shore of Whidbey Island he could see ships turning in or out of the Strait of Juan de Fuca and cross the inlet to clear them.

With ships required to stop, Port Townsend readily grew as a supply center. Its legal services included banking and merchandising and also consul representation by Great Britain, France, Norway, Sweden, Germany, and the independent kingdom of Hawaii. Illicit services included notorious "recruitment" of loggers turned into sailors by means of "deep sleep drinks" laced with knockout drops. Water level doors in brick buildings, intended for cargo handling, and trap-doors in the wharfs behind saloons simplified loading comatose crewmen-to-be into rowboats and delivering them to waiting ships. Many a young man who remembered going to Water Street to celebrate payday woke up somewhere off Cape Flattery.

Port Townsend's 1850s economy at first depended largely on San Francisco's gold rush appetite for Puget Sound timber. By 1858 and into the 1860s it benefited from gold discoveries on the Fraser River and in the Cariboo District of British Columbia; thousands of miners streamed north. Through the 1870s Port Townsend grew steadily but unspectacularly. For a while it expected to be the West Coast terminus of the transcontinental railroad, a vain hope fostered by the appointment of Judge James Swan as Northern Pacific agent. The tracks stopped at Tacoma instead. Nonetheless, Port Townsend burgeoned, boosted by the population surge and overall optimism that rode the rails across the entire state in the 1880s.

An unusual feature during this period was the growth of Port Townsend's Chinese community, sorely beleaguered elsewhere. A dozen or more Chinese mercantile firms advertised items such as tea, rice, imported crockery, and opium—a legal substance carrying a duty of $12 per pound and therefore often actually smuggled in from Canada. Several firms also acted as labor contractors supplying workmen and ships' crews, some legal and some illegal.

Federal laws changed every few years but in general prohibited Chinese laborers from entering the country after 1882, although merchants, scholars, and diplomats were still allowed to come in. As a result Port Townsend companies such as Yet Wo and Get Kee had minuscule shops of only a few square feet with inventories not over $500, but on paper they had 10 to 20 partners. Since merchants did not need to live in the town where they did business, the Port Townsend Wing Sing Company had 13 partners who listed addresses from Seattle and Portland to Philadelphia.

Discussing labor contracting, Ng June, of the prosperous and respected Zee Tai Company, in 1890 testified before a Congressional committee:

I take contracts to supply labor. My profits lie in keeping the men in supplies. . . . I have never smuggled, but have heard it stated that for $20 a head Chinamen can be gotten from British Columbia.

Railroad fever continued through the 1880s with boosters reasoning that a line from the Columbia River to Port Townsend was likely, since international connections were already well established here. They demonstrated their conviction by forming the Port Townsend and Southern Railroad and laying a mile of track. In 1889 the Oregon Improvement Company (a Union Pacific subsidiary) bought that token track. They promised to continue it to Portland and accepted land donated for a Port Townsend terminus. Town fathers celebrated with a massive building spree that produced six banks, three hotels, and numerous commercial buildings within a single year. Small lots sold for inflated prices and financed mansions. Population shot close to 7,000, and buildings and municipal systems such as streetcar lines were adequate for 20,000.

Port Townsend is one of the West Coast's major centers of ornate Victorian architecture.

The Union Pacific, however, proved more interested in selling the land it had been given than in grading roadbed. (It stirred similar hopes—and profits—in Anacortes.) A crew of 1,500 men laid 20 miles of track, and by August 1890 trains shuttled back and forth between Port Townsend and Leland Lake, south of Discovery Bay. But nothing happened on the Portland end of the line. In 1895 the Oregon Improvement Company went bankrupt. Its receivers continued the tracks almost 5 miles to Quilcene and stopped. Optimism drained from Port Townsend. Speculators folded their dreams and moved elsewhere, banks closed, creditors towed a huge, new drydock to Vashon Island (see p. 300), and the owners of a nail works junked their equipment and reopened in Everett.

Port Townsend slumbered without a major industry until 1927, when a pulp mill opened. In one way, the long lull was a blessing: handsome commercial buildings and homes were neither altered nor razed. They remain as a remarkably intact legacy from the past.

Two military establishments—from different eras—flank Port Townsend. **Fort Townsend** was established in 1856 (on a 1-mile spur road off State Route 20, about a mile south of town). Formal battles between Puget Sound natives and whites were newly ended but settlers continued

to feel nervous, particularly because of raids made by warriors from northern British Columbia and Alaska (see EBEY'S LANDING, p. 266, and PORT GAMBLE, p. 375).

Troops at Fort Townsend built barracks of logs chinked with mortar made from clamshells out of a beach midden. To reduce desertions during the British Columbia gold rush, Major Granville O. Haller hired ex-miners to work at the fort and dampen gold fever by describing realities along the Fraser River and in the Cariboo. When the "Pig War" boundary dispute with England broke out in 1859 troops sailed for San Juan Island (see AMERICAN CAMP, p. 243).

Today no buildings remain at Fort Townsend. The property is a state park with an interpretive trail winding across the fort's former site.

North of Port Townsend, **Fort Worden** (accessible via Cherry Street) overlooks both the Strait of Juan de Fuca and Admiralty Inlet. In 1904 the government began building a battery here, which was intended to forestall hostile ships from entering Puget Sound. Buildings and gun emplacements are now part of a state park along with mooring buoys and windy beaches ideal for strolling. A lighthouse (built in 1914) tips Point Wilson. The fort commander's house has been restored and is open to the public. Other officers' row houses are rented to vaca-

PANIC OF 1893

From the American Revolution in the 1770s until the Great Depression of the 1930s, economic busts followed booms in a relentless cycle. By the late 1880s, another depression was in the making. For years investors had been sinking money in railroads that spanned an unpopulated continent; yet the railroads had no hope of profit until more cities and farms and industries lined their routes. In the West, private debt was particularly high. Farmers borrowed money for the machines and the larger acreages they needed for profitable production. Lumbermen went into debt to acquire steam donkeys, logging railroads, and modern sawmills. Mining consortiums borrowed money to build concentrators and to tunnel deeper into the earth.

Meanwhile, knowledgeable people worried about the federal treasury's gold reserves. The 1890 McKinley Tariff Act meant a reduction of customs receipts, at the time a major source of revenue, and thus less gold flowing into the country. Furthermore, the Sherman Silver Purchase Act, also passed in 1890, obligated the government to buy 4,500,000 ounces of silver each month—usually paying in gold, a further drain on the nation's reserve.

Railroad magnate James J. Hill warned that the nation was headed for "a panic that it will take five years to get over." He was right. In 1893 the Baring Brothers Bank in London—deeply involved in international finance—suspended payment on its obligations, and U.S. Treasury gold reserves fell below $100 million, the level that common wisdom deemed minimal for economic safety. Depositors stormed bank doors and withdrew their funds to the greater safety of sugar jars and mattresses. Banks foreclosed mortgages and, in the depressed economy, found themselves holding unsalable properties. Nervous investors in the East withdrew support. Factories and sawmills closed, leaving thousands of workers unemployed. Many used their last wages for a ticket "back home"; others dug clams, grew vegetables, and hung on. Men laying track for the Port Townsend and Southern Railroad, supposedly on its way to Portland, got as far as Quilcene—25 miles—and stopped. Handsome brick commercial buildings in Port Townsend, and elsewhere, suddenly stood vacant; the upper floors of many are still not finished.

For four years Washington—and the rest of the country—lay throttled by depression. Jacob Coxey of Ohio led a protest march to Washington, D.C., and inspired other "armies" of unemployed men to head East to demand public works projects. Their desperation expressed the national mood.

In 1897 economic recovery for western Washington steamed from Alaska into Seattle as the S.S. *Portland* brought gold from the Klondike. Miners stampeded north. A crop failure in Europe that same year stimulated grain sales for eastern Washington farmers. The next year the Spanish-American War stimulated industry and brought additional relief. The panic was over.

tioners; (reserve ahead through the state park office). The private Centrum Foundation, which leases Fort Worden buildings, presents year-round arts workshops, seminars, and classes that range from drama and poetry to music, painting, weaving, wood carving, and various other arts. Musicals and theater performances are often open to the public, particularly in summer. The huge old World War II balloon hangar at the beach has been remodeled into a performing arts pavilion.

SEQUIM (Skwim), a modern town popular as a retirement center, lies in the rain shadow of the Olympic Mountains. Its annual precipitation is about 16 inches, compared with twice that for

Seattle and a full 140 inches for the Hoh Rain Forest south of Forks. Every May since 1896 an Irrigation Festival has celebrated agriculture—and the need to irrigate crops here. A museum (175 W. Cedar) exhibits local pioneer memorabilia and tusks from an archaeological excavation of where hunters killed a mastodon 11,000 years ago. The discovery site is one of a half dozen such ancient sites known in the entire Northwest.

Prairies here attracted settlers beginning in the mid-1850s. Farmers sold potatoes, wheat, oats, peas, and hay in Victoria. By the mid-1890s enough people had arrived that a group of visionaries, led by James W. Grant, decided to irrigate their fields with water from the Dungeness River. They formed the Sequim Prairie Ditch Company and hired a surveyor, who agreed to accept potatoes as part of his wage when the newly irrigated crop had been harvested. Neighbors worked together to dig a ditch and cut and mill timber for a flume. On May 1, 1896, water flowed into the ditch for the first time, celebrated with band music and speeches.

In time, 25,000 acres came under cultivation, the largest irrigated acreage in western Washington. Real estate developments now occupy much of that land, but the beauty and openness remain and make exploring the flats north of U.S. 101 a scenic joy. The outer ramparts of the Olympic Mountains rise as a snow-crowned wall and provide constant orientation for anyone wandering the maze of (otherwise confusing) roads.

The appeal of **SOL DUC HOT SPRINGS** (12 miles south of U.S. 101 near the west end of Lake Crescent) has endured for nearly a century. Mineral water cooled to 105 degrees Fahrenheit still flows into pools, and visitors drive the narrow, beautifully forested Soleduck Valley to soak away cares. In the mid-1980s the National Park Service completely refurbished the resort, which today includes three large outdoor soaking pools, cabins, and a campground.

From 1890 to 1920 a whirlwind of resort-building activity swept over the northern Olympic Peninsula. Around Lake Crescent homesteaders took in paying guests and, at Olympic Hot Springs in the Elwha Valley, proprietors provided guests with hand-carved wooden bathtubs and tent cabins. At Sol Duc,

A Sequim landowner digging a pond for ducks found the tusks of a mastodon killed by hunters.

Michael Earles implemented a far grander dream. A dynamic lumberman and entrepreneur, he bought the hot springs property in 1910, built a road, hauled in a small sawmill, and set 200 workers to building what he termed the West's most elaborate spa.

Two years later Earles' fabulous resort staged a grand opening. A four-story, 165-room hotel offered every convenience—hot and cold running water, telephones, electric lights—and diversions from billiards to golf and tennis. Fountains splashed in the manicured grounds. Masseurs stood ready to work their magic. And renowned chefs gratified "the veriest epicure's every whim." A sanitarium equipped as a creditable small hospital cared for health seekers. The moneyed elite flocked to this enclave of luxury in the hinterland; at its peak, 10,000 guests per season visited Sol Duc Hot Springs. On May 26, 1916, fire engulfed the resort. For a few seasons, guests still came to stay in the former "health house," but three years later Michael Earles died, and his heirs sold the property.

Below the resort, watch for a short path that leads from the Sol Duc road to a cascade where salmon leap the abrupt falls to continue their spawning run. (Best from mid-August into October; accessible from a pullout about 7 miles from U.S. 101.) Sometimes the fish succeed in gaining the next higher pool, sometimes they fall back to try again. Huge Douglas firs and scolding squirrels—and, often, deer—enhance watching for the salmon.

Hood Canal

Hood Canal edges the east side of the Olympic Peninsula as a narrow saltwater channel 40 miles long, lying at the base of glacier-clad peaks. Forested valleys with cascading rivers lead from the shore, and trails climb to subalpine flower meadows and lakes. Public beaches offer clamming and oystering (the oysters simply lie on the flats exposed at low tide; for digging clams, an ordinary shovel suffices). Check current shellfish seasons and regulations. If possible, make the drive in May or June when native rhododendrons, dogwoods, and madronas are in blossom.

British explorer Captain George Vancouver named the "canal" in 1792. He wrote in his journal: "Early on Sunday morning the 13th of May we again embarked, directing our route down the inlet, which, after the Right Honorable Lord Hood, I called Hood's Channel." ("Channel" became "canal" on Vancouver's chart.)

BRINNON is a small residential community offering a variety of services. A 15-mile road turns off U.S. 101 near the village center and winds along the Dosewallips River (Doh-see-wah′-lips), which flows bank-to-bank with clear, bubbling water. A 2-mile trail—that seems straight up—leads to Lake Constance, an exceptionally beautiful alpine lake ringed by high peaks. Three miles south of the Dosewallips, another forest-and-river drive threads for 7 miles up the Duckabush Valley. It passes Interrorem Guard Station (4 miles from U.S. 101; built in 1906), a classic ranger station still in use and the oldest remaining building in Olympic National Forest. A trail three quarters of a mile long leads from the station through dense forest to cascades and a small waterfall.

The community of Brinnon is named for Elwell P. Brinnon, who took a donation land claim at the river's mouth in 1860 and married the sister of Chetzemoka, a Klallam headman who lived near Port Townsend. Since Dosewallips had various spellings, early settlers decided on the name Brinnon for their post office. Mail came by rowboat from Seabeck, brought by a retired whaling captain; later it

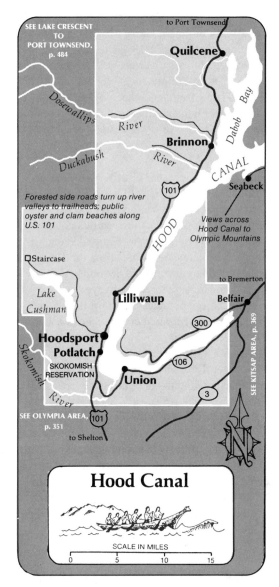

SEE LAKE CRESCENT TO PORT TOWNSEND, p. 484

to Port Townsend

Quilcene

Dosewallips River

Brinnon

Dabob Bay

Duckabush River

CANAL

101

Seabeck

Forested side roads turn up river valleys to trailheads; public oyster and clam beaches along U.S. 101

Views across Hood Canal to Olympic Mountains

HOOD

☐ Staircase

to Bremerton

Lake Cushman

Lilliwaup

Belfair

300

SEE KITSAP AREA, p. 369

Hoodsport
Potlatch
SKOKOMISH RESERVATION

Skokomish River

106

Union

3

SEE OLYMPIA AREA, p. 351

101

to Shelton

N

Hood Canal

SCALE IN MILES

0   5   10   15

came on the steamer serving the Quilcene-to-Union route.

In 1890 the prospect of a rail connection from Hood Canal to Portland stimulated settlement and logging at Brinnon and led to construction of a wagon road to Quilcene, 12 miles north. By 1907 Brinnon had a population of 120, amenities such as a hotel and a justice of the peace, and an economic base that included a creamery and a shingle mill. For awhile log drives on the Dosewallips and Duckabush rivers moved timber from the forest to salt water; railroad logging had taken over by the 1920s. Families subsisted well on farm produce plus oysters, clams, crabs, fish, shrimp, berries, and venison. Part-time work at a logging camp or mill provided cash.

Today's state park at the mouth of the Dosewallips is the best place on all of Hood Canal to dig for geoducks—the notorious two- to four-pound clams most accessible on minus tides (which are lowest during the bone-chilling nights of midwinter but—for the hardy— provide lantern-lit joy). Most public beaches are open for clam digging and oyster picking; ask about season and current regulations. Be sure to fill in holes after digging; otherwise, craters may expose creatures that need to be buried, and mounds may kill clams by making it impossible for them to extend their siphons to the surface to feed. Also, shuck oysters and return shells to the beach for the larvae of the next generation to attach to.

HOOD CANAL BRIDGE. (See p. 377.)

HOODSPORT (15 miles north of Shelton) is one of present-day Hood Canal's larger communities. A state hatchery beside U.S. 101 raises young salmon in saltwater ponds and releases them directly into Hood Canal, eliminating the usual stream migration. A joint National Park Service/National Forest Service information station is just off the highway on the Dosewallips road.

Captain G. K. Robbins settled here about 1880. He knew Hood Canal well, having sailed it for five years, transporting lumber. At first the Robbins family lived without neighbors, but others soon arrived. Most built houses without going through a preliminary log-cabin stage: logs littering beaches could be salvaged and towed to a mill to be sawn into boards. At the time all logs moved by water and many broke loose and washed ashore. Farming and logging provided a livelihood, and one man—Torval Nordby—operated a tannery near his farm, soaking hides in handmade vats sealed with pitch and bound with wooden bands. For a tanning agent, he used hemlock. (See also SEKIU, p. 482.)

Hoodsport was platted in 1890 by the Mason County Mine and Development Company, which owned manganese mines above Lake Cushman. Copper mines in the same area also drew men. Their efforts continued for 50 years with more than 400 claims filed. Some ore was shipped, but the main results were mine tunnels and tailings—and disappointment.

LAKE CUSHMAN—since the 1920s, enlarged as a hydropower reservoir for Tacoma—fills a forested valley at the base of high peaks. Summer homes and a state park line the

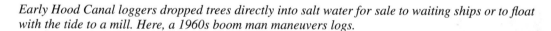

Early Hood Canal loggers dropped trees directly into salt water for sale to waiting ships or to float with the tide to a mill. Here, a 1960s boom man maneuvers logs.

lakeshore; the road ends at Staircase, 16 miles from U.S. 101 inside Olympic National Park.

People have been using the area for at least 5,000 to 6,000 years: archaeologists have found several dozen basalt projectile points and hundreds of finely crafted knives, scrapers, and other tools, along with thousands of flakes left as debris. The material lies in separate clusters, which apparently represent a series of occupations over time. Doubtless the people lived by hunting, fishing, and gathering plant foods, experiencing a climate that was warmer and drier than our present climate.

The broad expanses of open land that attracted these early people also drew white settlers. When the O'Neil Expedition came through in July 1890 they reported "no section of land not taken up or squatted on." The settlers included Fred Ault, a "bee man" who set out hives among the fireweed blooming in the logged-over country behind Potlatch. (He quit when bears started raiding his honey.) There also were several bachelors who trapped and hunted meat. Families farmed. And—as early as 1890— tourism began.

The first "hotel" was no more than a big tent dignified by the name Cushman House. By its second summer the hotel became a frame building of split cedar with rooms partitioned by muslin sheeting and, by the sixth summer, the hotel hired a Swiss chef. William Putnam began the hotel while on a trip to the Pacific Northwest soon after finishing college in the East. He met two Seattle men wanting to find homesteads and with them traveled by steamer to Shelton, walked to Union City, then rowed to Lilliwaup, and hiked the final 5 miles to the lake.

Cushman House attracted the attention of a high school classmate of Putnam's who belonged to Seattle's Rainier Club. Through him, other wealthy Easterners heard of the hotel and came on vacation. Two of them—Russell Homan and Stanley Hopper, an heir of the Singer Sewing Machine fortune—were so charmed by the lake they decided in 1898 to build a resort of their own. It became the elegant, log Antlers Hotel, where guests were treated each evening to an organ prelude, then led into the dining room by Homan and his widowed mother. Formal attire was required.

Entering the mountains from Lilliwaup in 1890, explorers with the O'Neil expedition were the first to climb 7,965-foot Mount Olympus. O'Neil recommended a national park.

Urban stress had created an urge to escape to quiet, wild places—especially to wilderness complete with physical comfort and social nicety.

In 1920 the Phoenix Logging Company of Potlatch began clearing the banks above the lake in preparation for the coming reservoir. In 1989 logging crews salvaged huge red-cedar stumps from that time, exposed during winter draw-downs of the lake.

LILLIWAUP (Lil´-li-wahp) dots the head of a narrow, deep bay with buildings on all flat land. Settlers came as early as 1854, but no town plat was filed until 1890. Rumors that the Union Pacific might soon reach the base of Hood Canal boosted population enough that 50 men found work grading streets, quarrying rock, and build-ing houses. (Also see under PORT TOWNSEND on p. 500.)

The same year that the boom got under way—1890—Lieutenant Joseph O'Neil started from Lilliwaup for an exploration of the inner Olym-pics. It was his second expedition; in 1885, curious about the "seemingly impenetrable barrier" of the mountains, he had started to explore the mountains behind Port Angeles with seven men. After only about six weeks, however, a courier brought orders to report immediately to Fort Leavenworth, Kansas. O'Neil sailed from Port Angeles.

Five years later he returned, intent on cutting a trail across the mountains from Hood Canal to the Pacific Ocean. Other parties were in the mountains that same summer. In fact, Private Harry Fisher, with O'Neil, commented that the expeditions might "jostle against each other in their quest of the secrets of the mountains." A party sponsored by the *Seattle Press* had started up the Elwha Valley a few months earlier (see p. 488), and Charles and Samuel Gilman, father and son, planned additional treks, having already explored the upper Quinault Valley and recon-noitered the entire length of the peninsula from the Strait of Juan de Fuca to Grays Harbor (see LAKE QUINAULT, p. 470; and QUEETS, p. 480).

The second O'Neil Expedition was jointly sponsored by the U.S. Army and the Oregon Alpine Club (a hiking club with O'Neil as secretary). Ten enlisted men and five civilians comprised O'Neil's party. Half of them were to build a trail adequate for pack animals; the others—including a botanist, geologist, and naturalist/cartographer—were to study "all phases of the country." The combination promised to make the Olympics both accessible and known.

The men arrived at Lilliwaup by stern-wheeler, anchored in shallow water, and used rowboats and canoes to carry supplies and gear ashore. Their mules had to jump overboard and swim to shore. Assembled, the party "pushed through the heavy timber" to Lake Cushman following a route long used by Native Ameri-cans but made suitable for pack animals only by slow, hard work. At Lake Cushman, O'Neil began sending out small, separate parties to investigate the jagged peaks and valleys of the inner Olympics. One such party was the first to climb Mount Olympus, at 7,965 feet the highest peak on the peninsula. Others explored and mapped the drainages leading east, south, and west from the inner crests of the mountains.

The expedition began in late June 1890. In early October its main contingent arrived at Hoquiam, having completed the first crossing of the Olympic Mountains from Hood Canal to the Pacific. Parts of the trails they blazed are still in use within Olympic National Park. Indeed, O'Neil reported to Congress in 1896 that the peninsula's interior "is useless for all practical purposes . . . [but] would serve admirably for a national park." Louis Henderson, the expedition botanist from Cornell University, had summa-rized the impression while scouting above Lake Cushman in the first month:

Canyon mingled with canyon, peak rose above peak, ridge succeeded ridge, until they culminated in old Olympus far to the northwest. . . . [With] the fast descending sun bringing out the gorgeous colors of pale-blue, lavender, purple, ash, pink and gold . . . one can form some slight idea of the reasons that compelled us to gaze and be silent.

In early summer, when the expedition first arrived, Private Fisher had described Lilliwaup as "a town with one house." In September he again traveled to Lake Cushman and commented that what had been "a howling wilderness" three months earlier now presented "an air of civiliza-tion." More than 30 new families had moved in, and Lilliwaup soon had a store and two hotels (one advertising "Meals at all hours; table supplied from Hotel Garden"). But the "civilization" did not last long. The townsite company went bankrupt and most families moved away.

Tourism came next. By the 1920s it included promises of a Lilliwaup summer retreat for movie stars. The prospect began when two men from Los Angeles—A. W. Layne and M. J. Keeley—bought eight acres and began landscaping and building a trail to Lilliwaup Falls. Reportedly, such Hollywood greats as Jackie Coogan, Mary Pickford, Douglas Fairbanks, and Charlie Chaplin expressed interest in buying homes here. They never came. The Lilliwaup Land and Resort Company folded and vanished—and left behind little except local disappointment and an aborted bulkhead intended to protect the stars' yachts.

POTLATCH (about 13 miles north of Shelton) is characterized by a state park, a powerhouse, and a slight increase in the density of houses and gasoline stations lining Hood Canal. The community began in 1900. That year French-Canadian Thomas Bordeaux, who had begun logging with a team of oxen, became the president of the newly incorporated Potlatch Commercial and Terminal Company. They immediately started building a logging railroad to tap newly acquired timber holdings, and at Potlatch they built a company town.

By 1920 Tacoma's utility department—which eight years previously had completed a hydro dam on the Nisqually River at LaGrande—found itself unable to meet the escalating demand for electricity. Engineers investigated various sites for an additional dam and decided the North Fork of the Skokomish River offered the best possibilities. Seattle had claimed the site in 1912, but released it. The editor of the *Shelton Journal* was not pleased with the new plans for a dam; he wrote that the project would put "not one dime in [Mason] County coffers." Shelton's Commercial Club felt differently; they supposed that transmission lines to Tacoma would circle around the lower end of the sound and bring power to Shelton. Matters did not work out that way, however. To save money, the city built a direct line spanning Puget Sound at the Narrows. Turbines at the Potlatch powerhouse began generating power in early 1926.

With low-cost power available, several industries opened plants in Tacoma and, within five years, City Light built a second, higher dam on the Skokomish a few miles downriver from their original dam. Huge pipes, conspicuous for miles, bring water from this reservoir to the powerhouse.

QUILCENE today straddles U.S. 101, a modern community with a handful of venerable buildings. Its center formerly stood closer to the bay, which is reached by 2-mile Linger Longer Road. The drive leads to the estuary of the Quilcene River, a small marina, rotting pilings from a railroad trestle, and an idyllic oyster farm that grows its oysters for four years before marketing them, an assurance of top quality.

Five miles south of town, a spur road off U.S. 101 climbs 5 miles to the summit of 2,750-foot Mount Walker (or a trail leads 2 miles to the top). The view is one of the peninsula's best. The high peaks of the Olympics stretch to the west, snowcapped all year; the blue water of Hood Canal and Puget Sound lie to the east with Mount Baker, Glacier Peak, and Mount Rainier soaring above the rest of the Cascade Range. Rhododendrons bloom at the summit in June.

Hampden Cottle, a logger from Maine, settled at Quilcene in 1860. He made his living "digging and cutting ships' knees," which entailed digging at the base of trees and cutting out the angled junction of trunk and root for use as ribbing in ships. That first industry was small scale; twin expectations of later economic bases involved a railroad and then a mine.

The railroad was to have been part of the Union Pacific network (see PORT TOWNSEND, p. 498). Work began in 1890, but the Union Pacific soon developed financial problems. In 1891 Judge James Swan, ardent railroad advocate, wired the editor of the *Quilcene Bugler* from Port Townsend, sadly announcing:

The jig is up. Reliable word reached me that Portland court today appointed receiver for O. I. Co. [Oregon Improvement Company, a Union Pacific subsidiary.] This kills all hope that road will be extended.

Mining expectations centered on the Tubal

Cain Mine, begun in 1902 near the headwaters of the Big Quilcene River. Backers claimed it would make Quilcene a smelting center to rival Tacoma. In 1905 the *Port Townsend Weekly Leader* reported an east tunnel for manganese with Tull City nearby—a camp with two bunkhouses, a cookhouse, and a blacksmith shop. There was also a west tunnel expected to produce copper. The camp there included guest house, barn, sawmill, powder house, and a snowshed from tunnel to buildings. Effort and money continued going into the ground until the 1920s but, unfortunately, little ore ever came out.

Farming and logging determined the actual economy for Quilcene, as for most Olympic Peninsula towns. In 1983 Robert Worthington, whose father had come to Quilcene a century earlier, reminisced about logging before the arrival of steam power:

The man to credit with starting logging is the man with just the axe, not the saw. He'd chip the hell out of trees, and they fell into the water. Next came men with logging jacks: turn the jack a little bit; roll the log till it gets into the water.

Later on there were skid roads. First they'd put down crosspieces and that'd be the skid road. Later on they used them fore and aft and that was called a tram road. There were four wheels on a tram car. The rim was concave so it fit over the rails. Horses pulled them. It was always downgrade; horses aren't power-ful enough to pull uphill.

Splash dams [see p. 456] were the fashion before the railroads went in. . . . On these small streams with heavy timber, it was well to use a dam to raise the water supply. Just an extra push to the current was needed, so they'd build a dam. There were some on the Dosewallips and I think earlier on the Duckabush. On the Big Quil there was a dam that gave force to the water and swept shingle bolts out to the bay. . . . Before there were steam tow boats, they'd use the tides and hoist a sail on the log boom.

The heyday of logging is now long past. A small-scale forest harvest, however, is still a sizeable local industry: sprays of sword fern, evergreen huckleberry, and salal two feet long are shipped from Quilcene to florists across the nation. An experienced picker working under lease agreements with various landowners points

Brushpicking, a frequent peninsula occupation, provides greenery to florists.

out: "Brush picking lets you get out in the woods, and make money, too. I like the peace and quiet."

The **SKOKOMISH RESERVATION** (Skoh-koh′-mish) was established in 1855 following the Point No Point treaty council (see HANSVILLE, p. 373). Agreements set aside about 5,000 acres of land at the mouth of the Skokomish River for the Twana people—of whom the Skokomish were one band—and also for the Klallams and Chimacums who lived along Hood Canal and the Strait of Juan de Fuca. Only about a sixth of the Native Americans the government expected to move onto the reservation actually did so. Land there was entirely forested except for some that was swampy; it lacked the range of resources needed for traditional life and was ill suited for farming.

The economy today is based on fishing and logging. A tribal program keeps the Twana language alive, and a tribal center includes displays open to the public.

UNION's setting—at the great bend of Hood Canal—epitomizes western Washington scenery; the view is across salt water and up forested slopes to lofty snow peaks. The community business district hugs the beach; residential streets are steep enough to make San Franciscans feel at home. Twanoh State Park (8 miles east of Union) offers a place to gaze at the scene and walk the beach and the forest; otherwise, pullouts are virtually nonexistent, and the road is narrow, curving, and lined with beach houses. (The situation on the opposite shore—State Route 300 to Tahuya—is much the same.)

Immediately west of Union the highway loops across the tidal flat of the Skokomish River mouth, a sample of the flat, open country that attracted settlers here to farm. An early survey describes the township as "mostly gravelly rolling table land," half of it with bunchgrass—an extraordinary break in the overall carpet of evergreens. Thomas Webb filed a donation land claim near the river mouth in 1855. For cash, he paddled to Port Gamble or Port Ludlow and worked at a mill through the winter, then spent the rest of the year proving up on his farm. In time the Webbs pastured logging companies' horses on their land through the winter, when work in the woods closed down.

Businesses began at Union in 1859 with the opening of a trading post that also served as a hotel—for guests who brought bedding. Within a decade 50 logging camps sprouted in the forest near Union, and the store was supplying most of them. The settlement was also a transportation hub. Steamers serving Puget Sound called here, and by 1887 a wagon road to Shelton and then south to Kamilche connected with a logging railroad that provided passenger service to Montesano. There, riverboats connected with Grays Harbor.

In 1890 rumors flew that Union would be the terminus for a Union Pacific rail line from Portland (see under PORT TOWNSEND on p. 500; and under QUILCENE on p. 508). A boom began instantly. Tent stores lined the beach and tent homes sheltered hopeful townsmen while the whirring saw of a hastily built mill produced boards for houses. Nine saloons opened along with a newspaper, a shoemaker, a photography shop, a boatyard, a broom handle factory, a salmon saltery, and an oyster business. Promises prevailed over progress, however, and it was 1893 before a Union Pacific crew with horses and a scraper arrived to start clearing a right-of-way. A similar crew was said to be working north from Olympia.

The work had little more than begun when London's Baring Brothers Bank collapsed in financial ruin and touched off the Panic of 1893 (see sidebar, p. 502). Union's boom busted. Tranquillity replaced it, treasured by local people and outsiders alike. Union is a pinprick village, yet also a microcosm of the state: its roots span from the days of Washington Territory to the present; tribal land adjoins, and archaeologists find that people have been in the area for thousands of years (see under LAKE CUSHMAN on p. 506). Furthermore, the setting remains intact.

In the late 1800s logging companies wintered their horses at a large ranch near Union; today a Christmas tree plantation crowds against the slowly collapsing house.

PHOTO CREDITS

All photographs by Ruth and Louis Kirk except for those on the following pages:

Juanita Walter Therrell, i; Eastern Washington State Historical Society, 20 (L87–1,5651–35), 44 (287); Special Collections Division, University of Washington Libraries, 23 (Cress 9283), 150, 164 (UW 11496), 229 (UW 5705), 262 (Robertson NA 1498), 275 (UW 14848), 286 (UW 5804), 298 (Nowell 1289), 315 (UW 894), 321 (UW 526), 355 (UW 9282), 371 (Curtis 19206), 454 (UW 188), 498 (UW 5065); Oregon Historical Society, 37 (OrHi 4729); Pacific Northwest National Parks and Forests Associations, 42; Betty Jo Bouska Neils, 53, 54; Washington State Historical Society, 43, 72, 78, 81, 86, 132, 162, 168 (Curtis 13369), 275 (Curtis 50246), 276 (Curtis 48511), 284 (Curtis), 299, 303, 310 (Curtis 47871), 331, 342, 344, 345, 380, 386, 448, 453 (Curtis 58969), 493 (Curtis 38414); *Wenatchee Daily World,* 111; Carmela Alexander, 142; U.S. Army Corps of Engineers, Walla Walla District, 170; Harvey S. Rice, 190; Special Collections, University of Idaho, 202; Alex McGregor, 209; Whatcom Museum Archive, 216 (10157–A), 230 (7296), 280 (20680); *Seattle Times* (Barry Wong), 253; Port of Seattle, 283; Mary Randlett, 292 (198); Bob and Ira Spring, 295, 320 (14,164.V); Larry Bullis, 337; Museum of History and Industry, 347 (2137); Murray Pacific Corporation, 364, 442; Kitsap County Historical Museum, 379 (B. Torvanger); Lewis County Historical Museum, 388, 437; U.S. Forest Service, 389; Sisters of Providence Archives, Seattle, 409 *(bottom)*; Columbia River Maritime Museum, 426 (Rolf Klep); Cowlitz County Historical Museum, 427; Montesano and Grays Harbor *Vidette*, 455 (Dean Photo Co.), 456; Michael Sullivan, 521

A SELECTIVE CHRONOLOGY OF WASHINGTON STATE

Glen W. Lindeman

1775   Spanish maritime explorers from Mexico land at Point Grenville on the Olympic Peninsula; a second landing party is destroyed by Quinault warriors; commanders Heceta and Bodega y Quadra confirm existing Spanish claims to the region.

1778   Captain James Cook, famed British naval explorer, sails along the Washington coast. He names Cape Flattery but misses the Strait of Juan de Fuca because of poor weather; his explorations fortuitously result in opening a maritime fur trade.

1785   Captain James Hanna, a British trader, pioneers the development of a lucrative fur trade with China; as a result, dozens of British, American, Spanish, Portuguese, and French vessels soon ply coastal Northwest waters.

1787   Captain Charles Barkley of England explores inside the Strait of Juan de Fuca while bartering for sea otter pelts; at Hoh River (on the outer coast) natives attack a landing party from his ship and, in retaliation, he burns a village.

1792   Captain Robert Gray, an American trader, explores Grays Harbor and the Columbia River mouth. Captain George Vancouver, a British mariner, explores and maps Puget Sound, and his party also reconnoiters up the Columbia River. Spaniards establish—and soon abandon—a fortified village at Neah Bay, which they call Nuñez Gaona.

1805   Captains Meriwether Lewis and William Clark, leading the Corps of Discovery, enter Washington from the east; they canoe down the Snake and Columbia rivers, winter south of Astoria, and return to St. Louis the following year.

1810   North West Company fur traders from Canada establish Spokane House at the junction of the Spokane and Little Spokane rivers; the site is occupied until 1826.

1811   John Jacob Astor's Pacific Fur Company founds Fort Astoria at the mouth of the Columbia; American and Canadian fur hunters open competing posts throughout the region.

1818   Great Britain and the United States agree to a joint occupancy of the Pacific Northwest; through diplomacy, they eliminate Spanish and Russian claims within a few years.

1825   The British Hudson's Bay Company establishes Fort Vancouver on the lower Columbia River and Fort Colvile on the upper river; their traders dominate the entire Pacific Northwest.

1836   Protestant missionaries Marcus Whitman and Henry Spalding and wives begin ministering to native people near Walla Walla and Lewiston; their success in getting a wagon as far west as Fort Boise encourages immigrants. Pioneering Jesuits and Oblates do not arrive in the region until the 1840s.

1841   The Wilkes expedition, exploring for the U.S. Navy, reaches Puget Sound and sends an overland party into the interior. Congress passes the Pre-emption Act, destined to remain in force for 50 years; it permits adult male citizens and women who head families or are widowed to claim 160 acres of the public domain for farm purposes, providing they live on and improve the land.

1843   The first large American migration—about 900 pioneers—arrives in the Northwest via the Oregon Trail; most claim land in the Willamette Valley. American settlement from north of the Columbia River to the southern end of Puget Sound begins two years later. The settlers' arrival causes the Hudson's Bay Company hegemony to wane.

1846   A treaty divides the Oregon Country and establishes the forty-ninth parallel as international boundary between Canada and the United States. England holds the land that is now British Columbia, the rest becomes American.

1847   Three years of intermittent hostility east of the Cascade Range begin when a party of Cayuse men destroy Whitman Mission in the Walla Walla valley and kill 14 whites there.

1848 Congress creates Oregon Territory, retaining the name used by fur traders; boundaries embrace present-day Washington, Oregon, Idaho, and western Montana and Wyoming.

1850 Congress passes the Donation Land Law, which grants 320 acres to single adult male citizens who settled before December 1, 1846 (640 acres, if married). Later settlers can claim 160 acres (320, if married). The act applies only to Oregon Territory; it expires in 1855.

1853 Congress establishes Washington Territory by dividing Oregon Territory. President Franklin Pierce appoints Isaac I. Stevens, a West Point graduate and Mexican War veteran, as Washington's first territorial governor; Stevens also serves as the head surveyor for a northern transcontinental railroad route and as superintendent of Indian Affairs.

1855 Hostilities between native tribesmen and whites erupt into the Yakima War following a treaty council held by Governor Stevens in the Walla Walla Valley. A series of pitched battles begins east of the Cascades; settlers west of the mountains build fortifications.

1856 Native warriors attacking Seattle are repulsed. To ease tension with Columbia Plateau tribes, the U.S. Army closes eastern Washington to settlement; this disgruntles territorial officials.

1858 Lieutenant Colonel Edward Steptoe's command barely escapes annihilation at the hands of Spokane, Coeur d'Alene, and other tribesmen near today's Rosalia; Colonel George Wright's troops are victorious at Four Lakes and Spokane Plains; and this ends the three-year Yakima War. Native people are largely confined to reservations although some choose instead to live under special provisions that grant individual allotments of land away from reservations.

1861 A territorial university (now the University of Washington) opens in Seattle with one instructor and one collegiate student; it all but flounders in bankruptcy and indifference, then begins anew and in 1895 moves to its present location.

1862 Congress passes the Homestead Act, which grants 160 acres to individual U.S. citizens; the law encourages white Americans to settle throughout the American West, including Washington.

1873 Congress institutes the Timber Culture Act, which allows homesteaders to claim an additional 160 acres of treeless land, providing they plant trees on a quarter of it within four years; Washingtonians east of the Cascades make widespread use of this act. The Northern Pacific completes tracks from Kalama to Tacoma, thereby technically meeting a congressional deadline for rails to reach the Pacific by December 31 (although a 1,500-mile gap remains between Dakota Territory and the Columbia River).

1878 Washington's first attempt to gain statehood proves unsuccessful; the proposed constitution framed in Walla Walla is not approved by Congress. A new, national Timber and Stone Act allows individuals to buy up to 160 acres of land unfit for agriculture; they must swear the land is for personal use—but most actually transfer title to lumbering interests, which build immense holdings in this way.

1881 Winter weather on the Columbia Plateau delivers a devastating blow to the open range livestock industry; eastern Washington agriculture as a whole—and particularly on the rolling grasslands of the eastern plateau—shifts overwhelmingly to grain production.

1883 The Northern Pacific Railroad and the Oregon Railway and Navigation Company complete the first northern transcontinental rail connection; the Union Pacific system soon follows. Arrival of the railroads triggers three decades of unprecedented economic and social growth and, by 1910, Washington's population reaches 1,141,990; this is 15 times greater than the 1880 population total of 75,116. Furthermore, whereas the 1880s population was largely rural, more than half of the state's people are living in cities by 1910. In 1883 women are allowed to vote in state elections; four years later the law is rescinded as unconstitutional, then is re-enacted in 1888 and again declared unconstitutional.

1885　Agitation and riots against Chinese labor begin in Washington's mines, mills, and orchards and then spread to urban areas, particularly Seattle and Tacoma.

1887　The Dawes Severalty Act, newly passed by Congress, requires Native people to select individual 160-acre claims, after which it opens reservations to white settlers. The traditional lifeways and customs of many Native Americans are changed forever as a result of this law and of a requirement that children attend government or mission schools—often boarding schools far from home.

1889　Congress passes an Omnibus Bill that grants statehood to Washington, Montana, North Dakota, and South Dakota; on November 11, 1889, Washington becomes the forty-second state.

1890　The state legislature authorizes what are now Washington State University in Pullman, Eastern Washington University in Cheney, and Central Washington University in Ellensburg; Western Washington University in Bellingham is founded three years later.

1893　A major economic panic grips the nation; Washington immigration and growth are stalled. The Great Northern Railroad is completed with depots at Everett and Seattle.

1895　A federal "Barefoot Schoolboy Law" authorizes state support for public schools; it brings uniformity and higher standards to Washington classrooms.

1897　The Klondike gold rush helps return boomtime prosperity to Seattle and the Pacific Northwest, much as gold strikes in Idaho, British Columbia, and Montana stimulated growth in earlier supply centers like Walla Walla and Spokane.

1899　Mount Rainier is designated as the first national park in the state (and the fifth in the nation).

1902　Extensive federal irrigation projects begin in the Yakima and Okanogan valleys and soon transform these areas into valuable orchards, hopyards, and croplands; to discourage vast land holdings, water for only 160 acres per owner is allowable from federally sponsored projects, no matter how much land a farmer or company may own.

1909　Seattle hosts the Alaska-Yukon-Pacific Exposition celebrating regional boosterism and growth. The "Milwaukee Road" is completed to Puget Sound—the fourth, and last, major northern transcontinental railroad. In a "free speech" campaign, the Industrial Workers of the World (or Wobblies), the Northwest's most radical labor union, protest a Spokane ban of street speakers; 600 are arrested.

1910　Washington voters approve women's suffrage; it becomes the fifth amendment to the state constitution and greatly encourages national supporters of women's rights. (Nine years later Congress approves the nineteenth amendment to the U.S. Constitution, which grants the vote to all female U.S. citizens.)

1914　The Panama Canal opens and significantly increases shipments to the Atlantic seaboard, particularly of Washington lumber and grain.

1915　The historic John R. Jackson log cabin north of Toledo is donated as Washington's first state park.

1916　The "Everett Massacre" occurs when the steamer *Verona* arrives at the Everett docks bringing Wobblies from Seattle; they are met by armed deputies, and an ensuing shootout accounts for at least seven dead and 51 wounded.

1917　Fort Lewis, near Tacoma, becomes a major army training center after the United States joins the Allies and enters World War I. In Seattle the Lake Washington ship canal is completed.

1919　A general strike in Seattle contributes to a nationwide specter of a "Red Revolution." Continuing economic problems within the state culminate in the "Centralia Massacre" as members of the American Legion storm an Industrial Workers of the World union hall during an Armistice Day parade; four Legionnaires are killed and a Wobbly is subsequently lynched—a sensational tragedy that stuns the nation.

1928　The state capitol at Olympia is completed.

1933　Rock Island Dam is built on the Columbia

River below Wenatchee; it is the first in a series of major Columbia and Snake River dams to be built over the next four decades.

1934 Boeing Airplane Company of Seattle completes the design of Project 299, prototype for the B-17 that will become the crucially important American bomber of World War II; ten years later Boeing alone is employing 50,000 workers, indication of the overall stimulus of the wartime economy.

1938 President Franklin D. Roosevelt signs a bill creating Olympic National Park from part of the land originally set aside in 1897 as a forest reserve. The lower Columbia River's Bonneville Dam is dedicated.

1941 Grand Coulee Dam is completed on the upper Columbia River; it supplies electric power essential for the burgeoning wartime industry that follows the Japanese attack on Pearl Harbor.

1943 The Hanford Project is started in central Washington to produce plutonium for an atomic bomb.

1948 As part of the Columbia Basin Project, irrigation water diverted by Grand Coulee Dam begins to transform dry sagebrush flats into valuable cropland. A Seattle broadcast station (KRSC) introduces television to the state, airing the West Seattle–Wenatchee high school football game.

1962 "Century 21"—the Seattle World's Fair—runs from April 21 to October 21.

1964 Congress passes the National Wilderness Preservation Act to protect pristine wilderness areas; in Washington this primarily affects the Cascade Range (and later also the Olympics).

1966 Congress passes the National Historic Preservation Act; it establishes a National Register of Historic Places, which recognizes and to some extent protects sites historically important to local communities.

1968 Washington's third national park—North Cascades—is established.

1974 Expo 74 opens in Spokane, converting a rundown industrial district into a riverside park.

1980 Mount St. Helens erupts on May 18, and its ash blankets much of eastern Washington; additional eruptions occur in the following months.

1989 Washington celebrates a century of statehood.

Centennial canoes approach Seattle, one typical of outer-coast Washington canoes, the other of northern British Columbia waters.

Suggested Reading

General

Anglin, Ron. *Forgotten Trails: Historical Sources of the Columbia's Big Bend Country.* Pullman: Washington State University Press, 1995. Early eastern Washington travel routes as recorded by diaries, drawings, and maps.

Bennett, Robert A., ed. *We'll All Go Home in the Spring: Personal Accounts and Adventures as Told by the Pioneers of the West.* Walla Walla, Washington: Pioneer Press Books, 1984. Oregon immigrants' letters and journals.

Blair, Karen J., ed. *Women in Pacific Northwest History: An Anthology.* Seattle: University of Washington Press, 1988. Twelve essays on topics from suffrage to World War II, factory work to Scandinavian and Japanese immigrants; illustrated with snapshots and portraits.

Brewster, David, and David Buerge, eds. *Washingtonians: A Biographical Portrait of the State.* Seattle: Sasquatch Books, 1988. The state's leading personages of all eras and backgrounds.

Cox, Thomas R. *Mills and Markets: A History of the Pacific Coast Lumber Industry to 1900.* Seattle: University of Washington Press, 1974. Economic impact of lumber industry on development of West; transition from cargo trade to railroads; historic photographs.

Dodds, Gordon B. *The American Northwest: A History of Oregon and Washington.* Arlington Heights, Illinois: The Forum Press, 1986. Excellent summation of Northwest prehistory and history with special attention to economic, cultural, and social changes; suggestions for further reading with each chapter; historic sketches and photographs.

Ficken, Robert E. *The Forested Land: A History of Lumbering in Western Washington.* Seattle: University of Washington Press, 1987. From the spar trade to World War II, emphasizing the individuals who made it happen; illustrated with portraits of magnates and loggers.

Ficken, Robert E., and Charles P. LeWarne. *Washington: A Centennial History.* Seattle: University of Washington Press, 1988. Concise introduction to state history; written as part of the centennial celebration.

Hitchman, Robert. *Place Names of Washington.* Tacoma: Washington State Historical Society, 1985. Extensive compilation of communities and geographical sites.

Keith, Thomas B. *Horse Interlude: A Pictorial History of Horse and Man in the Inland Northwest.* Moscow: University of Idaho Press, 1976. Chronicles the mid-1850s to the 1930s, describing the use of horses to pull simple McCormick reapers, then the multiple-hitch teams that made large-scale farming possible and led to development of movable combines; stunning photographs show details of machinery and hitches.

Kirk, Ruth, with Richard Daugherty. *Exploring Washington Archaeology.* Seattle: University of Washington Press, 1978. Highlights the diversity and richness of more than 10,000 years of Washington pre-history; many photographs.

Lavendar, David. *Land of Giants: The Drive to the Pacific Northwest, 1750–1950.* New York: Doubleday, 1958. Excellent summation of early exploration by sea and land; immigration and settlement.

LeWarne, Charles Pierce. *Washington State.* Rev. ed. Seattle: University of Washington Press, 1993. Excellent story of the state from pre-American settlement to the present; a widely used—and applauded—text.

MacFarlane, Robert S. *Henry Villard and the Northern Pacific.* New York: Newcomer Society in North America, 1954. A 28-page pamphlet detailing Villard's early life and character and his challenges as the head of a financially struggling railroad.

Margaret, Helene. *Father DeSmet: Pioneer Priest of the Rockies.* Milwaukee: Bruce Publishing Company, 1940. The story of an adventurous missionary, who dreamed of peaceful missions here, like those in Paraguay.

Martin, Albro, *James J. Hill and the Opening of the Northwest.* New York: Oxford University Press, 1976. Personal and public life of a railroad magnate who built a transcontinental line without benefit of land grants.

Meinig, Donald. *The Great Columbia Plain: A Historical Geography, 1805–1910.* Seattle: University of Washington Press, 1968; paperback ed., 1995. An authoritative and enjoyable account of the interplay of eastern Washington's geography and land use.

Newman, Peter C. *Caesars of the Wilderness.*

Markham, Ontario: Viking, 1987. Middle volume of a trilogy portraying the "feisty characters and remarkable circumstances" behind the Hudson's Bay Company's North American empire; illustrated with sketches, photographs, portraits; scholarly, yet highly readable.

Richards, Kent. *Isaac Stevens: Young Man in a Hurry.* 1979. Reprint, Pullman: Washington State University Press, 1993. Washington Territory's energetic first governor, from West Point to his death on the Civil War battlefield at Chantilly.

Ruby, Robert H., and John A. Brown. *A Guide to the Indian Tribes of the Pacific Northwest.* Norman: University of Oklahoma Press, 1986. Alphabetical listing of each group with historical and contemporary data.

Schlissel, Lillian. *Women's Diaries of the Westward Journey.* New York: Schocken Books, 1982. Historical introduction, four complete diaries, and quotes from a hundred others: heartaches, fear, courage, patience, adventure; 26 photographs.

Schwantes, Carlos. *Railroad Signatures across the Pacific Northwest.* Seattle: University of Washington Press, 1993. Lore and significance of the coming of the railroad. Striking illustrations.

Scott, James W., et al. *Washington: A Centennial Atlas.* Bellingham: Center for Pacific Northwest Studies, Western Washington University, 1989. Analytical summaries of state's population growth, political development, economy, and natural environment. Remarkably readable; ample maps, charts, and historic photographs.

Washington Atlas and Gazetteer. 2d ed. Freeport, Maine: DeLorme Mapping, 1992. Accurate maps of entire state, detailing topography and roads.

White, Richard. *"It's Your Misfortune and None of My Own": A New History of the American West.* Norman: University of Oklahoma Press, 1991. Fresh view of regional history evoking the essential self-centeredness and short-range viewpoints of the successive groups who have shaped the West.

Winthrop, Theodore. *Canoe and Saddle.* 1862. Reprint, Portland, Oregon: Binfords and Mort, 1956. Musings on a journey through Washington Territory in 1853.

Woodbridge, Sally B., and Roger Montgomery. *A Guide to Architecture in Washington State: An Environmental Perspective.* Seattle: University of Washington Press, 1980. Excellent field guide to Washington's buildings; illustrated with photographs.

Peoples of Washington

Capoeman, Pauline K., ed. *Land of the Quinault.* Taholah: Quinault Indian Nation, 1990. The people's own account of their past and present; generously illustrated.

Cole, Douglas, and Ira Chaikin. *An Iron Hand upon the People: The Law against the Potlatch on the Northwest Coast.* Seattle: University of Washington Press, 1990. History and effects of the antipotlatch law that greatly affected native peoples in both Canada and the United States.

Elmendorf, William W. *The Structure of Twana Culture.* 1960. Reprint, Pullman: Washington State University Press, 1992. Classic account of Salish life along Hood Canal.

Fahey, John. *The Kalispel Indians,* Vol. 180 of Civilization of the American Indian Series. Norman: University of Oklahoma Press, 1986. An account of how the Kalispel kept their sense of identity despite missionaries and alternating governmental neglect and harassment; historical photographs.

Hilbert, Vi, ed. and trans. *Haboo: Native American Stories from Puget Sound.* Seattle: University of Washington Press, 1985. Stories and legends of the Lushootseed-speaking people, translated by a Skagit elder.

Hunn, Eugene S., with James Selam and Family. *Nch'i-Wana, "The Big River": Mid-Columbia Indians and Their Land.* Seattle: University of Washington Press, 1990. Unique summation of Sahaptin culture, historical experience, values, and outlook.

Keyser, James D. *Indian Rock Art of the Columbia Plateau.* Seattle: University of Washington Press, 1992. A valuable reference and guidebook; line drawings, photographs, and maps provide a guide to sites where petroglyphs and pictographs can be viewed.

Kirk, Ruth. *Tradition and Change on the Northwest Coast: The Makah, Nuu-chah-nulth, Southern Kwakiutl, and Nuxalk.* Seattle: University of Washington Press in association with the Royal British Columbia Museum, 1986. Richly illustrated account of Native American life along the coast, from the ancient past to the present.

Mumford, Esther H. *Seattle's Black Victorians 1852–1901.* Seattle: Ananse Press, 1980. Black immigrants' experience in Washington Territory, including the gradually increasing repression up to the time of the Civil Rights movement; photographs of individuals and reprints of handbills and advertisements.

Powell, Jay, and Vickie Jensen. *Quileute: An Introduction to the Indians of LaPush.* Seattle: University of Washington Press, 1976. Brief history of Quileutes prepared under the auspices of the tribal council; abundant photographs.

Rasmussen, Janet E. *New Land, New Lives: Scandinavian Immigrants to the Pacific Northwest.* Seattle: University of Washington Press, 1993. Based on oral histories; highlights the experiences and emotions of forty-five immigrants in the early 1900s.

Suttles, Wayne. *Coast Salish Essays.* Seattle: University of Washington Press, 1987. Detailed and clear ethnography of Salish-speaking people; photographs.

Taylor, Quintard. *The Forging of a Black Community: Seattle's Central District from 1870 through the Civil Rights Era.* Seattle: University of Washington Press, 1994. Addresses not only a particular city in the Pacific Northwest but also the process of political change in black America.

Uebelacker. Morris L. *Time Ball: A Story of the Yakima People and the Land.* Toppenish, Washington: The Yakima Nation, 1984. An account of the Yakima people as they see themselves.

Valle, Isabel. *Fields of Toil: A Migrant Family's Journey.* Pullman: Washington State University Press, 1994. Inside view of migrant workers' lives and aspirations, told by a journalist who traveled with the Martinez family from Texas to the onion and asparagus fields near Walla Walla and Pasco.

Veirs, Kristina, ed. *Nordic Heritage Northwest.* Seattle: Writing Works, 1982. Beautifully illustrated summary of the contributions of Scandinavians to Washington culture.

White, Sid, and Sam Solberg, eds. *Peoples of Washington: Perspectives on Cultural Diversity.* Pullman: Washington State University Press, 1989. Essays by recognized scholars, written for lay readers. Focuses on the shared experience of immigration into Washington. Photographs.

Wright, Robin K., ed. *A Time of Gathering: Native Heritage in Washington State.* Seattle: Burke Museum and University of Washington Press, 1991. History and ethnography of Washington's diverse native peoples, past to present; abundant photographs, many in color.

Northeast Region

Becher, Edmund T. *Spokane Corona: Eras and Empires.* Spokane, Washington: C. W. Hill Printers, 1974. Lively, anecdotal reminiscences of early days in the Spokane area.

Fahey, John. *Inland Empire: D. C. Corbin and Spokane.* Seattle: University of Washington Press, 1965. The story of Corbin's railroads and their role in transforming Spokane into the hub of the inland Northwest.

———. *Inland Empire: Unfolding Years, 1879–1929.* Seattle: University of Washington Press, 1986. Mining, lumbering, and agriculture woven together to convey the flavor and history of small towns, farms, and lumber camps.

North Central Region

Fries, U. E. *From Copenhagen to Okanogan: The Autobiography of a Pioneer.* 1949. Reprint, Portland, Oregon: Binfords and Mort, 1984. Reminiscences of an early rancher.

Pitzer, Paul C. *Harnessing a Dream.* Pullman: Washington State University Press, 1994. The complete story of Grand Coulee Dam, including the 1990s economic and environmental debate concerning completion of its land reclamation potential.

Roe, JoAnn. *Frank Matsura: Frontier Photographer.* Seattle: Madrona Publishers, 1981. Account of a late-1800s Japanese American photographer who traveled through the Okanogan; outstanding photographs.

Ruby, Robert, and John A. Brown. *Half-Sun on the Columbia: A Biography of Chief Moses.* Norman: University of Oklahoma Press, 1965. The story of a commanding personality who, in his middle years, was a powerful force for peace during the period of white invasion.

Waring, Guy. *My Pioneer Past.* Boston: B. Humphries, 1936. The reminiscences of an Okanogan rancher whose Duck Brand Saloon in Winthrop, Washington, served only the best whiskey—and had no chairs.

Wilson, Bruce. *Late Frontier: A History of Okanogan County, Washington, 1800-1941.* Okanogan: Okanogan County Historical Society,

1990. Delightful summation and sampling of places, events, and people, from Salish-speaking Native Americans to Chinese miners and Euro-American settlers.

South Central Region

Helland, Maurice. *They Knew Our Valley*. Yakima, Washington: Maurice Helland, 1975. Historical vignettes of Yakima region notables by local journalist.

McCoy, Keith. *The Mount Adams Country: Forgotten Corner of the Columbia River Gorge*. White Salmon, Washington: Pahto Publications, 1987. History of individuals and events; large size, well-printed photographs.

Mills, Randall. *Stern-wheelers Up Columbia: A Century of Steamboating in the Oregon Country*. Palo Alto, California: Pacific Books, 1947. The boats that opened the interior to settlement, including dramatic incidents at various rapids and tales of corporate finagling; enticing photographs, including the boats' exteriors, cabins, and engine rooms.

Prater, Yvonne. *Snoqualmie Pass: From Indian Trail to Interstate*. Seattle: The Mountaineers, 1981. How Puget Sound settlers gained their most direct route over the Cascade Mountains; a story of cattle drives, tourist lodges, the nation's first transcontinental automobile race.

Relander, Click. *Drummers and Dreamers: The Story of Smowhala the Prophet and His Nephew, Puck-Hyah-Toot, the Last Prophet of the Nearly Extinct River People*. Caldwell, Idaho: Caxton Printers, 1956. Poignant tale of a movement to revive traditional native beliefs as a reaction to pressure by whites.

Shideler, John. *Coal Towns in the Cascades: A Centennial History of Roslyn and Cle Elum, Washington*. Spokane, Washington: Melior Publications, 1986. Describes the towns and their roles in Washington's development.

Vogel, Leo. *Years Plowed Under*. Spokane, Washington: University Press, 1977. A rambling, personal history of childhood on an irrigated farm near Attalia, Washington, and the middle years as a 1940s pioneer on the Columbia Basin Project near Connell, Washington; delightfully written.

Southeast Region

Bennett, Robert A. *Walla Walla: Portrait of a Western Town, 1804-1898*. Walla Walla, Washington: Pioneer Books, 1980. Portrays the development of eastern Washington's first city, which began as a mine supply center and became a rich wheat-growing area.

Drury, Clifford. *Marcus and Narcissa Whitman and the Opening of Old Oregon*. Glendale, California: A. H. Clark Company, 1973. Marcus and Narcissa as seen in the context of the American religious and social movements of the 1830s and 1840s.

———. *Elkanah and Mary Walker: Pioneers among the Spokanes*. Caldwell, Idaho: Caxton Printers, 1940. The story of missionaries who arrived in 1838; journals and letters reveal personal foibles as well as details of daily life.

Fryckman, George A. *Creating the People's University: Washington State University, 1890-1990*. Pullman: Washington State University Press, 1990. Scholarly assessment of administrative, faculty, and legislative policies in shaping "Wazzu's" major academic and research presence.

Gerber, Michele. *On the Home Front: The Cold War Legacy of the Hanford Nuclear Site*. Lincoln: University of Nebraska Press, 1992. Exposition of wartime and Cold War nuclear production and experimentation at Hanford, together with environmental/cleanup consequences.

McGregor, Alexander C. *Counting Sheep: From Open Range to Agribusiness on the Columbia Plateau*. Seattle: University of Washington Press, 1982. The story of the four McGregor brothers who immigrated to Washington and founded a sheep empire, which continues as a prominent third-generation business.

Peterson, Keith. *River of Life/Channel of Death: Fish and Dams on the Lower Snake*. Lewiston, ID: Confluence Press, 1995. Clear and balanced in presentation, epic in sweep, the book ranges from the Bretz Floods that carved the canyons and coulees and the people that began inhabiting them 10,000 years ago to the politics and construction of today's dams, and the continuing—but threatened—salmon runs that are basic both to biome and to economy.

Trafzer, Clifford E., and Richard D. Scheuerman. *Renegade Tribe: The Palouse Indians and the Invasion of the Inland Pacific Northwest*. Pullman:

Washington State University Press, 1986. Oral tradition and written accounts woven together to tell the story of the Palouse people from their point of view.

Woolston, Bill. *Harvest: Wheat Ranching in the Palouse*. Genesee, Idaho: Thorn Creek Press, 1982. A professional photographer and onetime farmhand highlights the men, women, and machines of a representative Palouse wheat farm; reality not romance .

Statesman. Seattle: University of Washington Press, 1994. The tale of how the Weyerhaeuser Company bought almost one million acres of Washington timberland and opened operations at Everett.

White, Richard. *Land Use, Environment, and Social Change: The Shaping of Island County, Washington*. Seattle: University of Washington Press, 1980. Land use by natives, early settlers, and latecomers, with implications much broader than Whidbey and Camano islands alone.

Northwest Region

Clark, Norman. *Milltown: A Social History of Everett, Washington, from Its Earliest Beginnings on the Shores of Puget Sound to the Tragic and Infamous Event Known as the Everett Massacre.* Seattle University of Washington Press, 1970. Everett, where intransient millowners and a brutal sheriff set the scene for a labor showdown.

Jenkins, Will. *Last Frontier in the North Cascades: Tales of the Wild Upper Skagit.* Mount Vernon, Washington: Skagit County Historical Society, 1984. Tales of isolated homesteaders on the upper Skagit.

Judson, Phoebe. *A Pioneer's Search for an Ideal Home: A Book of Personal Memoirs.* Tacoma: Washington State Historical Society, 1966. First published when the author was in her nineties, this reminiscence tells of crossing the plains by wagon and settling in the wilderness of the Nooksack Valley.

Keith, Gordon, ed. *The James Francis Tullock Diary: The True Story of the Ups and Downs of James and Annie Tulloch and Their Nine Children, All of Whom Were Born on Orcas Island in Washington State's San Juan Islands.* Portland, Oregon: Binfords and Mort, 1978. Vivid record of early years on Orcas, written at the request of the author's daughter.

Murray, Keith. *The Pig War.* Tacoma: Washington State Historical Society, 1968. Jurisdictional dispute between England and the United States over the San Juan Islands.

Roe, JoAnn. *The North Cascadians.* Seattle: Madrona Publishers, 1980. Rugged country and rugged individualists who mined and settled the foothills on both sides of the Cascades.

Twining, Charles E. *George S. Long: Timber*

Puget Sound Region

Berner, Richard C. *Seattle in the 20th Century.* Vol. 1, *Seattle, 1900-1920: From Boomtown, Urban Turbulence, to Restoration.* Seattle: Charles Press, 1991. Vol. 2, *Seattle, 1921-1940: From Boom to Bust.* Seattle: Charles Press, 1992. A detailed history by the well-known archivist.

Chew, Ron, ed. *Reflections of Seattle's Chinese Americans: The First 100 Years.* Seattle: Wing Luke Asian Museum with University of Washington Press, 1995. Memories of 71 pioneers from China.

Conant, Roger. *Mercer's Belles.* Pullman: Washington State University Press, 1992. Reprint of a journal of shipboard travel with the "Mercer Girls" who came from New York to Seattle as brides in 1866.

Denny, Arthur A. *Pioner Days on Puget Sound.* 1908. Reprint, Fairfield, Washington: Ye Galleon Press, 1979. Personal reminiscences by Seattle's founding father.

James, Dave. *Grisdale, Last of the Logging Camps: A Photo Story of Simpson Camps from 1890 into 1896.* Belfair, Washington: Mason County Historical Society, 1986. Chronicles Simpson Timber Company, detailing both the reality and the folklore of logging-camp life; abundant historical photographs, including superb images by Clark Kinsey (brother of better-known Darius).

LeWarne, Charles. *Utopias on Puget Sound 1885–1915.* 1975. Reprint, with a New Preface by the author, Seattle: University of Washington Press, 1995. Social reform in America as represented by five communitarian settlements in Washington; highly readable.

McDonald, Richard K., and Lucile McDonald. *The*

Coals of Newcastle: A Hundred Years of Hidden History. Renton, Washington: Issaquah Alps Trails Club, 1987. From coal-mining days—and fueling Seattle's early growth—to present status within a county park.

Meeker, Ezra. *Ventures and Adventures of Ezra Meeker or Sixty Years of Frontier Life.* Seattle: Rainier Printing Company, 1909. The personal story of western Washington's best-known pioneer who, late in life, retraced the Oregon Trail by both ox-drawn wagon and airplane.

Moore, Ernest. *The Coal Miner Who Came West.* (City not listed): Ernest R. Moore, 1982. A Black family memoir of life at Franklin.

Morgan, Murray. *Puget's Sound: A Narrative History of Early Tacoma and the Southern Sound.* Seattle: University of Washington Press, 1979. The Tacoma-to-Olympia area from wilderness beginnings to railroad boom and present-day lumber-and-military status quo.

———. *Skid Road: An Informal Portrait of Seattle.* 1951. Reprint, Seattle: University of Washington Press, 1982. Rollicking portrayal of an exuberant city.

Ochsner, Jeffrey Karl, ed. *Shaping Seattle Architecture: A Historical Guide to the Architects.* Seattle: University of Washington Press, 1994. Profiles of the architects and firms that built Seattle from a late 1800s town to a late 1900s urban center.

Ripley, Thomas E. *Green Timber: On the Flood Tide to Fortune in the Great Northwest.* Palo Alto, California: American West Publishing Company, 1968. A sparkling, vivid account of Tacoma from 1890 to 1893 by a young college man who entered the family lumber business.

Sale, Roger. *Seattle, Past to Present.* Seattle: University of Washington Press, 1976. Highlights what was most important in each of the city's major periods from the founding through the early 1970s.

———. *Seeing Seattle.* Photographs by Mary Randlett. Seattle: University of Washington Press, 1994. A series of walking tours of the city, in which Sale invites the reader to join him in looking, asking, and forming opinions and judgments.

Southwest Region

Bradley, Lenore K. *Robert Alexander Long: A Lumberman of the Gilded Age.* Durham, N.C.: Forest History Society, 1989. Story of the Long-Bell Lumber Company, originator of Longview, Washington.

Copeland, Tom. *The Centralia Tragedy of 1919: Elmer Smith and the Wobblies.* Seattle: University of Washington Press, 1993. The story and aftermath of the Armistice Day confrontation between veterans and members of the IWW, focusing on the lawyer who advised the Wobblies.

DeVoto, Bernard, ed. *The Journals of Lewis and Clark.* Boston: Houghton Mifflin, 1953. A blending of the two captains' journals together with an analysis of their contribution. The journals of Lewis and Clark are also available in the highly praised multivolume edition edited by Gary Moulton and published by the University of Nebraska Press.

Espy, Willard. *Oysterville: Roads to Grandpa's Village.* New York: C. N. Potter, 1977. One family's odyssey as Willapa Bay pioneers; delightfully written.

Irving, Washington. *Astoria, or Anecdotes of an Enterprise Beyond the Rocky Mountains.* 1849. Reprint, Philadelphia: Lippincott, 1961. The adventures of Pacific Fur Company men who established the first American-owned trading post on the West Coast.

Martin, Irene. *Legacy and Testament: The Story of Columbia River Gillnetters.* Pullman: Washington State University Press, 1994. The salmon story as told by a woman who fishes with her husband; draws on oral histories and unpublished materials as well as personal experience.

Morrison, Dorothy N. *The Eagle and the Fort: The Story of John McLoughlin.* 1979. Reprint, Portland: Oregon Historical Society, 1984. A particularly readable account of Fort Vancouver's renowned factor.

Nelson, Thomas Strong. *Cathlamet on the Columbia.* Portland, Oregon: Binfords and Mort, 1906. Heartfelt, simply told recollections of pioneer life along the lower Colombia.

Pyle, Robert. *Wintergreen: Rambles in a Ravaged Land.* New York: C. Scribner, 1986. Written by an insider who honors his corner with a poetic portrayal of place and people; optimism in an abused landscape.

Swan, James. *The Northwest Coast, or Three Years' Residence in Washington Territory.* 1857. Reprint, Seattle: University of Washington Press, 1972. Life on Willapa Bay in the 1850s, including a perceptive record of native customs and amusing accounts of often lackadaisical white neighbors.

Olympic Peninsula Region

Castile, George Pierre, ed. *Indians of Puget Sound: The Notebooks of Myron Eells.* Seattle: University of Washington Press with Whitman College, 1985. Missionary Eells' 1870s account of the Salish people with whom he lived and worked.

Fletcher, Elizabeth Huelsdonk. *The Iron Man of the Hoh.* Port Angeles, Washington: Creative Communications, 1979. A homestead daughter's account of pioneer life in the rain forest, complete with family snapshots.

Morgan, Murray. *The Last Wilderness.* New York: Viking, 1955. Delightful portrayal of the Olympic Peninsula as evoked through accounts of events and personalities.

Simpson, Peter, ed. *City of Dreams: A Guide to Port Townsend.* Port Townsend, Washington: Bay Press, 1986. Alphabetical entries that form a convenient historical summation of Port Townsend and its surrounding area.

Van Syckle, Edwin. *The River Pioneers: Early Days on Grays Harbor.* Seattle: Pacific Search Press, 1982. An account of the settlement and development of the beaches and rivers at the southern base of the Olympic Peninsula.

————. *They Tried to Cut It All: Grays Harbor— Turbulent Years of Greed and Greatness.* Seattle: Pacific Search Press, 1981. Lumbering lore and history written by a former logger-millhand-journalist; photographs.

Weinstein, Robert A. *Grays Harbor, 1885–1913.* New York: Viking Press, 1978. Fascinating compilation of high-quality photographs, plus informative text.

Wood, Robert L. *Men, Mules and Mountains: Lieutenant O'Neil's Olympic Expeditions.* Seattle: The Mountaineers, 1976. The 1885 and 1890 U.S. Army explorations of the Olympic Peninsula, including the first recorded ascent of Mount Olympus.

————. *Across the Olympic Mountains: The Press Expedition, 1889–1890.* 1976. Reprint, Seattle: The Mountaineers, 1988. Amusingly told tale of the "grit and manly vim" demonstrated by a newspaper-sponsored party that crossed the Olympics from the Elwha Valley to the Quinault.

Corner notching, cedar cabin.

INDEX

Boldface numbers refer to main entries.

mas trees, 319, 321; gardens, 351, 369, 411–12; wild plants used by florists, 509

Horton, Dexter, 123, 282

Horton, John, 80

Hot springs, 157, 444, 493, 503

Houchen, Alfred, 418

Houghton, 278

Houser, John, 180

Hovander, Hokan, 226

Howard, Oliver, 117, 118, 403

Howard Hanson Dam, 272–73

Howse, Joseph, 27

Hubbard, Gardiner, 139

Hubbs, Paul, 249

Huckleberries, 119, 166, 314

Hudson, Holden and Phoebe, 227

Hudson's Bay Co.: trading posts/forts of, 9, 31, 38, **40–41**, 45, 48, 106, 174, 302, **308–9**, 339, 401–3; merger with North West Co., 20, 59, 383, 436, 445; farms of, 40–41, 106, 309, 384, 396–97, 403, 409; and U.S.–Canadian border, 41, 108; and Native Americans, 45, 308–9, 311–328, 402, 463; employees of, 48, 141, 305, 402, 403, 404, 420; promotion of Christianity by, 48; competition in fur trade, 58, 59; Columbia River navigation rights, 108; architecture, 174, 308; and gold rushes, 217, 403; steamboats of, 232, 248, 486; salmon salteries of, 247–48, 423–24; land claims of, 248, 309, 323, 401; and "Pig War," 246, 268; bateaux of, 348, 389; and U.S. Army, 311, 403; "profits and peace" policy of, 402; and fishing industry, 423–24; capital punishment by, 424; jury trials of, 424; mentioned, 21, 49, 244–45, 250, 265, 304, 311, 312, 313, 323, 367, 368, 398, 410, 411, 445, 471, 485, 486. *See also* Fort Colvile; Fort George; Fort Nez Perce; Fort Nisqually; Fort Okanogan; Fort Vancouver; MacDonald, Archibald; McLoughlin, John; Puget's Sound Agricultural Company; Red River, Manitoba; Simpson, George

Hulda Klager Lilac Gardens, 398, **411–12**

Hume, George, 417, 450

Hume, William, 414, 417

Humes brothers, 425

Humes Ranch, 488

Humptulips River, **456**

Hunt, Leigh S. J., 275, 278

Hunt, T. Dwight, 397

Hunter, James, 43

Hunters (town), **43**

Hurricane Ridge, 484, **495**

Hutterites, 96

Hutton, May Awkright and Levi, 13

Hydroelectric power: export of, 4; record output, 7; waterfalls used for, 75, 350; first project on Columbia River, 108; used for Stevens Pass tunnels, 109; and Columbia River, 114, 157, 159; in nineteenth century, 127; history of, in displays, 213; publicly owned, 331; engineering of projects, 444, 508; mentioned, 22, 52, 89, 98, 124, 132, 234, 235, 303, 330–31, 332, 489, 506. *See also* Columbia Basin Project; Dams; Electricity; Puget Sound Power and Light Co.; Seattle City Light; Tacoma Public Utilities; Washington Water Power Co.

Hypotheekbank, 11, 18, 207

Ice, dry, 160

Ice caves, 166

Ice Harbor Dam, **169**

Icelandic Americans, 223, 296

Icemaking, 142, 403

Idaho and Washington Northern Railroad, 22, 25, 26

Ignatius, Saint, 25

Ilwaco, 414, **421–22**

Ilwaco Railway and Navigation Company, 431

Immigrants, 70–71, 187, 191; quarantine of, 422–23, 487. *See also* Railroads: promotion by; *specific nationalities*

Inchelium, 42, **43–44**

Index, **259**

Indian Island, 490, 494

Indians. *See* Native Americans

Indian Wars. *See* Battles; Wars

Industrial Workers of the World (IWW), 11, 254, **255**, 387, 451, 491. *See also* Labor; Strikes

Ingalls, Rufus, 403

Insane, treatment of, 7–8, 242, 310, 442

International border. *See* U.S.–Canadian border

Ione, 22, **24**, 28

Irish Americans, 3, 12, 42, 48, 210, 399

Iron, 124, 132, 278, 346; bog, 490; smelter, 490

Irondale, **490–91**

Iron Horse State Park, 133

Iron Springs, 451–52

Iroquois tribe, 3, 27, 48, 174, 403, 445

Irrigation: Grand Coulee Dam and, 3, 22, 28, 43, 90; Columbia Basin Irrigation Project, 27–28, 85, **88–89**,

95, 97, 98, 116, 168, 205, 211, 212; flumes, 43, 52, 61, 105, 108, 446, 503; Chief Joseph Dam, 52–53; engineering of, 52, 56–57, 89, 103, 107–8; Conconully Dam, 56–57; by Native Americans, 62, 143; Okanogan Irrigation Project, 67; circle, 100; in Quincy, 104–5; and orchards, 106–7, 113, 138, 141, 154, 177, 190; Highland Canal, 110–11, 113; in Beverly, 115; and vineyards, 116; Roza Canal, 140, 143, 154; early, 143, 151, 168, 172, 174, 177, 203; Sunnyside Canal, 144–45; Yakima Project, 151; Yakima Valley Canal, 154; museums, 204; Palouse Irrigation Project, 209, 214; in Western Washington, 503; mentioned, 7, 61, 75, 125, 134, 138, 147, 153, 155, 159, 170, 171, 174, 178. *See also* Dams; Flumes

Isaacs, H. P., 185

Issaquah, 285, 342, **346**

Italian Americans, 3, 11, 26, 132, 177, 322, 343, 353, 399, 426

Jackson, Henry M., 255

Jackson, John R. and Matilda, 393

James, Anna Marie, 362

James, Mary Ann, 353

James, Samuel, 352–53, 362

Jameson Lake, 94

Jamestown, **491**, 493

Japan: castaways from, 36; nineteenth-century, 36–37; trade with, 285

Japan Airlines, 95

Japanese Americans, 33, 294; internment of, 95, 147, 149, 273, 274, 277, 292, 302, 321–22, 372; as farm workers, 100, 136, 147, 202; as miners, 154; festivals of, 272; as farmers, 273, 274, 277, 292, 371–72, 382; neighborhoods of, 293; as mill workers, 349, 440

Jaussaud, Leon, 210

Jeffcoat, P. R., 228

Jefferson, Thomas, 58

Jenny (ship), 402, 415, 416

Jensen, Nez, 131

Jerisich, Samuel, 314

Jesuits. *See* Missionaries, Catholic

Jetty, 416, 435, 459

Jewish Americans, 12

Jim, Elowahka, 421

Jim Crow Point, 421

Joerk, August W., 445

John Day Dam, **159**

Johnson, Andrew, 433

John Wayne Pioneer Trail, 133

Peanuts, 139
Pears, 103, 107, 136, 151, 180, 190
Pearsall, Joseph, 259
Pearson, D. O., 270
Pearson Airpark, 409
Peas, 124, 179, 202; dry, 188
Pe Ell, **440**
Pellegrini, Angelo, 353
Penawawa, 188, **197**
Pend Oreille, Lake, 27
Pend Oreille Railway, 22
Pend Oreille River, 3, 22, 27, 90
Pend Oreille tribe, 5
Pendleton Mill, 411
Penitentiaries. *See* Prisons
Penn Cove, 264–65, 326
Peopeo Moxmox, Chief, 148, 173
Percival, Samuel, 357
Pérez, Juan, 475–76
Perkins, Blanche, 118, 146–47
Perkins, James, 190–91
Perkins, Lorenzo, 118, 146–47
Pérouse, I. F. G. de la, 460
Perrijo, Will, 344
Perry, Matthew, 37, 297
Peruvian Americans, 421
Peshastin, 76, **107–8**
Peshastin Creek, 130
Peterson, Hans, 414
Peterson, Minnie Nelson, 465
Petroglyphs, 158, 159, 165
Pettygrove, Francis, 500
Pflug, John, 71
Phelps and Wadleigh, 61
Phinney, Guy, 297
Pickernell, John, 421
Pickett, George E., 222, 246
Pierce, Henry H., 36, 61–62, 79
Pierce, Franklin, 322
Pigs. *See* Swine
"Pig War," 222, 243–44, 245–47, 249, 268, 313, 319, 501
Pike Place Market, 291–92
Pilkington, James, 452, 453
Pillar Rock, 414, **423–24**
Pinkney City, 38, 40, **47**
Pioneer Farm Museum, 306, 319
Pioneer Square, 338
Plamondon, Simon, 396, 445
Plante's Ferry, **8**, 17
Plummer, Alfred, 500
Plums, 190. *See also* Prunes
Plymouth, **171–72**
Pna village, 117
Poe, Manton, 211
Pogue, J. I., 67
Point Defiance (tribal land), 322
Point Defiance Park, 310, 338–39
Point Elliott Treaty, 225, 226, 242, 260, 263, 382
Point Grenville, **460**, 468

Point Mitchell, 378
Point No Point, **373**
Point No Point Treaty, 373, 491, 493, 509–10
Point of Arches, 474
Point Roberts, **229–30**
Point Wilson, 502
Polish Americans, 343, 433, 440
Polk, James, 187
Pomeroy, 175, **180–81**
Pond, Peter, 58
Pope and Talbot Company, 262, 376, 453, 497, 498
Porpoise (ship), 314, 328
Port Angeles, 465, 484, 485, **494–97**
Port Blakely, 281, **370–71**, 382
Port Blakely Mill Company, 364
Port Columbia, 52
Port Crescent, 465
Port Discovery, 491
Port Gamble, 268, 270, 324, 369, 370, **375–77**, 382, 493, 497
Port Hadlock, 380
Port Ludlow, 270, 382, **497–98**
Port Madison, 370, 371, 374, 377, 382
Port Madison Reservation, 260, **382**
Port of Seattle, 291
Port of Tacoma, 334
Port Orchard, **377–78**
Port Townsend, 243, 247, 269, 429, 465, 484, 494, 495, 496, **498–503**
Port Townsend and Southern Railroad, 500
Porter, 355
Portland, 11, 383, 500
Portland, S.S., 286, 291, 502
Portland–Port Angeles and Victoria Railroad, 481
Ports, 253, 285, 291, 333–34, 358, 390, 404; of entry, 495–96, 500
Potatoes, 42, 62, 89, 100, 144, 210, 211, 212, 266, 267, 270, 463, 477; Native American, 119, 266–67, 268, 477; seed, 228
Potholes Reservoir, 97
Potlatch, **508**
Poulsbo, 369, 374, **378–79**
Poultry, 42, 133, 218, 269, 278, 301, 381, 397, 484
Press Exploring Expedition, 488, 493, 507
Preston, **349**
Preston (ship), 232
Priest Point, 356
Priest Rapids, 115, **116–17**, 119
Pringle, Matilda Sager, 194
Prisons, 180, 259, 351–52, 463
Priteca, Marcus, 151
Progressive Brethren, 145
Prohibition, 34, 136, 237, 241, 252.

See also Smuggling
Prosser, 135, **141–42**
Protection Island, **487**
Protestants. *See* Missionaries, Protestant
Prunes, 191, 249, 314, 406, 410
Puffer Butte, 176
Puget Island, **424**
Puget Sound, 45, 297; area, 148, 498
Puget Sound and Grays Harbor Railroad, 365
Puget Sound Cooperative Colony, 496–97
Puget Sound Mill Company, 374, 376
Puget Sound Naval Shipyard, 268, 372–73, 379, 485, 494
Puget Sound Power and Light Company, 108, 234, 303, 350
Puget Sound War, 273, 282–83, 313, 318, 325, **326–27**, 428
Puget's Sound Agricultural Company, 309, 396–97
Pullen, Dan, 473, 481
Pullman, 188, **197–98**
Putnam, William, 506
Puyallup, 302, 319, **320**, 321, 322
Puyallup Reservation, **322**, 327, 355
Puyallup River, 272, 322, 327, 328
Puyallup tribe, 313, 318, 322
Pysht, 485

Quadra, Bodega y, 460, 468, 477
Qualchin, 10, 62
Qual-qual-blue, 381
Quarantine stations, 422–23, 457, 487
Quarries, 180, 194, 195, 234, 361; basalt, 151, 406; limestone, 245, 250; granite, 259; sandstone, 341, 365, 366
Quartermaster Harbor, 300
Quathlpotl, 406
Queets, **480–81**
Queets tribe, 460, 461
Quiemuth, 311, 326
Quilcene, **508–9**
Quileute Reservation, 473
Quileute tribe, 452–53, 461, 467, 473, 478
Quillayute Prairie, 465
Quimper, Manuel, 476
Quinault, Lake, **470–73**
Quinault Reservation, 453, 460, 467, 480
Quinault tribe, 448, 452–53, 460, 461
Quinault Valley, 470, 489, 507
Quincy, 89, **97–98**

Rabbeson, A. B., 365
Race (Ski to Sea), 228–29
Rafts, oceangoing, 427
Railroads: electric, 5, 7, 8, 19, 20,

263, 274, 418, 439, 441, 461, 505;
spawning runs, 220, 230, 466, 503;
salteries, 248, 282, 423–24, 425;
reef netting, 252; shipping, 282;
traps, 230, 418, 421; sport fishing
for, 461. *See also* Canneries;
Fishing; Native Americans: fishing
Salmon la Sac, **132–33**
Salmon Valley, 56
Salt Creek, 485, 486
Salt Water State Park, 276
Samish Island, 224, 242
Samish tribe, 224, 242
Sammamish River, 218, 275, 301
San De Fuca, **265**
Sand Island, 415
Sandspits, 487, 488, 494, 495–96
Sandstone, 341, 365, 366
Sanford, DeForest, Emily, and
William, 269
San Francisco: trade with, 281, 285,
303, 331, 347–48, 379–80, 383,
452; lumber market in, 380
San Juan Island, 229, 243, 245–47,
248, 250, **251–52**
San Juan Island National Historic
Park, 243–44, 245–47
San Juan Islands, 215, 243–52
San Juan Town, 247
Sanpoil River, 29, 34
Sanpoil tribe, 27, 31, 42, 140
Sappho, **481–82**
Sarsapkin, Chief, 57, 61
Satsop Railroad, 365
Satsop River, 352
Satsop Valley, **458**
Satulick, Henry, 305
Sauk City, **240**
Saunders, Schuyler S., 388
Sawmills: Boise Cascade Mill, 151;
pine lumber produced by, 160;
Whitman Sawmill site, 187; largest
in world, 254, 332, 370–71;
organized labor in, 255, 256; steam,
283; machinery, 314, 365, 368;
labor conditions in, 353, 370–71,
453; Port Blakely Mill, 370–71;
museums, 375; Seabeck mill, 380;
historic, 407; timber for railroad
construction, 426; Port Ludlow
mill, 497–98. *See also* Boise
Cascade Co.; Lumber industry;
Pope and Talbot Co.; Yesler, Henry
Sayward, W. F., 497
Scammon, Isaiah and Lorinda, 457
Scandinavian Americans, 97, 296–97,
305, 314, 426, 469; museums, 272,
296. *See also* Danish Americans;
Finnish Americans; Norwegian
Americans; Swedish Americans
Scarborough. James, 419

Schafer, John, 458
Schanewah, Chief, 445
Scheffer, Victor, 354
Schmidt, Leopold, 222, 366
Schmidt, Vitus, 280
Schupp, William, 274
Schweighbardt, Mrs. John, 93
Schweikert, Martin, 59
Scotch-Irish Americans, 442
Scottish Americans, 174, 207–9, 366,
396–97
Scranton, S., 9, 16
Seabeck, 370, 377, **379–80**
Seals, fur, 291, 473
Sealth, Chief, 260, 381–82; Chief
Seattle Days, 369
Sea otters, 291, 458; pelts of, 58, 476
Seaton, Thomas, 34
Seattle, **282–300**; fire, 251; name of,
260, 381; steamboat service to,
269; as "livable" city, 272; anti–
Chinese riots in, 285; Pioneer
Square, 287–88, 291, 338;
International District, 293, 294;
Discovery Park, 295–96; Ballard,
296–97; in 1855, 323; compared
with other early towns, 323, 328,
370; effect of gold rush on, 331–32;
fort in, 370; rainfall in, 503;
hydropower for, 508
Seattle, Chief. *See* Sealth, Chief
Seattle and Northern Railroad, 233,
240, 241
Seattle and Walla Walla Railroad and
Construction Company, 284, 348
Seattle Aquarium, 291
Seattle Center, 293
Seattle City Light, 26, 98, 235, 238–
39, 240, 241
Seattle Lake Shore and Eastern
Railroad, 87, 233, 241, 275, 279,
281, 297, 301, 346, 349, 350
Seattle Press. See Press Exploring
Expedition
Seaview, **433**
Second Beach, 473
Sedro Woolley, **241–42**
Sehome, 217
Sekiu, **482–83**
Selah, 134, 140, **144**, 153
Selleck, **349–50**
Semiahmoo Spit, 216, 223
Semple, Eugene, 488
Sentinel Peak, 114
Sequalitchew, 314
Sequalitchew tribe, 308
Sequim, 484, **503**
Seven Devils, 178
Seventh Day Adventists, 96, 194
Shaker religion, 154, 263, 354–55
Shannon, Lake, 234

Sharp, S. Price, 480, 481
Shaw, Benjamin, 382
Shaw, George, 344
Shaw Island, 243, **252**
Shead, Oliver, 352
Sheep: massacre of, 57; vs. cattle, 57,
85, 86, 113, 116; drives, 75, 88,
133; vs. farms, 75, 99; shearing, 99,
209; grazing, 113, 206, 207;
shipping, 192, 202; diet of, 207;
mentioned, 28, 33, 98, 103, 138,
144, 151, 246, 251, 252, 309, 444.
See also Wool
Shellfish, 276, 431
Shellgren, Ernest, 314
Shelton, 351, 353, **363–66**
Shephard, Mary Ann James, 362
Sheridan, Philip, 146
Sherling, Harry, 63
Sherman, William T., 36, 45, 403
Sherman Pass, **36**
Shi Shi Beach, 474
Shields, J. M., 238
Shipbuilding: stern-wheelers, 110,
111, 300, 382; riverboats, 251;
naval, 278, 369, 372, 406–7;
fishing boats, 300, 338; schooners,
300, 371, 382, 454; barks, 371;
barkentines, 371; museums, 372;
battleship repair, 373; lumber, 380;
ships' knees, 508; mentioned, 279,
285, 314, 433, 450
Shipping. *See* Railroads; Steamboats;
Trade; *and specific products*
Ships: historic, 295, 296; replicas of,
449; replacement by railroads, 213.
See also Boats; Steamboats;
Submarines
Shipwrecks, 416–17, 429–30, 478–79
Shipyards. *See* Shipbuilding
Shoalwater Bay. *See* Willapa Bay
Shoalwater Reservation, **433–34**
Shobert, Frederick, Henry, Napoleon,
and Stephen, 406
Short, Amos, 410
Shotwell, Jacob, 110
Shoudy, John, 123, 126
Shrimp, 418
Shushuskin Road, 144
Shute, Nevil, 370
Si, Mount, 345, **348**
Sidney, B.C., 243
Sierra, Benito, 460
Silcott, John, 177
Silica Road, 116
Silicosaska, 76
Silk, 330
Silver. *See* Mining
Silverdale, 369, **381**
Silverton, **260**
Similkameen River, 56, 61, 68, 261